D0983018

fine Cooking

2009

The Taunton Press
Inspiration for hands-on living®

©2009 by The Taunton Press, Inc.

All rights reserved.

Printed in the United States of America
ISBN: 978-1-60085-291-6

Fine Cooking, The Taunton Press, Inc.,
63 South Main Street, PO Box 5506,
Newtown, CT 06470-5506
e-mail: fc@taunton.com
www.finecooking.com

Taunton Product # 051011

Dear *Fine Cooking* reader,

Welcome to the eleventh annual volume of *Fine Cooking,* all issues from 2009 gathered together in one handsome edition. This was an exciting year for us, one in which we celebrated our fifteenth anniversary with a new look. While we haven't strayed from our core mission—to be "not just another" food magazine, but to be about the hows and whys of cooking—we have made some exciting changes to our logo and our columns and features. Here's a taste of the delicious stories you'll find in the pages that follow:

- Homemade Croissants (February/March)—We debut our new "Weekend Project" feature, which takes you step by step through a challenging and richly rewarding recipe—in this case the classic French pastry (tips, timelines, and tools included).

- Best-ever Roast Chicken (April/May)—In a new column called "Repertoire," we feature simple, classic recipes presented in an easy-to-follow format. Discover the tips and tricks to perfectly cooked roast chicken.

- Cooking without Recipes: Ice Cream (June/July)—One easy method, countless incredible ice creams, including chocolate peppermint stick and double vanilla bourbon.

- Cook Once/Eat Twice (August/September)—Make a big pot of fresh tomato sauce on the weekend, and then turn it into imaginative leftovers during the week, including summer vegetable stew and spiced lamb meatballs in tomato sauce.

- French Onion Soup (October/November)—The ultimate version of this bistro favorite goes up against a chef's inspired take on the dish (think: soup dumplings) in our Classic/Classic Update feature.

These are just a few of the stories and recipes that fill this special edition. You won't want to miss our beautiful ingredient features, which have highlighted everything from oranges to corn to green beans. And be sure to check out our other new columns, including Preserving the Season, Food Geek, and The Good Life (with contributing editor Ellie Krieger).

Happy cooking!

Laurie Glenn Buckle, Editor

The Taunton Press, 63 S. Main St., PO Box 5506, Newtown, CT 06470-5506 (203) 426-8171 E-mail: fc@taunton.com

SPECIAL RECIPE PULLOUT: quick & easy 5-ingredient appetizers

fine
Cooking

JANUARY 2009 NO. 96

FOR PEOPLE WHO LOVE TO COOK

Holiday Party Guide
22 pages of recipes, menus & more

HOW TO:
Baking with dark chocolate

Soup suppers from your pantry

Cold-weather cocktails

A gift for every cook on your list

www.finecooking.com

$7.99 can $8.99

Chocolate-Pomegranate Torte, p. 88

He made California a world-renowned
destination for wine.

Maybe he can do the same for your house.

Skeptics laughed when Robert Mondavi doggedly set out
to prove that California wines could be quality wines.
But today a glass of Woodbridge by Robert Mondavi may
make you smile in a totally different way.

His name is on the bottle. His story is in it.

WOODBRIDGE

by Robert Mondavi

fine Cooking

DECEMBER 2008/JANUARY 2009   ISSUE 96

46   54

20

The Taunton Press
Inspiration for hands-on living®

visit our web site: **www.finecooking.com**

60   68   72   78

Whole-Wheat Pasta
with Pancetta,
Greens & Garlic

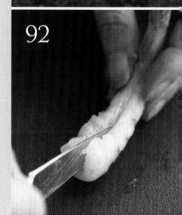
92

index

◆ **QUICK**
Under 45 minutes

◆ **MAKE AHEAD**
Can be completely prepared ahead but may need reheating and a garnish to serve

◆ **MOSTLY MAKE AHEAD**
Can be partially prepared ahead but will need a few finishing touches before serving

◆ **VEGETARIAN**
May contain eggs and dairy ingredients

recipes

Photos: Scott Phillips

AUSTRALIAN LAMB

Easy. Any Day.

cranberry-marinated rack of aussie lamb with almond wild rice

 FAMILY FAVORITE 6 SERVINGS

Sure, Australian Lamb is great for the holidays. It's also perfect for quick-and-easy everyday meals. Lean and rich in nutrients, with a mild taste and delicious flavor, it's a smart choice everyone at your dining table will love — which makes any day a great day to enjoy Australian Lamb!

Australian Lamb

Fresh, Easy and Delicious.

Visit **www.australian-lamb.com/fc** for this recipe and to order a **FREE** copy of our new cookbook, *Easy. Any Day.* featuring 28 pages of seasonal recipes your whole family will love!

Winter on the Menu

Recipes from this issue and from our Web site (FineCooking.com) come together here in meals for the season

New Year's Eve Dinner

Rosemary's Pink Diamond Fizz, *from FineCooking.com*

Prosciutto-Wrapped Mozzarella & Basil, *pullout*

Sweet & Spicy Roasted Nuts, *pullout*

Bourbon-Orange-Glazed Ham, *p. 50*

Roasted Fingerling Potatoes, *p. 52*

Sautéed Shredded Brussels Sprouts with Fresh Herbs & Crisp Shallots, *from FineCooking.com*

Ginger Cake Trifles with Caramelized Apples, Cranberries & Whipped Cream, *p. 66*

Brunch

Champagne Cosmo, *p. 62*

Artichoke & Smoked-Mozzarella Frittata, *p. 114a*

Mixed Green Salad with Red-Wine & Dijon Vinaigrette, *from FineCooking.com*

Sour Cream Coffee Cake with Toasted Pecan Filling, *p. 70*

Weeknight Combos: Soup and Salad

Spiced Tomato & Red Lentil Soup, *p. 82*

Baby Greens with Chicken, Dried Cherries, Pears & Pecans, *p. 114a*

Pasta e Fagioli, *p. 80*

Arugula, Carrot & Celery Root Salad with Almonds, *p. 58*

Root Vegetable & Barley Soup with Bacon, *p. 80*

Watercress Salad with Steak, Sautéed Shallots & Stilton, *p. 114a*

Friday Night Supper

Blackened Tilapia with Cilantro Lime Slaw, *p. 114a*

Lemon-Thyme Spinach, *p. 64*

Broiled Grapefruit with Honey, Vanilla & Cardamom, *p. 28*

Night Cap and a Snack

Hot Buttered Rum, *p. 41*

Triple-Shot Eggnog, *p. 40*

Orange-Scented Mulled Wine, *p. 41*

Ginger Cake, *p. 67*

Honey Shortbread, *p. 77*

Orange-Hazelnut Olive Oil Cookies, *p. 76*

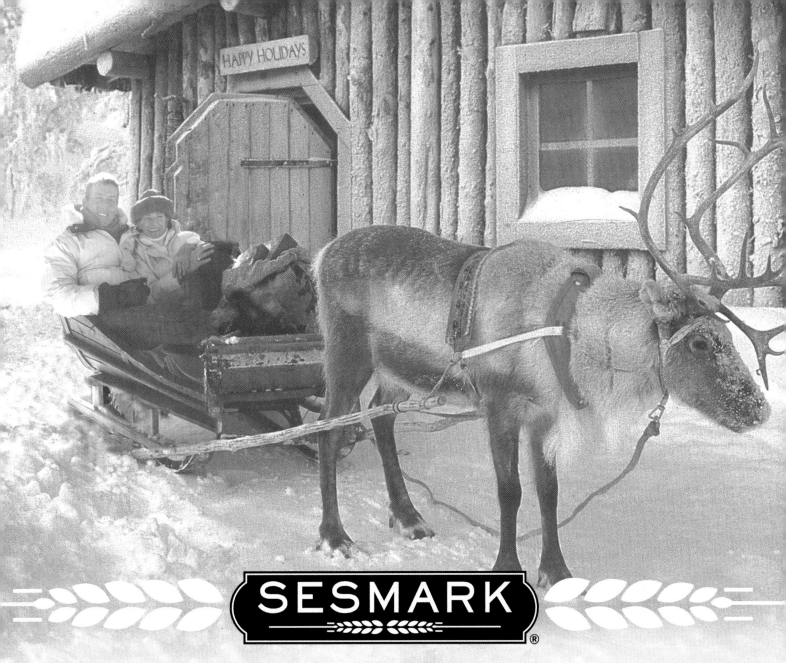

SESMARK®

HEARTLAND TASTE PERFECT FOR YOUR HOLIDAY GUESTS

SERVE WITH CABOT Vermont · WORLD'S BEST CHEDDAR ·

Entertaining with genuine heartland products, like baked, all natural Sesmark crackers and award-winning Cabot cheeses is a holiday tradition guaranteed to satisfy whoever you have stopping by.

SESMARK.COM

from the editor

Memory Lane

More food, more fun

In addition to this, our biggest holiday issue ever, you'll find several other special editions of *Fine Cooking* on newsstands now and in the next couple of months. *Roasting*, which comes out in early December, is filled with the best kind of satisfying, cold-weather cooking, and *Cookies*, available now, is packed with recipes for that favorite holiday activity—baking cookies. In addition, *How to Cook a Turkey* offers up a classic holiday menu along with a DVD of step-by-step videos of the techniques that will guarantee success with the bird and beyond.

I don't know about you, but I always think I'm going to remember: every baby, every vacation, every celebration. But time passes, and I can't necessarily tell you exactly which newborn that might be in the fading Polaroid, or what beach that was in the background of the annual family Christmas card. Instead, I rely on photographs taken around the table at our holiday dinners to spark my memory and deliver up the past in a kind of delicious detail. Roast beef with a good-size hunk of Yorkshire pudding, creamed Brussels sprouts, lard-roasted potatoes, and crisp bacon rolls—these are some of the things I remember as I flip through old snapshots, watching as the children grow up and the adults grow a little older.

Traditions are the perfect backdrop for change, familiar routines against which time comes better into focus. And food is a wonderful part of tradition, whether that's latkes for Hanukkah, cookies for Christmas, or any other dish that has some special meaning for you and the holidays you celebrate. We've got best-ever versions of those favorite recipes, both in this issue, and on our Web site (FineCooking.com), along with a few surprises that will keep the cook in you entertained, too.

And speaking of surprises, we have a couple up our sleeve, beginning with a new look and a new Web site, both debuting at the start of the New Year. While we're sticking with the traditions we hold dear—like triple-tested recipes, technique-rich stories, and gorgeous food photography—we're also embracing change and its myriad opportunities. Keep an eye out for our classy new logo, and then be sure to let me know what you think.

Here's to a festive holiday season filled with memorable things to eat, the company of family and good friends, and the promise of change.

—Laurie Buckle, editor
fc@taunton.com

6̲0̲% Caca̲o̲. 1̲00̲% Impr̲e̲s̲sive.

BAKE WITH OUR DEEP, INTENSE CHOCOLATE FOR PURE PLEASURE IN EVERY BITE.

GHIRARDELLI® INDIVIDUAL CHOCOLATE LAVA CAKES

Yield - 6 servings

Center: 1/2 bar (2 oz) 60% Cacao Bittersweet Chocolate Baking Bar
1/4 cup heavy cream

Cake: Nonstick cooking spray
1 bar (4 oz) 60% Cacao Bittersweet Chocolate Baking Bar
8 Tbsp. (1 stick) unsalted butter
2 whole eggs
2 egg yolks
1/3 cup sugar
1/2 tsp. vanilla extract
1/4 cup cake flour

Raspberries and whipped cream for garnish

To make centers, melt chocolate and cream in double boiler. Whisk gently to blend. Refrigerate about 2 hours or until firm. Form into 6 balls; refrigerate until needed.

To make cake, heat oven to 400°F. Spray six 4-ounce ramekins or custard cups with cooking spray. Melt chocolate and butter in double boiler; whisk gently to blend. With an electric mixer, whisk eggs, yolks, sugar, and vanilla on high speed about 5 minutes or until thick and light. Fold melted chocolate mixture and flour into egg mixture just until combined. Spoon cake batter into ramekins. Place a chocolate ball in the middle of each ramekin.

Bake about 15 minutes or until cake is firm to the touch. Let it sit out of the oven for about 5 minutes. Run a small, sharp knife around inside of each ramekin, place a plate on top, invert and remove ramekin. Garnish with raspberries and a dollop of whipped cream.

MOMENTS OF TIMELESS PLEASURE.®

Visit your local grocery store for a complete range of delectable Ghirardelli baking chips, bars and cocoa.   www.ghirardelli.com

from our readers

Cartoon cheer

I just wanted to let you know that I enjoyed the short cartoon in the "Letters" section of the September issue (*Fine Cooking* #94). I could certainly relate to the frustration of seeing an ingredient dozens of times and then not being able to find it when you need it for a particular recipe. I now find myself frequenting the artist's blog, and I hope that you are considering running a cartoon on a regular basis.

—*Frank Zuccarini, via email*

To stuff or not to stuff

I loved your Thanksgiving menu in your November issue (*Fine Cooking* #95). I am, however, a big fan of cooking the stuffing in the turkey. Could I stuff my turkey with the Rustic Bread Stuffing with Dried Cranberries, Hazelnuts & Oyster Mushrooms instead of baking it in the oven? Do I need to make any adjustments?

—*Sara Colodny, via email*

Senior food editor Jennifer Armentrout responds: Yes, you can cook this stuffing in your turkey, though you won't get a nice golden crust on the surface of the stuffing. You'll want to cut back on the liquid so the stuffing can absorb juices from the turkey without getting too soggy. Moisten the stuffing only enough that it barely clings together when mounded on a spoon. The stuffing will expand a bit as it absorbs turkey juice, so don't overstuff the turkey; leave enough room to fit your extended hand into the top of the cavity.

If you can't fit all of the stuffing in the bird, toss the extra with more liquid—just enough to fully moisten it but not so much that it seems soggy—and bake it separately in a foil pouch or a baking dish.

Finally, be sure the stuffing in the bird reaches at least 160°F; if the turkey is done before the stuffing is hot enough, spoon the stuffing into a baking dish and finish heating it while the turkey rests.

From CooksTalk,
Fine Cooking's online forum

Foam roller feedback

CooksTalk members had some things to say about the winning tip in the "Readers' Tips" column of *Fine Cooking* #95: Using a 3-inch foam paint roller for coating phyllo sheets with melted butter.

From: *Flapjack66*
To: *All*

I hope the urethane foam roller featured in the winning tip is food safe. Sure wasn't designed for food.

From: *Florida2*
To: *Flapjack66*

While I am so very glad that our own Tracy got the winning tip award, I understand your concern, and I do not think it's alarmist, as some others have suggested. It's a legitimate question. I wonder what the tool is made of.

From: *Denise Mickelsen,*
assistant editor
To: *Flapjack66*

Hi, Flapjack66 (and others). As editor of the Tips column, I thought I would post to let you know that before printing the winning tip about the foam pastry roller, I contacted the USDA to verify the tip's safety. The USDA had no problem with using a foam roller to apply melted butter to phyllo; their concern was for the possible bacterial growth inside the foam if all of the butter didn't come out after washing. We tried washing the buttered roller by hand and running it through the dishwasher on the sanitize cycle, but both methods left butter trapped inside. Our solution was to recommend that readers freeze the roller in between uses to avoid any bacterial contamination. I hope this sets any fears to rest. And thanks, as always, for your tips.

Correction

In *Fine Cooking* #94, we mistakenly identified the "Readers' Tips" prize as an Emile Henry flame-top brazier. It was actually Emile Henry's 4.2-quart flame-top round stewpot, which retails for $150. ◆

EDITOR
Laurie Glenn Buckle

ART DIRECTOR
Annie Giammattei

SENIOR FOOD EDITOR/TEST KITCHEN MANAGER
Jennifer Armentrout

SENIOR EDITOR
Rebecca Freedman

ASSOCIATE EDITORS
Laura Giannatempo, Lisa Waddle

ASSISTANT EDITOR **Denise Mickelsen**

MANAGING WEB EDITOR **Sarah Breckenridge**

ASSISTANT WEB EDITOR **Sharon Anderson**

SENIOR COPY/PRODUCTION EDITOR
Enid Johnson

ASSOCIATE ART DIRECTOR **Pamela Winn**

ASSISTANT TEST KITCHEN MANAGER/
FOOD STYLIST
Allison Ehri Kreitler

RECIPE TESTER **Dabney Gough**

EDITORIAL ASSISTANT **Julissa Roberts**

PHOTO COORDINATOR **Kelly Gearity**

TEST KITCHEN INTERNS
Will Moyer, Joy Braddock

EDITOR AT LARGE **Susie Middleton**

CONTRIBUTING EDITORS
**Pam Anderson, Abigail Johnson Dodge,
Maryellen Driscoll, Tim Gaiser, Sarah Jay,
Kimberly Y. Masibay, Tony Rosenfeld,
Molly Stevens**

PUBLISHER **Maria Taylor**

ASSISTANT PUBLISHER **Karen Lutjen**

CONSUMER MARKETING DIRECTOR
Beth Reynolds, ProCirc

VICE PRESIDENT, SINGLE COPY SALES **Jay Annis**

BUSINESS MANAGER **David Pond**

DIRECTOR OF ADVERTISER MARKETING
Kristen Lacey

ADVERTISING SALES MANAGER
Patrick J. O'Donnell

SENIOR NATIONAL ACCOUNT MANAGER
Judy Caruso

ADVERTISING SALES ASSOCIATE **Stacy Purcell**

Fine Cooking: (ISSN: 1072-5121) is published six times a year by The Taunton Press, Inc., Newtown, CT 06470-5506. Telephone 203-426-8171. Periodicals postage paid at Newtown, CT 06470 and at additional mailing offices. GST paid registration #123210981.

Subscription Rates: U.S. and Canada, $29.95 for one year, $49.95 for two years, $69.95 for three years (GST included, payable in U.S. funds). Outside the U.S./Canada: $36 for one year, $62 for two years, $88 for three years (payable in U.S. funds). Single copy, $6.95. Single copy outside the U.S., $7.95.

Postmaster: Send address changes to *Fine Cooking,* The Taunton Press, Inc., 63 South Main St., P.O. Box 5506, Newtown, CT 06470-5506.

Canada Post: Return undeliverable Canadian addresses to *Fine Cooking,* c/o Worldwide Mailers, Inc., 2835 Kew Drive, Windsor, ON N8T 3B7, or email to mnfa@taunton.com.

Printed in the USA.

The Taunton Press
Inspiration for hands-on living®

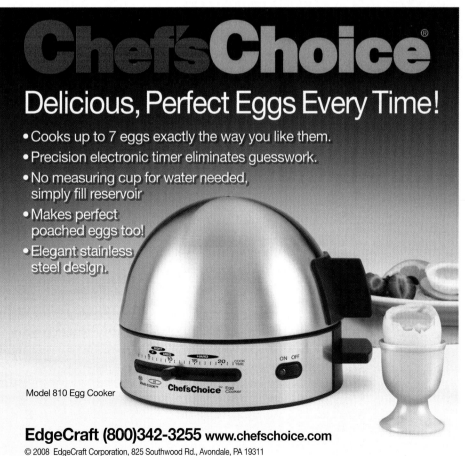

Meet our authors

Kate Hays ("Open House," p. 46) has cooked professionally in the Burlington, Vermont, area for more than 20 years. As chef-owner of Dish Catering, she's entertained crowds large and small. Besides planning ahead ("I'm a control freak," she admits), Kate says her best advice to a party host is to remain flexible and not let on when something goes wrong.

When she's not developing recipes and food styling for publications like *Food & Wine, Bon Appétit,* and *O, The Oprah Magazine,* Heidi Johannsen Stewart ("Dinner with Friends," p. 54) is cooking for family and friends in her Brooklyn brownstone. She has also begun working on a new line of tabletop items.

"When I was fresh out of culinary school, my holiday menus were way over the top," says former *Fine Cooking* editor Susie Middleton ("Modern Christmas," p. 60). "I've since learned that what everyone really wants is great takes on familiar classics." Susie, now editor at large and a contributor to FineCooking.com's Farm to Fork blog, is writing her first cookbook, on quick vegetable side dishes. When she's not in the kitchen, you'll most likely find her volunteering in support of local farmers and sustainable agriculture on Martha's Vineyard. She's a blue ribbon graduate of the Institute of Culinary Education and a member of its Alumni Hall of Achievement.

Carole Walter ("Coffee Cakes," p. 68) is the author of *Great Coffee Cakes,* which is based on years of studying with pastry chefs in France, Austria, Italy, Denmark, and the United States, and two decades of teaching baking classes. "Nothing sets my mind at ease like having one of these coffee cakes in the freezer,

especially when people pop in during the holidays," says the northern New Jersey resident. "Plus, I love knowing I have a stash of something sweet for breakfast anytime."

David Crofton ("Cookies," p. 72) met his wife and business partner, Dawn Casale, when he was looking for both a room to rent (she had one to let) and a day job as a baker while attending culinary school in the evenings. Dawn took him on as an employee to help with her wholesale cookie enterprise, rather than as a roommate. Two years later, they were married and together opened their Brooklyn bakery, One Girl Cookies. Recently, Dawn and Dave opened an evening dessert bar, called Confection, in the same space.

To pull together a weeknight meal in no time, Lori Longbotham ("Soups," p. 78) has an easy strategy: Stock the pantry, fridge, and freezer with lots of ingredient staples and use them in delicious, hearty soups. Lori is a food writer and recipe developer and the author of several cookbooks. Her latest, *Luscious Creamy Desserts,* was published in March.

"I grew up in the '50s on tall, fluffy American chocolate cakes made with shortening instead of butter," says Alice Medrich ("Chocolate," p. 84). "Then I went to Paris and had my first experience with 'adult' chocolate in the form of luscious truffles and buttery flourless cakes. It was an epiphany." Since then, Alice has been perfecting the art of baking with chocolate: first, at her pastry shop Cocolat, in Berkeley, California, where she became known for incredible French-inspired cakes and truffles, and then as a teacher and prolific cookbook author. Her books include *Chocolate Holidays, Pure Dessert,* and *Bittersweet: Recipes and Tales from a Life in Chocolate.* ◆

New books from our contributing editors

Abigail Johnson Dodge's *Around the World Cookbook,* her third children's title, came out last summer, bringing food from across the globe to young chefs. The recipes, with easy-to-follow instructions, are adventurous yet accessible, and sidebars on culinary techniques and cultural traditions from the countries of origin are informative and fun. On the adult front, *The Weekend Baker,* Abby's popular baking book (which was named an IACP cookbook finalist), was released in paperback last summer.

Pam Anderson's most recent cookbook, *The Perfect Recipe for Losing Weight and Eating Great,* was published in the spring. In it, Pam shares her secrets for losing weight (without dieting) by being active and eating often but healthfully to curb cravings. As always, her recipes are thoroughly tested to work every time.

Sarah Jay's new book, *Knives Cooks Love: Selection, Care, Techniques, Recipes,* appears on bookshelves this fall. It's an all-you-need-to-know guide to the most common tool in the kitchen, including how knives are made, how to shop and care for them, step-by-step instructions on essential knife skills, and an entire section of recipes that allow you to practice what you've learned.

Heidi Johannsen Stewart

David Crofton

Alice Medrich

Photos, from top: courtesy of the author, Kathi Littwin, Abigail Huller

Make every day a holiday with illy

Treat yourself or the coffee lover in your life to the joy of starting each day with authentic Italian espresso or cappuccino at home. With the illy a casa[SM] espresso membership program, coffee lovers receive everything they need to make the consistently flawless espresso served in the world's finest cafés and restaurants.

Give an illy a casa espresso membership featuring the Francis Francis X5 holiday introductory kit.

Yours for $150 (a value of $737).*

Members receive the state-of-the-art Francis Francis X5 espresso machine, perfect for E.S.E. pods or ground coffee, and available in 3 colors. We'll also include 4 illy logo cappuccino cups, a latte art steaming pitcher, and 18 individually wrapped E.S.E. pods.** As a member, purchase any 4 cans of illy each month for 12 months, and enjoy convenient home delivery. Make every day feel like a holiday. Spread the joy with illy.

30-day risk-free trial

Order by 12/31/08. **1 877 469 4559** or go to **illyusa.com/cooking**
Use offer code **PFCN8**

What not to miss this month on
FineCooking.com

Upload family recipes to your MyFineCooking recipe file and organize your holiday menus.

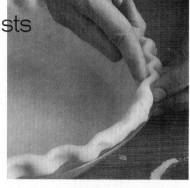

Learn how to **roll and flute piecrusts** in our step-by-step videos.

Discover what's on our holiday wish lists in the editors' blog, **The Kitchen Sink.**

Find inspiration for **edible gifts,** from recipes to wrapping ideas.

Get **on-demand answers** to your holiday cooking and baking questions in our Ask the Expert Forum.

Share your favorite cookies with friends and family— send a cookie e-card today.

Find holiday **menus for every occasion,** from a lazy family breakfast to a dazzling New Year's Eve party.

free email newsletter

Sign up at FineCooking.com to get great recipes, techniques, tips, and videos delivered directly to your inbox twice a month.

Does everything but cut the crust off.

$100 instant savings

The Viking Professional Toaster takes breakfast to new heights with automatic lift, professional-style control knobs, extra wide slots, heavy-duty stainless steel construction, plus even, consistent toasting. Shop quickly, this savings is a limited time offer. Price after instant savings: 2 slot - $150, 4 slot - $200.

To find a dealer near you, visit vikingrange.com/wheretobuy.

Great Finds

Gift ideas for every cook on your list

BY REBECCA FREEDMAN

FOR YOUR WEEKEND HOSTS

Maple syrup

Aged in bourbon barrels, these rich maple syrups—one infused with vanilla—will make anyone's breakfast special. **$49.95 (Two 375 ml bottles) at Blisgourmet.com.**

FOR THE PARTY PLANNER

Table centerpieces

As a crowning touch for your holiday table, fill one of these with fruit or flowers. **Mercury cachepots, $14 to $59 at Potterybarn.com; 888-779-5176.**

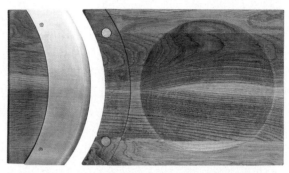

FOR THE COOK WHO HAS EVERYTHING

Mezzaluna and board

Storage made simple: Sagaform's oval oak mezzaluna fits right into the side of its board. **$29.95 at Halls.com; 800-624-4034. (Available December 7.)**

FOR THE NEWLYWEDS

Recipe boxes

Choose from a range of patterns and monogram styles to customize these cards. **$80 (includes fifty 4x6-inch cards, box, and monogramming) at Dabneyleeathome .com; 718- 596-4169.**

FOR THE MINIMALIST

Oil and vinegar pourers

Wrap these up along with a bottle of high-quality extra-virgin or balsamic. **Double-walled pourers, $23.99 to $28.99 at Tribbleshomeandgarden.com; 877-965-8742.**

THIS HOLIDAY, YOUR SOURCE FOR TRUE FLAVOR IS ALSO YOUR SOURCE FOR TRUE COMPLIMENTS.

The Spice Hunter sources its herbs and spices from the world's best growing regions, then bottles them at the peak of flavor. Now you can create holiday meals that are as tasteful as they are memorable. For recipes and more, visit spicehunter.com.

Your source for true flavor.™ The Spice Hunter®

FOR A COCKTAIL CONNOISSEUR
Ginger liqueur
Domaine de Canton's amazing liqueur blew us away with its sweet, gingery flavor—try it on the rocks or in a cocktail. **$33.99 (750 ml)** at Bevmo.com.

FOR THE GREEN THUMB
Herb stand
It's all here for you kitchen gardeners; grow your herbs and snip away. **Normann Copenhagen herb stand, $63** at Zincdetails.com.

FOR THE NEW COUNTRY KITCHEN
Jute placemats
Made with natural fibers, these playful mats are perfect for the everyday table; use them both indoors and out. **Set of four Grey Farmyard placemats by Simrin, $39.95** at Thebrooklynkitchen.com; 718-389-2982.

FOR THE MIXOLOGIST
Drink jigger
This contemporary jigger measures liquid amounts from ½ oz. to 2¼ oz. on each of its six sides. **$25** at Momastore.org.

FOR FUN
Butter dish
Our new favorite from Jonathan Adler, known for his whimsical retro designs. **$68** at Jonathanadler.com; **800-963-0891.**

FOR THE MODERNIST
Small serving bowls
Available in four colors, Le Creuset's wok-shaped stoneware bowls are both oven and microwave safe. **$30 each** at Amazon.com.

FOR THE ELEGANT ENTERTAINER
Black goblets
Juliska's gorgeous, dark glasses add a dash of drama to any table. **$65 each at Juliska.com; 888-414-8448.**

FOR THE CHEESE LOVER
Cheese accessories
An elegant wooden board and a bamboo-handled knife make a perfect pair. **Boards, $65 and $95, and knife, $60, Takashimaya-ny.com.**

FOR YOUR FAVORITE COOK
Dutch oven
Staub's Dutch ovens are coveted in our test kitchen, and now they come in a new color—this stunning, shiny titanium. **$192 to $265 at ChefsResource.com; 866-765-2433.**

FOR A DESIGN BUFF
Bread baskets
No need to pass the bread—just set each place with its own mini basket. **$87 each at Alessi.com; 877-253-7747.**

FOR THE FOODIE'S STOCKING
Candy canes
The quintessential holiday candy goes organic, with natural color and no artificial flavors. **Pure Fun candy canes at Whole Foods markets or Allergygrocer.com, about $4 for a box of 12.**

FOR THE CAFFEINE ADDICT
Portable espresso maker
Can't live without your daily espresso? Take this compact, single-serve machine with you on the road. **Handpresso handheld espresso maker, $160 at Neimanmarcus .com; 888-888-4757.** ◆

Books for Cooks
Give the gift of a good read

BY KIMBERLY Y. MASIBAY

Fat: An Appreciation of a Misunderstood Ingredient, with Recipes
**by Jennifer McLagan
(Ten Speed Press, $32.50)**

One of the season's more unusual titles, *Fat* isn't simply a cookbook; it's a celebration of the ingredient that makes everything we eat taste better. Chapters explore butter, pork, poultry, beef, and lamb fat, offering history, lore, and more than 100 sweet and savory recipes that range from the expected (Sweet Butter Pastry and Braised Pork Belly) to the surprising (Brown Butter Ice Cream and Bacon Baklava).

A Platter of Figs and Other Recipes
by David Tanis (Artisan, $35)

In this collection of 24 seasonal menus, chef David Tanis (of Berkeley's famed Chez Panisse) celebrates the simple grace of family-style eating. If many of the menus seem suited for special occasions—take, for example, the wonderfully wintry Slow Beef menu, which includes Watercress, Beet, and Egg Salad; Braised Beef with

Celery Root Mashed Potatoes; and Roasted Apples—that's because Tanis thinks everyday eating is a special occasion. With a disarming blend of seriousness and whimsy, Tanis nudges the reader toward spending and enjoying more time, not less, in the kitchen.

Jamie at Home: Cook Your Way to the Good Life
by Jamie Oliver (Hyperion, $37.50)

For this cookbook, his eighth, celebrity chef Jamie Oliver found all the inspiration he needed right in his own back yard (where he happens to have an amazing vegetable garden), and his jovial zeal for seasonal cooking just might inspire you to cook your way through the entire book. Look to the fall chapter for game, mushroom, orchard fruit, and pickle recipes and to the winter chapter for winter salad, pastry, leek, and squash recipes. Oliver's instructions are always generously detailed, and his chummy prose makes him as good a kitchen companion as one might hope to find in a book.

A16: Food + Wine
**by Nate Appleman and Shelley Lindgren
(Ten Speed Press, $35)**

A16 is the acclaimed San Francisco restaurant devoted to the foods and wines of southern Italy, but this is not just a feast-for-the-eyes restaurant cookbook. It's a book you really can cook and learn from. Written by the restaurant's chef and its wine director, the book is part cookbook and part wine guide, with comprehensive profiles of regional grapes (Fiano, Trebbiano, Aglianico, Montepulciano d'Abruzzo, and Primitivo, to name a few) and plenty of rustic, approachable recipes for antipasti, pizza, soup, pasta, seafood, meat, and vegetables.

Hometown Appetites: The Story of Clementine Paddleford, the Forgotten Food Writer Who Chronicled How America Ate
by Kelly Alexander and Cynthia Harris
(Gotham Books, $27.50)

In the 1950s and '60s, jet-setting Clementine Paddleford was the country's best-known food editor, a tireless roving reporter who wrote with style and wit about America's regional foodways. So why is it that her name and her work have been all but forgotten? This engrossing biography, sprinkled with recipes throughout, answers that question and in doing so returns Paddleford to her rightful place among the culinary elite.

Olives & Oranges: Recipes & Flavor Secrets from Italy, Spain, Cyprus & Beyond
by Sara Jenkins and Mindy Fox
(Houghton Mifflin, $35)

There's no shortage of Mediterranean-inspired cookbooks out there, so kudos to chef Sara Jenkins and food writer Mindy Fox for delivering one that's full surprises. It's a delight to discover that there are plenty of new dishes and cooking techniques to try, such as a surprisingly delicious Strawberry Risotto that's deeply flavored and not at all sweet, and a multigrain tabbouleh in which the bulgur is softened in lemon juice rather than cooked. These recipes, like all the others in this appealing book, are guided by simplicity—further proof that humble ingredients produce the most amazing fare.

BakeWise: The Hows and Whys of Successful Baking
by Shirley O. Corriher
(Scribner, $40)

Here it is—the long-awaited follow-up to Corriher's award-winning book, *Cookwise*. And once again, Corriher, a food scientist and gifted teacher, walks you through each of her no-fail recipes, explaining all the hows and whys of cakes, pies, cookies, meringues, soufflés, and much more. Packed with more than 200 tempting recipes, this book will satisfy your curiosity as much as your sweet tooth—and make you a better baker to boot.

Eat Me: The Food and Philosophy of Kenny Shopsin
by Kenny Shopsin and Carolynn Carreño
(Alfred A. Knopf, $24.95)

Kenny Shopsin is the eccentric chef-owner of a legendary Greenwich Village diner, Shopsin's General Store. His mind-boggling book, like Shopsin himself, may not be to everyone's taste (profanity alert!), but it's a definitely a gem. In it, you'll find some 100 recipes as well as insightful advice on griddling pancakes, blending milk shakes, making burgers, and roasting turkey. And if you read Shopsin's rants closely, you might even discover the secrets to happiness.

The Paris Neighborhood Cookbook: Danyel Couet's Guide to the City's Ethnic Cuisines
by Danyel Couet
(Interlink Books, $35)

Most of us will never have the opportunity to explore the City of Lights as widely or know it as intimately as does award-winning restaurateur Danyel Couet, but losing yourself in this enchanting book is the next best thing. Here, Couet reveals the gastronomic secrets of Paris's ethnic neighborhoods through a tantalizing collection of recipes and photographs. The recipes are invitingly brief, and many of them—for example, the fragrant Punjabi Lentil Curry and the paprika and cumin-tinged Quick Couscous—are wonderfully simple. But the truth is, this is one of those books you needn't even cook from to thoroughly enjoy.

Kimberly Y. Masibay is a Fine Cooking *contributing editor.* ◆

Grapefruit

BY RUTH LIVELY

I love the zing of plain, unadulterated grapefruit for breakfast. But the juicy flesh and perfumed zest of this sweet-tart fruit add a real spark to all kinds of dishes, from salads and salsas to desserts.

Although you see it at grocery stores year-round, grapefruit tastes best (and is least expensive) at its peak, which is from early winter through spring. In the United States, grapefruit is grown in Florida and Texas (which provide the bulk of the winter crop), while California and Arizona produce most of the spring supply.

Picking the best

Grapefruit falls into two basic types, based on the color of the flesh: white and pink (which includes red). This flesh color is not an indication of sweetness, which is more attributed to the season—fruits picked early are sour, but the same variety will turn sweeter as the season progresses. Regardless of color, the varieties are all similar, with the main difference being the number (or lack) of seeds.

In the store, look for firm fruit that feels heavy for its size, with plump, glossy skin. Store it at room temperature for up to a week, or up to three weeks in the produce drawer of your refrigerator.

Flavor pairings

Grapefruit's refreshing, tart flavor makes it a superb companion to fish; it's also very good with chicken and pork. Spices that marry well with grapefruit include cardamom, nutmeg, cloves, and cinnamon; salt intensifies its sweetness. Fresh ginger and herbs such as mint, basil, tarragon, and rosemary are also good pairings. A surprisingly pleasant marriage comes with chile peppers, both hot and mild.

Grapefruit zest is bitterer than other citrus skin, so you may want to blanch it several times to tame the harshness before adding it to your recipe. And beware of the pith, which is intensely bitter (it's used to flavor tonic water). A twist of grapefruit zest makes a nice change from lemon or lime in drinks where a little bitterness is welcome.

Photos: Scott Phillips

Savory and sweet ideas for grapefruit

Savory

Grapefruit, cabbage, and avocado salad

For a perfect side dish with Mexican food or sweet-hot Asian barbecue, toss finely shredded cabbage with kosher salt, a little grapefruit juice, and thinly sliced jalapeño. Let sit about 30 minutes, until the cabbage is slightly wilted, and then top with grapefruit segments and avocado slices that have been drizzled with olive oil.

Sauce for fish

For a mild fish, add a little blanched grapefruit zest (see blanching directions under Candied Grapefruit Peel, below right) and a spoonful or two of juice to a beurre blanc (see FineCooking.com for a recipe). For an oily fish such as salmon, tuna, swordfish, or mackerel, try a punchier pan sauce of sautéed minced ginger and garlic, blanched grapefruit zest, and thinly sliced scallion, with soy sauce and grapefruit juice.

Tropical salsa

Stir together grapefruit sections, avocado, mango, chile peppers, lime and grapefruit juice, olive oil, and lots of chopped herbs (basil, cilantro, or mint). Use with fish, chicken, or simply for scooping up with bread or chips.

Sweet

Winter citrus compote

Make a simple syrup (equal parts sugar and water) infused with vanilla bean, lemon zest, and a little grapefruit zest. Poach whole kumquats in this syrup just until tender; then pour over grapefruit and orange segments (include some blood oranges if you can) and let steep until time to serve. Serve with a dollop of softly whipped cream or mascarpone and garnish with chopped candied grapefruit peel.

Salted grapefruit granita

Stir together 3 cups of fresh grapefruit juice, the juice of half a lemon, and a generous pinch of sea salt. Add a simple syrup made from ¾ cup each of sugar and water, and 2 Tbs. finely minced unblanched grapefruit zest. Freeze in a shallow container, stirring every 30 minutes or so to separate the ice crystals.

Candied grapefruit peel

Remove the peel in large sections from organic grapefruits. Trim away as much of the pith as you can. Blanch 5 times in simmering water (10 minutes at a time) and then scrape away any remaining pith. Cut the zest into strips, simmer in 2 parts sugar to 1 part water for about 45 minutes; let cool. Remove from the syrup, arrange on a lined baking sheet, and let dry overnight. The next day roll the strips in sugar and store in an airtight container. Use as a garnish for iced tea, lemonade, or cocktails, or chop and add to cake batter, fillings, frostings, salad dressing, pan sauces, braises, or stews.

Broiled Grapefruit with Honey, Vanilla & Cardamom

Serves four.

Grapefruit halves are a breakfast classic, but adding just a few intense flavorings and then broiling elevates them to a whole new level of deliciousness.

2 large grapefruit
2 Tbs. honey
1 tsp. pure vanilla extract
**Seeds of 1 cardamom pod, ground in a mortar
  (or a pinch of ground cardamom)**

Position an oven rack about 4 inches below the broiler and heat the broiler on high. With a serrated knife, cut the grapefruit in even halves. Using a small paring knife or a grapefruit knife, cut each section away from the surrounding membrane. Set the grapefruit halves in a shallow broiler-safe pan (such as an enameled baking dish or a heavy-duty rimmed baking sheet). If necessary, trim a thin slice off their bottoms so they sit level.

In a small bowl, stir together the honey and the vanilla extract. Drizzle the honey mixture over the grapefruit halves. Dust each with a bit of cardamom. Broil until bubbling and lightly browned in spots, 4 to 6 minutes. Remove from the oven and let cool slightly. Serve warm or at room temperature.

Ruth Lively trained at La Varenne in France and was senior editor at Kitchen Gardener. ◆

what's new

Shake, then strain

While they excel as hip accessories, cocktail shakers often fail when it comes to function. Not so this new FlipTop shaker from Metrokane. It has just two pieces, a double-wall stainless body and a black screw-on lid. With a finger push, you can open or close the top, and the built-in strainer means truly one-handed operation. Plus, it's dishwasher safe. The shaker is $30 at Winestuff.com.

Sharply beautiful

This is one pricey knife, but when you use it you'll see why. The 1893 series from German knife maker F. Dick features Damascus steel, hot-forged and patterned with a grain that lends the 33-layered stainless steel a depth of beauty. We liked the heft and balance of the 8-inch chef's knife, which made easy work of chopping onions, mincing herbs, and cutting root vegetables. The layered plastic handle looks like leather but is waterproof and nicely nonslip. The chef's knife is $340 at Greatknives.com.

Twice-as-nice ice cream

This double-bowl electric ice cream maker from Cuisinart appeals to our dual nature: The glutton in us likes the idea of making two flavors of ice cream at once; the portion-control freak likes the option of making one quart at a time. Both sides love how fast the Flavor Duo churns and freezes cream, milk, and sugar. In less than 20 minutes we had scoopable ice cream. A simple switch lets you choose whether to make one or two quarts of ice cream, and the nonstick coating on the bowls makes cleanup easy. The Flavor Duo from Cuisinart is $80 at Amazon.com.

Photos: Scott Phillips

A LITTLE INSPIRATION. A LOT OF INNOVATION.

MOKONA
THE ITALIAN ORIGINAL REINVENTED.

MOKONA EXEMPLIFIES BIALETTI'S TRADITION AND EXPERTISE IN ITALIAN ESPRESSO AND CAPPUCCINO. ITS PERSONAL AND ELEGANT SHAPE IS INSPIRED BY THE MOKA EXPRESS, THE ORIGINAL ITALIAN STOVETOP ESPRESSO MAKER – A TRUE ICON OF STYLE INVENTED BY BIALETTI IN 1933.

MOKONA'S INNOVATIVE BREWING SYSTEM CREATES PERFECT ITALIAN COFFEE VIA GROUNDS, CAPSULES OR PODS. THE PREMIUM BUILT-IN STEAMER PROVIDES OPTIMUM FROTHING FOR CAPPUCCINO OR BREWING DELICATE TEAS. TRUE TO ITS HERITAGE, THE WELL BUILT, EASY TO USE MOKONA INCLUDES CRITICAL PARTS THAT ARE MADE IN ITALY.

AVAILABLE AT BIALETTISHOP.COM

Dried and true

Drying fruits and vegetables is a space-saving way to preserve the season, but we've always been put off by tying up our oven for the long-time-at-low-heat process. This electric countertop dehydrator from Nesco/American Harvest is so hands-off it makes dehydrating easy (and even fun). The fan and heater fit compactly in the top of the unit. Hot air is forced horizontally across each tray, so you don't need to rotate trays and can dry beef jerky and apple slices at the same time, with no flavor-mingling. Nesco makes a line of dehydrators that range from $39 to $150. We tested the Snackmaster Pro, which comes with five drying trays and costs $80 at Nesco.com. Most models are expandable, meaning you can buy extra trays to handle more fruits, vegetables, and herbs—up to 30 trays on the largest models.

The freshest flour

Grinding your own flour is one of those kitchen tasks that sounds smart—it tastes fresher, has no additives, and is less expensive—but also arduous. This countertop electric mill from L'Equip takes all the intimidation out of the process. You pour whole grains into the top compartment, adjust a dial to deliver coarse- or fine-ground flour, and up to 20 cups fill the bottom bin—it's as simple as a giant coffee grinder, fast, and (with the cover on) not terribly loud. We loved how you could adjust the fineness of the milling: We poured in supermarket popcorn and dialed up fine cornmeal for muffins; then we switched to coarser cornmeal for pizza dough. And the Nutrimill goes beyond grains, milling rice and dried beans (split peas, soybeans, pinto, and mung). Best of all, it comes with a lifetime warranty, so you can mill to your heart's content. It costs $300; find a local or online dealer at Kitchenresource.com.

See this grain mill in action at finecooking.com/extras

Smarter toasting

We never thought we'd get excited about toast, but that changed when the Smart Toaster from Breville entered our kitchen. It has a groovy push-button control that lowers and lifts the bread as if on an elevator—no more spring-loaded levers that need to be forced or that send the toast airborne. A microchip delivers precise browning control and regulates a lift-and-look button, which lets you check the toast without canceling the cycle. In brushed stainless with a blue-background LED control panel, the Smart Toaster comes in two-slice ($130) and four-slice ($180) models at Brevilleusa.com.

The big squeeze

Juicers deliver the essence of fruits and vegetables

BY NICKI PENDLETON WOOD

Nothing can match the intense flavor of fresh juice, whether squeezed from a peach to make a Bellini or from a carrot to make a sauce reduction. But the world of countertop electric juicers is complex, with confusing jargon (designs include centrifugal, pulp ejection, and masticating), different functions (some can't handle grasses or leafy greens), and a wide range in price ($50 to more than $2,200).

We set out to identify the type of juicer most useful for the cook in producing beverage-quality juices as well as vegetable and fruit extractions for reduction sauces, sorbets, and cold soups. Centrifugal juicers ended up being the best all-around choice for almost any fruit or vegetable and for getting the job done easily and quickly.

After narrowing the field, we tested 13 centrifugal juicers, both with and without pulp ejection (see "How centrifugal juicers work," below). All the juicers we tested produced juice efficiently from vegetables, fruit, and greens. Our top five choices boasted features and functionality that lifted them above the competition.

How centrifugal juicers work

Think of these juicers as a washing machine on the spin cycle. The vegetable or fruit is pushed against a rotating grater disk and shredded to a pulp. This pulp falls into a basket, spins at high speed, and centrifugal force throws the pulp against a basket screen, straining out the juice. The pulp builds up in the basket, which needs to be emptied after every half-dozen fruits or vegetables.

Centrifugal juicers that have a pulp ejection feature discharge the pulp into a separate container, so you can juice continuously without having to stop and empty the basket. But the pulp bin adds to the juicer's size and is an additional item to wash.

What to look for

❖ If space is an issue, choose a centrifugal juicer without pulp ejection, as these machines tend to be smaller.

❖ If you expect to juice large amounts of fruits or vegetables, get a model with pulp ejection.

❖ Steel construction is preferable over plastic, for both sturdiness and stain resistance.

❖ The width of the feed chute will determine how much chopping you need to do.

❖ Warranties range from 90 days to 15 years. If you're planning to use your juicer often, it makes sense to spend more for more coverage.

Juicers: top picks

Breville Juice Fountain Elite

$290, Chefcentral.com
Pulp ejection: Yes

With die-cast steel construction, a generous 3-inch feed tube, superior juicing performance, and sleek good looks, the Juice Fountain lives up to its name. Feed in the produce and a torrent of juice with only a trace of pulp pours from the spout. The Breville has two speeds: low for juicing soft fruits and greens, and high for hard foods. It comes with a one-year warranty and carries an additional three-year warranty on the motor.

Omega O2

$100, Juicersforless.com
Pulp ejection: Yes

Most pulp-ejection juicers take up a lot of space because of the pulp bin, but the Omega O2 has been designed to produce just a few servings of juice. It proved to be our favorite among the smaller juicers because it performed well in a compact space. The feed tube is 2½ inches wide, requiring you to cut up most produce. The O2 juices hard food beautifully and extracts juice from soft foods well, though it didn't produce as much juice from leafy greens as the other units tested. It comes with a five-year warranty. If you'll be juicing just two or three servings at a time, the O2 will likely provide enough juicing power and capacity, in a compact unit.

How we tested

❖ We juiced apples, beets, carrots, and ginger to assess how each machine's motor handled hard fruits and vegetables. We wanted maximum juice extraction with minimal noise and vibration.

❖ Soft foods can be a challenge for some juicers, which spin the food so fast that it is slung, unjuiced, into the pulp bin. We juiced peeled watermelon and sliced, pitted peaches, looking for relatively dry pulp, which indicates that the maximum amount of juice has been extracted.

❖ We juiced large leaves of kale, which typically are more difficult to juice than hard food because of the supple texture.

❖ Each machine was rated for ease of assembly and use, including cleanup.

L'Equip XL 215

$140, Harvestessentials.com
Pulp ejection: Yes

The L'Equip is a good mid-range juicer made affordable by plastic parts. The 3-inch feed tube gives just enough extra room that you can juice small apples and beets without cutting them first, saving on prep time. It performed well on hard and soft foods and extracted a surprising amount of juice from leafy greens. The food pusher comes with a locking safety feature to prevent items that are too large from going down the feed tube, but we found it didn't work well, instead stopping food halfway down the chute. The L'Equip comes with a six-year warranty on the motor and one-year warranty on the blade.

Omega 1000

$200, Cookware.com
Pulp ejection: No

This Omega model and the Waring Pro (at right) are nearly identical, except that this one has a plastic top and a slightly larger feed tube, at 2½ inches. Both have commercial-grade construction and powerful but quiet motors. Be sure to buy the paper basket liners that both Waring and Omega offer. When the basket is ready for cleaning, just lift out the liner and the pulp comes with it. The result is easier cleanup and pulp-free juice. It comes with an impressive 10-year warranty.

Waring Pro Juicing Center

$260, Lowes.com
Pulp ejection: No

A sturdily constructed juicer, the Waring is powerful yet quieter than the other juicers. It has a particularly narrow feed tube of only 2 inches, so apples, beets, and even large carrots must be cut into pieces before juicing. It's one of the largest juicers we tested and not as intuitive to use as the others (we had to reread the manual to figure out how to remove the basket). This model comes with a citrus press attachment, so you can juice oranges and lemons without peeling. It has a five-year motor warranty.

Nicki Pendleton Wood is a cook-book editor who lives in Nashville, Tennessee. ◆

See how these juicers work at
finecooking.com/extras

Start Your Party

Three new ideas for pre-dinner drinks

BY TIM GAISER

This year, it's time to move beyond bubbly. There are lots of festive apéritif options other than Champagne, so why not give one of these suggestions a try? Cheers to a new holiday drink.

VERMOUTH

Vermouth may be best known as an ingredient in that quintessential cocktail, the martini. But several high-quality vermouths are excellent sipped solo. Essentially an "aromatized" wine (a wine that has been fortified to around 18% alcohol with the addition of a neutral spirit and then infused with aromatic herbs), vermouth can be either dry or sweet. The **Noilly Pratt Dry** ($10) from France is one of the finest dry vermouths, with a balance of citrus and herbal notes and a pleasant, crisp acidity. For a good sweet vermouth, try **Carpano Antica** ($25 for a liter). Modeled after Carpano's original 18th-century recipe, it offers a seamless balance of bittersweet fruit flavors and spicy vanilla. Also worth seeking out is a relative newcomer from California, **Vya Sweet Vermouth** ($18), a delicious blend of spicy citrus and bitter herb flavors.

Regardless of style, serve vermouth chilled in a martini glass with a lemon twist or in an old-fashioned glass over ice with a slice of orange.

DRY MADEIRA

Though not much of a tradition in the United States, sipping dry Madeira as an apéritif has long been a ritual in many parts of Europe. Like sherry, Madeira is a fortified wine made in both dry and sweet styles, though arguably, the best apéritif Madeiras are dry versions, such as Sercial and Verdehlo. While both are known for their rich, nutty flavor, smooth texture, and tart acidity, Madeiras made from the Sercial grape are lighter and more citrusy, while Verdehlo versions tend to be richer and fuller in body. Look for either **Leacock's 5-Year Sercial** ($20) or **Blandy's 5-Year-Old Verdehlo** ($18). Serve chilled in a white wine glass.

PASTIS

The original pastis, a French anise-flavored liqueur, was once known as absinthe. This much-maligned spirit, referred to as "the green fairy" because of its color, contained wormwood, a hallucinogenic plant once believed to be highly addictive. When absinthe was banned in most of Europe and the U.S. in 1915, French absinthe distillers Pernod and Ricard concocted milder versions without wormwood and with much less alcohol, creating what we know today as pastis. The intense licorice and citrus flavors of pastis are best enjoyed over ice with a splash of water, which makes the liqueur appear characteristically cloudy. **Pernod Liqueur d'Anis** ($30) and **Ricard Pastis de Marseille** ($30) are both excellent, as is the American **Herbsaint Liqueur d'Anis** ($21).

Tim Gaiser is a contributing editor and a master sommelier.

Holiday in a Glass

Classic cold-weather cocktails—think hot buttered rum,
light and airy eggnog, and spicy mulled wine—get flavor updates

BY ALLISON EHRI KREITLER

Have you ever been to a holiday party where the host hands you a steaming mug of hot buttered rum topped with a spoonful of whipped cream as you walk in the door? It really sets the tone for a festive celebration. These modern takes on traditional cocktail recipes will do the same for your winter get-togethers.

Triple-Shot Eggnog

Yields about 6 cups; serves eight.

In this version of the holiday classic, three traditional spirits come together for a cocktail with a kick. Whisking frothy beaten egg whites into the eggnog base makes for a much lighter and less cloying drink than those found in containers at the supermarket.

3 large eggs, preferably pasteurized, separated
½ cup granulated sugar
Kosher salt
½ cup dark rum
¼ cup bourbon
2 Tbs. brandy
2 cups whole milk
1 cup heavy cream
½ tsp. freshly grated nutmeg, plus extra for garnish
½ tsp. pure vanilla extract

Whisk the egg yolks in a large bowl until they just begin to turn a lighter shade of yellow. Add the sugar and a pinch of salt and whisk until thick and pale yellow. Whisk in the rum, bourbon, and brandy until well combined and then whisk in the milk, cream, nutmeg, and vanilla until blended. Chill the mixture, covered, for 4 hours or overnight. Keep the egg whites chilled separately in a medium bowl.

Before serving, whip the egg whites to stiff peaks with a hand-held electric mixer. Fold the whipped egg whites into the chilled yolk mixture. Serve immediately, sprinkled with a little freshly grated nutmeg, or chill for up to 4 hours. Whisk the eggnog until smooth before serving.

Note: The risk of salmonella infection from consuming raw eggs is very low—only about 1 in 20,000 is contaminated—but you can eliminate the risk entirely by using pasteurized eggs.

Hot Buttered Rum

Yields about ³/₄ cup butter, enough for 10 to 12 drinks.

Dark brown sugar and a dollop of whipped cream give this buttered rum a deep, rich flavor. The trick to this recipe is to use the best-quality rum you can find. The spiced butter is also delicious spread onto fresh, crusty bread.

¾ cup lightly packed dark brown sugar
½ cup (8 Tbs.) unsalted butter, at room temperature
1 tsp. pure vanilla extract
½ tsp. ground cinnamon
¼ tsp. ground cloves
¼ tsp. freshly grated nutmeg
¼ tsp. ground allspice
2½ to 3 cups high-quality dark rum, preferably Gosling's
Whipped heavy cream for garnish

In a small bowl, mash the sugar, butter, vanilla, cinnamon, cloves, nutmeg, and allspice with a fork until well combined. The spiced butter can be made ahead and refrigerated for up to 3 weeks. Bring the butter to room temperature before using.

Bring a kettle of water to a boil; you'll need ½ cup of water for each drink. Fill mugs or heat-proof glasses with hot tap water to warm them. Once the water in the kettle boils, empty the warm mugs and fill each with ½ cup boiling water and ¼ cup rum. Stir a generous tablespoon of the spiced butter into each mug until melted. Garnish with a small dollop of whipped cream.

Orange-Scented Mulled Wine

Yields about 6 cups; serves eight.

This traditional cold-weather drink is just what its name implies (to mull means to warm and spice): wine, usually red, infused with sugar, citrus, and spices, served warm. A seasonal clementine adds a sweet fruit note.

10 cloves
Three 3-inch cinnamon sticks
2 star anise
1 whole nutmeg, cracked with the side of a chef's knife into a few pieces
1 tsp. coriander seeds
½ tsp. whole black peppercorns
Two 750-ml bottles or one 1.5-liter bottle medium- to full-bodied fruity red wine, such as Merlot, Shiraz, or Zinfandel
1 clementine or tangerine, washed and cut in half crosswise (seeded if necessary)
⅓ cup granulated sugar; more to taste
¼ cup brandy
1 Tbs. Grand Marnier (optional)
½ tsp. pure vanilla extract

Toast the cloves, cinnamon, star anise, nutmeg, coriander, and peppercorns in a medium (4-quart) saucepan over medium heat, stirring occasionally, until aromatic, 1 to 2 minutes. Transfer the spices to a 6x6-inch piece of cheesecloth and set the pan aside to cool slightly. Gather the corners of the cheesecloth and tie with butcher's twine to make a sachet.

Put the wine, clementine, and sugar in the slightly cooled pan along with the sachet. Heat the wine mixture uncovered over low heat for 1 hour to infuse it with the spices. Do not let the mixture boil.

Using a pair of tongs, gently and carefully squeeze the juice from the clementine or tangerine into the wine mixture. Discard the juiced citrus halves and the sachet. Stir the brandy, Grand Marnier (if using), and vanilla into the wine and taste. Add more sugar if needed—use just enough to smooth out the flavors but not so much that it actually tastes sweet. Serve hot.

Make ahead note: If you want to infuse the wine a day before serving it, go right ahead. Just make sure to remove the spice sachet before storing it for the night. Gently reheat the wine in a medium pot over low heat and then add the brandy, Grand Marnier, and vanilla.

Allison Ehri Kreitler is Fine Cooking's *assistant test kitchen manager.* ◆

Grinding spices with salt

I love the burst of flavor that comes from freshly ground spices, and the best way to achieve this is with a heavy mortar and pestle *and* a pinch of kosher salt. Instead of popping out of the mortar, cardamom pods and coriander seeds, for instance, are quickly reduced to a powder by the sharp edges of the salt crystals. I simply reduce the salt in the recipe by a pinch and proceed with my fragrant ground spice and salt mixture. This method also works wonders with garlic and citrus zest.

—*Ann Huber, West Lafayette, Indiana*

No-mess whipped cream

When whipping heavy cream with my hand mixer, some of the cream always splatters onto the counter (and me). The solution? I set the bowl in my sink and whip away. A rubber mat underneath protects the sink, and any splatters hit the sink walls and are easily rinsed away. Best of all, my clothes and countertops stay clean. This is also great for beating in dry ingredients like flour when making cakes or cookies.

—*Nancy Adams,*
Hancock, New Hampshire

Trimming with kitchen scissors

I was recently making the Grilled Five-Spice Chicken Thighs from *Fine Cooking* #87, and instead of using a knife to trim the thighs, or trying to pull off the slippery fat with my fingers, I used my kitchen scissors. They worked perfectly, gripping and cutting the chicken with ease; scissors would also work for trimming meat and fish.

—*Barb Driewer, York, Nebraska*

Spin cycle

The key to a great salad, in my opinion, is to dry washed salad greens completely before tossing them with vinaigrette. But my salad spinner rarely does the job to my satisfaction. Now I add a paper towel to the basket of the spinner along with the greens. The towel efficiently absorbs the excess moisture, and it's easy to spin until dry.

—*Robert Galford,*
Concord, Massachusetts

**THE PRIZE FOR
THIS ISSUE'S WINNER:**
Swiss Diamond wok/saucepan;
retail value, $190.

Easy onion soup cleanup

I love making Molly Stevens's French Onion Soup from *Fine Cooking* #47, but I always dreaded the heavy-duty cleaning job required to remove the crusted cheese from my soup crocks. I've started lightly greasing the inside of the crocks with olive oil before adding the soup, and now cleanup is a breeze. No scrubbing required.

—*Judy McBride, Harlingen, Texas*

Toasting ahead

To save time and get ready for my holiday baking, I like to toast large batches of nuts and store them in the freezer. They keep for up to three months, and all I have to do is measure out the amount I need and let the nuts come to room temperature before adding them to my recipe.

—*Karen Tannenbaum, Rhinebeck, New York*

Hold the anchovies

One day, in the midst of a Caesar salad craving, I realized that we were out of anchovies for the dressing. As I scoured my refrigerator for a substitute, I spied a bottle of fish sauce, and voilà! A few drops of the fish sauce, which is made from fermented anchovies, made a fabulous Caesar dressing, and my craving was satisfied.

—*Rosemary Love, North Vancouver, British Columbia*

Olive oil on hand

I tend to buy olive oil for cooking in large containers, but they are too heavy and unwieldy to pour from every day. I used to decant the oil into a smaller glass bottle, but recently I discovered that pouring the oil into a small plastic squeeze bottle works best of all. It's light and easy to handle and is great for filling a measuring spoon worth of oil without spills, coating a piece of parchment, or drizzling oil over food before or after cooking. When I'm not using the squeeze bottle, I store it in a cool, dark place to prolong the shelf life of the oil.

—*Susan Evans, Martha's Vineyard, Massachusetts*

Creative potato ricer

I adore potatoes, especially when mashed or in gnocchi. But due to limited kitchen space, I don't have room for a potato ricer. Instead, I press cooked potatoes through a small-holed colander with a rubber spatula with very satisfactory results.

—*Jennifer Charlton, Fountain Valley, California*

TOO GOOD TO FORGET
From *Fine Cooking* #20

Cut a cake in small portions

At a dessert party, guests may wish to sample many tarts and cakes, so they may want only a small serving of each. A good way to deal with this is a traditional Scandinavian technique: Cut a cylinder from the center of a round cake, using a small pot lid or saucer as a guide. Cut the outside ring into wedges about 1½ inches wide. When the outside of the cake is gone, you're left with a smaller round cake for tea time, another use, or more small pieces.

—*Lilia Dvarionas, Kanata, Ontario* ◆

FORGET LAST NIGHT'S WINE. YOU PROBABLY ALREADY DID.

Forgettable wines are so yesterday. For something a little bolder, pour yourself some Ravenswood. Our wines are complex, vivid and expressive. And above all, memorable.

RAVENSWOOD
NO WIMPY WINES

RAVENS
WOOD

Open House for a Crowd

The big buffet: It's as easy as two do-ahead mains and a grab bag of sides

BY KATE HAYS

Yes, you can pull off this impressive buffet for 24, featuring a slow-roasted ham, salmon, and crowd-pleasing favorites like biscuits, broccoli, and potatoes.

I f you're cooking for a crowd, I have three words of advice: open house buffet. Give guests a window of time to drop by, start with a festive cocktail, and fill your biggest table with scrumptious dishes that are mostly make-ahead. The result is an elegant yet low-key party that takes the stress out of entertaining.

As a party pro, I've developed a foolproof strategy for building a crowd-friendly buffet. I always suggest that people start with a couple of main dishes that taste great at room temperature, supplement them with simple side dishes, and then fill out the table with store-bought extras that you arrange on your own serving dishes. Festive yet relaxed, this buffet allows you to leave the kitchen and enjoy your own party.

Buffet for 24

PEAR SIDECAR

BOURBON-ORANGE-GLAZED HAM

PINEAPPLE-BOURBON CHUTNEY

HERB-BUTTERMILK-MARINATED SALMON WITH CUCUMBER SALAD

ROASTED FINGERLING POTATOES

BROCCOLI WITH SPICY GREMOLATA

Filling out the buffet

SPICED OR CANDIED MIXED NUTS*
Cashews, almonds, walnuts, hazelnuts

CRUDITÉ PLATTER
Baby and heirloom varieties of carrots, celery, green beans, cucumbers, and radishes served with a buttermilk and fresh herb dip*

BISCUITS*
Offer ham sandwiches with orange-maple mustard and horseradish cream (recipes on p. 50)

CHEESE PLATE
Camembert, Roquefort, fresh chèvre, Parmigiano-Reggiano, and other varieties along with fresh figs, grapes, dried apricots, and fig-almond cake

DESSERT
Make it easy on yourself by letting guests contribute cookies and other bite-size sweets

Wine suggestions

A vibrant Sauvignon Blanc with citrus and herb notes, like the 2006 Geyser Peak, California ($10) and a robust, youthful Zinfandel, like the Rosenblum Vintner's Cuvée XXX, California ($11)

*Visit FineCooking.com for recipes

Pear Sidecar

Serves two.

½ cup pear brandy
(like Poire Williams)
¼ cup triple sec
(like Cointreau)
2 Tbs. fresh lime juice
2 thin strips lime zest

Combine the brandy, triple sec, and lime juice in a cocktail shaker and fill with ice. Shake well and strain into two chilled martini glasses. Twist the lime zest into spirals and drop one in each glass.

Bourbon-Orange-Glazed Ham

Serves twenty-four.

¾ cups high-quality orange marmalade
¼ cup pure maple syrup
¼ cup whole-grain mustard
¼ cup bourbon or dark rum
2 Tbs. fresh lemon juice
Kosher salt and freshly ground black pepper
1 smoked half-ham, preferably a bone-in butt half (8 to 9 lb.), trimmed of skin and excess fat

In a medium bowl, mix the marmalade, maple syrup, mustard, bourbon or rum, and lemon juice. Season to taste with salt and pepper.

Position a rack in the lower third of the oven and heat the oven to 325°F. Brush the ham all over with ½ cup of the glaze and wrap loosely in foil. Put it on a large rimmed baking sheet and bake until an instant-read thermometer inserted into the center of the ham registers 125°F, 17 to 19 minutes per pound, for a total of 2¼ to 2¾ hours. (The ham will continue to rise in temperature during the glazing and resting.) Remove the ham from the oven and raise the oven temperature to 425°F. Peel back the foil from the top and sides of the ham; brush the ham with 6 Tbs. of the glaze and return it to the oven. Bake, brushing the ham again after 5 and then 10 minutes, using 6 Tbs. more glaze each time, until the glaze is shiny and golden, about 20 minutes total (keep a close eye on the ham so that the glaze doesn't burn).

Remove the ham from the oven and tent loosely with foil. Let rest at least 20 minutes and up to 2 hours before slicing.

SANDWICH FIXINGS

The glazed ham here also makes great sandwiches. To give your guests that option, add biscuits (store-bought are fine) and these two spreads to the buffet.

Horseradish cream

Mix 2 cups sour cream with ½ cup prepared horseradish (or very finely grated fresh horseradish), 2 tsp. white vinegar, ½ tsp. kosher salt, and ⅛ tsp. freshly ground black pepper. Add more horseradish, salt, or pepper to taste. Refrigerate until serving. Can be made up to 3 days ahead.

Orange-maple mustard

Reserve 3 Tbs. of the marmalade mixture from the Bourbon-Orange-Glazed Ham recipe and mix with 1 cup of grainy mustard.

Pineapple-Bourbon Chutney

Yields about 3 cups.

This sweet-tangy condiment provides a wonderful balance to bites of smoky ham, and it's also delightful on its own.

1 fresh pineapple, peeled, cored, and diced (about 4 cups)
1 large yellow onion, chopped (about 1½ cups)
1 cup packed light brown sugar
¾ cup apple cider vinegar
¼ cup bourbon or dark rum
3 Tbs. finely chopped fresh ginger
1 Tbs. lightly packed finely grated lemon zest
1 Tbs. fresh lemon juice
½ tsp. ground cloves
Kosher salt and freshly ground black pepper

In a 4-quart saucepan over medium-high heat, combine all the ingredients with ¼ tsp. salt and a few grinds of pepper. Bring to a boil and reduce the heat to low. Simmer, stirring occasionally, until most of the liquid has evaporated, about 1¼ hours. Add more salt and pepper to taste.

Make ahead: Can be made up to 3 days ahead and stored in the refrigerator.

Herb-Buttermilk-Marinated Salmon with Cucumber Salad

Serves twenty-four.

The salmon is delicious either warm or at room temperature.

FOR THE SALMON:
2 cups buttermilk
½ cup lightly packed fresh basil leaves, coarsely chopped
½ cup lightly packed fresh cilantro leaves, coarsely chopped
½ cup thinly sliced scallions (about 6 medium scallions)
¼ cup white vinegar
2 Tbs. honey
1 Tbs. ground ginger
Kosher salt and freshly ground black pepper
2 sides of salmon (3 lb. each), skin and pin bones removed

FOR THE CUCUMBER SALAD:
3 large English cucumbers, cut in half lengthwise, seeded, and sliced crosswise (about 9½ cups)
1 large red onion, cut in half and thinly sliced (about 2 cups)
1 cup pitted Kalamata olives, cut in half
1 cup crumbled feta cheese
Kosher salt and freshly ground black pepper

Get a head start

UP TO 3 DAYS AHEAD
❖ Make the chutney and horseradish cream
❖ Position the buffet table and set with linens, serving platters, utensils, and decorations (candles, flower vases)

4 HOURS BEFORE GUESTS ARRIVE
❖ Bake the ham
❖ Mix the orange-maple mustard

3 HOURS BEFORE
❖ Make the buttermilk marinade and prep the ingredients for the cucumber salad; refrigerate
❖ Cook the broccoli and prep the gremolata ingredients

1½ HOURS BEFORE
❖ Roast the potatoes

1 HOUR BEFORE
❖ Marinate the salmon

½ HOUR BEFORE
❖ Roast the salmon

JUST BEFORE SERVING
❖ Salt and dress the cucumber salad
❖ Mix the gremolata with the broccoli
❖ Slice the ham
❖ Platter the salmon

Broccoli with
Spicy Gremolata

Bourbon-Orange-Glazed Ham

Roasted Fingerling Potatoes

Cucumber Salad

Marinate and roast the salmon: In a food processor, combine the buttermilk, basil, cilantro, scallions, vinegar, honey, ginger, 1 tsp. salt, and 1/8 tsp. pepper. Process until smooth, about 30 seconds. Set aside 3/4 cup for the salad.

Thirty minutes before roasting the salmon, pour the remaining marinade over the salmon in a large rimmed dish and let sit at room temperature. (For the best texture, don't marinate longer than 30 minutes.)

While the salmon is marinating, position a rack in the center of the oven and heat the oven to 400°F. Line a large rimmed baking sheet with foil. When ready to roast the salmon, remove it from the marinade and set on the baking sheet. Bake until just firm to the touch and opaque in the center (use a paring knife to peek), 20 to 25 minutes. Remove from the oven and let rest in the pan for 10 minutes.

Make the salad: In a medium bowl, mix the cucumbers, onion, olives, cheese, and 1 1/2 tsp. salt. Toss with the reserved buttermilk dressing and season to taste with more salt and pepper.

Serve: Use two large spatulas to carefully move the salmon to a platter. Spoon some of the cucumber salad around the salmon and serve the rest in a bowl on the side.

Make ahead: Prep the cucumber salad up to 3 hours ahead, but do not add the salt or dressing until just before serving.

Roasted Fingerling Potatoes

Serves twenty-four.

If you have trouble finding fingerling potatoes, you can substitute baby red-skin potatoes; just cut any large ones in half.

8 lb. small fingerling potatoes, washed and scrubbed, skin on
3/4 cup extra-virgin olive oil
Fine sea salt and freshly ground black pepper
6 Tbs. thinly sliced chives
1/4 cup white truffle oil (optional)

Position racks in the top and bottom thirds of the oven and heat the oven to 425°F. Put two large rimmed baking sheets in the hot oven. In a large bowl, toss the potatoes, olive oil, 1 1/2 tsp. salt, and several grinds of pepper. When the pans are hot, divide the potatoes between the pans in a snug single layer (they should sizzle). Roast for 20 minutes, stirring occasionally, and then rotate the pans. Continue to roast, stirring occasionally, until

they are browned in spots and tender when pierced with a fork, about 40 minutes longer. Return the potatoes to the large bowl, add the chives and truffle oil, if using, and toss. Season to taste with more salt and pepper and pour onto a serving platter (make sure to pour all the oil in the bowl over the potatoes). Keep warm until ready to serve.

Broccoli with Spicy Gremolata

Serves twenty-four.

Traditional gremolata (garlic, parsley, and lemon zest) is given a spicy twist with the addition of crushed red pepper flakes.

1 cup chopped fresh flat-leaf parsley
1/2 cup extra-virgin olive oil
1/2 cup fresh lemon juice
3 Tbs. finely grated lemon zest
1 Tbs. minced garlic
1 tsp. crushed red pepper flakes; more to taste
Kosher salt and freshly ground black pepper
6 lb. fresh broccoli, trimmed and cut into 1/2-inch florets

In a large bowl, combine the parsley, olive oil, lemon juice, zest, garlic, pepper flakes, 1/2 tsp. salt, and a few grinds of pepper.

Bring a large pot of well-salted water to a boil over high heat. Add half of the broccoli and cook until crisp-tender, about 2 minutes. With a slotted spoon or strainer, transfer the broccoli to a colander, rinse with cold water to stop the cooking, and drain again. Repeat with the remaining broccoli. Add the broccoli to the gremolata and toss to combine. Season to taste with salt and pepper and transfer to a serving bowl.

Make ahead: You can prep the gremolata ingredients and cook the broccoli up to 3 hours ahead. Do not mix the gremolata or combine it with the broccoli until just before serving, as the lemon juice will eventually cause the broccoli and parsley to turn a dull green.

Kate Hays is chef-owner of Dish Catering in Shelburne, Vermont. ◆

Find an audio slide show that will walk you through building a holiday buffet at **finecooking.com/extras**

Building the buffet

❖ START BY CHOOSING A TABLE. A 6- or 8-foot dining table is a good choice, but you can also push two square tables together or set up two separate round tables.

❖ PULL THE TABLE AWAY FROM THE WALL so guests can serve themselves from both sides. Don't put the buffet near the front door or you'll create a bottleneck with arriving and departing guests.

❖ STRATEGIZE HOW TO FIT ALL THE FOOD by putting out empty serving dishes labeled with what they will hold.

❖ STACK PLATES ON ONE END of the buffet, but put drinks and glasses on a separate table. Guests can't serve themselves while juggling a plate and a glass.

❖ OFFER SILVERWARE AT THE BEGINNING OR END of the buffet table. It's nice to roll it in a napkin, which makes it easier to manage while carrying a full plate.

❖ ELEVATE SOME DISHES with cake stands or books stacked under a tablecloth. This creates more room on the table and keeps the overall spread from looking flat.

❖ TWO SERVING UTENSILS for each dish will keep the buffet line moving.

❖ POSITION CANDLES AND FLOWERS where they can't be knocked over.

Flaky cheese biscuits

Crudités with buttermilk-herb dip

Cheese and fruit platter

Spiced mixed nuts

dinner
with
friends

The one party menu you need for any night of the season

BY HEIDI JOHANNSEN STEWART

In a month filled with big celebrations (like the other two in this party guide), it can be easy to forget the simple pleasures of having a few friends over for dinner. This hearty, fireside supper is a good reminder. It's easy to pull together and packed with do-ahead tips (the main course gets even better if it spends a couple of days in the fridge). And it's a great excuse to pause, enjoy the season with your favorite people, and cook up some memories.

It's not a party without
something good to drink.
For suggestions, see p. 59.

Chicken, Lemon & Olive Stew

Serves ten to twelve.

Warm, earthy spices infuse this savory stew, and olives and lemon add brightness. It's perfect for casual entertaining because it tastes even better a day or two after it's made.

6 lb. boneless, skinless chicken thighs (about 25 thighs), trimmed of excess fat
Kosher salt and freshly ground black pepper
¼ cup extra-virgin olive oil
3 large yellow onions, thinly sliced
8 cloves garlic, crushed and peeled
1 Tbs. ground turmeric
2 tsp. ground cumin
2 tsp. ground coriander
3 small dried red chiles, preferably chile de Arbol, stemmed and crumbled
Two 3-inch cinnamon sticks
2 fresh bay leaves or 1 dried
1 quart lower-salt chicken broth
Finely grated zest and juice of 4 lemons
2 cups canned chickpeas, rinsed and drained
2 cups small pitted green olives, such as picholine or manzanilla
Saffron Couscous (see recipe at right)
3 Tbs. chopped fresh cilantro or mint

Season the chicken all over with 2 tsp. salt and 2 tsp. pepper. Heat the oil in an 8-quart Dutch oven over medium-high heat. Working in batches so as not to crowd the pan, brown the chicken well all over, about 3 minutes per side, transferring each batch to a plate or bowl—it'll take about 4 batches and 24 minutes total to brown all the chicken. The bottom of the pan will be brown, but that's OK.

Reduce the heat to medium, add the onions and garlic and cook, stirring occasionally until the onions are softened and golden brown, 5 to 6 minutes. Add the turmeric, cumin, coriander, chiles, cinnamon sticks, and bay leaves and cook, stirring constantly, until fragrant, about 1 minute more. Add the chicken broth, lemon zest, and ½ cup of the lemon juice. Cover and simmer over medium-low heat for 30 minutes.

Return the chicken and any accumulated juices to the pot. Carefully stir in the chickpeas and olives. Increase the heat to medium high and simmer uncovered, stirring occasionally, until the sauce has thickened somewhat and the chicken is cooked through, 6 to 8 minutes more. Stir in 1 Tbs. of the remaining lemon juice and season to taste with salt and pepper. Serve over the Saffron Couscous, sprinkled with the cilantro or mint.

Make ahead: This stew can be prepared and refrigerated up to 3 days ahead or frozen up to 1 month in advance. Reheat gently over medium-low heat, adding ½ cup water if the stew seems too thick.

Saffron Couscous

Serves ten to twelve.

Baking the couscous helps it cook evenly and frees up your stovetop too.

3 cups (1½ lb.) couscous
3 cups lower-salt chicken broth
4 Tbs. unsalted butter
½ tsp. saffron threads, crumbled
Kosher salt
¼ cup extra-virgin olive oil

Position a rack in the center of the oven and heat the oven to 350°F. Put the couscous in a 9x13-inch baking dish; set aside.

In a small saucepan, heat the chicken broth, butter, saffron, and 1 tsp. salt over medium-high heat until the butter is melted and the broth is hot. Pour the mixture over the couscous and mix well.

Cover the baking dish with foil and bake until the liquid has been absorbed by the couscous, 10 to 12 minutes. Let sit at room temperature, covered, for 5 minutes. Drizzle the olive oil over the couscous. Using a fork or your fingers, gently mix to coat the couscous in oil and break apart any clumps. Transfer to a serving dish. If not serving immediately, loosely cover the dish and keep warm for up to 30 minutes.

Easy Dinner for 12

Chicken, Lemon & Olive Stew

Saffron Couscous

Arugula, Carrot & Celery Root Salad with Almonds

Ginger Crème Brûlée

Arugula, Carrot & Celery Root Salad with Almonds

Serves ten to twelve.

This salad has everything going for it—spicy arugula, sweet grated carrots and celery root, crunchy almonds—all topped off with a vibrant honey-mustard vinaigrette.

2 Tbs. apple cider vinegar
2 Tbs. honey
1 tsp. Dijon mustard
6 Tbs. extra-virgin olive oil
Kosher salt and freshly ground black pepper
6 medium carrots (1 lb.)
1 medium celery root (¾ to 1 lb.)
6 lightly packed cups baby arugula (about 6 oz.)
¾ cup sliced almonds, toasted
⅓ cup chopped fresh cilantro

In a small bowl, whisk the vinegar, honey, and mustard. Whisk in the oil and season with ½ tsp. salt and a few grinds of pepper.

Peel and trim the carrots and celery root and then grate them in a food processor fitted with a medium grating disk. Transfer to a large bowl. Add the arugula, half of the almonds and half of the cilantro; toss with the vinaigrette. Season to taste with salt and pepper. Sprinkle with the remaining almonds and cilantro and serve.

Make ahead: You can make the dressing and prep the almonds and arugula up to a day ahead. Grate the carrots and chop the cilantro an hour or two ahead, but grate the celery root shortly before serving, as it may oxidize and turn brown if done earlier.

Ginger Crème Brûlée

Serves twelve.

Rich and creamy, these gingery custards can be prepared and baked a day or two ahead, but wait until you're ready to serve them to caramelize the sugar topping. You'll need a mini blowtorch for this step; see Where To Buy It on p. 104.

4 cups heavy cream
¼ cup plus 2 Tbs. minced fresh ginger
¾ cup plus 2 Tbs. granulated sugar
1 Tbs. pure vanilla extract
¼ tsp. table salt
10 large egg yolks

Put the cream, ginger, ¼ cup of the sugar, the vanilla, and salt in a medium saucepan and bring to a simmer over medium-high heat, stirring until the sugar dissolves. Cover, remove from the heat, and steep for 20 minutes.

Position a rack in the center of the oven and heat the oven to 350°F. Bring a kettle of water to a boil. Put twelve 4-oz. ramekins or teacups in a roasting pan or baking dish that's at least as deep as the ramekins.

In a medium bowl, whisk the yolks and ¼ cup of the sugar until smooth and combined. Lightly whisk about ½ cup of the warm cream mixture into the yolk mixture and then gradually whisk in the remaining cream mixture. Stir rather than whip with the whisk—you don't want a frothy mixture, or the baked custards will have a foamy-looking surface. Strain the mixture through a fine sieve into a large Pyrex measuring cup or a heatproof bowl with a spout.

Divide the custard among the ramekins. Slowly pour hot water from the kettle into the baking pan (don't get any water in the ramekins) until it comes about two-thirds of the way up the sides of the ramekins. Carefully transfer the pan to the oven and bake until the custards are set around the edges but still slightly jiggly (like Jell-O) in the center, 30 to 35 minutes. Transfer the ramekins to a cooling rack and let cool at room temperature for 30 minutes. Then refrigerate the custards uncovered. Once the custards are refrigerator-cold, wrap each ramekin with plastic wrap. Refrigerate for at least 3 hours or up to 2 days before proceeding.

To serve, sprinkle 1½ tsp. of the remaining sugar evenly over each custard. Wipe any sugar off the rim of the ramekins. Light a mini blowtorch and hold the flame 2 to 3 inches from the top of the custard, slowly gliding it back and forth over the surface until the sugar melts and turns a deep golden brown. Allow the sugar to cool and harden for a few minutes, and then serve immediately.

Heidi Johannsen Stewart is a food editor, recipe developer, and food stylist living in Brooklyn, New York, with her husband and 3-year-old son. ◆

See a video on making a brûlée topping at **finecooking.com/extras**

Good ideas for what to drink

For this menu, master sommelier Tim Gaiser suggests two bottles: a rich Mediterranean white wine with vivid citrus and mineral notes, like the 2007 Domaine Sigalas Assyrtiko, Santorini ($22) and a full-bodied Sicilian red with spicy cherry/plum fruit and savory earth notes, like the 2006 Planeta Cerasuolo di Vittoria, Sicily ($26).

For a nonalcoholic pairing, the complex, not-too-sweet herbal flavors of Fentiman's botanically brewed beverages are a perfect match. In particular, Fentiman's Ginger Beer and Mandarin and Seville Orange Jigger ($33 for a case of 12) go beautifully with the stew and couscous; see Where to Buy It, p. 104.

Slow-Roasted Beef Tenderloin
with Double-Mushroom Ragoût

Photos: Scott Phillips

A Modern Christmas

All the classics—roast beef and trifle included—get a fresh, new look in this festive holiday dinner

BY SUSIE MIDDLETON

I t's all fine and good to say you're not going to get caught up in the holiday madness this year. "No last-minute shopping," you swear. "Only one batch of cookies." And best of all, "I'll keep the meal simple." There's only one problem with this picture: You actually *like* to buy presents, bake cookies, and, well, cook.

Instead, what about a holiday meal that's fun to make and impressive to serve? It's got all the classics you want for the ultimate Christmas dinner (including a juicy roast beef), updated with a stylish, modern flare.

And never mind the 12 days of Christmas. We have an easy plan (see p. 66) that gets you started three days ahead, so you have lots of time to do the cooking—and enjoy your eggnog, too.

Champagne Cosmo

Serves eight.

Sip this festive sparkler—a Champagne twist on a Cosmopolitan—before dinner or while you enjoy the first course.

1½ cups cranberry juice cocktail, chilled
½ cup Grand Marnier
3 Tbs. fresh lime juice
8 thin strips of lime zest (from 2 limes), each about ¼ inch wide and 3 inches long
2 bottles (750 ml) brut sparkling wine or Champagne, chilled

Combine the cranberry juice, Grand Marnier, and lime juice in a small pitcher and mix well. Hold a lime strip over a tall Champagne flute, twist or tie it into a single knot to release the essential oils, and drop the zest into the flute. Repeat with the remaining zest and seven more flutes. Divide the juice mixture equally among the flutes. Top each flute with the sparkling wine (depending on the size of your flutes, you may not need all of the wine). Serve immediately.

Crab & Scallion Stuffed Shrimp

Serves eight.

For this recipe, avoid shrimp that's already been deveined; because it's been slit down the back, it can't be butterflied properly.

3½ Tbs. unsalted butter; more for the baking sheet
⅓ cup thinly sliced scallions (white and light-green parts only; from 5 to 6 scallions)

Kosher salt
½ tsp. Worcestershire sauce
Two drops Sriracha hot sauce (or other Asian chile sauce)
⅓ cup mayonnaise
2 Tbs. coarsely chopped fresh parsley, plus 20 whole leaves or small sprigs
1½ tsp. fresh lemon juice
1 tsp. finely grated lemon zest
½ tsp. Dijon mustard
Freshly ground black pepper
½ lb. backfin crabmeat, drained and picked over for shells
1¼ cups fine fresh breadcrumbs
16 jumbo shrimp (16 to 20 per lb.), butterflied (see From our Test Kitchen, p. 92)
1 small head frisée lettuce, torn into bite-size pieces
1½ tsp. extra-virgin olive oil

Make the stuffing: In a small saucepan, melt 2 Tbs. of the butter over medium-low heat. Add the scallions and a pinch of salt and cook, stirring, until softened, 3 to 4 minutes (don't brown). Take the pan off the heat and stir in the Worcestershire sauce and hot sauce. Cool to room temperature.

In a medium bowl, combine the mayonnaise, 1 Tbs. of the chopped parsley, 1 tsp. of the lemon juice, the lemon zest, the mustard, ¼ tsp. salt, and a few grinds of pepper. Stir in the cooled scallion mixture. Add the crab and mix gently but thoroughly.

In a 10-inch skillet, melt the remaining 1½ Tbs. butter over medium heat. Add the breadcrumbs and cook, stirring, until light golden brown, about 4 minutes. Transfer to a medium bowl and mix in the remaining 1 Tbs. chopped parsley and ¼ tsp. salt.

Stuff the shrimp: Line a rimmed baking sheet with parchment and rub lightly with butter. Arrange the butterflied shrimp on the baking sheet. Using a spoon or your hands, mound a heaping tablespoon of the crab mixture onto each shrimp. Sprinkle and pat the breadcrumbs over the crab. (This will be messy; don't worry if there are crumbs on the baking sheet.) Flip the tail of each shrimp up and over the crab.

Bake the shrimp: Position a rack in the center of the oven and heat the oven to 400°F. Bake until the shrimp are cooked through, the crabmeat is hot, and the crumbs are golden brown, 12 to 14 minutes.

While the shrimp are in the oven, toss the frisée and the whole parsley leaves with the remaining ½ tsp. lemon juice, the olive oil, and a pinch of salt. On 8 small plates, arrange a small pile of the salad and two shrimp. Serve right away.

Make ahead: You can butterfly the shrimp, make the stuffing and breadcrumb topping, and stuff the shrimp up to a day ahead. If stuffing ahead, don't top with the crumbs or flip up the tails until ready to bake. Cover and refrigerate the shrimp and stuffing; store the crumbs airtight at room temperature. Remove the stuffed shrimp from the fridge while the oven is heating.

Christmas Dinner for 8

Champagne Cosmo

❧

Crab & Scallion Stuffed Shrimp

❧

Slow-Roasted Beef Tenderloin
with Double-Mushroom Ragoût

❧

Lemon-Thyme Spinach

❧

Individual Savory Horseradish
Bread Puddings

❧

Ginger Cake Trifles with
Caramelized Apples, Cranberries
& Whipped Cream

❧

What to drink:
1995 Château Simard,
Saint-Emilion ($38)
or for a splurge, 2002 Seña,
Aconcagua, Chile ($80)

Slow-Roasted Beef Tenderloin with Double-Mushroom Ragoût

Serves eight.

Roasting the beef at a low temperature cooks the meat slowly and evenly and gives you time to finish preparing the other dishes.

2 Tbs. extra-virgin olive oil
2 tsp. coarsely chopped fresh thyme
2 tsp. minced garlic
Kosher salt and freshly ground black pepper
4-lb. beef tenderloin roast, preferably from the thicker end, trimmed of silver skin and chain (see From Our Test Kitchen, p. 92)
1 recipe Double-Mushroom Ragoût (see recipe below)

Position a rack in the center of the oven and heat the oven to 250°F.

In a small bowl, combine the olive oil, thyme, garlic, 1 tsp. salt, and several generous grinds of black pepper. Put the tenderloin on a heavy-duty rimmed baking sheet or in a small roasting pan and rub the oil mixture all over it.

Roast the tenderloin until an instant-read thermometer inserted in the thickest part reads 130°F for medium rare, about 1 hour. Transfer to a carving board, tent with foil and let rest for at least 20 minutes before serving.

Cut the tenderloin crosswise into ½-inch slices. Serve with the ragoût.

Make ahead: You can season the tenderloin up to 6 hours ahead and refrigerate.

Double-Mushroom Ragoût

Yields 2 to 2½ cups.

1 oz. dried porcini mushrooms (about 1 cup)
3 Tbs. unsalted butter
2 Tbs. extra-virgin olive oil
20 oz. cremini (baby bella) mushrooms, sliced ¼ inch thick
Kosher salt
⅓ cup finely chopped shallot
⅓ cup dry Marsala
1 Tbs. coarsely chopped fresh thyme
¾ cup heavy cream; more for reheating
Freshly ground black pepper
2 Tbs. chopped fresh parsley

Soak the porcini in 1½ cups very hot water, stirring occasionally, until they're rehydrated, about 20 minutes. With a slotted spoon, transfer them to a cutting board and chop coarsely. Strain the soaking liquid through a coffee filter into a small bowl and set aside.

In a 10-inch straight-sided sauté pan, heat 2 Tbs. of the butter with the olive oil over medium heat. Add the cremini and 1 tsp. salt and cook, stirring occasionally, until the

mushrooms have softened and released their liquid, 5 to 8 minutes. Increase the heat to medium high and cook, stirring more frequently, until the mushrooms are shrunken and very well browned, 8 to 10 minutes more.

Reduce the heat to medium, add the shallots and the remaining 1 Tbs. butter and cook, stirring, until the shallots are softened, 1 to 2 minutes. Add the Marsala, thyme, porcini, and ¼ cup porcini-soaking liquid (reserve the remaining soaking liquid if making ahead). Cook and stir until most of the liquid evaporates, 1 to 2 minutes. Add the cream and cook until reduced to a saucy consistency, 1 to 2 minutes. Stir in the parsley and season to taste with salt and pepper.

Make ahead: You can make and refrigerate the ragoût up to 2 days ahead. Just before serving, reheat it in a medium saucepan over medium heat. Stir in 1 or 2 Tbs. of the reserved mushroom-soaking liquid and 1 or 2 Tbs. heavy cream, letting both reduce slightly until the ragoût is just loose and saucy enough to spoon around the tenderloin. Stir in the parsley.

Lemon-Thyme Spinach

Serves eight.

A generous amount of lemon zest adds a touch of brightness to sautéed spinach.

6 Tbs. unsalted butter, softened
4 tsp. coarsely chopped fresh thyme
2 tsp. lightly packed finely grated lemon zest
½ tsp. minced garlic
Kosher salt
2 lb. stemmed spinach (from 2½ lb. bagged spinach or 5 lb. bunched spinach; see From Our Test Kitchen, p. 92)

In a small bowl, combine the butter, thyme, lemon zest, garlic, and a generous pinch of salt and mash with a fork or spoon until well blended.

Put several large handfuls of the spinach in a 12-inch nonstick stir-fry or sauté pan. Season with ½ tsp. salt. Turn the heat to medium high and cook, stirring frequently, until the spinach is mostly wilted, 1 to 2 minutes. Add another few handfuls of spinach and another ½ tsp. salt, and continue to cook, tossing, until wilted. Repeat until all of the spinach is wilted. Turn off the heat, but leave the pan on the burner. Add the butter mixture and toss just until it melts and coats the spinach. Season to taste with salt and serve immediately.

Make ahead: You can make the butter mixture up to 2 days ahead (cover and refrigerate), and you can wilt the spinach up to 2 hours before dinner. Reheat it gently with the butter before serving.

Individual Savory Horseradish Bread Puddings

Yields 12 individual puddings.

For this menu, you will need only 8 puddings, but you'll have 4 extra for anyone who wants seconds.

2 tsp. unsalted butter, softened
1¼ cups heavy cream
6 large eggs, at room temperature
¼ cup prepared white horseradish
Kosher salt and freshly ground black pepper
3 cups small-diced white sandwich bread, such as Pepperidge Farm Original (about 5 slices), with crusts
1 cup freshly grated Parmigiano-Reggiano
3 Tbs. thinly sliced fresh chives

Position a rack in the center of the oven and heat the oven to 400°F. Grease a 12-cup nonstick muffin tin with the butter.

In a 4-cup liquid measuring cup, thoroughly whisk the cream and eggs. Whisk in the horseradish, 1 tsp. salt, and a few grinds of pepper and set aside. Portion half of the bread cubes evenly among the 12 muffin cups. Portion half of the parmigiano and half of the chives evenly among the cups. Repeat with the remaining bread, cheese, and chives.

Whisk the custard again and carefully pour it into the muffin cups, distributing it evenly. Refrigerate for at least 30 minutes.

Bake until the puddings are set and the tops are nicely browned and puffed, 18 to 22 minutes. Let cool in the pan for 20 minutes. Carefully remove the puddings from the pan, running a paring knife around the edge of the puddings if they stick.

Make ahead: The puddings can be assembled and refrigerated up to 6 hours before baking. They can also be baked a day ahead, refrigerated, and reheated, wrapped in foil, in a low oven.

Beef Tenderloin with
Double-Mushroom Ragoût,
Lemon-Thyme Spinach, and Savory
Horseradish Bread Pudding

The Three Days of Christmas

No, you don't need 12 days. Here's a three-day plan that takes you from start to finish with ease.

3 days ahead

❖ Do the shopping, including wine and Champagne

❖ Buy decorations and centerpiece

2 days ahead

❖ Make ragoût and lemon-thyme butter

❖ Choose wine glasses, trifle glasses, and plates

❖ Stem and wash spinach

1 day ahead

❖ Stuff shrimp

❖ Make and bake bread puddings, if planning to reheat

❖ Make cake and apple mixture for trifles

❖ Set table and decorate room

Christmas day

In the morning:

❖ Assemble bread puddings (if not already made)

❖ Trim tenderloin, season, and refrigerate

Up to 2 hours before serving:

❖ Whip cream and assemble trifles

❖ Wilt spinach

❖ Prepare juice mixture for cocktail

❖ Roast beef, tent, and let rest

❖ Bake bread puddings (if not already cooked)

❖ Pour yourself a glass of wine (!)

Just before serving:

❖ Finish cocktails

❖ Bake shrimp

❖ Reheat ragoût and sides

Find a shopping list for this menu at
finecooking.com/extras

Ginger Cake Trifles with Caramelized Apples, Cranberries & Whipped Cream

Serves eight.

While these trifles are delicious made with warm gingerbread and warm apples, they are equally good made a few hours ahead and chilled, which makes serving dessert a snap.

FOR THE APPLES AND CRANBERRIES:
3 Tbs. unsalted butter
1½ lb. Granny Smith apples (about 4 small), peeled and cut into large dice
Kosher salt
1½ cups fresh (or frozen) cranberries
½ cup pure maple syrup
¼ tsp. ground cinnamon
2 Tbs. finely chopped crystallized ginger

FOR THE WHIPPED CREAM:
1½ cups heavy cream, chilled
1 tsp. pure vanilla extract
2 Tbs. granulated sugar

1 recipe Ginger Cake (opposite)

Cook the apples and cranberries: In a 10-inch straight-sided skillet, melt the butter over medium-high heat. Add the apples and ¼ tsp. salt and cook, stirring occasionally at first and then more frequently, until the apples are nicely browned and tender, about 10 minutes. Add 3 Tbs. water to the pan, remove it from the heat, and stir to incorporate some of the brown bits from the bottom of the pan.

Add half of the cranberries, the maple syrup, cinnamon, a pinch of salt, and 2 Tbs. water. Bring to a boil over medium-high heat, lower the heat to medium low, and simmer until the syrup has thickened a little and most of the cranberries have popped, about 2 minutes. Add the other half of the cranberries and simmer until about half of the new cranberries have popped, 2 to 3 minutes more. Take the pan off the heat and stir in the ginger. Let cool to room temperature.

Make the whipped cream: Using a chilled bowl and beaters, whip the heavy cream and vanilla with a hand-held or stand mixer on medium speed until it begins to thicken, about 1 minute. Slowly sprinkle in the sugar and continue whipping until soft peaks form, another 1 to 2 minutes. Refrigerate if not using right away.

Assemble: Using a serrated knife, cut the ginger cake into ¾-inch cubes. Portion about half of the cake among eight 10-ounce glasses. Portion about half of the whipped cream among the glasses, spooning it over and around the cake, and top with about half of the apple mixture. Repeat with another layer of cake, whipped cream, and apples. (You may have some leftover cake.)

Make ahead: The apple mixture can be made a day ahead and refrigerated (return it to room temperature before using). The cream can be whipped an hour before using. The trifles can be assembled and refrigerated up to 2 hours ahead.

Ginger Cake

Yields one 8x8-inch cake; serves eight.

This cake is very much like a traditional gingerbread, except that it's made with buttermilk and is extra tender and moist.

4 oz. (½ cup) unsalted butter, at room temperature; more for the pan
6¾ oz. (1½ cups) unbleached all-purpose flour
2 tsp. ground ginger
1 tsp. ground cinnamon
½ tsp. baking soda
¼ tsp. ground cloves
¼ tsp. table salt
1 Tbs. minced fresh ginger
¼ cup granulated sugar
¼ cup packed dark brown sugar
1 large egg, at room temperature
½ cup unsulfured mild molasses
½ cup buttermilk, at room temperature

Position a rack in the center of the oven and heat the oven to 350°F. Butter the sides of an 8x8-inch square cake pan and line the bottom of the pan with parchment. In a medium bowl, mix the flour, ground ginger, cinnamon, baking soda, cloves, and salt. Set aside.

Using a hand mixer or a stand mixer fitted with the paddle attachment, beat the butter on medium speed until light and fluffy, about 1 minute. Add the fresh ginger and mix until just combined. Add both sugars and beat on medium speed until well combined and fluffy, about 1 minute. Stop the mixer and scrape down the sides of the bowl. Add the egg and mix on medium speed until well combined. Turn the mixer to low and slowly add the molasses. Add about one-third of the dry ingredients and mix until just combined. Add one-third of the buttermilk and mix until just combined. Add the remaining dry and wet ingredients in four more additions, finishing with the buttermilk and mixing until just combined after each addition. Scrape the batter into the cake pan and spread it evenly.

Bake the cake until a skewer inserted into the center comes out clean, 30 to 35 minutes. Let the cake cool completely in the pan, at least an hour.

Make ahead: The cake can be made a day ahead and stored at room temperature.

Susie Middleton is editor at large for Fine Cooking. ◆

One Master Recipe, Three Irresistible coffee cakes

BY CAROLE WALTER

Every cook needs to know how to make a killer sour cream coffee cake, and this is that one recipe. It bakes up moist and buttery and looks impressive to boot. I have yet to serve this cake and be greeted with anything but raves—and crumb-filled plates thrust my way, with requests for another wedge.

As delectable as it is, this cake is not difficult. It hinges on three important techniques (see below), and it needs no icing. It also lends itself to variation, which means you get the bonus of adding three cakes to your repertoire with this one classic recipe.

Good to know

Master these three key techniques, and impressive results are guaranteed.

Layering the batter and filling

Layers are key to this cake's great flavor and sublime appearance. There are four layers of batter and three of filling. Using a large soupspoon for the batter, start by smoothing it to the sides of the pan and then work towards the center tube. Don't lift the spoon, or you'll disturb the filling.

Marbling the batter

Once the layers are complete, run a table knife through the batter in two circles around the tube, spacing them about an inch apart, without lifting up the blade. This distributes the filling but still keeps it clearly defined.

Forming the streusel

For the topping, form streusel clumps by squeezing the mixture together and breaking the mass into smaller pieces to sprinkle evenly over the top of the batter. Press the streusel lightly into the batter.

Sour Cream Coffee Cake with Toasted Pecan Filling

Serves sixteen.

1 Tbs. softened unsalted butter

FOR THE STREUSEL TOPPING:
2 oz. (4 Tbs.) unsalted butter
3 oz. (⅔ cup) all-purpose flour
¼ cup toasted pecans,
 coarsely chopped
2 Tbs. granulated sugar
2 Tbs. light brown sugar
½ tsp. ground cinnamon
¼ tsp. baking powder
¼ tsp. table salt

FOR THE FILLING:
1 cup toasted pecans
3 Tbs. granulated sugar
3 Tbs. light brown sugar
1½ tsp. ground cinnamon
1 tsp. Dutch-processed or natural
 cocoa powder

FOR THE CAKE:
11¼ oz. (3 cups) sifted cake flour
1½ tsp. baking powder
1 tsp. baking soda
¾ tsp. table salt
10 oz. (1¼ cups) unsalted butter,
 slightly softened
11½ oz. (1⅔ cups) superfine sugar
 (see sidebar on sugar, opposite)
4 large eggs
2 tsp. pure vanilla extract
16 oz. (2 cups) sour cream

Position a rack in the center of the oven and heat the oven to 350°F (325°F if using a dark nonstick pan). Generously butter a 10-inch tube pan with a removable bottom.

Make the topping: In a 2-quart saucepan, heat the butter over medium heat until almost melted. Remove from the heat and cool to tepid. In a medium bowl, combine the flour, pecans, both sugars, cinnamon, baking powder, and salt and stir with a fork. Add the flour mixture to the butter and stir until evenly moistened and crumbly.

Make the filling: In a food processor, pulse the pecans, both sugars, cinnamon, and cocoa 4 to 6 times to combine and chop the pecans.

Make the cake: In a medium bowl, whisk the flour, baking powder, baking soda, and salt. In the bowl of a stand mixer fitted with the paddle attachment, beat the butter on medium speed until smooth and creamy, 1 to 2 minutes. Add the sugar slowly, beating until combined. Scrape the bowl. Beat in the eggs one at a time, blending each one completely before adding the next. Scrape the bowl and blend in the vanilla. On low speed, alternate adding the dry ingredients and the sour cream, adding the flour in four parts and the sour cream in three parts, beginning and ending with the flour, and scraping the bowl as needed.

Layer and marble the batter and filling: Spoon 2 generous cups of the batter into the prepared pan. Smooth with the back of a soupspoon, spreading the batter to the side of the pan first and then to the center. Sprinkle about ½ cup of the filling evenly over the batter. Cover the filling with about 2 cups of batter, dropping dollops around the pan and smoothing with the spoon. Sprinkle another ½ cup

filling evenly over the batter and cover with 2 more cups batter. Layer on the remaining filling and then the remaining batter. (You'll have four layers of batter and three layers of filling.) Insert a table knife 1 inch from the side of the pan straight into the batter going almost to the bottom. Run the knife around the pan two times, without lifting up the blade, spacing the circles about 1 inch apart. Smooth the top with the back of the soupspoon.

Top and bake the cake: Take a handful of the streusel crumbs and squeeze firmly to form a large mass. Break up the mass into smaller clumps, distributing the streusel evenly over the batter. Repeat with the remaining streusel. Press the streusel lightly into the surface of the cake.

Bake until the top of the cake is golden brown, the sides are beginning to pull away from the pan, and a wooden skewer inserted into the center of the cake comes out clean, 70 to 75 minutes. Transfer to a wire rack and let cool for at least an hour before removing from the pan.

For tips on turning out the cake, see From Our Test Kitchen, p. 92.

Make ahead: This cake keeps at room temperature, well wrapped or under a cake dome, for up to 5 days; you can freeze it for up to 3 months.

Variations

Follow the directions for preparing the Sour Cream Coffee Cake at left, with these modifications:

Chocolate Ripple

½ cup toasted pecans
6 oz. coarsely chopped bittersweet chocolate
3 Tbs. granulated sugar
3 Tbs. light brown sugar
3 Tbs. Dutch-processed or natural cocoa powder

Prepare the streusel topping from the main recipe without any changes. Substitute the ingredients above for the filling ingredients, and pulse them in a food processor until the chocolate is finely chopped, 12 to 14 pulses. Reserve ½ cup as an additional topping and proceed with the layering instructions, using one-third of the remaining mixture for each filling layer. After topping the batter with the streusel crumbs, clump the reserved chocolate mixture together with your hands and sprinkle over the streusel, pressing lightly. Bake as directed.

Ginger & Marcona Almonds

1 cup coarsely chopped salted Marcona almonds
½ tsp. of ground ginger
3 Tbs. granulated sugar
3 Tbs. light brown sugar
⅛ tsp. freshly ground nutmeg
½ cup of very finely chopped crystallized ginger

Prepare the streusel topping from the main recipe, substituting ¼ cup of the almonds for the pecans and the ground ginger for the cinnamon. Substitute the remaining ingredients above for the filling ingredients: Pulse the remaining ¾ cup almonds with both sugars and the nutmeg in a food processor until the almonds are finely ground, 10 to 12 pulses. Empty the mixture into a medium bowl and mix in the crystallized ginger. Proceed with the layering and baking instructions, using one-third of the filling for each layer.

The sugar secret

It may seem silly that I call for three types of sugar in this recipe (superfine, granulated, and light brown), but there is a reason for each. Superfine is used in the batter, which is dense and doesn't get hot enough in the center during baking to dissolve the larger crystals in granulated sugar. Superfine ensures a fine crumb and lighter texture. You don't have to buy a special package of it, though—make your own by spinning granulated sugar in a food processor until it is as fine as sand. Granulated sugar adds a nice texture to the topping and filling, and the molasses in the brown sugar adds depth of flavor.

The right pan

Key to this cake's success is the pan it's baked in. You need a shiny aluminum tube pan (also known as an angel food cake pan). Don't use a Bundt or a fluted pan, because they have rounded bottoms and are meant for cakes that will be served inverted. Dark nonstick tube pans are not a good choice for a cake like this; because it bakes for more than an hour, over-browning or burning may result. If that is all you have, reduce the oven temperature by 25°F.

Carole Walter is a master baker and cooking instructor whose most recent cookbook is Great Coffee Cakes, Sticky Buns, Muffins & More. ◆

Smart Cookies

Spices and herbs, nuts and honey, coffee and chocolate— contemporary flavors make the classics new

BY DAVID CROFTON

Lemon-Rosemary Christmas Trees

Orange-Hazelnut Olive Oil Cookies

Chocolate-Mint Thumbprints

Honey Shortbread

Honey-Nut Bars

Mocha Sandwich Cookies

Pine Nut Wedding Cookies

Mocha Sandwich Cookies

Yields about 5 dozen cookies.

Delicate chocolate cookies stack up with a mocha-cream-cheese filling in these sweet little sandwiches.

FOR THE COOKIES:
7½ oz. (1⅔ cups) unbleached all-purpose flour
¾ oz. (¼ cup) Dutch-processed cocoa
½ tsp. baking soda
¼ tsp. table salt
4 oz. (½ cup) unsalted butter, at room temperature
½ cup plus 2 Tbs. granulated sugar
6 Tbs. packed light brown sugar
1 large egg
1 tsp. pure vanilla extract

FOR THE MOCHA FILLING:
1 Tbs. instant espresso
2 oz. (4 Tbs.) unsalted butter, at room temperature
2 oz. (4 Tbs.) cream cheese
6 oz. (1½ cups) confectioners' sugar, sifted
1 tsp. pure vanilla extract
¾ oz. (¼ cup) Dutch-processed cocoa powder, sifted

Make the cookies: In a medium bowl, whisk the flour, cocoa, baking soda, and salt. With a hand mixer or a stand mixer fitted with the paddle attachment, cream the butter and sugars on medium speed until light and fluffy, about 2 minutes. Add the egg and vanilla and continue beating until blended and smooth, about 30 seconds. Reduce the speed to low and slowly add the dry ingredients, mixing until the dough is just combined. Divide the dough in half. Wrap one half of the dough in plastic and refrigerate.

Roll the other half of the dough between two sheets of parchment to an even ⅛-inch thickness. Slide the dough onto a cookie sheet and freeze until cold and firm, about 30 minutes. Repeat with the remaining dough.

Position a rack in the center of the oven and heat the oven to 350°F. Line two cookie sheets with parchment.

Using 1½-inch round cookie cutters, cut out the dough and arrange the rounds 1 inch apart on the prepared sheets. If the dough gets too soft, return it to the freezer for a few minutes. Carefully press the scraps together, reroll, and cut. Repeat with the other half of the dough, and then gather all the scraps together, reroll, and cut one more time.

Bake in batches, two sheets at a time, until the tops look dry, about 6 minutes. Let the cookies cool on their pans for a minute and then let them cool completely on racks.

Make the filling: In a small bowl, dissolve the espresso in 2 Tbs. hot water. Let cool slightly, 5 minutes.

With the mixer, cream the butter and cream cheese on medium speed until light and smooth, about 1 minute. Reduce the speed to low and slowly add half of the sugar, mixing until just combined. Add the coffee mixture and vanilla, and mix until just incorporated. Gradually mix in the remaining sugar and the cocoa. Increase the speed to medium and beat until the filling is light and fluffy, about 1 minute more.

To assemble, transfer the cooled cookies to a work surface, flipping half of them over. With an offset spatula or butter knife, spread a thin layer of the filling onto each turned-over cookie. Set another cookie on top of each filled cookie, pressing gently to spread the filling. The cookies will keep at room temperature for up to 3 days or in the freezer for up to 1 month.

Make ahead: The filling can be made up to 3 days ahead and refrigerated. For the best texture, assemble the sandwiches as close to serving as possible.

Pine Nut Wedding Cookies

Yields about 3 dozen cookies.

2 cups pine nuts, toasted
10 oz. (2¼ cups) unbleached all-purpose flour
½ tsp. table salt
8 oz. (1 cup) unsalted butter, at room temperature
¼ cup granulated sugar
1 tsp. pure vanilla extract
4 oz. (1 cup) confectioners' sugar, sifted

In a food processor, pulse the pine nuts and 1 cup of the flour until finely ground. Add the remaining flour and the salt and pulse to blend.

With a hand mixer or a stand mixer fitted with the paddle attachment, beat the butter and granulated sugar on medium speed until light and fluffy, about 2 minutes. Add the vanilla and mix on medium until combined, about 15 seconds. Reduce the speed to low and gradually add the dry ingredients, mixing until the dough is just combined. Cover with plastic and refrigerate until firm, about 1 hour.

Position racks in the upper and lower thirds of the oven and heat the oven to 350°F. Line two cookie sheets with parchment or nonstick baking liners.

Using your palms, roll heaping tablespoonfuls of the dough into 1½-inch balls. Arrange them 1 inch apart on the lined sheets. Bake until golden around the edges and light golden on top, 19 to 21 minutes, rotating and swapping the sheets halfway through for even baking. Transfer the cookies, still on their parchment, to a rack and let cool for 5 to 10 minutes, or until they have firmed up a bit and are cool enough to handle.

Put the confectioners' sugar in a small bowl. Gently toss the cookies in the sugar to coat; let them cool completely on racks. Toss them again in the sugar. The cookies will keep in an airtight container at room temperature for up to 1 week.

Lemon-Rosemary Christmas Trees

Yields about 3 dozen 3½-inch cookies.

Rosemary gives these holiday cutout cookies a subtle piny touch, and lemon adds brightness.

FOR THE COOKIES:

15 oz. (3⅓ cups) unbleached all-purpose flour
1 tsp. table salt
8 oz. (1 cup) unsalted butter, at room temperature
¾ cup granulated sugar
1 Tbs. finely grated lemon zest
1 Tbs. finely chopped fresh rosemary
1 large egg
1 tsp. pure vanilla extract

FOR THE ICING:

1 large egg white (see note below)
6½ oz. (1½ cups plus 2 Tbs.) confectioners' sugar; more as needed
½ tsp. fresh lemon juice
Decorating sugar or edible dragées (optional)

Make the cookies: In a medium bowl, whisk the flour and salt. With a hand mixer or a stand mixer fitted with the paddle attachment, cream the butter and sugar on medium speed until light and fluffy, about 2 minutes. Mix in the lemon zest and rosemary. Add the egg and vanilla; continue beating until well blended and smooth, about 30 seconds more. Reduce the speed to low and gradually add the dry ingredients. Mix until the dough is just combined; don't overmix. Divide the dough into 2 equal portions.

Roll one half of the dough between two sheets of parchment to an even ³⁄₁₆-inch thickness. Slide the dough and parchment onto a cookie sheet and refrigerate until firm, about 30 minutes. Repeat with the remaining dough.

Position racks in the upper and lower thirds of the oven and heat the oven to 350°F. Line four cookie sheets with parchment.

Using a 3½-inch (or similar) Christmas tree cookie cutter, cut out the cookies and arrange them 1 inch apart on the cookie sheets. Press the scraps together, reroll, and cut (if the dough becomes too soft to handle,

chill until firm). Repeat one more time and then discard the scraps. Repeat with the remaining dough.

Bake two sheets at a time until the cookies' edges are golden brown, 10 to 12 minutes, rotating and swapping the sheets' positions halfway through for even baking. Cool the cookies on racks.

Make the icing: In a medium bowl, whisk the egg white, sugar, and lemon juice until smooth. If not using immediately, transfer the icing to a small bowl and press plastic wrap directly onto the surface of the icing to prevent it from drying out.

Decorate the cookies: Spoon some of the icing into a small pastry bag with a small (³⁄₁₆ inch) plain tip. (Or use a small plastic bag and cut a tiny bit off a bottom corner of the bag.) Pipe the icing onto the cookies to outline the rim. (If the icing is too thick to pipe, put it back in the bowl and stir in water, a drop at a time, until it pipes easily but still retains its shape. If the icing is too thin, add confectioners' sugar, 1 tsp. at a time.)

If using decorating sugar or dragées, apply them while the icing is wet. Once the icing is completely dry and hard, store the cookies in airtight containers in the refrigerator for up to 5 days.

Note: The risk of salmonella infection from consuming raw eggs is very low, but you can eliminate it entirely by using pasteurized eggs.

Honey-Nut Bars

Yields 16 bar cookies.

FOR THE CRUST:
Nonstick cooking spray
½ cup whole blanched almonds, toasted
½ cup granulated sugar
11¼ oz. (2½ cups) unbleached all-purpose flour
½ tsp. baking powder
½ tsp. table salt
6 oz. (¾ cup) cold unsalted butter, cut into ½-inch pieces
1 large egg, lightly beaten

FOR THE TOPPING:
¾ cup packed light brown sugar
3 oz. (6 Tbs.) unsalted butter
⅓ cup clover honey
½ tsp. table salt
2 Tbs. heavy cream
3 cups whole unsalted mixed nuts, toasted

Make the crust: Position a rack in the center of the oven and heat the oven to 350°F. Spray a 9x13-inch baking pan with cooking spray and line the bottom with parchment.

In a food processor, finely grind the almonds and sugar. Add the flour, baking powder, and salt and pulse to blend. Add the butter and pulse until it's the size of small peas, 5 to 6 one-second pulses. Add the egg and pulse just until the dough begins to gather into large clumps.

With your fingertips, press the dough into the bottom of the prepared pan and about 1 inch up the sides to form a ¼-inch-thick side crust. Using the tines of a fork, dock the crust evenly all over.

Bake until light golden brown on the edges and the center looks dry, 15 to 20 minutes. Cool the crust on a rack.

Make the topping: Bring the sugar, butter, honey, and salt to a boil in a medium saucepan over medium-high heat, stirring often. Slowly and carefully add the cream and return to a boil. Remove from the heat and carefully add the nuts, stirring to coat. Pour the nut mixture over the crust and spread evenly with a spatula. Tilt the pan to help spread the liquid to the edges and corners. Bake until the topping has just started to bubble slowly in the center, about 20 minutes. Let cool on a wire rack for 10 minutes and then run a knife around the inside edge of the pan to loosen the crust from the sides. Let the bars cool completely.

Invert the pan onto a flat surface and peel off the parchment. Reinvert onto a cutting board and cut into 16 bars with a sharp knife.

The cookies will keep in an airtight container at room temperature for 3 to 5 days.

Orange-Hazelnut Olive Oil Cookies

Yields about 6 dozen cookies.

Reminiscent of biscotti in texture, these not-too-sweet cookies are a perfect dipper for after-dinner coffee.

2 cups toasted and skinned hazelnuts
10 oz. (2¼ cups) unbleached all-purpose flour
1 tsp. baking powder
¼ tsp. table salt
¾ cup plus 2 Tbs. granulated sugar
½ cup extra-virgin olive oil
2 large eggs
Finely grated zest of 2 medium oranges (about 1½ packed Tbs.)
1 tsp. pure vanilla extract

Finely grind the hazelnuts in a food processor. In a medium bowl, whisk the hazelnuts, flour, baking powder, and salt to blend. With a hand mixer or a stand mixer fitted with the paddle attachment, beat the sugar, oil, eggs, zest, and vanilla on low speed until the sugar is moistened, about 15 seconds. Increase the speed to high and mix until well combined, about 15 seconds more (the sugar will not be dissolved at this point). Add the dry ingredients and mix on low speed until the dough has just pulled together, 30 to 60 seconds.

Divide the dough in half. Pile one half of the dough onto a piece

of parchment. Using the parchment to help shape the dough, form it into a log 11 inches long and 2 inches in diameter. Wrap the parchment around the log and twist the ends to secure. Repeat with the remaining dough. Chill in the freezer until firm, about 1 hour.

Position racks in the upper and lower thirds of the oven and heat the oven to 350°F. Line four cookie sheets with parchment or nonstick baking liners.

Unwrap one log of dough at a time and cut the dough into ¼-inch slices; set them 1 inch apart on the prepared sheets. Bake two sheets at a time until light golden on the bottoms and around the edges, about 10 minutes, rotating and swapping the sheets halfway through for even baking. Let cool completely on racks. The cookies will keep in an airtight container at room temperature for up to 1 week.

Make ahead: The unbaked logs of dough may be frozen for up to 1 month.

To skin hazelnuts: Toast the nuts in a single layer on a baking sheet in a 375°F oven until the skins are mostly split and the nuts are light golden brown and fragrant, about 10 minutes. Wrap the hot nuts in a clean dishtowel and let them sit for 5 to 10 minutes. Then vigorously rub the nuts against themselves in the towel to remove most of the skins.

Honey Shortbread

Yields 12 cookies.

Nonstick cooking spray
7½ oz. (1⅔ cups) unbleached all-purpose flour
⅓ cup granulated sugar
6 oz. (¾ cup) cold unsalted butter, cut into 1-inch pieces
3 Tbs. honey
1 tsp. kosher salt

Spray a 9½-inch tart pan with removable bottom with cooking spray.

In a food processor, briefly pulse the flour and sugar. Add the butter and pulse until incorporated and the mixture is sandy and uniform. Press the dough evenly into the prepared pan with your fingers. There will be some loose crumbs around the edges, but most of the dough should be solid and compact. Refrigerate until chilled, least 30 minutes.

Position a rack in the center of the oven and heat the oven to 350°F. Using the tines of a fork, dock the dough evenly all over. Bake the shortbread until golden in the center, 40 to 45 minutes.

Heat the honey in the microwave until warm and liquid but not boiling, about 10 seconds. Pour the honey over the shortbread and spread with a pastry brush over the entire surface. Sprinkle the salt evenly over the honey. Return the pan to the oven and bake for 3 minutes more.

Transfer the pan to a rack and let the shortbread cool slightly, about 15 minutes. While still warm, remove the tart pan ring and cut the shortbread into 12 wedges with a sharp knife. Cool completely before serving or storing. The cookies will keep in an airtight container at room temperature for 1 week.

Chocolate-Mint Thumbprints

Yields about 3 dozen cookies.

FOR THE COOKIES:
5¼ oz. (1 cup plus 2½ Tbs.) unbleached all-purpose flour
¾ oz. (¼ cup) Dutch-processed cocoa
6 oz. (¾ cup) unsalted butter, at room temperature
2 oz. (½ cup) confectioners' sugar, sifted
1½ tsp. pure vanilla extract
¼ tsp. table salt

FOR THE MINT FILLING:
4 oz. (¾ cup) chopped semisweet chocolate (or chocolate chips)
1½ oz. (3 Tbs.) unsalted butter, cut into 6 pieces
Scant ¼ tsp. pure peppermint extract

Make the cookies: Sift the flour and cocoa together into a medium bowl. With a hand mixer or a stand mixer fitted with the paddle attachment, cream the butter and sugar on medium speed until light and fluffy, about 2 minutes. Add the vanilla and salt; continue beating until blended and smooth, about 1 minute more. Add the flour-cocoa mixture and mix on low speed until a soft dough forms, about 1 minute. Chill the dough in the refrigerator until firm enough to roll into balls, 40 to 60 minutes.

Position a rack in the center of the oven and heat the oven to 350°F. Line two cookie sheets with parchment or nonstick baking liners.

Using your palms, roll heaping teaspoonfuls of the dough into 1-inch balls. Arrange them 2 inches apart on the lined sheets. With a lightly floured thumb or index fingertip, press straight down into the middle of each ball almost to the cookie sheet to make a deep well. (Or use the end of a thick-handled wooden spoon.)

Bake one sheet at a time until the tops of the cookies look dry, 8 to 9 minutes. Gently redefine the indentations with the end of a wooden spoon. Let the cookies cool on the sheet for 5 minutes and then let them cool completely on racks.

Make the filling: Put the chocolate and butter in a heatproof bowl set in a wide skillet of almost simmering water. Stir with a heatproof spatula until almost melted, 2 to 4 minutes. Remove the bowl from the heat and stir until melted and smooth, about 30 seconds more. Stir in the mint extract. Let the filling cool, stirring occasionally, until slightly thickened and a bit warmer than room temperature, 30 to 40 minutes. Spoon the filling into a small pastry bag with a small plain tip. (Or use a small plastic bag and cut a tiny bit off a bottom corner of the bag.) Pipe the filling into the center of each cookie. Cool completely before serving or storing. The cookies will keep in an airtight container at room temperature for 4 to 5 days.

David Crofton is the pastry chef and co-owner of One Girl Cookies bakery in Brooklyn, New York. ◆

Soup Suppers

Turn to the pantry for a satisfying one-pot meal

BY LORI LONGBOTHAM

Pasta e Fagioli

The pantry—with a little planning—is a great source of quick weeknight meals. And soup is one of the easiest things to whip up if you have the right ingredients at the ready. The trick is to keep the cupboard, fridge, and freezer stocked so that all you need is on hand—no last minute grocery runs required.

Stock up

With these items in your kitchen, you'll have everything you need to make the soups here, and do a little improvising, too.

In the pantry

Canned or boxed chicken broth

Canned diced tomatoes

Canned beans and dried lentils

Dried herbs and spices

Small pasta shapes like orzo, tubettini, acini de pepe, and ditalini

Quick-cooking grains like rice, pearl barley, and bulgur

Tomato paste

Onions

Garlic

Potatoes

Winter squash

Coconut milk

Thai curry paste

Dried chiles

Chile pastes, hot sauces

Canned chipotle chiles in adobo

Canned roasted green chiles

Dried mushrooms

Canned straw mushrooms

Sun-dried tomatoes

In the fridge

Hard cheeses like Parmigiano-Reggiano and Pecorino Romano

Citrus fruit like lemons, oranges, and limes

Root vegetables like carrots, parsnips, and turnips

Celery

Crème fraîche, sour cream, plain yogurt, and buttermilk

Flavorful oils like chile oil, nut oils, and sesame oil

In the freezer

Homemade vegetable, chicken, and beef broths

Bread (for croutons or for thickening)

Bacon

Shrimp

Small stuffed pastas like raviolini and tortellini

Corn

Peas

Edamame

Pasta e Fagioli

Yields 16 cups; serves eight.

This Italian soup—which has as many variations as there are cooks—is chock full of pasta, beans, and vegetables, making it a hearty one-dish meal.

8 slices bacon, cut crosswise into ¼-inch-wide strips
3 medium red onions, finely chopped
3 medium cloves garlic, minced
½ tsp. dried rosemary
2 quarts lower-salt chicken broth
Two 15½-oz. cans chickpeas, rinsed and drained
14½-oz. can petite-cut diced tomatoes
**4 medium carrots, peeled, halved lengthwise, and
    thinly sliced**
**3 medium celery ribs with leaves, thinly sliced
    crosswise**
1 slender 3-inch cinnamon stick
Kosher salt and freshly ground black pepper
1 cup tubettini (or other small pasta)
1½ tsp. red-wine vinegar; more to taste
Grated or shaved Parmigiano-Reggiano for garnish

In a 6-quart (or larger) Dutch oven over medium heat, cook the bacon, stirring occasionally, until partially crisp, about 7 minutes. With a slotted spoon, transfer the bacon to a paper-towel-lined plate. Add the onions to the pot and cook, scraping up any browned bits and stirring occasionally, until softened, 6 to 8 minutes. Add the garlic and rosemary and cook, stirring constantly, until fragrant, about 1 minute. Add the chicken broth, chickpeas, tomatoes and their juices, carrots, celery, cinnamon stick, ¾ tsp. salt, ½ tsp. pepper, and 1 cup water. Bring to a boil over high heat; skim any foam as necessary. Reduce the heat and simmer, stirring occasionally, until the carrots and celery are very tender, about 30 minutes.

Meanwhile, cook the tubettini according to the package directions and drain.

Discard the cinnamon stick and add the pasta. Stir in the bacon and vinegar. Season to taste with salt, pepper, and more vinegar. Serve garnished with the Parmigiano-Reggiano.

You can store leftovers in the refrigerator for up to 2 days.

Root Vegetable & Barley Soup with Bacon

Yields 13 cups; serves six to eight.

If you store this for more than a day, the barley will absorb some of the liquid and you'll need to thin it with a little water when you reheat it.

1 oz. dried porcini mushrooms
2 medium cloves garlic
Kosher salt
4 slices bacon, cut in half crosswise
2 medium red onions, chopped
2 small bay leaves
¾ tsp. caraway seeds
½ tsp. dried thyme
Freshly ground black pepper
2 quarts lower-salt chicken broth
5 medium carrots, peeled and cut into small dice
**2 medium purple-top turnips, peeled and cut
    into small dice**
**2 medium Yukon Gold potatoes, peeled and cut
    into small dice**
**¾ cup pearl barley, picked over, rinsed, and
    drained**
4 tsp. fresh lemon juice

In small bowl, soak the mushrooms in 1 cup boiling water for 20 minutes. Remove the mushrooms and pour the liquid through a fine strainer to remove any grit. Reserve the liquid. Rinse the mushrooms, chop them, and set aside.

Chop the garlic, sprinkle it with ¾ tsp. salt, and then mash it to a paste with the side of a chef's knife. Set aside.

In a 6-quart (or larger) Dutch oven, cook the bacon over medium heat until crisp, about 8 minutes. Transfer to a paper-towel-lined plate, crumble when cool, and set aside.

Add the onions and 1 tsp. salt to the bacon fat and cook, stirring occasionally, until softened, 6 to 8 minutes. Stir in the garlic paste, bay leaves, caraway seeds, thyme, and ¼ tsp. pepper and cook, stirring constantly, until fragrant, about 1 minute. Add the chopped mushrooms, mushroom liquid, chicken broth, carrots, turnips, potatoes, barley, and 1½ cups water. Bring to a boil over high heat; skim any foam as necessary. Reduce the heat, cover, and simmer, stirring occasionally, until the barley and vegetables are tender, 20 to 25 minutes. Add the lemon juice, season with salt and pepper, and discard the bay leaves. Serve garnished with the bacon.

You can store leftovers in the refrigerator for up to 2 days.

Root Vegetable &
Barley Soup with Bacon

Spiced Tomato & Red Lentil Soup

Yields about 14 cups; serves eight.

Curry powder and garam masala are both Indian spice blends, which vary in flavor from blend to blend. Experiment to see which you prefer.

3 Tbs. vegetable oil
2 medium yellow onions, chopped
Kosher salt
2 tsp. Madras curry powder or garam masala
2 quarts lower-salt chicken broth or homemade vegetable broth
Two 14.5-oz. cans petite-diced tomatoes
1 lb. (2⅓ cups) dried red lentils, picked over, rinsed, and drained
2 medium celery ribs, cut into small dice
1 medium carrot, peeled and cut into small dice
2 medium cloves garlic, peeled and chopped
⅛ to ¼ tsp. cayenne

Heat the oil in a 6-quart (or larger) Dutch oven over medium heat. Add the onions and a generous pinch of salt and cook, stirring occasionally, until the onions are softened and just starting to brown, 6 to 8 minutes. Add the curry powder or garam masala and cook, stirring constantly, until fragrant, 30 seconds to 1 minute.

Add the broth, tomatoes and their juices, lentils, celery, carrot, garlic, cayenne, ¾ tsp. salt, and 2 cups water. Bring to a boil over high heat, stirring frequently to keep the lentils from sticking; skim any foam as necessary. Reduce the heat and simmer uncovered, stirring occasionally, until the lentils, carrots, and celery are tender, 35 to 40 minutes. Season to taste with salt.

You can store leftovers in the refrigerator for up to 5 days.

Black Bean Soup with Sweet Potatoes

Yields about 14 cups; serves eight.

The sweet potatoes in this soup contrast nicely with the tang of the yogurt and the tartness of the lime. Aniseed lends an unusual hint of licorice flavor.

2 Tbs. vegetable oil
2 medium yellow onions, chopped
3 medium cloves garlic, coarsely
  chopped
1½ tsp. ground coriander
1 tsp. ground cumin
¼ tsp. aniseed
Freshly ground black pepper
2 quarts lower-salt chicken broth
  or homemade vegetable broth
Four 15.5-oz. or two 29-oz. cans
  black beans, rinsed and drained
2 medium sweet potatoes, peeled
  and cut into medium dice
Kosher salt
½ cup plain yogurt
8 paper-thin lime slices

Heat the oil over medium heat in a 6-quart (or larger) Dutch oven. Add the onions and cook, stirring occasionally, until starting to soften and brown slightly, about 8 minutes. Add the garlic, coriander, cumin, aniseed, and ¼ tsp. pepper and cook, stirring constantly, until fragrant, about 30 seconds. Add the broth, beans, sweet potatoes, and ¾ tsp. salt and bring to a boil over high heat; skim any foam as necessary. Reduce the heat and simmer, uncovered, stirring occasionally, until the sweet potatoes are tender, about 15 minutes.

Using a slotted spoon, set aside 3 cups of the beans and potatoes. Purée the remaining soup in batches in a blender. Return the solids to the soup and season to taste with salt and pepper. Serve topped with a dollop of the yogurt and a lime slice.

You can store leftovers in the refrigerator for up to 5 days.

Lori Longbotham is a New York-based cookbook author and freelance recipe developer. ◆

The big chill

These soups freeze easily, so they're great instant meals for busy nights.

Chill soup thoroughly before freezing; this allows it to freeze faster. The ice crystals that form will be smaller, so your soup will have better texture and flavor.

Freeze soup in plastic containers, leaving about a half inch at the top to allow for expansion. Or fill plastic freezer bags about three-quarters full and squeeze out as much air as possible.

Freeze soups in large amounts or in smaller, portion-size containers that are ready to heat and serve. The smaller the container, the quicker it will freeze and defrost.

Before freezing, cover, label, and date your soup. As a general rule, stocks and broths can be frozen for up to six months; vegetable soups, about four months; meat, fish, or chicken soups, about three months; and soups with egg and cream, about two months.

Keep a thermometer in the freezer to make sure the temperature remains constant at 0°F. If you're freezing a large quantity at once, turn the thermostat to its coldest setting until the soup freezes.

Leave the soup in its container and defrost in the refrigerator, microwave oven, or under cold running water. You can also remove it from the container and reheat the frozen soup in a saucepan over low heat. A microwave oven is better for small amounts of soup.

Serve soup as soon as possible after defrosting.

Don't be alarmed if puréed soup separates after defrosting. To fix it, just whisk it back together.

Be aware that soups containing cream, wine, or lemon juice (or those thickened with eggs or flour) don't always freeze well. When reheating, simmer gently and whisk constantly to prevent curdling. Or better yet, add these ingredients after reheating.

Find menus for quick soup and sandwich suppers at
finecooking.com/extras

the
dark side
of chocolate

A chocolate expert unlocks
the secrets to baking with
dark chocolate in three
showstopping desserts

BY ALICE MEDRICH

Cinnamon-Caramel-Ganache
Layer Cake

Chocolate: a question of percentages

Master baker and chocolate guru Alice Medrich calls for chocolates with specific cacao percentages, all in an effort to balance flavor and texture. We asked Alice what the percentages mean and why you should care.

Q. What exactly are cacao percentages?

A. The cacao percentage on a chocolate bar indicates the percentage of the bar (by weight) that is pure cacao, or cocoa bean. Cocoa beans are composed of cocoa butter (fat) and dry cocoa solids (think fat-free cocoa powder).

Since the best bittersweet and semisweet chocolates are composed almost entirely of cocoa beans (often including some extra cocoa butter) and sugar, with just tiny amounts of optional vanilla and lecithin, the cacao percentage indirectly tells us the sugar content as well: A bar of semisweet or bittersweet chocolate marked 55% cacao therefore contains 45% sugar, while a bar labeled 70% cacao contains 30% sugar.

As the cacao percentage increases, the chocolate itself will taste more intensely chocolatey and less sweet. The effect on recipes is a little more complex, however, because cacao percentage affects texture as well as the flavor and sweetness of cakes and desserts.

Q. Why do these recipes call for chocolates with specific cacao percentages?

A. Not even 10 years ago, most bittersweet and semisweet chocolates available to home cooks contained less than 60% cacao, and most recipes were developed accordingly.

Today, supermarkets and specialty shops offer semisweet and bittersweet chocolates that range from 54% to more than 70% cacao. The choice is exciting, but chocolates with radically different cacao percentages can produce radically different results. Substituting chocolate with significantly higher cacao (70% instead of 54% or even 60%, for example) has an effect similar to subtracting sugar and replacing it with unsweetened cocoa powder. Cakes will be dry and crumbly and might taste bitter, mousses will have a grainy texture, and ganaches and sauces will almost certainly curdle.

Since I love the flavor and complexity of modern high-cacao chocolates, I often create recipes specifically for them. To ensure success for the home cook, I always specify chocolates with the cacao percentage (or range of percentages) that will result in the right balance of flavor, texture, and sweetness.

Q. Why use chocolates with different percentages in the same dessert?

A. I love using a variety of chocolate elements in the same dessert—not just chocolates with different cacao percentages but also cocoa powder or ground chocolate—because it allows me to create contrasts in sweetness, flavor intensity, and texture.

Cinnamon-Caramel-Ganache Layer Cake

Serves twelve to sixteen.

Make the filling and the frosting first, letting the former chill and the latter thicken slightly at room temperature while the cake is baking and cooling.

FOR THE FILLING:
2 cups heavy cream
3-inch cinnamon stick, lightly crushed
¼ tsp. table salt
4½ oz. semisweet chocolate (up to 62% cacao), coarsely chopped
½ cup granulated sugar

FOR THE FROSTING:
6 oz. bittersweet chocolate (70% or 72% cacao), chopped medium fine
2 oz. (4 Tbs.) unsalted butter, cut into 4 pieces
1 Tbs. light corn syrup
Pinch table salt

FOR THE CAKE:
1½ oz. (½ cup) unsweetened natural cocoa powder
½ cup buttermilk, at room temperature
6 oz. (1½ cups) cake flour
¾ tsp. baking soda
¼ tsp. table salt
4 oz. (8 Tbs.) slightly softened unsalted butter, cut into 4 pieces
1 cup granulated sugar
½ cup packed light brown sugar
2 large eggs, lightly beaten and at room temperature

Easy Bittersweet Chocolate Shards, for garnish (optional; see From Our Test Kitchen, p. 92)

Make the filling: In a medium saucepan, bring the cream, cinnamon, salt, and 2 Tbs. water to a simmer over medium-high heat. Off the heat, cover and steep for 15 minutes. Meanwhile, put the chocolate in a medium bowl and set a fine strainer over it.

Pour ¼ cup water into a heavy-duty 3-quart saucepan. Pour the sugar in the center of the pan and pat it down until evenly moistened (there should be clear water all around the sugar). Cover the pan and cook over medium-high heat until the sugar dissolves, 2 to 4 minutes. Uncover and cook without stirring until the syrup begins to color slightly, about 1 minute. Reduce the heat to medium and continue to cook, swirling the pot gently if the syrup colors unevenly.

When the caramel turns reddish amber, 1 to 2 minutes longer, take the pan off the heat and immediately stir in the cream mixture. Simmer over low heat, stirring constantly, until the caramel is completely dissolved, 1 to 3 minutes.

Pour the caramel cream through the strainer onto the chocolate and discard the cinnamon. Whisk until the chocolate melts and the mixture is smooth. Scrape into a wide, shallow bowl, cover loosely, and refrigerate until thoroughly chilled, at least 4 hours and up to 3 days.

Make the frosting: Put the chocolate, butter, corn syrup, and salt in a heatproof bowl set in a skillet of barely simmering water. Stir gently until the chocolate melts and the mixture is perfectly smooth. Off the heat, stir in 6 Tbs. cool water. Let cool and thicken at room temperature without stirring for at least 3 hours. The consistency should be like chocolate pudding.

Make the cake: Line the bottoms of three 9x2-inch round cake pans with parchment.

Position a rack in the lower third of the oven if the three pans will fit on it. Otherwise, position racks in the upper and lower thirds of the oven. Heat the oven to 350°F.

In a small bowl, whisk the cocoa and 1/2 cup lukewarm water. In a liquid measuring cup, mix the buttermilk with 1/2 cup cool water.

In a medium bowl, whisk the flour, baking soda, and salt and sift them three times onto a sheet of parchment.

In a stand mixer fitted with the paddle attachment, beat the butter on medium speed until creamy, about 15 seconds. Add the sugars gradually, beating until the mixture lightens in color and appears sandy but fluffy, about 5 minutes total. Dribble the eggs in a little at a time, taking a full minute to add them. Continue to beat for a few seconds until the mixture is smooth and fluffy.

Stop the mixer and add the cocoa mixture. Beat on medium speed just until combined. Stop the mixer and, using the parchment as a chute, add about one-quarter of the flour. Mix on low speed just until incorporated. Stop the mixer and add one-third of the buttermilk. Mix just until blended. Repeat, stopping the mixer between additions and scraping the bowl as necessary, until the remaining flour and buttermilk are mixed in.

Divide the batter evenly among the pans. Bake until a toothpick inserted in the center of each cake comes out clean, 17 to 20 minutes (if baking on two levels, rotate the upper and lower pans halfway through baking). Cool the cakes on racks for 5 minutes and then turn onto the racks, remove the parchment, and cool completely.

Assemble the cake: Beat the chilled filling in a stand mixer fitted with the paddle attachment at medium speed until it's very thick and stiff enough to hold a shape but still spreadable, 1 to 2 minutes. Don't over beat.

Put a cake layer upside down on a cardboard cake circle or tart pan bottom. Spread half of the filling evenly all the way to the edge of the layer. Top with a second upside-

down layer and gently press in place. Spread with the remaining filling. Top with the third layer, again upside down. Smooth any filling protruding from the sides.

Frost the cake: With an offset spatula, spread a very thin layer (about 1/2 cup) of frosting evenly over the top and sides of the assembled cake to smooth the surface, glue on crumbs, and fill cracks. (Stirring the frosting more than necessary dulls the finish and makes it set up too hard.) Spread the remaining frosting all over the top and sides of the cake, swirling the surface with the spatula if desired. Top with the chocolate shards (if using) and serve at room temperature.

Chocolate-Pomegranate Torte

Serves twelve to fourteen.

For the best flavor and texture, make the cake and spread it with the jelly a day or two before serving. Glaze it on the day you serve it.

FOR THE CAKE:
2 oz. (4 Tbs.) softened unsalted butter, cut into 4 pieces; more for the pan
6 oz. bittersweet chocolate (70% or 72% cacao)
3 large eggs, separated
¾ cup granulated sugar
¼ tsp. table salt
⅛ tsp. cream of tartar
2¼ oz. (½ cup) unbleached all-purpose flour

FOR THE POMEGRANATE JELLY:
1 medium **Pink Lady** or **Braeburn** apple
1½ cups pure unsweetened pomegranate juice
¼ cup plus 2 Tbs. granulated sugar
12 fresh or frozen cranberries

FOR THE GLAZE:
6 oz. bittersweet chocolate (70% or 72% cacao), chopped medium fine
3 oz. (6 Tbs.) unsalted butter, cut into 6 pieces
1 Tbs. honey or light corn syrup
Pinch table salt

Fresh pomegranate seeds, for garnish (optional)

Make the cake: Position a rack in the center of the oven and heat the oven to 350°F. Lightly grease the sides of a 9x2-inch round cake pan and line the bottom with parchment.

Finely grate 2 oz. of the chocolate and set aside. Coarsely chop the remaining chocolate and combine with the butter and 3 Tbs. water in a heat-proof bowl. Set the bowl in a skillet of barely simmering water and stir frequently until the mixture is melted and smooth. Set aside.

In a large bowl, whisk the egg yolks with ½ cup of the sugar and the salt until thick and lightened in color.

In a stand mixer fitted with the whisk attachment, beat the egg whites and cream of tartar at medium-high speed to soft peaks,

about 2 minutes. With the motor running, gradually add the remaining ¼ cup sugar, beating to stiff peaks, 1 to 2 minutes more.

Whisk the warm chocolate and the flour into the yolk mixture. With a rubber spatula, fold one-quarter of the whites into the chocolate batter. Scrape the remaining whites into the chocolate mixture and sprinkle the grated chocolate on top. Fold together. Pour the batter into the prepared pan and spread it evenly.

Bake until a toothpick inserted in the center of the cake comes out smudged with a few moist crumbs, about 25 minutes. Cool in the pan on a rack for 10 minutes. Run a knife around the edge of the cake and invert it onto another rack. Remove the pan and parchment and invert the cake onto the first rack (it's normal for the cake to have a crusty exterior that may crack with handling). Let cool completely.

Make the pomegranate jelly: Grate enough of the apple (including the peel) to yield ¾ cup. In a medium saucepan, bring the grated apple, pomegranate juice, sugar, and cranberries to a simmer over medium heat. Simmer, covered, until the apple is softened and the mixture has thickened a little, about 10 minutes. Uncover and continue to simmer, stirring occasionally at first and then constantly towards the end, until the liquid has evaporated and the mixture is reduced to ¾ cup, about 5 minutes.

With a rubber spatula, press the pulp through a medium-mesh strainer into a bowl until you can't get any more juice out of the pulp. Scrape all of the juice clinging to the bottom of the strainer into the bowl and discard the pulp in the strainer.

Brush away any loose crumbs and easily detachable crusty pieces from the sides and top of the cake. Transfer the cake to a cardboard circle or tart pan bottom.

Stir the jelly to blend it, scrape it onto the cake, and spread it evenly over the top. Let the jelly cool until it's set, about 1 hour. At this point, the cake may be covered with an inverted cake pan, wrapped in plas-

tic (the pan keeps the plastic from touching the cake), and stored at room temperature for up to 2 days.

Make the glaze: Put the chocolate, butter, honey, and salt in a heatproof bowl set in a skillet of barely simmering water. Stir gently until the chocolate melts and the mixture is perfectly smooth. Remove from the heat and stir in 2 Tbs. cool water. Let cool to room temperature without stirring. If not using right away, cover and store at room temperature.

Set the cake on a rack set over a baking sheet. With an offset spatula, spread ⅓ cup of the glaze around the sides of the cake and on top of the gel (be careful not to disturb the gel) to smooth the surfaces and glue on any crumbs. Re-warm the remaining glaze gently to 90°F in a skillet of barely simmering water—the glaze should have the consistency of thick, pourable cream.

Scrape all of the glaze onto the top of the cake. Spread the glaze over the top and all around the sides. For the shiniest glaze, work quickly and use as few strokes as possible. Scoop up any excess glaze from the baking sheet and use it to cover bare spots.

Garnish with pomegranate seeds (if using) and let the cake rest on the rack for 10 minutes. Transfer to a cake plate and let sit at room temperature until set, 15 to 30 minutes, or up to several hours before serving.

Bittersweet Chocolate Tart with Salted Caramelized Pistachios

Serves twelve to fourteen.

This buttery shortbread tart crust is filled with rich, dark chocolate and garnished with salty-sweet caramelized nuts and sea salt.

FOR THE TART SHELL:
4 oz. (8 Tbs.) unsalted butter, melted
¼ cup granulated sugar
1 tsp. finely grated orange zest
¾ tsp. pure vanilla extract
⅛ tsp. table salt
4½ oz. (1 cup) unbleached all-purpose flour

FOR THE FILLING:
1 cup half-and-half
2 Tbs. granulated sugar
Pinch table salt
7 oz. semisweet chocolate (up to 64% cacao), coarsely chopped
1 large egg, lightly beaten

1 recipe Salted Caramelized Pistachios (at right)
Fleur de sel or other flaky sea salt

Make the tart shell: In a medium bowl, combine the butter, sugar, zest, vanilla, and salt. Add the flour and mix just until well blended. If the dough seems too soft to work with, let it sit for a few minutes to firm up. Press the dough into a 9½-inch fluted tart pan with a removable bottom. Start with the sides, making them about ¼ inch thick, and then press the remaining dough evenly over the bottom, pressing well into the corners.

Let rest at room temperature for 30 minutes or chill until ready to bake (you can make the crust up to 3 days ahead).

Position a rack in the lower third of the oven and heat the oven to 350°F. Put the pan on a cookie sheet and bake until the crust is a deep golden brown, 20 to 25 minutes, checking after about 15 minutes to see if the dough has puffed. Press the dough down with the back of a fork and prick a few times if necessary.

Meanwhile, make the filling: In a small saucepan bring the half-and-half, sugar, and salt to a simmer. Off the heat, add the chocolate and stir with a whisk until completely melted and smooth. Cover to keep warm.

Just before the crust is ready, whisk the egg thoroughly into the chocolate mixture. When the crust is done, lower the oven temperature to 300°F. Pour the filling into the hot crust. Return the tart (still on the baking sheet) to the oven and bake until the filling is set around the edges but still jiggles a little in the center when you nudge the pan, 10 to 15 minutes. Cool on a rack.

Serve at room temperature or slightly cool. Garnish each slice with crushed Salted Caramelized Pistachios and a light sprinkling of fleur de sel.

The tart is best on the day it's made but may be refrigerated for 2 to 3 days. Once the tart is completely chilled, cover it, but make sure no plastic wrap touches the surface by first putting the tart pan in a larger cake pan. Or cover the tart with an overturned plate.

Salted Caramelized Pistachios

Yields 1 cup.

You can make these up to a week in advance. Store in an airtight container while still warm to prevent the caramel from becoming sticky.

½ cup salted whole roasted shelled pistachios
½ cup granulated sugar
⅛ tsp. fine sea salt

Line a baking sheet with foil.

Microwave the nuts on high for 1 minute so they will be warm when you add them to the caramel. Alternatively, heat them in a 200°F oven while you make the caramel.

Pour ¼ cup water into a heavy 3-quart saucepan. Pour the sugar and salt in the center of the pan and pat it down just until evenly moistened (there should be clear water all around the sugar). Cover the pan and cook over medium-high heat until the sugar dissolves, 2 to 4 minutes. Uncover and cook without stirring until the syrup begins to color slightly, about 1 minute. Reduce the heat to medium and continue to cook, swirling the pot gently if the syrup colors unevenly.

When the caramel is a pale to medium yellow, less than 1 minute more, add the warm nuts. With a heatproof silicone spatula, stir gently and slowly to coat the nuts with caramel. Continue to cook until a bead of caramel dribbled onto a white plate is reddish amber, about 1½ minutes more. Immediately scrape the mixture onto the baking sheet and spread it as thin as you can before it hardens. When the caramel is slightly cooled but still warm, slide the foil with the caramel nuts into a zip-top plastic bag and seal the bag. Cool completely. Chop or crush.

A better way to melt chocolate

The goal of melting chocolate is to make it fluid and warm (or very warm, depending on the recipe) to the touch without overheating or scorching it.

While most recipes call for a double boiler (a bowl set over a pan of simmering water), I much prefer a wide, shallow skillet of water with a stainless-steel bowl of chocolate sitting directly in it. The open bath lets me see and adjust the water if it begins to boil or simmer too actively, whereas the water in a double boiler is usually out of sight and thus trickier to monitor. Just as chocolate in a double boiler will scorch if the cook is inattentive, chocolate in an open bath must also be watched carefully, stirred frequently, and removed from the bath when melted.

Chocolate expert Alice Medrich is the author of several books, including, most recently, Bittersweet: Recipes and Tales from a Life in Chocolate *and* Pure Dessert: True Flavors, Inspiring Ingredients, and Simple Recipes. ◆

Cooking with spinach

At the supermarket, we have a choice when it comes to spinach: baby, bagged, or bunched. When we tested the Lemon-Thyme Spinach on p. 64, we decided to try each kind to see how different they were after cooking. Here's what we found:

Bunched

spinach had the best, most spinachy flavor and tender texture of those we tried—it was the favorite among our tasters. It had a couple of drawbacks, though: By weight, about 60% of our spinach was stem, so it took 5 pounds to yield the 2 pounds of trimmed leaves we needed—that's a lot of waste. It's also usually pretty sandy, so it takes some time to stem and wash the leaves.

Bagged

spinach had solid spinach flavor, but it wasn't quite as good as the bunched spinach. What's nice about bagged spinach is that it's fairly well trimmed—only about 20% of the weight is stem. It's also a little quicker to clean because it's "triple-washed." It still needs rinsing (we've seen plenty of sandy triple-washed spinach), but not as many times as bunched spinach. For the Lemon-Thyme Spinach, we consider bagged spinach to be the best all-around option: good taste, less waste.

Baby

spinach has small, delicate leaves that wilt to a slippery mass when cooked, making the texture slightly less desirable. The flavor of baby spinach is also much milder than that of mature bagged and bunched spinach. On the upside, bagged baby spinach is ready to use as is—it's usually well washed and the stems can be left on—so if you're crunched for time, it's a reasonable option.

—Dabney Gough, recipe tester

Turmeric

The Chicken, Lemon & Olive Stew on p. 56 owes its bright yellow color to turmeric, a relative of ginger. Both the rhizome and the leaves of the turmeric plant are edible, but it's the rhizome that's most widely used. The small, knobby rhizome looks like a cross between a knob of ginger and a carrot, and it tastes that way too. It's slightly bitter and metallic in flavor and ranges in color from sunny yellow to a saturated, Technicolor orange.

In Vietnam, turmeric is paired with fish or used in savory crêpe batter. In India, it's a component of curries. Turmeric is also used as a natural food coloring (sometimes as a stand-in for pricey saffron) and is employed in ayurvedic medicine as an antiseptic.

Fresh turmeric is relatively hard to come by in this country, though you might get lucky at Asian or Indian markets or especially well-stocked health food stores. If you find some, use it as you would fresh ginger: peeled and minced or grated. It'll keep in a plastic bag in the refrigerator for at least two weeks.

Dried, ground turmeric is easy to find in the spice aisle of the supermarket, but we recommend looking for it at a Vietnamese or Indian grocer. There, you'll get more for your money and are likely to find a fresher product. Like any dried spice, ground turmeric should be stored in a tightly sealed container in a cool, dry place, where it should last six months to a year. —D.G.

Easy bittersweet chocolate shards

The delicate chocolate shards decorating the Cinnamon-Caramel-Ganache Cake on p. 86 are dead easy to make with this simple technique from contributor Alice Medrich.

Melt 4 oz. chopped bittersweet chocolate in a clean, dry heatproof bowl set in a wide pan of nearly simmering water, stirring frequently with a dry spatula until smooth. Remove the bowl from the water and wipe the bottom dry.

1 Tear off two 16-inch-long sheets of waxed paper. Scrape the melted chocolate onto one sheet and spread with an offset metal spatula in a thin, even layer to within about 1/3 inch from each edge. Cover the chocolate with the second sheet of waxed paper.

2 Starting at one short edge, roll the paper and chocolate into a narrow tube about 1 inch in diameter. Refrigerate the tube seam side down on a baking sheet for at least two hours.

3 Remove the tube from the fridge and quickly unroll it while the chocolate is still cold and brittle to crack it into long curved shards. Peel back the top sheet of waxed paper.

4 Immediately slide a metal spatula under the chocolate to release it from the waxed paper, and then slide the shards onto a rimmed baking sheet. Refrigerate until ready to use. Warm fingers will melt the shards, so handle them with a spatula or tongs.

See this technique in action at
finecooking.com/extras

1

2

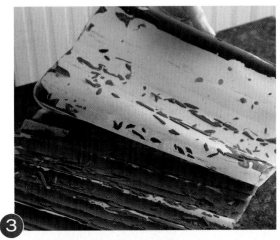

3

4

Inverting cakes with streusel toppings

Carole Walter's coffee cakes (pp. 68–71) offer a special challenge when the time comes to turn them out of their pans: How do you keep the streusel topping from falling off when you invert the cake? Here's the solution:

1 Gently lift up the center tube while carefully pushing the bottom upward with your opposite hand. If the cake doesn't release easily, run a thin knife between the cake and the tube and between the cake and the outer wall of the pan. Once the cake is out, run the knife under the bottom, too.

2 Fold a 12-inch square of aluminum foil into quarters. Measure 1¼ inches from the inside tip of the foil and cut an arc (this will become a hole for the tube when you unfold the foil). Unfold the foil and place over the cake, pressing gently onto the top of the cake and molding the foil around its sides to hold in the streusel.

3 Invert the cake onto a plate and remove the center tube.

4 Invert the cake onto a rack, remove the foil, and cool right side up.

Chop vs. dice

Of all the instructions you're likely to see in a recipe, "chop" and "dice" are two of the most common. Lots of people think they're the same thing, but between these two similar concepts lie important differences. This chart explains what we mean by each.

—*D.G.*

CUT	LOOKS LIKE	FOUND IN	HOW TO
CHOP	Similarly sized but irregularly shaped pieces.	Rustic dishes, mixtures that will be puréed, or ingredients that are small or unusually shaped, like olives or parsley.	Cut the ingredient into somewhat large, coarse pieces. Group the pieces and rock a chef's knife back and forth through them. Work randomly and in different directions. Fineness is relative to the original size of the ingredient, so "finely chopped" parsley should be smaller than "finely chopped" onions.
DICE	Cubes or squares, all the same size.	Dishes that are more refined in style or where even cooking is especially important.	For most ingredients, start by cutting lengthwise into sticks (or similar long, slender shapes). For onions, halve and slice them lengthwise, leaving the root end intact to help hold the slices together. Then hold the item together as you make neat, even crosswise cuts. Small dice is ¼ inch, medium dice is ½ inch, and large dice is ¾ inch.

FOR GOOD MEASURE:
Why you need a kitchen scale

Baking is just as much a science as an art. A delicate, fluffy cake is the result of many chemical reactions, and when one element is off, the result can fall flat—literally. A small digital kitchen scale truly is a baker's best friend. Here's why:

MEASURING INGREDIENTS

Depending on what scooping method you use, a leveled cup measure can hold anywhere from 3.5 to 5.5 weight ounces of flour. A fluffy ingredient like powdered sugar or cocoa can be even more variable. Weighing these ingredients eliminates the inconsistencies. It's also much faster and makes for less dishwashing; rather than measuring one cup at a time in a cup measure, you can weigh your ingredients right in the mixing bowl.

DIVIDING BATTER EVENLY

A scale is also helpful if you need to divide batter between two or more baking pans, as in the Cinnamon-Caramel-Ganache Layer Cake, on p. 86. Weighing the batter ensures that each layer is uniform, both in quantity and in baking time.

Even if you don't do a lot of baking, a scale is a worthwhile investment. You'll find yourself pulling it out again and again to weigh all sorts of things, like 12 ounces of pasta, a pound of potatoes, or even a letter that seems a little heavy for regular postage. Our favorites include models made by Salter, Soehnle, and Oxo (see Where to Buy It, p. 104).
—D.G.

Butterflying shrimp

Editor at large Susie Middleton uses an unusual technique for preparing the shrimp in her Crab & Scallion Stuffed Shrimp (p. 62): she butterflies them from underneath. This way, she's able to flip the tails up on the shrimp before baking, giving them a jaunty look. The technique is simple, but it's a good idea to buy a few extra shrimp in case you rip one or two while getting the hang of it. Be careful not to buy "easy-peel" shrimp, because they've already been deveined from the top side and won't work for this technique. Start by rinsing the shrimp and peeling them down to the section closest to the tail. Then follow the directions at right.

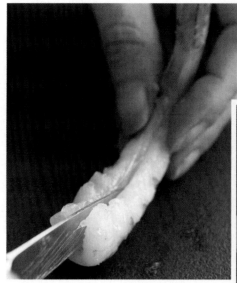

With a paring knife, slit the under-side of a shrimp down the middle, cutting almost but not all the way through to expose the vein that runs along the top of the shrimp.

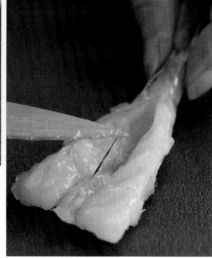

Open the shrimp like a book and use the knife to lift out the vein.

Decoding **crabmeat** labels

Backfin

Colossal or Jumbo Lump

Claw

Special

The holidays all but beg for splurgy ingredients like crab. You're likely to find several kinds of crabmeat at your market, each labeled to indicate what part of the crab the meat comes from.

COLOSSAL OR JUMBO LUMP crab consists of the two big muscles that help power the crab's back (swimming) legs. These luxuriously large lumps come at a premium price, so use them in recipes where you'll showcase them whole.

SPECIAL crab comes from other areas of the crab's body and consists of smaller pieces of meat. It's just as flavorful as the Colossal or Jumbo Lump and is the best, least-expensive choice for recipes that don't require large pieces of crab (such as the Crab & Scallion Stuffed Shrimp, on p. 62).

BACKFIN is a mixture of Special and (sometimes broken) Jumbo Lump pieces. This is another option for the stuffed shrimp.

CLAW meat, which can be from any of the legs (not just the claws), is darker than the body meat. It's also more robust in flavor, making it a good match for spicy or other strongly flavored recipes.

—D.G

How to trim a beef tenderloin

When it comes to beef, tenderloin is one of the priciest cuts. Our recipe for Slow-Roasted Beef Tenderloin, on p. 64, calls for a tenderloin roast that's been trimmed of its silverskin and "chain," or side muscle. If you want to purchase the roast completely trimmed and don't mind paying top dollar for it, just ask your butcher to prepare the roast "side muscle off and skinned." But if you'd rather save some money and you're up for a little knife work, ask for a "peeled, side muscle-on" roast, and trim it yourself as shown at right. You'll need to start with about 4¾ pounds to make up for the trim, but the price difference should still be worth it. Our untrimmed roast cost $6 less per pound, saving us about $15 in the end. Another bonus: You can save the chain for cooking another night (think stir-fry). It's perfectly tasty beef, just not as tender as the rest of the tenderloin.

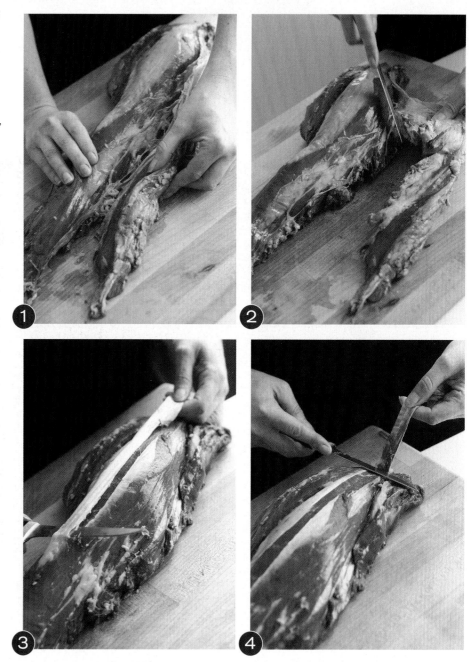

1 Locate the chain, the long piece of muscle that runs the length of the tenderloin. (The fatter, shorter, smooth muscle on the other side is part of the loin—leave that on.) Using your fingers, gently separate the chain from the tenderloin as much as possible.

2 With a boning knife, start at the narrow end of the chain and cut along the seam, making several long, shallow cuts rather than one or two deep ones. This way, you have more control over the path your knife takes and less chance of cutting too far in. You don't have to trim every bit of the chain from the wider end; it's fine to leave a narrow strip attached to the loin.

3 Starting about 1 inch from one end of the silverskin, push the tip of your knife under a strip of silverskin about ½ inch wide. Using your free hand to hold the silverskin taut, angle the knife slightly up toward the silverskin as you slide the knife down the tenderloin, freeing the silverskin.

4 Turn the knife around and cut off the end of the silverskin that's still attached. Repeat until all the silverskin is gone.

—Jennifer Armentrout, test kitchen manager, and Dabney Gough ◆

Sugar
more than just sweet

BY KIMBERLY Y. MASIBAY

We all know that sugar is essential for baking—after all, it's what makes sweets taste sweet. But thanks to its unique chemical nature, sugar also performs many other essential functions in cookies, cakes, and other baked goods.

Just to be clear, I'm talking about the kind of sugar we use most in baking: the dry, crystalline sugars that are collectively referred to as table sugar. (It comes in several forms, such as granulated, brown, powdered, and turbinado.) When you understand how this ingredient behaves in recipes, you'll be on your way to becoming a better baker, because many baking disasters can be traced to one little mistake: tinkering with sugar. Using less (or more) sugar than a recipe calls for (or even substituting honey for table sugar) can really affect your results.

Sugar stabilizes meringues

Whip egg whites with sugar and what do you get? Meringue. More than just a fluffy, white pie topping, meringue gives lightness and loft to mousses, sweet soufflés, angel food cakes, and even some frostings.

Sugar stabilizes meringue in two ways. First, it protects the egg whites from being overbeaten. As you whip air into egg whites, the egg proteins bond and form thin, strong sheets that stretch around the tiny air bubbles, creating foam. Adding sugar slows down this foaming, so you're less likely to overbeat the egg whites.

Second, sugar protects the foam from collapse. The sugar dissolves in the water in the bubbles' walls, forming a syrup that surrounds and supports the bubbles.

Sugar affects texture

When sugar molecules meet water molecules, they form a strong bond. This union of sugar and water affects the texture of baked goods in two important ways.

It keeps baked goods soft and moist. The bond between sugar and water allows sugar to lock in moisture so that items such as cakes, muffins, brownies, and frostings don't dry out too quickly.

It creates tenderness. Baked goods get their shape and structure from proteins and starches, which firm up during baking and transform soupy batters and soft doughs into lofty muffins and well-formed cookies. But because they build structure, proteins and starches can potentially make baked goods tough, too. The sugar in a batter or dough snatches water away from proteins and starches, which helps control the amount of structure-building they can do. The result? A more tender treat.

It is here that tinkering with a recipe's sugar can have a dramatic effect. When, for example, a loaf of pound cake has a nice shape and an appealing texture, the sugar, proteins, and starches are in balance. But if you tip that balance by using more or less sugar than the recipe calls for, the result could be so tender that it lacks the structure to hold its shape, or it could be shapely but too tough.

Tip: It's best to dust moist cakes with confectioners' sugar right before serving, because over time the sugar will attract even more moisture and become sticky.

Sugar leavens

No doubt you've noticed that cake and quick bread batters rise during baking. Well, sugar helps make this happen. When you mix up a cake batter and beat sugar into fat, eggs, and other liquid ingredients, the sugar crystals cut into the mixture, creating thousands of tiny air bubbles that lighten the batter. During baking, these bubbles expand and lift the batter, causing it to rise in the pan.

Sugar deepens color and flavor

Thank sugar for the appealing golden-brown color of many baked desserts. As sugar gets hot, it undergoes a cascade of chemical reactions called caramelization. In this process, sugar molecules break down into smaller and smaller parts and begin to turn deeper shades of brown and develop more complex flavors.

Sugar adds crunch

In the heat of the oven, moisture evaporates from the surface of baked goods, allowing dissolved sugars to re-crystallize. This creates the crunchy, sweet crust that you've probably enjoyed on such items as brownies, pound cakes, and some kinds of muffins and cookies.

Kimberly Y. Masibay is a Fine Cooking *contributing editor.* ◆

Browne Trading
Company

Russ &
Daughters

Tracklement's

Taku

Smoked Salmon

BY DENISE MICKELSEN

Smoked salmon is a holiday favorite, an indulgence served at parties and breakfasts. Often mislabeled as lox (which is unsmoked, wet-cured salmon), or gravlax (unsmoked and dry-cured), smoked salmon is actually fresh salmon—either farmed Atlantic salmon (*Salmo salar*) or one of five wild Pacific salmon species (chum, coho, pink, sockeye, or Chinook)—that is cured with salt, sugar, and seasonings and then cold-smoked at temperatures below 80°F. Unlike hot-smoking, cold-smoking doesn't cook the fish, so the result is the silky, delicate texture we expect from smoked salmon.

But which brand to buy? To find out, we tried eight of the country's top mail-order cold-smoked salmons in a blind taste test. We were looking for pleasantly smoky, not too salty succulent smoked salmon that we'd be happy to serve at our holiday celebrations. The four here fit the bill.

Browne Trading Company's

Scotch-cured smoked Scottish salmon ($23 for 8 oz., sliced; $45 for 1 lb., sliced; Brownetrading.com; 800-944-7848) comes from farmed Atlantic salmon wet-cured with Scotch whisky and smoked over Maine fruitwoods. We found it a touch sweet, a touch salty, and nicely smoky. Its texture was very close to that of raw salmon, which was a plus for several tasters.

Russ & Daughters'

Gaspé Nova ($30 per lb., sliced; Russanddaughters.com; 800-787-7229) was incredibly smooth and rich, starting out with a salty bite but finishing with gentle smoke. This salmon originates in the Gaspé Bay of Quebec, Canada. It's called Nova as shorthand for the traditional Nova Scotia nomenclature for smoked Atlantic salmon originating from fisheries in that area. Also wet-cured in brine, this style of smoked salmon would make a lovely canapé topping or a lush partner for crackers, crème fraîche, and capers.

Tracklement's

Original Highland Smoked Salmon ($59 for 1½ lb., unsliced; Tracklements.com; 800-844-7853) is made from fish from the Bay of Fundy, near Nova Scotia. Tasters noted its oily appearance, but after the salmon's cure in brown sugar and salt and hardwood-smoking, the nuanced balance of sweetness, salt, and smoke was perfect, and the texture was luscious and tender. To preserve quality and freshness, Tracklement's doesn't slice its salmon for you, so be ready with a sharp knife to carve the thinnest possible slices.

Taku Wild Alaska Seafood

was our favorite wild Pacific salmon ($61 for 1½ lb., sliced; Takustore.com; 800-582-5122). The intense red coloring of the sockeye salmon surprised some tasters, but its fresh flavor won us over. Lightly smoky and mild in flavor, the naturally dense fish had a less delicate texture than farmed varieties, but we felt good knowing we were enjoying a truly wild product.

White Smoked Salmon

For a real treat, seek out the rare—and absolutely delicious—silky smooth white smoked salmon. The same Atlantic species as pink-colored salmon, these fish live in the Baltic Sea on a diet devoid of shrimp or krill, which lend their pink hues to the fish that eat them. **Cap'n Mike's Holy Smoke** Northwest-style white salmon lox ($54.95 per lb., sliced; 707-585-2000) is a great product, even if it is misleadingly called lox. **Petrossian** (800-828-9241) and **Nantucket Wild Gourmet & Smokehouse** (508-945-2700) also carry white smoked salmon from time to time, so call to check for availability. It's well worth the effort. ◆

where to buy it

In Season, *p. 26*

It isn't crucial to have a special knife to separate the flesh from the membrane of a grapefruit; a small stainless paring knife will do the trick. But a good grapefruit knife—a thin, narrow, usually serrated blade that's curved at the tip—will help you cut close to the membrane, leaving less flesh attached to the rind. Look for one with very fine serrations on both edges of the blade. Amazon.com carries many brands, ranging in price from $2.59 to $19.45.

Open House, *p. 46*

The candlesticks in the photo on pp. 46–47 range in price from $5.95 to $17.95 at CB2.com (800-606-6252), except the one in the foreground, which is $150 at Juliska.com (888-414-8448). The bowl for the chutney ($59), the Champagne saucers for the mustard and horseradish cream ($85), the cake pedestal for the biscuits ($220), and the compote bowl for the nuts ($240) are also from Juliska. The white tureen holding the broccoli is $40 at Potterybarn.com (888-779-5176). On p. 52, the birch box ($13) is from Shopfete.com (203-263-6448), and the linen napkins, from Matteo, are available at J. Seitz & Co., New Preston, Connecticut (a set of four is $65; for more information, call 860-868-0119 or email info@jseitz.com).

Dinner with Friends, *p. 54*

You'll need a mini blowtorch for the ginger crème brûlée; try the Messermeister Cheflamme, available at Chefstools.com (866-716-2433) for $42.99. For information on the 9-inch "low bowls" on pp. 56–57 (about $60 each), visit Alexmarshallstudios.com or call 530-824-3800.

We love the complex, not-too-sweet flavors of ❶ Fentiman's botanically brewed beverages (think sodas). In particular, Fentiman's Ginger Beer and Mandarin and Seville Orange Jigger pair beautifully with the Chicken, Lemon & Olive Stew and Saffron Couscous. Look for these all-natural sodas at select retailers (Dean & Deluca, Fairway, Cost Plus World Market) or online at Chelseamarketbaskets.com (888-727-7887), where a case of 12 bottles is $33.

For information on buying a Dutch oven (you'll need an 8-quart version for the stew in this story), see the source under Soup Suppers.

The square, etched platter by Terra Firma on p. 58 is $75 at Shopfete.com (203-263-6448).

Holiday Menu, *p. 60*

Visit Surlatable.com (800-243-0852) for 8-inch square cake pans ($15.95), 12-cup nonstick muffin pans ($26), and heavy-duty rimmed baking sheets (Chicago Metallic's commercial jelly roll pan set is $27 for a set of two).

To find the placemats ($6.95), chargers ($19.95), dinner plates ($38.95), medium plates ($14.95), and napkins ($3.95) on pp. 60–61, visit Crateandbarrel.com (800-967-6696). The glass votives ($25 to $55) are from Simonpearce.com (800-774-5277). The trifle on p. 67 is pictured in a water glass from Match Italian pewter, $69.96 at Woodbury Pewter (Woodbury pewter.com; 800-648-2014).

Coffee Cakes, *p. 68*

For best results, use a 10-inch angel food cake pan, preferably shiny aluminum. Nonstick is fine as long as it has a light interior. A removable bottom makes it easier to get the cake out of the pan. Try Nordicware's, which is $19.99 at Pans.com (888-827-3960).

Spanish Marcona almonds are available at Whole Foods Markets or at Tienda.com (800-710-4304), where they're $9.95 for 5.3 oz.

Cookies, *p. 72*

Visit Sugarcraft.com for a wide variety of decorating sugars and pastry bags, as well as a 3/16 (#7) piping tip for 95¢. For a ❷ 3 1/2x4 1/2-inch Christmas tree-shaped cookie cutter, look to Coppergifts.com (620-421-0654).

Soup Suppers, *p. 78*

To make these soups, you'll need a 6-quart (or larger) ❸ Dutch oven. Chefsresource.com (866-765-2433) carries both Le Creuset and Staub brands in a range of colors and sizes.

The sterling silver ladle on p. 81 came to us from Country Loft Antiques in Woodbury, Connecticut (203-266-4500; Countryloftantiques.com).

Chocolate Desserts, *p. 84*

Cooking.com (800-663-8810) carries a 9 1/2-inch fluted tart pan with a removable bottom for $10.95, as well as a wide selection of 9-inch cake pans ($6.95 to $17.95). Arte Italica's Tesoro cake stand (on pp. 84–85) sells for about $226. For stores, visit Arteitalica.com.

From Our Test Kitchen, *p. 92*

Look for Soehnle's digital kitchen scales at Soehnleusa.com (866-695-3434), where prices start at $31.99. Metrokitchen.com (888-892-9911) carries a nice selection of Salter scales, from $39.95. And Oxo's food scale is $49.99 at Oxo.com (800-545-4411). ◆

Recipes, listed by title only, from *Fine Cooking* issues 90–96. For a free printout of the full 2008 index, call customer service at 800-888-8286. For a full searchable index, visit www.finecooking.com.

APPETIZERS

BEANS

BEEF & LAMB

BEVERAGES

BREADS & SANDWICHES

BREAKFAST

Stuffed Blue Cheese Burgers, 94:48

BURGERS

CHICKEN & TURKEY

Roasted Turkey with Juniper-Ginger Butter & Pan Gravy, 95:46

Rosemary-Garlic Chicken with Apple & Fig Compote, 95:66

Sautéed Chicken Paillards with Herb Salad & White Balsamic Vinaigrette, 92:90a

Sautéed Chicken with Sherry & Olive Pan Sauce & Toasted Almonds, 92:90a

Sesame Noodles with Chicken, 92:90a

Spanish Chicken with Chickpeas & Chorizo, 95:94a

Turkey Tacos, 95:94a

Vietnamese-Style Caramel-Braised Chicken, 92:90a

Vietnamese-Style Chicken Salad, 94:82a

Village-Style Greek Salad with Chicken & Lemon-Mint Vinaigrette, 92:90a

EGGS

Artichoke & Smoked Mozzarella Frittata, 96:114a

FISH & SHELLFISH

Blackened Tilapia with Cilantro-Lime Slaw, 96:114a

Brazilian Chicken & Shrimp Stew, 91:65

Broiled Miso-Marinated Halibut, 90:86a

Chinese Five-Spice Halibut with Pickled Red Pepper & Ginger, 92:47

Cod with Mushrooms, Garlic & Vermouth, 90:86a

Crab & Scallion Stuffed Shrimp, 96:62

Crabmeat Empanadas with Grilled Corn Salsa & Poblano Cream Sauce, 94:61

Cumin-Rubbed Tuna with Roasted-Jalapeño Tartar Sauce, 90:86a

Fire-Roasted Red Pepper & Shrimp Fettuccine with Toasted Garlic Breadcrumbs, 93:61

Fresh Tuna Burgers with Ginger & Cilantro, 94:48

Garlicky Shrimp with Basil, 92:61

Grilled Shrimp & Calamari Salad with Arugula & Orange Vinaigrette, 93:86a

Herb & Parmigiano-Crusted Tilapia with Quick Tomato Sauce, 90:86a

Herb-Buttermilk-Marinated Salmon with Cucumber Salad, 96:50

Hoisin-Glazed Scallops with Spinach & Cilantro, 96:114a

Lemon-Ginger Poached Halibut with Leeks & Spinach, 95:94a

Linguine with Shrimp, Caramelized Onion, Pancetta & Peas, 95:94a

Mussels Steamed with Leeks, Tomatoes & Garlic, 90: 86a

Pan-Seared Salmon with Plum-Cucumber Salad, 94:82a

Pea & Shrimp Penne with Basil, 92:55

Poppy Tooker's Seafood Gumbo, 90:54

Risotto with Scallops, Pancetta & Spinach, 91:86a

Roasted Salmon with Shiitake, Leek & Arugula Salad, 95:back cover

Salmon Seared on Bacon with Balsamic Vinegar, Honey & Rosemary, 90:86a

Scallop & Mushroom Rosemary Kebabs, 95:69

Seared Scallops with Golden Shallot & Grapefruit Sauce, 90:86a

Seared Scallops with Pea Purée, Crisp Pancetta & Gremolata, 92:back cover

Sear-Roasted Haddock or Cod with Horseradish Aïoli & Lemon-Zest Breadcrumbs, 92:48

Sear-Roasted Halibut with Tomato & Capers, 93:86a

Shrimp Roasted with Potatoes & Prosciutto, 90:back cover

Shrimp Salad Rolls with Tarragon & Chives, 94:82a

Shrimp Stew with Coconut Milk, Tomatoes & Cilantro, 91:86a

Shrimp with Spicy Asian Peanut Dipping Sauce, 96:pullout

Spice-Rubbed & Sear-Roasted Salmon with Honey-Glazed Fennel, 92:49

Thai Green Curry Shrimp, 96:114a

Vietnamese Tilapia with Turmeric & Dill, 95:94a

MEATLOAVES

Bacon-Wrapped Meatloaf, 91:37

Fried Meatloaf, 91:77

Glazed Meatloaf with Peppers & Warm Spices, 91:39

Meatloaf with Fresh Scallions & Herbs, 91:38

PASTA & GNOCCHI

Classic Baked Macaroni & Cheese, 91:49

Fire-Roasted Red Pepper & Shrimp Fettuccine with Toasted Garlic Breadcrumbs, 93:61

Fregola with Wild Mushrooms, Sherry & Cream, 90:42

Gnocchi with Creamy Gorgonzola Sauce, 90:64

Gnocchi with Sausage & Leek Ragù, 90:65

Israeli Couscous with Saffron, Toasted Pine Nuts & Currants, 90:45

Linguine with Roasted Red Peppers, Tomatoes & Toasted Breadcrumbs, 94:82a

Linguine with Shrimp, Caramelized Onion, Pancetta & Peas, 95:94a

Linguine with Zucchini, Pancetta & Parmigiano, 93:86a

Orecchiette with Fennel, Sausage & Tomatoes, 93:86a

Orzo with Lemon, Garlic, Parmigiano & Herbs, 90:44

Pan-Seared Gnocchi with Browned Butter & Sage, 90:64

Pasta with Roasted Cauliflower, Arugula & Prosciutto, 96:back cover

Pea & Shrimp Penne with Basil, 92:55

Potato Gnocchi, 90:62

Spaghetti alla Carbonara, 92:57

Spaghetti with Garlic & Spinach, 92:61

Spaghetti with Mushroom Cream Sauce, 95:94a

Whole-Wheat Pasta with Pancetta, Greens & Garlic, 96:114a

PIZZA, CALZONES & STROMBOLI

Basic Pizza Dough, 92:68

Better than Pepperoni Pizza, 92:69

Calzones with Sausage & Peppers, 92:70

Classic Margherita Pizza, 92:69

Stromboli with Salami, Ham & Cheese, 92:71

White Pizza, 92:69

PORK & SAUSAGE

Apple-Bacon Barbecued Ribs, 93:48

Bourbon-Orange-Glazed Ham, 96:50

Chicken-Andouille Filé Gumbo, 90:55

Chinese Pork & Mushroom Wraps, 90:40

Double-Fennel Pork Chops, 96:114a

Grilled Roast Pork Cubano Sandwiches, 90:39

Grilled Sausage with Summer Squash, Fresh Herbs & Olives, 94:back cover

Hoisin Barbecued Ribs, 93:48

Mediterranean Kale & White Bean Soup with Sausage, 91: 25

New Mexican Pork & Green Chile Stew, 90:41

Pork Chops with Mustard Sauce, 95:94a

Roasted Pork Loin with Maple-Mustard Crust, 90:38

Pan-Seared Gnocchi with Browned Butter & Sage, 90:64

Sesame Noodles with Chicken, 92:90a

Soy-Braised Kabocha Squash, 95:57

Roasted Baby Red, White & Purple Potatoes with Rosemary, Fennel & Garlic, 91:41

Roasted Beets with White Balsamic & Citrus Dressing, 90:25

Roasted Fingerling Potatoes, 96:52

Rustic Bread Stuffing with Dried Cranberries, Hazelnuts & Oyster Mushrooms, 95:46

Saffron Couscous, 96:56

Sautéed Broccoli Raab with Chile, Garlic & Lemon, 95:25

Sherry Baked Beans with Chorizo, 93:54

Shredded Carrots with Jalapeño, Lime & Cilantro, 93:52

Soy-Braised Kabocha Squash, 95:57

Spaghetti Squash with Indian Spices, 95:56

Spicy Red-Eye Baked Beans, 93:56

Spicy Slaw with Radicchio & Green Mango, 93:52

Spinach with Yogurt & Chickpeas, 90:60

Zucchini & Yellow Squash Ribbons with Daikon, Oregano & Basil, 93:51

Zucchini Fritters, 93:67

SOUPS, STEWS & STOCKS

Asparagus Soup with Saffron Croutons, 92:42

Black Bean Soup with Sweet Potatoes, 96:83

Brazilian Chicken & Shrimp Stew, 91:65

Chicken-Andouille Filé Gumbo, 90:55

Chicken Broth, 91:74

Chilled Oven-Roasted Yellow Pepper Soup, 93:60

Classic Tomato Soup, 91:55

Creamy Tomato Soup with Basil Coulis, 91:57

Curried Carrot Soup with Cilantro, 91:86a

Golden Turkey Broth, 95:84

Mediterranean Kale & White Bean Soup with Sausage, 91:25

New Mexican Pork & Green Chile Stew, 90:41

Pasta e Fagioli, 96:80

Pea & Mint Soup with Lemon Cream, 92:54

Poppy Tooker's Seafood Gumbo, 90:54

Quick Chicken Chili, 91:86a

Roasted Hubbard Squash Soup with Hazelnuts & Chives, 95: 5

Root Vegetable & Barley Soup with Bacon, 96:80

Sausages & White Bean Stew with Tomatoes, Thyme & Crisp Breadcrumbs, 91:86a

Shrimp Stew with Coconut Milk, Tomatoes & Cilantro, 91:86a

Southwest Tomato & Roasted Pepper Soup, 91:56

Spiced Tomato & Red Lentil Soup, 96:82

Summer Vegetable Soup with Dill, 94:82a

Tomato Soup with Fennel, Leek & Potato, 91:back cover

Winter Vegetable Soup with Coconut Milk & Pear, 91:63

Desserts & Pastry

Cakes

Angel Food Cake with Strawberries & Whipped Cream, 92:45

Blueberry-Lime Pound Cake, 93:73

Caramelized Pear Upside-Down Cake, 95:74

Chocolate Ripple Sour Cream Coffee Cake, 96:71

Cinnamon-Caramel-Ganache Layer Cake, 96:86

Cinnamon-Walnut Shortcakes with Caramelized Plums, 94:67

Ginger Cake, 96:67

Plum Coffee Cake with Brown Sugar & Cardamom Streusel, 94:65

Sour Cream Coffee Cake with Ginger & Marcona Almonds, 96:71

Sour Cream Coffee Cake with Toasted Pecan Filling, 96:70

Cookies & Bars

Apricot & Pistachio Baklava with Orange-Cardamom Syrup, 92:64

Blueberry Streusel Bars with Lemon-Cream Filling, 93:71

Caramel-Pecan Brownies, 95:75

Chocolate-Mint Thumbprints, 96:77

Classic Baklava, 92:64

Hazelnut & Chocolate Baklava with Espresso-Frangelico Syrup, 92:64

Honey-Nut Bars, 96:76

Honey Shortbread, 96:77

Lemon-Rosemary Christmas Trees, 96:75

Mocha Sandwich Cookies, 96:74

Orange-Hazelnut Olive Oil Cookies, 96:76

Pine Nut Wedding Cookies, 96:74

Truffles, 91:70

Fruit Desserts

Broiled Grapefruit with Honey, Vanilla & Cardamom, 96:28

Peach & Blueberry Crisp with Spiced-Pecan Topping, 93:72

Frostings & Sauces

Basic Caramel, 95:72

Basic Ganache, 91:68

Caramelized Plums, 94:67

Hot Fudge Sauce, 91:70

Rich Caramel Sauce, 95:73

Pies, Tarts & Tortes

Bittersweet Chocolate Tart with Salted Caramelized Pistachios, 96:90

Black & Blueberry Pie with Lemon-Cornmeal Crust, 93:70

Chocolate Caramel-Almond Tart, 95:76

Chocolate-Espresso Mousse Torte, 91:69

Chocolate Pomegranate Torte, 96:88

Plum Tart with Lemon-Shortbread Crust, 94:64

Sugar & Spice Pumpkin Pie with Brandied Ginger Cream, 95:50

Puddings & Parfaits

Apricot-Almond Bread Pudding, 90:67

Crème Caramel, 95:73

Espresso Crème Caramel, 95:73

Ginger Cake Trifles with Caramelized Apples, Cranberries & Whipped Cream, 96:66

Ginger Crème Brûlée, 96:59

Individual Toasted Coconut & Lemongrass Bread Puddings, 91:64

Lemon-Buttermilk Pudding Cakes, 93:45

Lemon-Coconut Bread Pudding, 90:67

Mango Lassi Parfait, 90:60

Orange Crème Caramel, 95:73

Rum-Raisin Bread Pudding, 90:67

Triple-Berry Bread Pudding, 90:67

Truffles, 91:70

Blueberry-Lime Pound Cake, 93:73

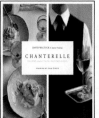

Statement of Ownership, Management, and Circulation

1. Publication title: *Fine Cooking.* **2.** Publication no. 1072-5121. **3.** Filing date: September 29, 2008. **4.** Issue frequency: Bimonthly. **5.** No. of issues published annually: 6 as of Feb/Mar 08. **6.** Annual subscription price: $29.95. **7.** Complete mailing address of known office of publication: 63 S. Main St., PO Box 5506, Newtown, Fairfield County, CT 06470-5506. **8.** Complete mailing address of headquarters or general business office of publisher: 63 S. Main St., PO Box 5506, Newtown, CT 06470-5506. **9.** Publisher: Maria Taylor, address same as 8. Editor: Laurie Buckle, address same as 8. Managing Editor: Rebecca Freedman, address same as 8. **10.** Owner: The Taunton Press, Inc., address same as 8. Stockholders owning or holding 1% or more of total amount of stock: Taunton, Inc., address same as 8. **11.** Known bondholders, mortgagees, and other security holders: None. **12.** Not applicable. **13.** Publication title: *Fine Cooking.* **14.** Issue date for circulation data below: August/September 2008. **15.** Extent and nature of circulation:

	Average no. copies each issue during preceding 12 months	No copies of single issue published nearest to filing date
A. Total number copies (net press run)	478,088	484,674
B. Paid circulation (by mail & outside the mail)		
1. Mailed outside-county paid subscriptions stated on PS form 3541	146,666	147,500
2. Mailed in-county paid subscriptions stated on PS form 3541	0	0
3. Paid distribution outside the mails including sales through dealers & carriers, street vendors, counter sales & other paid distribution outside USPS	111,476	90,350
4. Paid distribution by other classes of mail through USPS	0	0
C. Total paid distribution (Sum of 15B 1, 2, 3 & 4)	258,142	237,850
D. Free or nominal rate distribution (by mail & outside the mail)		
1. Outside-county copies on PS form 3541	3,622	5,415
2. In-county copies on PS form 3541	0	0
3. Other classes through USPS	0	0
4. Outside the mail	6,462	6,301
E. Total free or nominal rate distribution (Sum of 15D 1, 2, 3 & 4)	10,084	11,716
F. Total distribution (sum of 15C & 15E)	268,226	249,566
G. Copies not distributed	209,862	235,108
H. Total (sum of 15F & 15G)	478,088	484,674
I. Percent paid (15C ÷ 15F x 100)	96.2%	95.3%

16. This statement of ownership will be printed in the Dec/Jan 2009 issue of this publication. **17.** I certify that all information on this form is true and complete. I understand that anyone who furnishes false or misleading information on this form or who omits material or information requested on the form may be subject to criminal sanctions (including fines and imprisonment) and/or civil sanctions (including civil penalties). Signature: Laurie Buckle, editor.

Appliances

Chef's Choice *p. 15* Woo 'em with waffles! Prepare the world's most delicious waffles in 90 seconds! The Chef's Choice® unique Quad® baking system lets you choose the ideal flavor, texture, and color.
800-342-3255
www.chefschoice.com

The Chef's Resource *p. 103* Serious tools for serious chefs! The Chef's Resource offers the highest-quality handpicked items for the serious home chef.
www.chefsresource.com

Earthstone Wood-Fire Ovens *p. 111* Wood-fired brick ovens for indoor and outdoor use. Can double as a fireplace. Great for baking, grilling, and roasting.
800-840-4915
www.earthstoneovens.com

Mugnaini Imports *p. 97* Mugnaini, exclusive importers of Italian wood-fired ovens. Italian tradition, American technology. Dedicated to customer service in design, building support, and oven use.
888-887-7206
www.mugnaini.com

Viking Range Corporation *p. 19* If cooking is everything, the complete Viking kitchen offers everything you need - professional performance and impeccable design.
888-845-4641
www.vikingrange.com/wheretobuy

Zojirushi America Corporation *p. 43* Zojirushi manufactures top-of-the-line cooking appliances from rice cookers to breadmakers. Focusing on how our appliances fit into everyday lives for nearly 90 years.
www.zojirushi.com

Bakeware

A Cook's Wares *p. 111* We have what you need for your kitchen: The finest cookware, bakeware, cutlery, utensils and small appliances. Since 1981.
800-915-9788
www.cookswares.com

Emile Henry *p. 13* Beautiful, scratch-proof, naturally nonstick, and easy to clean. French-made Emile Henry® ovenware and bakeware heats evenly for perfect cooking. It does more, so you do less.™
www.emilehenryusa.com

LaPrima Shops *p. 111* Come discover the finest-quality selection of gourmet and European-style merchandise—from the finest espresso to the future in silicone baking and cooking tools.
www.laprimashops.com

Nordic Ware *p. 33* Nordic Ware is America's favorite manufacturer of bakeware, cookware, and kitchenware. Our famous Bundt® pans are found in well-equipped kitchens all around the world.
www.nordicware.com

Pillivuyt USA, Inc. *p. 101* Over 400 porcelain items for cooking and serving. Virtually nonstick with easy-to-clean impenetrable glaze. Durable, versatile, and a joy to use.
www.pillivuytus.com

Books

Cookbook Publishers *p. 111* Cookbook Publishers, Inc.: Raise money with your custom community fundraising cookbook. Great for churches, schools, or organizations. Free kit.
800-227-7282
www.cookbookpublishers.com

Jessica's Biscuit *p. 100*
www.ecookbook.com

Cookware

DeBuyer Industries *p. 101* French manufacturer since 1830, de Buyer offers professional high-quality cooking and pastry utensils for lovers of flavor and gastronomy.
www.debuyer.com

Fagor Cookware *p. 97* Manufacturer of stainless steel pressure cookers, specialty cookware, and kitchen accessories. Sold at fine retail stores nationwide. Shop online for parts and accessories.
www.fagoramerica.com

Falk Culinair *p. 15* Fine cookware for fine cooks. Stainless lined, solid copper cookware from Belgium. No other cookware conducts heat more efficiently or evenly than Falk.
www.copperpans.com

Kuhn-Rikon Corporation *p. 14* Kuhn Rikon offers the finest in pressure cookers, specialty cookware, and distinctive kitchen tools to make a cook's life easier.
800-924-4699
www.kuhnrikon.com/fine

MetroKitchen.com *p. 99* Metrokitchen.com, top brands for the professional chef in each of us. Free shipping, the web's best prices. Friendly, expert service on-line since 1998.
www.metrokitchen.com

Swiss Diamond Cookware *p. 103* Swiss manufacturer of patented diamond reinforced non-stick cookware, up to 200,000 real diamonds per pan. Diamonds guarantees lifetime non-stick performance, oven, dishwasher, metal utensil safe.
www.swissdiamondusa.com

Swissmar Imports, Ltd. *p. 39* For all your entertaining needs, find some of the finest houseware products in the world at Swissmar, Contact us Today!
877-947-7627
www.swissmar.com

The Chef's Resource *p. 33* Serious tools for serious chefs! The Chef's Resource offers the highest-quality handpicked items for the serious home chef.
www.chefsresource.com

The Chef's Resource *p. 39* Serious tools for serious chefs! The Chef's Resource offers the highest-quality handpicked items for the serious home chef.
www.chefsresource.com

Cutlery

The Chef's Resource *p. 97* Serious tools for serious chefs! The Chef's Resource offers the highest-quality handpicked items for the serious home chef.
www.chefsresource.com

Friedr. Dick Corp. *p. 103* Made in Germany since 1778. The only manufacturer worldwide who offers a complete range of knives, sharpening steels, ancillary items for chefs.
www.fdick.com

Japanese Chefs Knife *p. 43* Your online source for Japanese chef's knives for home cooking and the professional chef. Finest selections from the top brands: Masahiro, Misono, Fujiwara Kanefusa, Glestain.
www.japanesechefsknife.com

Japanese Chefs Knife *p. 99* Your online source for Japanese chef's knives for home cooking and the professional chef. Finest selections from the top brands: Masahiro, Misono, Fujiwara Kanefusa, Glestain.
www.japanesechefsknife.com

MetroKitchen.com *p. 101* Metrokitchen.com, top brands for the professional chef in each of us. Free shipping, the web's best prices. Friendly, expert service on-line since 1998.
www.metrokitchen.com

Sointu USA *p. 39* Sointu USA created the market for Japanese knives in the US. Its collection of brands represents the very best of what is manufactured in Japan.
www.sointuusa.com

Gourmet Foods

Avocado of the Month Club *p. 111* Your online source for gourmet avocados you won't find in grocery stores. Delicious premium avocados delivered straight to your front door—order today!
866-714-9921
www.aotmc.com

Beverages Direct *p. 110* Beverages Direct has been shipping unique and hard to find gourmet sodas, specialty waters, iced teas, etc. Direct to your door since 1997.
www.beveragesdirect.com

Chestnut Growers of America *p. 101* Your source for fresh chestnuts and chestnut products from orchards in the U.S.A. Order now for the holidays.
www.chestnutgrowers.com

Ghirardelli Chocolate Co. *p. 11* The luxuriously deep flavor and smooth texture of Ghirardelli Premium Baking Chocolate delivers the ultimate chocolate indulgence. Visit www.ghirardelli.com for great holiday recipe ideas!
www.ghirardelli.com

Illy Espresso USA, Inc. *p. 17* Full selection of expertly roasted coffee, home-delivery coffee subscription programs, artist cup collections, and exceptional accessories and gifts. Free shipping on coffee orders over $50.
www.illyusa.com

John Wm. Macy's Cheesesticks *p. 95* Enrich any occasion with our all-natural sourdough CheeseSticks, CheeseCrisps and SweetSticks, made with fine aged cheeses and choice seasonings, then baked twice to "the perfect crunch!"
www.cheesesticks.com

La Tienda *p. 110* A window to the best of Spain. America's most comprehensive inventory of quality Spanish food selected by a knowledgeable and dedicated family. Immediate delivery.
888-472-1022
www.tienda.com

Ladd Hill Orchards *p. 110* Premium, Oregon-grown fresh or dried chestnuts and chestnut flour Gluten free. Certified organic by guaranteed organic certification agency.
www.laddhillchestnuts.com

nutrition

Recipe	Page	Calories total	Calories from fat	Protein (g)	Carb (g)	Fats total	Fats sat	Fats mono	Fats poly	Chol. (mg)	Sodium (mg)	Fiber (g)	Notes
In Season	26												
Broiled Grapefruit with Honey, Vanilla & Cardamom		90	0	1	22	0	0	0	0	0	0	2	
Drinks	38												
Orange-Scented Mulled Wine		220	0	0	15	0	0	0	0	0	10	0	
Triple-Shot Eggnog		270	130	5	16	15	9	4.5	1	125	80	0	
Hot Buttered Rum		250	90	0	14	10	7	3	0	30	10	0	
Open House	46												
Pear Sidecar		280	0	0	36	0	0	0	0	0	0	0	
Bourbon-Orange-Glazed Ham		230	90	25	10	9	3	4	1.5	75	940	0	
Pineapple-Bourbon Chutney		50	0	0	13	0	0	0	0	0	15	0	per 2 Tbs.
Herb-Buttermilk-Marinated Salmon with Cucumber Salad		230	60	27	4	7	1	2.5	2	80	340	0	
Roasted Fingerling Potatoes		190	80	3	24	9	1	6	2	0	160	3	
Broccoli with Spicy Gremolata		80	45	3	9	5	0.5	3.5	0.5	0	320	4	
Dinner with Friends	54												
Chicken, Lemon & Olive Stew		490	220	48	18	25	6	12	5	150	860	4	without couscous
Saffron Couscous		250	80	7	34	9	3	4.5	1	10	115	2	
Arugula, Carrot & Celery Root Salad with Almonds		130	90	2	10	10	1	7	1.5	0	110	2	
Ginger Crème Brûlée		380	300	4	18	33	20	10	1.5	280	85	0	
Holiday Dinner	60												
Champagne Cosmo		210	0	0	16	0	0	0	0	0	0	0	
Crab & Scallion Stuffed Shrimp		210	130	15	6	14	4.5	4	4.5	125	370	1	
Slow-Roasted Beef Tenderloin with Mushroom Ragoût		670	430	47	9	48	20	20	2.5	190	390	2	
Lemon-Thyme Spinach		100	80	3	4	9	5	2	0.5	25	230	3	
Individual Savory Horseradish Bread Puddings		170	120	5	7	14	7	4	0.5	145	220	1	
Ginger Cake Trifles with Apples & Cranberries		630	300	5	81	34	21	9	1.5	130	240	3	
Ginger Cake		320	120	4	48	13	8	3.5	0.5	60	190	1	
Coffee Cake	68												
Sour Cream Coffee Cake with Toasted Pecan Filling		500	280	6	51	32	16	10	3	115	300	2	
Sour Cream Coffee Cake with Ginger & Marcona Almonds		520	270	7	57	30	16	10	2.5	115	300	2	
Chocolate Ripple Sour Cream Coffee Cake		600	330	7	64	37	18	12	4	115	310	3	
Cookies	72												
Chocolate-Mint Thumbprints		80	50	1	7	6	3.5	1.5	0	15	15	0	per cookie
Honey Shortbread		200	100	2	23	12	7	3	0.5	30	95	0	per wedge
Orange-Hazelnut Olive Oil Cookies		60	35	1	6	4	0	3	0	5	15	0	per cookie
Pine Nut Wedding Cookies		130	90	2	10	10	3.5	2.5	3	15	35	0	per cookie
Mocha Sandwich Cookies		60	25	1	9	3	2	1	0	10	25	0	per cookie
Honey-Nut Bars		460	260	8	45	30	11	13	4	50	170	3	per bar
Lemon-Rosemary Christmas Trees		130	50	2	18	5	3.5	1.5	0	20	70	0	per cookie
Soup Suppers	78												
Root Vegetable & Barley Soup with Bacon		210	30	11	37	3.5	1	1.5	0.5	5	450	7	
Pasta e Fagioli		370	70	21	59	7	1.5	2.5	2	5	720	11	
Spiced Tomato & Red Lentil Soup		320	70	22	45	8	1	3	2.5	0	480	9	
Black Bean Soup with Sweet Potatoes		310	50	17	51	6	1	2.5	2	0	370	11	
Chocolate Desserts	84												
Cinnamon-Caramel-Ganache Layer Cake		430	240	4	49	26	16	8	1	90	190	3	
Bittersweet Chocolate Tart with Caramelized Pistachios		260	140	4	31	15	8	5	1	40	95	2	
Chocolate-Pomegranate Torte		350	180	5	41	20	11	6	2.5	70	105	3	
5-Ingredient Appetizers	pullout												
Warm Spinach & Artichoke Dip		230	200	4	5	22	6	5	9	20	280	1	
Shrimp with Spicy Asian Peanut Dipping Sauce		160	80	15	5	9	1	0	0	110	135	1	
Greek Salad Skewers		110	90	3	3	10	3.5	5	1	15	340	0	
Baked Brie with Dried Cherries & Thyme		150	90	6	6	11	6	3.5	0	30	200	0	
Prosciutto-Wrapped Mozzarella & Basil		180	130	11	1	15	7	5	0.5	45	540	0	
Warm Cheese & Mushroom Toasts		130	80	7	4	9	6	3	0	30	220	1	
Smoked Salmon & Cucumber Tea Sandwiches		150	60	6	16	7	4	2	0.5	15	540	2	
Sweet & Spicy Roasted Nuts		220	180	5	9	20	3	11	4.5	5	85	3	per ¼ cup
Endive Spears with Sweet Potato, Bacon & Chives		50	35	1	3	4	2	1.5	0	10	100	1	
Spicy Spanish Olives		100	70	0	4	8	0.5	6	2	0	660	0	
Quick & Delicious	114a												
Double-Fennel Pork Chops		520	310	39	13	35	13	14	5	140	750	6	
Baby Greens with Chicken, Cherries, Pears & Pecans		250	150	14	14	16	2.5	10	3.5	35	180	4	
Hoisin-Glazed Scallops with Spinach & Cilantro		210	70	21	13	9	1	3.5	3.5	40	570	4	
Blackened Tilapia with Cilantro-Lime Slaw		370	220	31	9	25	7	6	10	95	500	3	
Watercress Salad with Steak, Sautéed Shallots & Stilton		260	170	18	4	19	6	10	1.5	45	420	0	
Thai Green Curry Shrimp		510	380	25	14	42	36	2	1	170	1380	4	
Whole-Wheat Pasta with Pancetta, Greens & Garlic		520	200	22	62	22	8	9	2.5	40	1410	8	
Artichoke & Smoked-Mozzarella Frittata		260	160	18	9	17	5	7	2	435	420	5	
Back Cover													
Pasta with Roasted Cauliflower, Arugula & Prosciutto		530	150	23	73	16	3.5	8	2	20	1100	7	

The nutritional analyses have been calculated by a registered dietitian at Nutritional Solutions in Melville, New York. When a recipe gives a choice of ingredients, the first choice is the one used. Optional ingredients with measured amounts are included; ingredients without specific quantities are not. When a range of ingredient amounts or servings is given, the smaller amount or portion is used. When the quantities of salt and pepper aren't specified, the analysis is based on ¼ teaspoon salt and ⅛ teaspoon pepper per serving for entrées, and ⅛ teaspoon salt and ¹⁄₁₆ teaspoon pepper per serving for side dishes.

Hoisin-Glazed Scallops with Spinach & Cilantro

Serves four.

For the best results, use "dry" scallops rather than "wet" scallops, which have been soaked in a sodium solution that prevents them from browning well.

16 all-natural "dry" sea scallops (about 1 lb.)
Kosher salt
⅛ tsp. cayenne pepper
2 Tbs. vegetable oil
1 Tbs. hoisin sauce
3 thin scallions, very thinly sliced
10 oz. baby spinach (10 loosely packed cups)
1 cup coarsely chopped fresh cilantro
½ tsp. Asian sesame oil

Dry the scallops well with paper towels and season with ½ tsp. salt and the cayenne. In a 12-inch cast-iron skillet, heat 1 Tbs. of the oil over high heat until hot. Cook the scallops, turning once with tongs, until golden brown and just opaque throughout, 3 to 4 minutes per side. As they finish cooking, transfer the scallops to a large plate and brush the top of each with hoisin sauce.

Wipe out the skillet and then heat the remaining 1 Tbs. oil over medium-high heat. Add about two-thirds of the scallions and cook, stirring constantly, until softened, about 30 seconds. Add the spinach, cilantro, and ¼ tsp. salt and cook, tossing constantly with tongs, until just barely wilted, about 2 minutes. Remove the skillet from the heat, drizzle the spinach mixture with the sesame oil, and toss to combine well.

Serve the scallops with the spinach, sprinkled with the remaining scallions.

—*Lori Longbotham*

Watercress Salad with Steak, Sautéed Shallots & Stilton

Serves four.

This salad is heavier on greens than on steak, making it a lighter meal.

3 Tbs. extra-virgin olive oil
1 Tbs. fresh lemon juice
½ tsp. Worcestershire sauce
½ tsp. Dijon mustard
Kosher salt
12- to 14-oz. strip steak or rib eye (1 inch thick)
Freshly ground black pepper
4 large shallots, sliced ¼ inch thick (about 1½ cups)
6 cups (lightly packed) small watercress sprigs (about 2 bunches trimmed of lower stems), torn into bite-size pieces
2 oz. Stilton, crumbled (about ½ cup)

In a small bowl, whisk 2 Tbs. of the olive oil, the lemon juice, Worcestershire sauce, mustard, and a generous pinch of salt. Season both sides of the steak with ½ tsp. salt and ¼ tsp. pepper.

In a 10-inch straight-sided sauté pan, heat the remaining 1 Tbs. oil over medium-high heat until hot. Cook the steak, without disturbing, swirling the oil in the pan occasionally, until the bottom of the steak is deeply browned, about 5 minutes. Flip and cook until the other side is nicely browned, about 3 minutes more. Transfer the steak to a cutting board.

Turn the heat to low and cook the shallots, stirring frequently, until softened and lightly browned, 5 to 8 minutes. (Use a spatula or spoon to break apart the shallot slices and to incorporate some of the browned bits from the pan.) Remove from the heat and let cool slightly.

Slice the beef thinly. Fan an equal number of slices on each of 4 dinner plates. Rewhisk the dressing if necessary. In a large bowl, toss the shallots, watercress, and Stilton with a generous pinch of salt and just enough of the dressing to coat. Season with more salt and pepper and arrange the salad over the beef slices.

—*Susie Middleton*

Photos: Eddie Berman, except two at far right, Scott Phillips

Thai Green Curry Shrimp

Serves four.

This is even faster than take-out from your local restaurant. The only fresh ingredient you'll need to grab is basil—all of the others can be stored in your pantry or freezer.

Two 13½- or 14-oz. cans unsweetened coconut milk
¼ cup Thai green curry paste
2½ Tbs. Asian fish sauce
1 tsp. firmly packed light brown sugar
1 lb. large shrimp (31 to 40 per lb.), shelled and deveined
1 cup lightly packed fresh basil leaves, torn into bite-size pieces
1 cup frozen green peas, thawed

Spoon ½ cup of the thick coconut cream from the tops of the cans of coconut milk into a large, heavy saucepan and heat over medium heat. Add the curry paste and cook, whisking constantly, until heated through and smooth, 2 to 3 minutes. Whisk in the remaining coconut milk and bring to a boil over high heat, whisking frequently. Reduce the heat to low, add the fish sauce and sugar and simmer gently for 5 minutes, whisking occasionally.

Increase the heat to medium high, stir in the shrimp, and cook, stirring occasionally, just until the shrimp are opaque throughout, 2 to 3 minutes. Stir in the basil and peas and cook, stirring, until the peas are heated through, about 1 minute.

Serving suggestion: Serve with steamed jasmine rice.

—Lori Longbotham

Baby Greens with Chicken, Dried Cherries, Pears & Pecans

Serves four to six.

Rotisserie chicken is the time saver in this salad. Feel free to substitute your favorite lettuces for the herb salad or mixed greens.

1 medium clove garlic
Kosher salt
3 Tbs. extra-virgin olive oil
1 Tbs. red-wine vinegar
1 tsp. fresh thyme leaves
Freshly ground black pepper
1 medium firm-ripe pear, peeled, cored, and cut into ½-inch dice
⅓ cup dried tart cherries
8 oz. packaged herb salad or mixed baby greens (8 loosely packed cups)
2 cups shredded cooked chicken
½ cup pecans, toasted

Chop the garlic, sprinkle with ½ tsp. salt, and mash to a paste with the flat side of a chef's knife. Put the paste in a large serving bowl and whisk in the olive oil, vinegar, thyme, and ¼ tsp. pepper. Gently stir in the pear and cherries. Add the greens, chicken, and pecans and toss to coat. Season to taste with more salt and pepper and serve immediately.

—Lori Longbotham

Double-Fennel Pork Chops

Serves four.

Both fennel seed and sautéed fresh fennel bring big flavor to simple pork chops.

2 tsp. fennel seed
Kosher salt and freshly ground black pepper
Four 1-inch-thick center-cut bone-in pork loin chops (about 12 oz. each), trimmed
3 Tbs. unsalted butter
2 medium fennel bulbs (2 lb.), trimmed, cored, and cut into ¼-inch-thick strips, plus ¼ cup coarsely chopped fronds
¾ cup lower-salt chicken broth
3 Tbs. coarsely chopped fresh flat-leaf parsley
2 Tbs. vegetable oil

Lightly crush the fennel seed in a mortar and pestle or with the bottom of a small skillet. Transfer to a small bowl and stir in 2 tsp. salt and ¼ tsp. pepper. Season the pork chops with 3 tsp. of the spice mixture.

Melt the butter over medium heat in a 12-inch skillet. Stir in the fresh fennel, ½ cup of the broth, and the remaining spice mixture.

Cover the skillet, increase the heat to medium high, and cook, stirring occasionally, until the fennel begins to soften and brown, 8 to 10 minutes (reduce the heat if the fennel browns too quickly).

Uncover, reduce the heat to medium, and add the remaining ¼ cup broth and 2 Tbs. of the parsley. Cook, stirring frequently and scraping up any browned bits, until tender, 1 to 2 minutes. Stir in the remaining parsley and the fronds, season to taste with salt and pepper, and transfer to a medium bowl.

Wipe out the pan, add the oil, and heat over medium-high heat. Add the pork chops and cook, turning once with tongs, until well browned and cooked through, 10 to 12 minutes. (To check for doneness, make a small cut near the bone and look inside—the pork should still have a hint of pinkness.) Serve the pork chops with the fennel.

—Lori Longbotham

Artichoke & Smoked-Mozzarella Frittata

Yields one 10-inch frittata; serves four.

8 large eggs
½ cup grated smoked mozzarella
1 Tbs. extra-virgin olive oil
½ cup diced yellow onion
10 oz. frozen artichoke hearts, thawed, and roughly chopped (1⅔ cups)
2 Tbs. chopped fresh flat-leaf parsley
Kosher salt and freshly ground black pepper

Position a rack in the center of the oven and heat the oven to 400°F.

In a medium bowl, whisk the eggs and mix in the cheese.

Heat the olive oil in a well-seasoned 10-inch cast-iron skillet (or ovenproof nonstick skillet) over medium-high heat. Add the onions and cook, stirring frequently, until golden around the edges,

2 to 3 minutes. Stir in the artichoke hearts, parsley, ½ tsp. salt, and ¼ tsp. pepper.

Remove from the heat and add the egg mixture. Stir just until the vegetables and herbs are distributed evenly. Transfer to the oven and bake until the eggs are set and firm to the touch, 13 to 14 minutes. Let the frittata rest in the pan for 2 minutes.

Run a knife or spatula around the edge of the pan to loosen the frittata and slide it out onto a cutting board. Slice the frittata into wedges and serve hot or at room temperature.

—Jessica Bard

quick & **delicious**

Blackened Tilapia with Cilantro-Lime Slaw

Serves two.

½ **small clove garlic**
Kosher salt
1 medium lime
3 Tbs. mayonnaise
¼ **medium head Savoy cabbage, cored and thinly sliced (about 2 cups)**
2 scallions, thinly sliced
2 Tbs. chopped fresh cilantro leaves
Freshly ground black pepper
½ **tsp. chili powder**
¼ **tsp. ground cumin**
Two 5-oz. tilapia fillets, cut in half lengthwise
1 Tbs. unsalted butter

Chop the garlic, sprinkle it with a pinch of salt, and mash it into a paste with the side of a chef's knife. Finely grate the zest from half of the lime and then juice the whole lime. In a medium bowl, whisk the garlic, lime zest, 1 Tbs. of the juice, and the mayonnaise. Toss in the cabbage, scallions, and cilantro. Season with ¼ tsp. salt and several grinds of pepper.

In a small bowl, mix the chili powder, cumin, ¼ tsp. salt, and several grinds of pepper. Sprinkle the spice rub all over the tilapia.

Melt the butter in a 10-inch cast-iron or nonstick skillet over medium-high heat. Cook the tilapia on both sides until browned and cooked through, about 3 minutes total for the small pieces and 5 minutes total for the large pieces. Transfer to a plate. Toss the slaw and add more lime juice, salt, and pepper to taste. Serve the tilapia with the slaw.

—Allison Ehri Kreitler

Whole-Wheat Pasta with Pancetta, Greens & Garlic

Serves two to three.

Kosher salt
1 large clove garlic
8 oz. dried whole-wheat linguine or spaghetti
1 Tbs. olive oil
4 oz. thinly sliced pancetta, finely diced (about 1 cup)
¼ **tsp. crushed red pepper flakes**
1 pint grape tomatoes, halved
6 cups (lightly packed) small watercress sprigs (about 2 bunches trimmed of lower stems), torn into bite-size pieces
½ **cup lightly packed finely grated Pecorino Romano**

Bring a large pot of well-salted water to a boil. Meanwhile, chop the garlic, sprinkle with ½ tsp. salt, and mash to a paste with the flat side of a chef's knife. Set aside.

Cook the pasta according to the package directions until al dente. Reserve about ⅓ cup of the cooking water, drain the pasta in a colander, and return to the pot.

While the pasta cooks, heat the oil in a 12-inch cast-iron or nonstick skillet over medium heat until hot. Add the pancetta and cook, stirring frequently, until the fat is rendered, 4 to 6 minutes. Stir in the garlic and pepper flakes and cook, stirring constantly, until fragrant, about 30 seconds. Stir in the tomatoes and cook, stirring frequently, until softened, 3 to 5 minutes. Remove the skillet from the heat and add the watercress; stir until wilted, 1 to 2 minutes.

Add the watercress mixture and pecorino to the pasta. Stir to combine, adding the reserved water 1 Tbs. at a time as needed to moisten. Season to taste with more salt and serve.

—Lori Longbotham

A dessert that feeds your soul deserves the sweet, aromatic cinnamon of Saigon.

For more great-tasting recipes, visit mccormickgourmet.com

Molten Spiced Chocolate Cabernet Cakes
(Makes 4 servings)

Ingredients:
- 4 oz. semi-sweet baking chocolate
- 1/2 cup (1 stick) butter
- 1 tbsp. Cabernet Sauvignon or other wine
- 1 tsp. McCormick® Pure Vanilla Extract
- 1 cup confectioners' sugar
- 2 eggs
- 1 egg yolk
- 6 tbsp. flour
- 1/4 tsp. McCormick® Gourmet Collection™ Saigon Cinnamon
- 1/4 tsp. McCormick® Gourmet Collection™ Ground Ginger

Directions:

BUTTER 4 (6-oz.) custard cups or soufflé dishes. Place on baking sheet.

MICROWAVE chocolate and butter in large microwaveable bowl on HIGH 1 minute or until butter is melted. Whisk until chocolate is completely melted. Stir in wine, vanilla, and sugar until blended. Whisk in eggs and yolk. Stir in remaining ingredients. Spoon evenly into prepared dishes.

BAKE in preheated 425°F oven 15 minutes or until sides are firm but centers are soft. Let stand 1 minute. Loosen edges with knife. Invert onto serving plates. Sprinkle with confectioners' sugar, if desired.

Pasta with Roasted Cauliflower, Arugula & Prosciutto

Serves four.

Kosher salt
One-half medium head cauliflower, cored
   and cut into ¾-inch florets (3½ cups)
1 pint grape tomatoes
3 Tbs. extra-virgin olive oil
Freshly ground black pepper
9 large fresh sage leaves
4 large cloves garlic, peeled
6 thin slices prosciutto (about 4 oz.)
12 oz. dried orecchiette
5 oz. baby arugula (5 lightly packed cups)
¾ cup grated Parmigiano-Reggiano

Position a rack in the lower third of the oven and heat the oven to 425°F. Bring a large pot of well-salted water to a boil.

Toss the cauliflower, tomatoes, oil, ¾ tsp. salt, and ½ tsp. pepper on a rimmed baking sheet; spread in a single layer. Roast, stirring once or twice, until the cauliflower begins to turn golden and tender, about 15 minutes.

Meanwhile, pulse the sage and garlic in a food processor until minced. Add the prosciutto and pulse until coarsely chopped.

Once the cauliflower is golden, toss the herb mixture into the vegetables and continue to roast until fragrant and the cauliflower is golden brown, 5 to 7 minutes.

Boil the orecchiette until al dente, 9 to 10 minutes. Reserve 1 cup pasta-cooking water. Drain the pasta and return it to the pot. Stir in the roasted cauliflower mixture, arugula, cheese, and enough pasta water to moisten. Season to taste with salt and pepper.

—by Pam Anderson, contributing editor

fine
Cooking

WE BRING OUT THE COOK IN YOU

Hearty soups & stews
to make now

Ellie Krieger gives
fried rice a
fresh makeover

CLEVER COOK
One delicious
roast, inspired
leftovers

NEW SECTION!
Marketplace
Shop smarter, eat better

MAKING CROISSANTS
FROM SCRATCH

B/MAR 2009 • No.97
w.finecooking.com

6.95 CAN $7.95

03

74470 56529 1

Wine-Braised Chicken with
Shallots and Pancetta, page 8

WE'VE GONE FROM THE FIRE TO THE FRYING PAN.

The same professional performance of the Viking range is also available in Viking cookware. Handcrafted in Belgium from an exclusive 7-ply material, Viking cookware offers the exceptional cleanability of stainless steel and the even heat distribution of aluminum.

VIKING ®

Visit vikingrange.com/wheretobuy to find a dealer near you.

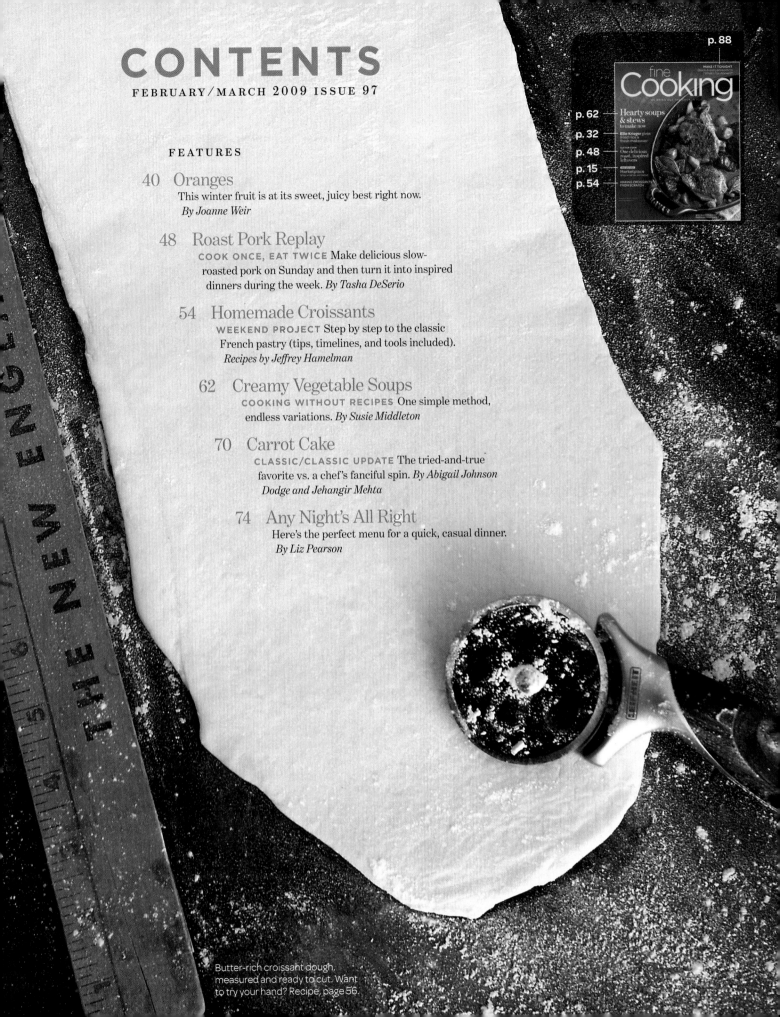

CONTENTS

FEBRUARY/MARCH 2009 ISSUE 97

Butter-rich croissant dough, measured and ready to cut. Want to try your hand? Recipe, page 56.

CONTENTS

FEBRUARY/MARCH 2009 ISSUE 97

Cover and contents photographs by Scott Phillips

Smoked Paprika Roasted Salmon with Wilted Spinach

(Makes 8 servings)

Ingredients:

1/4 cup orange juice

2 tablespoons plus 1 teaspoon olive oil, divided

2 teaspoons McCormick® Gourmet Collection™ Thyme Leaves, divided

2 pounds salmon fillets

1 tablespoon brown sugar

1 tablespoon McCormick® Gourmet Collection™ Smoked Paprika

1 teaspoon McCormick® Gourmet Collection™ Saigon Cinnamon

1 teaspoon grated orange peel

1/2 teaspoon McCormick® Gourmet Collection™ Sicilian Sea Salt

1 bag (10 ounces) spinach leaves

Directions:

MIX orange juice, 2 tablespoons of the oil and 1 teaspoon of the thyme in small bowl. Place salmon in large glass dish. Add marinade; turn to coat well. Cover. Refrigerate 30 min. or longer for extra flavor.

MIX sugar, smoked paprika, cinnamon, orange peel, remaining 1 teaspoon thyme and sea salt in small bowl. Remove salmon from marinade. Place in greased foil-lined baking pan. Discard any remaining marinade. Rub top of salmon evenly with smoked paprika mixture.

ROAST salmon in preheated 400°F oven 10 to 15 min. or until fish flakes easily with a fork. Meanwhile, heat remaining 1 teaspoon oil in large skillet on medium heat. Add spinach; cook and stir

Same Great Taste

"Fine Cooking is not just another food magazine. It's about the hows, and more important, the whys of cooking."

Remains of the day: the cover recipe, enjoyed by me.

THAT'S A QUOTE FROM the publisher's letter in the first issue of *Fine Cooking,* which made its debut in 1993. It's never been more true. And while we are not changing our core mission—the one we've held tight to for 15 years now—we have changed a few other things with this anniversary issue. Well, OK, we've changed quite a few things, including our logo, which now looks more like us in the year 2009: authoritative and authentic, modern but still classic (not unlike the new take on coq au vin on our cover—see the recipe on page 8), smart, and fun. And did I mention gorgeous?

In the past 15 years, a lot has changed in the world of food and cooking. Food is front-page news now; cookbooks and food literature top the bestseller lists; food TV attracts vast audiences; chefs are celebrities. In fact, food has become a lot more important to a lot more people: Local, sustainable, and renewable are the buzzwords of a back-to-the-earth movement that's inspired a passion for fresh, locally grown food.

This is all good news, especially for the cook, who has more access to better ingredients than ever before. As a magazine, we're embracing the thrill of that hunt and dedicating a good chunk of our pages to stories about buying the best ingredients, and ideas and recipes for cooking with them. Start your shopping lists with Marketplace, a new section that begins on page 15.

We also like to think we've broadened our horizons, reaching out to those cooks who are anxious to learn and are looking for a place to begin (try Repertoire, page 22). And we're linking in with those kitchen adventurers who like a challenge (homemade croissants, anyone? See Weekend Project, page 54).

In addition, we're getting real. We know what it's like to live a crazy life but still want to cook dinner at the end of the day—for you, for your family, for the sake of something good to eat. Good food fast is more than an equation of cans and frozen goods; it's simple and ingredient-focused, like the recipes you'll find in Make It Tonight on page 88.

Recipes are great tools, but we like to teach too, to explain the "why" behind "how" something works. We even have a feature called "Cooking Without Recipes," which begins with a basic technique and then lets you take it from there.

As for our new look, suffice it to say we really cleaned out the closet. Don Morris (see page 10 for more about him) spent months listening to me talk about the magazine and its opportunities, our plans and goals and ideas. His vision distills the best of our past while embracing our greatest hopes for the future—all in one stylishly timeless package.

Of course, we won't be stopping here. That's one of the benefits of magazine work: the chance to keep at it constantly, reassessing and rethinking as we get to the next better, ever-more-articulate iteration of the world as we see it. Your thoughts and opinions will make this process even more interesting; please write, call, or email me. Can't wait to hear from you.

Laurie Buckle, editor
fc@taunton.com

FINECOOKING.COM

what's for dinner?

I don't know about you, but that's the question of the day at my house. A hunch tells me it's a favorite subject for a lot of you.

So we decided to tackle the topic on our newly redesigned Web site. But since there's no one-size-fits-all answer, we've got any number of ways for you to find just what you're looking for. Some suggestions:

● Find the answer by clicking on the **recipes** icon (plenty of quick and easy options included).

● Got leftover produce? Hit the **ingredients** icon and discover great ways to use up the last of those carrots (or anything else you might have around).

● Want a good tip? Go to the **how-to** icon for great ideas and now-I-get-it videos.

● If you could use a little advice, click on the **CooksTalk** icon, where you'll find like-minded cooks sharing their ideas.

One burning question; thousands of delicious answers. All at the new FineCooking.com.

Photographs by Scott Phillips

Continued on page 8

wine-braised chicken with shallots and pancetta

In this modern take on coq au vin, Riesling subs for the usual red wine.

Serves 4

- ¼ **cup olive oil**
- 4 **bone-in, skin-on chicken thighs (about 1½ lb.)**
- 4 **chicken drumsticks (about 1½ lb.)**
  Kosher salt and freshly ground black pepper
- 7 **oz. pancetta, cut into ¾-inch dice (1 heaping cup)**
- 8 **medium shallots, lobes separated, large lobes halved through the core**
- 4 **medium carrots, cut into ¾-inch-thick slices, large slices cut in half**
- 1 **small bulb fennel, trimmed, cored, and cut into ¾-inch dice**
- 1 **large clove garlic, finely chopped**
- 4 **sprigs fresh flat-leaf parsley**
- 4 **sprigs fresh thyme**
- 1 **bay leaf**
- 2 **cups dry fruity white wine, preferably Alsatian or German dry Riesling**
- 3 **cups lower-salt chicken broth**
- ¼ **tsp. finely grated lemon zest**
- 1 **Tbs. chopped fresh flat-leaf parsley**

Position a rack in the bottom third of the oven and heat the oven to 300°F.

Heat 2 Tbs. of the oil in a 7- to 8-quart Dutch oven over medium-high heat. Season the chicken all over with 1 tsp. salt and ½ tsp. pepper. Arrange the chicken skin side down in the pot in a snug single layer and sear, flipping once, until golden brown all over, 10 to 13 minutes. Transfer to a plate.

Cook the pancetta in the pot until well browned all over, 5 to 8 minutes. Transfer with a slotted spoon to paper towels to drain. Pour off and discard the fat.

Heat the remaining 2 Tbs. oil in the pot over medium-high heat. Cook the shallots, carrots, and fennel, stirring occasionally, until lightly browned, about 7 minutes. Add the garlic and cook, stirring frequently, until its aroma subsides, 1 to 2 minutes.

Tie the parsley sprigs, thyme sprigs, and bay leaf together with twine (or tie them in a small cheesecloth sachet). Add the herb bundle to the pot, along with the wine. Simmer briskly, scraping the bottom of the pot to loosen the brown bits. Add the broth and return the chicken and pancetta to the pot, arranging the chicken in a single layer. Bring to a simmer, cover and transfer to the oven.

Braise the chicken until the meat is fork-tender and just starting to come away from the bone, 35 to 45 minutes.

Transfer the chicken and vegetables to a serving platter with a slotted spoon and tent with foil. Discard the herb bundle. Bring the sauce to a boil over high heat and reduce to 2 cups, about 15 minutes. Stir in the lemon zest and season with salt and pepper. Pour the sauce over the chicken and serve sprinkled with the chopped parsley.

Make ahead: This dish may be made up to 2 days ahead. Let the sauce cool before adding the chicken and vegetables and refrigerating. Reheat gently over medium-low heat before serving.

—Allison Ehri Kreitler

fine Cooking®

Editor	Laurie Glenn Buckle
Art Director	Annie Giammattei
Senior Food Editor/ Test Kitchen Manager	Jennifer Armentrout
Senior Editor	Rebecca Freedman
Associate Editors	Laura Giannatempo Lisa Waddle
Assistant Editor	Denise Mickelsen
Managing Web Editor	Sarah Breckenridge
Assistant Web Editor	Sharon Anderson
Senior Copy/ Production Editor	Enid Johnson
Associate Art Director	Pamela Winn
Assistant Test Kitchen Manager/Food Stylist	Allison Ehri Kreitler
Recipe Testers	Dabney Gough Melissa Pellegrino
Editorial Assistant	Julissa Roberts
Photo Coordinator	Kelly Gearity
Test Kitchen Intern	Joy Braddock
Editorial Intern	Sophy Bishop
Editor at Large	Susie Middleton
Contributing Editors	Pam Anderson Abigail Johnson Dodge Maryellen Driscoll Tim Gaiser Sarah Jay Ellie Krieger Kimberly Y. Masibay Tony Rosenfeld Molly Stevens
Senior Managing Editor, Books	Carolyn Mandarano

Fine Cooking: (ISSN: 1072-5121) is published six times a year by The Taunton Press, Inc., Newtown, CT 06470-5506. Telephone 203-426-8171. Periodicals postage paid at Newtown, CT 06470 and at additional mailing offices. GST paid registration #123210981.

Subscription Rates: U.S. and Canada, $29.95 for one year, $49.95 for two years, $69.95 for three years (GST included, payable in U.S. funds). Outside the U.S./Canada: $36 for one year, $62 for two years, $88 for three years (payable in U.S. funds). Single copy, $6.95. Single copy outside the U.S., $7.95.

Postmaster: Send address changes to *Fine Cooking*, The Taunton Press, Inc., 63 South Main St., P.O. Box 5506, Newtown, CT 06470-5506.

Canada Post: Return undeliverable Canadian addresses to *Fine Cooking*, c/o Worldwide Mailers, Inc., 2835 Kew Drive, Windsor, ON N8T 3B7, or email to mnfa@taunton.com.

Printed in the USA.

THE WINNER

Reader tip: Easier stock

I enjoyed the recipe for Golden Turkey Broth in your October/ November issue (*Fine Cooking* #95). I've found that when making stock, my large stockpot with the pasta insert works great. I throw all the ingredients into the insert, cover with water, and when finished cooking, lift out the insert and dispose of the ingredients. No more messy spills or fumbling with a colander in the sink.

—*Lori W., via email*

Write a winning tip

We want to hear from you. Give us your best tip and we'll reward you with a fabulous kitchen prize. Lori is the winner of a knife sharpener from Chef's Choice.

CALL OR WRITE: *Fine Cooking*, The Taunton Press, 63 S. Main St., P.O. Box 5506, Newtown, CT 06470-5506. Tel: 203-426-8171. Send an email: fc@taunton.com.

Making the most of every recipe

I just made your most beautiful cover recipe (Chocolate-Pomegranate Torte, *Fine Cooking* #96). It came out gorgeous. But rather than throw out the pulp after straining the pomegranate jelly, I rescued it to spread on my English muffin in the morning. This stuff is fabulous; try it. Thanks for all the good work and inspiration, I love your magazine.

—*Catherine McAvoy, via email*

Bring it on...

First of all, I love your magazine. I just renewed my subscription and added my parents to the list. But I agree with reader Dolores B. LiSooey (Letters, *Fine Cooking* #95) in that I want to see recipes that are challenging and appeal to the wannabe gourmet in me. Maybe you could have a section for "amateur gourmets" like me, where you feature more complex recipes, techniques, and even plating tips.

—*Rebecca Shinduke*
Calgary, Alberta

I agree with Ms. LiSooey. Give us challenging recipes. Don't bother competing with run-of-the-mill "women's service" magazines. Give us the meals that we and our friends are eating in the finest restaurants.

—*Karen Phillips, via email*

...or not

I disagree with Ms. LiSooey. My apologies to her, but there are plenty of difficult, hard-to-understand cookbooks out there that are more appropriate to the century in which we all *used* to live. Now we live in a much faster-paced world in which we need clear and concise directions that get to the point and get results. You guys at *Fine Cooking* just get it. Keep changing with the times and we'll keep cooking along with you.

—*Kerry O'Farrell*
Studio City, California

Gumbo go-alongs?

I've been a fan of *Fine Cooking* for years, and I've read each issue cover to cover. I want to serve the Chicken-Andouille Filé Gumbo from the January 2008 issue (*Fine Cooking* #90) to a crowd of about 30 people and was wondering what you would suggest as a side dish?

—*Debbie Enssle, via email*

Author Poppy Tooker replies: Everyone will be so impressed with your gumbo, you won't need much else. It's traditionally ladled over cooked white rice, making it a hearty, one-dish meal. I like to serve crusty bread alongside, to sop up any leftovers in the bowl. Offer folks a leafy, fresh green salad, and you won't have any complaints.

Induction info, please

We were excited to see the review on stockpots (Equipment, *Fine Cooking* #95) but were disappointed that you didn't note which ones are induction compatible. We are replacing our cooktop with an induction unit and in the process buying new induction-friendly cookware. We have had trouble finding replacements for our 12- and 16-quart stockpots. Any advice?

—*Michael Mendelsohn*
Chapel Hill, North Carolina

Contributing editor Maryellen Driscoll responds: Space restricts us from including as much information as we'd like to about every piece of equipment we review. Of the four stockpots we featured, all but the All-Clad are induction compatible. However, we reviewed the All-Clad LTD line; the company's stainless and brushed-stainless professional lines *are* induction compatible.

Great gratins

From the moment I saw "Cooking without Recipes: Potato Gratin" in the November 2008 issue (*Fine Cooking* #95), I knew my friend and I would have to make one the next time we got together to cook dinner for our families. That opportunity came last Friday night. We made the version with shallots and Gruyère and agreed that it was the best potato dish we had ever had. Indeed, I found myself making the same version again only two nights later. Thank you for a fabulous article.

—*Kathryn Morris*
Indianapolis, Indiana

CORRECTION

In our last issue, Melissa Feldman produced our Great Finds holiday shopping gift guide, and Michelli Knauer was the food stylist for our Smart Cookies feature. Their names were inadvertently omitted.

Don Morris owns Don Morris Design, a Manhattan studio that has orchestrated redesigns and launches for *PC World, Budget Travel,* and *Smithsonian* and has produced special issues for *Entertainment Weekly* and *In Style.* Along with art director **Tannaz Fassihi,** Don brought his 28 years of experience to modernizing and energizing the pages of *Fine Cooking.*
- The last thing I cooked was... blueberry pancakes.
- My resumé highlight is... designing for the Sundance Film Festival.
- My guilty-food pleasure is... pie.

Stefan Dziallas, who lives in Bremen, Germany, created the charming icons for our department pages. His company, Iconwerk, has designed custom icons for AOL, Cisco, American Airlines, and *ESPN The Magazine.*
- The last thing I cooked was... spaghetti with jarred Arrabbiata sauce, topped with grilled vegetables.
- My drink of choice is... apple juice from local farmers.
- I think the next food trend will be... food matched by color to fashion.

Brian Geiger ("Why the Chicken Comes Before the Lemon," page 22) started down the path of food geekdom after attending cooking school in Tuscany. A robotics project manager by day, he blogs at thefoodgeek.com on nights and weekends.
- I'm currently obsessed with... baking bread.
- My guilty-food pleasure is... a BBB sandwich—a BLT without the extraneous vegetables and fruits.
- My resumé highlight is... helping build a car that can drive itself in traffic.

Registered dietician **Ellie Krieger** ("Fried Rice Gets Fresh," page 32) is the author of *The New York Times* bestseller *The Food You Crave;* she also hosts the Food Network's *Healthy Appetite.*
- My guilty-food pleasure is... french fries and chocolate molten cake. Although not together, of course.
- I think the next food trend will be... closer to home. People will be cooking more and buying food more locally—even growing it themselves.

Born in Australia, photographer **Quentin Bacon** ("Any Night's All Right," page 74) now makes New York City his home. He has shot for British and American magazines as well as for cookbooks by Gordon Ramsay, Jean-Georges Vongerichten, and Mario Batali.
- I'm currently obsessed with... vanilla ice cream with a shot of espresso on top.
- The last thing I cooked was... fudge.
- I think the next hottest drink trend will be... pisco sours.

Christopher Silas Neal's illustrations ("Why the Chicken Comes Before the Lemon," page 22) regularly appear in *The New York Times Review of Books, The New Yorker,* and *Time* magazine. He exhibits at galleries across the country and teaches illustration at Brooklyn's Pratt Institute.
- The last thing I cooked was... ribollita [a soup of cannellini beans, cabbage, and greens over grilled peasant bread].
- My drink of choice is... Guinness in the winter, acqua frizzante in the summer.

Jim Meehan ("Shaken or Stirred?" page 38) is a contributing editor for *Mr. Boston: Official Bartender's and Party Guide.* He has been a mixologist at Manhattan's Gramercy Tavern and Pegu Club and is now manager at the bar PDT (Please Don't Tell) in New York.
- My drink of choice is... a latte made from Stumptown Coffee at Ninth Street Espresso.
- My resume highlight is... I'm still employed.
- I think the next food trend will be... low-fat, decaf, gluten-free, free-range, organic, sustainably raised rabbit jerky.

Jehangir Mehta ("Carrot Cake," page 70) is chef and owner of New York's Graffiti restaurant. Previously pastry chef at Jean-Georges, Mercer Kitchen, and Aix, he recently came out with his first cookbook, *Mantra,* featuring ingredient-inspired avant-garde sweets.
- The last thing I cooked was... toast.
- The one food I'd like to see banished is... meatloaf.
- I'm inspired by... my wife's inability to cook.

Josh Darden is chief designer at Darden Studio, in Brooklyn. He developed *Fine Cooking*'s new typeface, called FC Omnes, which features rounded characters and an open, inviting feel.
- The last thing I ate was... a burger on ciabatta with grilled pineapple and a fried egg.
- My drink of choice is... bitters and tonic.
- I think the next food trend will be... locavores rising.

contributors' update

Former *Fine Cooking* editor Martha Holmberg has a new cookbook out called *Puff,* with recipes for puff pastry. She is food editor for *The Oregonian* and editor of its magazine, *MIX.*

Regular contributor Nicole Rees's new book, *Baking Unplugged,* features simple recipes for basic baked goods that don't require fancy ingredients or equipment.

fine Cooking®

Publisher	Maria Taylor
Assistant Publisher	Karen Lutjen
National Advertising Manager	Patrick J. O'Donnell 203-304-3250 podonnell@taunton.com
Senior National Account Managers:	
East	Judy Caruso 203-304-3468 jcaruso@taunton.com
Midwest	Mark Adeszko 312-629-5222 madeszko@aol.com
West	Chuck Carroll 818-972-9650 cwcarroll@earthlink.net
Advertising Sales Associate	Stacy Dejulio 203-304-3231 sdejulio@taunton.com
Advertising Inquiries:	800-309-8940 fcads@taunton.com

Member Audit Bureau of Circulation	The Audit Bureau
Director of Advertiser Marketing	Kristen Lacey
Senior Consumer Marketing Director	Beth Reynolds, ProCirc
Circulation Manager	Noelia Garcia, ProCirc
Business Managers	David Pond Megan Sangster

The Taunton Press
Inspiration for hands-on living®

Independent publishers since 1975

Founders	Paul & Jan Roman
President	Suzanne Roman
EVP & CFO	Timothy Rahr
SVP, Operations	Thomas Luxeder
SVP, Creative & Editorial	Susan Edelman
SVP, Technology	Jay Hartley
SVP & Group Publisher	Paul Spring
SVP & Publisher, Book Group	Donald Linn
SVP, Advertising Sales	Karl Elken
SVP & Group Publisher	Janine Scolpino
VP, Human Resources	Carol Marotti
VP & Controller	Wayne Reynolds
VP, Fulfillment	Patricia Williamson
VP, Finance	Kathy Worth
VP, Taunton Interactive	Jason Revzon
VP, Single Copy Sales	Jay Annis

Publishers of magazines, books, videos and online
Fine Woodworking • Fine Homebuilding
Threads • Fine Gardening • Fine Cooking
www.taunton.com

FINECOOKING.COM

Question of the Day

One reader ponders "What's for dinner?" and then begins her search for an answer at FineCooking.com. Oh, the places you can go!

Cook the Issue

Ever thought about cooking your way through an entire issue of *Fine Cooking*? Take the CooksTalk challenge at FineCooking.com: Post photos of what you make, tell us what you love, what you don't, and what else you want to know. Cook the whole issue and you could win a cookware shopping spree.

SLOW DAY AT WORK

Hmm, what's for dinner? I've got salmon and mushrooms in my fridge.

RECIPE SEARCH

Asian Glazed Salmon with Roasted Mushroom Salad. Do I have everything I need? Scallions, check. Ginger, check. It calls for mirin. What exactly is mirin?

INGREDIENT DISCOVERY

A Japanese sweet rice wine for cooking. Says here it's available in some grocery stores. OK, I'll check it out.

No mirin at my supermarket, but Ingredient Discovery says I can substitute white wine plus a little sugar.

RATE & REVIEW RECIPES

Mirin or no mirin, the glazed salmon was delicious. I'm posting my review on FineCooking.com

What's new at FineCooking.com?

 What We're Cooking Now
Like the column (see page 18)? Follow the blog. Seasonal inspiration straight from our editors' home kitchens.

 Ingredient Discovery
Pump up your ingredient IQ with the curious cook's guide to everything from asafetida to ziti.

 Test Kitchen Blog
Learn all the right moves with our test kitchen experts. Find recipe hints, video tips, and great advice.

 Weekend Project
Get your hands even doughier (see page 54). Find more croissant how-tos, with audio slide shows and plenty of step-by-step photos.

 Food Geek Blog
Why did my cake fall? Follow the Food Geek (see page 22) as he gets to the bottom of culinary mysteries every week.

Sign up for the **free** FineCooking.com eLetter for a weekly look at what's newest and hottest on the Web. Get exclusive **Web-only recipes**, how-to **videos**, and advice from the experts.

Photographs by Scott Phillips

fine Cooking®

To contact us:
Fine Cooking,
The Taunton Press,
63 South Main Street,
P.O. Box 5506, Newtown,
CT 06470-5506
Tel: 203-426-8171
fc@taunton.com

Visit:
www.finecooking.com

To submit an article proposal:
Write to *Fine Cooking* at the address above or
Call: 800-309-0744
Fax: 203-426-3434
Email: fc@taunton.com

To subscribe or place an order:
Visit www.finecooking.com/fcorder
or call: 800-888-8286
9am-9pm ET Mon-Fri;
9am-5pm ET Sat

To find out about *Fine Cooking* products:
Visit www.finecooking.com/products

To get help with online member services:
Visit www.finecooking.com/customerservice

To find answers to frequently asked questions:
Visit www.finecooking.com/FAQs

**To speak directly to a customer service
professional:**
Call 800-477-8727 9am-5pm ET Mon-Fri

To order products for your store:
Send an email to magazinesales@taunton.com

To advertise in *Fine Cooking*:
Call 800-309-8940
Or send an email to fcads@taunton.com

Mailing list:
We make a portion of our mailing list available
to reputable firms. If you would prefer that
we not include your name, please visit:
www.finecooking.com/privacy
or call: 800-477-8727 9am-5pm ET Mon-Fri;

For employment information:
Visit www.careers.taunton.com

The Taunton guarantee:
If at any time you're not completely satisfied with
Fine Cooking, you can cancel your subscription and
receive a full and immediate refund of the entire
subscription price. No questions asked.

MARKETPLACE

Shop Smarter, Eat Better

TRY THIS

Escarole

YOU PROBABLY SEE THEM all the time—those heads of escarole tucked in among the other lettuces and leafy greens in your grocery store's produce section. But maybe you pass them by, choosing the more familiar spinach and romaine instead. Here's why you should give escarole another look. *Continued on page 16*

What it is

Escarole goes by a few aliases, including Batavian endive, common chicory, or broad chicory. Whatever you call it, escarole is a bitter leafy green that's part of the chicory genus, so it's closely related to frisée, radicchio, curly endive, and Belgian endive. It grows into an open, somewhat flat head of broad, crumpled-looking, light- to dark-green leaves with wide, fleshy stems.

Why we love it

Compared to that of its other chicory cousins, escarole's bitterness is relatively mild, and you can eat it raw or cooked. Raw escarole has a crisp texture and a slightly sweet flavor that tempers the bitterness, making it a perfect choice for winter salads. It's especially delicious paired with apples, pears, cheeses (blue or goat), olives, and nuts. Once cooked, escarole develops a tender, melting texture, and its bitterness becomes a little more pronounced. It's great in soups or sautéed with other strong flavors, like capers and garlic, as a side dish. Escarole and white beans is a classic pairing.

How to buy and store it

Choose heads of escarole with perky, fresh-looking leaves. Avoid any with tough-looking outer leaves, especially if there are signs of browning around the tops of the leaves. Store escarole in a plastic bag in your refrigerator's crisper bin for up to three days.

How to cook it

To use escarole in a soup, simply chop it up, stems and all, and add it to the soup in the last 15 or 20 minutes of cooking—enough time to become very tender. If you're planning to sauté the escarole, it's worth taking the extra step of blanching it in boiling water for a couple of minutes first. Though there are plenty of recipes out there that call for sautéing escarole without blanching, we've found that this approach results in a tough-textured dish that looks like wilted lettuce. In comparison, blanched and sautéed escarole has a succulent texture and a brighter green color.

—*Jennifer Armentrout*

sautéed escarole with raisins, pine nuts, and capers

You can blanch the escarole up to one hour ahead. Wait until just before serving to add the lemon juice, though, as the acid in the juice will dull the escarole's color if it sits too long.

Serves 4

Kosher salt

2 lb. escarole (about 2 heads), trimmed, rinsed, and cut into roughly 2-inch pieces

2 Tbs. extra-virgin olive oil

3 large cloves garlic, smashed and peeled

2 Tbs. pine nuts

2 Tbs. raisins

1 Tbs. capers, rinsed

Pinch of crushed red pepper flakes

1 tsp. fresh lemon juice

Bring a large pot of well-salted water to a boil over high heat. Add the escarole and cook until the stem pieces start to soften, about 2 minutes (the water needn't return to a boil). Drain, run under cold water to cool, and drain again.

In a 12-inch skillet, heat the olive oil and garlic over medium heat, stirring occasionally, until the garlic browns lightly, 2 to 3 minutes. Remove the garlic with tongs and discard. Add the pine nuts, raisins, capers, and pepper flakes and cook, stirring, until the pine nuts are golden and the raisins puff, about 1 minute. Add the escarole, increase the heat to medium high, and cook, tossing often, until heated through and tender, 3 to 4 minutes. Sprinkle with the lemon juice and season to taste with salt.

Photographs by Scott Phillips

Radishes, Avocados, and Cabbage

Nine ways to use three seasonal ingredients we can't get enough of. *Fine Cooking* editors share some delicious ideas.

Avocados

Dabney Gough: I got addicted to avocado shakes when I was in Indonesia—ripe avocados, plenty of sweetened condensed milk, and ice puréed in a blender. The result is almost like a milkshake but a bit more refreshing.

Rebecca Freedman: Caterer Tasha DeSerio gave me this easy idea for avocado toast, and I've been obsessed with it ever since—especially when I get home from work and am too tired to make anything else. I mash an avocado, spread it on slices of toasted crusty bread, sprinkle with sea salt, and drizzle with good-quality olive oil.

Denise Mickelsen: My friend and former colleague Avery Wittkamp told me about this twist on classic tuna salad, and now this is the way I always make it. Skip the mayo and smash up some avocados instead. Add tuna, salt and pepper, and your favorite tuna fixings—I like fresh dill and finely chopped red onion.

Cabbage

Allison Ehri Kreitler: I sauté thinly sliced Savoy cabbage over high heat until nicely browned and then use it as a bed for sautéed white fish, with an Asian dipping sauce poured over the whole dish.

Laura Giannatempo: To make a mock sauerkraut, cook some diced bacon in a large skillet, set the bacon aside, add a little oil to the bacon fat, and cook some mashed garlic in the fat to flavor it. Remove the garlic and sauté sliced napa cabbage in the fat until just wilted. Then add some water or broth, cover, and cook until it's very tender. Next add a generous amount of red wine vinegar (a good ⅓ cup for a full pan) and let it evaporate uncovered. To finish, toss the bacon back in and season with salt and pepper.

Denise Mickelsen: For a wintery slaw-like salad, I steam shredded green cabbage in water with a touch of cider vinegar until wilted, then throw it into a colander with thinly sliced red onion and toss while still hot. After it's cooled a bit, I add a vinaigrette of orange juice, lemon juice, cider vinegar, chopped fresh dill, grainy mustard, and olive oil, along with some poppyseeds and thinly sliced apple.

Radishes

Allison Ehri Kreitler: Try making a radish raita by mixing coarsely grated radishes with whole-milk yogurt, thinly sliced chives, a little mashed garlic, salt, and pepper. It's delicious with salmon and boiled baby potatoes.

Denise Mickelsen: Braised radishes make a lovely side dish for roasted meats. I gently simmer whole radishes in a little broth with olive oil or butter until crisp-tender, and then sprinkle with sea salt and thinly sliced chives.

Laura Giannatempo: I love adding thinly shaved radishes to a classic wintery Mediterranean salad of shaved raw fennel, orange segments, and black olives dressed with a citrus vinaigrette.

Photographs, both pages, by Scott Phillips

Lemons

LEMONS NEVER TASTE BETTER than they do right now, so it's the perfect time to stock up and "put up" lemons in the form of marmalade.

Here's a method for making marmalade that uses just about the entire fruit—from zest to juice. Powdered pectin shortens the cooking time and eliminates the guesswork behind gauging the correct consistency. Easy and foolproof, this marmalade is a sure-fire way to enjoy lemons now and long after the season is gone.

lemon-ginger marmalade

This golden-hued marmalade is right at home on toast, but it's also divine stirred into plain yogurt or dolloped on coconut ice cream. Find pectin where canning supplies are sold—try supermarkets or hardware stores—or see page 92 for a mail-order source.

Yields 5½ to 6 cups

- 1½ to 2 lb. lemons (6 to 8 medium)
- ½ cup finely chopped fresh ginger
- 1 1¾-oz. package powdered pectin
- 6½ cups granulated sugar

Peel the zest from the lemons with a vegetable peeler, avoiding as much of the white pith as possible. Slice the zest strips crosswise very thinly at an angle to make strips about ¹⁄₁₆ inch wide by 1 inch long—you'll need 1 cup of zest strips. Put the zest in a 4-quart (or larger) saucepan.

Trim the ends from the zested lemons to expose the flesh. With one cut side down on the cutting board, trim the pith off the lemon all the way around and discard the pith. Quarter the lemons lengthwise and remove any visible membranes and seeds. Slice the wedges crosswise ¼ inch thick—you'll need about 1½ cups.

Add the sliced lemons, ginger, and 2 cups water to the lemon zest. Bring to a boil over medium-high heat, adjust the heat to maintain a simmer, and cook until the zest is soft and the membranes start to break down, 6 to 8 minutes.

Whisk the pectin into the mixture. Increase the heat to high, add the sugar, and bring to a boil, whisking constantly to smooth lumps. Boil vigorously for 1 minute, whisking constantly (move the pan off the burner momentarily if it threatens to boil over). Remove the pan from the heat and let sit undisturbed for 5 minutes.

Skim any foam and seeds off the surface of the marmalade. Stir gently to redistribute the solids. Transfer the marmalade to heatproof storage containers, let cool to room temperature, and then refrigerate for up to 1 month.

Note: For longer storage at room temperature, can the marmalade. Transfer the hot marmalade to clean, hot canning jars, leaving ½ inch of headspace in each jar, and follow the canning directions at FineCooking .com, processing the marmalade for 10 minutes.

—*Dabney Gough*

 It's lime season, too. Find a bonus recipe for Lime-Tequila Marmalade at **FineCooking.com/extras.**

A Fishy Guide

You're standing at the seafood counter, on your way home to make dinner—good luck remembering whether Atlantic cod or bluefish is the better sustainable choice. The Seafood Watch guides from the Monterey Bay Aquarium make it easy. (Answer: bluefish.) They're updated every January and June, so now's the time to go to montereybayaquarium .org to download and print out your card, order free guides, or download the guide to your cell phone.

Cookies That Count

Delectable flavors, unusual ingredients, and adorable size would be reason enough to buy the shortbread and granola squares from the Khaya cookie company. But the Cranberry Rooibos Shortbread and Granola Fruit Krunchi taste even better when you know that every batch is made by hand in South Africa, creating jobs for local women. Buy online for $5.75 a box at www.khayacookies.com.

White Cheddar

Making the most of a favorite food find from a warehouse store.

BY ALLISON EHRI KREITLER

HERE'S A SECRET: Foodies love shopping at the big box stores (delicious finds, bargain prices). The challenge? Not letting any of that big buy go to waste. The solution? Great recipes like these. Consider the two-pound brick of Cheddar. Sure, it's great for snacking and making old favorites like mac and cheese and grilled cheese sandwiches, but we've taken it a step further—soufflé, soup, and cheese-stuffed chiles, to be specific. Before you know it, that hunk of cheese will be gone—and you'll be going back for more.

The Big Buy

What: Sharp or extra-sharp white Cheddar
How much: Two pounds
How to store: Remove the plastic wrapper and loosely rewrap the cheese in waxed paper or parchment, and then in plastic wrap or foil. Store in the refrigerator crisper drawer and change the wrapping every few days. Or store the un-wrapped cheese in a sealed, paper-towel-lined storage container anywhere in the fridge. The cheese will keep for several weeks. If it develops mold, cut into the cheese ½ inch below the mold to remove it. The remaining cheese is still good to eat. Discard the cheese if it develops any off-odors or becomes slimy or overly dry.

cheddar and cauliflower soup

Yields 8 cups; serves 6 to 8

	Kosher salt
½	head cauliflower (about 1 lb.), cored and cut into 1½-inch florets
2	Tbs. unsalted butter
1	medium yellow onion, small diced
1	medium clove garlic, minced
2	Tbs. all-purpose flour
¼	tsp. packed, freshly grated nutmeg
⅛	tsp. cayenne
2	cups lower-salt chicken broth
½	cup heavy cream
3	sprigs fresh thyme
4	cups grated sharp or extra-sharp white Cheddar (about 14 oz.)
	Freshly ground black pepper

Bring a large pot of salted water to a boil. Boil the cauliflower until tender, about 4 minutes. Drain and let cool slightly. Trim the stems from 18 of the cauliflower pieces and cut the crowns into mini florets about ½ inch wide; set aside. Reserve the trimmed stems with the remaining larger pieces.

Melt the butter in a 4-quart saucepan over medium-low heat. Add the onion and ¼ tsp. salt and cook, stirring frequently, until soft, 10 to 12 minutes.

Add the garlic and cook until the aroma subsides, 2 to 3 minutes. Increase the heat to medium, add the flour, nutmeg, and cayenne and cook for 3 minutes, stirring constantly. Whisk in the broth, cream, and 2 cups water. Add the thyme and bring to a

Photographs by Scott Phillips

simmer. Stir in the cheese until melted and simmer for 5 minutes to develop the flavors.

Remove and discard the thyme stems and stir in the larger cauliflower pieces and reserved stems. Working in batches, purée the soup in a blender. Return the soup to the pot, season with salt and black pepper to taste. Add the mini cauliflower florets and reheat gently before serving.

Variation: To dress up this rustic soup for a special occasion, garnish with a combination of 3 Tbs. toasted chopped walnuts, 1 Tbs. chopped fresh parsley, and 1½ tsp. finely grated lemon zest.

baked cheddar grits with bacon

Whipped egg whites lighten the grits, giving them a soufflé-like texture.

Serves 6

    Kosher salt
1   cup hominy grits (not instant or quick), such as Quaker Old Fashioned
1½ cups grated sharp or extra-sharp white Cheddar (about 5 oz.)
1   Tbs. all-purpose flour
1   tsp. chopped fresh thyme
    Freshly ground black pepper
1   medium clove garlic
6   strips bacon (about 6 oz.), cooked until crisp and chopped into small bits
3   large eggs, separated
¼   cup heavy cream

Position a rack in the center of the oven and heat the oven to 350°F.

Put 4½ cups water and ½ tsp. salt in a 4-quart saucepan, cover, and bring to a boil. Whisk the grits into the pan in a slow stream. Reduce the heat to medium low, cover, and simmer, whisking occasionally, until thickened, 12 to 15 minutes.

In a large bowl, toss 1¼ cups of the cheese, the flour, thyme, and several grinds of pepper. Chop the garlic, sprinkle with a generous pinch of salt, and mash it into a paste with the side of a chef's knife. Whisk the mashed

garlic, the cheese mixture, and the bacon into the grits until blended and the cheese is melted. Season to taste with salt and pepper.

Scrape the grits into the large bowl. In a medium bowl beat the egg whites and a pinch of salt with a hand mixer until they just hold stiff peaks. In a small bowl, whisk the yolks and cream; whisk this mixture into the grits. With a large spatula, gently stir one-third of the whites into the grits to lighten them and then fold in the remaining whites. Scrape the grits into an 8x8x2-inch glass or ceramic baking dish.

Sprinkle the remaining ¼ cup cheese evenly over the grits. Bake until puffed, browned, and bubbling, 50 minutes to 1 hour.

poblanos stuffed with cheddar and chicken

Serves 4

4   large poblano chiles
2   medium tomatoes, chopped
½   medium white onion, chopped
1   large clove garlic, chopped
1   tsp. dried oregano, crumbled
1   tsp. ground cumin
    Generous pinch ground cinnamon
    Kosher salt
1   Tbs. olive oil
2   cups shredded cooked chicken, preferably dark meat
1½ cups cooked brown or white rice
2   cups grated sharp or extra-sharp white Cheddar (about 7 oz.)

¼   cup chopped fresh cilantro (including some tender stems)
1   Tbs. lime juice

Position an oven rack about 4 inches from the broiler and heat the broiler on high. Line a large rimmed baking sheet with foil.

Slit the chiles from stem to tip and set on the baking sheet. Broil, turning every few minutes, until blackened all over, 5 to 8 minutes. Let cool slightly, peel off the skins, and cut out the seed cores, leaving the stems on. Turn the chiles inside out, flick out any remaining seeds, and turn right side out. Return the poblanos to the baking sheet.

Purée the tomatoes, onion, garlic, oregano, cumin, cinnamon, and ½ tsp. salt in a food processor. Heat the oil in a 12-inch skillet over medium heat. Add the purée and cook, stirring frequently, until the liquid has evaporated and the mixture looks thick and pulpy, 8 to 11 minutes. Remove the pan from the heat. Stir in the chicken and rice, and then 1 cup of the cheese, the cilantro, and the lime juice. Season to taste with salt. Divide the filling among the peppers, wrapping the sides of the peppers up and around the filling, some of which will still be exposed.

Broil the peppers until the cheese is melting and the top is beginning to brown, about 4 minutes. Top with the remaining 1 cup cheese and broil until the cheese is completely melted, about 2 minutes.

Why the Chicken Comes Before the Lemon

Or the science behind making a meal taste better. BY BRIAN J. GEIGER

I'VE ALWAYS LOVED EXPERIMENTING. In my day job, I mess around at a robotics firm. When I get home, I do my experimenting in the kitchen. And because I'm a geek (I admit it), when I get interested in something, I tend to go into it a bit further than a normal person. The good news is that my all-consuming focus doesn't just lead to interesting discoveries— it also results in better-tasting food.

Take, for example, a recent trip to the grocery store, where I saw lemons on sale. My first thought on seeing a whole bag of lemons was one you've probably had as well: "Wow, I could make a lot of chicken piccata." No? Well, to me, the sight of all those lemons made me want to play around with my standard recipe, to see if I could improve on a weeknight staple. Here's what I found out.

Chicken piccata is a fast, easy recipe— you flatten chicken cutlets, dredge them in flour, sauté until brown, and then make a pan sauce with some lemon juice added for tang. I thought to myself, Wouldn't it be an awfully good idea to use lemon earlier in the cooking, to infuse the chicken with lemony goodness? Might not even need a sauce at that point. Crazy thinking, I know.

So I added an extra bowl at the beginning of my dredging station and put lemon juice in it. I dipped the flattened chicken breast into the lemon juice, then in flour, then into a hot skillet. The odd thing was that the chicken didn't cook quite right. It was mostly fine, but the browning was uneven.

I wondered if the problem was that the chicken was too wet (because of the added

amp up the flavor

As our Food Geek learns, browning chicken and other foods creates intense flavors. His conclusions point to two good tips:

● For meat to brown, it must be heated hotter than 230°F.
● Too much acid (like lemon juice) will result in less browning.

lemon juice), so I made two cutlets side by side, dipping one in lemon juice at the beginning and one in water. Strangely, the lemony chicken browned unevenly and didn't have as complex a flavor as the one dipped in water.

What was going on? I concluded that the results had something to do with the Maillard reactions. These are a series of chemical reactions that cause browning and amp up the flavor when you cook meat, vegetables, or anything that isn't mostly sugar. A French scientist named Louis-Camille Maillard discovered these reactions in 1913 when researching cell biochemistry, and most of the research

browning occurs at 230°F. Water normally boils at 212°F. Therefore, if you have too much water, you'll be steaming whatever you're cooking, and it will never have the chance to brown.

PH The environment should not be acidic. Aha! This is when I realized that too much lemon juice was throwing off the pH balance of my chicken piccata. That's why it wasn't browning. You know how if you put sliced apples in water with lemon juice, they won't turn brown? That's because the browning of fruit is a Maillard reaction as well, albeit one

Aha! I realized that too much lemon juice was throwing off the pH balance of my chicken piccata. That's why it wasn't browning.

had to do with diabetes, not cooking. But that doesn't mean we can't use what scientists have learned in order to make better food.

Here's what we know about Maillard reactions: Heat + amino acids + sugar + water in a pH-neutral to somewhat alkaline environment will make food taste better. Too much to take in at once? Let's break it down.

HEAT This is the easy one. Not all that much heat is necessary for the golden-brown deliciousness of the Maillard reactions—generally, about 230°F. This is significantly lower than is needed to caramelize sugar, which is good because otherwise, meat would dry out while you're trying to bring out the flavor. Another way to encourage browning is to cook at a lower heat for a longer time.

AMINO ACIDS Proteins, like the ones found in meat and gluten, are composed of building blocks of about 20 amino acids. In addition, there are hundreds of other amino acids running around doing things that are unrelated to making protein. The important thing is that some of them are on the surface of the food you're cooking; otherwise, it won't brown. Usually, you get these amino acids from proteins that start to break down when you cook them.

SUGAR You don't need much, and it doesn't have to be table sugar. Starches are made of sugar molecules, and when you heat the starches, some of them break down into sugars and fuel the tasty chemical reactions.

WATER Again, not a lot of water. You may recall from the heat discussion that

that happens without heat. The acid in the lemon juice prevents browning there, and it will prevent browning in other circumstances as well.

So the key to tasty chicken piccata is not the lemon (although that adds a nice sharpness) but the fact that the whole recipe is geared towards maximizing the Maillard reactions (which translates into maximum flavor). Here's why:

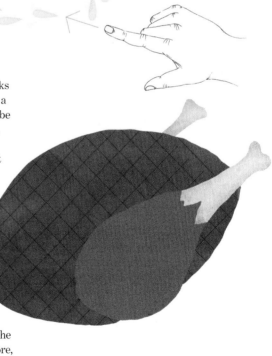

● **First, you flatten the chicken.** This creates more surface area, so there's more browning. More browning means more flavor.

● **Second, you dredge in flour.** The flour soaks up moisture from the surface and imparts a bunch of handy proteins that are ready to be broken apart and turned into amino acids.

● **Third, you make a pan sauce.** Scrape up the bits of whatever you were cooking that were changed by the Maillard reactions but were left in the pan, dissolve those bits in liquid, and get a delectable sauce.

By adding lemon juice at the beginning, I was interfering with the Maillard reactions. Even though the resulting chicken was infused with lemony flavor, I don't think I'll make this modification permanent for my standard chicken piccata. It's not worth losing the tasty browning. Instead, the next time lemons go on sale at my local store, I'll just get out my juicer and make lemonade.

Brian J. Geiger is a project manager for a robotics company in Charlottesville, Virginia. His alter ego is thefoodgeek.com.

Illustrations by Christopher Silas Neal

HOW TO MAKE

Chocolate Mousse

It's surprisingly simple to prepare this classic, oh-so-decadent dessert.
What's hard is not eating it all in one sitting. BY DABNEY GOUGH

RICH, INDULGENT, LIGHT AS AIR.
Chocolate mousse is all of those
things. And given how easy it
is to make, it's a dessert that
should have prime real estate in
your recipe box. With our basic
recipe, the right tools, and a little
know-how, you'll soon be on your
way to sweet success.

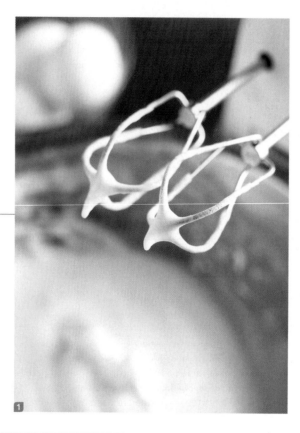

cook's tips

1 **Knowing when to stop
beating your egg whites is key.**
Soft peaks barely hold their shape;
the peaks flop over when the beaters are lifted. Stiff peaks (like those
at right) stand up when the beaters
are lifted.

2 **For an airy mousse** (after all,
mousse means foam in French),
use a light touch and a large rubber
spatula to fold the egg whites and
whipped cream into the chocolate.

No cooking class required

Making this classic French dessert is as easy as the tools you need and
the tricks you know. Check out our flavor twists to expand your repertoire.

TOOLS
A few standard kitchen
utensils are all you'll need:

- 3 bowls
- a skillet
- a large heatproof
  rubber spatula
- an electric hand mixer
  or a balloon whisk

TRICKS
Use the best-quality semisweet or bittersweet chocolate
you can find, preferably with
60 to 62 percent cacao for
the smoothest texture and
best flavor.

Serve your mousse right away
for a slightly looser texture or
chill it for a firmer result.

TWISTS
For something a little different,
add:

- **Hazelnut:** 3 Tbs. Frangelico.
- **Bourbon:** 1 Tbs. bourbon.
- **Coconut:** ½ cup toasted
  sweetened coconut (serve
  immediately to retain texture).

real chocolate mousse

Serves 4

- 6 oz. semisweet or bittersweet chocolate, preferably 60% to 62% cacao, chopped
- 2 Tbs. unsalted butter, cut into 8 pieces
- 3 large egg whites
  Pinch of table salt
- 3 Tbs. granulated sugar
- ¾ cup cold heavy cream
  Chocolate shavings for garnish (optional)

Put the chopped chocolate in a medium heatproof bowl and set the bowl in a skillet of barely simmering water. Stir the chocolate with a heatproof spatula just until it is melted. Remove the bowl from the skillet, add the butter to the chocolate, and stir until the butter is completely melted and the mixture is smooth.

In a medium bowl with an electric hand mixer on medium-high speed (or with a balloon whisk), whip the egg whites and salt until they barely hold soft peaks. While whipping, gradually sprinkle in the sugar—go slowly, as adding it too fast may cause the whites to fall. Continue whipping until the whites just start to hold stiff peaks (see photo 1 opposite). Don't overbeat or the dissolved sugar may weep out of the whites.

Wipe the beaters (or whisk) clean and then whip the cream in a large bowl until it's fairly thick and holds a soft peak when the beaters are lifted.

With a large spatula, gently fold about one-third of the egg whites into the chocolate until the mixture is no longer streaky. Fold in the remaining whites. Scrape the chocolate mixture into the whipped cream. Add a flavoring, if using (see sidebar opposite). Fold gently until the mixture is uniform in color and texture.

Divide among 4 dessert dishes and serve immediately, or refrigerate for at least 30 minutes for a slightly firmer texture. Garnish with chocolate shavings, if using.

Note: The risk of salmonella infection from consuming raw egg whites is low, but the only way to be completely safe is to use pasteurized egg whites.

Great Finds

Our latest buys for the kitchen and table.

BY DENISE MICKELSEN

The New Doily
Modern Twist's silk-screened silicone Doileez protect your furniture while adding a decorative touch. They're food safe, so you can use them to line platters, too. **$22 to $25 for a set of two 10-inch Doileez; modern-twist.com for stores.**

One of a Kind
A woodgrain pattern gives these gorgeous handcrafted bowls a rustic look, while their free-form shapes make them modern. dbO Home's Burl Collection dinnerware (available in chocolate, lettuce, and oyster shown here, as well as honey, truffle, and steamer), **$24 to $80 at dbohome.com; 860-364-6008.**

Grind to Go
Particular about your s&p? Take your own on the road with this stylish stainless-steel mini salt and pepper grinder travel set. **$45 (includes leather pouch) at grindpepper.com; 888-514-7463.**

Rustic and Refined
This elegant wine chiller offsets hammered stainless steel with a leopard wood base, to lovely effect. **$180; atticus home. com for stores.**

Sweet Ending
Fifty-year-old Mercer's Dairy of New York state makes these luscious ice creams with wines from the oldest vineyard in the country, Brotherhood Winery. We liked all six flavors, but Red Raspberry Chardonnay, Chocolate Cabernet, and Ala Port were our favorites. **$6 per pint at mercersdairy .com; 866-637-2377.**

History in the Baking
We love the swirling shape of NordicWare's Heritage Bundt pan—inspired by an eastern European kugelhopf pan but cool now in a Frank Gehry kind of way. **$34 at williams-sonoma.com; 877-812-6235.**

Photographs by Scott Phillips

Subscribe and save up to $55*

TREAT YOURSELF

☐ 1 year just $29.95 — **Save 28%***
☐ 2 years just $49.95 — **Save 40%***
☐ 3 years just $69.95 — **BEST BUY! Save 44%***

Send no money now. We will bill you later.

N509760N

MR. / MRS. / MS.

ADDRESS _____ APT. #

CITY

STATE   ZIP   EMAIL (OPTIONAL)

fine Cooking®
FineCooking.com/order

The Taunton Press will send you occasional notices about noteworthy products and exclusive offers.

*Savings off U.S. newsstand price. Above prices for U.S. and Canada (GST included). Payable in U.S. funds. International customers, visit FineCooking.com/order

Treat a friend to *Fine Cooking*

☐ 1 year just $29.95 — **Save 28%***
☐ 2 years just $49.95 — **Save 40%***
☐ 3 years just $69.95 — **BEST BUY! Save 44%***

Send no money now. We will bill you later.

A great gift idea!

N509761N

YOUR NAME: _____   **SEND GIFT TO:** _____

ADDRESS _____   ADDRESS _____

APT. #   CITY _____   APT. #   CITY _____

STATE   ZIP _____   STATE   ZIP _____

EMAIL: (OPTIONAL) _____

The Taunton Press will send you occasional notices about noteworthy products and exclusive offers.

fine Cooking®
FineCooking.com/order

*Savings off U.S. newsstand price. Above prices for U.S. and Canada (GST included). Payable in U.S. funds. International customers, visit FineCooking.com/order

The Taunton Press
Inspiration for hands-on living®

BUSINESS REPLY MAIL
FIRST-CLASS MAIL   PERMIT NO. 6   NEWTOWN CT

POSTAGE WILL BE PAID BY ADDRESSEE

fine
Cooking®

63 S MAIN ST
PO BOX 5507
NEWTOWN, CT 06470-9879

The Taunton Press
Inspiration for hands-on living®

BUSINESS REPLY MAIL
FIRST-CLASS MAIL   PERMIT NO. 6   NEWTOWN CT

POSTAGE WILL BE PAID BY ADDRESSEE

fine
Cooking®

63 S MAIN ST
PO BOX 5507
NEWTOWN, CT 06470-9879

Luxe for Less

Rich faux leather croc-odile coasters bring a touch of luxury to your table, without a hefty price tag (available in black, cinnamon, chest-nut, and cream). **$20 for a set of 6; to order, call Vietri at 866-327-1279.**

Form Meets Function

Miam.Miam's sleek new 4-cup Emperor French press is double walled to keep your morning coffee piping hot. **$44; unitedbrands.us for stores; 800-500-0583.**

Modern Vintage

Beautiful and functional, this handcast polished aluminum lemon juicer has real heft. It also makes a great gift. **$36 at beehivekitchenware .com; 508-678-4335.**

The Perfect Snack

Like a cross between a cookie and a cracker, these super-light, not-too-sweet olive oil tortas are made with all natural ingredients. They also happen to be impossible to resist. **Ines Rosales Sweet Olive Oil Tortas, $11.95 for 2 packs of 6 at tienda.com; 800-710-4304.**

Easy as A-B-C

Handmade porcelain alphabet napkin rings let you customize your table with style. They also make a great gift when paired with the hem-stitched linen napkins. **$10 each or $125 for a set of 8 with napkins at dinner-ware.com; 718-593-4097.**

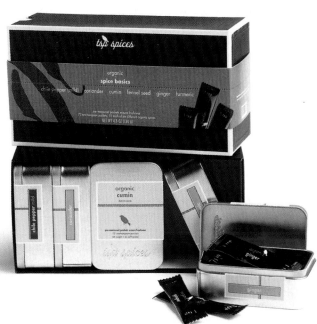

Keeping It Fresh

Organic spices, individually wrapped in one-teaspoon packets and sold in sets, are easy to use and stay fresh longer; plus their cute tins are stackable for storage. **$42 for a collection of 6 tins with 12 packets in each at tspspices.com; 877-511-8777.**

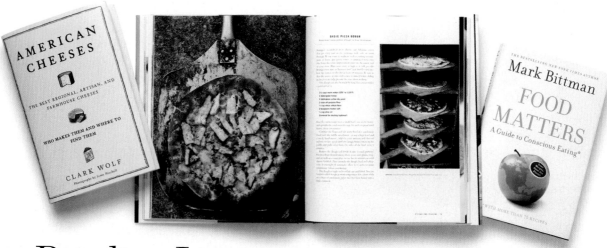

The Reading List

New must-buys for food lovers. BY KIMBERLY Y. MASIBAY

American Cheeses

The Best Regional, Artisan, and Farmhouse Cheeses; Who Makes Them, and Where to Find Them
by Clark Wolf
(Simon & Schuster, $25)

Clark Wolf had been meaning to write about his adventures sleuthing out this country's most amazing cheeses for almost 30 years. It's good news for all of us that he has finally gotten to it. In this delightful book, Wolf travels from West to East, stopping often along the way to introduce us to his favorite cheeses and the artisans who make them. It's hard to imagine a better guide.

Wolf, who has run multiple cheese shops and served as the executive director of the American Cheese Society, is generous, knowledgeable, charming, and chatty. He starts by walking us through cheese basics in depth: how it's made, how to store and serve it, what to eat and drink with it, where to buy it, and a whole lot more. Next come intimate profiles of cheesemakers, organized by region (the Northeast and New England, the South, the Middle West, and the Wild West), along with an eclectic mix of recipes

from top American chefs. Taken together and illustrated with lovely black-and-white photographs, it's a fascinating overview of a particular sliver of our national food culture.

Frank Stitt's Bottega Favorita

A Southern Chef's Love Affair with Italian Food
(Artisan Books, $40)

Back in 1988, Frank Stitt, a third-generation Alabamian, opened Bottega Italian Restaurant in Birmingham. Blending southern ingredients with Italian culinary techniques, Stitt's Bottega was a delicious success, as is his inspiring new book. It's filled with evocative photos that capture the restaurant's spirit and energy, plus 150 tantalizing recipes—you'll find Venetian risottos, Tuscan grilled and roasted meats, Piedmontese braises, Neapolitan grilled and stewed seafood, hearty Roman pastas and wood-fired pizzas, and spicy Sicilian couscous. Bottega's fare is straightforward —fresh, humble ingredients, harmoniously combined and simply presented—so you really can cook Stitt's recipes at home.

Food Matters

A Guide to Conscious Eating, with More Than 75 Recipes
by Mark Bittman
(Simon & Schuster, $24)

Food lovers have plenty to ponder these days. A trip to the supermarket can stir up a stew of questions about where our food comes from; how animals and crops are raised; how our choices affect our health and our planet; and, increasingly, why food costs so darn much.

In his new book, award-winning cookbook author Mark Bittman efficiently investigates these tough questions and proposes an eating plan to improve the health

of people, planet, and pocketbook. It's simple: Cut out the junk. Eat fewer animals. Feast on lots of real whole foods—fruits, veggies, grains. But Bittman's not about to deprive anyone of good food. Rather, in a direct, appealing style, he unravels a tangle of information about diet, health, agriculture, government, and climate change, illustrating the links between our eating habits and the environment. Bittman foresees a brighter future as he offers solutions in the form of meal plans, menus, and more than 75 well-crafted recipes.

Kimberly Y. Masibay is a Fine Cooking *contributing editor.*

what we're reading now

A recent stroll though a sidewalk book sale turned up a 1949 edition of James Beard's *The Fireside Cookbook*. And while I've been a fan of Beard's since the first time I made his pot roast from *American Cookery* (despite the salt typo!), this was a first experience with this charming book. I won't be trying Duchess Soup (an odd mix of tapioca, milk, and grated American cheese), but the Whitebait Pancakes sound like a good bet. Beard's unique voice is a big part of this book's appeal, but it's the vintage illustrations that take the cake. —*Laurie Buckle*

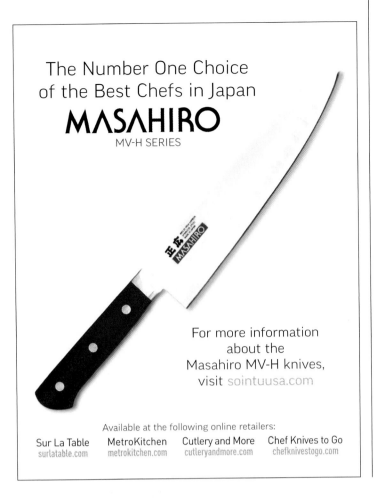

Bronze Is the New Stainless

What's new in kitchen design. BY LISA WADDLE

SHINY STAINLESS-STEEL KITCHENS ARE far from over, but we're predicting a warm-up. The new metal in the mix: bronze. Happily, bronze blends well with stainless, so you don't have to overhaul your entire kitchen at once—but consider the trend a good excuse to go for an update, if you're looking for one. Several manufacturers have introduced bronze finishes for appliances large and small; here are a few of our favorites.

start small

Anolon has unveiled a new Advanced Bronze collection of cookware, bakeware, tools, and cutlery (available at potsandpans.com; cookware and bakeware range from $15 to $120).

let it flow

Moen now offers many of its kitchen faucets in an oil-rubbed bronze finish, including this Woodmere model ($760 at showhouse .moen.com).

trash it

Oxo's Good Grips Touch Can is a tall and narrow column of bronze ($130 at oxo.com).

go big

Jenn-Air offers wall ovens, refrigerators, dishwashers, microwaves, warming drawers, and chimney hoods in oiled bronze. Visit jennair.com for details.

Fried Rice Gets Fresh

Nutritionist **Ellie Krieger** takes a less-than-healthy favorite and gives it a veggie-full makeover.

IT STARTED WITH SOME BROCCOLI. My daughter eats only the florets, so as usual, I went to cut them off to steam for her, throwing away the stalks in the process. But this time I stopped myself. I had read some shocking news recently that made me think twice: Americans waste a whopping 25 percent of available food. That's the equivalent of one pound per person every day, a number that accounts for not only broccoli stalks tossed at home but also unsold rotisserie chickens dumped at the market and half-eaten trays of lasagne discarded after a catered affair. With the cost of food making a bigger dent in everyone's pocketbook, wasting less at home seems like a no-brainer. Plus, it turns out that wasting less has been identified as the number one way to reduce your carbon "food" print. So I rescued the broccoli stalks—a drop in the stockpot for saving the planet, but a drop nonetheless. Surely I could find some way to use them.

Treasure hunting

Little did I know that the nearly rejected broccoli would lead me on a fantastic culinary journey. While pondering its possibilities, I found myself thinking about the odds and ends in my fridge that were in danger of being tossed—the last of a bag of baby carrots, most of a red bell pepper. I could make a fabulous omelet or frittata, or perhaps some kind of chopped salad. With a different mindset, I saw all of these discardable bits as treasures waiting to be turned into something satisfying and scrumptious. But what? The light bulb came in the form of leftover rice from Chinese takeout. Fried rice! Just those words get my mouth watering. And what better way to use all those little leftovers? It's the very reason fried rice was invented.

The trouble with fried rice is that it's usually pretty greasy and salty, with more

Continued on page 34

For Ellie, a fridge cleanout yields some tasty ideas.

five-treasure fried rice

This recipe is easily adaptable, so feel free to substitute other vegetables you might have in the fridge—asparagus, zucchini, peas, mushrooms, bok choy, bean sprouts, and jícama are all possibilities.

Serves 4

- 2 Tbs. canola oil
- 1 cup peeled, finely diced broccoli stems (from about 1¼ lb. broccoli)
- ¾ cup finely diced carrots
- ¾ cup finely diced red bell pepper
- ¾ cup frozen shelled edamame
- ¾ cup corn kernels, fresh or frozen
- 4 scallions (both white and green parts), thinly sliced
- 2 Tbs. finely grated fresh ginger
- 2 large cloves garlic, minced
- 4 cups very cold cooked brown rice
- ¾ cup finely diced Canadian bacon (4 oz.)
- 2 large eggs, lightly beaten
- ¼ cup lower-sodium soy sauce

Heat all but 1 tsp. of the oil in a large nonstick skillet or stir-fry pan over medium-high heat. Add the broccoli stems, carrots, and bell pepper and cook, stirring frequently, until the vegetables begin to soften, 3 to 5 minutes. Add the edamame and corn and cook until the edamame is thawed, about 1 minute. Add the scallion, ginger, and garlic and cook, stirring, until the raw garlic aroma subsides, about 1 minute. Add the rice and Canadian bacon and cook, stirring, until heated through, 3 to 5 minutes.

Make a 3-inch well in the center of the rice mixture. Add the remaining 1 tsp. oil, then the eggs, and cook, stirring, until the eggs are almost fully scrambled. Stir the eggs into the rice mixture. Stir in the soy sauce and serve.

good to know

- Brown rice is a better bet than white.
- More vegetables means a healthier dinner.
- There's big flavor in a small amount of meat.

From left to right: To give fried rice a healthy spin, Ellie uses lots of vegetables (including broccoli stems, carrots, and corn). She sprinkles in fresh aromatics like scallions, ginger, and garlic as flavor boosters and cooks the rice mixture with just a little canola oil to keep things light. Best of all, her fried rice comes together in less than 15 minutes, pan to bowl.

Photographs by Scott Phillips

cons than pros nutritionally. Not something you would consider healthful. But a few tweaks to the standard dish and you can keep all the crave-able deliciousness without the downsides.

Healthy upgrades

First, upgrade the rice from white to brown. I love brown rice's nutty taste and slight chewiness. And you just can't argue with its whole-grain antioxidant power and fiber. My favorite route to brown rice is to order it with Chinese food, but you can certainly cook some up yourself. Either way, bear in mind that the cooked rice has to be well chilled so the starch hardens and makes it fry-able. Use fresh rice and you wind up with a gummy mess.

Next, load the fried rice up with vegetables (and even fruit like pineapple or mandarin oranges) to get a big satisfying portion full of color and texture and nutrients.

To make it a complete meal in a bowl, add lean protein—Canadian bacon (which gives classic smoky pork flavor with very little fat), chicken, shrimp, ham, and tofu all work

wonderfully. And instead of relying on salt for flavor, amp up with healthful seasonings like fresh ginger, scallions, garlic, sesame oil, and chile peppers. Go easy on the salt by using lower-sodium soy sauce. Cook it all in

just a little canola oil, which is ideal for Asian-style cooking because it's neutral in flavor and takes the heat well. It's also rich in heart-healthy monounsaturated and omega-3 fat.

My broccoli-stalk-inspired treasure hunt ultimately led me to a collection of five freezer and fridge finds for my fried rice. Besides the broccoli, carrots, and red bell pepper, a peek in the freezer revealed half-full bags of corn and edamame. Perfect. The ideal ingredients for a satisfying, one-bowl meal studded with tasty goodies. I named it Five-Treasure Fried Rice.

It's amazing how simply thinking about food differently can do so much. With a fresh look, you can use the last of your week's produce to help you save money and eat greener and more healthfully. Not to mention the fact that you get to indulge in fried rice.

Registered dietician Ellie Krieger is a Fine Cooking *contributing editor.*

Nonstick Skillets

Time to buy a new one? Here are our top choices for this kitchen essential. BY MARYELLEN DRISCOLL

NONSTICK PANS USED TO BE considered disposable: toss when chipped. But that throw-it-away mentality has given way to a smarter, more eco-conscious way of thinking, and manufacturers are beginning to reformulate the way they make their nonsticks. The pans may cost a little more, but they're meant to last longer.

That's why, although you can get a large nonstick skillet for under $30, we chose to test pans priced between $50 and $80. In this range, we found four skillets that not only lived up to their nonstick claims but also delivered stellar performances. They're keepers.

Play it safe

Nonstick tops cookware sales, yet there remain concerns over its safety. Although nonstick coatings begin to break down and release potentially toxic fumes when heated above 500°F, experts confirm that cooking with nonstick is safe, provided it's used properly. To be safe:

- Don't heat a nonstick when it's empty.
- Don't use heat higher than medium high.
- Replace pans that begin to flake.

Also of concern is the toxic effect of nonstick's manufacturing process on the environment. Some manufacturers, including Cuisinart and Scanpan, have introduced pans made from PFOA-free technologies. (Perfluorooctanoic acid, or PFOA, is a man-made chemical identified by the Environmental Protection Agency as a likely carcinogen.) PFOA isn't used to make nonstick cookware but to make materials which are then used to create most nonstick surfaces. Even though there's no indication that people are exposed to PFOA through the use of nonstick, more companies are expected to follow suit in introducing PFOA-free cookware.

TOP CHOICE
Cuisinart Green Gourmet nonstick skillet
$70, homeandbeyond.com
Weight: 3 lb. 8 oz.

While this 12-inch pan was one of two "eco-friendly" pans in our review (along with the Scanpan), it was the performance and construction that made it our favorite. There was no sticking, and the aluminum core conducted heat in a controlled and even manner. Well balanced, the pan is classically shaped with gently sloping sides and a rolled edge for easy pouring. The riveted stay-cool handle is comfortable, and the opposing helper handle is a bonus. The exterior comes in hard anodized or stainless steel.

MOST COMFORTABLE
Scanpan Professional fry pan
$80, metrokitchen.com
Weight: 2 lb. 9 oz.

This 11-inch pan was a standout for its easy maneuverability. Substantial but lighter than most, it's well balanced, with a handle that's rounded and tapered in just the right places. The sloping sides are short, which made food feel readily accessible. The pressure-cast-aluminum disk base conducted heat evenly, and the ceramic titanium nonstick surface meant no sticking of fish fillets or fried eggs cooked without oil.

Photographs by Scott Phillips

LARGEST COOKING SURFACE
Swiss Diamond fry pan

$84, parkers-pantry.com
Weight: 2 lb. 9 oz.

We can't vouch for whether fusing nonstick compounds with diamond crystals is what makes the difference for this pan, but we can testify that sticking wasn't an issue. The straight sides of this 11-inch pan give it a roomy 9½-inch flat cooking surface. Eggs fried with no oil flipped with ease and slid out of the pan. The pressure-cast-aluminum disk base conducted heat evenly and browned foods beautifully. The small helper handle is a nice aid in lifting.

DEEPEST
Anolon Advanced French nonstick skillet

$70, cutleryandmore.com
Weight: 4 lb.

This 12-inch pan's hard-anodized aluminum construction delivered the kind of heat conduction you'd expect from a high-quality, traditionally surfaced fry pan. It browned pork chops as well as a traditional pan did, and the nonstick properties were flawless. This is a substantial pan, with 3-inch-high sides, which make it feel more suited to containing a simmering sauce than slipping out an omelet. The one downside: This pan is oven-safe to no more than 400°F; the others are safe up to 500°F.

how we tested

We put 10 widely available 11- to 12-inch nonstick skillets through the following tests:

- Cooked multiple batches of pancakes to see how evenly each pan cooked over time.
- Sautéed boneless pork chops to test how well each pan could brown.
- Cooked fish fillets and eggs without any fat to test release.

what to look for

All four of these pans heated evenly and were beautifully nonstick. Which you choose comes down to the following features:

Shape If you plan to cook mainly eggs or fish, a pan with low sides like Scanpan's or Swiss Diamond's lets you easily slide out delicate foods. For a wider variety of cooking tasks, such as stir-fries or sauces, the deeper Cuisinart or Anolon might be better.

Grip The pan should feel comfortable and secure.

Balance While lifting it or swirling oil, the pan should not strain your wrist or forearm.

Oven safe If high-heat oven use is in your future, make sure your pan's handle can take the heat.

Storage Most nonsticks get scratched when stacked with other pans. Look for a handle with a hole or loop so you can hang it.

Maryellen Driscoll is a Fine Cooking *contributing editor.*

Shaken or Stirred?

A New York City mixologist gives us the lowdown on the proper way to prepare classic cocktails. BY JIM MEEHAN

BEFORE WE CONSIDER THE question of whether to shake or stir, let's pause to consider a certain fictional spy's influence on the answer. Here's James Bond ordering a martini in Ian Fleming's *Casino Royale* (1953):

"A dry martini," he said. "One. In a deep Champagne goblet."

"Oui, monsieur."

"Just a moment. Three measures of Gordon's, one of vodka, half a measure of Kina Lillet. Shake it very well until it's ice-cold, then add a large, thin slice of lemon peel. Got it?"

Ordering a custom-made martini—shaken, not stirred—would have turned heads in the 1950s, when martinis were customarily stirred to preserve the drink's clarity. That, presumably, is why Bond did it. But before we blame the man for altering the course of 20th-century cocktails, it's important to understand that drink preparation, and the methodologies behind it, have varied over time. After ice became widely available in the latter half of the 19th century, cold drinks of all types were mixed and chilled according to the wisdom—and trends—of the day. Some bartenders shook; some stirred.

The big chill

Bond seemed more concerned about the temperature of his cocktail than its appearance; hence his unusual request. Let's just say he was smarter about outsmarting the bad guy than he was about ordering a drink. You don't have to shake a martini to get it good and cold. In fact, the temperature of a cocktail is determined by everything the liquid comes in contact with, from the moment it leaves the bottle until it's served. A cocktail served in a chilled glass and made with well-chilled equipment results in an ice-cold drink, whether it's shaken or stirred.

Shake it up

Cocktails containing citrus, cream, or eggs should be shaken. Sure, shaking liquids with ice chills them, but shaking also mixes the ingredients thoroughly and incorporates air for a frothy texture and opaque appearance. There is one key point to remember: As soon as you add ice to your shaker the clock starts ticking, so it's best to have a chilled serving glass with fresh ice and any garnishes ready before you shake the drink.

My method for shaking is simple. After combining the ingredients in a chilled cocktail shaker, add ice and the top of the shaker. If shaken for too long, the ice will overdilute the drink, so shake hard for 7 to 10 seconds; then immediately strain the cocktail into a chilled glass over fresh ice. A great shaken drink is the Whiskey Smash, a spicy-sweet mix of rye whiskey, simple syrup, lemon, and mint (recipe at right). The crushed lemon and mint give the drink a cloudy look, but the flavors are smooth and true.

Create a stir

I'd never stirred my drinks properly until Audrey Saunders taught me how to prepare a martini at her New York City cocktail bar, Pegu Club. She showed me that stirring properly, with the right equipment, yields a cold, beguilingly clear martini—among other drinks—and I've never looked back. The best cocktails for stirring are those composed entirely of spirits (no juices or other ingredients added to the mix). Stirring helps achieve even dilution and a crystal-clear presentation.

Again, the method is straightforward. Pour the ingredients into a chilled mixing glass or shaker and add ice. Hold the glass at the base with your index finger and thumb. Insert a long-handled spoon into the glass, grip the spoon like a pencil, and stir quickly for about 10 seconds. Stir in a fluid motion that won't agitate the liquid or create air bubbles. Then strain the drink into a chilled glass (over fresh ice, if appropriate) and serve.

The Martinez is one of my favorite stirred cocktails (recipe, opposite). A predecessor of the dry martini, it combines gin and sweet vermouth with maraschino liqueur and bitters. One of the first mentions of The Martinez appeared in the 1887 edition of *Jerry Thomas' Bar-Tenders Guide.* Thomas called for it to be shaken in accordance with the trend of his time. I don't know how Bond would feel about it, but I'm glad we know better now.

whiskey smash, shaken

This Whiskey Smash update was created by Dale DeGroff at the Rainbow Room in the early 1990s. Today, he makes his Smash with Curaçao instead of simple syrup, but I like the drink more true to form.

Serves 1

- 6–8 fresh mint leaves; plus 1 sprig for garnish
- ½ small lemon, quartered and seeded
- ¾ fl. oz. (4½ tsp.) simple syrup
- 2 fl. oz. (¼ cup) rye whiskey

Put the mint leaves, lemon, and syrup in a chilled cocktail shaker. Gently crush with a muddler or the end of a wooden spoon until the lemon wedges have released their juice. Add the whiskey and fill the shaker with ice. Put the lid on the shaker and make sure you have a tight seal. Shake as hard as you can for 7 to 10 seconds and then strain into a small chilled rocks glass filled with fresh ice. Garnish with the mint sprig and serve.

Note: To make simple syrup, heat equal parts sugar and water until the sugar dissolves. Refrigerated, simple syrup keeps indefinitely.

the martinez, stirred

The original Martinez (from which the dry martini likely evolved) called for Old Tom Gin and Boker's Bitters, neither of which has been available in the United States for decades. In 2007, I created this adaptation.

Serves 1

- 1½ fl. oz. (3 Tbs.) gin
- 1½ fl. oz. (3 Tbs.) sweet vermouth
- ¼ fl. oz. (1½ tsp.) maraschino liqueur
- 2 dashes orange bitters
  Lemon twist, for garnish

Combine the gin, vermouth, maraschino liqueur, and orange bitters in a chilled mixing glass or cocktail shaker. Fill the glass almost to the top with ice. Hold the glass at the base with your index finger and thumb and insert a long spoon (such as an iced tea spoon) into the glass. Grip the spoon like a pencil and stir the drink for about 10 seconds, pressing the back of the spoon against the glass as you rotate the spoon around the circumference of the glass. The idea is to stir quickly in a fluid motion that doesn't agitate the liquid or create air bubbles. Strain the drink into a chilled martini glass or coupe, garnish with the lemon twist, and serve immediately.

Jim Meehan is manager of PDT (Please Don't Tell) in New York City.

Oranges

A supermarket staple? Sure. Delicious year-round? Not even close. That's why we love oranges in winter, when they're at their sweet, juicy best.

BY JOANNE WEIR

sear-roasted halibut with blood orange salsa

Serves 4

FOR THE SALSA

- ¾ cup fresh navel or Valencia orange juice (from 2 medium oranges)
- 3 small blood oranges, cut into segments (see Test Kitchen, p. 83), segments cut in half
- 2 Tbs. minced red onion
- 1 Tbs. chopped fresh cilantro
- 1 Tbs. extra-virgin olive oil
- 1 Tbs. finely grated navel or Valencia orange zest (from 2 medium oranges)

   Kosher salt and freshly ground black pepper

FOR THE HALIBUT

- 1 tsp. finely grated navel or Valencia orange zest (from 1 small orange)
- 1 tsp. chopped fresh thyme

   Kosher salt and freshly ground black pepper

- 4 6-oz. skinless halibut fillets
- 3 Tbs. olive oil

Position a rack in the center of the oven and heat the oven to 425°F.

MAKE THE SALSA

In a small saucepan, boil the orange juice over medium heat until reduced to ¼ cup, 8 to 10 minutes. Let cool.

In a medium bowl, combine the reduced orange juice, blood orange segments, onion, cilantro, olive oil, and orange zest. Season to taste with salt and pepper.

COOK THE HALIBUT

In a small bowl, mix the orange zest, thyme, 1½ tsp. salt, and ½ tsp. pepper. Rub the mixture all over the halibut fillets. Heat the oil in a 12-inch ovenproof skillet over medium-high heat. When the oil is shimmering hot, arrange the fillets in the pan. Sear for about 2 minutes without moving; then use a thin slotted metal spatula to lift a piece of fish and check the color. When the fillets are nicely browned, flip them and put the pan in the oven.

Roast until the halibut is just cooked through, 3 to 5 minutes. Remove the pan from the oven and transfer the halibut to serving plates. Spoon some of the salsa over each fillet.

blood orange and radicchio salad with hazelnuts and shaved parmigiano

Serves 6

- 5 medium blood oranges
- ¼ cup extra-virgin olive oil
- 1 Tbs. white wine vinegar
   Kosher salt and freshly ground black pepper
- 1 medium (12-oz.) head radicchio, washed, cored, and cut into 1- to 2-inch pieces (about 5 loosely packed cups)
- 1 medium (6-oz.) head butter lettuce, washed, cored, and cut into 1- to 2-inch pieces (about 4 loosely packed cups)
- ¾ cup blanched hazelnuts, toasted and coarsely chopped
- 1½ oz. chunk Parmigiano-Reggiano or aged goat cheese

Finely grate 1 tsp. of zest and then squeeze 2 Tbs. juice from one of the oranges. In a medium bowl, whisk the zest and juice with the olive oil, vinegar, ½ tsp. salt, and a few grinds of black pepper.

Using a sharp knife, trim off the peel and white pith from the remaining 4 oranges and cut crosswise into ¼-inch slices; remove any seeds. (See Test Kitchen, page 83, for more information.)

In a large bowl, toss the radicchio and butter lettuce with the hazelnuts and just enough dressing to lightly coat (about ¼ cup). Season to taste with salt and pepper. Divide the salad among 6 serving plates and top each with 3 or 4 blood orange slices. With a vegetable peeler, shave a few shards of cheese over the top.

 For more orange-centric recipes, go to **FineCooking.com/extras.**

Photographs by Scott Phillips

Sear-Roasted Halibut
with Blood Orange Salsa

Pan-Roasted Chicken Breasts
with Orange-Brandy Sauce

pan-roasted chicken breasts with orange-brandy sauce

A quick soak in an orange juice brine infuses the chicken with lots of flavor. You'll need a total of about 9 medium oranges for this recipe.

Serves 6

FOR THE CHICKEN

- **2** cups fresh navel or Valencia orange juice
- **2** Tbs. finely grated orange zest
  Kosher salt
- **6** 6- to 7-oz. boneless, skin-on chicken breast halves (see Test Kitchen, p. 83)
- **2** Tbs. extra-virgin olive oil
  Freshly ground black pepper

FOR THE SAUCE

- **3** Tbs. unsalted butter
- **1** medium shallot, minced
- **2** Tbs. brandy
- **1** cup fresh navel or Valencia orange juice
- **½** cup lower-salt chicken broth
- **1** navel or Valencia orange, cut into segments (see Test Kitchen, p. 83), segments cut into thirds
- **1** Tbs. chopped fresh flat-leaf parsley
  Kosher salt and freshly ground black pepper

BRINE THE CHICKEN

Combine the orange juice, zest, 6 Tbs. salt, and 4 cups water in a large bowl or pot; stir to dissolve the salt. Add the chicken breasts and refrigerate for 2 to 3 hours.

COOK THE CHICKEN

Position a rack in the center of the oven and heat the oven to 400°F.
Remove the chicken from the brine and pat it dry with paper towels.
Heat the olive oil in a 12-inch oven-proof skillet over medium-high heat until shimmering hot. Add the chicken skin side down in a snug single layer and cook until the skin is golden brown, 3 to 5 minutes. Turn the chicken, season with ¼ tsp. salt and a few grinds of pepper, and put the pan in the oven. Roast the chicken until an instant-read thermometer registers 165°F in the center of the thickest breast, about 15 minutes. Remove from the oven, transfer the chicken to a carving board, tent with foil, and let rest while you make the sauce.

MAKE THE SAUCE

Pour the juices from the skillet into a heatproof measuring cup. Let the fat rise to the surface and then spoon it off.
Melt 2 Tbs. of the butter in the skillet over medium-high heat. Add the shallot and cook, stirring, until soft, 1 to 2 minutes. Off the heat, add the brandy. Return the pan to the heat and cook, scraping the bottom of the pan, until the brandy has almost evaporated, about 30 seconds. Increase the heat to high and add the orange juice. Boil until thick and syrupy and reduced to about ⅓ cup, about 5 minutes. Add the chicken broth, pan juices, and any juices from the carving board. Boil until reduced to about ¾ cup, about 3 minutes.
Swirl in the orange segments. Then, off the heat, swirl in the remaining 1 Tbs. butter and the parsley until the butter is melted. Season to taste with salt and a few grinds of pepper.
To serve, cut the chicken on the diagonal into thin slices and arrange on 6 serving plates. Drizzle with the sauce.

Shop and Store

Buying info
To ensure that they'll be juicy, look for oranges that are firm and heavy for their size. Choose oranges with no blemishes or soft areas and avoid ones that look dry.

Storing info
Keep oranges in a cool place, and use them within a week or two. Good to know: Oranges don't continue to ripen once picked.

a buyer's guide

Here's a brief guide to the most common orange varieties—Valencia, navel, and blood oranges. With a few exceptions (see below), most subvarieties of these oranges aren't labeled at the market. That's because the differences have little to do with flavor and more to do with when the fruit matures during the year—only a grower would know one from the other.

Valencia
Valencia oranges— originally from Spain—are thin-skinned and almost seedless. They're your best bet when you need lots of juice. But Valencia oranges are also a great choice for any recipe that calls for sweet oranges.

Navel
Originally from Brazil, navel oranges get their name from a second, smaller orange that develops at the base. (This un-developed twin looks a little like a belly button.) Seedless, with thick skins, navels are the best eating oranges around. Though a little less juicy than Valencias, they're virtually interchange-able when it comes to cooking. At the store, most navels are labeled simply "navel," but you might see some called Cara Cara; these have dark-pink flesh, an orange exterior, and a sweet, mildly acidic flavor.

Blood oranges
Blood oranges have a much sweeter flavor and less acidity than navels or Valencias, with overtones of raspberries or strawberries. Their thin skins may be blushed with red, and the flesh is a distinctive blood-red. If you want sweetness, blood oranges are the way to go, especially if paired with slightly bitter ingredients, as in the radicchio salad on page 42. At the market, you might find varieties like Moro or Tarocco. Moros have dark-purple flesh and a deep-reddish rind. Taroccos (sometimes called half-blood oranges because they aren't as red as the Moro) have a blushed rind.

disk, and wrap in plastic. Refrigerate for 30 minutes.

Press the dough evenly into the bottom and sides of a 9½-inch fluted tart pan with a removable bottom—the dough sides should be ¼ to ⅜ inch thick. To smooth the bottom, cover with plastic wrap and press with a flat-bottom measuring cup or glass. Freeze the covered shell for 30 minutes. Meanwhile, position a rack in the center of the oven and heat the oven to 400°F.

Remove the plastic, line the dough with parchment and fill with dry beans or pie weights. Bake the tart shell until the top edges are light golden, about 15 minutes. Carefully remove the parchment and beans, reduce the heat to 375°F, and continue to bake until the shell is golden all over, about 15 minutes. Cool on a rack.

MAKE THE FILLING

In a small saucepan, heat the butter over medium-high heat until it melts and the milk solids turn brown, swirling the pan occasionally for even browning, about 3 minutes. Immediately pour into a small heatproof bowl to stop the cooking.

In a medium bowl, whisk ¼ cup of the milk with the cornstarch. Whisk in the eggs.

In a medium saucepan, bring the remaining 1¾ cups milk, the sugar, and salt to a boil over medium heat. Take the pan off the heat, whisk about ¼ cup of the hot milk into the egg mixture, and then whisk the egg mixture into the hot milk. Return to medium heat and continue whisking until the filling boils and becomes very thick, 30 seconds to 1 minute. Off the heat, whisk in the brown butter and vanilla.

Spread the filling evenly in the tart shell and set aside at room temperature while you prepare the topping.

MAKE THE TOPPING

Using a sharp knife, trim off the peel and pith from the oranges. (See Test Kitchen, page 83, for more.) Halve the oranges lengthwise and then slice them thinly crosswise and remove any seeds. Arrange the orange slices on the top of the tart in concentric, slightly overlapping circles.

Stir the marmalade in a small saucepan over medium heat until melted, 30 to 60 seconds. Strain and then stir in the Cointreau. Brush enough of the mixture on the oranges to give them a shine (you may not need it all). Refrigerate for 1 hour before serving so the filling can set up.

orange and brown-butter tart

Serves 8

FOR THE TART SHELL

5	oz. (1¼ cups) unbleached all-purpose flour
1	Tbs. granulated sugar
	Pinch of table salt
5	oz. (10 Tbs.) cold unsalted butter, cut into small pieces
1	tsp. finely grated orange zest

FOR THE FILLING

3	Tbs. unsalted butter
2	cups whole milk
3	Tbs. cornstarch
2	large eggs
½	cup granulated sugar
	Pinch of kosher or table salt
¼	tsp. pure vanilla extract

FOR THE TOPPING

3	large navel or blood oranges, or a combination
½	cup orange marmalade
1	Tbs. orange liqueur, such as Cointreau

MAKE THE TART SHELL

In a food processor, pulse the flour, sugar, and salt a few times to combine. Add the butter and orange zest and pulse until the mixture resembles cornmeal, six to eight 1-second pulses. A teaspoon at a time, pulse in up to 1 Tbs. water until the dough just holds together in clumps. Press the dough together, shape into a 6-inch

Perfect Pairs

Even just a strip of orange zest adds amazing flavor to steamed rice, custard, hot chocolate, a cup of tea, crème anglaise, or a pot of tomato soup. And oranges match up well with a range of ingredients that might surprise you; experiment with any of the following.

Asparagus	Ginger
Basil	Grapefruit
Cardamom	Lemon
Chives	Lettuces
Chocolate	Lime
Cilantro	Mint
Cinnamon	Oregano
Cloves	Saffron
Coriander	Sugar snap peas
Endive	Tomatoes

blood orange and mango sorbet

Yields about 1 quart; serves 8

3	medium ripe mangos, peeled and cut into chunks
2½	cups blood orange juice (from 7 to 8 medium blood oranges)
1	cup granulated sugar
1	Tbs. fresh lemon juice
1	Tbs. finely grated blood orange zest

Purée the mango and blood orange juice in a blender on high speed until smooth. Strain through a fine strainer into a large measuring cup. You should have about 4 cups.

Combine the sugar and about one-quarter of the purée in a medium saucepan; cook over medium heat, stirring until the sugar has dissolved completely, about 2 minutes. Stir into the remaining purée and add the lemon juice and blood orange zest. Refrigerate until thoroughly chilled.

Freeze in an ice cream maker according to the manufacturer's instructions.

Joanne Weir is a cooking teacher, cookbook author, and host of the PBS show, Joanne Weir's Cooking Class. ◘

SLOW-ROASTED PORK SHOULDER
WITH CARROTS, ONIONS, AND GARLIC

Roast Pork Replay

Eat delicious slow-roasted pork on Sunday and then turn it into inspired dinners during the week.

BY TASHA DeSERIO

A SUCCULENT ROAST WITH meltingly tender vegetables, slow-cooked for hours in the oven—it's a dish I affectionately call "housewife pork." That's because it reminds me of the roasts my mother used to make when I was young. She would season the roast the night before, pop it in the oven in the morning, and let it cook slowly all day long. In the afternoon, she'd add some vegetables and continue to cook the roast until dinnertime. The result: meat with an amazing fall-off-the-bone texture.

Now that I'm a mom, I've learned to appreciate this simple slow-cooking technique, and I still love the delicious results. Occasionally, I tinker with the basic recipe—adding crushed fennel seed and hot pepper flakes to the seasoning, or a few dried chipotles to the vegetables—but the premise remains the same. I also appreciate this recipe for its promise of leftovers. The shredded pork easily becomes another delicious meal or two later in the week—a kind of dinner "insurance" for the modern mom.

PULLED-PORK
SANDWICHES

PORK RAGOUT
WITH SOFT POLENTA

PORK AND POTATO HASH
WITH POACHED EGGS

MASTER RECIPE

slow-roasted pork shoulder with carrots, onions, and garlic

Start this recipe at least a day ahead. Serve the pork and vegetables with mashed potatoes or with beans (like cranberry or cannellini) seasoned with pounded garlic, extra-virgin olive oil, and sage.

Serves 4 with leftovers (or 8 without)

	Kosher salt and freshly ground black pepper
1	6¾- to 7-lb. boneless pork shoulder roast
1	large yellow onion, cut into ½-inch-thick rings
3	medium carrots, cut into sticks ½ inch wide and 2 to 2½ inches long
10	cloves garlic, peeled
1	cup dry white wine

Combine 2 Tbs. salt and 2 tsp. pepper in a small bowl and rub the mixture all over the pork. Put the pork, fat side up, in a large roasting pan (about 12x16x3 inches). Cover and refrigerate overnight or for up to 3 days.

Remove the pork from the refrigerator and let sit at room temperature for 1 to 1½ hours before cooking.

Position a rack in the center of the oven and heat the oven to 300°F. Uncover the pork and roast until tender everywhere but the very center when pierced with a fork, 4 to 4½ hours. Add the onion, carrots,

garlic, wine, and 1 cup water to the roasting pan and continue to roast, stirring the vegetables occasionally, until the pork is completely tender, about 1 hour more.

Remove the roast from the oven and raise the oven temperature to 375°F. Using tongs, separate the pork into 8 to 10 large, rustic chunks and spread out on the pan. If most of the liquid has evaporated, add a splash more water to the pan to create a little more juice. (It shouldn't be soupy.) Return the pork to the oven and continue to roast until nicely browned on the newly exposed surfaces, about 15 minutes. Remove the pan from the oven, transfer the meat and vegetables to a serving platter, and tent loosely with foil. Let rest for 20 minutes. Skim the excess fat from the juices and serve the juices with the vegetables and meat.

Shredding the evidence

After dinner, pull (or hand-shred) the leftover pork. To do this, cut the chunks of pork across the grain into about 1-inch widths and pull the pork apart into pieces. Save any leftover juices separately. Well-wrapped leftovers will keep in the refrigerator for 3 to 4 days, or in the freezer for up to 2 months.

pulled-pork sandwiches with cabbage, caper, and herb slaw

For these sandwiches, the bread should be very lightly toasted so that it's soft and warm but not dry. Be sure to use every last bit of the juices and drizzle every last drop of vinegar onto the sandwich. Both steps improve the flavor and moisten the bread, which is key.

Serves 4

- 1½ Tbs. capers, preferably salt-packed
- 2 cups very thinly sliced green cabbage
- ¼ small red onion, very thinly sliced
- ¼ cup chopped fresh flat-leaf parsley
- 3 Tbs. thinly sliced fresh chives
- 1½ tsp. finely chopped fresh oregano
- 1–2 tsp. finely chopped preserved red chiles, such as cherry peppers or Calabrian peppers, or substitute Asian chile sauce (optional)
- 2 Tbs. red wine vinegar
- Kosher salt
- 3½ cups leftover shredded Slow-Roasted Pork Shoulder (recipe opposite)
- 1 baguette
- 3 Tbs. extra-virgin olive oil; more to taste

Position a rack in the center of the oven and heat the oven to 350°F.

Rinse the capers well. If using salt-packed capers, soak them in warm water for at least 5 minutes. (They should taste capery rather than salty; if not, continue soaking for a little longer.) Drain the capers and, unless they're very small, coarsely chop them.

Combine the capers, cabbage, red onion, parsley, chives, oregano, and chiles (if using). Add the vinegar and ¼ tsp. salt, toss well, and let sit at room temperature for at least 30 minutes. Toss again and season to taste with more salt or chile.

Meanwhile, put the pork in a small baking dish. (If you have any juices left, scrape them into the dish, skimming and discarding as much of the congealed fat as possible.) Cover with foil and bake the pork until warmed through, 10 to 15 minutes. Remove the pork from the oven, position a rack 6 inches from the broiler, and heat the broiler to high.

Cut the baguette crosswise into 4 equal portions (each 5 to 6 inches long) and then slice each piece horizontally so that it opens like a book. Just before serving, put the baguette pieces on a baking sheet, opening each as much as possible, and toast very lightly under the broiler, 2 to 3 minutes. Divide the pork into 4 equal portions and mound on the bottom half of each piece of baguette. Drizzle any pan juices over the pork and then pile on the cabbage slaw. Drizzle the olive oil over the slaw. If any vinegar has collected on the bottom of the slaw bowl, distribute it among the sandwiches, and serve.

pork ragout with soft polenta

This recipe is comfort on a plate; it's reason enough to make the slow-roasted pork in the first place.

Serves 4

2	cups whole milk; more as needed
	Kosher salt
1	cup yellow stone-ground cornmeal
¼	cup freshly grated Parmigiano-Reggiano; more for sprinkling
1½	Tbs. unsalted butter
2	Tbs. extra-virgin olive oil
2	medium carrots, cut into small dice
2	medium ribs celery, cut into small dice

1	medium yellow onion, cut into small dice
	Pinch of crushed red pepper flakes
3	canned tomatoes, drained and cut into medium dice
3	cloves garlic, finely chopped
3	cups leftover shredded Slow-Roasted Pork Shoulder (recipe, p. 50)
3	cups lower-salt chicken broth
	Freshly ground black pepper
2	Tbs. chopped fresh flat-leaf parsley

Combine the milk with 2 cups water in a medium heavy-duty saucepan and bring to a boil over medium-high heat (watch carefully to prevent a boilover). Add 1½ tsp. salt and whisk in the cornmeal in a fine stream. Continue to whisk until the polenta begins to thicken, 1 to 3 minutes. Reduce the heat so that the polenta slowly bubbles and cook, uncovered, stirring frequently, until tender and no longer gritty, 20 to 40 minutes, depending on the cornmeal. If the polenta becomes too thick in the process, add milk, a little at a time, to maintain a soft consistency. When the polenta is done, stir in the Parmigiano and ½ Tbs. of the butter and season to taste with salt. Keep warm until serving. (The polenta will thicken as it sits. If necessary, add a splash of milk to thin it just before serving.)

Heat the oil in a 10-inch straight-sided sauté pan over medium heat. Add the carrots, celery, onion, pepper flakes, and a generous pinch of salt and cook, stirring often, until tender and starting to brown, 8 to 10 minutes. Add the tomatoes and garlic and cook, stirring, for another minute. Add the pork and chicken broth. Bring to a boil and then lower the heat to maintain a simmer. Cook until the broth has reduced by half, about 10 minutes. Stir in the remaining 1 Tbs. butter. Season to taste with salt and pepper.

Spoon the polenta into shallow bowls and then spoon the ragout on the top and to one side, with the broth pooling around the polenta. (Make sure each portion gets a fair share of broth.) Sprinkle each portion with parsley and Parmigiano and serve immediately.

pork and potato hash with poached eggs and avocado

For a finishing touch, sprinkle this hash with cilantro and piment d'Espelette (see Test Kitchen, page 83, for more about this ingredient).

Serves 4

1½	lb. russet potatoes, peeled and cut into small dice (about 3¾ cups)
	Kosher salt
2	Tbs. extra-virgin olive oil; more as needed
1	medium yellow onion, cut into small dice (about 1¼ cups)
2¼	cups leftover finely shredded Slow-Roasted Pork Shoulder (recipe, p. 50)
2	medium cloves garlic, finely chopped
½	tsp. white wine vinegar or lemon juice
4	large eggs
1	large ripe avocado, sliced
¼	cup coarsely chopped fresh cilantro
	Piment d'Espelette or other medium-hot red chile flakes, to taste (optional)

Put the potatoes in a medium saucepan, add water to cover by about ¾ inch, and add 1 Tbs. salt. Bring to a boil over high heat, reduce the heat to maintain a simmer, and cook until the potatoes are tender but not falling apart, about 5 minutes. Drain the potatoes, transfer to a plate, and set aside.

Heat the oil in a 10-inch straight-sided sauté pan over medium-high heat. Add the onion and ½ tsp. salt and cook, stirring occasionally until soft, 5 to 7 minutes. Add the pork and continue to cook until the pork is warm, about 3 minutes. Add the garlic and cook, stirring, until the raw garlic aroma subsides, about 1 minute. Add the potatoes, toss gently to combine, and continue to cook, stirring, until heated through, 1 to 3 minutes more. Season to taste with salt. If the hash is a little dry, add a drizzle of olive oil. Keep warm.

Fill a medium saucepan with 3 inches of water. Add the vinegar and a pinch of salt, and bring the water to a simmer. Crack the eggs one at a time into a small bowl or teacup and then gently slide each egg into the water. Poach the eggs, gently turning once or twice until the whites are completely opaque but the yolks are still soft, 3 to 4 minutes. Using a slotted spoon, remove the eggs from the water and gently blot dry with a towel.

Evenly distribute the hash among 4 plates. Prop a poached egg and a few slices of avocado next to each portion. Sprinkle the egg and avocado with salt. Sprinkle the cilantro and piment d'Espelette (if using) over the hash, and serve immediately.

Tasha DeSerio is co-proprietor of Olive Green Catering in Berkeley, California. ❑

Homemade Croissants

Step by step to the classic French pastry (tips, timelines, and tools included). RECIPES BY JEFFREY HAMELMAN

TO TELL HOW WELL A CROISSANT IS MADE, take a bite and look at your shirt: If it's covered with flakes of golden pastry that shatter from each bite, you know it's a good one. A crisp brown crust and airy insides, rich with buttery flavor and aroma—these are the hallmarks of a beautifully made croissant.

Making your own croissants is not difficult; there's no special equipment or hard-to-find ingredients required. What is necessary is good technique—and that's where this recipe from a master baker comes in. Once you understand the basics of creating multilayered dough like this, you'll be well on your way to wowing friends and family with delicious croissants that make a mess of whatever they're wearing.

classic croissants

Yields 15

FOR THE DOUGH

1	lb. 2 oz. (4 cups) unbleached all-purpose flour; more for rolling (see Flour Know-How, p. 58)
5	oz. (½ cup plus 2 Tbs.) cold water
5	oz. (½ cup plus 2 Tbs.) cold whole milk
2	oz. (¼ cup plus 2 Tbs.) granulated sugar
1½	oz. (3 Tbs.) soft unsalted butter
1	Tbs. plus scant ½ tsp. instant yeast
2¼	tsp. table salt

FOR THE BUTTER LAYER

10	oz. (1¼ cups) cold unsalted butter

FOR THE EGG WASH

1	large egg

MAKE THE DOUGH

Combine all of the dough ingredients in the bowl of a stand mixer fitted with the dough hook. Mix on low speed for 3 minutes, scraping the sides of the mixing bowl once if necessary. Mix on medium speed for 3 minutes. Transfer the dough to a lightly floured 10-inch pie pan or a dinner plate. Lightly flour the top of the dough and wrap well with plastic so it doesn't dry out. Refrigerate overnight.

MAKE THE BUTTER LAYER

The next day, cut the cold butter lengthwise into ½-inch-thick slabs. Arrange the pieces on a piece of parchment or waxed paper to form a 5- to 6-inch square, cutting the butter crosswise as necessary to fit. Top with another piece of parchment or waxed paper. With a rolling pin, pound the butter with light, even strokes **1**. As the pieces begin to adhere, use more force. Pound the butter until it's about 7½ inches square and then trim the edges of the butter. Put the trimmings on top of the square and pound them in lightly with the rolling pin. Refrigerate while you roll out the dough.

LAMINATE THE DOUGH

(For a definition of laminating, see page 85.) Unwrap and lay the dough on a lightly floured work surface. Roll into a 10½-inch square.

Brush excess flour off the dough. Remove the butter from the refrigerator—it should be pliable but cold. If not, refrigerate a bit longer. Unwrap and place the butter on the dough so that the points of the butter square are centered along the sides of the dough. Fold one flap of dough over the butter toward you, stretching it slightly so that the point just reaches the center of the butter. Repeat with the other flaps **2**. Then press the edges together to completely seal the butter inside the dough. (A complete seal ensures butter won't escape.)

Lightly flour the top and bottom of the dough. With the rolling pin, firmly press the dough to elongate it slightly and then begin rolling instead of pressing, focusing on lengthening rather than widening the dough and keeping the edges straight **3**. Roll the dough until it's 8 by 24 inches. If the ends lose their square

A Baker's Tool Kit

Kitchen scale (optional but highly recommended; weighing both liquid and dry ingredients will yield consistent results)

Stand mixer with a dough hook attachment

Photographs by Scott Phillips

shape, gently reshape the corners with your hands. Brush any flour off the dough. Pick up one short end of the dough and fold it back over the dough, leaving one-third of the other end of dough exposed. Brush the flour off and then fold the exposed dough over the folded side 4. Put the dough on a baking sheet, cover with plastic wrap, and freeze for 20 minutes to relax and chill the dough.

Repeat the rolling and folding, this time rolling in the direction of the two open ends until the dough is about 8 by 24 inches. Fold the dough in thirds again, as shown in photo 4 above, brushing off excess flour and turning under any rounded edges or short ends with exposed or smeared layers. Cover and freeze for another 20 minutes.

Give the dough a third rolling and folding. Put the dough on the baking sheet and cover with plastic wrap, tucking the plastic under all four sides. Refrigerate overnight.

DIVIDE THE DOUGH

The next day, unwrap and lightly flour the top and bottom of the dough. With the rolling pin, "wake the dough up" by pressing firmly along its length—you don't want to widen the dough but simply begin to lengthen it with these first strokes. Roll the dough into a long and narrow strip, 8 inches by about 44 inches. If the dough sticks as you roll, sprinkle with flour. Once the dough is about half to two-thirds of its final length, it may start to resist rolling and even shrink back. If this happens, fold the dough in thirds, cover, and refrigerate for about 10 minutes; then unfold the dough and finish rolling. Lift the dough an inch or so off the table at its midpoint and allow it to shrink from both sides—this helps prevent the dough from shrinking when it's cut. Check

that there's enough excess dough on either end to allow you to trim the ends so they're straight and the strip of dough is 40 inches long. Trim the dough 5.

Lay a yardstick or tape measure lengthwise along the top of the dough. With a knife, mark the top of the dough at 5-inch intervals along the length (there will be 7 marks in all).

Position the yardstick along the bottom of the dough. Make a mark 2½ inches in from the end of the dough. Make marks at 5-inch intervals from this point all along the bottom of the dough 6. You'll have 8 marks that fall halfway between the marks at the top.

Make diagonal cuts by positioning the yardstick at the top corner and the first bottom mark. With a knife or pizza wheel, cut the dough along this line. Move the yardstick to the next set of marks and cut. Repeat until you have cut the dough diagonally at the

Recipe continues on next page

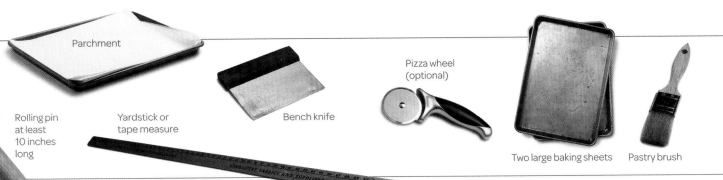

Parchment

Rolling pin at least 10 inches long

Yardstick or tape measure

Bench knife

Pizza wheel (optional)

Two large baking sheets

Pastry brush

For sources, see Where to Buy It, page 92.

same angle along its entire length—you'll have made 8 cuts. Now change the angle of the yardstick to connect the other top corner and bottom mark and cut the dough along this line to make triangles **7**. Repeat along the entire length of dough. You'll end up with 15 triangles and a small scrap of dough at each end.

SHAPE THE CROISSANTS

Using a paring knife or a bench knife, make a ½- to ¾-inch-long notch in the center of the short side of each triangle. The notch helps the rolled croissant curl into a crescent.

Hold a dough triangle so that the short notched side is on top and gently elongate to about 10 inches without squeezing or compressing the dough—this step results in more layers and loft **8**. Lay the croissant on the work surface with the notched side closest to you. With one hand on each side of the notch, begin to roll the dough away from you, towards the pointed end **9**. Flare your hands outward as you roll so that the "legs" become longer. Press down on the dough with enough force to make the layers stick together, but avoid excess compression, which could smear the layers. Roll the dough all the way

down its length until the pointed end of the triangle is directly underneath the croissant. Now bend the two legs towards you to form a tight crescent shape and gently press the tips of the legs together (they'll come apart while proofing but keep their crescent shape) **10**.

Shape the remaining croissants in the same manner, arranging them on two large parchment-lined rimmed baking sheets (8 on one pan and 7 on the other). Keep as much space as possible between them, as they will rise during the final proofing and again when baked.

Flour Know-How

Protein content differs among types (and brands) of flour and is an important consideration in baking—the higher the protein, the stronger the gluten. Gluten translates into structural support, necessary to give croissants and other yeast-raised breads their loft

and chew. But too much protein would lead to a tough croissant.

Most flours don't list protein content on the package. **Cake flour,** made from soft wheat, has the lowest amount of protein, 6 to 8 percent, depending on brand. **Bread flour** has the high-

est, at 12 to 14 percent. **All-purpose flour** falls in the middle, with a protein content of 10 to 12 percent. That makes it ideal for this recipe, with just enough protein to encourage maximum volume in the croissants. Use the highest-quality flour you can.

PROOF THE CROISSANTS
(For a definition of proofing, see page 85).
Make the egg wash by whisking the egg with
1 tsp. water in a small bowl until very smooth.
Lightly brush it on each croissant . Refrigerate
the remaining egg wash (you'll need it again).
Put the croissants in a draft-free spot at
75° to 80°F. Wherever you proof them, be
sure the temperature is not so warm that the
butter melts out of the dough. They will take
1½ to 2 hours to fully proof. You'll know they're
ready if you can see the layers of dough when
the croissants are viewed from the side, and

if you shake the sheets, the croissants will
wiggle. Finally, the croissants will be distinctly
larger (though not doubled) than they were
when first shaped 12.

BAKE THE CROISSANTS
Shortly before the croissants are fully
proofed, position racks in the top and lower
thirds of the oven and heat it to 400°F
convection, or 425°F conventional.
Brush the croissants with egg wash a
second time. Put the sheets in the oven.
After 10 minutes, rotate the sheets and swap
their positions. Continue baking until the

bottoms are an even brown, the tops richly
browned, and the edges show signs of coloring, another 8 to 10 minutes. If they appear to
be darkening too quickly during baking, lower
the oven temperature by 10°F. Let cool on
baking sheets on racks.

MAKE AHEAD
The croissants are best served barely
warm. However, they reheat very well,
so any that are not eaten right away
can be reheated within a day or two
in a 350°F oven for about 10 minutes.
They can also be wrapped in plastic or
aluminum foil and frozen for a month
or more. Frozen croissants can be
thawed overnight prior to reheating or
taken from the freezer directly to the
oven, in which case they will need a few
minutes more to reheat.

Butter Matters

● **Quality** Use the
highest-quality unsalted
butter you can find.
European-style butters
have higher butterfat
content (82 percent and
up) than most super-
market brands have—the
extra butterfat not only
provides superior flavor
but also encourages
better lamination.

● **Temperature** The
temperature of the
butter is crucial when
you laminate the dough.
Too cold and hard, and
the butter will break into
small shards; too warm
and soft, and the layers
will not be distinct. To
test, press a finger into
the butter slab—it should
feel pliable and cold.

Find more step-by-step photos
at **FineCooking.com**.

Variations: the classic made sweet and savory

Chocolate Croissants Chop some good-quality bittersweet chocolate and distribute it along the length of the notched end of the dough triangle after you've stretched it—use about ½ oz. or 1½ Tbs. for each one. Roll it up just like a plain croissant but without stretching out or bending the legs. Proof and bake the same.

Ham and Cheese Croissants After stretching but before rolling up each croissant, put a thin layer of sliced ham on the dough at the notched end. Tuck it in if it lies more than a little outside the surface of the dough. Put a layer of thinly sliced or grated cheese—good Cheddar or Gruyère is best—on top of the ham. Without stretching or bending the legs, roll the dough tightly. Proof and bake the same.

Timeline: making croissants

The three-day method used in our classic croissant recipe gives the dough maximum fermentation time for flavor to develop. But if time is tight, you can use the shortcut two-day method (below right) instead. The active work time is exactly the same in both scenarios; choose whichever fits your schedule.

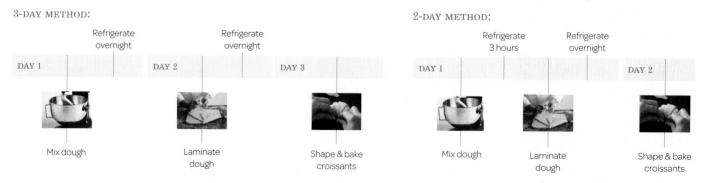

3-DAY METHOD:

Refrigerate overnight
Refrigerate overnight

DAY 1   DAY 2   DAY 3

Mix dough   Laminate dough   Shape & bake croissants

2-DAY METHOD:

Refrigerate 3 hours
Refrigerate overnight

DAY 1   DAY 2

Mix dough   Laminate dough   Shape & bake croissants

Jeffrey Hamelman bakes croissants weekly as bakery director at King Arthur Flour in Vermont.

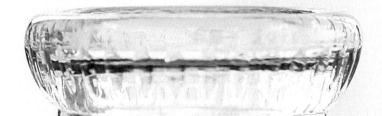

One simple method,
endless variations.

BY SUSIE MIDDLETON

MAKING SOUP is the
best kind of kitchen alchemy:
You start with a few humble
ingredients and wind up with a gem.
That's why I love making these puréed
vegetable soups; the components and
technique are simple, but the result is a
silky, delicious soup that's refined enough
for any elegant first course. • The technique is straightforward. First, cook some
aromatics (like carrots, onion, celery, garlic,
and leeks) to start building the soup's flavor
base. Next, add your favorite vegetable plus
some liquid and simmer until tender. Finally, just
purée everything in a blender. You won't believe
how easy it is to make something so lovely.

Creamy Vegetable Soups

Photographs by Scott Phillips

STEP 1

CHOOSE YOUR INGREDIENTS

Read the method from start to finish and then choose and prep your ingredients.
All soups serve 8 as a starter.

STEP 2

COOK THE AROMATICS

In a 4- to 5-quart saucepan or Dutch oven, heat the cooking fat over medium-low heat. When hot, add the 1¼ cups aromatics and a pinch of kosher salt. Stir well, cover, reduce the heat to low, and cook, stirring occasionally, until the aromatics are softened, 8 to 10 minutes. Stir in 1 tsp. kosher salt, as well as an optional spice, if using.

Cooking Fat

Use 1 or a combination for a total of 2 Tbs.

- **Unsalted butter**
- **Extra-virgin olive oil**
- **Vegetable oil**

Spices (optional)

These soups are delicious without any embellishment, but you can add a spice to give your soup a global twist. Choose 1 of the following.

- **Curry powder, 1½ tsp.**
- **Crushed fennel seed, 1 tsp.**
- **Garam masala, 1 tsp.**
- **Ground cumin plus ground coriander, 2 tsp. total**

- **Mustard seed, 2 tsp.**
- **Saffron threads, big pinch, lightly crushed and mixed with some of the liquid**
- **Smoked paprika, ½ to 1 tsp.**

 Build and save your own creamy soup recipes with our interactive feature at **FineCooking.com.**

Aromatics

Choose any combination of 2 to 5 from the list below for a total of 1¼ cups.

- **Onions, cut into medium dice**
- **Leeks, thinly sliced and washed**
- **Shallots, finely chopped**
- **Carrots, peeled, halved or quartered lengthwise, and thinly sliced**
- **Celery, halved lengthwise and thinly sliced (no more than ¼ cup)**
- **Fresh ginger, minced (no more than 1 Tbs.)**
- **Garlic, minced (no more than 2 tsp.)**

Good to Know

Aromatic vegetables become the flavor foundation of your soup. The best blend of aromatics starts with garlic and includes some onions, leeks, or shallots. From there, move on to your other choices, selecting those that are most complementary to your main vegetable.

TOMATO-FENNEL SOUP WITH ORANGE

Choose these:

- Onions, shallots, carrots, celery, garlic
- Crushed fennel seeds
- Tomatoes
- Vegetable broth, orange juice
- Heavy cream, rice vinegar, croutons

CARROT-GINGER SOUP

Choose these:

- Leeks, onions, celery, garlic, ginger
- Carrots
- Vegetable broth, orange juice
- Yogurt, lime, chives

STEP 3

SIMMER THE VEGETABLES

Add your choice of **vegetables** and **liquids**, stir well, and bring to a simmer over medium heat. Cook, uncovered, stirring occasionally, until the vegetables are very tender and the soup is full-flavored, 7 to 20 minutes, depending on the vegetable.

Vegetables

Choose 1 or more of the following for a total weight of 1½ lb. prepped vegetables.

- **Asparagus, bottom of stems trimmed, cut into ½-inch pieces**
- **Broccoli, bottom of stems trimmed, florets coarsely chopped, stems sliced very thinly**
- **Butternut squash, peeled, seeded, and cut into ½-inch dice**
- **Carrots, peeled, cut in half or quartered lengthwise if thick, and sliced ¼ inch thick**
- **Cauliflower, trimmed, cored, and coarsely chopped**
- **Mushrooms (combination of cremini or baby bella and white button), halved and thinly sliced**
- **Canned whole tomatoes (two 28-oz. cans) drained and coarsely chopped or crushed**

Liquids

Broth makes up the body of the soup, while liquids like wine and juice add extra flavor.

Choose 1 of the following for a total of 5 cups liquid.

- **Lower-salt chicken broth, 2½ cups, plus 2½ cups water**
- **Vegetable broth, preferably homemade (see FineCooking.com for a recipe), 5 cups**

Choose 1 of the following (3 Tbs.).

- **White wine**
- **Dry vermouth**
- **Dry sherry**
- **Apple cider**
- **Orange juice**

How Much Do I Buy?

When shopping for your main vegetable, you'll need to buy extra to account for the weight you lose when you trim. To yield 1½ lb. trimmed vegetables, start with:

- 2¼ lb. asparagus
- 1¾ lb. broccoli
- 2 lb. butternut squash
- 1¾ lb. carrots
- 2 lb. cauliflower
- 1½ lb. mushrooms

STEP 4
PURÉE

Take the pan off the heat and let the soup cool for 5 minutes. Working in batches, purée the soup in a blender (see Test Kitchen, page 83, for safety tips). Wipe the pan clean and put the soup back in the pan.

STEP 5
FINISH

Season the soup to taste with salt and pepper and add your choice of **dairy**, if using, and **acid**; start with ½ tsp. lemon or lime juice or vinegar, and add up to 1½ tsp. as needed. Ladle into 8 soup bowls and sprinkle a **garnish** over each serving, if using.

Acid

A bit of citrus juice or a dash of vinegar will give your soup an additional touch of brightness and bring out the vegetable flavor. Choose 1 of the following (up to 1½ tsp.).

- **Fresh lemon or lime juice**
- **Vinegar, such as red or white wine vinegar, cider vinegar, sherry vinegar, balsamic vinegar, or rice vinegar**

Storing Soups

Most of these soups are best eaten within a day, as the vegetables tend to separate from the liquids. Carrot, butternut squash, and tomato soups can last up to 2 days in the refrigerator and up to a month in the freezer; if frozen, reheat slowly and whisk if separated.

Dairy (optional)

If you like, you can finish your soup with some dairy (though some vegetables, especially cauliflower, carrots, and butternut squash, make such silky purées on their own that I sometimes leave the dairy out completely). While cream is nice, I often prefer the results I get with whole yogurt or buttermilk, since their slightly tangy flavor brightens the soup. Choose 1 of the following (¼ cup).

- **Heavy cream**
- **Buttermilk**
- **Thick whole yogurt, preferably Greek**

Garnishes (optional)

Add a finishing touch for extra flavor and texture. Choose 1 of the following.

- **Crumbled cooked bacon or pancetta, 2 tsp. per serving**
- **Chopped fresh herbs (basil, chives, cilantro, mint, or parsley), 1 to 2 tsp. per serving**
- **Homemade croutons, 1 to 2 Tbs. per serving** (see recipe at FineCooking.com)
- **Nuts (almonds, peanuts, pecans, pine nuts, or walnuts), toasted and finely chopped, 1 tsp. per serving**
- **Flavored oil (your choice of nut, spiced, sesame, or truffle oil), ½ tsp. per serving**

More Soups to Make

Mix and match ingredients for a delicious soup your way. Here are two more ideas we like.

ASPARAGUS SOUP WITH LEEKS AND MUSTARD SEED

Choose these:
- leeks, garlic
- mustard seed
- asparagus
- chicken broth, white wine
- cream, lemon juice, croutons

BUTTERNUT SQUASH SOUP WITH GARAM MASALA, YOGURT, AND LIME

Choose these:
- leeks, shallots, celery, garlic
- garam masala
- butternut squash
- vegetable broth, apple cider
- yogurt, lime juice, cilantro

Susie Middleton is Fine Cooking's *editor at large.* ❏

BROCCOLI SOUP WITH BACON

Choose these:

- Onions, leeks, garlic
- Broccoli
- Chicken broth, white wine or vermouth
- Cream, lemon juice, bacon

Carrot Cake

In this corner, the all-American favorite, and in that corner, a fanciful carrot-topped wonder. It's going to be one delicious smackdown.

BY ABIGAIL JOHNSON DODGE AND JEHANGIR MEHTA

the classic....

Back Story

Carrot cake came onto the American cookbook scene in 1929 in *The Twentieth Century Bride's Cookbook.*

Top It Off

For a match made in heaven, cream cheese frosting was married with carrot cake in the 1960s.

Usual Suspects

This cake is chock full of shredded carrots, chopped walnuts, and raisins, plus all the expected spices (think cinnamon, ginger, nutmeg, and cloves).

Health Food?

With chopped nuts, dried fruit, and Vitamin A-rich carrots in the mix, is carrot cake good for you? Not if you figure in the sugar, oil, and cream cheese frosting.

Photographs by Scott Phillips

EVERYONE LOVES CARROT CAKE. We like it so much we decided to track down the best-ever classic version and the most innovative variation we'd come across, and do a little comparison tasting. Abby Dodge, *Fine Cooking* contributing editor and baker extraordinaire, gave us the ultimate recipe for the classic (she got it from her mother). Jehangir Mehta, pastry chef and owner of Graffiti, a food and wine bar in New York City, created an inspired update. Let the bake-off begin.

....the update

Carrot Top
Spiced candied carrot ribbons add a cool look and exciting texture.

Think Again
No shredded carrots or walnuts here. A sweet carrot juice reduction flavors these little cakes, and a pistachio garnish brings color and crunch to the party.

Got Sugar?
During lean times, bakers sweetened desserts with carrots instead of costly sugar. In a nod to the past, our update uses much less sugar.

Double Duty
After candying carrots in a sweet syrup for the topping, the cakes are dunked into the syrup for an extra dose of carrot goodness.

I'm all for change when necessary, but don't mess with my mom's carrot cake. It's perfect just the way it is. —ABBY DODGE

classic carrot cake with vanilla cream cheese frosting

The flavors of this moist cake only improve with time, so feel free to bake and frost the cake up to a few days ahead.

**Yields one 9-inch layer cake;
Serves 12 to 14**

FOR THE CAKE

- 1 cup canola, corn, or vegetable oil; more for the pans
- 2 cups (9 oz.) unbleached all-purpose flour; more for the pans
- 2 tsp. ground cinnamon
- 1¾ tsp. baking soda
- ¾ tsp. ground nutmeg
- ¾ tsp. ground ginger
- ¾ tsp. table salt
- 4 large eggs
- 2½ cups (8¾ oz.) lightly packed, finely grated carrots
- 2 cups packed light brown sugar
- ¾ cup chopped walnuts, toasted
- ½ cup raisins
- 1½ tsp. pure vanilla extract

FOR THE FROSTING

- 1 lb. cream cheese, softened
- 12 oz. (1½ cups) unsalted butter, softened
- 1 lb. (4 cups) confectioners' sugar
- 4 tsp. pure vanilla extract
- ¾ tsp. table salt

MAKE THE CAKE

Position a rack in the center of the oven and heat the oven to 350°F. Lightly oil and flour the sides of two 9x2-inch round cake pans, tapping out any excess flour. Line the bottoms of the pans with parchment.

In a medium bowl, whisk the flour, cinnamon, baking soda, nutmeg, ginger, and salt. In a large bowl with a hand mixer or in a stand mixer fitted with the paddle attachment, mix the oil, eggs, carrots, brown sugar, walnuts, raisins, and vanilla on medium speed until well blended, about 1 minute. Add the dry ingredients and mix on low speed until just blended, about 30 seconds. Divide the batter evenly between the prepared pans.

Bake until the tops of the cakes spring back when lightly pressed and a cake tester inserted into the centers comes out clean, 28 to 30 minutes.

Let cool in the pans on a rack for 15 minutes. Run a knife around the inside edge of the pans to loosen the cakes, invert them onto the rack, remove the pans, and carefully peel away the parchment. Set the cakes aside to cool completely before frosting.

MAKE THE FROSTING

In a large bowl, beat the cream cheese and butter with the mixer on medium speed until very smooth and creamy, about 1 minute. Add the confectioners' sugar, vanilla, and salt and beat on medium high until blended and fluffy, about 2 minutes. Cover the frosting and set aside at room temperature until the layers are completely cool.

ASSEMBLE THE CAKE

Carefully set one cake upside down on a large, flat serving plate. Using a metal spatula, evenly spread about 1½ cups of the frosting over the top of the cake. Top with the remaining cake layer, upside down. Spread a thin layer (about ⅓ cup) of frosting over the entire cake to seal in any crumbs and fill in any gaps between layers. Refrigerate until the frosting is cold and firm, about 20 minutes. Spread the entire cake with the remaining frosting. For more tips on how to frost a layer cake, see Test Kitchen, page 83.

Refrigerate the cake for at least 4 hours or up to 2 days. The cake is best served slightly chilled or at room temperature.

spiced carrot cakes with candied carrots and pistachios

Candied carrots and a finer crumb set this variation apart from traditional carrot cake.

Serves 8

FOR THE CAKES

- 2 cups carrot juice
- 1 1-inch piece fresh ginger, peeled and finely grated
- 3 oz. (6 Tbs.) unsalted butter, softened; more for the molds
- 6¾ oz. (1½ cups) unbleached all-purpose flour; more for the molds
- 1½ tsp. ground allspice
- 1 tsp. ground cinnamon
- ½ tsp. ground star anise
- ½ tsp. baking soda
- ¼ tsp. table salt
- ¼ cup packed light brown sugar
- 2 large eggs
- ¼ cup chopped unsalted pistachios (for garnish)

FOR THE CANDIED CARROTS

- 2 cups granulated sugar
- 2 large carrots, peeled and cut into long julienne strands to yield 1 cup (see Test Kitchen, p. 83)
- 1 cinnamon stick
- 1 whole star anise

MAKE THE CAKES

Combine the carrot juice and ginger in a medium saucepan and bring to a boil over medium heat. Boil until reduced to ¾ cup, about 25 minutes. Let cool to room temperature.

Position a rack in the center of the oven and heat the oven to 325°F. Butter and flour 8 baba au rhum molds (2¼ to 2½ inches tall; see Where to Buy It, p. 92). Set aside on a large rimmed baking sheet.

In a medium bowl, whisk the flour, allspice, cinnamon, star anise, baking soda, and salt. In a large bowl with a hand mixer or in a stand mixer fitted with the paddle attachment, cream the butter and brown sugar on medium speed until light and fluffy, 1 to 2 minutes. On medium-low speed, add one of the eggs, mix until mostly blended, and then add the second egg. On low speed, alternate adding the flour mixture and the carrot reduction in two additions each. Mix each addition until just combined.

Spoon the batter into the prepared molds, filling each a little more than half full. Swirl the batter with a skewer to smooth the tops. Bake the cakes until a cake tester inserted into the centers comes out clean, 20 to 22 minutes.

People's tastes have changed—sugar is out and spices are in. That's change we can believe in.

—JEHANGIR MEHTA

Cool the cakes on a rack for 10 minutes and then carefully invert to remove from the molds. Cool the cakes upright on the rack. The cakes may be served warm or at room temperature.

MAKE THE CANDIED CARROTS

Bring the sugar and 2 cups of water to a boil in a medium saucepan over high heat. Add the carrots, cinnamon stick, and star anise. Reduce the heat to maintain a simmer; simmer gently, stirring occasionally, until the carrots are translucent, soft, and slightly sticky to the touch, about 30 minutes. Discard the cinnamon and star anise. Remove the carrots with a slotted spoon and set aside. Reserve the syrup.

To serve, dip each cake in the syrup for about 3 seconds, put it on a dessert plate, and drizzle with about 1 tsp. syrup. Garnish with the candied carrots and pistachios.

Make ahead: You can make the cakes up to 1 day ahead and the candied carrots up to 2 hours ahead.

Abby Dodge lives in Southport, Connecticut, and Jehangir Mehta, in New York City. ◻

Pan-Seared Skirt Steak with
Warm Radish and Red Onion Pickle

any night's all right

For celebrating with good friends
and great food.

BY LIZ PEARSON

menu

*Creamy White Bean
and Herb Dip*

*Pan-Seared Skirt Steak
with Warm Radish and
Red Onion Pickle*

*Broccolini with
Kalamata Dressing*

*Roasted Potato and
Mushroom Salad with
Mascarpone*

*Buttermilk Cake with
Spiced Vanilla Icing*

*The secret to entertaining
any night of the week?
A menu of mostly
make-ahead food.*

creamy white bean and herb dip

This new take on bean dip is equally good served cold or at room temperature.

Serves 6 to 8

- 2 15-oz. cans cannellini beans, rinsed and drained
- 4 oz. cream cheese (½ cup)
- ⅓ cup chopped yellow onion
- 2 Tbs. fresh lemon juice
- 1 anchovy fillet, rinsed and patted dry (optional)
  Kosher salt and freshly ground black pepper
- 2 Tbs. extra-virgin olive oil
- 3 Tbs. thinly sliced fresh chives
- 1 Tbs. chopped fresh marjoram or oregano
  Crudités, crusty sourdough bread, or crackers, for serving

Put the beans, cream cheese, onion, lemon juice, anchovy (if using), 1 tsp. salt, and ½ tsp. pepper in a food processor and process until smooth. With the motor running, drizzle in the oil. Transfer the spread to a large bowl and fold in 2 Tbs. of the chives and the marjoram. Season to taste with salt and pepper.

Transfer the spread to a serving bowl, garnish with the remaining 1 Tbs. chives, and serve with crudités, bread, or crackers.

Make ahead: May be made 1 day ahead and refrigerated.

pan-seared skirt steak with warm radish and red onion pickle

The quick vegetable pickle is a bright, tangy complement to marinated steak. If there's any left over, try it on a turkey sandwich.

Serves 6 to 8

FOR THE STEAK

- 2 lb. skirt steak
- ½ cup plus 2 Tbs. extra-virgin olive oil
- ½ cup fresh lemon juice
- 2 Tbs. Dijon mustard
- 2 tsp. finely grated lemon zest
- 2 tsp. honey
- 1 tsp. crushed red pepper flakes
- 4 medium cloves garlic, smashed and peeled
  Kosher salt and freshly ground black pepper

FOR THE PICKLE

- ¼ cup extra-virgin olive oil
- 3 Tbs. apple cider vinegar
- 1 Tbs. honey
- 1 Tbs. sherry vinegar
- 1 tsp. ground coriander
  Kosher salt and freshly ground black pepper
- 1 bunch red radishes (8 or 9), halved and thinly sliced
- 1 medium carrot, thinly sliced
- 1 small red onion, halved lengthwise and thinly sliced crosswise
- 1 small jalapeño, seeded and thinly sliced

MARINATE THE STEAK

Trim any large patches of fat from the surface. If necessary, cut the steak crosswise into pieces 8 to 10 inches long. In a 9x13-inch baking dish (or similar), whisk ½ cup of the oil, the lemon juice, mustard, lemon zest, honey, pepper flakes, garlic, 1½ tsp. salt, and ¼ tsp. pepper. Arrange the steak in the dish and turn to coat with the marinade. Cover with plastic and refrigerate for at least 2 hours but preferably overnight.

MAKE THE PICKLE

In a medium saucepan, stir together the oil, cider vinegar, honey, sherry vinegar, coriander, 1½ tsp. salt, and ¼ tsp. pepper. Bring to a simmer over medium-high heat. Add the radishes, carrot, onion, and jalapeño and toss gently to coat. Reduce the heat to medium low and cook, stirring occasionally, until the onions are wilted and the radishes are no longer crunchy but are still firm, 4 to 5 minutes. Give it one final stir and remove from the heat. Set aside, uncovered, while you cook the steak.

COOK THE STEAK

Remove the steak from the marinade and pat dry with paper towels. Season on both sides with ½ tsp. salt and a few grinds of pepper. Heat 1 Tbs. of the remaining oil in a large skillet over medium-high heat. Add half of the steak to the hot skillet in a single layer and cook, flipping once, until deeply browned on both sides and cooked to your liking—medium rare will take 5 to 7 minutes total. Transfer the steak to a carving board and set aside. Wipe out the skillet with a paper towel, heat the remaining 1 Tbs. oil, and cook the remaining steak as above.

Let the steaks rest for at least 5 minutes; then slice thinly across the grain and transfer to a large platter. Pour any accumulated juices over the steaks, top with the warm radish pickle, and serve.

Make ahead: The steak can be marinated and the pickle prepared up to 1 day ahead. Refrigerate both, and reheat the pickle before serving.

Steak, potatoes, and broccolini never had it so good. Small changes make for big flavors.

Broccolini with
Kalamata Dressing

broccolini with kalamata dressing

The olive dressing is also delicious on asparagus, carrots, and Brussels sprouts.

Serves 6 to 8

- ⅓ cup pitted Kalamata olives
- ¼ cup lightly packed fresh parsley leaves, plus 1 Tbs. roughly chopped
- ¼ cup mayonnaise
- 3 medium cloves garlic, peeled
  Kosher salt and freshly ground black pepper
- 2 lb. broccolini, trimmed (4 bunches)

Put the olives, parsley leaves, mayonnaise, garlic, ½ tsp. salt, and ¼ tsp. pepper in a food processor and pulse into a coarse paste.

Bring a large pot of well-salted water to a boil. Working in 3 batches, boil the broccolini until tender, about 5 minutes per batch. Drain each batch well and keep warm in a large bowl covered with foil.

Dab the olive mixture over the broccolini and toss well to combine. Season to taste with salt and pepper. Transfer to a platter, sprinkle with the chopped parsley, and serve.

Make ahead: The black olive dressing can be made 1 day ahead and refrigerated until ready to use.

drink up

Master sommelier Doug Frost suggests pairing both wine and beer with this rustic menu, so there's a little something for everyone. The crisp Ommegang Hennepin ($10 for 750 ml) has a bit of spice and fruit, while Anchor Steam ($8 for a six-pack) balances malty sweetness and hoppy tanginess. For the main course, Frost recommends a beer with some heft to it, such as the dark Samuel Smith's Imperial Stout ($10 for a four-pack).

St. Supéry Sauvignon Blanc 2006 ($20) is a fruity American white that's a great match for this menu. A bold red wine with rich blue and black fruit notes, such as the Trapiche Malbec Oak Cask 2006 ($12) or the Las Rocas de San Alejandro Garnacha 2007 ($12), is perfect for rounding out the meal.

 Get a shopping list and timeline for this menu at FineCooking.com/extras.

roasted potato and mushroom salad with mascarpone

Roasting the potatoes and mushrooms deepens the flavor of this warm salad, and the mascarpone dressing adds richness and tang.

Serves 6 to 8

- 6 Tbs. extra-virgin olive oil
- 2 lb. Yukon gold potatoes (about 6 medium), halved and cut into ¾-inch wedges
  Kosher salt and freshly ground black pepper
- ¾ lb. small to medium cremini or white mushrooms, quartered
- ½ cup mascarpone
- ¼ cup fresh orange juice
- 1½ tsp. red wine vinegar
- ⅓ cup thinly sliced scallions, white and green parts (about 4 small)

Position a rack in the center of the oven and heat the oven to 450°F. Coat a large rimmed baking sheet with 1 Tbs. of the oil.

In a large bowl, toss the potatoes, 2 Tbs. of the oil, 1 tsp. salt, and ½ tsp. pepper. Arrange in a single layer on the prepared baking sheet. Roast until barely tender, about 20 minutes, gently tossing with a spatula halfway through.

Meanwhile, toss the mushrooms, 1 Tbs. of the oil, ½ tsp. salt, and ¼ tsp. pepper in the bowl.

Gently toss the potatoes again, scatter the mushrooms evenly over the potatoes, and continue to roast until both the potatoes and mushrooms are tender and golden brown in spots, 10 to 15 minutes more.

Meanwhile, in a medium bowl, whisk the mascarpone, orange juice, vinegar, 1 tsp. salt, and ⅛ tsp. pepper. Drizzle in the remaining 2 Tbs. oil while whisking constantly; set aside.

Return the potatoes and mushrooms to the large bowl and add the mascarpone dressing. Toss gently to coat, season to taste with salt and pepper, and transfer to a large serving bowl. Garnish with the scallions and serve.

Nobody will be able to resist a slice of this rich cake (not even the resident dog).

buttermilk cake with spiced vanilla icing

The secret to this moist, tender cake is grated butternut squash, which is folded into the batter just before baking. Use the large holes on a box grater to grate the squash.

Serves 10 to 12

FOR THE CAKE

4	oz. (½ cup) unsalted butter, softened; more for the pan
13½	oz. (3 cups) unbleached all-purpose flour; more for the pan
1½	cups granulated sugar
½	cup canola oil
2	large eggs
1	Tbs. distilled white vinegar
2	tsp. pure vanilla extract
1	tsp. baking soda
1	tsp. table salt
½	tsp. ground ginger
¼	tsp. freshly grated nutmeg
¾	cup buttermilk
2¼	cups peeled and grated butternut squash (about 8 oz.)

FOR THE ICING AND GARNISH

9	oz. (2¼ cups) confectioners' sugar
3	Tbs. buttermilk; more as needed
1	tsp. pure vanilla extract
¼	tsp. freshly grated nutmeg
¼	tsp. table salt
¼	cup finely chopped crystallized ginger

MAKE THE CAKE

Position a rack in the center of the oven and heat the oven to 325°F. Butter and flour a 10-cup Bundt pan; tap out excess flour.

In a large bowl with a hand mixer or in a stand mixer fitted with the paddle attachment, beat the butter and sugar on medium speed until well combined, about 1 minute. Add the oil and beat until combined, about 15 seconds. Add the eggs one at a time, mixing well on low speed. Add the vinegar and vanilla and mix again until just combined. Add half of the flour and the baking soda, salt, ginger, and nutmeg, mixing on low speed until just combined. Add half of the buttermilk and mix until just combined. Repeat with the remaining flour and buttermilk.

Stir the squash into the batter and transfer the batter to the prepared pan; smooth the top with a rubber spatula. Bake until a cake tester inserted in the center comes out clean, about 1 hour. Cool on a wire rack for 30 minutes; then carefully invert the cake onto the rack and remove the pan. When the cake is completely cool, transfer it to a serving plate.

MAKE THE ICING

In a medium bowl, whisk the sugar, buttermilk, vanilla, nutmeg, and salt until smooth. Add more buttermilk, a few drops at a time, as needed, until the icing is pourable but still quite thick. Pour the icing back and forth in thick ribbons over the cooled cake. Sprinkle the ginger on top. Let the icing set at room temperature, about 45 minutes, before serving.

Make ahead: This cake can be made a day or two in advance. After the icing has set, wrap the cake in plastic and refrigerate. Let come to room temperature before serving.

Liz Pearson is a food writer and recipe developer based in Austin, Texas. ◻

Buttermilk Cake with
Spiced Vanilla Icing

TEST KITCHEN

Tips/Techniques/Equipment/Ingredients/Glossary

The secret to a beautifully frosted cake? A crumb coat. For exactly what that is, and how it works, see page 84.

Photographs by Scott Phillips

The icing on the cake

Knowing how to frost a layer cake like the one on page 72 can be both a blessing and a curse. On the one hand, it's not hard and your friends will be impressed. On the other hand, everyone will want you to make them a birthday cake.

1 Position and level your cake

Set a cake plate on a rotating cake stand or lazy Susan. Position your first layer of cake upside down on the plate. If necessary, level the cake layer with a long serrated knife. Slide strips of parchment or waxed paper under the edge of the cake to keep the plate clean as you frost.

2 Fill the layers

Gently brush any crumbs from the cake. Using an offset spatula, spread the recommended amount of frosting across the surface of the cake in an even layer (don't worry about getting the surface perfectly smooth).

Place the second cake layer on the frosting, aligning the layers in a perfectly vertical column. If using split layers that were cut unevenly, match up the layers so the cake stays flat. If the cake is three or more layers, continue to fill between the layers, ending with the top layer unfrosted.

3 Seal in the crumbs

Frosting the cake is easier if you first seal the crumbs in a thin layer of frosting, called a crumb coat. With an offset spatula, spread about ½ cup of frosting in a thin, even layer all over the cake. Smooth any frosting protruding between the layers and use that extra frosting as part of the crumb coat. It's fine if the cake is still visible through the thin crumb coat. Refrigerate the cake to firm up the crumb coat, about 20 minutes.

4 Finish with style

Spread the remaining frosting evenly over the chilled crumb coat. Once the cake is frosted, you can decorate the surface in a variety of ways, using a spoon or offset spatula to create swoops or stripes. If you prefer a smooth look, dip the spatula in hot water, wipe it dry, and hold it against the surface as you rotate the cake. Keep dipping the spatula in water and wiping it dry. —*Dabney Gough*

how to: split the layers

If your recipe calls for split cake layers, use a long serrated knife to gently "draw" a line all the way around the side of the cake at the center point. Turn the stand slowly, with your knife exerting gentle pressure on the cake. (If you aren't using a rotating stand, use a gentle sawing motion, giving the cake quarter turns as you go.) When you get back to where you started the cut, begin to cut horizontally through the cake, using the cut line as a guide. Focus on keeping the handle end of the knife in place; if you do this, the far end will follow naturally.

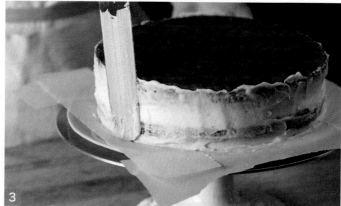

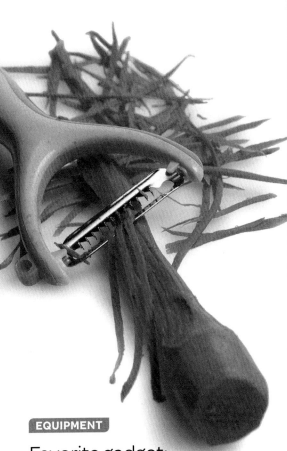

EQUIPMENT

Favorite gadget: the julienne peeler

TO MAKE THE CANDIED carrot strips for the Spiced Carrot Cakes on page 73, our gadget of choice is a hand-held julienne peeler. In one swoop, it shreds carrots, zucchini, and other fruits and vegetables into thin, delicate ribbons. It's quicker than a knife, and unlike a mandoline, which can also make julienne cuts, it fits neatly into the dishwasher. —*D. G.*

TIP

Don't get burned: safe soup puréeing

Haphazard blending of the creamy soups on page 62 can lead to serious burns (and really ruin a good cooking session). Taking a few precautions will save your skin—and your soup:

• **Chill out** Let the soup cool for 5 to 10 minutes before blending.

• **Pace yourself** Blend in batches, filling the jar halfway each time. More than that, and you run the risk of soup exploding from the jar with the initial whir.

• **Use the vent** Keeping the lid's vent open prevents steam buildup.

• **Take cover** Put a folded kitchen towel between your hand and the lid to protect yourself from hot splashes. —*D. G.*

Fully proofed croissants, ready for the oven.

GLOSSARY

Dough lingo

Two terms you'll be glad you know when it comes to making your own croissants (see page 54):

Proofing Yeasted breads, like croissants, are usually "proofed" after the dough has been shaped. The proofing step allows the dough to rise more and develop in flavor. Proofing is usually done in a warm environment—75° to 80°F—which encourages the yeast to grow and multiply.

Laminated dough Croissants, Danish, and puff pastry are all made from laminated dough—thin sheets of dough layered with thin sheets of butter. There are two steps to laminating dough: First, encasing butter in a dough "envelope," and second, rolling and folding the dough. Depending on the type of pastry, the rolling and folding step is repeated two to six times.

During baking, the steam generated by the moisture in the butter is trapped, lifting and separating the individual dough layers. The resulting lofty layers (as many as 1400 for classic French puff pastry) bring an airy lightness to the finished baked good.

—*D. G.*

Boning a chicken breast

FOR THE PAN-ROASTED CHICKEN breasts on page 45, you'll need boneless, skin-on chicken breasts. Unfortunately, these aren't readily available at many supermarkets, so for most of us, the only way to get this cut of chicken is to start with skin-on split breasts and bone them ourselves. Here's how:

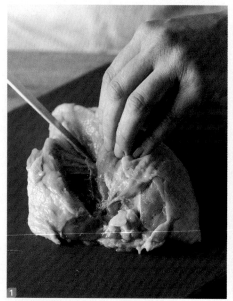

1 With a sharp boning knife, begin cutting between the meat and rib bones along the narrower edge of the breast. Gently pull back on the meat as you continue slicing the meat away from the bone.

2 When you reach the wing joint, maneuver the knife over and around the joint as you continue to pull back on the meat.

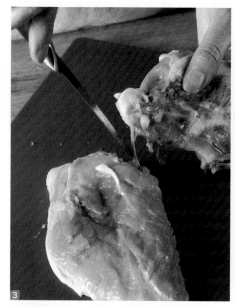

3 At this point, you should be able to feel a spur of the wishbone in the breast meat. Scrape and cut around the wishbone to free it from the meat and then, if necessary, finish cutting the breast completely free of all the bones.

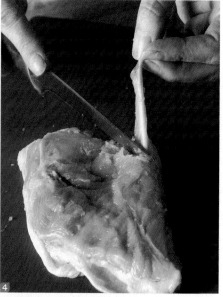

4 Remove the tendon that runs down the length of the breast by pinching the end and pulling it taut. Scrape the knife against it on either side until it pulls free.

—*Jennifer Armentrout*

Piment d'Espelette

Though you could use regular cayenne or chile flakes to garnish the Pork and Potato Hash on page 52, piment d'Espelette gives the dish an unusual Basque twist.

Piment d'Espelette chiles come from a group of ten villages (one of which is called Espelette) in the Basque region of southwestern France. After harvesting, the chiles are strung together and dried outside houses and shops in the villages—the image of a chile-festooned building is in the logo used to designate this product.

The slightly sweet, mildly spicy chiles are most commonly ground into a coarse powder. In the Basque region, the spice is often used in place of black pepper. In addition to using it as a finishing touch on dishes, we like to add it to spice rubs and sauces.

Piment d'Espelette is available at specialty markets and by mail order (see Where to Buy It, page 92). Store as you would any other spice: in an airtight container in a cool, dry place for up to six months.

—*D. G.*

Orange slices and segments

SEVERAL OF THE RECIPES in the "Oranges" feature on page 40 call for slices and segments. Here's how to make them.

Cut off the top and bottom of the orange, slicing off enough to expose a circle of the orange's flesh.

With a paring knife, slice off a strip of peel from top to bottom. Try to get all of the white pith, but leave as much of the flesh as possible. Continue all the way around.

To make segments (a.k.a. suprêmes), use a paring knife to cut on either side of each membrane, freeing the orange segment in between. Work over a bowl to catch the juice.

To make slices, cut the orange crosswise in the desired thickness.

—*D. G.*

Crumple it

The Orange and Brown-Butter Tart recipe on page 46 calls for lining the tart shell with parchment before blind baking. A crisp, new sheet of parchment doesn't snuggle into a tart shell very well, but if you first crumple the sheet into a ball and then unfold it, it'll fit easily. —*J. A.*

Make It Tonight

Just 30 minutes to dinner, start to finish.

spicy jerk pork chops

This recipe is based on the fiery Jamaican seasoning known as jerk, made of Scotch bonnet chiles, ground spices, garlic, and herbs. Serve with a cabbage slaw and buttered white rice.

Serves 4

- 2 Tbs. extra-virgin olive oil; more for the pan
- 4 bone-in center-cut pork chops (¾ inch thick, about 2 ½ lb. total)

  Kosher salt and freshly ground black pepper
- 4 medium scallions (white and green parts), coarsely chopped
- 2 small Scotch bonnet or habanero chiles, seeded and coarsely chopped (wear gloves)
- 2 small limes, 1 juiced and 1 cut into 8 wedges
- 2 large cloves garlic, coarsely chopped
- 2 Tbs. coarsely chopped fresh ginger
- 1 Tbs. coarsely chopped fresh thyme
- ¾ tsp. ground allspice
- ⅛ tsp. ground cinnamon

Position an oven rack about 4 inches from the broiler and heat the broiler to high. Lightly oil a broiler pan or a rack set over a large rimmed baking sheet.

Season the pork all over with 1 tsp. salt and ¾ tsp. pepper. In a food processor, purée the oil, scallions, chiles, lime juice, garlic, ginger, thyme, allspice, cinnamon, and 1 tsp. salt. Coat the chops on all sides with the mixture and set on the broiler pan or rack.

Broil until the pork begins to brown, about 7 minutes. Flip and cook until browned, the meat is firm to the touch, and an instant-read thermometer inserted close to (but not touching) the bone registers 145°F, about 7 minutes more. Serve with the lime wedges.

—*Tony Rosenfeld*

smoked turkey reubens

In this update on the classic, smoked turkey stands in for corned beef, while a fresh slaw and sun-dried tomato mayo take the place of sauerkraut and Thousand Island dressing.

Serves 4

- 2 **cups thinly sliced green cabbage (about 4 oz.)**
- ¾ **cup julienned kosher dill pickle (from 1 large)**
- 2 **tsp. cider vinegar**
  Kosher salt
- ½ **cup mayonnaise**
- 3 **oil-packed sun-dried tomatoes**
- 2 **Tbs. ketchup**
- 8 **slices whole wheat bread**
- 12 **thin slices smoked turkey**
- 8 **thin slices Swiss cheese**
- 2 **Tbs. unsalted butter, softened**

In a medium bowl, toss the cabbage and pickles with the vinegar and ½ tsp. salt. Transfer to a colander, set it in the sink, and let sit for 10 minutes. Meanwhile, pulse the mayonnaise, sun-dried tomatoes, and ketchup in a food processor until the tomatoes are finely chopped.

Squeeze the cabbage mixture to remove any excess liquid and return to the bowl. Toss the cabbage with 2 Tbs. of the mayonnaise.

Spread the remaining mayonnaise on one side of each slice of the bread. Assemble the sandwiches, layering the turkey, cabbage, and cheese over 4 slices of the bread and topping with the other 4 slices. Spread the outsides of the sandwiches with the butter.

Heat a large grill pan, skillet, or stovetop griddle over medium-low heat. Working in batches if necessary, put the sandwiches in the pan, top with a grill press or heavy skillet to weigh them down, and cook until browned, 2 to 4 minutes. Flip and cook the other side until browned and the cheese is melted, 2 to 4 minutes more. Cut the sandwiches in half and serve.

—Tony Rosenfeld

red-cooked tofu

Red-cooking is a traditional Chinese braising technique that uses soy sauce, sugar, and rice wine to flavor the food and give it a dark red color. This easy, aromatic stew is delicious served over cooked rice or mustard greens.

Serves 4

- 4 **medium scallions, thinly sliced (white and green parts separated)**
- 2 **medium carrots, cut into small dice**
- 1 **cup lower-salt chicken broth or (preferably homemade) vegetable broth**
- 6 **Tbs. reduced-sodium soy sauce; more as needed**
- ¼ **cup Shaoxing (Chinese cooking wine) or dry sherry**
- 1½ **Tbs. minced fresh ginger**
- 2 **tsp. granulated sugar**
  Freshly ground black pepper
- 2 **14-oz. packages firm tofu, cut into 1-inch pieces**
- 2 **Tbs. seasoned rice vinegar**
- 2 **tsp. arrowroot or cornstarch**

In a large saucepan, combine the scallion whites, carrots, broth, soy sauce, Shaoxing, ginger, sugar, and ¼ tsp. pepper. Bring to a simmer over medium-high heat, stirring once or twice. Cover, reduce the heat to low, and simmer gently for 5 minutes. Add the tofu, cover, and continue to simmer gently until the tofu is heated through and has absorbed some of the other flavors, 10 minutes.

In a small bowl, whisk the vinegar and arrowroot until smooth and then stir the mixture into the stew, taking care not to break up the tofu. Stir gently until thickened, about 1 minute. Add more soy sauce to taste, sprinkle with the scallion greens, and serve.

—Bruce Weinstein and Mark Scarbrough

Continued on page 90

chicken sauté with lemon, cumin, and parsley

Serve this brightly flavored dish over baby spinach, with crusty bread on the side.

Serves 2 to 3

- 1 medium lemon
- 3 Tbs. extra-virgin olive oil
- 1 large red onion, thinly sliced
- 1 medium clove garlic, smashed and peeled
- 6 boneless, skinless chicken thighs (1 lb.), trimmed and cut into ½-inch-thick strips
- ¾ tsp. ground cumin
  Kosher salt and freshly ground black pepper
- ¼ cup chopped fresh flat-leaf parsley

Finely grate 1 tsp. zest from the lemon and then juice the lemon.

Heat the oil in a 12-inch skillet over medium heat until shimmering hot. Add the onion and garlic and cook, stirring frequently, until the onion begins to soften, 3 to 5 minutes. Add the chicken, lemon zest, cumin, ½ tsp. salt, and ¼ tsp. pepper and cook, stirring, until the chicken is just cooked through, 4 to 6 minutes. Remove the skillet from the heat and stir in the parsley and 2 Tbs. of the lemon juice. Discard the garlic if you like. Season to taste with salt and pepper.

—Lori Longbotham

salt-and-pepper shrimp with garlic and chile

Using easy-peel shrimp will speed prep because the shells are slit open and they've been deveined. Steamed or stir-fried vegetables, jasmine rice, and lots of napkins are the perfect accompaniments.

Serves 4

- 2 Tbs. cornstarch
- 1 tsp. granulated sugar
  Pinch of Chinese five-spice powder
  Kosher salt and freshly ground black pepper
- 5 large cloves garlic, finely chopped
- 1 serrano chile, thinly sliced into rounds
- 4 large scallions (green parts only), sliced ¼ inch thick
- 1½ lb. large shrimp (26 to 30 per lb.), peeled and deveined, tails left on
- 3½ Tbs. peanut or canola oil
- 1 small lime, cut into 4 wedges

In a large bowl, mix the cornstarch, sugar, five-spice powder, 1 tsp. salt, and 1 tsp. pepper. In a small bowl, mix the garlic, chile, and scallions; set aside.

Pat the shrimp dry with paper towels. Line a small baking sheet or large plate with a double layer of paper towels. Add the shrimp to the cornstarch mixture and toss until evenly and thoroughly coated.

In a heavy-duty 12-inch nonstick skillet, heat 1½ Tbs. of the oil over medium-high heat until very hot. Add half of the shrimp in a single layer. Cook without disturbing until deep golden and spotty brown on one side, about 2 minutes. Using tongs, quickly flip each shrimp and continue to cook until the second sides are spotty golden brown, about 1 minute longer. (The shrimp may not be cooked through at this point.) Transfer the shrimp to the prepared sheet. Add another 1 Tbs. of the oil to the skillet and repeat with the remaining shrimp, transferring them to the sheet when done.

Reduce the heat to medium and add the remaining 1 Tbs. oil to the skillet. Add the garlic mixture and cook, stirring constantly, until the chile and scallions are softened and the garlic is golden and smells toasted, about 1 minute. Return the shrimp to the pan and stir to combine. Serve immediately, with the lime wedges.

—Dawn Yanagihara

beef picadillo

A Latin American and Caribbean favorite, picadillo is a savory-sweet ground beef filling that's delicious wrapped in lettuce leaves. It's also good in tacos, quesadillas, and omelets.

Serves 4 to 6

- 3 Tbs. extra-virgin olive oil
- 1½ lb. lean ground beef
- ⅓ cup dry red wine
- 1 small yellow onion, minced
- 3 cloves garlic, minced
- 1 cup canned crushed tomatoes
- ½ cup golden raisins
  Kosher salt and freshly ground black pepper
- 2 large hard-cooked eggs, finely chopped
- 6 Tbs. chopped pimiento-stuffed green olives
- ¼ cup minced fresh cilantro
- 1 small head Boston lettuce, cored and leaves separated

Heat the oil in a large skillet over medium heat. Add the ground beef and cook, stirring occasionally and breaking up the meat with the edge of a spoon, until done, about 5 minutes. Add the wine, onion, and garlic and cook, stirring occasionally, until the wine is almost evaporated, about 5 minutes.

Add the tomatoes and raisins and simmer, stirring occasionally, until the liquid has almost evaporated, 2 to 3 minutes. Season with 1½ tsp. salt and a few grinds of pepper.

Remove the skillet from the heat and stir in the chopped eggs, olives, and cilantro. Serve hot with the lettuce leaves for wrapping.

—Bruce Weinstein and Mark Scarbrough

fresh pasta with sausage and mushrooms

You can find fresh pasta in the refrigerated section of your supermarket. For a spicier dish, use hot Italian chicken sausage.

Serves 3 to 4

Kosher salt

2 Tbs. extra-virgin olive oil

¾ lb. sweet Italian chicken sausage, cut into 1-inch pieces

½ lb. mixed sliced mushrooms (like oyster, shiitake, and cremini)

4 medium scallions (white and green parts), trimmed and thinly sliced

2 tsp. chopped fresh rosemary

⅛ tsp. crushed red pepper flakes

Freshly ground black pepper

1 cup drained canned diced tomatoes

1 cup lower-salt chicken broth

1 12-oz. package fresh linguine or fettuccine

¾ cup freshly grated Parmigiano-Reggiano

Bring a medium pot of salted water to a boil. Meanwhile, heat the oil in a large,

heavy skillet over medium-high heat until shimmering hot. Add the sausage and cook, stirring occasionally, until browned,

about 3 minutes. Add the mushrooms, scallions, rosemary, red pepper flakes, ¾ tsp. salt, and ½ tsp. pepper and cook, stirring often, until the mushrooms soften and start to brown, about 3 minutes. Add the tomatoes and chicken broth, bring to a boil, and then cover and reduce to a gentle simmer. Cook until the sausage is heated through and the flavors are melded, about 5 minutes.

Meanwhile, cook the pasta according to package timing until it's just al dente. Drain well and add to the sauce along with half of the Parmigiano. Cook over medium heat, tossing for 1 minute. Serve sprinkled with the remaining Parmigiano and some black pepper.

—Tony Rosenfeld

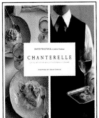

WHERE TO BUY IT

preserving the season, page 19

- **Ball fruit jell pectin,** $2.29, Canning Pantry, 435-245-6776.

repertoire, page 24

WE RECOMMEND:
- **Le Creuset super spatula,** $13.99, Chef Tools, 866-716-2433.
- **Best 12-inch balloon whisk,** $9.79, Chef Tools, 866-716-2433.

the good life, page 32

WE RECOMMEND:
- **Circulon 12-inch nonstick stir-fry pan,** $39.95, Macy's, 800-289-6229.

drinks, page 38

PICTURED IN THE STORY:
- **Vera Wang Duchesse double old-fashioned glass,** $120 for four, Macy's, 800-289-6229.

WE RECOMMEND:
- **24 oz. 3-piece wide-mouth stainless-steel shaker,** $16.45, Bar Store, 800-256-6396.
- **10-inch stainless-steel bar spoon,** $2.15, Bar Store, 800-256-6396.
- **Stock maraschino liqueur,** $14.99 for 750 ml, Witty's Fine Wine, 732-381-6776.

creamy soups, page 62

WE RECOMMEND:
- **All-Clad 4-quart stainless saucepan,** $184.95, Cooking.com, 800-663-8810.
- **5-quart Lodge enamel Dutch oven,** $166.15, Kerekes, 800-525-5556.

carrot cake, page 70

WE RECOMMEND:
- **Baba au rhum 2½-inch molds,** $4.99, Fante's, 800-443-2683.
- **Ateco revolving cake stand,** $19.95, Cooking.com, 800-663-8810.
- **Zyliss julienne peeler,** $6.95, Kitchen Store on 10th, 888-935-1999.

any night's all right, page 74

PICTURED IN THE STORY:
- **Chilewich bamboo runner in chalk color,** $47, Mod Decor, 866-729-1156.
- **Antiqued mercury-glass votive holders,** $24 for four, Pottery Barn, 888-779-5176.

WE RECOMMEND:
- **NordicWare fleur de lis Bundt pan,** $31.95, Cooking.com, 800-663-8810.

oranges, page 40

WE RECOMMEND:
- **Blood orange juice,** $12.50 for a half-gallon, LaVigne Organics, 760-723-9997.
- **SCI/Scandicrafts 9½-inch round tart pan,** $10.95, Cooking.com, 800-663-8810.

roast pork, page 48

WE RECOMMEND:
- **Piment d'Espelette,** $18.99 for 1.8 oz., Chefshop.com, 800-596-0885.
- **Mauviel stainless-steel roasting pan,** $179.9, Cooking.com, 800-663-8810.

make it tonight, page 88

- **Shaoxing cooking wine,** $14.99 for 640 ml, Kalustyan's, 800-352-3451.

food for thought, page 98

- **Steve Brill is the author of** *The Wild Vegetarian Cookbook* and two foraging field guides. Buy them or get information on Brill's tours at 914-835-2153.

croissants, page 54

PICTURED IN THE STORY:
- **Oxo multipurpose scraper and chopper,** $8.99, Chef Tools, 866-716-2433.
- **Organic bib apron,** $21.95, Chefwear, 800-568-2433.

WE RECOMMEND:
- **Salter Aquatronic scale,** $59.95, Cooking.com, 800-663-8810.
- **KitchenAid stand mixer,** $299.99 to $399.99, Cooking.com, 800-663-8810.
- **Maple French rolling pin,** $13.95, Cooking.com, 800-663-8810.
- **Parchment half-sheets,** $19.95 for 100, King Arthur Flour, 800-827-6836.
- **Upholstery ruler,** $21, Perfect Fit, 800-652-5202.
- **Bench knife,** $6.99, Ultimate Baker, 866-285-2665.
- **Leifheit pizza cutter,** $10.99, Amazon.com, 800-201-7575.
- **Aluminum half-sheet pans,** $19.95, King Arthur Flour, 800-827-6836.
- **Pastry brush,** 1½ inches wide, $6.45, Cooking.com, 800-663-8810.

For quick and easy online shopping go to **FineCooking.com/buy-it** to buy anything on this page.

Photographs by Scott Phillips

NUTRITION

Recipe	Calories (kcal)	Fat Cal (kcal)	Protein (g)	Carb (g)	Total Fat (g)	Sat Fat (g)	Mono Fat (g)	Poly Fat (g)	Chol (mg)	Sodium (g)	Fiber (g)
LETTER FROM THE EDITOR, p. 6											
Wine-Braised Chicken with Shallots and Pancetta	750	410	42	21	46	12	23	7	140	1440	4
ESCAROLE, p. 15											
Sautéed Escarole with Raisins, Pine Nuts, and Capers	140	90	3	11	10	1	6	2.5	0	530	6
MARMALADE, p. 19											
Lemon-Ginger Marmalade (per 1 Tbs.)	60	0	0	15	0	0	0	0	0	0	0
WHITE CHEDDAR, p. 20											
Baked Cheddar Grits with Bacon	340	170	16	24	19	10	6	1	160	490	1
Poblanos Stuffed with Cheddar and Chicken	510	250	37	28	28	14	9	2.5	125	570	5
Cheddar and Cauliflower Soup	340	250	17	7	28	17	8	1	90	540	2
CHOCOLATE MOUSSE, p. 24											
Real Chocolate Mousse	470	300	6	39	33	20	10	1	75	135	3
FRIED RICE, p. 32											
Five-Treasure Fried Rice	440	130	17	63	14	2	7	3.5	115	880	8
DRINKS, p. 38											
Whiskey Smash	170	0	0	11	0	0	0	0	0	0	0
The Martinez	180	0	0	8	0	0	0	0	0	0	0
ORANGES, p. 40											
Blood Orange and Radicchio Salad	250	170	5	19	19	2.5	13	2	0	120	5
Pan-Roasted Chicken Breasts with Orange-Brandy Sauce	380	180	38	9	20	7	9	3	120	550	1
Sear-Roasted Halibut with Blood Orange Salsa	380	160	37	18	18	2.5	11	2.5	55	510	3
Blood Orange and Mango Sorbet	180	5	1	47	0	0	0	0	0	0	2
Orange and Brown-Butter Tart	430	200	6	54	22	13	6	1	110	110	2
ROAST PORK, p. 48											
Slow-Roasted Pork Shoulder with Carrots, Onions, and Garlic	630	260	75	6	29	11	13	3.5	235	1090	1
Pork and Potato Hash with Poached Eggs and Avocado	510	230	27	43	26	6	15	3	265	910	8
Pork Ragout with Soft Polenta	550	240	35	44	27	10	12	3	95	1090	5
Pulled-Pork Sandwiches with Cabbage, Caper, and Herb Slaw	360	180	28	12	20	5	12	2.5	80	720	2
CROISSANTS, p. 54											
Classic Croissants	310	160	5	32	19	12	5	1	60	360	1
Chocolate Croissants	380	200	5	41	22	14	5	1	60	360	2
Ham and Cheese Croissants	380	210	10	33	23	14	6	1	80	600	1
CREAMY VEGETABLE SOUPS, p. 62											
Asparagus Soup with Leeks and Mustard Seed	100	60	4	8	7	3	2.5	0.5	15	200	2
Butternut Squash Soup with Garam Masala	80	30	1	13	3.5	1.5	1.5	0	5	260	2
Carrot-Ginger Soup	90	30	1	13	3.5	1.5	1.5	0	5	310	3
Tomato-Fennel Soup with Orange	110	60	2	13	6	3	2.5	0	15	540	2
Broccoli Soup with Bacon	120	70	6	9	7	3.5	3	0.5	15	300	3
CARROT CAKE, p. 70											
Classic Carrot Layer Cake with Vanilla Cream Cheese Frosting	840	480	8	86	54	22	20	9	150	550	2
Spiced Carrot Cakes with Candied Carrots and Pistachios	460	110	6	85	12	6	3.5	1	75	200	2
ANY NIGHT'S ALL RIGHT, p. 74											
Creamy White Bean and Herb Dip	170	80	5	16	9	3.5	4	1	15	300	4
Pan-Seared Skirt Steak with Warm Radish and Red Onion Pickle	320	190	24	6	22	5	14	1.5	65	490	1
Broccolini with Kalamata Dressing	120	60	4	9	7	1	2.5	3	5	530	2
Roasted Potato and Mushroom Salad with Mascarpone	320	210	6	24	23	8	11	1.5	35	380	3
Buttermilk Cake with Spiced Vanilla Icing	510	170	5	80	19	6	8	3	60	380	2
MAKE IT TONIGHT, p. 88											
Red-Cooked Tofu	350	160	34	20	18	2.5	4	10	0	960	6
Beef Picadillo	420	210	34	17	23	7	12	1.5	165	610	2
Chicken Sauté with Lemon, Cumin, and Parsley	370	220	28	7	25	5	14	4	100	280	1
Spicy Jerk Pork Chops	650	370	62	5	41	14	21	3.5	165	670	1
Smoked Turkey Reubens	660	420	30	33	46	17	12	13	90	1370	5
Fresh Pasta with Sausage and Mushroooms	490	150	30	55	17	4.5	5	1.5	115	1280	5
Salt-and-Pepper Shrimp with Garlic and Chile	270	120	28	9	13	2.5	6	4.5	250	580	1

The nutritional analyses have been calculated by a registered dietitian at Nutritional Solutions in Melville, New York. When a recipe gives a choice of ingredients, the first choice is the one used. Optional ingredients with measured amounts are included; ingredients without specific quantities are not. Analyses are per serving; when a range of ingredient amounts or servings is given, the smaller amount or portion is used. When the quantities of salt and pepper aren't specified, the analysis is based on ¼ tsp. salt and ⅛ tsp. pepper per serving for entrées, and ⅛ tsp. salt and ¹⁄₁₆ tsp. pepper per serving for side dishes.

MENUS

hearty breakfast

Baked Cheddar Grits with Bacon
page 21

Classic Croissants
page 56

Lemon-Ginger Marmalade
page 19

freestyle fajitas

Mojitos
FineCooking.com

Pan-Seared Skirt Steak
with Warm Radish and
Red Onion Pickle
page 76

Handmade Flour Tortillas
FineCooking.com

Cilantro-Lime Guacamole
FineCooking.com

Arroz Verde (Green Rice)
FineCooking.com

soup & salad night

Blood Orange and Radicchio Salad
page 42

Carrot-Ginger Soup
page 66

Free-Form Pear Tarts with
Almond and Cinnamon
FineCooking.com

indoor picnic

Smoked Turkey Reubens
page 89

Roasted Potato and
Mushroom Salad with
Mascarpone
page 79

Buttermilk Cake with
Spiced Vanilla Icing
page 80

game day

Whiskey Smash
page 38

Pulled-Pork Sandwiches
with Cabbage, Caper,
and Herb Slaw
page 51

Crispy Smashed Roasted
Potatoes, **FineCooking.com,** with
Orange and Chive Aïoli for dipping
FineCooking.com

Caramel-Pecan Brownies
FineCooking.com

fast friday

The Martinez
page 39

Creamy White Bean
and Herb Dip
page 76

Sear-Roasted Halibut
with Blood Orange Salsa
page 42

Basmati Rice Pilaf
FineCooking.com

Real Chocolate Mousse
page 25

Photographs by Scott Phillips, except center, Quentin Bacon

RECIPE INDEX

New ways to find your favorite recipes:

1. Get the 15th anniversary archive: all 96 issues on DVD.

2. Get the 15th anniversary index on CD.

Both at **FineCooking.com**

Icons by Olga Jakim

VEGETARIAN: May contain eggs and dairy ingredients

MAKE AHEAD: Can be completely prepared ahead (may need reheating and a garnish to serve)

QUICK: Under 30 minutes

"Wildman" Steve Brill

For 23 years, this self-taught forager has made New York City's Central Park his produce aisle. BY LISA WADDLE

Fine Cooking: What made you decide to start picking and cooking what many people dismiss as weeds?

Brill: My motivation was hunger. As a poor student in Queens, I was riding my bike past a park and noticed some Greek women gathering plants—grape leaves, as it turned out. I took some home and stuffed them. They were delicious. It was free food.

FC: We're guessing that not everyone agrees that plants in public parks are free food.

Brill: Back in 1986, I was arrested for picking dandelions in Central Park by undercover park rangers. They handcuffed and searched me, but I had eaten the evidence. In court they dropped the charges, and the Parks Department offered me a job as a naturalist. They realized they couldn't keep people from foraging and that it would be better to educate them. That launched my career.

FC: Besides the thrill of the hunt, why forage for food?

Brill: First of all, taste. The flavors of a wild mushroom or berry are so intense. Second is cost; especially with organic food being so expensive. Third, you can find foods only available in the wild, like Juneberries and goutweed.

FC: Isn't it risky to eat wild plants?

Brill: I don't fool around with anything I'm unsure about. The stuff you pick in Central Park isn't sprayed with pesticides. It has fewer chemicals than what's in processed food or even what's in a lot of the stuff in the produce aisles.

FC: Do you think foraging will become the next big thing?

Brill: Well, I've seen an exponential growth in interest lately. It used to be just hikers and tourists who signed up for my tours.

FC: Any advice for the neophyte forager?

Brill: Pick only wild foods you've identified with 100 percent certainty. Always collect at least 50 feet from heavy traffic, and wash all plants under running water. And I emphasize on all my tours that you shouldn't decimate a plant—leave enough for future reproduction, as well as future foragers.

FC: What's your favorite thing to make with what you find?

Brill: Nothing can match my Five-Borough Salad, filled with greenbrier shoots, blue violet leaves, ramp leaves, dandelion flowers, and black locust blossoms, all from New York City parks. I served it on the steps of the courthouse at my hearing, and the press ate it up.

FC: In all your years foraging, what's been your most prized find?

Brill: My wife. I met her in Central Park while foraging. We've been married six years and have a four-year-old daughter, Violet.

the dish

Name: Steve Brill

Age: 59

Job: Leads tours of public parks, teaching which wild edibles to pick and ways to cook them

Started: 1986

Where: New York City

Known for: Pith helmet, corny jokes

A penchant for: Soymilk smoothies with Juneberries from Central Park

 Watch a video of Brill foraging in Central Park at **FineCooking.com.**

PIAZZA DEL DUOMO

Barilla

FETTUCCINE

Searching for great food & scenery, a sense of tranquility quickly overtook my sense of direction.

Somewhere along a winding country road, the slow pace of Umbria set in. A land known for fertile farmland, Roman ruins and sacred shrines, spending time in Umbria feels less like a trip and more like a pilgrimage. And yet no matter how far we strayed from the beaten path, every restaurant featured at least one familiar favorite — Barilla pasta.

www.DiscoverBarilla.com

Barilla Fettuccine
with sausage and leeks

GENUINE BARILLA — Parma, Italy

Ingredients	
Barilla Fettuccine	1 box
Extra virgin olive oil	4 tbsp. divided
Italian sausage	1 lb. crumbled
Leeks	2, diced
Dry white wine	½ cup
Grated fresh Pecorino cheese	2 cups
Salt and black pepper to taste	

For the complete recipe visit
DiscoverBarilla.com

The Choice of Italy.

The function of a professional range.
The form of a work of art.

BEST-EVER ROAST CHICKEN
One easy technique,
perfect results every time

fine Cooking

WE BRING OUT THE COOK IN YOU

Serving up Spring!

mint strawberry shortcakes
peas & carrots with lemon
spicy lemongrass mussels

THINK FAST

Dinner in 30 minutes

Brisket done right
plus delicious leftovers

HOW TO CRACK A COCONUT

Pancakes for dessert
A new take on brunch

PR/MAY 2009 · No.98
ww.finecooking.com
$6.95 CAN $7.95

05

7 44470 56529 1

Spring Vegetable Ragout
with Fresh Pasta, page 7

He made California a world-renowned
destination for wine.

Maybe he can do the same for your house.

Skeptics laughed when Robert Mondavi doggedly set out
to prove that California wines could be quality wines.
But today a glass of Woodbridge by Robert Mondavi may
make you smile in a totally different way.

His name is on the bottle. His story is in it.

WOODBRIDGE

by Robert Mondavi

CONTENTS

APRIL/MAY 2009 ISSUE 98

CONTENTS

APRIL/MAY 2009 ISSUE 98

Cover and contents photographs by Scott Phillips; illustration by Ward Schumaker

WE'VE GONE FROM THE FIRE TO THE FRYING PAN.

 The same professional performance of the Viking range is also available in Viking cookware. Handcrafted in Belgium from an exclusive 7-ply material, Viking cookware offers the exceptional cleanability of stainless steel and the even heat distribution of aluminum.

Visit vikingrange.com/wheretobuy to find a dealer near you.

A night to remember

Clockwise, from left: Photographer Scott Phillips and contributing editor Abby Dodge; publisher Maria Taylor; art director Don Morris and photographer Frances Janisch; contributors (from left) Raquel Pelzel, Melissa Feldman, Ed Schoenfeld, Ellie Krieger, and me; staffers Jen Armentrout, Allison Kreitler, and Sharon Anderson.

Party People

THE MOST ENTHUSIASTIC COOKS are irrepressible in their efforts to find reasons to cook; they think even the most minor occasion (your half-birthday, the long-awaited ripening of a favorite tomato) is a fine excuse to make a cake or buy lobster or slow-smoke the better part of a pig. These are some of my favorite people: They're the best cooks I know, and they make occasions of days that might otherwise pass unnoticed.

We recently made an occasion of a couple of milestones at *Fine Cooking:* our fifteenth anniversary and the redesign of the February/March 2009 issue. Despite some wintry weather, we slipped away from the office early and joined contributors and friends at a restaurant on New York's Lower East Side (party photos above). It was, of course, a good excuse to eat well, but it was also a chance to thank everyone who had helped make those accomplishments possible.

There are any number of occasions to celebrate over the next couple of months— Easter, Passover, Mother's Day, and Memorial Day among them. Surely there are also birthdays, anniversaries, and other days special to you that might be made all the more special if you cooked. This issue is packed with ideas for doing just that, including our cover recipe (opposite), itself a celebration of the new season. Happy (fill in the blank anyway you like).

Laurie Buckle, editor
fc@taunton.com

more fine cooking

Web In case you haven't paid a visit yet, finecooking.com has a new look, new blogs, an incredibly useful ingredient guide, and a tool that takes our "Create Your Own Recipe" idea to the next level.

Books Fans of the *Fresh* special issues will want our new book of the same name. It's got 350 delicious seasonal recipes.

Special Issues Keep an eye out for our latest title, *Make It Tonight,* packed with 85 easy and tasty reasons to eat in. In addition, *Fine Cooking* contributing editor and best-selling cookbook author Ellie Krieger shares her simple recipes for healthy cooking from a well-stocked pantry in *Eat Smart with Ellie Krieger.*

Photographs by Genevieve Gearity

spring vegetable ragout with fresh pasta

Serves 4

Kosher salt

¾   lb. fresh pasta sheets

1   small clove garlic, minced

Freshly ground black pepper

3   cups mixed spring vegetables (such as medium-thick asparagus, baby carrots, baby turnips, spring onions, and sugar snap peas), trimmed and cut into 1- to 3-inch long by ½- to ¾-inch-wide pieces

½   cup shelled peas or peeled fava beans (see note)

⅓   cup loosely packed pea shoots or watercress sprigs; more for garnish

¼   cup loosely packed chopped mixed fresh herbs, such as basil, chervil, mint, parsley, and/or tarragon; more for garnish

4   Tbs. cold unsalted butter, cut into ½-inch pieces

1½   tsp. freshly grated lemon zest

Freshly grated Parmigiano-Reggiano for garnish (optional)

Bring a large pot of well-salted water to a boil. With a pizza cutter or chef's knife, cut the pasta sheets into rustic strips about ½ inch wide.

In a 10- to 11-inch straight-sided sauté pan, bring 2½ cups water, the garlic, 1 tsp. salt, and ¼ tsp. pepper to a simmer over high heat. Add the mixed vegetables and simmer briskly, adjusting the heat as necessary, until just crisp-tender, 3 to 4 minutes. With a slotted spoon, transfer to a large plate. If using peas, simmer them until barely tender, about 2 minutes, and transfer to the plate with the slotted spoon. (If using favas, skip this step.) Raise the heat to high and boil the liquid until reduced to 1 cup, 3 to 4 minutes.

Meanwhile, cook the pasta in the boiling water until barely al dente, 2 to 4 minutes. Drain.

Add the cooked pasta, vegetables, favas (if using), pea shoots or watercress, herbs, butter, and lemon zest to the broth. Toss over medium-high heat until the butter is melted, about 1 minute.

Season to taste with salt and pepper. Serve garnished with pea shoots or watercress, fresh herbs, and Parmigiano (if using).

Note: To peel fava beans, shuck them and cook them in boiling salted water until tender, 1 to 2 minutes, then rinse them with cold water and peel off the skin.

—*Allison Ehri Kreitler*

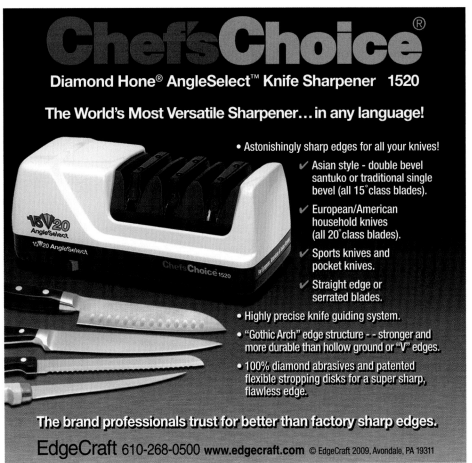

THE RESPONSE to our redesign issue (*Fine Cooking* #97, Feb/Mar 2009) was both big and opinionated, so we thought we'd share with you the good, the bad, and the constructive.

PROS...

My new issue of *Fine Cooking* came today and I heard my wife say, Wow, look at this. She was staring at the gorgeous photo on the front cover. What a beautiful, well-organized layout full of so many things I want to cook. Then I went back and read your letter, explaining the new design. I can't imagine how much work it took to reformat *Fine Cooking*. I have been a reader for a long time, and this is a winner.

—*Jim Blackman, Middleton, Idaho*

I love your magazine. It caters to every level of expertise; your explanations of techniques make it possible for anyone to get a great result. My two energetic boys love to cook and bake, and, together, we just successfully made the croissants from the latest issue. This magazine makes recipes from the cutting edge of cuisine seem easy. Keep up the exceptional work and thanks for a wonderful magazine. I can't wait to see what the next issue holds.

—*Kathryn, Adam, and Ryan Hull, Nova Scotia, Canada*

We received issue #97 today, and we were wowed by it. We love the new font on the cover and the new tag line. The photography inside is terrific. In fact, on page 72, I tried brushing the crumbs of carrot cake off the page. We also like the grouping of several recipes around one ingredient. The new icons are great. It was interesting to read about the team you assembled to pull this new look together. You're off to a good start; keep it up.

—*Barbara Peckenpaugh, via email*

I love, love, love the new look of *Fine Cooking,* and as a longtime subscriber, I have to say that the Feb/Mar issue is one of the best. I wanted to make everything in it and have set out to do so. The slow-roasted pork has been cooking all day, and my home smells wonderful. Thank you.

—*Holly Wenzl, via email*

I've subscribed to *Fine Cooking* for a number of years and have given gift subscriptions to many family members and friends. As a chef, I've also used it as a teaching tool for some of my young apprentices. I love the new look. Your publication is simply excellent. It is fresh, clean, updated, timely, easy to navigate, informative, and, most of all, fun to read.

—*Margot J. Bodchon, British Columbia, Canada*

I simply want to congratulate you for such a great magazine and Web site. The Feb/Mar issue has answered so many questions for me, including how to make soups without recipes and the difference between baking flours. The Web site was fast, and I loved the video on how to slice and dice onions. The new format is terrific.

—*Fabienne Melkanoff, via email*

CONS...

The Feb/Mar issue of *Fine Cooking* arrived and unfortunately, I was quite disappointed in the new format. The photos are great, but the layouts and recipes were very difficult to follow. What I liked best about *Fine Cooking* was the variety of recipes and simple directions, not to mention the fact that the results were always perfect. The magazine gave me the confidence to cook well, since the recipes were clear and concise. The new format makes it difficult to organize the ingredients and understand the process.

—*Roswitha Linde, Wolcott, Vermont*

I wanted to let you know that I am not a fan of the new format. In my opinion you have "dumbed down" the magazine with bigger pictures, less writing, and less of the content that I used to look forward to seeing.

—*Stuart Miller, via email*

When my Feb/Mar issue arrived I immediately loved the new look. But now that I'm reading the magazine, I'm wondering: Where are the words? I've learned a lot from the article introductions, but now most of them have been shortened to just a sentence or two. I hope that in the future you can balance the cool graphic design with a little more text.

—*Elana Gravitz, Minneapolis*

I loved the magazine as it was. The current issue doesn't have the clean, welcoming look and feel of former issues. Somehow, it seems disjointed. The paper feels flimsier, and it seems like there aren't as many nice photos, one of the hallmarks of the magazine. I used to look forward to sitting down with a new issue and thumbing through it before I read the editorial. This time, I found myself thinking, What's wrong with this issue?

—*Teresa Sanofsky, via email*

THE WINNER

Reader tip: Planing butter

When preparing breakfast for my family I often forget to take the butter out of the refrigerator to soften. In a pinch, I use a cheese plane to skim thin slices off the stick of butter. They melt instantly when applied to hot toast, bagels, or English muffins.

—*Kate Thomas, Lynnfield, Massachusetts*

Write a winning tip
We want to hear from you. Give us your best tip and we'll reward you with a kitchen prize. Kate is the winner of a 20x36-inch GelPro mat.

TO REACH US: *Fine Cooking,* The Taunton Press, 63 S. Main St., PO Box 5506, Newtown, CT 06470-5506. Telephone: 203-426-8171. Email: fc@taunton.com.

fine Cooking

Editor	**Laurie Glenn Buckle**
Contributing Art Director	**Don Morris**
Senior Food Editor/ Test Kitchen Manager	**Jennifer Armentrout**
Senior Editor	**Rebecca Freedman**
Associate Editors	**Laura Giannatempo** **Lisa Waddle**
Assistant Editor	**Denise Mickelsen**
Managing Web Editor	**Sarah Breckenridge**
Assistant Web Editor	**Sharon Anderson**
Senior Copy/ Production Editor	**Enid Johnson**
Associate Art Director	**Pamela Winn**
Contributing Designer	**Tannaz Fassihi**
Photo Coordinator	**Kelly Coughlan Gearity**
Assistant Test Kitchen Manager/Food Stylist	**Allison Ehri Kreitler**
Recipe Tester	**Melissa Pellegrino**
Editorial Assistant	**Julissa Roberts**
Test Kitchen Intern	**Joy Braddock**
Editorial Intern	**Sophy Bishop**
Editor at Large	**Susie Middleton**
Contributing Editors	**Pam Anderson** **Abigail Johnson Dodge** **Maryellen Driscoll** **Sarah Jay** **Ellie Krieger** **Kimberly Y. Masibay** **Tony Rosenfeld** **Molly Stevens**
Senior Managing Editor, Books	**Carolyn Mandarano**

Fine Cooking: (ISSN: 1072-5121) is published six times a year by The Taunton Press, Inc., Newtown, CT 06470-5506. Telephone 203-426-8171. Periodicals postage paid at Newtown, CT 06470 and at additional mailing offices. GST paid registration #123210981.

Subscription Rates: U.S. and Canada, $29.95 for one year, $49.95 for two years, $69.95 for three years (GST included, payable in U.S. funds). Outside the U.S./Canada: $36 for one year, $62 for two years, $88 for three years (payable in U.S. funds). Single copy, $6.95. Single copy outside the U.S., $7.95.

Postmaster: Send address changes to *Fine Cooking*, The Taunton Press, Inc., 63 South Main St., P.O. Box 5506, Newtown, CT 06470-5506.

Canada Post: Return undeliverable Canadian addresses to Fine Cooking, c/o Worldwide Mailers, Inc., 2835 Kew Drive, Windsor, ON N8T 3B7, or email to mnfa@taunton.com.

Printed in the USA.

San Francisco illustrator Ward Schumaker (Food for Thought, page 94) counts *The New York Times* and *Le Figaro* among his clients. His work has been exhibited at Shanghai's Stir Gallery and UC Berkeley's Townsend Center.

• **The last thing I ate was...** a rice cake with peanut butter.

• **My drink of choice is...** my wife's sun lemonade. It's like sun tea but with lemon and lime juice and crushed strawberries.

• **My guilty food pleasure is...** pie for breakfast. But without whipped cream; I was raised Protestant, after all.

Lauren Chattman ("Sandwiches," page 62) has written nine cookbooks, including *Panini Express: 70 Delicious Recipes, Hot off the Press,* with Daniel Leader, and *Dessert Express.* Her next book, *Cake Keeper Cakes,* comes out this fall.

• **I am currently obsessed with...** black licorice.

• **My least favorite food is...** cooked leafy greens. I know I should eat my veggies, but...

• **My culinary icon is...** Sheila Lukins.

One of only three people in the world who can claim both the master sommelier and master of wine titles, Doug Frost ("Riesling," page 32) is also an author and lecturer on wine, beer, and spirits. He is the beverage columnist for the *Kansas City Star* and has written for numerous publications, including the *San Francisco Chronicle* and *Santé.* Frost has also written two books, *On Wine* and *Uncorking Wine.*

• **The last thing I cooked was...** fresh salsa with heirloom peppers, onions, lime, cilantro. Ain't no tomato in my salsa.

• **I'm currently obsessed with...** mezcal.

• **My least favorite food is...** Brussels sprouts, unless they're smothered in butter and bacon.

Adam Kaye ("Sausage," page 68) is chef and kitchen director at Blue Hill at Stone Barns in Pocantico Hills, New York, where he also heads up the charcuterie program. He's cooked for more than 10 years in top restaurant kitchens, including Vidalia in Washington, DC, and Chanterelle in New York City.

• **Milk or dark chocolate...** I just like chocolate. Do I really have to choose?

• **The last thing I ate was...** curried chicken salad at our staff meal.

• **My guilty food pleasure is...** take-out General Tso's chicken.

The former chef-owner of Square One restaurant in San Francisco, Joyce Goldstein ("Brisket," page 56) is a frequent contributor to national magazines and newspapers and writes a monthly column for *Sommelier Journal* on pairing food and wine. Her most recent book is *Mediterranean Fresh: A Compendium of One-Plate Salad Meals and Mix-and-Match Dressings,* and her next book, coming out this spring, is called *Tapas, Sensational Small Plates from Spain.*

• **The last thing I cooked was...** a green lentil salad with beets and chopped hard-boiled eggs.

• **My drink of choice is...** coffee. My espresso machine is broken right now, and it's very frustrating.

• **The best part of my job is...** research. I love tracking down the origin of a dish.

Photographer Frances Janisch ("Brunch," page 34) shoots food for numerous American magazines (*More* and *House Beautiful* among them), and some British and Australian ones, too. Born in South Africa, she lives with her husband and daughter in New York City.

• **My least favorite food is...** licorice.

• **The last thing I cooked was...** pasta with avocado and peas for my daughter.

• **My guilty-food pleasure is...** Marmite on hot buttered toast.

fine Cooking®

Publisher	Maria Taylor
Assistant Publisher	Karen Lutjen
National Advertising Manager	Patrick J. O'Donnell 203-304-3250 podonnell@taunton.com
Director of Advertising Marketing	Kristen Lacey 203-304-3757 klacey@taunton.com
Advertising Sales East Coast	Judy Caruso 203-304-3468 jcaruso@taunton.com
	Margaret Fleming-O'Brien 203-304-3530 mflemingobrien@taunton.com
Midwest	Mark Adeszko 312-629-5222 madeszko@aol.com
West Coast	Chuck Carroll 818-972-9650 cwcarroll@earthlink.net
Advertising Sales Associate	Stacy DeJulio 203-304-3231 sdejulio@taunton.com
Advertising Inquiries	800-309-8940 fcads@taunton.com

Member Audit Bureau of Circulation — The Audit Bureau

Senior Consumer Marketing Director	Beth Reynolds, ProCirc
Circulation Manager	Noelia Garcia, ProCirc
Business Managers	David Pond, Megan Sangster

The Taunton Press
Inspiration for hands-on living®
Independent publishers since 1975

Founders	Paul & Jan Roman
President	Suzanne Roman
EVP & CFO	Timothy Rahr
SVP, Operations	Thomas Luxeder
SVP, Creative & Editorial	Susan Edelman
SVP, Technology	Jay Hartley
SVP & Publisher, Book Group	Donald Linn
SVP, Advertising Sales	Karl Elken
SVP & Group Publisher	Janine Scolpino
VP, Human Resources	Carol Marotti
VP & Controller	Wayne Reynolds
VP, Fulfillment	Patricia Williamson
VP, Finance	Kathy Worth
VP, Taunton Interactive	Jason Revzon
VP, Single Copy Sales	Jay Annis

Publishers of magazines, books, videos and online
Fine Woodworking • Fine Homebuilding
Threads • Fine Gardening • Fine Cooking
www.taunton.com

Enjoy café-quality espresso for less than $1 a cup

Why go out for coffee when you can enjoy an authentic Italian cappuccino or espresso at home, any time? Treat yourself to the illy a casa℠ membership program and receive everything you need to make the consistently flawless espresso served in the world's finest cafés and restaurants — for less than $1 a cup.

Join now to receive your exclusive introductory kit featuring the Francis Francis X5 and four illy logo cups.

Yours for 3 payments of $50 (a $678 value).*

You'll receive the state-of-the-art Francis Francis X5 espresso machine, available in 5 colors, four illy logo cappuccino cups, and more.** Perfect for E.S.E. pods or ground coffee, the X5 lets you make the highest quality espresso. As a member, just purchase four cans of illy coffee each month for one year to receive convenient home delivery. Order today to enjoy legendary illy coffee with this extraordinary offer.

> **30-day risk-free trial**

Order today. Call **1 877 469 4559** or go to **illyusa.com/finecook9**
Use promotion code **PFCA9**

Questions of the Day

A cook's favorite question—What's for dinner?—
often leads to even more questions. For answers, go to
FineCooking.com's Ingredient Discovery.

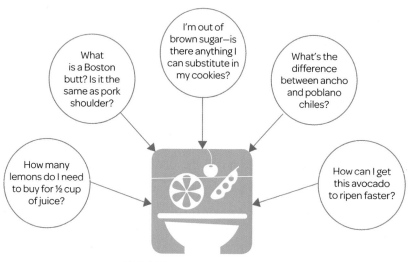

What
is a Boston
butt? Is it the
same as pork
shoulder?

I'm out of
brown sugar—is
there anything I
can substitute in
my cookies?

What's the
difference
between ancho
and poblano
chiles?

How many
lemons do I need
to buy for ½ cup
of juice?

How can I get
this avocado
to ripen faster?

INGREDIENT DISCOVERY

CooksClub

Online subscribers to FineCooking
.com are now charter members
of the CooksClub—a backstage
pass to the world of *Fine Cooking*.
Here's a taste of what's on offer:

Are pie crusts your undoing? This
month, enter our members-only
What Can't You Cook? contest:
Tell us what dish or technique
you struggle to master, and win a
personal, hands-on cooking class
with an expert on that topic.

Enter the contest by clicking
on the CooksClub logo at
FineCooking.com.

new kids
on the blog

The Good Life
Stay balanced with Ellie
Krieger's blog. Get video
tips, quick meal ideas, and
smart-eating strategies
from *Fine Cooking*'s healthy-
living expert.

The Eat Generation
Follow the foodie adventures
of blogger Dabney Gough as
she takes a bite out of life in
San Francisco.

Sign up for the **free** FineCooking.com
eLetter for a weekly look at what's newest
and hottest on the Web. Get exclusive
Web-only recipes, how-to **videos**, and
advice from the experts.

---

fine Cooking®

To contact us:
Fine Cooking,
The Taunton Press,
63 South Main Street,
P.O. Box 5506, Newtown,
CT 06470-5506
Tel: 203-426-8171
fc@taunton.com

Visit:
www.finecooking.com

To submit an article proposal:
Write to *Fine Cooking* at the address above or
Call: 800-309-0744
Fax: 203-426-3434
Email: fc@taunton.com

To subscribe or place an order:
Visit www.finecooking.com/fcorder
or call: 800-888-8286
9am-9pm ET Mon-Fri;
9am-5pm ET Sat

To find out about *Fine Cooking* products:
Visit www.finecooking.com/products

To get help with online member services:
Visit www.finecooking.com/customerservice

To find answers to frequently asked questions:
Visit www.finecooking.com/FAQs

**To speak directly to a customer service
professional:**
Call 800-477-8727 9am-5pm ET Mon-Fri

To order products for your store:
Send an email to magazinesales@taunton.com

To advertise in *Fine Cooking*:
Call 800-309-8940
Or send an email to fcads@taunton.com

Mailing list:
We make a portion of our mailing list available
to reputable firms. If you would prefer that
we not include your name, please visit:
www.finecooking.com/privacy
or call: 800-477-8727 9am-5pm ET Mon-Fri;

For employment information:
Visit www.careers.taunton.com

The Taunton guarantee:
If at any time you're not completely satisfied with
Fine Cooking, you can cancel your subscription
and receive a full and immediate refund of the
entire subscription price. No questions asked.

Photograph by Scott Phillips

AUSTRALIAN LAMB

Easy. Any Day.

moroccan-style australian lamb kabobs with red pepper puree

 GRIILL & ENJOY 6 SERVINGS

Sure, Australian Lamb is great for the holidays. It's also perfect for quick-and-easy everyday meals. Lean and rich in nutrients, with a mild taste and delicious flavor, it's a smart choice everyone at your dining table will love — which makes any day a great day to enjoy Australian Lamb!

Australian Lamb

Fresh, Easy and Delicious.

AUSTRALIAN LAMB

Easy. Any Day.

Visit www.australian-lamb.com/fc for this recipe and to order a **FREE** copy of our new cookbook, *Easy. Any Day.* featuring 28 pages of seasonal recipes your whole family will love!

MARKETPLACE

Shop Smarter, Eat Better

TRY THIS

Lemongrass

This citrusy plant plays a starring role in many Southeast-Asian cuisines, adding its unique flavor to everything from curries to cold drinks. Not long ago, it was nearly impossible to find, except in Asian markets. But these days, lemongrass is going mainstream, making its way into the produce section of your supermarket. Here's why you should give it a try.

Continued on page 16

Photographs by Scott Phillips

What it is

Evergreen in warm climates, lemongrass is a sharp-bladed, perennial, blue-green grass that grows in 3- to 6-foot-tall cascading clumps. In addition to its uses in the kitchen, it's valued medicinally as a remedy for a wide range of ailments, from stomach troubles and fever to depression.

Why we love it

In a word: fragrance. The ethereal aroma of lemongrass—redolent of tropical flowers, ginger, and all things citrus—is like a delicate perfume for food. Lemongrass pairs well with just about anything, though it's particularly good with seafood, chicken, and pork. It also has an affinity for coconut milk. Its most iconic use is in Thai curry pastes, where it's puréed with chiles, shallots, ginger, garlic, and spices to become an aromatic flavor base for all types of curries.

How to buy and store it

Much of lemongrass's flavor is concentrated in its lower, cane-like stalks, which is why most markets sell them already trimmed of their leafy tops, leaving just a few short, spiky blades still attached. Look for firm, pale-green stalks with fat, bulbous bottoms and reasonably fresh-looking tops (they may be a little dry but shouldn't be desiccated or yellowed). To store, wrap in plastic and refrigerate for two to three weeks, or freeze for up to six months.

How to cook it

There are two main ways to cook with lemongrass, and each determines how you handle it. To **infuse teas, broths, soups, and braising liquids**, trim off the spiky tops and the bases, crush the stalks with the side of a knife to release their aromatic oils, and then cut them into 1- or 2-inch pieces. Remove the pieces before eating (they tend to be woody) or eat around them, as in the recipe below.

To use lemongrass **in marinades, stir-fries, salads, spice rubs, and curry pastes**, trim the top and base of the stalks—you want to use only the bottom 4 inches or so. Then peel off any dry or tough outer layers before finely chopping or mincing. Lemongrass holds up to long cooking and gains intensity the longer it's cooked. If you'd like a strong lemongrass flavor, add minced lemongrass at the start of cooking, browning it along with the other aromatics. For a lighter, fresher lemongrass flavor, add it near the end of cooking.

—*Jennifer Armentrout*

spicy steamed mussels with lemongrass, chile, and basil

Serves 4

- 1   Tbs. vegetable oil
- 2   shallots, thinly sliced into rounds (¼ cup)
- 1   cup lower-salt chicken broth
- 3   stalks lemongrass, trimmed, cut into 2-inch pieces, and lightly smashed (¾ cup)
- 3   ⅛-inch-thick slices fresh ginger
-     Zest of ½ lime, peeled off in strips with a vegetable peeler (about 5 strips)
- 2   lb. mussels, scrubbed and debearded
- 1   red serrano (or other small hot red chile), sliced into thin rounds
- ½   cup chopped fresh basil
-     Asian chili sauce, such as Sriracha (optional)

Heat the oil in a large straight-sided sauté pan or pot over medium heat. Add the shallots and cook, stirring often, until browned, 2 to 3 minutes. Add the broth, lemongrass, ginger, lime zest, and 1 cup water. Bring to a boil over medium-high heat and then reduce to medium low; cover and simmer for 10 minutes.

Raise the heat to medium high and add the mussels and chile. Cover and simmer until the mussels open, 2 to 3 minutes. Transfer the mussels to serving bowls, discarding any that haven't opened. Add the basil to the broth and simmer for 1 minute. Add chili sauce to taste, if using. Ladle the broth over the mussels. Don't eat the lemongrass or the ginger.

Get the skinny on hundreds of ingredients at FineCooking.com/ingredients.

A homemade dish deserves only the most sensational flavor.

For more great-tasting recipes, visit mccormickgourmet.com

Mediterranean Pasta with Fire Roasted Tomatoes

(Makes 6 servings)

Ingredients:

2 pounds medium plum tomatoes (10-12), halved lengthwise

1/2 cup olive oil, divided

2 cloves garlic, minced

1 tbsp. McCormick® Gourmet Collection™ Italian Seasoning

1/2 tsp. McCormick® Gourmet Collection™ Crushed Red Pepper

1/2 tsp. McCormick® Gourmet Collection™ Sicilian Sea Salt

1/4 tsp. McCormick® Gourmet Collection™ Coarse Grind Black Pepper

8 ounces pasta, such as spaghetti

Directions:

PLACE tomato halves, cut-sides up, in foil-lined 15"x10"x1" pan sprayed with no stick cooking spray. Mix 1/4 cup oil, garlic and seasonings in small bowl. Spoon over tomatoes. Drizzle with 2 tablespoons of the remaining oil.

ROAST in preheated 400°F oven 45 to 60 minutes until tomatoes are soft and browned on top.

PREPARE pasta as directed on package. Drain well. Place 1/2 of the roasted tomatoes and remaining 2 tablespoons oil in large bowl. Coarsely mash tomatoes. Add pasta and remaining tomatoes; toss to mix well. Sprinkle with shredded Parmesan cheese and additional crushed red pepper, if desired.

Asparagus, Arugula, and Rhubarb

Nine ways to use three seasonal ingredients we can't get enough of.
Fine Cooking editors share some delicious ideas.

Asparagus

Allison Ehri Kreitler: I like to steam asparagus, then shave the stalks in fettuccine-like strips with a vegetable peeler, reserving the tips. I toss the asparagus "fettuccine" and tips with real fettuccine and a creamy sauce flavored with lemon zest and tarragon.

Rebecca Freedman: For a tasty salad, I start off by roasting some asparagus and cherry tomatoes in a hot oven until tender. Then I combine them with baby greens, goat cheese, toasted nuts, and a simple balsamic vinaigrette.

Jennifer Armentrout: My favorite way to prepare asparagus is to roast them in a hot oven and drizzle them with *takliah,* an easy-to-make Egyptian condiment. To make takliah, gently heat chopped garlic in olive oil until it begins to turn golden. Add a little ground coriander, let it heat briefly, and then pour the takliah into a small heatproof bowl. Drizzle it, along with a little lemon juice, over the roasted asparagus.

Arugula

Laura Giannatempo: I love to make a simple salad of baby arugula tossed with a lemony vinaigrette. I top it with thin shavings of Parmigiano-Reggiano and serve it over slices of bresaola for a quick and tasty weeknight meal.

Melissa Pellegrino: One of my favorite late-spring dishes is grilled lamb burgers topped with arugula, grilled red onion, and feta slices, accompanied by a rosemary aïoli.

Lisa Waddle: For a different kind of pesto, blend three parts arugula to one part spinach, a couple of garlic cloves, lemon juice, and toasted walnuts in a food processor. With the processor running, drizzle in extra-virgin olive oil and season with salt and pepper. It's a nice change from basil pesto on pasta or spread on crostini.

Rhubarb

Denise Mickelsen: What could be easier than a rhubarb fool? Cut 4 large rhubarb stalks into chunks and put them in a large saucepan. Add 1 packed cup light brown sugar, about ½ cup water, and a generous squeeze of lemon juice. Cook over medium heat, stirring, until the rhubarb is broken down and the mixture has thickened a little. Add more sugar or lemon juice to taste, then chill completely. Gently fold into cold whipped cream and serve in chilled wine glasses or small glass bowls.

Allison Ehri Kreitler: Try making a savory compote by sautéing chopped shallots in butter and then adding sliced rhubarb, red wine, sugar, black pepper, and a little star anise. Simmer until very soft, breaking it up with a wooden spoon. Add more sliced rhubarb and simmer until just barely tender to provide crunch. Serve with roasted or grilled meats.

Lisa Waddle: Make a rustic crumble by mixing 1½ lb. chopped rhubarb with ½ cup sugar, orange zest, and nutmeg. Pour it into a pie dish, then stir together 1 cup flour, ¾ cup dark brown sugar, ¾ cup oatmeal, and about 6 Tbs. canola oil and spread it over the rhubarb mixture. Bake the crumble at 375°F until the rhubarb is tender and bubbling.

Mushrooms

BEFORE SPRING HAS REALLY SPRUNG, it can feel like there isn't much in season. That's why we love mushrooms. From cremini and shiitake to portobellos and hens of the woods, cultivated mushrooms are often one of the few items in stores that haven't been flown in from across the globe. So buy a bunch and enjoy them for weeks to come by preserving them in olive oil.

These mushrooms get lots of flavor from a quick sear, although they keep a nice, chewy texture because they're not cooked all the way through. The wine-and-vinegar marinade infuses them with even more flavor and provides an acidic balance to the rich olive oil. Tastier and meatier than your average store-bought jarred mushrooms, these are delicious on crostini, over steak, pork, or chicken, and as a pita topping or omelet filling.

twice-marinated mushrooms

This recipe works well with a variety of mushrooms. The cooking time, however, varies slightly depending on the type you use (see sidebar below). You can marinate each mushroom variety separately, or if you want to marinate a mix of mushrooms, cook them separately and then marinate them together.

Yields about 2 cups

1½	cups dry white wine
½	cup white wine vinegar
3	medium cloves garlic, crushed
2	1x4-inch strips lemon zest, white pith removed
1	4-inch sprig rosemary
2	tsp. kosher salt
½	tsp. juniper berries (about 14), lightly crushed
½	tsp. fennel seed, lightly chopped
¼	tsp. crushed red pepper flakes
¼	tsp. coarsely ground black pepper
¾	cup extra-virgin olive oil (approximately)
1	lb. mushrooms, trimmed (see below)

Mix the wine, vinegar, garlic, lemon zest, rosemary, salt, juniper berries, fennel seed, red pepper flakes, and black pepper to make a marinade.

Heat 3 Tbs. of the olive oil in a 12-inch skillet over medium-high heat until very hot. Add the mushrooms and cook, stirring once or twice, until golden brown on one or two sides, 1½ to 4 minutes, depending on the type of mushroom—they should not be cooked all the way through. Spread on a plate to cool.

Add the marinade to the skillet. Bring to a boil, reduce the heat, and simmer for 5 minutes to infuse the flavors. Put the mushrooms and marinade in a heatproof container, such as a 1-quart Pyrex measuring cup. Let cool to room temperature, cover, and refrigerate overnight.

Drain the mushrooms, reserving the garlic and discarding the marinade and most of the aromatics (it's OK if some of the aromatics stick to the mushrooms). Pack the mushrooms and garlic into a pint jar with lid (or other sealable container). Add enough of the remaining oil to cover, and refrigerate at least overnight and up to 1 month.

—*Allison Ehri Kreitler*

Mushroom prep

Each type of mushroom requires slightly different trimming. Here's how to prepare some of our favorites:

Cremini Halve if large; cook 2 to 3 minutes.
Portobello Remove stem and gills and cut into ½-inch-thick slices; cook 1½ to 2 minutes.
Shiitake Remove stems and leave whole; cook 1½ to 2 minutes.

Oyster If large, separate lobes from bunches; if small, leave in little bunches ½ to ¾ inch thick; cook 1½ to 2 minutes.
Maitake/Hen of the woods Separate into little bunches with ½- to ¾-inch-thick stems; cook about 2 minutes.

Trumpet royale Leave whole or in little clumps if small; cut lengthwise into halves or thirds if large. The stems should be ½ to ¾ inch thick. Cook about 4 minutes.

Sun-Dried Tomatoes

Making the most of a favorite food find from a warehouse store.

BY ALLISON EHRI KREITLER

SO YOU COULDN'T RESIST buying that jar of sun-dried tomatoes—but now that you're home, what are you going to do with two pounds of them? Not to worry. With these tasty recipes—a punchy salad dressing, stuffed chicken breasts, and a creamy pasta sauce with a peppery kick—you'll have no problem using them up. That big jar will be empty before you can say "delicious."

The Buy

What: Sun Dried Tomatoes in 100% pure olive oil and herbs.

How much: Two-pound jar.

How to store: Refrigerate in their jar covered in their oil. They will keep for up to a month. To use the tomatoes, scrape them on the rim of the jar to remove some of the stuck-on cold oil. But don't bother to wipe them; the extra oil adds flavor.

sun-dried tomato and feta vinaigrette

Not only is this dressing great on salads, but it's also delicious on boiled peeled baby potatoes. The dressing keeps for up to 1 week in the refrigerator.

Yields about 1½ cups

- ⅓ cup drained oil-packed sun-dried tomatoes, coarsely chopped, plus ¼ cup oil from the jar
- ¼ cup plus 2 Tbs. sherry vinegar
- 1 small shallot, coarsely chopped (about 3 Tbs.)
- 1 Tbs. loosely packed chopped fresh oregano
- ¼ tsp. sweet pimentón (smoked paprika)
  Kosher salt and freshly ground black pepper
- ½ cup extra-virgin olive oil
- ¼ cup crumbled feta cheese

Put the tomatoes, vinegar, shallot, oregano, pimentón, 1 tsp. salt, ¼ tsp. pepper, and 2 Tbs. water in a blender and blend to combine (don't worry if it doesn't purée; it will when you add the oil). With the blender running, pour the olive oil and the tomato oil in a slow steady stream through the feed hole in the blender's lid. Transfer to a bowl or jar and stir in the feta. Season to taste with salt and pepper.

rigatoni with sun-dried tomato and fennel sauce

Serves 4

Kosher salt
2 Tbs. extra-virgin olive oil
1 cup chopped fennel
(about ½ medium bulb)
2 medium cloves garlic,
very coarsely chopped
1 cup heavy cream
1 cup lower-salt chicken broth
⅓ cup drained oil-packed sun-dried
tomatoes, very coarsely chopped
¼ tsp. crushed red pepper flakes
1 Tbs. Pernod (optional)
1 lb. dried rigatoni

Bring a large pot of well-salted water to a boil.

Meanwhile, heat the olive oil in a 10- to 11-inch straight-sided sauté pan over medium heat. Add the fennel and garlic and cook, stirring occasionally, until the fennel starts to soften and brown, about 5 minutes. Stir in 1 cup water and the cream, chicken broth, sun-dried tomatoes, pepper flakes, and 1 tsp. salt. Bring to a boil, reduce the heat, and simmer briskly, uncovered, until the tomatoes are plump and soft, about 15 minutes.

Remove from the heat and stir in the Pernod, if using. Let cool slightly and then purée in a blender until smooth. Wipe out the skillet, return the sauce to the skillet, season to taste with salt, and keep hot.

Photographs by Scott Phillips

Cook the rigatoni until just barely al dente, 1 to 2 minutes less than package instructions. Drain well and return to the pot. Add the sauce and toss over medium-low heat for a minute or two so the pasta finishes cooking and absorbs some of the sauce.

chicken breasts stuffed with sun-dried tomatoes and green olives

Serves 4

Pinch saffron (about 15 threads)
¼ cup extra-virgin olive oil
2½ tsp. fresh lemon juice
1½ tsp. mild honey, such as clover
½ tsp. freshly grated lemon zest
¼ tsp. crushed red pepper flakes
1 large clove garlic, crushed and
peeled
Kosher salt
¼ cup drained oil-packed sun-dried
tomatoes, very coarsely chopped
¼ cup pitted green olives, such as
manzanilla
¼ cup loosely packed fresh flat-leaf
parsley leaves, coarsely chopped
4 split skin-on bone-in chicken
breasts (3 to 3½ lb.)
Freshly ground black pepper

Position a rack in the middle of the oven and heat the oven to 425°F.

Soak the saffron in 2 tsp. hot water for 5 minutes. In a food processor, purée the saffron and soaking water with the olive oil, lemon juice, honey, lemon zest, red pepper flakes, garlic, and ½ tsp. salt. Add the sun-dried tomatoes, olives, and parsley. Pulse to form a coarsely chopped stuffing (it should be coarser than pesto).

If any of the backbone is still attached to the chicken, cut it off with poultry shears. Trim off the side flap with rib meat and bones. Use your finger to make a small opening between the skin and the flesh of the breasts. Run your finger under the skin to separate it from the breasts, making a pocket and being careful not to detach the edges of the skin. Stuff the tomato

mixture into the pocket, distributing it evenly over the chicken. Pat the skin back in place and season with 1 tsp. salt and ½ tsp. pepper. Line a heavy-duty rimmed baking sheet with aluminum foil. Roast the chicken on the baking sheet until the juices run clear and a meat thermometer registers 165°F, about 30 minutes.

For Butter or Worse

Clarifying how to make butter a more versatile player in the kitchen.
BY BRIAN GEIGER

Butter is...

4% milk solids
16% water
80% fat

I LOVE OLIVE OIL. It's versatile, it's easy to cook with, it's even potentially healthful. And yet, alas, even olive oil in all its extra-virgin splendor lacks something: It's not butter.

I really love butter. It's a magical emulsion of water, fat, sugar, and protein, with a taste and texture that makes me glad to be alive. One of the greatest compliments a cook can hear is that a creation is "buttery." (You never want to hear that something tastes "oily.")

But you can't cook with butter all the time. Magical though it may be, and as much as I love it, even I recognize butter's limitations. You would, too, if you'd ever tried to improve on a french fry's inherent goodness by deep frying it in butter. Sounds delicious, right? In

reality, though, heating butter to the point at which you can fry sliced potatoes will give you a burnt mess and a screeching smoke alarm.

So why won't butter cooperate? As with many things in life, the very attribute that makes butter so irresistible is also what makes it misbehave. Butter is about 80 percent fat, 16 percent water, and 4 percent milk solids. It's those milk solids, which are made of protein, sugar, and minerals, that give butter its rich flavor. But when those tasty milk solids get too hot, they start to smoke and burn.

The moment at which fats burn is called the "smoke point." For butter, the smoke point is 350°F. For vegetable oil, which doesn't have any milk solids, the smoke

point is around 450°F. All fats burn if heated enough, but the smoke point for each is different, depending on the amount of free fatty acids (found in all fats, as the name implies) and impurities. That's why light olive oil, which is purified olive oil, has a higher smoke point than extra-virgin olive oil. All of which is a technical way of explaining why you can deep-fry foods in oil but not butter.

Perhaps at some point you were told by a convincing TV chef or read in an otherwise trustworthy cookbook that if you mix butter with oil, it will raise its smoke point. Unfortunately, you were told a terrible lie. Combining butter with oil can be good for flavor purposes, but it does not raise its smoke point.

Adding oil to a pan of butter will spread out the milk solids, but they're still there and they're still going to burn. The myth persists that mixing butter and oil raises butter's smoke point for one simple reason: Since the milk solids are dispersed over a larger surface area, swimming in all that oil, it's not as obvious when they start to smoke and burn.

Before you despair too much over the fact that anytime you cook at 350°F or above you and butter must part ways, let me offer this one bit of encouragement: clarified butter.

Clarifying butter is a simple enough process that involves removing those troublesome milk solids along with much of the water. Then, butter behaves more like oil and can be heated to about 400°F without fear of smoke or burning.

Pick up a stick of butter and you may wonder how to take out the milk solids and water. But it's actually very easy. As we said before, butter is an emulsion.

If you've ever had a hard time making a Hollandaise sauce, now's your time to shine. Here's why: When you make an emulsified sauce, like Hollandaise, you are attempting to link oils and water-type liquids together, often with other flavors. If you don't do everything just so, the sauce breaks. When you clarify butter, you are intentionally breaking the emulsion.

Let the clarifying begin. Heat the butter in a small saucepan over medium-low heat. Simmer slowly to boil off the water, 10 to 15 minutes. The white foam that forms on the surface is the milk solids (some may also sink to the bottom). Skim off the foam and then strain the liquid through cheesecloth into a clean container to filter out the solids that have sunk. You can store your golden clarified butter in the refrigerator, and it will last even longer than regular butter if kept airtight.

You would think that being able to raise butter's smoke point would have me dancing in the streets. But the mixed blessing of clarifying is that removing the milk solids from butter also removes some of its delicious essence, the *je ne sais quoi* that gives it that wonderful, milky richness. Also, clarified butter can't be used in baking without making adjustments for the loss of water.

The process of clarifying does a good job of making butter a more versatile player in the kitchen (I use it for sautéing vegetables over high heat), but limitations persist—it can't be heated as high as many oils, isn't always at hand, and can be pricey if you buy it. That's why olive oil tends to be my go-to fat for cooking. Although the butter dish is never far away.

Brian J. Geiger is a robotics project manager by day and The Food Geek on nights and weekends. He blogs at FineCooking.com.

another butter

Store-bought clarified butter isn't widely available. What you're more likely to see in Asian food stores or online is ghee (pronounced GEE, with a hard G sound). A staple in Indian pantries, ghee is made from a cream that's encouraged to sour a bit, so it has some extra tang compared with clarified butter. Also, the milk solids are browned slightly before being strained out, for a nuttier flavor.

HOW TO MAKE

Roast Chicken

It's a classic all cooks need to have in their arsenals—and it's surprisingly simple. Here are the secrets to making the best bird ever. **BY SUSIE MIDDLETON**

what you need to know

Five essential tips to roasting a perfect chicken

1 Use high-quality chicken.
Starting with the best bird is the first step to tasty results (see Test Kitchen, page 77, for a chicken buying guide).

2 Start breast side down.
Positioning the chicken breast side down allows all the juices to gather in the breast meat during the

first half of cooking. When you flip the bird, those juices slowly redistribute but leave plenty of moisture behind to keep that white meat ultra juicy.

3 Use high heat.
Heat is roast chicken's best friend. A 450°F oven browns the skin quickly and keeps it nice and crisp.

4 Don't overcook.
An overcooked chicken is a dry chicken. To prevent overcooking, use an instant-read thermometer as your most reliable indicator of doneness (see the tip below for how to use it). It should read 165° to 170°F.

5 Let it rest.
Don't be tempted to cut into the chicken as soon as it's out of the oven. Resting for at least 15 minutes on the cutting board allows the juices to redistribute into the meat, making it moist and tender.

Tool Box

The simple utensils needed for this roast chicken are essential to any well-stocked kitchen:

- Medium flameproof roasting pan (about 9x13 inches)
- Medium roasting rack that fits in the pan
- Sturdy tongs
- Instant-read thermometer
- Carving board

cook's tip

To get the most accurate temperature reading, insert the instant-read thermometer in the thickest part of the thigh, toward the interior rather than the exterior of the bird. Make sure you don't touch the bone with the tip of the thermometer, or you'll get a higher reading.

Photographs by Scott Phillips

For sources, see Where to Buy It

best-ever roast chicken

Serves 4

1. 4-lb. roasting chicken, giblets removed
   Kosher salt and freshly ground black pepper
2. Tbs. extra-virgin olive oil

Position a rack in the center of the oven and heat the oven to 450°F.

Put the chicken breast side up on a roasting rack in a medium (9x13-inch or similar) flameproof baking dish or roasting pan. Tuck the wing tips behind the neck and loosely tie the legs together with a piece of kitchen twine. Season the breast all over with ½ tsp. each salt and pepper. Turn the chicken over. Season the back all over with ½ tsp. each salt and pepper. Drizzle the oil evenly over the back of the chicken.

Roast the chicken breast side down for 30 minutes. Turn it over by inserting sturdy tongs into the cavity and flipping it. Continue roasting until an instant-read thermometer inserted into the thigh reads 165° to 170°F, an additional 30 to 35 minutes (see the tip, opposite).

Transfer the chicken to a cutting board, loosely tent it with foil, and let it rest for 15 minutes. Snip the twine from the chicken's legs, carve the chicken (see Test kitchen, p. 77, for carving instructions), and serve.

Susie Middleton is Fine Cooking's *editor at large.*

 Take roast chicken to the next level with the Easy Pan Sauce at FineCooking.com.

Great Finds

Our latest buys for the kitchen and table. BY DENISE MICKELSEN

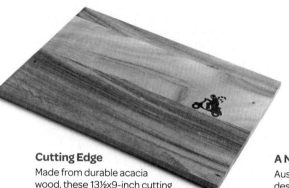

Cutting Edge

Made from durable acacia wood, these 13½x9-inch cutting boards have laser-engraved illustrations that interact with the natural grain of the wood to charming effect. Available in vespa, astronaut, skier, eskimo, and diver. **About $45 at uptoyoutoronto.com; 416-778-6487.**

A New Look

Aussie Lisa Vincitorio designed this new double-walled glass sugar caster to give the impression that the sugar inside is floating. **$49 at alessi-shop.com.**

Nature Comes Inside

Laura Zindel brings flora and fauna into the kitchen with her new Woodstock collection of dinnerware, including this splurge-worthy 17-inch platter. **$550; 802-254-8930.**

Feel-Good Honey

Buying these delicate, delicious Chilean raw honeys helps support the more than 30 beekeeping families in Temuco, Chile, who hand-harvest them. **About $9 at casaoliver.com; 888-807-7246.**

Oven to Table

Nambé's new line of alloy ovenware has it all: thick cast construction, nonstick interiors, and sleek good looks, which means you can bake and serve with style. Available in 1-, 2-, and 3-quart "Butterfly" covered casseroles and 1- and 2-quart bakers. **$200 to $300 at nambe.com; 800-443-0339.**

Back in Style

Dansk's Flamestone dinnerware line was originally released in 1957, but its recent return to the market shows that good taste never goes out of style. **Hot beverage server, $50; other pieces, $15 to $72 at dansk.com; 800-326-7528.**

The Right Stuff

Take good care of that stinky blue or runny Brie with cheese paper from the pros. A waxy exterior and plastic interior lets cheeses breathe so they stay fresh longer. **$5 for 15 sheets at murrayscheese.com; 888-692-4339.**

For more Great Finds, go to FineCooking.com/buy-it.

Subscribe and save up to $58*

TREAT YOURSELF

Reply today!

☐ 1 year just $29.95 — **Save 30%***
☐ 2 years just $49.95 — **Save 42%***
☐ 3 years just $69.95 — **BEST BUY! Save 45%***

Send no money now. We will bill you later.

N509860N

MR. / MRS. / MS.

ADDRESS   APT. #

CITY

STATE   ZIP   EMAIL (OPTIONAL)

The Taunton Press will send you occasional notices about noteworthy products and exclusive offers.

fine Cooking®
FineCooking.com/order

*Savings off U.S. newsstand price. Above prices for U.S. and Canada (GST included). Payable in U.S. funds. International customers, visit FineCooking.com/order

---

Treat a friend to *Fine Cooking*

☐ 1 year just $29.95 — **Save 30%***
☐ 2 years just $49.95 — **Save 42%***
☐ 3 years just $69.95 — **BEST BUY! Save 45%***

Send no money now. We will bill you later.

A great gift idea!

N509861N

YOUR NAME: SEND GIFT TO:

ADDRESS   ADDRESS

APT. #   CITY   APT. #   CITY

STATE   ZIP   STATE   ZIP

EMAIL (OPTIONAL)

The Taunton Press will send you occasional notices about noteworthy products and exclusive offers.

fine Cooking®

*Savings off U.S. newsstand price. Above prices for U.S. and Canada (GST included). Payable in U.S. funds. International customers, visit FineCooking.com/order

The Taunton Press
Inspiration for hands-on living®

BUSINESS REPLY MAIL
FIRST-CLASS MAIL   PERMIT NO. 6   NEWTOWN CT

POSTAGE WILL BE PAID BY ADDRESSEE

fine
Cooking®

63 S MAIN ST
PO BOX 5507
NEWTOWN, CT 06470-9879

The Taunton Press
Inspiration for hands-on living®

BUSINESS REPLY MAIL
FIRST-CLASS MAIL   PERMIT NO. 6   NEWTOWN CT

POSTAGE WILL BE PAID BY ADDRESSEE

fine
Cooking®

63 S MAIN ST
PO BOX 5507
NEWTOWN, CT 06470-9879

Mini Food, Big Rewards

From bite-size muffins to sliders, little is a big trend. Nutritionist **Ellie Krieger** thinks cooking and eating small is a smart thing.

THE OTHER DAY MY FRIEND WAS lamenting how much she misses bagels, especially just-baked ones—still warm, soft, and dense inside, crisp and chewy outside. Amazingly, she manages to resist them, sticking to her resolution to cut down on carbs. But it takes all her will power, and she feels deprived. When I mentioned that our local bagel store bakes fresh mini bagels, she jumped up and hugged me. Going mini is the perfect way for her to have her bagel and not overeat it, too.

Maybe that's why small is so big these days. It's the best way to eat what you crave without putting too much of a dent in your diet. Plus, there's something whimsical and fun about scaled-down versions of favorite foods. Who doesn't feel like a child when eating silver dollar pancakes? It's no wonder mini is everywhere—from the supermarket, with bite-size and mini pack versions of cookies, crackers, and candies, to restaurants, where sliders have slid on to every menu.

The irony is that typical serving sizes have gotten so out of hand that what's considered mini today is about the same as our grandparents' standard portion. That mini bagel my friend ran out to buy is just a tad smaller than the 3-inch bagel of 20 years ago.

So when you're out and about, ordering mini can be a great trick for beating portion distortion. And at home, going small is one way of having it all: enjoying indulgent, rich treats while staying healthy and balanced. It's instant portion control.

It can be as simple as cutting your tray of brownies into two-bite squares or using mini muffin tins to create the perfect party-size muffins or cupcakes. That way, each one is not as much an indulgence as a sweet amusement. Same goes for the tiny ice cream sandwiches I like to make with just a couple of tablespoons of ice cream between two vanilla wafer cookies. On the savory side, I use muffin tins for mini quiches or mac-and-cheese bites. And burgers and pizzas are even more fun when they're downsized. The trick—and this is crucial—is to eat just one or two instead of popping them like grapes.

Mini pizzas are a perennial favorite at my house. Their goodness—and wholesomeness—

In Ellie's kitchen, pizza gets a mini makeover.

builds from the base up, starting with a whole wheat crust (the dough is available frozen at most grocery stores). I douse the pizzas with an easy, fresh tomato sauce and then top them with a gorgeous pile of arugula, which wilts perfectly as the pizzas cook, and a few strips of sweet roasted peppers (both vegetables are powerhouses of vitamins and antioxidants). A little prosciutto sprinkled on top gives them

rich flavor, while just the right amount of cheese lends a melty finish. The result is fresh, colorful, and scrumptious. And the best part is that these pizzas are so small, you get to eat three.

I love how something as simple as downsizing your favorite foods allows you to have everything you want while keeping portions in check and eating more healthfully. That's a big payoff.

Photographs by Scott Phillips

mini pizzas with arugula, peppers, and prosciutto

You can find pizza dough at many supermarkets. If you have to buy more than the ¾ lb. needed for this recipe, you can freeze the leftover dough.

Yields 12 mini pizzas; serves 4 as a main course

5	tsp. extra-virgin olive oil
¾	lb. pizza dough, preferably whole wheat, thawed if frozen
1	14½-oz. can whole tomatoes, drained
1	tsp. dried oregano
1	large clove garlic, chopped
	Kosher salt and freshly ground black pepper
2	cups lightly packed arugula, chopped
½	cup thinly sliced roasted red peppers (rinsed if jarred)
1½	oz. thinly sliced prosciutto di Parma, cut into thin strips (about ½ cup)
1	cup grated part-skim mozzarella
¼	cup freshly grated Parmigiano-Reggiano
	Crushed red pepper flakes (optional)

Lightly coat a large bowl with 1 tsp. of the oil. Put the dough in the bowl, cover loosely, and let sit at room temperature until supple and relaxed, 45 minutes to 1 hour.

Position racks in the top and bottom thirds of the oven and heat the oven to 475°F. Meanwhile, put the tomatoes, oregano, garlic, 2 tsp. of the oil, and ½ tsp. each salt and pepper in a food processor; pulse to make a chunky sauce.

Lightly oil 2 baking sheets with the remaining 2 tsp. oil. Divide the dough into quarters. Divide each quarter into 3 equal parts; you'll have twelve 1-oz. pieces of dough. (Alternatively, use a scale to divide the dough.) Shape each piece of dough into a 3-inch round and put on the baking sheets.

Spread about 1 scant Tbs. of the sauce over each dough round, leaving a little border around the edge for the crust. Top each with a mound of arugula, then some strips of pepper and prosciutto. Sprinkle the mozzarella and Parmigiano on top.

Bake until the cheese is bubbling and the crust is browned, 12 to 14 minutes, rotating and swapping the pans' positions about halfway through for even baking. Sprinkle with crushed red pepper flakes (if using) and serve.

Registered dietician Ellie Kreiger is a Fine Cooking *contributing editor.*

good to know

- Whole wheat pizza dough is more nutritious and better for you (think more antioxidants and fiber) than white pizza dough.
- More vegetables than meat plus a fresh, homemade tomato sauce keep this pizza light and healthy.
- Three of these mini pizzas are as satisfying as two big slices of meat pizza, but with 100 fewer calories.

Meat Grinders

The best options for home use, from the basic manual to powerful electric models. BY MARYELLEN DRISCOLL

IF YOU'RE ONE OF THOSE PEOPLE who likes to know exactly where your food comes from and how it's prepared, then a meat grinder might be your next great purchase. Skip the prepackaged ground meats from the grocery and instead buy quality cuts and grind them yourself. You choose the meat, the amount of fat, and the grind, all of which means your hamburgers, meatloaf, sausages, meat-based sauces, and pâtés turn out the way you want them to. Opt for a big, electric meat grinder or a more compact, inexpensive option. Read on to find out which grinder is right for you, and which we liked best in each category. (For a sausage recipe and more information on grinders, see page 68.)

Three Ways to Grind

Before deciding on what kind of grinder to buy, consider how often you'll use it, how much meat you plan to grind, and your storage space. There are three choices:

1. **Manual grinders** make sense if you want to experiment with grinding meat but aren't ready to make a big investment. This style of meat grinder is perfect for modestly sized grinding tasks, such as a few pounds of meat at a time.
2. **Mixer attachment grinders** are the happy medium if you already own a stand mixer. The attachments fit right onto your mixer, and they offer the streamlined benefits of a motorized unit without the bulk and noise that comes with an electric grinder.
3. **Electric grinders** are great if you intend to regularly grind meat or make sausages. These grinders are about the size of a food processor and weigh nearly as much. And while noisy, they're designed for grinding meat quickly and cleanly, and they do it very well.

how we tested

A grinder's ability to grind several pounds of meat quickly without clogging, overheating, or smearing the fat is key. We ground about 5 pounds of cold, cubed boneless pork butt and pork fat back through nine widely available grinders (two manual, three mixer attachments, and four electric).

THE BEST MANUAL GRINDER

Weston Deluxe Manual Tinned Meat Grinder

$22.91; morningbite.com
Size: 11.75x4.25x8.5 inches

This size 10 cast-iron manual grinder is perfect for the home cook who wants to grind a few pounds of meat at a time. Its rubber-padded clamp was easy to secure to a countertop, and the 3x4-inch hopper opening was roomy and easy to load with the meat. Most important, both the hardened-steel grinding plates and blade were razor sharp and ground with ease.

Cuisinart Grinder Attachment

$128.95; cooking.com
Size: 10.5x6.5x8 inches

This grinder attachment is well constructed and efficient. It's smaller, easier to store, and much quieter than the electric models we tested and uses the power of the stand mixer's motor for more kick than a manual grinder. Simple to attach and operate, it has thick grinding plates and a sturdy, sharp blade. It comes with fine, medium, and coarse grinding plates, and the food pusher has a detachable lid to hold the extra accessories. (If you own a Viking stand mixer, their grinder attachment performed on par with Cuisinart's.)

Maverick Deluxe Food Grinder MM-5501

$89.95; comforthouse.com
Size: 12.5x7.5x9 inches

For a lower price tag, this model has a lot to offer (though it has a 90-day warranty and some plastic parts). It has a 575-watt motor with reverse capabilities, and a reset thermometer that automatically turns off the machine before the motor can overheat—a great feature that helps avoid smearing fat as you grind. The grinding plates and blade are made of stainless steel for rust-free storage.

Waring Pro's MG800 Professional Meat Grinder

$169.95; williams-sonoma.com
Size: 15.25x9x10.25 inches

This grinder is pricey but worth it. With a heavy-duty 450-watt motor, sturdy metal base, and extra-large hopper (not to mention a five-year warranty), it gets the job done right and quickly. It boasts a reverse function to help avoid clogging, and the food pusher has a compartment inside for storing attachments. But the best feature of this grinder is the toggle switch, a nice touch because you don't have to search for the on/off switch when you're in the middle of grinding.

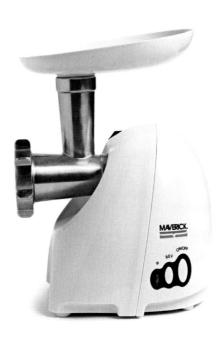

what to look for

All of these grinders worked well, but which you choose comes down to the following:

Manual grinders bolt or clamp to the edge of a countertop or a table. They come in numbered sizes, ranging from 5 to 31; for home use, sizes 8 and 10 are best because they're not too big yet can still grind 2 to 3 pounds of meat per minute. The most inexpensive choice, manual grinders require the most elbow grease.

Mixer attachments range in quality of construction; some are not as well built as their stand-alone counterparts. Check that the model that fits your stand mixer has a large hopper with plenty of room to feed meat through the machine. Also, look for sharp steel grinding plates and blades.

Electric grinders range in price depending on the power of the motor. Extra features like thermostats and reverse functions make grinding easy, but those features add to the price of the grinder, so assess your needs before buying.

Maryellen Driscoll is a Fine Cooking *contributing editor.*

Riesling, Changeling

The favorite new white comes from every corner, in styles from dry to sweet. How to choose?

BY DOUG FROST

RIESLING IS COMING OFF A BAD REP. It used to be thought of as a wine for beginners—a simple, sweet, easy-drinking German white. Those who drank it admitted to their liking only sheepishly. (It's a shame, really, because a well-crafted sweet Riesling was and is a wonderful thing.)

Fast forward a few years. Now, Riesling is the fastest growing white wine in the American marketplace and has been for nearly two years. So why this explosive growth in Riesling's popularity?

I have a theory. Riesling, a grape with multiple personalities (an unsettling trait in people, but rather likeable in wine), is appealing because it's a changeling of a wine, made from a malleable grape capable of all levels of sweetness and style. With Riesling, it's always possible to discover something new, and its flexibility is the key to its charm.

True to its terroir

These days, Riesling heralds from many lands (not just Germany) and exhibits more styles than ever before. France, Austria, Australia, New Zealand, North America, South America, and South Africa—not to mention Italy and southeastern Europe—are just a few of the countries and regions now growing this impressionable grape.

Depending on where it's from, Riesling can be juicy, floral, earthy, tangy, tart, or fruity. Don't be surprised to taste or smell lemons, limes, oranges, tangerines, grapefruits, peaches, nectarines, apricots, apples, pears, melons, bananas, papayas, mangos, or pineapples—the list goes on. Sometimes Riesling is sweet; sometimes it's dry. Just as often it's something in between.

Apart from Riesling's different flavor profiles, the wine's styles are as varied as its home countries: There are crisp and racy New Zealand versions; pungent, aromatic Aussie Rieslings; soft and delicate ones from New York and Michigan; powerful, dry Rieslings from Alsace and Austria. These enter a marketplace already con-fused by the myriad styles of German Rieslings, from lemon-lime tangy to pancake-syrup sweet.

Rieslings grown on the slate soils of some German and Alsatian vineyards smell intensely of honey, minerals, and beeswax (the Germans call the aroma *firne*). Far away in Australia's Clare and Eden Valleys, similar slate soils provide many of the same smells.

Other Riesling vineyards in Germany, Alsace, and Austria might have fewer slate rocks and express few of those notes. Rather, limestone, granite, alluvial, and volcanic soils bring their own flavors and aromas, each adding a distinct layer to Riesling's complex brew.

Lacy to racy, crisp to coy

Just as personality is dependent on terroir, so is a wine's potency. Alcohol levels in wine depend on how ripe the grapes are at crush. The warmer the climate, the riper the grapes and the more alcoholic the resulting wine. In the middle of Germany's relatively cool Mosel River Valley, Riesling has a lacy delicacy from very low alcohol levels (less than 10 percent). No other grape is as interesting at such timid levels. Rieslings in Austria and Alsace are often much bolder, with 14 percent alcohol or more. America's West Coast Rieslings are somewhere in between; Michigan and New York's versions, as well as New Zealand's, tend to be lower in alcohol, similar to Germany's.

To top it all off, Riesling labels don't help matters. German wine labels can be as confusing as an Umberto Eco plot synopsis. Sweetness information is scarce, though that may be changing.

A worldwide group of Riesling producers, under the rubric of the International Riesling Foundation, has devised a back label that provides some guidance. Participating wineries (producers everywhere have either signed up or are watching closely) will include a Riesling taste profile on their labels, and their wines will be designated as dry, medium dry, medium sweet, or sweet. With this new clarity, maybe some folks who haven't yet fallen in love with the grape will join the Riesling rush.

Riesling reconsidered

Its popularity may be on the rise, but who exactly is draining these Riesling bottles dry? It doesn't seem to be conservative wine buyers, who, put off by Riesling's reputation as a sweet wine, overlook its potential. It's got to be the foodies, chefs, and wine writers (yours truly included) who have been

insisting for years that the grape has been wrongly dismissed. After all, just because Riesling is easy to enjoy doesn't mean we should look down on it. Does great wine have to be difficult to drink?

Wine experts and chefs alike have long championed the Riesling grape for its flexibility and compatibility with a wide variety of cuisines. The tart-sweet nature of many Rieslings explains the grape's ability to pair well with food, especially spicy dishes that benefit from a touch of fruit or sweetness. Its gentle demeanor doesn't overwhelm lighter foods like shellfish (oysters and clams in particular), grilled fish, and pork, which can be overpow-

ered by or even taste slightly bitter with bigger, more buttery whites like Chardonnay.

Don't get me wrong. I'm not about to grill someone for pouring a Chardonnay with shellfish, roast beef, or anything else for that matter. But with robust growth, new countries, adventurous drinkers, chefs, and wine writers on Riesling's side, it seems clear that its Sybil-like nature is not a bad thing. Perhaps Riesling's many personalities—sweet, dry, fruity, soft, bold, intense, mild—have a little something for everyone.

Doug Frost is a wine consultant and writer based in Kansas City, Missouri.

Riesling: A Buying Guide

To really understand the range of Rieslings, consider trying bottles along the spectrum of dry to fruity.

DRY AND LIGHT   DRY AND TANGY   DRY AND EARTHY   FRUITY AND TANGY

Left Foot Charley Dry Riesling 2007, Michigan ($16) This remarkable winery in Michigan's Old Mission Peninsula lakeside vineyards produces great wines, but you need to shop in Michigan or call the winery to buy this beauty.

Standing Stone Riesling 2007, New York ($15) The Finger Lakes region has more Riesling producers than any other area in the U.S., and this rich, crisp bottle is a great introduction to these wines.

Trefethen Riesling 2007, California ($25) Refreshing, lemony, and tangy, this Napa Valley wine could last several years in the cellar.

Grosset Springvale Watervale Riesling 2007, Australia ($35) One of the country's top producers from the Clare Valley offers Riesling with richness, citric tartness, and distinctive earth flavors.

Trimbach Riesling 2006, France ($25) The Alsace region straddles Germany, and with its rocky soils, adds a few more juicy layers to Riesling's panoply of fruits.

Gunderloch Jean-Baptiste Kabinett 2007, Germany ($20) If I had a house wine, this Rhine River bottle would be it: green apples, peaches, and always bracingly tart, too.

Selbach-Oster Kabinett 2007, Germany ($22) From the Mosel River area, this is soft, delicate, only a bit sweet, and has a lovely, long finish. It's surprisingly age-worthy.

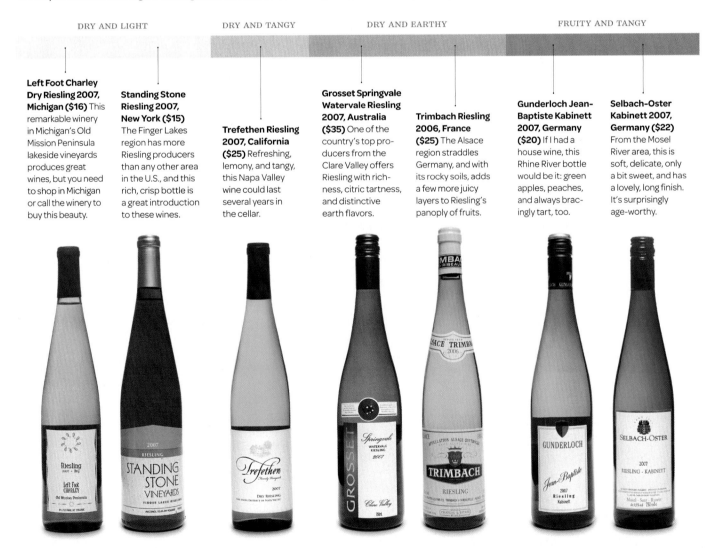

Rise & Party

Got a special occasion? Here's an
easy, elegant brunch menu that
works every time. BY MARTHA STAMPS

Smoked Salmon, Goat Cheese,
and Artichoke Quiche

menu for 8

Citrus Tea Punch

*Smoked Salmon,
Goat Cheese,
and Artichoke Quiche*

*Peas and Carrots with
Lemon, Dill, and Mint*

Fresh Fruit

*Wild Blueberry and
Ricotta Pancakes*

SPRING HOLIDAYS just seem to lend themselves to a brunch menu, especially one that makes the most of everything that's coming up fresh now. Brunch has a festive feel, too—a good excuse to set a lovely table and even dress up a little.

This menu runs with both of those ideas, getting its start with seasonal ingredients like baby carrots, sugar snap peas, and artichoke hearts, and giving them an elegant spin (don't miss the quiche, with its high-sided, free-form crust). And since we're celebrating, why not dust off the punch bowl and make the mint and citrus tea punch? It will give your party that extra something special.

Passionfruit, mini pineapples, and chunks of kiwi give the classic fruit platter a little edge.

smoked salmon, goat cheese, and artichoke quiche

If you can't find hot-smoked salmon, cold-smoked will also be scrumptious, although it will lose some of its silky texture once it's baked.

Serves 8

FOR THE CRUST

9	oz. (2 cups) all-purpose flour	
2	tsp. granulated sugar	
1	tsp. kosher salt	
8	oz. (1 cup) cold unsalted butter, cut into ½-inch cubes	
4-6	Tbs. ice water	

FOR THE FILLING

1	oz. (2 Tbs.) unsalted butter	
½	medium red onion, thinly sliced crosswise (1 cup)	
24	frozen artichoke heart quarters, thawed	
4	large eggs	
1	cup heavy cream	
½	cup whole milk	
1	Tbs. roughly chopped fresh dill	
	Kosher salt and freshly ground black pepper	
	Pinch nutmeg	
6	oz. hot-smoked salmon, skin removed and roughly broken into ½-inch pieces (1 cup)	
4	oz. fresh goat cheese, crumbled (¾ cup)	

MAKE THE CRUST

In a stand mixer fitted with the paddle attachment, mix the flour, sugar, and salt on low speed. Add the butter and mix until the largest pieces are the size of peas. With the mixer still on low, add the ice water 1 Tbs. at a time until the dough just begins to come together—you may not need all the water. Transfer the dough to a piece of plastic and shape it into a disk. Wrap in the plastic and refrigerate for at least 30 minutes.

Roll the dough on a lightly floured surface into a 15-inch circle about ¼ inch thick. Transfer to a 9-inch spring-form pan and press the dough into the bottom and up the sides, pressing any pleats flat against the sides. With scissors, unevenly snip any dough that overhangs the rim, to make a jagged edge. Prick the bottom of the crust all over with a fork. Freeze for 20 minutes.

Position a rack in the center of the oven and heat the oven to 350°F. Line the frozen crust with two overlapping sheets of parchment and fill two-thirds of the way with dried beans. Bake until the sides are set, about 25 minutes. Remove the beans and parchment and bake until the crust just begins to brown lightly, another 8 to 10 minutes. Remove from the oven and let cool on a rack. Meanwhile, raise the oven temperature to 400°F.

MAKE THE FILLING

Melt the butter in a 10-inch sauté pan over medium-high heat. Add the onion and cook, stirring occasionally, until soft and turning translucent, about 3 minutes. Add the artichoke hearts and cook until softened and slightly browned, another 3 to 4 minutes. Remove the pan from the heat.

Beat the eggs in a medium bowl with the cream, milk, 1 tsp. of the dill, ¼ tsp. salt, ¼ tsp. pepper, and the nutmeg.

Put the springform pan on a rimmed baking sheet. Pour about half of the egg mixture into the crust. Bake in the oven until the filling is partially set (it will still be slightly runny), about 20 minutes.

Scatter half of the onion and artichoke mixture over the partially set egg mixture. Distribute half of the salmon and goat cheese on top. Pour on the remaining egg mixture and then scatter the remaining onions, artichokes, salmon, and goat cheese over the egg. Sprinkle the remaining dill over the top.

Bake until the center is just set (use a paring knife to peek), another 40 to 50 minutes. Check about halfway through baking; if the crust seems to be browning too fast, shield it with strips of foil. Cool slightly on a wire rack.

To unmold, remove the springform ring and loosen the quiche from the pan's bottom by running a thin-bladed knife between the two. Slide the quiche off its base onto a serving plate. Serve warm or at room temperature, cut in wedges.

Make ahead: You can bake the crust up to a day ahead and the quiche up to 2 hours ahead.

Assistant prop stylist: Alexa Waterman

Smoked Salmon, Goat Cheese, and Artichoke Quiche and Peas and Carrots with Lemon, Dill, and Mint

Peas and Carrots with
Lemon, Dill, and Mint

peas and carrots with lemon, dill, and mint

Remember the frozen version of peas and carrots? The dish gets an update here: no square carrots in sight.

Serves 8

- 1-2 **medium lemons**
- ½ **cup extra-virgin olive oil**
- 1 **Tbs. minced fresh mint**
- 1 **tsp. minced fresh dill**
  Kosher salt and freshly ground black pepper
- 2 **bunches small young carrots, preferably with tops (about 2 lb.)**
- 8 **oz. fresh sugar snap peas, trimmed and strings removed**

Finely grate ½ tsp. zest from a lemon and then juice the lemon to yield ¼ cup (if it yields less, juice the second lemon). In a large bowl, whisk the zest, juice, oil, mint, dill, ½ tsp. salt, and ⅛ tsp. pepper.

Trim the tips and all but about ½ inch of the greens from the carrots and then peel them. In a large pot fitted with a steamer insert, bring an inch of water to a boil over high heat. Have ready a large bowl of ice water. Lay the carrots in the basket of the steamer, cover tightly, and steam until crisp-tender, 4 to 5 minutes. Cool the carrots in the ice water for a few minutes; then lift them out and add to the dressing.

Steam the peas in the same pot until barely tender, about 3 minutes. Cool them in the ice water for a few minutes, drain, and add to the carrots. Stir to coat the vegetables in the dressing. Taste and add more salt, if needed.

Let the vegetables sit for at least 30 minutes and up to 1 hour, tossing occasionally. With a slotted spoon, transfer the vegetables to a serving platter. Serve chilled or at room temperature.

Make ahead: You can make the entire dish up to 1 hour in advance.

citrus tea punch

Sweet iced tea is a southern staple. Adding fresh lemon and orange juice transforms it into a punch that can be made even more festive with a splash of vodka.

Yields 2 quarts

- 3 **oz. fresh spearmint (2 bunches)**
- 2 **large "pitcher-size" tea bags (for iced tea), such as Tetley or Lipton**
- 1½ **cups granulated sugar**
- 1 **cup fresh lemon juice (from 4 to 6 medium lemons)**
- 1 **cup fresh orange juice (from about 4 medium oranges)**
- 1 **cup vodka (optional)**
- 1 **lemon, thinly sliced or cut into wedges, for garnish**

Put the mint in a large heatproof pitcher and pour in 6 cups boiling water. Add the tea bags and let steep for 30 minutes. Remove the tea bags, strain out the mint, and stir in the sugar and juices. Let cool to room temperature and add the vodka (if using). Refrigerate until cold. Stir before serving. Serve over ice, garnished with the sliced lemon.

wild blueberry and ricotta pancakes

Ricotta makes these pancakes light and creamy. It's the perfect foil for the intense sweet-tart flavor of wild blueberries, which are widely available frozen. You can also use cultivated blueberries, which are larger but still sweet and delicious.

Yields about 18 pancakes

- 3 large eggs, separated
- ¾ cup part-skim ricotta, drained of excess liquid before measuring
- 2¼ cups buttermilk
- 5 Tbs. granulated sugar
- 1 Tbs. pure vanilla extract
- ¾ tsp. table salt
- 8 oz. (1¾ cups) all-purpose flour
- 1 tsp. baking powder
- ¼ tsp. baking soda
- 6 oz. frozen wild blueberries (don't thaw) or fresh wild or cultivated blueberries (1½ cups)
  Vegetable oil for the griddle
  Softened salted butter, pure maple syrup, and confectioner's sugar, for serving

In a large bowl, whisk the egg yolks and ricotta. Whisk in the buttermilk, sugar, vanilla, and salt.

In a small bowl, stir the flour, baking powder, and baking soda with a spatula. Fold into the egg yolk mixture until just combined.

Beat the egg whites in a clean, dry bowl until they hold firm peaks. Fold gently into the batter until just combined. Fold in the blueberries.

Lightly oil a griddle and set it over medium heat. The griddle is ready when water droplets dance briefly on the surface before disappearing. Ladle a scant ¼ cup batter per pancake onto the griddle. Cook until the undersides are nicely browned, the edges look set, and small bubbles appear on the surface, about 3 minutes. Flip and cook until the second sides are golden brown, about 3 minutes more. Repeat, re-oiling the griddle between batches, until all the batter is cooked. Serve at once with butter, maple syrup, and confectioners' sugar.

Martha Stamps is chef-owner of Martha's at the Plantation in Nashville, Tennessee, and the author of The New Southern Basics *cookbook.* ❏

Pancakes for dessert—why not? Once everyone has finished the main course, head for the kitchen to start batches of these blueberry-studded gems. Serve them with butter, maple syrup, and confectioners' sugar.

For sources, see Where to Buy It

Wild Blueberry and Ricotta Pancakes

mint condition

Spring's number one herb in six fresh recipes.

BY JESSICA BARD

Mint is mint is mint. Right? So it would seem, given that supermarkets carry only one kind (which is almost always spearmint). But go to a farmers' market in spring and you'll find small pots of fragrant orange, apple, and pineapple mint, zesty ginger mint, and even chocolate mint. The variety is mind-boggling, and the smells alone are enough to send you straight to the kitchen. And once you see these recipes, that will seem like an even better idea.

**Derby Day Mint Julep Cocktail,
recipe on page 48**

toasted israeli couscous salad with mint, cucumber, and feta

This refreshing pasta salad is a nice accompaniment to barbecued meats and a welcome contribution to a potluck.

Serves 4 to 6

Kosher salt
1 **cup Israeli couscous**
1 **medium English cucumber, peeled and finely diced (2 cups)**
½ **cup coarsely chopped fresh spearmint or pineapple mint leaves; additional sprigs for garnish**
¼ **cup extra-virgin olive oil**
2 **Tbs. fresh lemon juice; more as needed**
1 **tsp. finely grated lemon zest**
Freshly ground black pepper
1 **cup small-diced feta cheese**

In a large saucepan, bring 2 quarts well-salted water to a boil.

Meanwhile, in a medium skillet over medium heat, toast the couscous, stirring frequently, until golden-brown, about 7 minutes.

Cook the couscous in the boiling water until tender, about 10 minutes. Drain and rinse under cold running water until cool. Pour the couscous into a large mixing bowl. Stir in the cucumber and mint.

In a small bowl, mix the oil, lemon juice and zest, ¾ tsp. salt, and ¼ tsp. pepper. Stir in the feta. Add the feta mixture to the couscous, season to taste with salt, pepper, and lemon juice, and mix well. Transfer to a serving bowl and garnish with the mint sprigs.

Make ahead: You can refrigerate the salad for up to 4 hours; toss before serving.

a buyer's guide

There are more than 200 mint varieties, all of which fall into one of two categories: spearmint or peppermint. They're similar in taste and aroma, but peppermints contain menthol, which gives them a stronger character and a cooling sensation. Here's a guide for some of the common varieties.

SPEARMINT

The most versatile of mints, spearmint has a natural affinity with fruits and spring vegetables (think peas, asparagus, and artichokes), herbs like basil and cilantro, and spices like ginger, cumin, and cardamom. Its relatively mild flavor makes it ideal for a variety of savory dishes, including grilled and roasted meats.

Spearmint varieties:

Pineapple mint With a fruity scent reminiscent of pineapple and a flavor that's a bit sweeter than regular spearmint, pineapple mint complements other fresh, fruity flavors and livens up rich cheeses and meats.
Apple mint Its gentle spearmint flavor has a hint of green apple. It's lovely in iced tea.
Curly and smooth-leaf mint Both taste just like spearmint but have different textures. Curly mint is ruffled and a bit coarser, while smooth-leaf mint is soft and velvety. Use them to add textural variety to a dish.

PEPPERMINT

Peppermint is assertive enough to stand up to strong flavors, so it's ideal for chocolate desserts and boldly flavored dishes.

Peppermint varieties:

Orange mint Overtones of orange and sometimes bergamot make it a perfect choice when you want to add a citrusy note.
Chocolate mint This peppermint has an unmistakable hint of chocolate that makes it ideal for desserts featuring chocolate and berries.
Ginger mint The ginger notes complement dishes that use fresh or powdered ginger.
Grapefruit mint Hints of grapefruit set off anything with citrus zest.

Food styling, except pages 43 and 49, by Jessica Bard

Photographs by Scott Phillips

poached flounder with mint beurre blanc

This classic shallow-poached fish is served with a minty French butter sauce. It's delicious with a simple rice pilaf and tender green spring vegetables like peas or baby spinach.

Serves 4

- 6 **skinless flounder fillets (1½ lb. total)**
- ½ **tsp. ground ginger**
  Kosher salt and freshly ground black pepper
- 3½ **Tbs. coarsely chopped fresh spearmint or ginger mint leaves**
- ¼ **cup minced shallots**
- ¼ **cup dry white wine**
- 2 **Tbs. heavy cream**
- 2 **oz. (4 Tbs.) cold unsalted butter, cut into 8 slices**
- 1 **Tbs. thinly sliced chives**

Lay the fish fillets skinned side up on a cutting board. Slice each fillet in half lengthwise to make 12 strips. In a small bowl mix the ginger, ¼ tsp. salt, and ¼ tsp. pepper. Sprinkle the spice mixture evenly over all the fish and then sprinkle with 2 Tbs. of the chopped mint. Roll each strip into a coil, starting with the fatter end and aligning the roll along the cut edge. Secure with a toothpick, pushing it into the thin end and through the other side.

Sprinkle the shallots over the bottom of a 10-inch straight-sided sauté pan. Arrange the fish coils cut edge down in the pan. Pour in the wine and ⅓ cup water. Turn the heat to medium high and bring the liquid to a simmer. Adjust the heat to maintain a gentle simmer, cover, and poach the fish until cooked through, 4 to 8 minutes. Use a slotted spoon to transfer the fish to a warm plate. Tent with foil while finishing the sauce.

Increase the heat to high and boil the liquid until it's reduced to about 3 Tbs. (It should just barely cover the bottom of the pan.) Add the cream and boil for 30 seconds. Reduce the heat to low and whisk in 2 slices of the cold butter, the remaining 1½ Tbs. mint, and the chives. When the butter is almost melted, add another slice and whisk until mostly melted. Repeat with the remaining butter, 1 slice at a time. (Take care not to overheat the sauce or it will separate.) Season to taste with salt and pepper.

Remove the toothpicks from each piece of fish. Serve the fish (3 pieces per serving) drizzled with the sauce.

Roast Rack of Lamb with
Lemon-Mint Salsa Verde

roast rack of lamb with lemon-mint salsa verde

Plan ahead because the lamb needs to marinate for at least 8 hours. To serve, lean the cut chops up against a pile of roasted garlic mashed potatoes and a side of bright green beans.

Serves 8

- 2 medium lemons
- 1 cup packed fresh spearmint or grapefruit mint leaves (1 oz.)
- 2 Tbs. chopped garlic
  Kosher salt and freshly ground black pepper
- ½ cup extra-virgin olive oil
- 3 frenched racks of lamb (8 ribs and 1 to 1½ lb. each)

Finely grate 1 Tbs. zest from the lemons and then squeeze them to yield 3 Tbs. juice. Combine the zest and juice with the mint, garlic, 2 tsp. salt, and 1 tsp. pepper in a food processor. Pulse a few times and then with the motor running, add the oil. Reserve ¼ cup and refrigerate.

Trim the fat on the lamb racks to a ¼-inch-thick layer. Poke holes all over the lamb with a fork to help the marinade penetrate. Lightly score the fat layer about ⅟₁₆ inch deep in a ½-inch diamond pattern. Arrange the racks, fat side up, in a 9x13-inch baking dish, overlapping the bones if necessary to fit the racks in the dish. Brush the remaining salsa verde all over the racks. Cover and refrigerate for at least 8 hours and up to 24 hours.

Heat the oven to 425°F. Take the lamb out of the fridge and arrange the racks fat side up in a large roasting pan (or rimmed baking sheet)—they should fit in one layer. Brush the top and sides of each rack with 1 Tbs. of the reserved salsa verde. Roast for 15 minutes. Brush with 1 Tbs. more of the salsa verde and continue to roast to an internal temperature of 130° to 135°F for medium rare, an additional 15 to 20 minutes. Let the meat rest for 5 minutes before carving into chops. Drizzle the remaining salsa verde over each serving.

Find a bonus recipe for Date-Mint Chutney at FineCooking.com/extras.

white bean salad with mint and red onion

This is a flavorful bean salad that goes well with most meat and poultry, particularly roasted pork tenderloin or broiled lamb chops.

Serves 4

- ½ cup small-diced red onion
- 3 Tbs. sherry vinegar
- 1 15-oz. can white beans, drained and rinsed (like Great Northern)
- ½ cup roughly chopped fresh spearmint or smooth-leaf spearmint leaves
- ½ cup small-diced red bell pepper
- 2 Tbs. nonpareil (small) capers
- 2 Tbs. extra-virgin olive oil
  Kosher salt and freshly ground black pepper

In a small bowl, mix the onion and vinegar; let sit for 15 minutes. In a medium bowl, mix the onions and vinegar with the beans, mint, red pepper, capers, olive oil, and salt and pepper to taste.

keep it fresh

Make a bouquet Store mint bunches with the cut stems in a glass of water and cover the leaves with a plastic bag. Refrigerate, changing the water every couple of days. It should stay fresh for at least 1 week.

Be gentle Mint starts to blacken after it's cut, so wait until the last minute before chopping or tearing it and adding it to a dish. When appropriate, tear the leaves gently instead of cutting them, to help prevent blackening.

derby day mint julep cocktail

There are as many variations of the mint julep as there are thoroughbreds that have run in the Kentucky Derby, which is when this sweet concoction is traditionally served. It's often stirred with ice in a silver cup; this version calls for shaking with a slice of lemon for a frothy, refreshing drink.

Yields 14 cocktails

MINT SYRUP

- 25 fresh spearmint or apple mint leaves
- ¾ cup granulated sugar

FOR THE JULEPS

- 3½ quarts crushed ice
- 3½ cups bourbon (such as Maker's Mark or Knob Creek)
- 14 thin slices lemon
- 14 sprigs spearmint or apple mint

Make the mint syrup: In a small saucepan, stir the mint with the sugar and ¾ cup water, crushing the mint lightly with the spoon. Bring to a boil over medium-high heat and boil for 1 minute. Remove from the heat and let cool in the pan, about 30 minutes. Strain into a small container. Use immediately to make the cocktails or chill for up to 2 weeks.

For each cocktail: Have a chilled 8- to 10-oz. cocktail or wine glass ready. In a cocktail shaker, combine 1 Tbs. of the mint syrup with 1 cup ice, ¼ cup bourbon, and a lemon slice. Shake for 30 seconds; pour into the chilled glass. Garnish with a mint sprig.

strawberry-mint shortcakes

Minty sugar-crusted biscuits, strawberries, and sweetened sour cream come together for a new take on a traditional favorite. For the freshest color, slice the mint for the berries just before you need it.

Serves 8

- 3 Tbs. packed, finely chopped fresh spearmint, peppermint, or chocolate mint leaves, plus 1 Tbs. thinly sliced
- ¾ cup granulated sugar
- 9 oz. (2 cups) unbleached all-purpose flour; more for rolling the dough
- 2 tsp. baking powder
- 1 tsp. table salt
- 2 oz. (4 Tbs.) cold unsalted butter, cut into ½-inch pieces, plus 1 Tbs., melted, for brushing
- ⅔ cup half-and-half
- 1 quart strawberries, hulled and quartered lengthwise
- 1 cup sour cream

Position a rack in the center of the oven and heat the oven to 400°F. Draw or trace an 8-inch circle on each of two pieces of parchment and flip them over so you see the circle through the parchment.

In a small bowl, mix the finely chopped mint with 3 Tbs. of the sugar, gently pressing with the back of a spoon until the sugar becomes damp, like wet sand; set aside.

In a large bowl, mix the flour, 2 Tbs. of the sugar, baking powder, and salt. With a pastry blender, cut in the butter until the mixture resembles coarse cornmeal. Stir in the half-and-half and mix just until the dough comes together in a ball and all bits of flour have been incorporated.

Divide the dough in half and shape into two disks. Lightly flour one piece of parchment and roll out one disk into a 8-inch circle, using the parchment circle as a guide. Flour the surface as needed to keep the dough from sticking. Repeat with the remaining dough and parchment. Brush any excess flour off the parchment. Transfer one of the circles, still on its parchment, to a large rimmed baking sheet. Brush it with

half of the melted butter and spread with half of the remaining mint sugar.

Invert the second dough round onto the first and remove the top parchment. Brush the top with the remaining butter and spread with the remaining mint sugar. Cut the dough into 8 wedges (a pizza cutter works well). Use an off-set spatula to gently move the wedges at least 1 inch apart (keeping the tops and bottoms aligned). Bake until the biscuits are lightly browned and the sugar crust has set, 20 to 22 minutes—it's fine if they haven't risen much. Cool on a rack until ready to assemble.

While the biscuits bake, mix the strawberries with ¼ cup of the sugar in a medium bowl; let sit at room temperature. In a small bowl, stir the sour cream and the remaining 3 Tbs. sugar; refrigerate until ready to use.

TO ASSEMBLE EACH SHORTCAKE

Stir the thinly sliced mint into the strawberries. Gently twist (or pry with a fork) a biscuit to separate the top and bottom. Set the bottom on a serving plate and top with about ⅓ cup strawberries and some juice. Spoon on 1½ Tbs. sweetened sour cream and top with the other half of the biscuit. Add another small dollop of cream, if you like.

Jessica Bard is a food writer and recipe tester who teaches cooking classes at Warren Kitchen and Cutlery in Rhinebeck, New York. ◻

grow your own

The best way to try some of the more unusual varieties of mint is to grow them (you can find plants at most nurseries or online; see Where to Buy It, page 89). Mint is a quick and often rampant grower. It can be planted almost anywhere, though it does best with at least half a day's sunlight and plenty of water.

Strawberry-Mint Shortcakes

a sweet bite
of
Brazil

Class description: **Leticia Moreinos** reveals the secrets to brigadeiros, a classic candy from her native Brazil. Prerequisites: None (except maybe a sweet tooth).

COOKING TEACHER Leticia Moreinos has one thing on her mind: to put Brazilian cooking on the map. "Brazilian food is too often bunched in with other Latin American foods," says Leticia. "I want everyone to know that we have our own very distinctive cuisine."

A native of Rio de Janeiro, Leticia learned to cook from her family's housekeeper—and collected dozens of recipes in the process. As an adult, she moved to New York to go to culinary school and later worked at some of the city's most renowned French restaurants. But those childhood recipes haunted her, and it wasn't long before she gave up sauces and reductions to return to her roots. Now, she's spreading the word through her popular Brazilian cooking classes, including this one, on Brazil's national treat: the brigadeiro.

Brigadeiros, step-by-step. They may look like truffles, but they're more like little fudge balls made with sweetened condensed milk and covered not with cocoa powder but sprinkles. Leticia shows us how to make them, beginning to end (recipe, page 54).

1 Class begins with Leticia bringing condensed milk, butter, cream, and corn syrup to a boil before she whisks in chocolate and cocoa powder. "Traditionally, brigadeiros' flavor comes from cocoa powder," says Leticia. "But the way I figure it, why not make it with the real stuff? I like to use the best-quality dark chocolate."

2 As the brigadeiro mixture cooks over a medium-low burner, it slowly begins to thicken. "It starts to feel like fudge," says Leticia. "You know you're almost done when you see whisk trails in the batter."

3 "Learning when to stop cooking the batter is the trickiest part of making brigadeiros," Leticia warns. "If the batter is undercooked, your brigadeiros will be too soft; if the batter is overcooked, they will be hard and chewy." The batter is done when it slides to one side of the pan in a blob and leaves a thick residue on the bottom.

4 A small ice cream scoop (see Where to Buy It, page 89, for a source) is Leticia's tool of choice for scooping up the batter, but a melon baller or a teaspoon works just fine.

5 "Rolling the scooped-up batter between the palms of your hands is the best way to get a smooth, even ball," suggests Leticia.

6 To coat a brigadeiro evenly, Leticia covers it with sprinkles and then rolls it gently in her hands, exerting the slightest pressure to make sure the sprinkles adhere.

TOP TIP
Great texture is all about knowing just how long to cook the batter. It should slide out of the pan, leaving a thick residue behind.

Chocolate brigadeiros are classic, but coconut and pistachio are tasty variations.

the secret ingredient

Brigadeiros get their distinctive flavor and melt-in-your-mouth texture mainly from sweetened condensed milk, which is a bit of a national obsession in Brazil. It's used in hundreds of recipes and is the base for some of the most popular Brazilian sweets—brigadeiros included. Every cook has condensed milk stashed in the pantry. Most likely it's a can of Nestlé's Leite Moça ("the lady's milk"), Brazil's favorite brand since 1922.

chocolate brigadeiros

Like many Brazilian sweets, brigadeiros are named after a famous personality. Brigadier Eduardo Gomes was a well-known Brazilian Air Force commander who loved chocolate. Legend has it that chocolate brigadeiros were created for and named after him.

Yields about 3 dozen

- 1 14-oz. can sweetened condensed milk
- 2 Tbs. unsalted butter
- 2 Tbs. heavy cream
- 1 tsp. light corn syrup
- 1½ oz. semisweet or bittersweet chocolate (preferably 60% to 62% cacao), chopped
- 1 tsp. Dutch-processed cocoa powder
- 1 cup chocolate sprinkles (preferably Guittard)

Put the condensed milk, butter, cream, and corn syrup in a 3-quart heavy-duty saucepan and bring to a boil over medium heat, whisking constantly. Add the chocolate and cocoa powder and continue to whisk, making sure there are no pockets of cocoa powder. As soon as the mixture comes back to a boil, turn the heat to medium low and cook, whisking constantly, until the mixture thickens and pulls together into a dense, fudgy batter, about 8 minutes. When the mixture is ready, the whisk will leave trails in the batter, allowing you to briefly see the pan bottom, and when you tilt the pan, the mixture should slide to the side in a blob, leaving a thick residue on the bottom of the pan.

Slide the mixture into a bowl. (Don't scrape the pan—you don't want to use any of the batter stuck to the bottom.) Let the mixture cool to room temperature and then refrigerate uncovered until very firm, 3 to 4 hours.

Put the sprinkles in a bowl. Using a teaspoon or a melon baller, scoop the mixture by the teaspoonful, and with your hands, roll each into a ball about 1 inch in diameter. Drop each ball into the sprinkles as you finish rolling it. When you have 4 to 6 brigadeiros, toss them in the sprinkles to coat. You may need to exert a little pressure to ensure that the sprinkles stick.

Make them last

Store brigadeiros in a tightly covered container at room temperature for up to two days or in the refrigerator for up to two weeks. (If refrigerating, bring to room temperature before serving for the best flavor and texture.)

pistachio brigadeiros

Yields about 3 dozen

- 1   **14-oz. can sweetened condensed milk**
- ⅔   **cup heavy cream**
- ½   **cup plus 2 Tbs. finely ground pistachios**
- 2   **tsp. light corn syrup**
- 1   **tsp. unsalted butter**

Put the condensed milk, cream, 6 Tbs. ground pistachios, corn syrup, and butter in a 3-quart heavy-duty saucepan and bring to a boil over medium heat. Turn the heat to medium low, and cook, whisking constantly, until the mixture thickens and pulls together into a dense batter, about 12 minutes. When the mixture is ready, the whisk will leave trails in the batter, allowing you to briefly see the pan bottom, and when you tilt the pan, the mixture should slide to the side in a blob, leaving a thick residue on the bottom of the pan.

Slide the mixture into a bowl. (Don't scrape the pan—you don't want to use any of the batter stuck to the bottom.) Let the mixture cool to room temperature and then refrigerate until very firm, 3 to 4 hours.

Put the remaining ¼ cup ground pistachios in a bowl. Using a teaspoon or a melon baller, scoop the mixture by the teaspoonful, and with your hands, roll each into a ball about 1 inch in diameter. Drop each ball into the pistachios as you finish rolling it. When you have 4 to 6 brigadeiros, roll them in the pistachios and lift them out with your fingers semi-open, carefully shaking off the excess. If the pistachios don't stick to the outside, re-warm the balls by rolling them briefly between your hands and then try to coat them again.

coconut brigadeiros

Yields about 3 dozen

- 1   **cup sweetened condensed milk**
- ½   **cup coconut milk**
- 2   **Tbs. unsalted butter**
- 2   **tsp. light corn syrup**
- 1   **cup finely shredded, unsweetened coconut (toasted, if desired)**

Put the condensed milk, coconut milk, butter, corn syrup, and ½ cup of the coconut in a 3-quart heavy-duty saucepan and bring to a boil over medium heat. Turn the heat to medium low and cook, whisking constantly, until the mixture thickens and pulls together into a dense batter, about 8 minutes. When the mixture is ready, the whisk will leave trails in the batter, allowing you to briefly see the pan bottom, and when you tilt the pan, the mixture should slide to the side in a blob, leaving a thick residue on the bottom of the pan. (It's OK if the residue is slightly brown.)

Slide the mixture into a bowl. (Don't scrape the pan—you don't want to use any of the batter stuck to the bottom.) Let the mixture cool to room temperature and then refrigerate until very firm, 3 to 4 hours.

Put the remaining ½ cup coconut in a bowl. Using a teaspoon or a melon baller, scoop the mixture by the teaspoonful, and with your hands, roll each into a ball about 1 inch in diameter. Drop each ball into the coconut as you finish rolling it. When you have 4 to 6 brigadeiros, roll them in the coconut and lift them out with your fingers semi-open, carefully shaking off the excess.

Note: If you can't find finely shredded unsweetened coconut, you can buy coconut chips or flaked coconut and run it through a food processor until it looks like it was grated on the smallest holes of a box grater. Be sure it's unsweetened, or the brigadeiros will be much too sweet. If you're feeling adventurous, you can also buy a fresh coconut and crack and grate it yourself. See Test Kitchen, p. 77, to learn how.

Leticia Moreinos is a cooking teacher based in Weston, Connecticut. To get information on her classes, see page 89. ◻

RED-WINE-BRAISED BRISKET WITH
CREMINI, CARROTS, AND THYME

RIGATONI WITH
BRISKET AND
PORCINI RAGÙ

BRISKET AND
ROOT VEGETABLE
SALAD WITH
HORSERADISH
DRESSING

BRISKET AND
BEAN CHILI

Brisket
the real deal

An authentic, tried-and-true
recipe, plus three delicious ways
to use it up. BY JOYCE GOLDSTEIN

IT'S A FUNNY THING ABOUT BRISKET. Because I've
taught cooking for so long and have written a few Jewish
cookbooks, perfect strangers find me online or in the
phone book and call me at home with brisket questions.
I usually get these calls at Passover, just before the first
Seder. There are questions about timing, slicing, and
reheating, about tenderness, fat, tomatoes or not, about
how far in advance the brisket can be prepared. I don't
know these callers, but because they sound so stressed,
I answer their questions. The brisket doctor is in.

OK, so I'm not really a doctor. But I *have* been making
brisket for many years, so I've got pretty strong opinions
on how it should be made. While some cooks like to get
creative with their ingredients, flavoring their brisket with
anything from chili sauce to cranberry juice, I think the
best brisket is cooked the way my family has always done
it—with tons of onions, a little tomato, red wine, mushrooms, and carrots. It's a simple yet classic combination.

That simplicity also makes the leftovers (you'll have
lots of them) easy to transform into other delicious and
unexpected dishes later in the week. Combine brisket
with tomatoes, beans, and spices, and you've got a rich,
spicy chili; add some wine, porcini, and rigatoni, and you
have a hearty pasta dish; and brisket plus root vegetables, fresh herbs, and a creamy dressing add up to a fresh
spring salad—my prescription for easy weeknight meals.

MASTER RECIPE

red-wine-braised brisket with cremini, carrots, and thyme

To get a jump start on this recipe, you can season the brisket up to 1 day ahead.

Serves 12 (or 4 to 6 with enough leftovers to make 2 or 3 of the recipes that follow)

2	Tbs. sweet paprika
	Kosher salt and freshly ground black pepper
8½	to 9 lb. beef brisket (whole brisket or flat and/or point halves; see Test Kitchen, p. 77, for more information), untrimmed of fat
5	Tbs. vegetable oil
6	large yellow onions, diced (about 12 cups)
3	to 4 cloves garlic, thinly sliced
1	15-oz. can tomato purée
1	cup dry red wine
4	large sprigs fresh thyme
8	large carrots, cut into 2-inch pieces
10	oz. cremini or white button mushrooms, quartered if large, halved if small (3 cups)

In a small bowl, combine the paprika, 1 Tbs. salt, and 1 Tbs. pepper. Rub the mixture all over the brisket. Let rest at room temperature for two hours or cover and refrigerate overnight (bring the meat to room temperature before cooking).

Position a rack in the center of the oven and heat the oven to 350°F.

Meanwhile, heat the oil in a large pot over medium heat. Add the onions and garlic and cook, stirring occasionally, until very soft and pale gold, 15 to 20 minutes. Transfer the onions to a large heavy-duty roasting pan and spread them in an even layer. Set the brisket fat side up on the onions (it's OK if the pieces overlap), cover tightly with heavy-duty foil (or a double layer of regular foil), and braise in the oven for 1 hour. As the brisket cooks, it will give off quite a bit of liquid.

Pour the tomato purée and wine around the brisket and add the thyme sprigs. Cover and continue to braise the meat for 2½ hours.

Add the carrots and mushrooms and continue to braise, covered, until the meat is fork-tender, about 1 hour more.

Transfer the meat to a cutting board and trim the fat. If using a whole brisket or a point half, separate the two layers of meat and trim the fat. With a slotted spoon, move the vegetables to a serving bowl.

Skim the excess fat from the pan juices, strain 2 cups of the juices, and bring to a boil in a small saucepan over medium-high heat. Boil until reduced to about 1 cup; the sauce should be rich and flavorful. Season to taste with salt and pepper.

Slice as much brisket across the grain as you need for the meal and serve with the vegetables and reduced sauce. Wrap the leftover brisket, vegetables, and juices separately. Leftovers will keep in the fridge for 3 to 4 days, or in the freezer for up to 2 months.

Serving suggestion: Serve with potato pancakes (see FineCooking.com for a recipe) or mashed potatoes, and offer hot mustard, horseradish (or the horseradish sauce for the salad on p. 60), and applesauce at the table.

Food styling by Susan Sugarman

Photographs by Scott Phillips

Though this recipe calls for dried pasta, you can also use any shape of fresh pasta. Once you've drained it, just toss it with a few tablespoons of butter to prevent it from sticking together.

Serves 6

1 oz. dried porcini mushrooms (1 cup)
3 Tbs. extra-virgin olive oil
4 oz. pancetta, chopped (1 cup)
1 large celery stalk, chopped
1 large carrot, chopped
1 large yellow onion, chopped
 Kosher salt
3 large cloves garlic, minced
4 cups coarsely chopped leftover brisket (about 1 lb.; recipe opposite), plus 2 cups leftover brisket juices
2 cups dry red wine; more as needed
2 tsp. chopped fresh thyme
 Freshly ground black pepper
1 lb. dried rigatoni
 Freshly grated Parmigiano-Reggiano, for serving

Soak the porcini in 1 cup hot water for 30 minutes. Drain, straining and reserving the soaking liquid. Chop the porcini and set aside.

Heat the oil in an 11- to 12-inch straight-sided sauté pan over medium heat. Add the pancetta, celery, carrot, onion, and 1 tsp. salt; cook, stirring often, until the vegetables are soft and lightly golden, about 15 minutes. Add the garlic and cook, stirring, for 1 minute. Add the brisket and its juices, wine, thyme, and the porcini and their soaking liquid. Bring to a simmer, reduce the heat to low, and cook until the sauce is very thick, about 30 minutes. Season to taste with salt and pepper.

Meanwhile, bring a large pot of well-salted water to a boil. Cook the pasta in the boiling water until al dente. Drain and toss with most of the meat sauce. Top with the remaining sauce and pass the Parmigiano at the table.

TIP

no browning necessary

Some cooks brown their brisket before braising, but I don't—I've tasted it both ways and haven't noticed much of a flavor difference. Plus, without browning, the meat is more tender and easier to slice.

brisket and root vegetable salad with creamy horseradish dressing

Meat from the flat end of the brisket is best for this dish because it holds its shape better than brisket point. (For more information, see Test Kitchen, p. 77). Leave the brisket in long slices or cut it into wide strips, and be sure it's at room temperature so it won't be too dense.

Serves 4

4	small golden or red beets (about 2½ inches wide)
8	small red potatoes (about 2½ inches wide)
	Kosher salt
½	cup sour cream
¼	cup drained prepared horseradish
1	Tbs. distilled white vinegar; more as needed
½	medium tart apple, peeled, cored, and minced
2	Tbs. minced white onion (optional)
	Freshly ground black pepper
1	medium bulb fennel, cored and very thinly sliced or shaved with a mandoline or vegetable peeler (about 2½ cups; see Test Kitchen, p. 77, for more information)
½	cup fresh flat-leaf parsley leaves
1	Tbs. extra-virgin olive oil
16	thin slices leftover brisket (recipe, p. 58), at room temperature

Cut the tails and leaves from the beets but leave about 1 inch of the stems attached. Wash well and put them in a 2-quart saucepan with enough cold water to cover. Bring to a boil over high heat, reduce the heat to medium low, and simmer until tender when pierced with a skewer, 30 to 35 minutes. Drain and rinse with cold water to cool. When cool enough to handle, slip off the peels. Slice the beets ¼ inch thick.

While the beets cook, put the potatoes in a 4-quart saucepan with enough water to cover and 1 Tbs. salt. Bring to a boil over high heat, reduce the heat to medium low, and simmer until the potatoes are tender when pierced with a skewer, 20 to 25 minutes. Drain and rinse with cold water to cool. When cool enough to handle, peel and slice ¼ inch thick.

In a small bowl, whisk the sour cream, horseradish, and vinegar. Mix in the apple and onion, if using. Season to taste with salt, pepper, and vinegar.

In a medium bowl, toss the fennel and parsley with 2 Tbs. of the horseradish dressing, the olive oil, ¼ tsp. salt, and a pinch of pepper.

Arrange the brisket, potatoes, and beets on 4 large plates. Sprinkle lightly with salt and drizzle with some of the dressing. Pile the fennel on top and serve the remaining dressing on the side.

brisket and bean chili

Chunks of leftover brisket make this chili much more interesting than one made with ground beef. If you don't have time to cook beans, skip that step and use 3 cups drained and rinsed canned beans instead.

Serves 4 to 6

FOR THE BEANS

- 1 cup dried pinto or kidney beans
- 1 large yellow onion, chopped
- 2 large cloves garlic, minced
- 1 tsp. dried oregano
  Kosher salt

FOR THE CHILI

- 3 Tbs. olive oil
- 2 large yellow onions, chopped
- 4 large cloves garlic, minced
- 3 Tbs. ancho chile powder (see note)
- 1 Tbs. dried oregano
- 1 Tbs. ground cumin
- ¼ tsp. cayenne
  Kosher salt and freshly ground black pepper
- 1 28-oz. can diced tomatoes
- 1 12-oz. bottle lager beer (such as Corona)
- 1 6-oz. can tomato paste
- 1 lb. leftover brisket (recipe, p. 58), cut into ½-inch dice (about 4 cups), plus 1½ cups leftover brisket juices
  Dash balsamic or red wine vinegar (optional)

PREPARE THE BEANS

In a medium bowl, soak the beans in enough water to cover by at least 2 inches, and refrigerate overnight.

Drain the beans and put them in a medium saucepan. Cover with fresh cold water by about 1 inch. Add the onion, garlic, and oregano. Bring to a boil over high heat, lower the heat to a simmer, and cook for 30 minutes. Add 1 tsp. salt and continue to simmer until tender, about 30 minutes more. Drain and set aside.

MAKE THE CHILI

Heat the oil in a heavy-duty 6-quart pot over medium heat. Add the onions and cook, stirring occasionally, until soft and pale gold, about 15 minutes. Add the garlic, chile powder, oregano, cumin, cayenne, 1 tsp. salt, and 1 tsp. black pepper and cook for 1 to 2 minutes. Stir in the tomatoes and their juices, beer, and tomato paste.

Add the brisket and its juices, bring to a boil and then reduce the heat to low. Simmer, covered, until the meat is meltingly tender and the sauce is flavorful, about 30 minutes. Season to taste with salt, pepper, and vinegar, if the chili needs some acidity for balance.

Serve the beans on the side, or stir them into the chili and simmer for about 15 minutes before serving.

Serving suggestion: The garnishes are half the fun. Serve with warm corn tortillas, sour cream, sliced avocado, salsa, and minced onion and cilantro. If you're not from Texas, you may want to serve rice with the chili.

Note: If you can't find ground ancho chile powder, use regular chili powder instead and reduce the oregano and cumin to 1½ tsp. each. Add cayenne to taste.

Joyce Goldstein is the former chef-owner of San Francisco's Square One restaurant. Her latest book, Tapas: Sensational Small Plates from Spain, *is due out this spring.* ◻

SANDWICH MEETS GRILL

Pressed for time?
A few fresh ingredients
plus good bread make
a fast and easy dinner.

BY LAUREN CHATTMAN

If you think a sandwich is a step
down from dinner, think again. Taking their inspiration from everyone's
favorites—but taking them quite
a bit further—these fast and easy
recipes make the most of ingredients
you likely have on hand (bacon, tuna,
turkey). Add a fresh ingredient or
two (spinach, tomato, mushrooms)
and then cheese (mozzarella, sharp
Cheddar, provolone) for the "melt"
effect. In the few minutes it takes to
heat up a panini press or grill pan,
you're ready to go, and then dinner's
just minutes from done.

Grilled Mozzarella and Spinach BLT

grilled portobello and goat cheese sandwiches with green olive pesto

The earthy flavor of the portobellos goes well with the mild, tangy goat cheese and salty olive pesto.

Serves 4

- 1 cup tightly packed fresh basil leaves
- ½ cup pitted green olives, such as manzanilla, coarsely chopped
- 1 Tbs. walnuts or pine nuts
- 1 small clove garlic, coarsely chopped
- ½ cup plus 2 tsp. extra-virgin olive oil
  Kosher salt and freshly ground black pepper
- 8 small to medium portobello mushrooms, stemmed, gills removed, and wiped clean
- 4 soft round rolls, such as Portuguese or kaiser, split in half
- 4 oz. fresh goat cheese, crumbled

Heat a panini or sandwich press according to the manufacturer's instructions. (Alternatively, heat a nonstick grill pan over medium-high heat.)

While the press is heating, put the basil, olives, nuts, and garlic in a food processor and process until finely chopped. With the motor running, add 6 Tbs. of the olive oil in a slow, steady stream through the feed tube and continue to process until thick and smooth. Season to taste with salt and pepper.

Brush the mushrooms with 2 Tbs. of the olive oil and sprinkle with salt and pepper. Put them on the press, pull the top down, and cook until softened and browned, 3 to 5 minutes (or cook in the grill pan, flipping once). Transfer to a plate and let cool slightly.

Spread the pesto on the bottom halves of the rolls. Put 2 mushrooms on each and then some cheese. Top the sandwiches with the other halves of the rolls. Brush both sides of the sandwiches with the remaining 2 tsp. oil.

Put the sandwiches on the press pesto side up, pull the top down, and cook until browned and crisp and the cheese is melted, 5 to 7 minutes, depending on how hot your machine is. (If using a grill pan, put a heavy pan on top of the sandwiches and cook, turning the sandwiches over once.) Carefully remove from the press and serve.

grilled mozzarella and spinach blts

Creamy mozzarella is a good foil for the salty, smoky bacon in this grilled version of a BLT. Before cooking, remove any tough stems from the spinach.

Serves 4

- 12 slices thick-cut bacon
- 1 medium clove garlic, finely chopped
- 3 cups lightly packed baby spinach
  Kosher salt and freshly ground black pepper
- 8 slices country-style white bread
- 8 oz. fresh mozzarella, sliced
- 1 large tomato (about 8 oz.), cored and thinly sliced
- 1 Tbs. extra-virgin olive oil

Working in batches, cook the bacon in a 12-inch skillet over medium heat until crisp, about 8 minutes per batch. Transfer to a paper-towel-lined plate and drain off all but 1 Tbs. of the fat. Return the pan to medium heat, add the garlic, and cook until fragrant, about 30 seconds. Stir in the spinach and cook until just wilted, about 30 seconds longer. Season to taste with salt and pepper.

Heat a panini or sandwich press according to the manufacturer's instructions. (Alternatively, heat a nonstick grill pan over medium-high heat.)

While the press is heating, arrange the spinach on 4 pieces of the bread. Top each with some bacon, mozzarella, and tomato, sprinkle lightly with salt, and complete each sandwich with a slice of the remaining bread. Brush both sides of the sandwiches with the oil.

Put the sandwiches on the press, pull the top down, and cook until browned and crisp and the cheese is melted, 3 to 6 minutes, depending on how hot your machine is. (If using a grill pan, put a heavy pan on top of the sandwiches and cook, turning the sandwiches over once.) Carefully remove from the press and serve.

Grilled Portobello and Goat Cheese
Sandwich with Green Olive Pesto

grilled tuna and provolone sandwiches with salsa verde

For this recipe, steer clear of tuna packed in water; instead, choose good-quality tuna packed in olive oil.

Serves 4

- ½ cup packed fresh flat-leaf parsley leaves
- ¼ cup plus 2 tsp. extra-virgin olive oil
- 2 Tbs. fresh lemon juice
- 1 Tbs. capers, drained and rinsed
- 1 small clove garlic, chopped
- 1 anchovy fillet, rinsed and chopped
  Freshly ground black pepper
- 8 thin slices provolone (about 4 oz.)

- 4 4-inch squares focaccia (or substitute any soft roll), split in half
- 12 oz. tuna packed in olive oil, drained well

Heat a panini or sandwich press according to the manufacturer's instructions. (Alternatively, heat a nonstick grill pan over medium-high heat.)

While the press is heating, combine the parsley, ¼ cup of the olive oil, lemon juice, capers, garlic, anchovy, and a few grinds of pepper in a blender and blend until smooth.

Lay the cheese on the bottoms of the focaccia. Spoon the tuna over the cheese.

Spread some of the salsa verde over the inside tops of the focaccia and put the tops on the sandwiches salsa verde side down. Brush both sides of the sandwiches with the remaining 2 tsp. oil.

Put the sandwiches on the press salsa verde side up, pull the top down, and cook until browned and crisp and the cheese is melted, 5 to 7 minutes, depending on how hot your machine is. (If using a grill pan, put a heavy pan on top of the sandwiches and cook, turning the sandwiches over once.) Carefully remove from the press and serve.

grilled turkey and cheddar sandwiches with mango chutney

Naan is slightly puffy Indian-style flatbread. Other substantial flatbreads may be substituted, but avoid super-thin tortillas and lavash, which won't be sturdy enough to contain the filling. Major Grey's chutney, available in the condiment or Indian foods section of the supermarket, adds moisture, sweetness, and spice.

Serves 4

2	cups grated sharp Cheddar
¼	cup finely chopped fresh cilantro
½	cup Major Grey's mango chutney
4	naan breads
12	oz. sliced turkey breast
1	Tbs. unsalted butter, melted
⅛	tsp. ground cumin

No pan, no problem

If you don't have a panini or sandwich press, you can use a nonstick grill pan or skillet. Put a heavy pan on top of the sandwiches as they cook to press them, and flip once.

Heat a panini or sandwich press according to the manufacturer's instructions. (Alternatively, heat a nonstick grill pan over medium-high heat.)

While the press is heating, combine the cheese and cilantro in a small bowl and stir until well blended. Spread the chutney on one half of each of the naan breads. Top with the turkey. Spoon the cheese mixture over the turkey. Fold the naan in half to cover the sandwich filling. Combine the melted butter and cumin; brush on both sides of the sandwiches.

Put the sandwiches on the press, pull the top down, and cook until browned and crisp, 3 to 6 minutes, depending on how hot your machine is. (If using a grill pan, put a heavy pan on top of the sandwiches and cook, turning the sandwiches over once.) Carefully remove from the press and serve.

Lauren Chattman is the coauthor of Panini Express: 70 Delicious Recipes, Hot off the Press. ◘

Homemade Sausage

Embrace your inner butcher and learn how to grind, season, and stuff your own. BY ADAM KAYE

WHAT COULD BE MORE SATISFYING than biting into a juicy, meaty, perfectly seasoned sausage that you've made with your own two hands? The good news is that sausage-making is simple and fun. High-quality ingredients like sustainably raised meat are widely available, and online purveyors sell everything from seasonings to natural hog casings. With a little know-how and a home meat grinder and stuffer (see Test Drive, page 30), avid carnivores can make impressive butcher-shop-quality links right in their own kitchens. And we're going to show you how.

Photographs by Scott Phillips

Sage and Red Wine Pork Sausage, recipe page 70

sage and red wine pork sausage

For information about fat back, see Test Kitchen, p. 77; to buy a meat grinder, see Test Drive, p. 30.

Yields about 5 lb.

4½	lb. boneless pork butt
1	lb. pork fat back
1	oz. kosher salt (4 Tbs. Diamond Crystal brand or 2 Tbs. Morton brand)
2¼	tsp. fresh finely ground black pepper
1½	tsp. minced garlic
¼	cup chopped fresh sage
½	cup dry red wine, such as Cabernet Sauvignon, Chianti, or Merlot
12	feet small hog casings (32 to 35 mm diameter), cut into three 4-foot pieces (optional); see Where to Buy It, p. 89

MAKE THE SAUSAGE

Trim and discard any gristle or connective tissue from the pork. Cut the pork and pork fat back into 1-inch cubes **1**. Spread in an even layer on a rimmed baking sheet and put in the freezer, uncovered, until very cold (partially frozen on the edges but still soft in the center), about 1 hour **2**. Meanwhile, chill a large mixing bowl and the blade and ¼-inch grinding plate from your meat grinder.

Set up the meat grinder with the chilled parts according to manufacturer's instructions. Grind the pork and the fat together into the chilled bowl. The mixture should come off the grinder cleanly, and the fat should not appear warm or smeared **3**. If smearing occurs, return the meat and fat to the freezer until very cold.

Tricks of the trade

- **Chill out.** Keep the ingredients and equipment cold at all times. Partially freeze the meat and fat before you grind and mix to avoid "smearing" through the grinder, which yields a greasy, grainy-textured sausage.
- **Use your hands.** One of the many joys of sausage-making is the tactile experience of the process. Your hands make the best mixing tools, but be careful to use a light touch so you don't

overwork or overheat the sausage mixture.

- **The choice is yours.** One of the best things about this recipe is that you can shape the sausage mixture into patties, or you can stuff it into casings to make links.
- **Make room.** If stuffing, set up your sausage stuffer on a countertop or table with ample space so the sausages don't slide off the counter as you stuff them.

- **Stuff it.** Make sure the sausage mixture moves through the stuffer quickly enough to fill the casings firmly, but not so fast that they burst. Practice makes perfect.
- **Air dry.** Let fresh sausage links rest on a wire rack in the refrigerator for 24 hours before cooking or storing to allow the flavors to develop and the casings to dry out a bit (this produces the "snap" that you get when you bite into a great sausage).

In a small bowl, mix the salt, pepper, garlic, and sage. Add the seasonings and the wine to the ground meat and mix briefly but thoroughly with your hands. Don't overmix, or the fat could begin to melt **4**.

To taste for seasoning, make a small patty of the sausage mixture and cook it in a small skillet over medium-low heat **5**. Taste and adjust the seasoning to your liking. If not shaping the sausages immediately, refrigerate until you're ready to proceed.

SHAPE THE SAUSAGE: You can make patties, links, or some of both.

To make sausage patties, use your hands to shape the patties about 2½ to 3 inches in diameter and ¾ inch thick **6**. For cooking information, see p. 75; storage, p. 73.

To make links, turn the page.

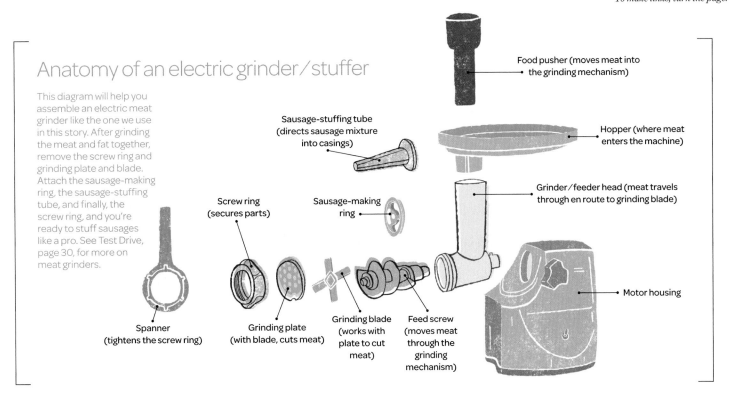

Anatomy of an electric grinder/stuffer

This diagram will help you assemble an electric meat grinder like the one we use in this story. After grinding the meat and fat together, remove the screw ring and grinding plate and blade. Attach the sausage-making ring, the sausage-stuffing tube, and finally, the screw ring, and you're ready to stuff sausages like a pro. See Test Drive, page 30, for more on meat grinders.

Food pusher (moves meat into the grinding mechanism)

Sausage-stuffing tube (directs sausage mixture into casings)

Hopper (where meat enters the machine)

Screw ring (secures parts)

Sausage-making ring

Grinder/feeder head (meat travels through en route to grinding blade)

Spanner (tightens the screw ring)

Grinding plate (with blade, cuts meat)

Grinding blade (works with plate to cut meat)

Feed screw (moves meat through the grinding mechanism)

Motor housing

To make sausage links, put the casings in a medium bowl and set it in the sink. Rinse the casings under cool running water: Hold one end of each piece of casing open under the tap and flush it out by gently running cool water through it **7**. (Once you fill part of the casing, use your hands to push the water through to other end.) Fill the bowl with fresh, cool water and let the casings soak for 10 minutes.

Attach a ⅝- or ¾-inch sausage-stuffing tube to the front of your grinder or to a sausage stuffer. (If using a grinder with a stuffing attachment, be sure to remove the grinding plate and blade first.) Splash cool water onto the tube to moisten it. Open an end of one piece of casing and pull it over the end of the tube. Push the rest of the casing onto the tube accordion-style, leaving 3 or 4 inches hanging off the end.

Fill the hopper with the sausage mixture and feed it through just until it reaches the end of the stuffing tube. Check with your finger to feel if the meat is flush with the opening. Tie the end of the attached casing into a knot, and slide it up over the tube until the knot hits the tip of the tube **8**.

Continue to feed the meat mixture through the tube to fill the casing, pressing your thumb and forefinger against the tip of the tube to control the rate and tightness of the filling **9**. Go slowly, don't overstuff (but do stuff firmly), and watch for air holes. When there are only 3 to 4 inches of empty casing left, stop the feeder, slip the casing off the tube and tie it in a knot about ½ inch from the end of the sausage filling—this extra space will fill in as you make links.

A sausage maker's tool kit

Sharp chef's knife

Mixing bowls (1 small, 1 medium, 1 large)

Cast-iron skillet

10

11

12

Use a skewer or toothpick to prick any air holes that have formed during stuffing 10. Repeat with the remaining casings and sausage mixture.

To make links, lay one sausage at a time on a clean work surface, with the front end of the sausage (the end where you began filling) in front of you and the rest of the sausage lying to the right. Measure 5 inches from left to right and pinch the casing at that spot between your thumb and forefinger. Twist the unlinked portion away from you at least 4 or 5 turns to bind off the link on the left. Measure another 5 inches and pinch and twist away from you to form another link. Repeat until you reach the end of the casing, always twisting in the same direction 11. Prick any remaining air holes.

Lay the links, uncovered, on a rack set over a rimmed baking sheet 12. Dry in the refrigerator for 24 hours to allow the flavors to meld and to give the casings a good bite when cooked. Drying will also reduce the amount of moisture in the meat, too much of which can steam and lead to bursting. For cooking information, see p. 75.

How to store: After drying, **sausage links** can be stored, covered, in the refrigerator for up to 2 days. Wrap **sausage patties** individually or separate them between squares of parchment or wax paper. Wrap well in plastic and refrigerate for up to 3 days. Both links and patties may be frozen for up to 3 months. Frozen sausages should be thawed overnight in the refrigerator prior to cooking.

tip: keeping casings

- Natural sausage casings come packed in salt or covered in brine. To store left-over salt-packed casings, squeeze out as much water as possible, and when fairly dry, cover them generously with kosher salt and refrigerate—they'll last for up to a year this way.
- Brined casings will keep in their brine for up to six months in the refrigerator.
- Whatever you do, don't freeze the casings—they'll break down and tear during stuffing.

Wood skewer

Ruler

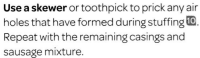

Large rimmed baking sheet

Wire rack

For sources, see Where to Buy It

Variations

The basic recipe takes on new flavors with a few ingredient substitutions.

Spicy Fennel Sausage
To add a bit of heat and that classic sausage flavor partner, fennel, omit the sage and add 2¼ tsp. fennel seeds, lightly crushed, and 2½ tsp. crushed red pepper flakes.

Apple and Madeira Sausage
For a sweet and savory combination, replace the red wine with Madeira (or another fortified wine like sherry) and add 1 cup finely chopped dried apple.

Smoked Paprika and Thyme Sausage
For a warm, smoky touch, omit the sage and add 2 Tbs. chopped fresh thyme, 2 tsp. ground cumin, and 1½ tsp. pimentón (smoked paprika).

Adam Kaye is chef and kitchen director at Blue Hill at Stone Barns in Pocantico Hills, New York, where he makes sausages every day. ◻

To sauté sausages, heat 2 tsp. oil in a large, preferably cast-iron, skillet over medium heat. Cook, turning as needed, until browned and cooked through, about 8 minutes for patties and 12 minutes for links.

TEST KITCHEN

Tips/Techniques/Equipment/Ingredients/Glossary

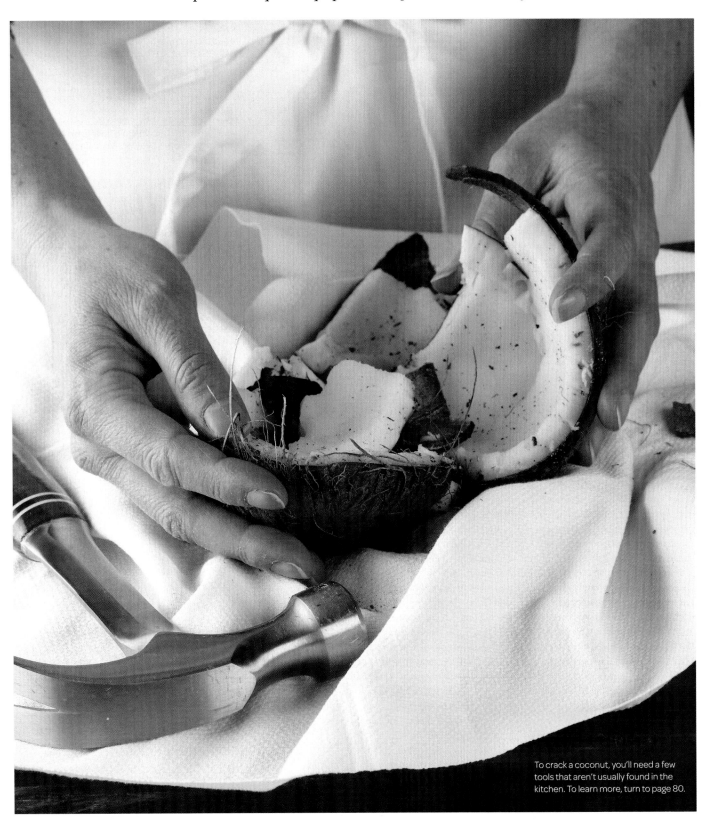

To crack a coconut, you'll need a few tools that aren't usually found in the kitchen. To learn more, turn to page 80.

Why Parmigiano-Reggiano?

HAVE YOU EVER WONDERED what distinguishes Parmigiano-Reggiano from Parmesan cheese? Genuine Parmigiano-Reggiano is made only in the Emilia-Romagna region of northern Italy, following stringent guidelines. The milk used to make the cheese comes from cows that spend most of their days grazing in grassy meadows. The farmers pay special attention to their animals, knowing that their reward will be a truly unique cheese, with an unrivaled texture and nutty taste. Each wheel is aged for at least 12 months before the Parmigiano-Reggiano stamp is imprinted on its rind and it's ready for the market.

Parmigiano-Reggiano is one of the most copied cheeses on the market, its imitators being Parmesan cheeses. These cheeses tend to be salt laden and mass produced from the milk of penned-in, grain-fed cows. There are no guidelines or rules to guarantee quality, and the cheese is often sold already grated or shredded.

Because Parmigiano-Reggiano is far superior, we make a point of calling for the genuine item in our recipes. We also recommend that you purchase a chunk of the cheese and grate it freshly yourself, rather than buying it already grated. When you buy pre-grated cheese, you have no way of knowing how long ago it was grated, and as the grated cheese sits, it loses moisture and flavor, eventually tasting more like sawdust than cheese. Grating the cheese yourself is well worth the small effort—the cheese will have more flavor and nuance, and your food will taste better for it.

—*Melissa Pellegrino*

How to Buy a Chicken

If you want the best-tasting, most humanely raised chicken with no unnatural additives, look for one or more of these labels on the wrapping:

Best bet

USDA Organic Certified The official organic seal means the chicken was raised under a specific set of humane guidelines, including requirements for shelter and an organic diet without antibiotics or synthetic pesticides.

Next best

No Antibiotics Used These chickens are not necessarily organic, but they have been raised without antibiotics of any kind.

Certified Humane Chickens with the Humane Farm Animal Care seal meet requirements for humane treatment, which include access to clean water, no antibiotics, and no cages.

Pastured Poultry or "Grass-Ranged" Poultry This term is most often used to label chickens that have been raised on small farms in un-crowded conditions and been allowed to feed on grass in addition to grain.

Keep an eye out for

Air-Chilled Most chickens are chilled in water, but a new process called air-chilling prevents them from absorbing excess water, which can mean a tastier, crispier bird. There are brands that are both air-chilled and certified organic.

Kosher Kosher chickens are slaughtered according to Jewish dietary laws. The process includes brining the chicken in a salt solution, which not only removes any remaining blood and bacteria but enhances flavor as well. There are brands that are both kosher and organic.

Don't be fooled by

100 % Natural This means nothing. Many of these birds are injected with saline solution to add weight. They may also contain "natural" additives, such as carrageenan, broth, tenderizers, or marinades.

Hormone-Free All chickens are hormone-free because the use of hormones in poultry is prohibited by law.

Cage-Free The birds may still be tightly packed into sheds without room to move, access to the outdoors, or clean surroundings.

Free-Range This popular label does not mean much other than the birds are "allowed" to wander outside the barn for a few short weeks of their lives.

—*Susie Middleton*

How to carve a roast chicken

There's more than one way to carve a roast chicken, but this technique is our favorite because it gives you boneless breast meat that you can slice across the grain, if you like.

FIRST THE LEGS
Forcefully bend a leg away from the body until the joint pops apart.

Use a sharp boning knife to sever the leg from the body, cutting through the joint. As you separate the leg, be sure to get the "oyster," a tasty nugget of meat toward the back of the chicken just above the thigh.

Separate the drumstick from the thigh by cutting through the joint. It should be fairly easy to cut through—if the knife meets resistance, reposition it slightly and try again.

THEN THE BREAST
Begin separating one side of the breast from the body by cutting along the breast bone with the tip of your boning knife.

When you reach the wishbone, angle the knife and cut down along the wishbone. Then cut down through the wing joint. Finish separating the breast by pulling back on the meat and using little flicks of the knife tip to cut the meat away.

Cut the wings from the breast. Trim off the wing tips, if you like. Slice the breast crosswise, in half, or in thin slices.
—*Jennifer Armentrout*

TECHNIQUE

Cracking a coconut

IF YOUR SUPERMARKET is anything like ours, the baking aisle offers lots of choices for sweetened shredded coconut. Unsweetened coconut, which you'll need if you're making the Coconut Brigadeiros on page 55, is harder to find—check health food stores, or consider starting with a fresh coconut from the produce section.

It does take more effort to crack and grate a coconut yourself, but you will be rewarded with great flavor. Choose one that's heavy for its size. Its three eyes should be dry, and it should slosh when shaken. Avoid coconuts that are gray in color or that show wet staining, a sign that the shell is deeply cracked. A cracked outer shell is fine as long as the coconut sloshes and doesn't look wet. To get cracking, follow the steps at right.

TIPS

How to toast and store coconut

Spread grated coconut on a baking sheet and toast in a 350°F oven until it's a rich golden-brown, 5 to 10 minutes. Stir every few minutes so the coconut toasts evenly, and watch carefully, as it can go from toasted to burnt very quickly. Cool on the baking sheet before using.

Grated coconut keeps in the refrigerator for about one week, or in the freezer for about three months.

1 With a Phillips screwdriver, probe the eyes until you find the one that yields easily. Push the screwdriver into this eye until you reach the liquid. Then pull it out and shake the coconut juice into a cup. You can drink the juice or discard it.

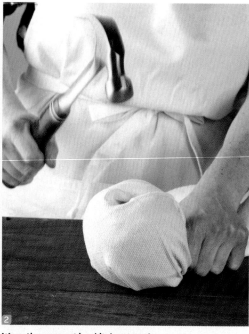

2 Wrap the coconut in a kitchen towel, set it on a sturdy surface, and bash it with a hammer until it cracks into several pieces.

3 With a regular screwdriver or an oyster knife, pry the coconut meat from the shells. If any pieces resist, bake them at 350°F for 10 to 15 minutes; they should then separate easily.

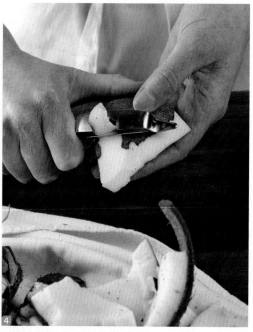

4 With a vegetable peeler, remove the brown skin from each piece of coconut. Now you're ready to grate the coconut. Use a box grater if you're up for a little arm workout, or a food processor if not.

—*Jennifer Armentrout*

The whole brisket

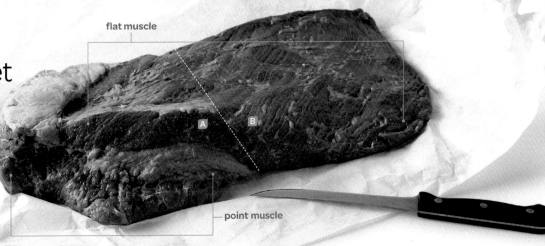

flat muscle

point muscle

WEIGHING IN AT ANYWHERE from 8 to 16 pounds, a whole brisket is a jumbo cut of meat. Brisket, which comes from the breast of the cow, comprises two distinct muscles: the flat muscle and the point muscle. The **flat muscle**, as its name implies, is flat, wide, and fairly lean; it tapers at one end. At that tapered end, separated by a thick layer of fat, the flat overlaps the smaller, fattier **point muscle**.

Unless you live in Texas barbecue country, where brisket is the meat of choice for slow-smoking, you're not likely to find a whole one in the meat case. Instead, you'll see brisket halves. The *point half* **A** (also known as the second cut, point cut, nose cut, front cut, or thick cut) includes the point muscle connected to the tapered end of the flat muscle by the layer of fat. The *flat half* **B** (also known as the first cut, flat cut, or thin

cut) is the wider side of the brisket flat—it doesn't include any of the point.

After cooking, the flat half holds together in neat slices, whereas the point half tends to shred. For our Braised Beef Brisket recipe on page 58, you can use two flats or two points, or one of each. And if a small whole brisket happens to be available (or you feel like special-ordering one), you could use that, too.

When deciding how much to buy, keep in mind that brisket exudes a lot of juice during cooking and may weigh 40 to 60 percent

less by the time it's done. We found, for example, that our brisket recipe yielded about 5¼ pounds of cooked meat from 9 pounds of raw brisket flat halves. To offset the moisture loss, it's important to choose briskets that aren't trimmed of too much fat and that have nice marbling (intramuscular fat). The fat bastes the meat as it cooks and enhances the flavor, and then you can trim it away before eating.

—*Jennifer Armentrout and Melissa Pellegrino*

Fat Back vs. Salt Pork

Fat back and salt pork look enough alike that they're sometimes confused, but they can't be used interchangeably.

SALT PORK is salt-cured fat from the belly and sides of the pig. It's mainly used in small amounts as a flavoring in dishes like Boston baked beans and fish chowder. The degree of saltiness varies, and it sometimes has to be blanched to remove some of the salt. Salt pork keeps for up to one month tightly wrapped in the refrigerator.

FAT BACK is a fresh, unsmoked, and unsalted layer of fat from a pig's back. It's used in a variety of ways. Thin sheets of fat back are used to line terrines and to wrap lean cuts of meat like pork loin roasts. It's also used to make lard, cracklings, pâtés, and all kinds of fresh sausages, like the Sage and Red Wine Sausage on page 70. Fat back keeps for up to one week tightly wrapped in the refrigerator or two months in the freezer.

—*Melissa Pellegrino*

SALT PORK   FAT BACK

Two tools for shaving fennel

RAW FENNEL ADDS GREAT FLAVOR TO SALADS like the Brisket and Root Vegetable Salad on page 60, but if it's too thickly sliced, it can be fibrous and tough to eat. By shaving fennel into very thin slices, you can showcase its best attributes—a mild licorice-like flavor and crisp texture. Fortunately, you don't need perfect knife skills to produce thin slices of fennel. The mandoline (or hand slicer) and the vegetable peeler can do it for you.

◀ **Mandoline or hand slicer**
Choose the thinness of the fennel shavings by adjusting the blade of the mandoline or hand slicer. Trim the base of the fennel bulb and then halve and core it. Position one fennel half base side down on the mandoline or slicer. Using a fluid motion, slide the fennel back and forth across the blade, allowing the shavings to fall on the cutting board. Keep going until the fennel becomes difficult to hold.

Vegetable peeler ▶
Trim the base of the fennel and cut the bulb into quarters. Remove the core from each quarter. Holding a fennel quarter in one hand, run the peeler lengthwise down a cut side of the quarter. Continue to shave the bulb in this manner until it becomes difficult to hold.

—*Melissa Pellegrino*

For sources, see Where to Buy It

Make It Tonight

Just 30 minutes to dinner, start to finish.

thai-style stir-fried chicken and basil

If you like, use a mix of fresh cilantro and mint instead of basil. Serve over cooked jasmine rice.

Serves 2 to 3

- 2 **Tbs. vegetable oil**
- 4 **medium shallots, peeled and thinly sliced**
- 2 **medium cloves garlic, thinly sliced**
- ¼ **tsp. crushed red pepper flakes**
- 1 **lb. chicken breast cutlets (about ¼ inch thick), cut crosswise into 1-inch-wide strips**
- 1 **Tbs. fish sauce**
- 1 **Tbs. fresh lime juice**
- 2 **tsp. packed light brown sugar**
- 1 **cup lightly packed fresh basil leaves**

Heat the oil in a well-seasoned wok or a heavy-duty 12-inch skillet over medium-high heat until shimmering hot. Add the shallots, garlic, and red pepper flakes; cook, stirring frequently, until the shallots start to soften but not brown, 1 to 2 minutes. Add the chicken and cook, stirring, until it's no longer pink and the shallots are beginning to brown, 2 to 3 minutes.

Add the fish sauce, lime juice, sugar, and ¼ cup water. Cook, stirring frequently, until the chicken is just cooked through and the liquid reduces to a saucy consistency, 2 to 3 minutes. (If the sauce reduces before the chicken is cooked through, add water, 1 Tbs. at a time.) Remove from the heat, add the basil, and stir to wilt it. —*Lori Longbotham*

quick beef enchiladas with salsa verde

An easy, homemade salsa verde adds a tangy kick to these hearty enchiladas.

Serves 4

- **Kosher salt**
- 1 **lb. tomatillos (about 15 medium), husked and rinsed**
- 3 **jalapeños, stemmed and halved lengthwise (seeded, if you like)**
- 1 **large yellow onion, half cut into 4 wedges, half chopped**
- ⅔ **cup roughly chopped fresh cilantro**
- 1½ **Tbs. canola oil**
- 1 **lb. lean ground beef**
- 2 **tsp. ground cumin**
- **Freshly ground black pepper**
- 8 **6-inch corn tortillas**
- 1½ **cups shredded Monterey Jack cheese**

Bring a medium pot of salted water to a boil. Add the tomatillos, jalapeños, and onion wedges; cover and simmer until tender, about 10 minutes. Drain well and transfer to a blender along with ⅓ cup of the cilantro. Purée until just slightly chunky and season to taste with salt.

Meanwhile, heat 1 Tbs. of the oil in a large skillet over medium-high heat. Add the beef, chopped onion, cumin, 1 tsp. salt, and ¼ tsp. pepper and cook, stirring occasionally to break up the meat, until cooked through, about 5 minutes. Stir ½ cup of the salsa verde into the beef.

Position a rack about 6 inches from the broiler and heat the broiler to high. Grease a 9x13-inch metal or ceramic baking dish with the remaining ½ Tbs. oil.

Wrap the tortillas in a few slightly damp paper towels and microwave on high until warm, 30 to 45 seconds. Working with one tortilla at a time, spoon some of the beef mixture down

Continued on page 86

Photographs by Scott Phillips

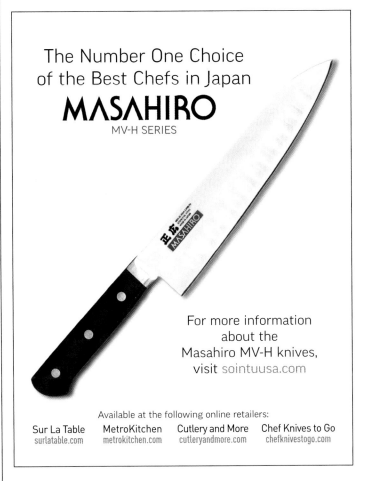

the center of the tortilla and sprinkle with 1 Tbs. of the cheese. Roll up snugly and transfer to the prepared baking dish, seam side down. Repeat with the remaining tortillas and beef mixture. Pour the remaining salsa verde over the enchiladas and sprinkle with the remaining cheese. Broil until golden brown and bubbly, 3 to 5 minutes. Garnish with the remaining cilantro and serve. —*Liz Pearson*

open-face brie, apple, and arugula sandwiches

A cup of hot soup turns this sandwich into a satisfying meal.

Serves 4

- 8 slices rustic artisan bread (about 2½ by 6 inches and ¾ inch thick)
- 8 tsp. Dijon mustard
- 4 cups packed baby arugula
- 1 medium Fuji apple, cored and thinly sliced
  Kosher salt and freshly ground black pepper
- 8 oz. Brie, thinly sliced

Position a rack 6 inches from the broiler and heat the broiler to high.

Put the bread slices on a rimmed baking sheet and set under the broiler. Broil until nicely toasted, 1 to 2 minutes.

Remove the pan from the oven, flip the bread over, and spread 1 tsp. of the mustard evenly on each untoasted side. Top with the arugula and then the apple slices. Season lightly with salt and pepper, and then arrange the Brie slices in a single layer over the apples.

Broil just until the Brie starts to melt, 1 to 2 minutes (don't let it melt too much or the apple will get warm and the arugula will wilt). Sprinkle with a little black pepper.

—*Dabney Gough*

minestrone with green beans and fennel

For a vegetarian version of this recipe, use vegetable broth—preferably homemade.

Yields about 8 cups; serves 4 to 6

- 3 Tbs. extra-virgin olive oil
- 2 medium cloves garlic, smashed
- ½ lb. green beans, trimmed and cut into 1-inch pieces
- 1 small fennel bulb, quartered, cored, and cut into ¼-inch dice
  Kosher salt
- 1 quart lower-salt chicken broth
- 1 14½-oz. can diced tomatoes
- 1 15½-oz. can cannellini beans, rinsed and drained
- ½ cup dried ditalini pasta or small elbows
- ½ cup freshly grated Parmigiano-Reggiano; more for sprinkling
- 6 large fresh basil leaves, coarsely chopped
  Freshly ground black pepper

Heat the oil and garlic in a medium sauce-pan over medium heat until the garlic begins to brown, 2 to 3 minutes; discard the garlic. Raise the heat to medium high, add the green beans, fennel, and ¾ tsp. salt, and cook, stirring, until the beans and fennel begin to soften and brown in places, 5 to 7 minutes. Add the broth and the tomatoes with their juices and bring to a boil. Add the cannellini beans and pasta and return to a boil. Reduce the heat to a simmer, cover, and cook until the pasta and green beans are completely tender, 10 to 12 minutes.

Stir in the cheese and basil and season to taste with salt and pepper. Serve sprinkled with additional cheese.

—*Tony Rosenfeld*

pan-seared salmon with spinach and shiitake

Be sure to ask your fishmonger to scale the salmon.

Serves 4

- 3½ Tbs. extra-virgin olive oil
- 2 medium shallots, finely chopped
- ½ lb. shiitake mushrooms, stemmed and sliced ¼ inch thick
- ½ cup heavy cream
- 1 tsp. chopped fresh thyme
  Kosher salt and freshly ground black pepper
- 2 cups lightly packed baby spinach leaves
- 4 6-oz. boneless, skin-on salmon fillets
- 3 Tbs. fresh lemon juice

Heat 2 Tbs. of the oil in a 12-inch nonstick skillet over medium-high heat. Add the shallots and cook, stirring often, until golden brown, about 2 minutes. Add the mushrooms and cook, stirring occasionally, until softened, 3 to 4 minutes. Stir in the cream, thyme, 1 tsp. salt, and ⅛ tsp. pepper. Reduce the heat to medium and cook, stirring often, until thickened, 1 to 2 minutes. Remove the skillet from the heat and stir in the spinach until wilted. Transfer to a bowl and cover with foil to keep warm. Clean the skillet and return it to the stove.

Heat the remaining 1½ Tbs. oil in the skillet over medium heat. Season the salmon fillets all over with 1 tsp. salt and ¼ tsp. pepper. Arrange the salmon in the skillet skin side up in a single layer and cook, turning once, until golden brown and just cooked through, 7 to 9 minutes total. Transfer the salmon to a large plate.

Mix the lemon juice with 1 Tbs. water, add to the skillet, and cook, scraping up any browned bits, until just thickened, about 30 seconds. Drizzle the pan juices over the salmon and serve with the warm shiitake mixture.

—*Liz Pearson*

pecan-crusted skirt steak

This main course is just right with coleslaw, or steamed broccoli served with a few lemon wedges on the side.

Serves 4

½	Tbs. olive oil
1½	lb. skirt steak, trimmed
	Kosher salt and freshly ground black pepper
¾	cup pecan pieces
2	Tbs. cold butter, cut into small pieces
2	tsp. honey
1½	tsp. roughly chopped fresh rosemary

Position an oven rack about 6 inches from the broiler and heat the broiler on high.

Line a large rimmed baking sheet with foil and grease the foil with the oil. If necessary, cut the steak crosswise into pieces 8 to 10 inches long. Arrange the steak on the baking sheet in a single layer and season with 1 tsp. salt and ¼ tsp. pepper. Put the pecans, butter, honey, rosemary, 1 tsp. salt, and ¼ tsp. pepper in a food processor and pulse until well combined and the pecans are finely chopped.

Broil the steak until lightly browned, 3 to 4 minutes. Flip it and broil until it's cooked nearly to your liking, about 3 minutes more for medium rare. Spread the pecan mixture over the steak, patting the mixture with the back of a spoon to help it adhere. Continue broiling until the pecan coating is toasted and fragrant, 1 to 2 minutes. Set the steak aside to rest for 5 minutes.

Thinly slice the steak against the grain and transfer to plates. If the pecan coating falls off the steak as you're slicing it, spoon it over the top.

—*Liz Pearson*

WHERE TO BUY IT

preserving the season, page 19

- **Bormioli Rocco Quattro Stagioni home-canning jars**, $2.49 to $3.99, containerstore.com, 888-266-8246.

repertoire, page 24

- **Le Creuset 12x9½-inch enameled cast-iron baking dish**, $39.95, cooking.com/fc, 800-663-8810.
- **Small (8x10-inch) roasting rack**, $5.95, kitchenworks.com, 800-967-9755.
- **CDN ProAccurate cooking thermometer**, $8.99, cooking.com/fc.

mint, page 42

- **Oyyo white small plate**, $17, teroforma.com, 877-899-9950.
- **24-oz., 3-piece, wide-mouth stainless-steel shaker**, $16.45, webtender.barstore.com, 800-256-6396.
- **For mint seedlings**, go to richters.com, 800-668-4372.

brunch, page 34

- **Large Shelbourne bowl**, $190, and **large stainless ladle**, $32, simonpearce.com, 800-774-5277.
- **Modern Twist gray floral placemat**, $17, heliotropehome.com, 404-371-0100.
- **Clear Elena goblet**, $10, potterybarn.com for stores, 888-779-5176.
- **Assorted fresh tropical fruit** from Melissa's World Variety Produce, melissas.com for prices, 800-588-0151.
- **Four-slat black Adirondack chair**, $550; **black rocker**, $570; and **white Satellite round table**, $149; lolldesigns.com, 877-740-3387.
- **Waramaug #2 black clay pot**, $16, benwolffpottery.com, 860-618-2317.
- **Calphalon 9-inch springform pan**, $19.95, cooking.com/fc, 800-663-8810.

For more kitchen tools, go to
FineCooking.com/buy-it

drinks, page 32

- **Riedel Ouverture white wine glass**, set of 4 glasses for $48, glassware.riedel.com, 888-474-3335.
- **TerraMagic globe**, $39.95, innovatoys.com.

grilled sandwiches, page 62

- **Le Creuset Flame square grill pan** with panini press, $184.95, cooking.com/fc, 800-663-8810.
- **Griddler panini & sandwich press**, $49.95, cuisinart.com, 800-211-9604.

test kitchen, page 77

- **Kyocera adjustable ceramic slicer**, $22.95, metrokitchen.com, 800-892-9911.

sausage, page 68

- **Natural salt-packed hog casings** (32/35 mm), $37.99, sausagemaker.com, 888-490-8525.
- **Lodge cast-iron skillets:** 6½ inch, $7.45, and 12 inch, $33.95, cooking.com/fc, 800-663-8810.
- **Stainless-steel mixing bowl set**, $14.95, cooking.com/fc, 800-663-8810.
- **Aluminum half-sheet pans**, $19.95, kingarthurflour.com, 800-827-6836.
- **Bamboo skewers**, $.85, cooking.com/fc, 800-663-8810.
- **Wusthof 8-inch classic cook's knife**, $119.95, cooking.com/fc, 800-663-8810.
- **Aluminum 12-inch ruler**, $2.49, dickblick.com, 800-828-4548.
- **WearEver commercial bakeware cooling rack**, $7.99, amazon.com, 800-201-7575.

brigadeiros, page 50

- **One-teaspoon round ice cream scoop**, $12.50, jbprince.com, 800-473-0577.

- **Guittard's bittersweet chocolate sprinkles**, $3.95, kingarthurflour.com, 800-827-6836.
- **For information on Leticia Moreinos's cooking classes**, visit chefleticia.com.

brisket, page 56

- **KitchenAid roasting pan with rack**, $59.95, cooking.com/fc, 800-663-8810.
- **McCormick ancho chile pepper**, $4.82, mccormickgourmet.com, 800-474-7742.

Appliances

Chef's Choice *p. 7* Woo 'em with waffles! Prepare the world's most delicious waffles in 90 seconds! The Chef's Choice® unique Quad® baking system lets you choose the ideal flavor, texture, and color.
800-342-3255
www.edgecraft.com

Earthstone Wood-Fire Ovens *p. 88* Wood-fired brick ovens for indoor and outdoor use. Can double as a fireplace. Great for baking, grilling, and roasting.
800-840-4915
www.earthstoneovens.com

Rangecraft Manufacturing, Co. *p. 85* Specializing in the manufacture of a wide selection of high-quality metal range hoods, including copper, brass, and stainless steel. Quality finishes include matte, brushed, antique, mirror, or hammered.
877-RCHOODS
www.rangecraft.com

Viking Range *p. 5* If cooking is everything, the complete Viking kitchen offers everything you need - professional performance and impeccable design.
888-845-4641
www.vikingrange.com/wheretobuy

Zojirushi America Corporation *p. 27* Zojirushi manufactures top-of-the-line cooking appliances from rice cookers to breadmakers. Focusing on how our appliances fit into everyday lives for nearly 90 years.
www.zojirushi.com

Books

Jessica's Biscuit *p. 88*
www.ecookbooks.com

The Kitchen Idea Book *p. 27*
www.taunton.com/books

Cookware

Kuhn-Rikon Corporation *p. 9* Kuhn Rikon offers the finest in pressure cookers, specialty cookware, and distinctive kitchen tools to make a cook's life easier.
800-924-4699
www.kuhnrikon.com/fine

Metrokitchen *p. 85* Metrokitchen.com, top brands for the professional chef in each of us. Free shipping, the web's best prices. Friendly, expert service on-line since 1998.
www.metrokitchen.com

Swissmar Imports, Ltd. *p. 85* For all your entertaining needs, find some of the finest houseware products in the world at Swissmar, Contact us Today!
877-947-7627
www.psp-peugeot-usa.com

Cutlery

Metrokitchen *p. 83* Metrokitchen.com, top brands for the professional chef in each of us. Free shipping, the web's best prices. Friendly, expert service on-line since 1998.
www.metrokitchen.com

Sointu USA *p. 85* Sointu USA created the market for Japanese knives in the US. Its collection of brands represents the very best of what is manufactured in Japan.
www.sointuusa.com

Gourmet Foods

John Wm. Macy's Cheesesticks *p. 81* Enrich any occasion with our all-natural sourdough CheeseSticks, CheeseCrisps and SweetSticks, made with fine aged cheeses and choice seasonings, then baked twice to "the perfect crunch!"
www.cheesesticks.com

La Tienda *p. 88* A window to the best of Spain. America's most comprehensive inventory of quality Spanish food selected by a knowledgeable and dedicated family. Immediate delivery. 888-472-1022
www.tienda.com

Sesmark *p. 95*
www.sesmark.com

Texas Black Angus.com *p. 88* Absolutely the finest beef your ever tasted! No Hormones. All Natural. Delivered to your doorstep.
www.texasblackangus.com

Ingredients

Australian Lamb *p. 13* Australian Lamb makes a delicious holiday highlight or an easy everyday meal. For a variety of lamb recipes, contests and a free cookbook, visit australian-lamb.com/fc
www.australian-lamb.com/fc

Bob's Red Mill Natural Foods *p. 23* Bob's Red Mill Natural Foods, Inc. is the nation's leading miller of stone ground whole grains. To learn more about our wholesome, delicious products visit:
www.bobsredmill.com/fc

Colavita USA *p. 14* Colavita Authentic Italian extra virgin olive oil is unmatched for freshness and flavor. Colavita's Italian vinegars, pasta, and sauces are available in food stores everywhere and at colavita.com, where *Fine Cooking* readers can save 10% with the code: FC
www.colavita.com

McCormick *p. 17* The elegant flavors of the McCormick Gourmet Collection help passionate cooks everywhere create uniquely delicious meals. Lovingly cultivated and harvested with care, the rich, enticing flavors of the Gourmet Collection will transform your meals into extraordinary feats of flavor. mccormickgourmet.com
www.mccormickgourmet.com

Plugra European Style Butter *p. 96*
www.plugra.com

Kitchen Design & Tableware

Dacor *p. 76* Since 1965, Dacor® has redefined the modern kitchen with a collection that offers the best balance of style and performance. Dacor is in the details.
800-793-0093
www.dacor.com/hot

Plum Pudding Kitchen *p. 9* Your online source for "irresistibly Italian" Vietri dinnerware, flatware, glassware, and much more. Let us help you set a special table!
888-940-7586
www.plumpuddingkitchen.com

Kitchen Tools & Utensils

A Cook's Wares *p. 88* We have what you need for your kitchen: The finest cookware, bakeware, cutlery, utensils and small appliances. Since 1981.
800-915-9788
www.cookswares.com

GelPro *p. 87* Stand in comfort! Let's Gel was started with one simple goal, to make the time you spend standing in your kitchen more comfortable.
866-GEL-MATS
www.gelpro.com

Kerekes *p. 88* Your complete online source for professional chef's tools, cookware, bakeware, and cake decorating supplies used by top chefs at the finest restaurants and kitchens.
www.bakedeco.com

Mugnaini's Wood-Fired Cooking *p. 88* Mugnaini, exclusive importers of Italian wood-fired ovens. Italian tradition, American technology. Dedicated to customer service in design, building support, and oven use.
888-887-7206
www.mugnaini.com

Schools, Travel & Organizations

Culinary Business Academy *p. 87* Extensive and comprehensive personal chef business knowledge and training from the world's recognized leader in the personal chef industry. Nobody offers what we offer.
800-747-2433
www.culinarybusiness.com

Greenwood CVB *p. 7* Indulge at our fabulous restaurants and take a cooking class at our famous cooking school. Treat yourself at our luxurious new spa and explore quaint shops, fascinating museums and historic tours.
800-748-9064
www.greenwoodms.org/fc

Zingerman's Bakehouse *p. 83* Long known for their full flavored, traditionally-made breads, and pastries, Zingerman's Bakehouse now offers BAKE!; a hands-on teaching bakery in Ann Arbor.
www.bakewithzing.com

Wines, Beverages & Accessories

Illy Espresso USA, Inc. *p. 11* Full selection of expertly roasted coffee, home-delivery coffee subscription programs, artist cup collections, and exceptional accessories and gifts. Free shipping on coffee orders over $50.
www.illyusa.com

Woodbridge Winery *p. 2* For 25 years, we have aged our wines in small oak barrels and handcrafted each vintage. Woodbridge: Taste our small winery tradition™.
www.woodbridgewines.com

NUTRITION

Recipe	Calories (kcal)	Fat Cal (kcal)	Protein (g)	Carb (g)	Total Fat (g)	Sat Fat (g)	Mono Fat (g)	Poly Fat (g)	Chol (mg)	Sodium (g)	Fiber (g)
LETTER FROM THE EDITOR, p. 6											
Spring Vegetable Ragout with Fresh Pasta	390	120	12	55	14	8	3	1.5	95	460	6
LEMONGRASS, p. 15											
Spicy Mussels with Lemongrass, Chile, and Basil	240	80	29	11	9	1.5	3	3	65	670	0
MUSHROOMS, p. 19											
Twice-Marinated Mushrooms (per ¼ cup)	200	180	2	3	20	3	15	2	0	75	1
SUN-DRIED TOMATOES, p. 20											
Sun-Dried Tomato and Feta Vinaigrette (per 1 Tbs.)	70	60	0	1	7	1	4.5	1.5	0	70	0
Rigatoni with Sun-Dried Tomato and Fennel Sauce	760	300	19	94	33	16	13	2.5	80	720	6
Chicken Breasts Stuffed with Sun-Dried Tomatoes	550	280	60	5	31	7	17	5	165	570	1
ROAST CHICKEN, p. 24											
Best-Ever Roast Chicken (with skin)	560	310	56	0	35	9	15	7	180	450	0
MINI PIZZAS, p. 28											
Mini Pizzas with Arugula, Peppers, Prosciutto (per pizza)	140	45	6	16	5	2	2	0.5	10	360	2
BRUNCH, p. 34											
Citrus Tea Punch (per 8 oz.)	240	0	0	46	0	0	0	0	0	5	1
Peas and Carrots with Lemon, Dill, and Mint	180	120	2	14	14	2	10	1.5	0	150	4
Smoked Salmon, Goat Cheese, and Artichoke Quiche	590	400	16	33	44	27	12	2.5	230	740	3
Wild Blueberry and Ricotta Pancakes (per pancake)	110	20	5	16	2	1	0.5	0	40	190	1
MINT, p. 42											
Derby Day Mint Julep Cocktail	160	0	0	8	0	0	0	0	0	0	0
Israeli Couscous Salad with Mint, Cucumber, and Feta	260	130	8	25	15	5	8	1	20	520	2
Poached Flounder with Mint Beurre Blanc	290	140	29	3	16	9	4	1.5	120	200	0
Roast Rack of Lamb with Lemon-Mint Salsa Verde	440	320	25	2	36	12	19	3	100	360	1
White Bean Salad with Mint and Red Onion	160	60	7	21	7	1	5	1	0	530	7
Strawberry-Mint Shortcakes	360	130	6	51	15	10	2.5	0.5	45	410	2
BRIGADEIROS, p. 50											
Chocolate Brigadeiros (per piece)	50	20	1	8	2.5	1.5	0.5	0	5	15	0
Coconut Brigadeiros (per piece)	50	30	1	6	3.5	2.5	0	0	5	10	0
Pistachio Brigadeiros (per piece)	70	35	1	7	3.5	2	1.5	0	10	15	0
BRISKET, p. 56											
Red-Wine-Braised Brisket with Cremini and Carrots	440	140	53	17	15	4	6	3	90	540	4
Brisket and Bean Chili	460	140	35	45	16	3	8	2.5	40	1240	12
Brisket and Vegetable Salad with Horseradish Dressing	640	180	43	72	20	7	8	3	70	1160	10
Rigatoni with Brisket and Porcini Ragù	700	190	39	68	22	5	11	3.5	55	1040	6
GRILLED SANDWICHES, p. 62											
Grilled Tuna and Provolone Sandwiches with Salsa Verde	650	350	42	34	39	13	18	4.5	65	1250	1
Grilled Mozzarella and Spinach BLTs	570	260	29	46	29	12	11	2	70	1510	5
Grilled Turkey and Cheddar Sandwiches with Chutney	660	240	36	67	27	15	6	1	105	1890	4
Grilled Portobello and Goat Cheese Sandwiches	590	370	15	40	42	9	26	6	15	1010	4
SAUSAGE, p. 68											
Sage and Red Wine Pork Sausage (per ¼ lb)	350	250	21	1	28	10	13	3	75	630	0
Spicy Fennel Pork Sausage (per ¼ lb)	350	250	21	1	28	10	13	3.5	75	630	0
Smoked Paprika and Thyme Pork Sausage (per ¼ lb)	350	250	21	1	28	10	13	3.5	75	630	0
Apple and Madeira Pork Sausage (per ¼ lb)	360	250	21	4	28	10	13	3	75	630	1
MAKE IT TONIGHT, p. 84											
Thai-Style Stir-Fried Chicken and Basil	280	110	32	8	13	2	5	5	85	540	0
Minestrone with Green Beans and Fennel	220	80	10	27	9	1.5	5	1.5	0	510	6
Pan-Seared Salmon with Spinach and Shiitake	530	320	41	13	35	10	16	7	150	680	2
Quick Beef Enchiladas with Salsa Verde	580	280	36	40	31	12	12	3.5	110	790	6
Open-Face Brie, Apple, and Arugula Sandwiches	380	160	17	37	18	10	4.5	0.5	55	1300	3
Pecan-Crusted Skirt Steak	510	350	36	6	39	11	20	6	100	680	2

The nutritional analyses have been calculated by a registered dietitian at Nutritional Solutions in Melville, New York. When a recipe gives a choice of ingredients, the first choice is the one used. Optional ingre- dients with measured amounts are included; ingredients without specific quantities are not. Analyses are per serving; when a range of ingredient amounts or servings is given, the smaller amount or portion is used. When the quantities of salt and pepper aren't specified, the analysis is based on ¼ tsp. salt and ⅛ tsp. pepper per serving for entrées, and ⅛ tsp. salt and ⅟₁₆ tsp. pepper per serving for side dishes.

MENUS

pronto italiano

Minestrone with Green
Beans and Fennel
page 86

Grilled Mozzarella
and Spinach BLTs
page 64

To drink:
Sangiovese or Sauvignon Blanc

Vanilla Ice Cream with
Espresso-Caramel Sauce
FineCooking.com

anytime thai

Spicy Steamed
Mussels with
Lemongrass,
Chile, and Basil
page 16

Steamed Rice

Spicy Slaw with
Radicchio
and Green Mango
FineCooking.com

To drink:
India pale ale
or white ale

friends' night

Brisket and Bean Chili
page 61

Tex-Mex Cornbread
with Cheese & Green Chiles
FineCooking.com

To drink: amber lager or dry stout

Brigadeiros,
page 54

passover supper

Red-Wine-Braised Brisket
with Cremini, Carrots, and Thyme
page 58

Crispy Potato Pancakes
FineCooking.com

To drink: kosher Syrah or Shiraz

Flourless Chocolate-Almond Cake
with Almond-Cherry-Caramel Glaze
FineCooking.om

chicken dinner

Best-Ever Roast Chicken
page 25

White Bean Salad with
Mint and Red Onion
page 47

To drink: Chardonnay or Riesling

Strawberry-Mint Shortcakes
page 48

mother's day breakfast

Wild Blueberry and
Ricotta Pancakes
page 40

Apple and
Madeira Pork Sausage
page 74

Melons with Ginger Syrup
FineCooking.com

easter feast

Roast Rack of Lamb with
Lemon-Mint Salsa Verde
page 47

Mashed Potatoes
with Caramelized Shallots
FineCooking.com

Mixed Greens Dressed
with Sun-Dried Tomato and
Feta Vinaigrette
page 20

To drink: Zinfandel or Shiraz

Classic Carrot Layer Cake with
Vanilla Cream Cheese Frosting
FineCooking.com

RECIPE INDEX

VEGETARIAN: May contain eggs and dairy ingredients

MAKE AHEAD: Can be completely prepared ahead (may need reheating and a garnish to serve)

QUICK: Under 30 minutes

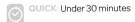

Adam Smith

Spreading the chocolate word, with a side of news.

BY LISA WADDLE

Fine Cooking: So you sell magazines and you sell chocolate, all in the same 1,000 square feet. Why?
Smith: Chocolate was never part of the equation. I set out to open the best newsstand on Market Street, with the usual candy by the cash register. Soon, my customers were asking why they could buy a French magazine but no French chocolate.

FC: How do you feel about mass-market chocolate?
Smith: I grew up eating the usual candy bars, like most Americans. The thing is, most of that is just chocolate-flavored sugar. I learned quickly that sweetness isn't the same thing as flavor. Once the light bulb came on, there was no going back.

FC: How did that candy epiphany change your business?
Smith: I became passionate about trying to sell only the best chocolate I could find and squeezing it in alongside the magazines. I started tasting everything I came across. And I still do; I taste every day.

FC: How do you keep it all straight?
Smith: We have a computer database with tasting notes on more than 2,000 chocolate bars.

FC: I take it your notes go beyond "yummy" or "yech."
Smith: You'd be surprised what you can taste: black cherry, vanilla bean, whipped cream, peach, licorice, wheat toast, dill; then there's an aftertaste of vanilla, cream cheese, buttermilk pancake, and clove—all that from Scharffen Berger's 70 Percent Cacao Bar.

FC: Say that again?
Smith: Really. We take three to seven minutes to taste a single piece.

FC: So out of the 225 different chocolate bars on your shelves, what's the best?
Smith: We don't use words like "best" or "worst." It's about flavor. We judge chocolate based on four flavor criteria: complexity, balance, length, and accuracy.

FC: Do you expect new employees to have chocolate "expertise"?
Smith: No. When they're first hired, new staffers think we have the greatest employee benefit—weekly chocolate tastings. Later, they curse me, because I've ruined them for the usual stuff.

FC: And your customers, can they keep up?
Smith: We have a frequent-buyer card, but it's not just "Buy 10 bars and get one free." It's buy 10 *different* bars. That way, they become experienced tasters, too.

FC: Some bars cost $13. Do customers balk at the prices?
Smith: We have two answers: Taste it and you'll see why, and Aren't you worth it?

FC: Do you ever get tired of chocolate?
Smith: Not at all. I have stashes of it at home and eat chocolate even when I'm not at work. It's a lifestyle.

FC: Anyone ever call you a chocolate snob?
Smith: Not to my face.

the dish

Name: Adam Smith
Age: 40-something
Job: Newsstand owner, chocolate fiend
Started: 1999
Where: San Francisco
Known for: Defending milk chocolate
Find out more: fogcitynews.com

Illustration by Ward Schumaker

Your famous raspberry streusel just became legendary.

Culinary bliss awaits with Plugrá® European-Style Butter as your secret ingredient. Create higher cakes and flakier pastries for *pâtisserie* that are truly *magnifique*.

PLUGRÁ
EUROPEAN STYLE BUTTER

Discover inspiration from the masters at www.plugra.com.

THE COMPLETE GUIDE
to freezing summer's
best produce

fine
Cooking

WE BRING OUT THE COOK IN YOU

A new way to grill!

Sear, braise & glaze
your way to the best
ibs, chicken & more

Make your own
ice cream
1 easy technique,
18 luscious flavors

CRAB CAKE
COOK-OFF

IT'S ALL LIGHT

Fast & fresh
salad suppers

NE/JULY 2009 • No. 99
/w.finecooking.com

6.95   CAN $7.95

07

Barbecue-Braised Vietnamese
Short Ribs, page 61

Heavy-duty smoothies. $25 instant savings.

The Viking Professional Blender combines a rugged high-torque motor with commercial style to deliver all the power and features

to crush a block of ice or purée a papaya. Shop quickly, this is a limited time offer. Price after savings: $125.

To find a dealer near you, visit vikingrange.com/wheretobuy.

CONTENTS

JUNE/JULY 2009 ISSUE 99

Fresh crab becomes a classic
summer favorite: crab cakes.
Recipe on page 72.

CONTENTS

JUNE/JULY 2009 ISSUE 99

p. 20
p. 54
p. 46
p. 70
p. 74

Cover and Contents photographs by Scott Phillips, except faucet, courtesy of the manufacturer; food styling, cover, by Michelli Knauer and Susan Sugarman; illustration by Steven Salerno

THE RULES FOR OUR INGREDIENTS ARE SIMPLE. YOU SHOULD BE ABLE TO TASTE THEM. AND PRONOUNCE THEM.

Shown: summer vegetable sauté with roasted garlic sausage.

We've spent years in the kitchen—finding the perfect combinations of fresh, all natural ingredients—so that you only need minutes to turn our fully cooked, all natural chicken sausage into a healthy, delicious meal that you and your family will love. In fourteen gourmet flavors.

For healthy and delicious meal ideas from al fresco, including the recipe shown, go to:

alfrescoallnatural.com

al fresco®

live life with flavor

70% less fat than pork sausage   ✳   *All natural*   ✳   *No artificial ingredients or preservatives*

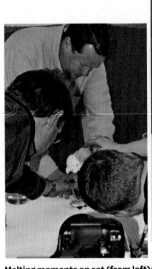

Melting moments on set (from left): How many men does it take to shoot an ice cream cone? The star cone, holding up well, and her stunt double, made with instant mashed potatoes (which you definitely wouldn't want to eat). Oh, the mix-in options!

Ice Cream Season

RELOCATING FROM THE WEST COAST to the East required a few adjustments on my part (those first snow days, to begin with). But there was no way I was giving in to the concept of "seasonal" ice cream. Who knew that ice cream shops closed in the fall? It's a well-known fact that I have something of an ice cream habit; in fact, it's a rare night when we don't meet at the same bowl. What to do?

The solution to the local ice cream shortage arrived in the form of David Lebovitz's feature in this issue. The Paris-based cooking teacher and award-winning cookbook author brings his expertise to our Cooking Without Recipes feature and teaches us how to make a simple custard that easily freezes into any number of different ice creams. We tested our way through some two dozen variations, 18 of which make up our idea of a centerfold (pages 52–53). Getting all of those flavors to pose was something of a challenge; I'll let the photos above tell that story.

Of course, that's just one of the many stories that make up this start-of-summer issue. We've also got a picnic that bears no resemblance to the expected sandwich-and-chips menu, some exciting recipes for all the different beans that are hitting farmers' markets now, dueling crab cakes, and much more. And whatever you do, don't miss the ground-breaking feature we're calling "A New Way to Grill." I don't want to give it all away here, but I'd wager you've never tried braising on your barbecue. Let's just say there's a first time for everything.

Laurie Buckle, editor
fc@taunton.com

more *Fine Cooking*

AWARDS
We're excited to report that three of our contributors recently received book award nominations from the International Association of Culinary Professionals (IACP). Contributing editor Ellie Krieger won in the health category for her best-selling book, *The Food You Crave*. Others nominated were contributing editor Pam Anderson for her new title, *The Perfect Recipe for Losing Weight and Eating Great*, and Martha Holmberg for her first book, *Puff.*

WEB
Is there one dish or technique you've never been able to really master? (Crusty bread? A high-rising soufflé?) Members of our new Cook's Club can share their pain, and enter to win a one-on-one tutorial with a *Fine Cooking* expert—we come to you! Go to FineCooking.com for more info.

SPECIAL ISSUES
For fans of our special *Fresh* issues, the newest edition is out now. It's a great mix of spring-into-summer recipes. Also, keep an eye out for this summer's *Grilling* issue, which hits newsstands in mid-June. It's the one source you'll need for delicious cookouts all summer long.

Discover the next generation of espresso from illy.

Purchase the Francis Francis X8 for only $150* (a $445 value)

Introducing iperEspresso — the extraordinary innovation that combines state-of-the-art technology and legendary illy coffee to make the joy of savoring authentic Italian espresso an even greater pleasure. And when you take advantage of this remarkable offer, you'll also delight in the convenience of receiving illy a casa℠ automatic coffee capsule deliveries. There's no commitment and you can cancel any time.

The revolutionary iperEspresso capsule system lets you make perfect espresso with a single touch.

The iperEspresso method uses a two-stage extraction process that produces an intensely aromatic, full-bodied espresso with velvety, long-lasting crema. Designed exclusively for iperEspresso capsules, the X8 is wonderfully simple to use — just insert a capsule and turn the dial for easy, no mess preparation. Cappuccino aficionados will adore its auto-frothing wand that lets anyone steam like a pro.

Order today to enjoy legendary illy coffee with this limited-time offer.

30-day risk-free trial

METODO
IPERESPRESSO

Order by July 15 using promotion code **PFC59** to receive this exclusive offer.

Go to **illyusa.com/finecook5** or call **1 877 469 4559**

THE WINNER

Reader tip: Measuring a reduction

When a recipe called for reducing a sauce or stock by a fraction, say by half, I always ended up measuring it with a cup several times and making a mess. To avoid this, I now prepare whatever I need to reduce in a straight-sided saucepan and dip a bamboo skewer straight into the sauce. I score the skewer with my knife at the height of the sauce, then the halfway mark (or whatever the recipe calls for) to note where my sauce should be. I continue to dip the skewer in every so often to see how much the sauce has reduced until I get to the amount I need.

—*Ken Erdman,*
Hydesville, California

We want to hear from you. Give us your best tip and we'll reward you with a kitchen prize. Ken is the winner of this Swiss Diamond shallow grill pan.

Beating us to the punch

This year, I'm planning my garden with the idea of canning or freezing some of my produce. Since I've never attempted this before, you are my first "go-to" resource. I think a special issue on this topic would be really great.

—*Jane Amoruso, via email*

Editors' reply: We're on it, Jane. This issue contains a handy guide to freezing all the great summer fruits and vegetables you will be harvesting. Plus, you can find several canning recipes online at FineCooking.com.

Quick & Delicious dilemma

I hope that you are not eliminating the Quick & Delicious section of *Fine Cooking*. That is my favorite part of the magazine and most of the recipes I use are from that section. While I like the changes, I miss Quick & Delicious.

—*Merle Lewis, via email*

Editors' reply: Quick & Delicious has a new name: Make It Tonight. The column is still packed with fast and easy recipes for weeknight cooking, but now they're faster

than ever: Every Make it Tonight recipe has to clock in at under 30 minutes, start to finish. We've also decided to focus on main course recipes, since that's the "main" question for most of us when time is of the essence.

Cook the issue

I'm thrilled to be a runner-up in the Cook the Issue Challenge on your Web site. It was a lot of fun, and I tried recipes I may have otherwise skipped over. Thanks for a great magazine. I love *Fine Cooking*.

—*Lucinda Sears,*
Acton, Massachusetts

The gift that keeps on giving

I was given your magazine as a gift two years ago. It is absolutely my favorite cooking magazine. I'm a competent cook, and I find your recipes very easy to follow. More important, most are geared to a kitchen stocked with the basics, so they don't require the purchase of a lot of exotic ingredients. Keep up the great work.

—*Robert Hundt, via email*

To heat or not to heat

In Maryellen Driscoll's article on nonstick skillets (Test Drive, *Fine Cooking* #97), she says not to heat a nonstick pan when it is empty. That runs counter to what I've always been taught: To get a good sear on meat you should heat a dry skillet for two or three minutes before adding the meat. What is the proper way to get a good sear?

—*Walter Tower, via email*

Contributing editor Maryellen Driscoll replies:
I wouldn't recommend using a nonstick pan to sear a steak or, for that matter, even brown a pork chop. For such a task, preheating a traditionally surfaced pan, such as stainless steel, over high or medium-high heat, without oil, until hot is the proper technique. If you get distracted and the pan overheats, you can just pull it off the heat momentarily to let it cool slightly. Nonstick isn't that resilient. When heated above 500°F, the nonstick coating begins to break down or degrade.

If you're set on using your nonstick pan for this kind of cooking, avoid anything higher than medium-high heat, and add a little oil, which will provide a good visual cue for how hot your nonstick pan is. Vegetable oil's smoke point is around 450°F. So if the oil starts to smoke, you know your nonstick pan is getting too hot for its own good.

CORRECTIONS

In our last issue, in Test Drive, we mistakenly published a photo of a Viking meat grinder attachment instead of a Cuisinart attachment. The Cuisinart attachment is pictured here.

In Where to Buy It, an 8x10-inch roasting rack was listed as available from kitchenworks.com; the correct Web site is kitchenworksinc.com. Also, the phone number for Teroforma is 877-899-1190. The correct retail price for the Le Creuset enameled-cast-iron rectangular baking and roasting dish is $184.95

We regret these errors.

Photographs by Scott Phillips

fine Cooking®

Editor	Laurie Glenn Buckle
Contributing Art Director	Don Morris
Senior Food Editor/ Test Kitchen Manager	Jennifer Armentrout
Senior Editor	Rebecca Freedman
Associate Editors	Laura Giannatempo Lisa Waddle
Assistant Editor	Denise Mickelsen
Managing Web Editor	Sarah Breckenridge
Assistant Web Editor	Sharon Anderson
Senior Copy/ Production Editor	Enid Johnson
Associate Art Director	Pamela Winn
Contributing Designer	Tannaz Fassihi
Photo Coordinator	Kelly Coughlan Gearity
Assistant Test Kitchen Manager/Food Stylist	Allison Ehri Kreitler
Recipe Tester	Melissa Pellegrino
Editorial Assistant	Julissa Roberts
Test Kitchen Intern	Joy Braddock
Editorial Intern	Sophy Bishop
Editor at Large	Susie Middleton
Contributing Editors	Pam Anderson Abigail Johnson Dodge Maryellen Driscoll Sarah Jay Ellie Krieger Kimberly Y. Masibay Tony Rosenfeld Molly Stevens
Senior Managing Editor, Books	Carolyn Mandarano

Fine Cooking: (ISSN: 1072-5121) is published six times a year by The Taunton Press, Inc., Newtown, CT 06470-5506. Telephone 203-426-8171. Periodicals postage paid at Newtown, CT 06470 and at additional mailing offices. GST paid registration #123210981.

Subscription Rates: U.S. and Canada, $29.95 for one year, $49.95 for two years, $69.95 for three years (GST included, payable in U.S. funds). Outside the U.S./Canada: $36 for one year, $62 for two years, $88 for three years (payable in U.S. funds). Single copy, $6.95. Single copy outside the U.S., $7.95.

Postmaster: Send address changes to *Fine Cooking,* The Taunton Press, Inc., 63 South Main St., P.O. Box 5506, Newtown, CT 06470-5506.

Canada Post: Return undeliverable Canadian addresses to Fine Cooking, c/o Worldwide Mailers, Inc., 2835 Kew Drive, Windsor, ON N8T 3B7, or email to mnfa@taunton.com.

Printed in the USA.

Chef and meat guru Bruce Aidells ("A New Way to Grill: Barbecue-Braising," page 54) has written more than 10 cookbooks and is a frequent guest on TV and radio cooking shows. He lives in the Bay Area with his wife, Nancy Oakes, who is the chef at Boulevard restaurant in San Francisco.

• **To a summer cookout, I would bring...** homemade sausages.

• **My latest food discovery is...** these wonderful spice mixes from Whole Spice, a Middle Eastern spice shop in Napa.

• **My culinary icon is...** Loni Kuhn.

Eric Ripert ("Crab Cakes," page 70) is the executive chef and co-owner of Le Bernardin in New York City, and the chair of City Harvest's Food Council. He has co-written three cookbooks, including *On the Line* and *A Return to Cooking,* which was recently released in paperback. This fall, he will star in his own PBS television series, *Avec Eric.*

• **My top food destination is...** Puerto Rico.

• **My least favorite food is...** brains.

• **My guilty food pleasure is...** I don't feel guilty about the things I eat, but does dark chocolate at 3:00 in the morning count?

Maria Helm Sinskey ("Spill the Beans," page 38), former award-winning executive chef at Plump-Jack Café in San Francisco, is now the culinary director of Robert Sinskey Vineyards, which she co-owns with her husband. Her new book, *Williams-Sonoma Family Meals: Creating Traditions in the Kitchen,* was published in March.

• **Three items always in my shopping cart are...** extra-virgin olive oil, a loaf of fresh bread, and Champagne.

• **My guilty food pleasure is...** iceburg lettuce.

• **My favorite aspect of my job is...** nurturing people with food.

St. John Frizell ("Pleased as Punch," page 36) is a food, drink, and travel writer whose work has appeared in *Oxford American, Edible Brooklyn,* and *Edible Manhattan,* as well as on epicurious.com. This spring, he will put his former bartending experience at New York's Pegu Club to good use in his own café-bar, Fort Defiance, in the Red Hook neighborhood of Brooklyn.

• **To a summer cookout, I would bring...** a pitcher of margaritas or mojitos. Everyone loves them, and they go down easy.

• **My go-to weeknight dinner is...** chicken under a brick.

• **My favorite thing about my job is...** talking to people. As a writer and bartender, you have license to ask anyone anything.

Susan Sugarman's food styling ("A New Way to Grill," page 54; "Splendor in the Grass," page 62; and "Crab Cakes," page 70) regularly appears in *O, The Oprah Magazine, The New York Times Magazine,* and *Martha Stewart Living,* where she was a food editor for 13 years.

• **For breakfast, I eat...** roasted, unsalted cashews and freshly squeezed Satsuma mandarin orange juice.

• **The last thing I cooked was...** jerk-rubbed hanger steak.

• **My culinary icon is...** Italy.

Avid food blogger, cooking teacher, and critically acclaimed cookbook author David Lebovitz ("Scooped!," page 46) is a veteran of Chez Panisse, where he was a baker. His newest book, *The Sweet Life in Paris,* was published this spring.

• **The last thing I ate was...** a black radish dipped in fleur de sel.

• **The dish I most want to learn to cook is...** Girl Scouts' Thin Mints.

• **My drink of choice is...** sparkling fermented cider, because you can drink a lot of it without getting trashed.

fine Cooking®

Publisher	Maria Taylor
Assistant Publisher	Karen Lutjen
National Advertising Manager	Patrick J. O'Donnell 203-304-3250 podonnell@taunton.com
Director of Advertising Marketing	Kristen Lacey 203-304-3757 klacey@taunton.com
Advertising Sales East Coast	Judy Caruso 203-304-3468 jcaruso@taunton.com
	Margaret Fleming-O'Brien 203-304-3530 mflemingobrien@taunton.com
Midwest	Mark Adeszko 312-629-5222 madeszko@aol.com
West Coast	Chuck Carroll 818-972-9650 cwcarroll@earthlink.net
Advertising Sales Associate	Stacy DeJulio 203-304-3231 sdejulio@taunton.com
Advertising Inquiries	800-309-8940 fcads@taunton.com
Member Audit Bureau of Circulation	The Audit Bureau
Senior Consumer Marketing Director	Beth Reynolds, ProCirc
Circulation Manager	Noelia Garcia, ProCirc
Business Managers	David Pond, Megan Sangster

The Taunton Press
Inspiration for hands-on living®
Independent publishers since 1975
Founders, Paul & Jan Roman

President	Suzanne Roman
EVP & CFO	Timothy Rahr
SVP, Operations	Thomas Luxeder
SVP, Creative & Editorial	Susan Edelman
SVP, Technology	Jay Hartley
SVP & Group Publisher	Paul Spring
SVP & Publisher, Book Group	Donald Linn
SVP, Advertising Sales	Karl Elken
SVP & Group Publisher	Janine Scolpino
VP, Human Resources	Carol Marotti
VP & Controller	Wayne Reynolds
VP, Fulfillment	Patricia Williamson
VP, Finance	Kathy Worth
VP, Taunton Interactive	Jason Revzon
VP, Single Copy Sales	Jay Annis

Publishers of magazines, books, videos and online
Fine Woodworking • Fine Homebuilding
Threads • Fine Gardening • Fine Cooking
www.taunton.com

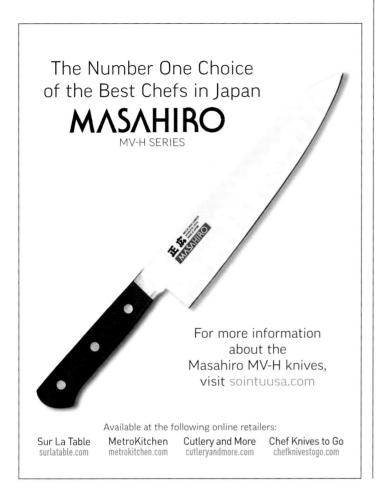

Questions of the Day

A cook's favorite question—What's for dinner?—doesn't need to be answered solo. Not when there are so many ways to join the community of cooks at FineCooking.com's CooksTalk.

Rate and review recipes.
Tell us what you like, what you don't, and what you changed.

Get inspired.
Need a tip or a recipe suggestion? Visit the forum and ask other readers.

Brag.
Post a photo of a dish you're proud of in the gallery.

Speak out.
Comment on our blogs or add your two cents to a member's blog.

Play.
Test your foodie knowledge in the trivia quiz in our games section.

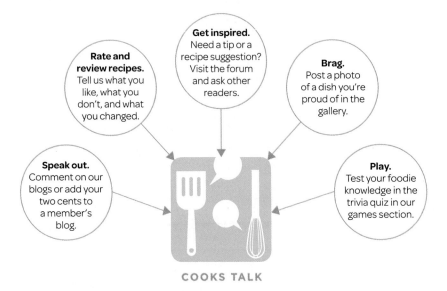

COOKS TALK

the farm report

What's in season near you? Share pictures of the fruits and vegetables you're finding at your local farmers' market or pulling from your own garden, and tell us what you're making with them in our new members' blog, **Farm to Fork.**

Winner's Spotlight

Congratulations to Barbara Jacobson (left), the winner of our first **Cook the Issue Challenge**. Barbara cooked and photographed all the recipes in our February/March issue, many of them more than once. Then she improvised and posted several variations, including a blood-orange marmalade and a chocolate-mousse tart.

Barbara wins a $200 Cooking.com gift card. Check out FineCooking.com for our latest contest.

fine Cooking®

To contact us:
Fine Cooking,
The Taunton Press,
63 South Main Street,
P.O. Box 5506, Newtown,
CT 06470-5506
Tel: 203-426-8171

Send an e-mail to:
fc@taunton.com

Visit:
www.finecooking.com

To submit an article proposal:
Write to *Fine Cooking* at the address above or
Call: 800-309-0744
Fax: 203-426-3434
Email: fc@taunton.com

To subscribe or place an order:
Visit www.finecooking.com/fcorder
or call: 800-888-8286
9am-9pm ET Mon-Fri
9am-5pm ET Sat

To find out about *Fine Cooking* products:
Visit www.finecooking.com/products

To get help with online member services:
Visit www.finecooking.com/customerservice

To find answers to frequently asked questions:
Visit www.finecooking.com/FAQs

To speak directly to a customer service professional:
Call 800-477-8727 9am-5pm ET Mon-Fri

To order products for your store:
Send an email to magazinesales@taunton.com

To advertise in *Fine Cooking*:
Call 800-309-8940
Or send an email to fcads@taunton.com

Mailing list:
We make a portion of our mailing list available to reputable firms. If you would prefer that we not include your name, please visit:
www.finecooking.com/privacy
or call: 800-477-8727 9am-5pm ET Mon-Fri

For employment information:
Visit www.careers.taunton.com

The Taunton guarantee:
If at any time you're not completely satisfied with *Fine Cooking*, you can cancel your subscription and receive a full and immediate refund of the entire subscription price. No questions asked.

Photographs, from top, by Pamela Winn, Martin Jacobson

Simply sensational!

Locally grown has never tasted this good.

fine Cooking fresh

350 Recipes that Celebrate the Seasons

350 TESTED RECIPES

Fresh is the long-awaited cookbook collection of the best recipes from *Fine Cooking* that feature fresh ingredients. It's a delicious way to eat healthy and make the most of farm-stand produce and organic foods at peak season.

- 350 recipes that work
- Proven how-to techniques
- #1 cooking authority

Fresh lets you create fabulous dishes with what's in the market with a minimum of fuss. So don't miss out!

Paperback, Product #071261
ISBN: 978-1-60085-109-4
$19.95

Order yours today!

Call toll free: 800-888-8286, mention offer: MC80031
Go to: www.Taunton.com/Fresh-Book

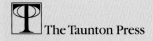
The Taunton Press

Shipping and handling extra. Payable in US funds.

© 2009 The Taunton Press

Photographs by Scott Phillips; food styling by Michelli Knauer

MARKETPLACE

Shop Smarter, Eat Better

TRY THIS

Kohlrabi

With its curious, Sputnik-like shape, kohlrabi has no trouble standing out among the more familiar vegetables in the produce aisle. But what exactly is it? And, most important, how do you cook with it? Read on for some answers.

What it is

It may look like a turnip, but kohlrabi is a type of cabbage related more to broc-coli and cauliflower than to any kind of root vegetable. It's a bulbous stem that grows just above ground, with leafy stalks protruding upward from various parts of the bulb. Both bulb and leaves are edible and are best cooked separately. You can find purple and green kohlrabi, although both are white inside and taste essentially the same.

Continued on page 17

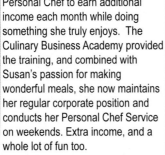

Why we love it

We can't get enough of kohlrabi's crisp, juicy texture and unusual flavor, which combines the earthy sweetness of cabbage and the crunchy bite of a turnip, with a hint of radish-like heat. Kohlrabi is delicious paired with chives, watercress, radishes, tomatoes, carrots, apples, and bacon as well as with seasonings like horseradish, sesame, ginger, and mustard. You can pickle it or use it as you would cabbage in your favorite slaws.

How to buy and store it

Look for bulbs 3 inches in diameter or less (about the size of a medium turnip). They're more tender and delicate in flavor than larger ones and usually don't require peeling. Large bulbs tend to be tough and woody, with a hard outer layer. Cut the leafy stalks off the bulbs and refrigerate them separately in zip-top bags. If stored properly, the bulbs can last a few weeks. The leaves, however, should be consumed within two or three days.

How to cook it

Use kohlrabi bulbs raw—shredded or thinly sliced—to add crunch to slaws and salads. Or cook them in a variety of ways. They're tasty sautéed or roasted (cut them into thin slices or bite-size wedges first) or added to your favorite braises and stews. You can also boil the bulbs until tender and mash them. When cooked, kohlrabi retains some of its crunchy texture, but the flavor mellows quite a bit. Treat the leafy tops as you would kale or collard greens: Sauté them in oil or add them to soups and stews in the last 15 minutes or so of cooking (trim off the stalks before cooking).

—*Melissa Pellegrino*

NEWS BITE

Politics of the plate

The laws governing food policy are complex and political, encompassing agribusiness, the obesity epidemic, and food safety. Expect the issue to come to a head this summer as Congress debates reauthorization of the Child Nutrition Act. This governs the school lunch program, but at stake are changes in the very way America's food system works. Go to the Food Research and Action Center (frac.org) for details.

kohlrabi-radish slaw with cumin and cilantro

To speed up the vegetable prep, use the grating and slicing blades on a food processor for the radishes, carrots, and cabbage, and the julienne cutter on a mandoline for the kohlrabi.

Serves 8

- 3 Tbs. white wine vinegar
- 1 tsp. Dijon mustard
- 1 tsp. clover honey
- ¼ tsp. cumin seeds, toasted, coarsely ground in a mortar and pestle

  Kosher salt and freshly ground black pepper
- 5 Tbs. canola oil
- 5 radishes, grated (about 1 cup)
- 3 medium carrots, grated (about 1½ cups)
- 2 small unpeeled kohlrabi bulbs (purple, green, or both), trimmed and cut into ⅛-inch-thick matchsticks (3 cups)
- ½ medium head green cabbage (about 1 lb.), thinly sliced (5 cups)
- ⅓ cup chopped fresh cilantro

In a small bowl whisk the vinegar, mustard, honey, cumin, ¼ tsp. salt, and a pinch of pepper. Gradually whisk in the canola oil until combined. **Put the radishes,** carrot, kohlrabi, cabbage, and cilantro in a large bowl. Pour in the dressing and gently toss to combine. Season to taste with salt and pepper.

Leeks, Peas, and Strawberries

Nine ways to use three seasonal ingredients we can't get enough of. *Fine Cooking* editors share some delicious ideas.

Peas

Laura Giannatempo: I love to quick-braise peas in good chicken or vegetable broth and then finish them with butter and lots of chopped fresh herbs. Mint is a natural, but I also like thyme or basil.

Denise Mickelsen: Treat peas like fava beans and make a tasty fresh pea spread (it's especially delicious early in the season, when the peas are tiny and sweet). Blanch peas in salted water for a minute or so, drain, and then mash them with grated pecorino, extra-virgin olive oil, a touch of lemon juice, salt, and pepper. Spread thickly on toasted baguette slices.

Lisa Waddle: For a great quick pasta, start by cooking a minced shallot in a little olive oil until soft and then add some grated lemon zest. Meanwhile, cook the pasta shape of your choice in boiling salted water and add peas in the last two minutes. Drain, saving some of the water, and then add the pasta and peas to the shallots, along with some of the pasta water and a squeeze of lemon juice. Top with grated Parmigiano-Reggiano and torn fresh mint leaves.

Leeks

Sarah Breckenridge: Make a melted-leek-topped flatbread by slicing leeks into half-moons and then cooking them slowly in butter and olive oil until completely tender. Stir in a little crème fraîche, spoon the mixture on top of a stretched round of pizza dough, and bake on a pizza stone (or on the grill).

Allison Ehri Kreitler: In France, it's very common to halve trimmed small leeks lengthwise (white and light-green parts), steam them until completely tender, and toss them with a Dijon vinaigrette.

Jennifer Armentrout: Chef and cookbook author David Tanis gave me the idea to use leeks as a bed for baked fish. Slowly cook thinly sliced leeks in butter or oil with lots of minced garlic, chopped fresh thyme and sage, salt, and pepper until soft but not brown. Spread in a baking dish and arrange skinless fish fillets on top. Drizzle the fish with a little oil and then sprinkle with finely grated lemon zest, salt, and pepper. Bake at 400°F.

Strawberries

Sarah Breckenridge: One of my favorite strawberry desserts is as simple as setting out whole ripe berries with a bowl of sour cream (or crème fraîche) and a bowl of brown sugar and letting people dip away. For a tidier presentation, stir together the brown sugar and sour cream and drop a dollop over sliced berries.

Juli Roberts: For a fast dessert, I macerate strawberry quarters in balsamic vinegar (preferably authentic Aceto Balsamico di Modena) and a bit of sugar and serve over vanilla ice cream.

Melissa Pellegrino: Try making a spinach salad with sliced strawberries, blue cheese, toasted almonds, and a balsamic vinaigrette.

Photographs by Scott Phillips

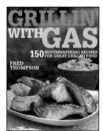

The Big Freeze

BY ABIGAIL JOHNSON DODGE

IF YOU HAVE A VEGETABLE GARDEN in the back yard, or even if you're just a farmers' market junkie, you know you can't possibly use up the season's bounty of fruits and vegetables. It's just too much in too little time. If jams and preserves are not your thing, think about freezing, which is a great way to preserve the fresh flavors of fruits and veggies at their peak. And it's easy—all you need is a baking sheet, heavy-duty freezer bags, and the best your summer garden has to offer (oh, and a freezer, of course). Here's a handy guide for freezing all the season's favorites.

how to freeze
Three easy steps from fresh to frozen

1. Create a level area in your freezer to fit a rimmed baking sheet. If you're strapped for space, use something smaller—like a cake pan—and repeat the freezing steps below as needed.

2. Line the baking sheet with parchment, foil, or waxed paper. Arrange the prepared fruits or vegetables in a single layer, making sure they don't touch (see chart opposite for prep directions). Freeze until solid, 60 to 90 minutes, depending on size and freezer temperature.

3. Transfer to heavy-duty freezer bags. Press out as much air from the bag as possible (if you have a vacuum sealer, use it), seal, and store in the back of the freezer (the coldest part) until ready to use. To thaw, transfer the amount you need to a bowl or plate and thaw in the refrigerator.

from freezer to table

Freezing is a great way to preserve flavor, but don't expect fruits and vegetables that have been frozen to have the same texture as fresh ones. That's why it's better to cook with them than eat them out of hand. Here's how:

FRUITS

Frozen: Use in pie or galette fillings and in smoothies.
Partially frozen (5 to 10 minutes out of the freezer at room temperature): Use in sauces, smoothies, cake batters, and pancakes, and as garnishes.
Thawed: Use in sauces, smoothies, and jams.

VEGETABLES

Frozen: Use in soups, braises, and stews, and steamed.
Thawed: Use in sautés, stir-fries, and purées.

A couple of exceptions: Tomatoes should always be thawed and drained before using in soups, braises, stews, and sauces (don't use in sautés or stir-fries). Corn on the cob can be steamed frozen but should be thawed before grilling.

freezer basics

Freezer temp Set your freezer at 0°F or colder (use a freezer thermometer to check). Many home freezers are opened and closed frequently, causing the temperature to fluctuate. This makes fruits and vegetables thaw slightly and refreeze—not ideal for texture and taste. To prevent this, stash frozen fruits and veggies as far from the door as possible.

Freezing time Stand-alone freezer (infrequently opened chest or upright): 10 to 12 months. Frequently opened freezer compartment: 3 months.

Photographs by Scott Phillips

How to prep 20 fruits and vegetables for freezing

VEGETABLES		PREP	BLANCH
English peas		Shell peas	Yes (1 to 1½ minutes)
Snap peas and snow peas		Trim strings	Yes (1 to 1½ minutes)
Wax or green beans		Trim stem ends	Yes (1 to 2 minutes)
Bell peppers		Remove stem and seeds and cut into 4 pieces or into strips or dice	No
Asparagus		Trim woody bottoms	Yes (1 to 2 minutes)
Spinach		Wash and trim	Yes (1 to 1½ minutes)
Tomatoes		Peel (you'll need to blanch them first), seed, and cut into chunks	Yes, to remove the peel (30 seconds)
Broccoli and cauliflower		Remove stems and cut florets into 1½-inch pieces	Yes (2 to 3 minutes)
Corn		Remove husks and leave the cob whole	Yes (3 to 5 minutes); cut kernels off after blanching, if needed
Rhubarb		Cut into 2-inch chunks	Not necessary but can help retain the vivid color
FRUITS		**PREP**	**BLANCH**
Raspberries, blueberries, blackberries		Leave whole, wash, and dry well	No
Strawberries		Remove hull, wash, and dry well	No
Cherries		Leave whole, wash, and dry well; remove the pit, if you like	No
Peaches and nectarines		Peel (the peel hardens during freezing) and remove the pit; then cut into 1-inch wedges	No
Apricots		Remove the pit and cut in half, or in quarters if large	No

why blanch?

Most vegetables benefit from blanching before freezing. The process stops the enzymes' aging action while slowing vitamin and nutrient loss. It also brightens and sets the vegetables' color. In general, fruits don't need blanching (unless it's to remove the peel). Here's how to blanch:

1. Bring a large pot of water to a rolling boil (about 2 quarts per 2 to 3 cups of vegetables).

2. Working in small batches, add the vegetables. Allow the water to return to a boil and cook very briefly (see the chart for blanching times).

3. Using a large slotted spoon, scoop out the veggies and immediately immerse them in a large bowl of ice water to stop the cooking. Remove and dry thoroughly before freezing.

Abigail Johnson Dodge is a Fine Cooking *contributing editor.*

Hearts of Palm

Making the most of a favorite food find from a warehouse store.

BY ALLISON EHRI KREITLER

YOU LOVE THE SOFT CRUNCH and mild artichoke flavor of hearts of palm, so you buy a big jar—or two. (We know! We do the same.) But what else can you do with these beauties besides toss them in salads? We have some ideas. Here are three amazing dishes—an hors d'oeuvre, a starter, and a side—that take this summer favorite to a whole new level.

hearts of palm and radish coins with shrimp

Yields 24 hors d'oeuvres

3-4	hearts of palm (1- to 1½-inch diameter), rinsed and cut into ¼-inch-thick coins (you'll need 24)
2	Tbs. plus ¼ tsp. fresh lime juice
2	Tbs. extra-virgin olive oil
	Pinch of granulated sugar
	Kosher salt
1	Tbs. mayonnaise, preferably Hellmann's or Best Foods brand
¼	tsp. coriander seeds, toasted and coarsely ground in a mortar
¼	tsp. freshly grated lime zest
	Pinch of cayenne
	Freshly ground black pepper
48	small peeled and deveined cooked shrimp (71 to 90 or 100 to 150 per lb.)
5-6	radishes (1 to 1½ inches wide), sliced into ¼-inch-thick coins (you'll need 24)
24	fresh cilantro leaves for garnish

Lay the palm coins in a single layer in a nonreactive dish. Drizzle with 2 Tbs. of the lime juice, 3 Tbs. water, and the olive

The Big Buy

What: Hearts of palm packed in water.
How much: Two 25-oz. jars.
How to store: Once opened, refrigerate them in their jar, covered in the water they come in. They will keep for up to two weeks. Hearts of palm benefit from quick rinsing and drying before using, which helps remove some of the jarred flavor.

oil. Sprinkle evenly with sugar and a generous pinch of salt. Shake the dish to coat the palm coins and let sit while preparing the remaining ingredients.

In a medium bowl, mix the remaining ¼ tsp. lime juice with the mayonnaise, coriander seeds, lime zest, cayenne, a generous pinch of salt, and a pinch of pepper. Toss the shrimp with the mayonnaise and season to taste with salt and pepper.

Carefully drain the hearts of palm and pat dry with paper towels. Top each radish coin with a palm coin of similar size, two shrimp, and a cilantro leaf.

arugula with hearts of palm, grapefruit, and oil-cured olives

Serves 4 as an appetizer

1	large Ruby Red grapefruit
¼	cup extra-virgin olive oil
1½	Tbs. Champagne vinegar
1	tsp. finely chopped fresh rosemary
¼	tsp. crushed red pepper flakes
	Kosher salt and freshly ground black pepper
3	hearts of palm, rinsed, halved lengthwise, and cut on a diagonal into ¾-inch pieces (about ¾ cup)
¼	cup pitted black oil-cured olives, halved lengthwise
7	oz. arugula (preferably bunched), trimmed (about 5 loosely packed cups)
¼	cup loosely packed fresh flat-leaf parsley leaves

Finely grate ½ tsp. zest from the grapefruit; set aside. Slice just enough off the top and bottom of the grapefruit to expose the fruit. Stand the grapefruit on one cut end and slice away all of the peel and white pith. Working over a bowl, cut the segments away from the membranes, letting them fall into the bowl. Then, over another bowl, squeeze the membranes to get any remaining juice. Cut each segment into thirds.

In a small bowl, whisk 2 Tbs. of the reserved grapefruit juice and the zest with the oil, vinegar, rosemary, red pepper flakes, ¼ tsp. salt, and a pinch of pepper.

In a small bowl, mix the grapefruit segments, hearts of palm, and olives with 2 Tbs. of the dressing.

Toss the arugula and parsley in a large bowl with a generous pinch of salt and 3 Tbs. of the dressing. Divide the arugula among 4 plates, top with the hearts of palm mixture, and drizzle with the remaining dressing, if desired.

grilled hearts of palm, radicchio, and asparagus

This makes a great accompaniment to grilled chicken or pork. Use a vegetable peeler to shave the Parmigiano.

Serves 4 as a side dish

5	hearts of palm, rinsed and patted dry
½	head radicchio, halved lengthwise (about 4 oz.)
½	bunch asparagus, ends trimmed (about 8 oz.)
¼	cup extra-virgin olive oil
	Kosher salt and freshly ground black pepper
1	Tbs. fresh lemon juice
½	tsp. finely grated lemon zest
	Pinch of granulated sugar
3	very thin slices prosciutto di Parma, torn into strips (about 1¾ oz.)
1	oz. shaved Parmigiano-Reggiano (scant ½ cup)

Heat a gas grill on high or prepare a hot charcoal grill fire.

In a large bowl, toss the hearts of palm, radicchio, and asparagus with

2 Tbs. of the olive oil, ¼ tsp. salt, and several grinds pepper. Grill, flipping as needed, until nicely marked all over and tender, 4 to 5 minutes total. Set aside until cool enough to handle.

Meanwhile, in a small bowl, whisk the remaining 2 Tbs. olive oil with the lemon juice, zest, sugar, ¼ tsp. salt, and a pinch of pepper.

Core the radicchio. Cut the radicchio, asparagus, and hearts of palm into pieces about 3 inches long by ½ inch wide. Return to the large bowl and toss with the prosciutto, Parmigiano, and 2 Tbs. of the vinaigrette. Serve drizzled with the remaining vinaigrette, if desired.

The Myths of Marinating

Before firing up the grill, get the facts on what this technique can (and can't) do. **BY BRIAN GEIGER**

DRAGONS. SWIMMING JUST AFTER EATING. The number of calories in cake eaten on your birthday. The tenderizing effect of a marinade. What's the connection? All of these things are surrounded in mythology.

With grilling season upon us, I thought I'd put aside my dragon sword and tackle some of the more widely held beliefs about marinades to see how they hold up to Food Geek scrutiny.

MYTH 1: A marinade will infuse a steak completely if you let it soak long enough. (Or if you vacuum seal it. Or if you inject the marinade into the steak.)

FACT: Whether three minutes or three days, a marinade penetrates the meat by only a fraction of an inch. Here's an easy experiment you can do to prove this. Take a steak, plop it in a zip-top bag with some marinade, squeeze out as much of the air as possible, and put it in your refrigerator for 3 days. Take it out, cut the steak in half, and see where the meat is darker. You'll find the marinade has perme-

ated about ⅛ inch. The reason: Meat is made up of bundles of muscle fibers, which are packed densely together. That density blocks the marinade from getting through.

Those vacuum sealers that claim to help the marinade drill down deeper and faster don't do anything to pull apart the cells and let the marinade (or any other liquid) in.

You could inject some marinade deeper into the meat using a syringe sold specifically for that purpose. This would give you pockets of flavor below the surface. The problem is that the syringe punctures the surface of the meat,

creating little escape hatches for the juices during cooking. After all, what lets liquid in also lets it out, and while the steak is cooking and shrinking, the moisture is going to look for any way it can to get out. A dry steak is the opposite of what you're going for, so resist the temptation.

Besides, you don't really want your entire steak to taste like the marinade. The goal is to enhance the flavor of the meat, not cover it up.

THE LESSON: Marinades may never penetrate deeply into a piece of meat, but they do flavor the surface.

MYTH 2: A marinade will tenderize a tough piece of meat.

FACT: Not exactly. As I explained above, a marinade doesn't penetrate very deeply into a piece of meat, so it can't transform its makeup. Some chemical tenderizing does take place on the surface, because the acids in a marinade break down muscle tissue, a process called denaturing. Let it go too long, though, and the muscle tissue will coagulate, squeezing out water molecules and resulting in mushy yet tough meat.

How long is too long? Depends on what you're marinating and how strong an acid you're using. A relatively tough cut of meat like flank steak can handle a more acidic marinade (say one part acid to two parts oil) longer than delicate shrimp (which would be better served with an acid-to-oil ratio of one

to four). The acid in yogurt and buttermilk is far milder than that in wine, vinegar, and lemon juice. Yogurt and buttermilk also contain calcium, which activates enzymes in meat that break down muscle fibers. So dairy products are a better choice for delicate proteins.

But the only way to tenderize meat beyond the surface is through cooking slowly in a liquid (also known as braising) or through aging. In aging, natural enzymes in the meat break down the tough connective tissues all the way through the meat. Wet aging is done by sealing the meat air-tight in the fridge; dry aging involves a controlled rotting in a cool, well-ventilated environment. It causes molds and yeasts to grow on the surface, which are cut off before cooking.

In olden days, people left meats in an acidic marinade for days or weeks, and the acid in the marinade protected the surface of the meat from spoiling while the rest of the meat matured. (Of course, the surface texture of the meat suffered.) As a result, many people think it's the marinade that leads to tender meat, when it's really time that does the work.

THE LESSON: Aging, not marinating, is the key to tender meat.

MYTH 3: Marinating always takes place before cooking.

FACT: Sometimes, a marinade can *do* the cooking. As explained in Myth 2, the acid in a marinade denatures a food's proteins. Heat does the same thing. So when a delicate protein like fish is bathed in an acid, such as lemon juice, the proteins will be denatured and then coagulate (technically, the acid is unraveling the molecules and altering their

chemical and physical properties). This causes raw foods to firm up and appear more opaque, as in ceviche.

THE LESSON: A marinade can take the place of cooking.

MYTH 4: Some marinades can make grilled foods healthier.

FACT: This one is true, actually. If you cook red meat at a high enough temperature, you can create heterocyclic amines, or HCAs. HCAs are carcinogenic, so you'd be smart to avoid them. However, herbs in the mint family, such as sage, thyme, rosemary, and, er, mint, contain phenolic compounds, which are impressive antioxidants. It's believed that the phenolic compounds keep the HCAs from forming, according to a study published by a team of food researchers at Kansas State University. A marinade with oil allows those herbs to stick to the surface of the meat and do their antioxidant best.

THE LESSON: Some myths are true.

MYTH 5: A marinade adds flavor to meat.

FACT: This one is true as well. Restrained marinating adds a layer of flavor to meats and vegetables that can elevate a simple steak or chicken leg. Think about your last grilling adventure. An average steak is received with a chorus of "Great steak!" and promptly forgotten. A steak marinated briefly in a balanced mixture of wine, spices, and oil and then grilled perfectly haunts the eater, even when the days of summer have waned. The memory may have your guests digging out their grills in winter in an attempt to recapture that taste experience.

THE LESSON: A marinade is the secret to creating a steak of legend.

You can almost certainly swim after eating without getting cramps, and cake eaten on your birthday probably has some calories after all. But there is still magic in the way a marinade adds flavor to grilled foods. With science as your guide, you can bring a mythical experience to your backyard grilling party every time.

Brian Geiger is a robotics project manager by day and The Food Geek at night and on weekends. He blogs at FineCooking.com.

anatomy of a marinade

A marinade has three essential elements. Here's what they do:

ACID
Whether vinegar, citrus juice, wine, buttermilk, or yogurt, acid breaks down the protein on the surface of the meat, allowing it to initially absorb moisture and flavor.

AROMATICS
Herbs, spices, chile peppers, garlic, ginger, and onion provide most of the flavor.

OIL
This is the flavor delivery system. Because it is more viscous than water, oil helps hold herbs and aromatics to the surface of the meat or vegetable.

HOW TO MAKE

Vichyssoise

This chilled potato-leek soup is an elegant summer classic.

BY JAMES PETERSON

SMOOTH, CREAMY, AND COLD, classic French vichyssoise is the perfect hot-weather soup. And it's so easy to make, it should be in every cook's recipe box. The technique is straightforward: Leeks and potatoes are simmered in milk and then puréed in a blender. The challenge is to get the smoothest, silkiest texture possible—because that's what vichyssoise is all about.

Need to Know

Four essential tips for perfect texture

1 Choose the right potatoes.
With their rich flavor and medium starch content, Yukon Gold potatoes are the best choice. Russets are too starchy and can make the soup mealy, while waxy potatoes like Red Bliss can turn it gluey and gelatinous.

2 Purée in a blender.
For the absolute finest texture, purée in a regular blender; an immersion (hand) blender won't give you as smooth a result.

3 Strain well.
To get rid of any residual coarseness, strain the soup through a fine sieve, using the back of a spoon or ladle to push the soup through (as shown in the photo below).

4 Add water.
If the soup is too thick, add a little cold water to thin it before serving. The consistency should be that of heavy cream.

COOK'S TIP

To clean a leek

Leeks grow with soil piled around them, so grit and dirt accumulate between their layers. To clean a leek thoroughly, trim the root end and cut off the dark-green top. Then, slit the leek lengthwise, without cutting all the way through. Open it like a book and hold it root end up under cold running water, riffling through the layers until it is completely clean.

tool box

The simple utensils needed for vichyssoise are essential to any well-stocked kitchen:
- 4-quart pot
- Blender
- Fine sieve

Photographs by Scott Phillips; food styling by Michelli Knauer

For sources, see Where to Buy It

classic vichyssoise

Serve this refreshing cold soup as a first course or as a light lunch, accompanied by a green salad.

Yields about 6 cups; serves 6

- 4 medium leeks, trimmed and washed as directed opposite, sliced ⅛ inch thick (about 3 cups)
- 2 large Yukon Gold potatoes, peeled and sliced ⅛ inch thick (about 4 cups)
- 2 cups whole milk
  Kosher salt
- 1 cup heavy cream
- 1 Tbs. thinly sliced fresh chives, for garnish

Combine the leeks, potatoes, milk, and 2 cups water in a 4-quart pot.
Bring to a simmer over medium-high heat. Add 1½ tsp. salt, reduce the heat to medium low, and simmer until a potato slice falls apart when you poke it with a fork, about 20 minutes. Remove from the heat, stir in the cream, and let cool briefly.
Purée the soup, preferably using a regular blender and working in batches, filling it only half way each time.

Strain the puréed soup through a fine sieve. Let cool to room temperature, stirring occasionally (stirring prevents a skin from forming), and then refrigerate until thoroughly chilled.
Before serving, thin the soup with water if necessary—it should be the consistency of heavy cream. Season to taste with salt. Serve cold in chilled bowls, garnished with the chives.

James Peterson is a cooking teacher and award-winning cookbook author.

Great Finds

Our latest buys for the kitchen and table. BY DENISE MICKELSEN

Three in One

Sagaform's sleek new pasta tool can be used three ways: you can measure dried pasta, serve it after cooking, and even grate cheese to finish the dish. **$18 at conranusa.com; 866-755-9079.**

Sweet Treats

Husband-and-wife team Don and Sue Morris began selling their all-natural, buttery madeleines from the back of their Volkswagon bus in 1976; today, the tender cakes are a bit easier to get (even Whole Foods sells them), and we can't stop eating them. Available in five flavors (lemon zest is our favorite); prices vary. **Donsuemor.com; for stores, call 888-420-4441.**

Family Affair

These artisanal preserves, made in small batches from fruits produced on an organic family farm in Ortezzano, Italy, are intensely flavorful and have just the right touch of sweetness. **Muccichini preserves, $9.95 to $18.95 a jar, assorted flavors (apricot is shown here) at formaggiokitchen.com; 888-212-3224.**

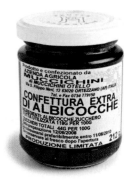

Take It Outside

It's easy to enjoy your wine in the sunshine with this all-in-one picnic carrier, which includes tumblers, a corkscrew, and an insulated bag to keep your bottle cool. **Enid wine picnic tin, $130 at picnicfun.com; 800-706-3981.**

Eco-Chic

The stylish designs that decorate these stainless-steel water bottles are just part of their appeal—they're also BPA-free and come in three sizes. **$16 to $21; earthlust.com for stores; 415-252-5878.**

Natural Elegance

Made from fallen Pennsylvania hardwood trees, these graceful serving utensils were designed after model airplane propellers. **Spoon, fork, and spreader set, $55 at teroforma.com; 877-899-1190.**

Photographs by Scott Phillips

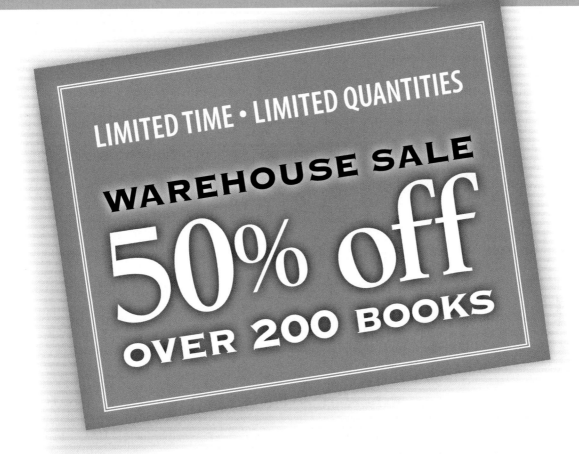

The Reading List

New must-buys for food lovers. BY KIMBERLY Y. MASIBAY

Well-Preserved

Recipes and Techniques for Putting Up Small Batches of Seasonal Foods

**By Eugenia Bone
(Clarkson Potter, $25)**

In these waste-not, want-not times, it's no surprise that canning and preserving are staging a big comeback. What is surprising, though, is how elegant and accessible these endeavors are in the hands of food writer Eugenia Bone.

Bone has perfected simpler techniques for putting up small amounts of seasonal foods using low-tech options like freezing, curing, and oil-preserving. Though she does cover traditional canning and pickling methods, this book isn't the place to look for old-fashioned jams for your morning toast. Bone treats her urbane alcohol-, vinegar-, and herb-spiked preserves like condiments, brushing Apricot-Amaretto Jam over a garlic-studded pork roast, and stirring Pear, Port, and Thyme Conserve into silky butternut squash soup.

Bone puts up far more than fruit, though, and offers recipes for pickled and marinated vegetables; nut, bean, and mushroom sauces; and cured, smoked, and oil-preserved meats, poultry, and

fish. If, like Bone, you can't seem to stop overbuying at the farmers' market, then this captivating book just might prove to be your saving grace.

Seven Fires, Grilling the Argentine Way

By Francis Mallmann with Peter Kaminsky (Artisan Books, $35)

Judging from this glorious book, Patagonian chef Francis Mallmann, one of Buenos Aires's most celebrated restaurateurs, is nothing less than a poetic genius of the flame. His recipes—from Pork Loin Chops Wrapped in Crisped Prosciutto and Sage, to Caramelized Apple Pancakes, to simple "Burnt" Tomato Halves—are completely approachable. And his cooking is utterly unpretentious, a cuisine "of wood fire and cast iron" inspired by his Andean heritage.

Throughout the book, Mallmann details his seven fiery techniques for grilling. You could amuse yourself all summer long exploring his methods, from the massively hot *infiernillo*, in which large cuts of salt-encrusted meat roast between two fires, one above and one below, to the gentle *rescoldo*, where whole pumpkins, potatoes, or unhusked

ears of corn cook beneath the embers and ashes of a slowly dying fire.

Try Mallmann's recipe for A Perfect Steak. Then try it again. And again. The ingredients couldn't be simpler: rib-eye steak, coarse salt. Attaining perfection—that heavenly confluence of seared crust and rosy succulence—may require some practice. But that's just part of the fun.

I Loved, I Lost, I Made Spaghetti

By Giulia Melucci (Grand Central Publishing, $23.99)

When life gives you lemons, why not write a cookbook? That's just what former publishing exec Giulia Melucci has done in this lighthearted memoir about her fruitless attempts to cook her way to happily ever after.

Melucci weaves together her dating history with mirthful tales of love and loss, from her first romance (Kit, a cuddly but clueless alcoholic) to her last (Lachlan, an impotent novelist who takes off after she scores him a lucrative book deal). In your hurry to follow the story, you may be tempted to whiz past the recipes that pepper the narrative, but don't. Many of them are gems and as amusing to read as they are delicious to eat (like Lachlan's Farfalle with Zucchini and Egg). Melucci may not have found her man (yet), but her recipes are keepers.

Kimberly Y. Masibay is a Fine Cooking *contributing editor.*

Find more reviews and editor picks at our new Books That Cook blog at FineCooking.com.

what we're reading now

A family friend gave me my copy of *The Art of Fine Baking* by Paula Peck when I was still in high school. It may be an old (from 1961) paperback without any photos, but I was instantly captivated—and remain so—by Peck's matter-of-fact writing, which erases any fear of attempting a challenging or unfamiliar recipe (like her incredible chestnut buttercream). —*Lisa Waddle*

Go with the Flow

What's new in kitchen faucet design. BY DENISE MICKELSEN

KITCHEN FAUCETS HAVE COME A LONG WAY. These days, it's not enough to spout hot or cold water on command. New models twist and turn to dispense water in any direction (even outside the sink), color the water according to its temperature, and even turn on and off with the tap of a finger. Here are a few of our favorites.

stay put

Kohler's Karbon articulated faucet, available in both sink- and wall-mount models, is jointed so it stays in the exact position you want it, either inside or outside the sink (wall mount, shown, available in polished chrome for $1,300, and vibrant stainless for $1,625; go to kohler.com for stores).

lighten up

New from the Gessi Just Color faucet line, this model emits water lit by a concealed colored LED (water goes red for hot, purple for warm, blue for cold) without using a drop of electricity—turbines power the light as water passes through them (available in chrome for $2,150, and satin nickel for $2,795; call 714-808-0099 for stores).

the ultimate

The Kizoku faucet from Swiss-based Mec Electronics AG has it all—touch technology to turn the faucet on and off and to control water flow rate, a retractable, flexible spout, LED lights to indicate water temperature, and a sleek design to boot. The Kizoku, which costs about $1,095, isn't available in the United States, but if you have to have it, you can call Mec directly at 011-4191-835-0105 to place an order, or visit mec-ag.ch for more details.

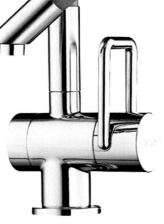

super flex

Arwa of Switzerland's Twinflex faucet offers a flexible spout system, and the spout comes in four great colors: orange, pigeon blue, beige-gray, and black ($950 at geminibkp.com; 520-770-0667).

soft touch

Delta's Pilar faucet boasts touch 2.0 technology, which means you can start or stop the flow of water by tapping anywhere on the handle or spout. It also sports a magnetic retractable spray head (available in polished chrome for $337, or stainless steel for $426 at efaucets.com).

Photographs courtesy of the manufacturers

Plenty Fresh

Nutritionist **Ellie Krieger** uses fresh herbs to amp up flavor in a healthful way.

AS A NUTRITIONIST AND A BORN FOOD LOVER, I'm a walking contradiction to many people. How do I reconcile a foodie's focus on flavor and indulgence with the nutritional wisdom that I should cut back on such flavor builders as butter, cream, cheese, and bacon? Well, I don't always have to—I use healthier flavor boosters instead. Think chile peppers, ground spices, fresh aromatics like ginger and garlic, and my absolute favorites: fresh herbs.

Herbs are one of those magical ingredients that have the power to transform a dish. Not only do they add tremendous flavor, but they also infuse food with enticing aromas and beautiful color. And if that weren't enough, they're full of health-protective antioxidants and are a surprisingly rich source of vitamin A.

A Major Player While it's easy to think of herbs as a garnish or a subtle hint in a dish, I encourage you to take a new look at them as a major player. A generous dose of basil, mint, dill, or parsley can make any hum-drum green salad burst with flavor. Add fresh mint to a standard turkey sandwich, and it's like hitting the refresh button. A bunch of basil, parsley, or cilantro puréed with olive oil and a touch of lemon juice makes a vibrant salsa verde that's great for drizzling over scallops or grilled fish or meat. And heartier herbs like rosemary, thyme, and sage make terrific rubs and marinades for roasted meats and poultry.

Such herbal abundance translates well into many grain dishes, too. In traditional Middle-Eastern tabbouleh, for example, fresh, grassy flat-leaf parsley is a dominant ingredient, held aloft by robust bulgur wheat. In the same vein, I love making light, summery pastas that rely heavily on a combination of aromatic fresh herbs for flavor impact. The recipe here is a go-to summer dish for me that's simple, fresh, and full of flavor. It takes advantage of the bounty of zucchini and leaves it to the herbs to deliver the freshness of the season right to the plate—no cream or butter required.

Nutritional Wisdom That's not to say we should ban butter and other flavor standbys. I use all those ingredients in my own cooking, but strategically and in small amounts for maximum effect (a little freshly grated Parmigiano, for instance, goes a long way in this penne dish). But a liberal amount of fresh herbs sprinkled on a dish just before serving gets the job done in a way that tastes good and is good for you. That's my kind of nutritional know-how.

good to know

- Fresh herbs are full of antioxidants and vitamin A.

- Let herbs be a major player in a dish, not just a garnish—think cups, not teaspoons.

- Swap ⅓ cup Parmesan sprinkled on pasta for a handful of fresh herbs, and keep the big flavor while saving about 100 calories.

For Ellie, there's big flavor in fresh herbs.

Photographs by Scott Phillips; food styling by Susan Sugarman

penne with zucchini, fresh herbs, and lemon zest

Serves 4 (serving size, 2¼ cups)

Kosher salt

¾ **lb. whole wheat penne**

¼ **cup extra-virgin olive oil**

2 **medium zucchini (8 oz. each), cut in half lengthwise and sliced crosswise into ¼-inch-thick half moons**

4 **large cloves garlic, thinly sliced**

2 **tsp. finely grated lemon zest**

Freshly ground black pepper

¼ **cup freshly grated Parmigiano-Reggiano**

3 **Tbs. coarsely chopped fresh mint**

3 **Tbs. coarsely chopped fresh basil**

3 **Tbs. coarsely chopped fresh flat-leaf parsley**

Bring a large pot of well-salted water to a boil over high heat. Add the penne and cook according to package instructions until al dente. **Meanwhile,** heat the oil in a 12-inch skillet over medium-high heat. Add the zucchini and cook, stirring occasionally, until barely tender and just starting to brown, about 3 minutes. Add the garlic and cook, stirring occasionally, until the garlic is soft and fragrant, an additional 2 to 3 minutes. Remove from the heat. Stir in the lemon zest, ¾ tsp salt, and ¼ tsp. pepper. **Reserve ½ cup** pasta cooking water and drain the pasta. Add the pasta to the zucchini mixture along with the Parmigiano, mint, basil, and parsley. Season to taste with salt and pepper. Toss to combine, adding some of the reserved water if necessary to moisten the pasta, and serve immediately.

Registered dietitian Ellie Krieger is a Fine Cooking *contributing editor.*

Toaster Ovens

These days, the latest models do much more than toast your morning bagel. Here are our top picks for this handy countertop appliance. BY NICKI PENDLETON WOOD

FOR MANY, THE TOASTER OVEN bell signals that breakfast is ready. Ideal for heating morning pastries and turning out golden bagels, toaster ovens are also great for reheating, defrosting, toasting nuts, broiling, baking, and even roasting fish fillets, chops, and chicken breasts. And depending on the job at hand, they can be more practical than a standard oven because they heat quickly, cook faster, and use less energy. Here are our favorite models.

toast points

With many models to choose from, each offering different features, there are a few things to keep in mind when shopping for a new toaster oven.

Construction Look for sturdy construction. Besides promising a longer, repair-free life, an oven with thick walls, good door fit, and smoothly operating hinges also offers heat efficiency.

Size Rather than eyeball it or buy on a hunch, measure the counter space you have and buy accordingly. Some toaster ovens have an upper and lower rack for extra vertical space, while others use the "pizza bump" (a bulge at the back of the oven) to maximize interior space but keep a modest footprint.

Function If you use your toaster oven only to toast bread and maybe melt cheese, avoid the extra features of more complex ovens.

Safety Consider models with an automatic shut-off function (that is, a timer), audible ticking, and a bell that signals the oven's task is complete. Some models also offer a cool-to-the-touch exterior.

THE POWERHOUSE

KitchenAid countertop oven, KC01005

$130; macys.com
Size: 18 x 10 x 11½ inches

If you're looking for a sturdy, powerful toaster oven that can tackle any kitchen task you throw at it, this is the one for you. It doesn't offer a lot of bells and whistles (the two rack positions are a nice feature, though), but it has reassuringly heavy construction (backed up by a one-year warranty), intuitive functioning, and a large interior space so you can cook bigger items. It heats quickly, but the heat is well controlled—a frozen pizza left in the 350°F oven for nearly 20 minutes didn't burn. It broiled burgers and toasted nuts and bread very well.

Two rack positions

how we tested

We tested 14 ovens, all designed primarily as toasters but capable of performing other cooking tasks such as baking and broiling. We chose ovens with small to medium footprints, without convection, and with analog dials to control the functions.

We toasted bread, browned nuts, made cheese toast, and baked croutons and frozen pizzas, all the while looking for even browning, speed, and good heat control. We also baked a small batch of cookies or homemade pretzels, broiled a burger, baked a potato, and roasted sweet potato fries.

FORM AND FUNCTION

Cuisinart toaster oven, TOB 50

$100; cuisinart.com
Size: 16 x 9¼ x 12¼ inches

This toaster oven has both looks and smarts, so to speak. The sleek, almost retro design is attractive, and it offers a spacious ½-cubic-foot interior. The smarts come from this oven's extra features and all-around good performance. It heats evenly and did a great job baking a pizza and a sweet potato, and toasting nuts. Start and stop buttons offer easy control over your cooking. A pierced metal broiler tray makes broiling meats and fish easy, and the exterior stayed cool even when the oven was blazing hot inside. The three-year warranty is another bonus. One puzzling feature: the crumb tray is removed from the back, inconvenient if the oven is pushed against a wall.

Start and stop buttons

BEST FEATURES

DeLonghi toaster oven with broiler, EO-1200B

$60; delonghi.com
Size: 17¼ x 8¾ x 12¾ inches

This oven has a lot to offer besides the basics of toasting, baking, and broiling (in fact, toasting was probably its weakest point). There are two positions for the wire rack, and it baked crisp chicken fingers, a beautiful tray of cookies, and homemade pretzels. But its best aspect is a "pizza bump"—a pushed-out back to accommodate a 12-inch pizza—which gives the oven a bit more room inside (this model had the smallest interior of those tested). There's also a "stay-on" feature for regular baking, an automatic shut-off function so your toast doesn't burn, and a "slow bake" setting, meaning that the heat radiates gently from only the bottom heating element. It comes with a one-year warranty.

"Pizza bump"

Nicki Pendleton Wood is a cookbook editor who lives in Nashville.

Pleased as Punch

Perfect for warm-weather celebrations, this old-time cocktail-for-a-crowd is making a delicious comeback. BY ST. JOHN FRIZELL

IN THE CLASSIC WORLD WAR I FILM *Grand Illusion,* German Captain von Rauffenstein walks into the officers' mess hall, fresh from a flying mission, and says to one of his officers, "Freisler, make us one of your famous fruit punches to celebrate the downing of my twelfth plane." Freisler reads off a list of necessary ingredients to the barman as the camera pans away: "Three bottles of Moselle, two Rhine, half a bottle of Martell, three bubbly, two seltzer, pineapple…" In the next scene, two captured French airmen are offered punch from a spherical crystal bowl filled with slices of fresh fruit. War may have been hell, then as now, but at least somebody was tending bar.

The art of punch

For centuries, bowls of punch have marked special occasions, from feats of military daring to, much later, the passage of children into adulthood—your high school prom, for example. But those super-sweet candy-colored concoctions ladled out in school gymnasiums bear about as much resemblance to old-fashioned punch as a "fruit cocktail" does to a dry martini.

Punch's heyday was 18th-century England, where punch was a celebration of the breadth of the Empire, combining tea and spices from Asia with the spirits and wines of Europe and the New World. The British probably learned the art of punch in India, where the Hindi word *panch* means five, corresponding to the traditional five ingredients of the most basic punch: strong (spirits like brandy and rum), weak (water or tea), sour (citrus), sweet (sugar), and spice (which could be just about anything else added to the mix, from nutmeg and coriander to ambergris, a musky, waxy substance harvested from sperm whales).

When the custom was imported by the American colonists, punch became the centerpiece of the tavern table, where people gathered to talk taxes and treason in the days before the Revolution. In time, punch would fall out of fashion, as the great-grandchildren of the founding fathers just didn't have the time to drink to the bottom of the bowl. They preferred the short, quick, made-to-order cocktails that took American barrooms by storm in the late 1800s. And so punch bowls were packed away on high, dusty shelves, only to be brought down for special occasions, like weddings, holidays, or high-school dances.

Life of the party

Thanks to today's history-obsessed mixologists, vintage punches are on the menu in some of the nation's hippest cocktail dens, from San Francisco to Boston, and punch bowls have replaced speakeasy-style arm garters and turn-of-the-century bar manuals as the bartender's must-have accessory. The trend has trickled down to the amateur entertainer as well, for punch remains the most efficient and elegant way to serve a party crowd, no matter the season or occasion. For the time-strapped host of today, it's a godsend. Punch is, by necessity, prepared in advance, allowing the host to cook or decorate in the hours before a party. Guests can serve themselves, eliminating the need for a bartender. Most important, a well-made punch appeals to everyone. It's not too strong, not too sweet, and after an initial sip, those tipplers who instinctively reach for wine, Champagne, or vodka-soda highballs will likely compete to drain the bowl dry.

Last, there's something grand and romantic about punch; the sight of the flowing bowl marks an occasion as special indeed. In his 1939 book, *The Gentleman's Companion,* the American writer and world-traveler Charles H. Baker Jr. recorded drink recipes from three trips around the world, including punch recipes from San Salvador, Vienna, Punjab, and Santiago de Cuba. He wrote: "Few things in life are more kind to man's eye than the sight of a gracefully conceived punch bowl… enmeshing every beam of light, and tossing it back into a thousand shattered spectra to remind us of the willing cheer within." Through the centuries of war and peace, that light has not dimmed.

St. John Frizell is a freelance writer and bartender. He lives in Brooklyn, New York.

punch rules

Charles H. Baker Jr., an American food, drink, and travel writer, proposed a "few—but inflexible" rules for punch makers, which are as apt today as they were in 1930s, when he wrote them.

- **Wait for it.** Add sparkling wine, sparkling water, or any other bubbly beverage to your punch just before serving. "The whole object to a sparkling punch is to have it sparkle."

- **Chill out.** Use big blocks of ice, not small cubes. Cubes melt quickly and "dilution beyond a certain point courts sure disaster." **Making ice blocks is simple:** fill metal bowls or cake pans with water and freeze them overnight. To unmold, briefly dip the bottom of the bowl or pan into warm water to release the ice.

- **Plan ahead.** Chill all of the punch ingredients at least a few hours before adding them to your punch bowl. "Pouring room temperature liquids on any sort of ice is a withering shock to the ice itself." If possible, chill the punch bowl too, either in the refrigerator or with bags of ice.

For sources, see Where to Buy It

st. cecilia society punch

This punch is named for a famously private and exclusive social organization founded in Charleston, South Carolina, in the 18th century. The recipe can easily be doubled.

Serves 6 to 8

- 2 medium lemons, thinly sliced
- ¾ cup brandy
- ¾ cup granulated sugar
- 2 tea bags green tea
- ¾ cup dark rum, such as Gosling's
- ½ small pineapple, peeled, cored, sliced ½ inch thick, and cut into small wedges
- 1 750-ml bottle dry sparkling wine, such as Domaine Ste. Michelle Brut, chilled
- 6 cups sparkling water, chilled

Put the lemon slices in a large bowl and pour the brandy over them. Let macerate at room temperature overnight.

In a small saucepan, combine the sugar with ¾ cup water and bring to a boil over high heat. Cook, stirring occasionally, until the sugar dissolves, 2 to 3 minutes. Remove from the heat, add the tea bags, and steep for 2 to 3 minutes. Discard the tea bags and let the syrup cool.

At least 3 hours and up to 6 hours before serving, combine the lemons, brandy, syrup, rum, and pineapple in a large pitcher or bowl. Chill in the refrigerator.

Just before serving, pour the punch into a large chilled punch bowl with a block of ice. Add the sparkling wine and sparkling water, and gently stir.

tenant's harbor punch

This punch is named for a quiet, windswept point on the rocky coast of Maine. I made this punch there for the summer wedding of two friends. The caraway-flavored aquavit was made in Norway, near the bride's hometown.

Serves 10 to 12

- 4-5 medium lemons
- ¾ cup granulated sugar
- 3 750-ml bottles off-dry white wine (such as Riesling Spatlese, Vouvray, or Chenin Blanc), chilled
- 1½ cups aquavit, preferably Norwegian, such as Linie, chilled
- 2 pints fresh strawberries, hulled and halved
- 1 English cucumber, washed and sliced about ⅛ inch thick
- 4 cups sparkling water, chilled

Using a peeler, remove the zest from the lemons, avoiding the white pith. In a medium bowl, combine the lemon zest and the sugar, stirring with a wooden spoon until the sugar is fragrant and has the texture of soft, fresh snow, about 10 minutes. Add ¾ cup boiling water to the bowl and stir to dissolve the sugar. Strain the syrup and let cool.

Juice the lemons and strain the juice —you'll need 1 cup plus 2 Tbs. juice.

At least 3 hours and up to 6 hours before serving, combine the syrup, lemon juice, wine, aquavit, strawberries, and cucumbers in a large bowl or pot. Chill in the refrigerator.

Just before serving, pour the punch into a large chilled punch bowl or dispenser, with a block of ice. Add the sparkling water and gently stir.

spill the beans

Go green (and yellow and purple). Now is when summer beans of all colors are at their crispest, sweetest best. BY MARIA HELM SINSKEY

BEANS ARE AN ESSENTIAL on my summer table. Versatile enough to roast, sauté, or braise, they also shine with just a quick boil or steam, a slick of butter, and a sprinkle of salt. And although you can find them in the market year-round, eaten at the start of their season (right now), green beans of all varieties and colors are smaller, sweeter, and more velvety than they'll be all year. So go ahead and give in to those piled-high bushel baskets at farmers' markets. Here's a handful of delicious ways to get them on your table.

A World of Beans

"Green bean" is a generic term used for the skinny, long green beans almost universally available canned, frozen, and fresh. But the world of beans is much wider (and more colorful), as a trip to a farmers' market will attest. The five bean varieties used in these recipes have subtly different textures, colors, and tastes but can all be used interchangeably.

1. Green, string, wax, or snap beans: Long and rounded, these are most often bright green but also come in yellow and purple. The fibrous string that was once their trademark has been bred out of them, although you'll still find it in some heirloom varieties.

2. French green beans, haricots verts, or filet beans: These delicate, very thin beans come in green and yellow. Picked at their peak, they are the crème de la crème of beans, and priced accordingly.

3. Romano beans: Flat and wide, Romanos can be green or yellow. When young and short, they're tender, but they are often sold larger (as long as 6 inches), with visible bean seeds, at which point they need to be cooked longer.

4. Spanish Musica beans: Flat, green, and meaty, these look similar to Romanos but have a delicate nutty flavor.

5. Chinese long beans or yard-long beans: These giants belong to a completely different branch of the bean family. They are the immature pods of a variety of cowpea (an African bean variety that includes the black-eyed pea). These can grow to great lengths but are best between 12 and 18 inches. Similar in flavor to the string bean, these are softer and starchier.

roasted romanos and tomatoes with tapenade

Serves 4 to 6

Kosher salt

¾ lb. green or yellow Romano beans, trimmed and cut into 2-inch lengths (3 cups)

2 Tbs. extra-virgin olive oil

Freshly ground black pepper

1½ cups assorted-color cherry tomatoes

1 tsp. minced garlic

1 tsp. fresh thyme leaves

1 recipe Easy Tapenade (below)

Bring a large pot of well-salted water to a boil. Cook the beans in the water until crisp-tender, 4 to 6 minutes. Drain and run under cold water to cool. Drain well.

Position a rack in the center of the oven and heat the oven to 425°F. Put the beans in a medium bowl, toss with 1 Tbs. of the olive oil, and season with ¼ tsp. salt and a few grinds of pepper. Spread the beans in one layer on a heavy-duty rimmed baking sheet, leaving space for the tomatoes.

In a small bowl, toss the tomatoes with the remaining 1 Tbs. oil, garlic, thyme, ¼ tsp. salt, and a few grinds of pepper. Spread the tomatoes on the baking sheet.

Roast the beans and tomatoes just until the tomatoes start to split, 7 to 10 minutes. Slide the beans onto a serving dish, top with the tomatoes, and dot liberally with the tapenade. Serve, with additional tapenade on the side.

EASY TAPENADE

Extra tapenade is delicious on crostini or spread on sandwiches.

Yields 1 scant cup

½ cup pitted Niçoise or Kalamata olives

2 Tbs. fresh lime juice

2 anchovy fillets, rinsed

1 medium shallot, quartered and peeled

1 large clove garlic, quartered and peeled

¼ cup extra-virgin olive oil

3 Tbs. finely chopped fresh flat-leaf parsley

Kosher salt and freshly ground black pepper

Put the olives, lime juice, anchovies, shallot, and garlic in a food processor and process until smooth, about 20 seconds. With the machine running, slowly add the olive oil through the feed tube and process until you have a smooth paste. Stir in the parsley and season to taste with salt and pepper.

spicy shrimp with ginger-garlic long beans

Scissors make snipping the beans into 4-inch lengths a breeze. Use plain sesame oil, not toasted.

Serves 4

- 1 lb. extra-large (16 to 20 per lb.) shrimp, peeled and deveined
- ¼ cup mirin (sweetened rice wine)
- 2 Tbs. soy sauce
- 1 large scallion, thinly sliced (both white and green parts)
- ¼ tsp. crushed red pepper flakes
- 2 Tbs. untoasted Asian sesame oil
- 2 tsp. minced garlic
- 2 tsp. minced fresh ginger
- ½ lb. Chinese long beans, trimmed and cut into 4-inch lengths

In a nonreactive medium bowl, combine the shrimp, mirin, soy sauce, scallion, and red pepper flakes. Marinate in the refrigerator for at least 1 hour and up to 6 hours.

Heat a 12-inch skillet over medium-high heat. Add the sesame oil and then the garlic and ginger, and cook, stirring, until the garlic begins to color, about 10 seconds. Add the beans and stir quickly to coat with the garlic and ginger. Continue to cook, stirring, until the beans start to turn bright green, 1 to 2 minutes. (If the garlic starts to burn, remove the pan from the heat and continue to stir quickly.)

Add the shrimp and the marinade (the liquid hitting the hot pan will create steam, so be careful). Cook, stirring constantly, until the juices have reduced and thickened slightly and the shrimp are pink and curled, an additional 3 to 4 minutes. Serve immediately.

Shop and Store

Avoid buying beans that look withered at either end—it means they've been sitting a while and are losing moisture. Beans relinquish sweetness the longer they're stored, so try to use them right away. If you can't, store them in the refrigerator for up to four days in a paper bag or a plastic bag with holes punched in it so the beans can breathe.

summer bean confetti salad with pickled red onion vinaigrette

Use a selection of beans for this salad. The colors, shapes, and textures will make it interesting and delicious.

Serves 4

> Kosher salt
> ¾ lb. beans, assorted sizes and varieties, trimmed and cut into 1- to 2-inch lengths (3 cups)
> ¼ cup red wine vinegar
> 2 tsp. granulated sugar
> ½ cup thinly sliced red onion
> 1 Tbs. extra-virgin olive oil
> ¼ cup loosely packed torn fresh basil
> ¼ cup pine nuts, toasted (optional)
> Freshly ground black pepper

Bring a medium pot of well-salted water to a boil. Cook the beans in the water until crisp-tender (cooking times of different types of beans will vary, so cook each variety separately). Drain and run under cold water to cool. Drain well and put the beans in a serving bowl.

In a small, nonreactive saucepan, combine the vinegar, sugar, and 1 tsp. salt. Bring the mixture to a boil over medium-high heat. Add the onion, return to a boil, and immediately pour the mixture into a nonreactive bowl to cool, about 15 minutes. Drain the onion and reserve the vinegar.

Toss the onion with the beans, add 1 Tbs. of the vinegar and the olive oil. Add the basil and pine nuts (if using), season to taste with salt and pepper and toss again. Add more of the vinegar if you'd like a little more tang.

haricots verts with toasted walnuts and chèvre

If you love goat cheese, feel free to add more to this simple dish.

Serves 4

> Kosher salt
> ¾ lb. haricots verts (green, yellow, or both), trimmed
> 1 Tbs. extra-virgin olive oil
> 2 Tbs. minced shallots
> ⅓ cup walnuts, lightly toasted and chopped
> 2 tsp. walnut oil
> Freshly ground black pepper
> 2 oz. fresh goat cheese, crumbled (⅔ cup)

Bring a medium pot of well-salted water to a boil. Cook the beans in the water until tender, 2 to 3 minutes. Drain and run under cold water to cool. Drain well.

Heat the olive oil in a 12-inch skillet over medium-high heat. Add the shallots and cook, stirring, until they begin to brown, about 30 seconds. Stir in the walnuts. Add the walnut oil and the beans and cook, stirring to heat through, 2 to 3 minutes. Season to taste with salt and pepper and transfer the beans to a serving dish. Sprinkle the goat cheese over the top and serve.

 Get buying, storing, and prepping tips for hundreds more ingredients at FineCooking.com/ingredients.

fusilli with green beans, pancetta, and parmigiano

The pasta's cooking water melts the cheese and turns it into a rich sauce that coats the beans and pulls everything together. If you can't find pancetta, substitute bacon.

Serves 2 to 3

> Kosher salt
>
> ½ lb. fusilli or other twisted pasta
>
> 4 oz. pancetta, sliced ¼ inch thick and cut into ½-inch squares (¾ cup)
>
> 1 large clove garlic, smashed and peeled
>
> ½ lb. green beans, trimmed and cut into 1-inch lengths (2 cups)
>
> Freshly ground black pepper
>
> 2 Tbs. unsalted butter, at room temperature
>
> 2 oz. finely grated Parmigiano-Reggiano (1 cup)

Bring a medium pot of well-salted water to a boil. Cook the pasta until just barely al dente, about 1 minute less than package timing. Reserve 1 cup of the cooking water, and drain the pasta.

While the pasta cooks, put the pancetta in a cold 10-inch skillet and set over medium-high heat. When the pancetta starts sizzling, add the garlic and cook, stirring constantly, until starting to brown, 1 minute. Reduce the heat to medium and continue to cook the pancetta until golden but still chewy at the center (taste a piece if you're not sure), an additional 2 to 3 minutes. If the pancetta has rendered a lot of its fat, spoon off all but 1 Tbs. of the fat from the pan.

Add the beans to the pan and cook, stirring constantly, until they're crisp-tender, 3 to 4 minutes. Remove the garlic and season the beans with salt and pepper. With the pan still over medium heat, add the pasta, ½ cup of the pasta water, and the butter. Toss to combine. Add another ¼ cup pasta water and ¾ cup of the Parmigiano. Stir well and season to taste with salt and pepper. If necessary, add a little more pasta water to loosen the sauce.

Transfer the pasta to a serving bowl. Grind black pepper over the top and sprinkle with the remaining cheese.

Maria Helm Sinskey is culinary director at Robert Sinskey Vineyards, the Napa Valley winery she owns with her husband, Robert. ❑

green beans with smoked paprika and almonds

If you don't like spicy heat, use sweet pimentón instead.

Serves 4

> Kosher salt
>
> ¾ lb. green beans, preferably Spanish Musica, trimmed and cut on the diagonal into 2-inch lengths (3 cups)
>
> ½ cup thinly sliced shallots (about 2 medium)
>
> 1 Tbs. extra-virgin olive oil
>
> 1½ tsp. granulated sugar
>
> ⅓ cup coarsely chopped Marcona almonds
>
> ¼ tsp. hot Spanish smoked paprika (pimentón de la Vera)

Bring a large pot of well-salted water to a boil. Cook the beans in the water until just tender, 4 to 5 minutes. Drain and run under cold water to cool. Drain well.

Put the shallots and olive oil in a cold 12-inch skillet and set the pan over medium-high heat. Cook until the shallots begin to turn golden, stirring to break them into rings, about 2 minutes. Sprinkle the sugar over the shallots and stir constantly until they are golden all over, about 45 seconds. Add the almonds, stir well, and immediately add the beans and smoked paprika. Cook, stirring, until heated through, 2 to 3 minutes. Season to taste with salt and serve.

Bean Basics: Prep and Cook

Green beans need just a quick rinse in a colander. Snap or cut off the stem end, which tends to be tough. (You can cut off the tails as well, although it's not necessary.) Note that beans react quickly to acidity, losing their bright color when you season them with lemon or vinegar. You can use the following cooking methods for all types of green beans.

Blanch: Immersing beans in a pot of salted water briefly and then removing them to a cold water bath sets their color and brings out their sweetness. I like to do this even if I plan to sauté or stir-fry them, especially with the meatier varieties, as they'll cook faster. The more delicate, thinner varieties (like haricots verts) need only a quick blanch before being tossed into salads or side dishes.

Steam: Cooking beans in water vapor in a closed vessel is the fastest method and doesn't leach out flavor or nutrients, as boiling can. Foods steam best in shallow layers, though, so unless you want to work in batches, you're better off boiling large amounts of beans.

Boil: All these beans taste delicious boiled in salted water until tender and served with butter or olive oil, a squeeze of lemon, and finished with a sprinkle of sea salt. Boiling softens vegetables faster and more thoroughly than steaming, because contact with hot water dissolves and extracts pectin and calcium from the plant's cells.

For sources, see Where to Buy It

Scooped!

One easy method, countless incredible ice creams. BY DAVID LEBOVITZ

UNLIKE A LOT OF OTHER DESSERTS, ice cream isn't one of the fussy ones. You start by making a basic custard and then you can steer off in many delicious directions to flavor your ice cream any way you like it.

The custard recipe is simple: egg yolks stirred over low heat with milk, sugar, and some cream. After cooking until silky smooth and slightly thickened, the custard gets strained into heavy cream and then chilled before churning.

The best part is choosing your flavors—and there are several options to consider along the way. First, you might infuse flavor into the custard. Tea, fresh ginger, coffee, citrus zest, and vanilla bean are all possibilities. After that, you can make additions to the cooked custard, including chocolate, berries, liquor, or even olive oil. Finally, after your ice cream is churned, you can mix in any variety of ingredients, from bite-size bits of candy and chocolate to chunks of cake or brownies. Try using any of the suggestions on pages 52–53, or be creative and make up your own flavors. Don't laugh, but once I even put bacon in a batch—it was a surprise hit!

Triple-decker
Strawberry Pound Cake, Double Ginger, and Rocky Road make for a new take on Neapolitan. Turn to pages 52–53 for more flavor options.

STEP 1

CHOOSE YOUR INGREDIENTS

Read the method from start to finish and then choose your flavors and prep all of your ingredients.

Yields about 1 quart

STEP 2 MASTER RECIPE

MAKE THE CUSTARD

Use this basic custard recipe as the starting point for all ice creams.

- 2 **cups heavy cream**
- 1 **cup whole milk**
- ¾ **cup granulated sugar**
  Table salt
- 5 **large egg yolks**

In a medium saucepan, mix 1 cup of the cream with the milk, sugar, and a pinch of salt. Warm the cream mixture over medium-high heat, stirring occasionally, until the sugar dissolves and tiny bubbles begin to form around the edge of the pan, 3 to 4 minutes.

To infuse a flavor (option 1), stir in your selection from the ingredient choices below. Cover, remove from the heat, and let sit for

Flavor Your Ice Cream

You have the option of flavoring the ice cream custard at two different steps: **INFUSE** it at the beginning of cooking or **ADD** flavors at the end of cooking. You can do just one or both.

OPTION 1:

Infuse

Choose one or two of these ingredients and add before warming the cream mixture.

Vanilla: 1 vanilla bean, split lengthwise and seeds scraped out (use both the split bean and seeds)

Lemon: Finely grated zest of 4 medium lemons

Tea: ¼ cup loose black tea leaves, such as jasmine, Earl Grey, or English breakfast

Orange: Finely grated zest of 4 medium oranges

Lavender: 2 Tbs. dried lavender

Coffee: 1½ cups coarsely crushed medium-roast coffee beans (seal the beans in a large zip-top bag and crush with a rolling pin or meat mallet)

Fresh herbs (basil, mint): 1 cup tightly packed, coarsely torn leaves

Toasted nuts (hazelnuts, pistachios, almonds, peanuts, etc.): 1½ cups coarsely crushed

Ginger: ½ cup peeled, thinly sliced fresh ginger

Pepper: 1 Tbs. black peppercorns, very coarsely ground

Cinnamon: Two 3- to 4-inch sticks (broken into large pieces)

Food styling by Brian Preston-Campbell

Photographs by Scott Phillips

1 hour. Taste and let sit longer if you want a stronger flavor. If not infusing, proceed with the recipe.

Prepare an ice bath by filling a large bowl with several inches of ice water. Set a smaller metal bowl (one that holds at least 1½ quarts) in the ice water. Pour the remaining cup of cream into the inner bowl (this helps the custard cool quicker when you pour it in later). Set a fine strainer on top. Whisk the egg yolks in a medium bowl.

If you have infused the cream mixture, re-warm it over medium-high heat until tiny bubbles begin to form around the edge of the pan, 1 to 2 minutes. In a steady stream, pour half of the warm cream mixture into the egg yolks, whisking constantly to prevent the eggs from curdling.

Pour the egg mixture back into the saucepan and cook over low heat, stirring constantly and scraping the bottom with a heatproof cooking spoon or rubber spatula until the custard thickens slightly (it should be thick enough to coat the utensil and hold a line drawn through it with a finger; see p. 83 for details), 4 to 8 minutes. An instant-read thermometer should read 175° to 180°F at this point. Don't let the sauce overheat or boil, or it will curdle. Immediately strain the custard into the cold cream in the ice bath. If using an infusion ingredient, press firmly in the strainer with the spoon or spatula to extract as much flavor as possible. If you want to **add** melted chocolate and cocoa (see below), do so now.

Cool the custard to below 70°F by stirring it over the ice bath. To **add** a flavor other than chocolate (see the **option 2** choices below), stir it into the cooled custard.

OPTION 2:

Add

Choose one or two of these ingredients and add after straining and cooling the cooked custard. (The exceptions are cocoa and chocolate, which should be added to the warm custard, or they will seize.)

Peach: 1½ lb. fresh (or 1⅓ lb. frozen) peaches, peeled, pitted, cooked to soften, and puréed

Mascarpone: 1 cup mascarpone

Raspberry: 12 oz. fresh or frozen raspberries, puréed, strained, and mixed with ⅓ cup sugar

Vanilla: 2 tsp. pure vanilla extract

Olive oil: ¼ cup fruity extra-virgin olive oil

Chocolate: 4 oz. bittersweet chocolate (at least 60% cacao), chopped and melted, plus ¼ cup Dutch-process cocoa

Lemon: ¼ cup strained fresh lemon juice

Orange: ¾ cup strained fresh orange juice

Liqueur/liquor: 3 to 4 Tbs. Grand Marnier, Cognac, Baileys, Frangelico, Kahlúa, amaretto, Armagnac, whiskey, rum, etc.

Strawberry: 1 lb. fresh or frozen strawberries, trimmed, puréed, strained, and mixed with ½ cup sugar

Passionfruit: ¼ cup passionfruit concentrate (see Where to Buy It, p. 89)

Double Down

Some flavors can be both infused and added. To double the flavor of citrus ice cream, for example, start by infusing the cream mixture with zest and add fresh juice to the custard. And for a stronger hit of vanilla, add extract to custard already infused with vanilla bean.

STEP 3

CHILL AND FREEZE THE CUSTARD

Refrigerate the custard until completely chilled, at least 4 hours. Then freeze the custard in your ice cream maker according to the manufacturer's instructions. If using **mix-ins** from the list at right, fold them into the just-churned ice cream. Transfer the ice cream to an air-tight container and freeze solid for at least 4 hours.

Ice Cream Tips

How to swirl

To swirl an ingredient like jam or Nutella into ice cream, let the swirling ingredient come to room temperature first. With a spoon, drop it in small dollops between layers of just-churned ice cream as you remove it from the machine. Gently drag a spatula to swirl the ingredient as best you can; to keep the swirls distinct, avoid vigorous stirring.

Fresh fruit rule

Resist the temptation to mix whole fresh berries or other fresh fruit chunks into your ice cream. Because they have a high water content, they're likely to freeze into hard, icy chunks.

How long to feeze

You can store ice cream in the freezer for up to two weeks; however, because homemade ice cream doesn't have any stabilizers, it's best eaten within a couple of days of making it.

No machine, no problem

If you don't have an ice cream maker, you can freeze the custard in a bowl in the freezer. Check after about an hour; once it starts freezing, blitz through it with a hand-held electric mixer and then return it to the freezer. Repeat every so often as the mixture is freezing, until the ice cream is completely whipped and frozen.

Mix In

Choose up to three ingredients for a total of up to 1 cup (optional).

Mini marshmallows or Marshmallow Fluff

Chocolate-covered coffee beans

Dried fruit (raisins, prunes, etc.), soaked in warm liqueur, liquor, or water until plumped

Crushed candy bars

Jam or marmalade

Crushed cookies

Chopped crystallized ginger (no more than ½ cup)

Chopped chocolate (no more than 6 Tbs.)

Nutella

Chunks of gingerbread, pound cake, brownies, or quick breads

Crushed peppermint candy or peppermint patties

Toasted nuts, chopped if large

Simple sundae
Scoop your favorite flavors, sprinkle on some chopped toasted nuts and chocolate, and top with a dollop of whipped cream.

What's the Scoop?

These are only some of the amazing flavor combinations you can create with this simple technique.

Hazelnut Chocolate Chunk
Infuse: Toasted hazelnuts
Mix in: Chopped chocolate

Passionfruit Macadamia
Add: Passionfruit concentrate
Mix in: Toasted macadamias

Whiskey Gingerbread
Add: Whiskey
Mix in: Gingerbread chunks

Raspberry Chambord
Add: Raspberry and Chambord

Olive Oil Pine Nut
Add: Olive oil
Mix in: Toasted pine nuts

Lavender Vanilla
Infuse: Lavender
Add: Pure vanilla extract

Double Vanilla Bourbon
Infuse: Vanilla bean
Add: Pure vanilla extract and bourbon

Rocky Road
Add: Chocolate
Mix in: Marshmallows or Fluff, toasted nuts, and chopped chocolate

Strawberry Pound Cake
Add: Strawberry
Mix in: Pound cake chunks

David Lebovitz is a pastry chef, cooking teacher, and cookbook author. His latest book is The Sweet Life in Paris: Delicious Adventures in the World's Most Glorious and Perplexing City. *He also writes a popular blog at davidlebovitz.com.* ◻

Peach Mascarpone
Add: Peach and mascarpone

Strawberry Basil
Infuse: Basil
Add: Strawberry

Irish Coffee
Infuse: Coffee
Add: Baileys

Rum Raisin
Add: Rum
Mix in: Raisins soaked in rum

Chocolate Peppermint Stick
Add: Chocolate
Mix in: Crushed peppermint sticks

Cinnamon Pecan
Infuse: Cinnamon
Mix in: Toasted pecans

Orange Earl Grey
Infuse: Orange zest and Earl Grey tea

Double Ginger
Infuse: Fresh ginger
Mix in: Chopped crystallized ginger

Armagnac Prune
Add: Armagnac
Mix in: Prunes soaked in Armagnac

Enter the Create Your Own Ice Cream Challenge at FineCooking.com, and you could win a Cuisinart ice cream maker.

1. SEASON
Apply a dry rub before cooking for an initial layer of flavor.

2. SEAR
Grill over the hottest part of the fire to create a flavorful browned crust.

A NEW WAY TO GRILL

Barbecue-Braising

Season, sear, braise, and glaze your way to slow-cooked flavor from the grill. BY BRUCE AIDELLS

COME SUMMER, not many cooks are thinking pot roast or short ribs. Who wants to heat up the kitchen? I don't. But I don't want to take a three-month pass on slow-cooked dishes, either. So I solved the problem by taking it outside. I call this new cooking method barbecue-braising.

Photographs by Scott Phillips

3. BRAISE
Move the meat to a covered pot on the cooler section of the grill so it cooks slowly and becomes infused with flavors from the braising liquid.

4. GLAZE
Quickly brown the tender meat over the hottest part of the grill to caramelize the glaze for a final layer of flavor.

Why braise on the barbecue? For the most part, you probably use your grill to quickly cook steaks, burgers, and chicken breasts over high heat. But the grill is great for braising, too. Traditionally, meat is braised by browning it in a Dutch oven, adding a flavorful liquid and aromatics, and cooking it slowly for several hours on the stovetop or in the oven until it's meltingly tender. (I actually prefer the oven method, since the heat source is more even.)

When barbecue-braising, the grill performs like an oven: You just put your pot on the grill, cover, and let the meat simmer for several hours. But with this method, you have two advantages over the indoor technique. First, before braising, you can brown the meat directly on the grill, which adds extra flavor. And after braising, you can brush the cooked meat with a tasty glaze (a part of each of these recipes) and finish it directly over the fire. The result: delicious, saucy, fall-off-the-bone meat.

barbecue-braised country spareribs with beer and mustard glaze

For this recipe, the German dark lager called bock beer is my top choice, but any dark lager works well. Serve with boiled new potatoes or potato salad.
Serves 4 to 6

FOR THE RIBS

- 1 Tbs. sweet Hungarian paprika
- 1 tsp. dark brown sugar
- 1 tsp. dry mustard (preferably Coleman's)
- 1 tsp. dried sage
  Kosher salt and freshly ground black pepper
- 3 lb. bone-in country style pork ribs (see Test Kitchen, p. 81, for more information)

FOR THE BRAISING LIQUID

- 4 strips bacon, cut crosswise into ½-inch-wide strips
- 2 medium yellow onions, thinly sliced (3 cups)
- 4 medium cloves garlic, chopped (1 Tbs.)
- 1 medium carrot, chopped (½ cup)
- 2 cups lower-salt chicken broth
- 1 12-oz. bottle bock beer or dark lager
- ¼ cup cider vinegar
- 2 bay leaves
- 1 tsp. caraway seeds

FOR THE GLAZE

- ¼ cup Dijon mustard
- ¼ cup light brown sugar
- ¼ tsp. Worcestershire sauce

SEASON In a small bowl, combine the paprika, brown sugar, dry mustard, sage, 1 tsp. salt, and 1 tsp. pepper. Set aside 2 tsp. to use in the braise and sprinkle the remaining rub all over the ribs. Cover and refrigerate for at least 2 hours but preferably overnight.

SEAR Prepare a gas grill for direct grilling over medium-high heat (see Grill Skills, p. 58). Grill the ribs until nicely browned, 3 to 5 minutes per side. Transfer to a platter, let cool briefly, and then tie each rib with 3 or 4 loops of butcher's twine.

BRAISE Prepare the grill for indirect grilling (see Grill Skills, p. 58). In an 8-quart heavy-duty pot, cook the bacon over medium heat, stirring occasionally, until it just starts to crisp, 2 to 3 minutes. Add the onions and cook, stirring occasionally, until soft and beginning to color, 6 to 8 minutes. Add the garlic, carrot, and the reserved spice rub and cook for about 1 minute more. Add the broth, beer, vinegar, bay leaves, and caraway seeds. Bring to a boil, reduce the heat, and simmer, uncovered, for 10 minutes.

Nestle the ribs into the braising liquid. Set the pot on the grill over the cool zone. Cover the pot, close the grill lid, and cook until fork-tender, about 1½ hours, turning the ribs halfway through cooking.

Transfer the ribs to a tray. Strain the braising liquid into a heatproof vessel, such as a Pyrex measuring cup, and let sit until the fat rises to the top. Discard the solids. Skim off and discard the fat. Keep warm.

GLAZE Prepare the grill for direct grilling over medium-low heat (see Grill Skills, p. 58). In a small bowl, stir the mustard, brown sugar, and Worcestershire sauce. Stir in just enough of the braising liquid, 1 Tbs. at a time, to produce a glaze thin enough to easily brush on the ribs. Brush one side of the ribs with the glaze and grill glazed side down until bubbly and beginning to darken, 3 to 5 minutes. Brush the other side, flip the ribs, and grill until the glaze is bubbly and beginning to darken, an additional 3 to 5 minutes.

Remove the string from the ribs, put them on a warm platter, and drizzle with the remaining braising liquid.

barbecue-braised thai chicken legs with lemongrass glaze

Lemongrass adds a wonderful fragrance to this dish. To prepare it, trim off the tops and enough of the bottoms that you no longer see a woody core and then remove the tough outer leaves. Thinly slice the remaining light-green stalks crosswise and then finely chop them. **Serves 6**

FOR THE CHICKEN

- 2 **tsp. ground turmeric**
- 1 **tsp. minced fresh ginger**
- ½ **tsp. ground coriander**
- ½ **tsp. cayenne**
  Kosher salt
- 6 **whole skin-on chicken legs**

FOR THE BRAISING LIQUID AND GLAZE

- 2 **tsp. peanut oil**
- 1 **cup finely chopped scallions (white and light-green parts only)**
- ⅓ **cup finely chopped lemongrass (1 to 2 large or 3 medium stalks)**
- 1 **Tbs. minced garlic**
- 2 **tsp. minced fresh ginger**
- 1 **Tbs. Thai green curry paste**
- 3 **cups lower-salt chicken broth**
- 2 **Tbs. Asian fish sauce**
- 1 **Tbs. granulated sugar**
  Kosher salt

FOR SERVING

- 1½ **cups Thai jasmine rice, cooked**

SEASON In a small bowl, combine the turmeric, ginger, coriander, cayenne, and 1 tsp. salt. Rub all over the chicken legs. Cover and refrigerate for at least 2 hours but preferably overnight.

SEAR Prepare a gas grill for direct grilling over medium heat (see Grill Skills, p. 58). Grill the legs until they begin to brown on both sides, 3 to 5 minutes per side (watch carefully for flare-ups). Set aside.

BRAISE Prepare the grill for indirect grilling (see Grill Skills, p. 58). In an 8-quart heavy-duty pot, heat the oil over medium heat. Add the scallions and stir for 1 minute. Add the lemongrass and stir for 1 minute. Add the garlic and ginger and stir for 1 minute. Stir in the curry paste until the vegetables are evenly coated. Add the broth, fish sauce, and sugar and bring to a boil. Remove from the heat.

Nestle the chicken legs into the braising liquid. Set the pot on the grill over the cool zone. Cover the pot, close the grill lid, and cook until the legs are tender, about 30 minutes. Transfer the chicken to a tray.

Pour the braising liquid into a heatproof vessel, such as a Pyrex measuring cup, and let sit until the fat rises to the top. Skim off and discard the fat.

GLAZE Prepare the grill for direct grilling over medium heat (see Grill Skills, p. 58). Strain enough of the braising liquid to yield 1 cup and boil over medium heat in a small saucepan until reduced to ¼ cup glaze, about 15 minutes. (Return the strained solids to the remaining cooking liquid).

Brush some of the glaze over one side of each chicken leg and grill glazed side down until the glaze begins to color, 2 to 3 minutes. Brush the other side of the legs with glaze and flip them over—the skin may stick to the grill a bit, so gently pry up any stuck areas before you flip. Grill until browned on the second side, 2 to 3 minutes.

To serve, reheat the remaining cooking liquid if necessary and season to taste with salt. Put some rice in each of 6 serving bowls, lean a leg against the rice, and ladle in some of the cooking liquid.

barbecue-braised moroccan lamb shanks with honey-mint glaze

Sweet and savory flavors—a hallmark of Moroccan food—combine in this dish. The vegetables and lamb are served over couscous. For more on harissa, including a recipe, see Test Kitchen, p. 81.

Serves 4

FOR THE LAMB

- 1 Tbs. sweet paprika
- 1 tsp. ground ginger
- 1 tsp. turmeric
- 1 tsp. cayenne
- 1 tsp. dried mint
- ½ tsp. ground coriander
- ½ tsp. ground cumin
  Kosher salt and freshly ground black pepper
- 4 meaty lamb shanks, trimmed (about 1 lb. each)

FOR THE BRAISING LIQUID

- 3 cups chopped yellow onion
- 1 cup chopped canned tomatoes
- ¼ cup finely chopped cilantro stems (save leaves for garnish)
- 2 Tbs. fresh lemon juice; more to taste
- 1 Tbs. chopped garlic
  Kosher salt
- 4 carrots, peeled and cut into 2-inch lengths, thicker pieces split lengthwise
- 2 medium purple turnips, peeled and cut into 1-inch pieces
- 2 cups chickpeas (freshly cooked or canned)
  Freshly ground black pepper

FOR THE GLAZE

- ¼ cup honey
- 2 tsp. fresh lemon juice
- 1 tsp. dried mint
- 1 tsp. harissa (optional; see Test Kitchen, p. 81, for more information)

FOR SERVING

- 1 cup couscous, cooked
  Reserved cilantro leaves
  Harissa (optional)

SEASON In a small bowl, combine the paprika, ginger, turmeric, cayenne, mint, coriander, cumin, 2 tsp. salt, and 1 tsp. pepper. Rub the shanks with 2 Tbs. of the spice mixture (save the rest for the braising liquid). Cover and refrigerate for at least 2 hours but preferably overnight.

SEAR Prepare a gas grill for direct grilling over medium heat (see Grill Skills, at left). Grill the lamb shanks until golden brown, about 4 minutes per side. Let cool briefly and then tie each shank with 3 or 4 loops of butcher's twine.

BRAISE Prepare the grill for indirect grilling (see Grill Skills, at left). In an 8-quart heavy-duty pot, combine the onion, tomatoes, cilantro stems, lemon juice, garlic, and the remaining spice mixture. Stir in 4 cups water and 1 tsp. salt. Nestle the lamb shanks into the pot in a single layer. Set the pot on the grill over the cool zone. Cover the pot and close the grill lid. After 1 hour, add the carrots, turnips, and chickpeas. Cover the pot and the grill, and braise until the lamb shanks and vegetables are fork-tender, an additional ½ to 1 hour.

Transfer the shanks to a tray. With a slotted spoon, transfer the vegetables and chickpeas to a bowl and keep warm.

Pour the braising liquid into a heatproof vessel, such as a Pyrex measuring cup, and let sit until the fat rises to the top. Skim off and discard the fat. Taste the liquid; if it's too watery, return to the pot and boil over high heat until flavorful. Season to taste with salt, pepper, and lemon juice. Keep warm.

GLAZE Prepare the grill for direct grilling over medium heat (see Grill Skills, at left). In a small saucepan, combine 3 Tbs. of the braising liquid with the honey, lemon juice, mint, and harissa (if using). Boil over medium heat until the mixture has the consistency of a light syrup, 1 to 2 minutes.

Brush the mixture on the shanks and then grill them, turning and basting until the glaze has bubbled and has a few black spots, about 5 minutes total.

To serve, remove the strings from the shanks. Mound the couscous in a large shallow serving bowl. Spoon the vegetables and chickpeas over the couscous. Set the shanks on top, and sprinkle with the cilantro. Season the remaining braising liquid to taste with harissa (if using) and serve on the side.

Grill Skills

A gas grill is best for barbecue-braising, because it's easy to control the grill's heat level for the two grilling techniques this method requires—direct and indirect.

If you consider yourself a fire master, though, you can make all these recipes on a charcoal grill. It takes a bit more attention and effort to maintain the fire, but cooking over charcoal delivers a nice, smoky flavor. Go to FineCooking .com/extras for instructions on how to set up your charcoal grill for this method.

Here's how to set up your gas grill to use direct heat for the initial sear and final glaze and indirect heat for the long braise.

Direct grilling means cooking food directly over the heat source. Turn on all the burners, setting them at the level indicated in the recipe, and let the grill heat for 10 to 15 minutes.

Indirect grilling means the heat source is around, but not directly under, the food. Turn all but one of the burners on medium heat. For a three-burner grill, leave the center burner off. Set an oven or grill thermometer (see Test Kitchen, p. 81) on the grate above the unlit burner and close the lid. Let it heat for about 10 minutes. Adjust the temperature of the burners as necessary until the thermometer reads 350°F. When ready, set the pot over the unlit burner.

Serve this incredibly tender pot roast with creamy polenta or thickly sliced roasted or grilled potatoes seasoned with olive oil, salt, and pepper.

Serves 6 to 8

FOR THE BEEF

- 2 tsp. chopped fresh thyme
- 2 tsp. chopped fresh rosemary
- 2 tsp. sweet Hungarian paprika
- 1 tsp. dry mustard (preferably Coleman's)
  Kosher salt and freshly ground black pepper
- 1 4-lb. boneless beef chuck roast

FOR THE BRAISING LIQUID

- 2 to 2½ cups lower-salt chicken broth
- ½ cup bourbon
- 1 Tbs. coarse-grain Dijon mustard
- 2 tsp. unsulphured molasses
- 2 large yellow onions, halved and thinly sliced (about 4 cups)
- 4 medium cloves garlic, peeled

FOR THE GLAZE

- 2 Tbs. smooth Dijon mustard
- 2 tsp. chopped fresh rosemary

SEASON In a small bowl, combine the thyme, rosemary, paprika, dry mustard, and 2 tsp. each salt and pepper. Sprinkle the spice blend all over the roast. Cover and refrigerate for at least 2 hours but preferably overnight.

SEAR Prepare a gas grill for direct grilling over medium heat (see Grill Skills, p. 58). Grill the roast until nicely browned on all sides, 4 to 6 minutes per side. Let cool briefly and then tie the roast with several loops of butcher's twine (see Test Kitchen, p. 81, for directions). Put the roast in an 8-quart heavy-duty pot.

BRAISE Prepare the grill for indirect grilling (see Grill Skills, p. 58). In a small bowl, whisk ½ cup of the chicken broth with the bourbon, mustard, and molasses and pour the mixture over the meat. Scatter the onions and garlic on top of the meat; it's fine if some fall off. Put the pot on the grill over the cool zone. Cover the pot, close the grill lid, and cook for 1 hour. **Uncover the pot** and turn the roast over so the onions are now on the bottom. Check the liquid level in the pot and add broth as necessary until there's about an inch of liquid in the pot. Continue to cook, pot uncovered, grill lid closed, for 1 hour, stirring the onions and checking the liquid level every 20 minutes and adding broth as needed to maintain about an inch of liquid.

Replace the lid on the pot and continue to cook the meat until fork-tender, about 1 hour more, checking after 30 minutes and adding more broth as needed to maintain 1 inch of liquid. Move the meat to a tray and pat dry. **Pour the onions** and juices into a heatproof vessel, such as a Pyrex measuring cup, and let sit until the fat rises to the top. Skim off and discard the fat. Keep warm.

GLAZE Prepare the grill for direct grilling over medium heat (see Grill Skills, p. 58). In a food processor, purée ¼ cup of the onion mixture with the mustard and rosemary. Brush about half of the glaze on one side of the meat and put the meat on the grill, glaze side down. Brush the top of the roast with the remaining glaze. When the glaze turns brown on the bottom, after 2 to 3 minutes, flip and brown the other side, an additional 2 to 3 minutes. **To serve,** remove the string and slice the meat into ½-inch-thick slices. Ladle the onion mixture over the meat and serve.

barbecue-braised vietnamese short ribs with sweet vinegar glaze

These ribs are great served with rice noodles or steamed rice.

Serves 4

FOR THE RIBS

- 1 Tbs. mild pure chile powder, such as ancho (or substitute hot Hungarian paprika)
- 1 tsp. five-spice powder
- 1 tsp. dark brown sugar
  Kosher salt and freshly ground black pepper
- 4 lb. English-style beef short ribs (see Test Kitchen, p. 81)

FOR THE BRAISING LIQUID AND GLAZE

- 2 Tbs. peanut oil
- 2 cups chopped yellow onion
- 1 Tbs. chopped garlic
- 2 tsp. minced fresh ginger
- 3 cups lower-salt chicken broth
- ¼ cup plus 2 tsp. rice vinegar
- 3 Tbs. dark brown sugar
- 2 Tbs. Asian fish sauce
- 1 Tbs. soy sauce
- 1 whole star anise

FOR SERVING

- 3 scallions, thinly sliced (¼ cup)
  Cilantro sprigs

SEASON In a small bowl, combine the chile powder, five-spice powder, brown sugar, 2 tsp. salt, and 1 tsp. pepper. Sprinkle generously all over the ribs. Cover and refrigerate for at least 2 hours but preferably overnight.

SEAR Prepare a gas grill for direct grilling over medium-high heat (see Grill Skills, p. 58). Grill the ribs until all sides are nicely browned, 1 to 2 minutes per side. Let cool briefly and then tie with a couple of loops of butcher's twine.

BRAISE Prepare the grill for indirect grilling (see Grill Skills, p. 58). Set an 8-quart heavy-duty pot over medium heat and when hot, add the oil. Add the onions and cook, stirring occasionally, until soft, about 5 minutes. Add the garlic and ginger and stir for 1 minute more. Pour in the chicken broth, ¼ cup of the vinegar, 1 Tbs. of the brown sugar, the fish sauce, and the soy sauce. Add the star anise, bring to a boil, and then remove from the heat.

Put the ribs in the pot and set the pot on the grill over the cool zone. Cover the pot, close the grill lid, and cook for 30 minutes. Check the ribs and rearrange so they remain submerged in the simmering liquid. Check the ribs again after 30 minutes and move them around if necessary. After another 30 minutes, check the ribs for tenderness.

apart. If they're not tender enough, continue to cook, checking every 15 minutes. Remove the ribs from the pot and set aside.

Pour the liquid into a heatproof vessel, such as a Pyrex measuring cup, and let sit until the fat rises to the top. Skim off and discard the fat. Taste the liquid; if it's too watery, return to the pot and boil over high heat until flavorful.

GLAZE Prepare the grill for direct grilling over medium-high heat (see Grill Skills, p. 58). Pour 1 cup of the braising liquid into a small saucepan and stir in the remaining 2 Tbs. brown sugar and 2 tsp. rice vinegar. Over medium-high heat, reduce the liquid until it becomes syrupy, about 12 minutes—you'll have about ⅓ cup.

Brush the glaze over one side of each short rib and grill glazed side down until the glaze begins to bubble and lightly darken, 2 to 3 minutes. Brush another surface with the glaze and turn the ribs. Continue to brush and glaze, turning frequently, until all sides are nicely glazed. Transfer the ribs to a warm platter, drizzle with the remaining braising liquid, and garnish with the scallions and cilantro.

Bruce Aidells is the author of nine cookbooks, including Bruce Aidells's Complete Book

Splendor in the Grass

BY TASHA DeSERIO • At long last, it's picnic season. And while it's true that many meals just seem to taste better outside, it's also true that much picnic fare tends toward the predictable. Not this menu.

This fair-weather feast is an imaginative mix of do-ahead dishes that taste great individually and even better when combined on the plate. The grilled, brined chicken breasts, for example, are served with a rich chile oil that adds a unique flavor to the bulgur salad when the two come in contact. Likewise, the garlicky yogurt sauce that accompanies the toasted pita chips makes a fine dip for the chicken as well. Go ahead, play with your food.

There's more fun to be had packing up this picnic. When every dish is boxed individually, and all picnickers get their own box of goodies, unwrapping and discovering what's to eat takes on the feel of a group birthday party. (For more on how to pack it up—and keep it green while you're at it—see pages 64 and 67.)

No fried chicken, no potato chips, no sandwiches (unless you count the impossibly delicious ginger and lemon sandwich cookies for dessert)—a picnic never tasted so good. Let the hunt for that perfect grassy spot begin.

Wrap It Up

- Start with large individual boxes with flap lids that can hold several containers snugly.

- Next, look for medium-size, rectangular boxes with flap lids to hold the chicken, the bulgur salad, and the pita.

- Pack the peppers and sauces in separate sealed plastic containers. They should be added to the plate just before eating; otherwise, they'll stain the other foods.

brined grilled chicken breasts with red chile oil

This brine not only keeps the chicken moist, but the sugar in it helps the chicken brown nicely on the grill.

Serves 6

FOR THE CHICKEN

2 Tbs. granulated sugar

2 Tbs. kosher salt

6 boneless, skinless chicken breast halves (preferably organic), tenders reserved for another use

FOR THE CHILE OIL

1 Tbs. cumin seeds

1 Tbs. coriander seeds

1 tsp. caraway seeds

3-4 dried New Mexico or Anaheim chiles

1 tsp. cayenne

2 medium cloves garlic, minced and mashed to a paste with a pinch of salt

Kosher salt

1 cup extra-virgin olive oil

½ tsp. red wine vinegar, or to taste

BRINE THE CHICKEN

In a large bowl, combine 2 cups boiling water with the sugar and salt and stir to dissolve. Let cool completely. Add the chicken breasts, cover, and refrigerate for 2 to 3 hours.

MAKE THE CHILE OIL

In a medium skillet, lightly toast the cumin, coriander, and caraway seeds over medium heat, stirring often, until fragrant, about 2 minutes. Grind the seeds to a powder in an electric spice grinder and transfer to a medium bowl. In the same skillet, toast the chiles over medium heat, pressing on them with a spatula, until fragrant and darker in spots, about 1 minute per side. Remove the stems and seeds and grind in the spice grinder—you'll need 3 Tbs. ground chile. Add the ground chile, cayenne, garlic, and 1 tsp. salt to the ground spices, and then stir in the oil and vinegar. Taste and adjust the season-ing with more salt or vinegar if necessary. Stir before using. (The chile oil can be made up to several hours in advance, or up to a day ahead and stored in the refrigerator.)

GRILL THE CHICKEN

Prepare a medium gas or charcoal grill fire. While the grill heats, remove the chicken from the brine, pat dry with paper towels, and let sit at room temperature.

Toss the chicken with 2 Tbs. of the chile oil. Grill the chicken without moving until golden brown grill marks form, 4 to 6 minutes. Flip the chicken and grill until just cooked through, 4 to 5 minutes. Transfer to a cutting board and let rest for a few minutes. Holding your knife at an angle, cut the breasts crosswise into ½-inch-thick slices and let cool to room temperature. Serve with the remaining chile oil on the side. (The chicken can be grilled up to 6 hours in advance. Refrigerate and return to room temperature for serving.)

Food styling by Susan Sugarman

Photographs by Scott Phillips

- Wrap the cookies in parchment or in a parchment bag and place them carefully in the box.

- If you aim to impress, glue a menu card to the lids of the boxes so people know what they're eating.

- To keep everything fresh, transport the picnic boxes in a cooler, with ice packs. Pack a tote bag with plates, forks, knives, and napkins (see page 67 for green options).

bulgur salad with wilted chard and green olives

Be sure to use good-quality olives and rinse them well before you remove the pits, or the salad will be too salty.

Yields about 6 cups; serves 6 to 8

- 1½ cups medium bulgur
  Kosher salt
- 1½ lb. green Swiss chard (about 1 large or 2 small bunches), stemmed
- ¼ cup fresh lemon juice (from 1 to 2 lemons)
- 2 medium cloves garlic, minced and mashed to a paste with a pinch of salt
- 1 large shallot, finely diced
- ½ lb. whole green olives, such as picholines, rinsed well in warm water, pitted, and very coarsely chopped (1 cup)
- ½ cup coarsely chopped fresh cilantro
- ½ cup coarsely chopped fresh flat-leaf parsley
- ½ cup extra-virgin olive oil
  Freshly ground black pepper

Bring a large pot of water to a boil. Put the bulgur and 1 tsp. salt in a large bowl. Add 2¼ cups of the boiling water and cover the bowl. Let sit until the water has been absorbed and the bulgur is tender, about 1 hour.

Add 1 Tbs. salt to the remaining boiling water, add the chard, and cook until tender, 2 to 3 minutes. Drain the chard and run under cold water to cool. Thoroughly squeeze the chard to remove the excess liquid and chop to the same size as the chopped herbs. Lightly toss the chard so it doesn't remain in clumps when combined with the bulgur.

Combine the lemon juice, garlic, and shallot and let sit for at least 15 minutes.

Gently fold the lemon juice mixture, chard, olives, cilantro, parsley, and olive oil into the bulgur. Season to taste with salt and pepper. (The salad may be made a day ahead and stored in the refrigerator. Taste and adjust the seasoning before serving.)

Picnic for Six

Brined Grilled Chicken Breasts with Chile Oil

Bulgur Salad with Wilted Chard and Green Olives

Toasted Pita with Black Sesame Seeds and Sumac

Garlic-Yogurt Sauce

Charred Peppers with Garlic and Sherry Vinegar

Ginger-Spice Sandwich Cookies with Lemon Cream

toasted pita with black sesame seeds and sumac

This recipe makes more than you need, but you won't regret it. The pita chips keep well in a sealed bag. Look for black sesame seeds and sumac in specialty stores (or see Where to Buy It, p. 89). The Garlic-Yogurt Sauce (below) makes a great dip.

Yields about 36 pieces

- 2 tsp. black sesame seeds
- 1 tsp. ground sumac
- ¼ tsp. cayenne; more to taste
  Kosher salt
- 6 whole wheat or white pita breads
- ⅓ cup extra-virgin olive oil, approximately

Position a rack in the center of the oven and heat the oven to 400°F.

In a small bowl, combine the black sesame seeds, sumac, cayenne, and 1½ tsp. salt.

Split each pita horizontally into 2 rounds and tear each round into 3 rustic pieces. Brush a large rimmed baking sheet with a generous amount of olive oil, and spread 12 of the pita pieces in a single layer, inner side down, on the sheet. Brush the outer side of the pita with additional olive oil and sprinkle evenly with about a third of the spice mixture. Toast the pita in the oven until golden brown and crisp, about 8 minutes. Repeat with the remaining pita and spice mixture in two more batches. (The chips may be made 1 day ahead.)

garlic-yogurt sauce

This very simple sauce combines beautifully with the other foods in this menu.

Yields about 1 cup

- 1 cup full-fat plain yogurt
- 2 Tbs. extra-virgin olive oil
- 1 medium clove garlic, minced and mashed to a paste with a pinch of salt
  Kosher salt to taste

Combine the yogurt, oil, and garlic in a small bowl and season to taste with salt. Refrigerate until shortly before serving. (The sauce may be made 1 day ahead.)

charred peppers with garlic and sherry vinegar

Serves 6

- 6 medium red bell peppers
- 3 Tbs. extra-virgin olive oil
  Kosher salt
- 4 medium cloves garlic, very thinly sliced (about 1 Tbs.)
- 3 Tbs. sherry vinegar
  Freshly ground black pepper

Prepare a medium gas or charcoal grill fire. Rub the peppers with 1 Tbs. of the oil, set them on the grill, and char on all sides, 8 to 12 minutes total. If the peppers still feel a bit firm, put them in a bowl and cover with plastic—the residual heat will finish cooking them. Or, if the peppers are tender, let them cool at room temperature.

When the peppers are cool enough to handle, skin, core, and seed them. Cut or tear the peppers into strips about ½ inch wide and put them in a medium bowl. Season with ½ tsp. salt.

Put the remaining 2 Tbs. oil and the garlic in a small skillet and cook over medium heat until the garlic begins to sizzle and turn golden brown, 1 to 2 minutes. Remove the pan from the heat and carefully add the vinegar. Pour the garlic mixture over the peppers, and let cool at room temperature. Season to taste with salt and pepper. (The peppers may be made up to 2 days ahead and kept in the refrigerator.)

Make It Green

For an eco-friendly picnic, use 100 percent post-consumer recycled boxes and clear containers made of corn-based plastic that are compostable. Look for bamboo plates and utensils and for unbleached, chemical-free napkins that can be composted. For sources, see page 89.

ginger-spice sandwich cookies with lemon cream

If you make these a day ahead of time, the cookies will soften a bit, and the flavors will mingle nicely. Fresh spices are key.
Yields about 30 sandwich cookies

FOR THE COOKIES

9	oz. (2 cups) unbleached all-purpose flour
2	tsp. ground ginger
1½	tsp. ground cinnamon
½	tsp. ground cardamom
½	tsp. baking soda
½	tsp. kosher salt
6	oz. (¾ cup) unsalted butter, softened
½	cup packed dark brown sugar
½	cup granulated sugar; more for rolling
¼	cup unsulphured molasses
1	large egg, at room temperature
½	tsp. pure vanilla extract

FOR THE LEMON CREAM

4	oz. cream cheese, at room temperature
1	Tbs. finely grated lemon zest (from 1 medium lemon)
6	oz. (1½ cups) confectioners' sugar

MAKE THE COOKIES

Position a rack in the center of the oven and heat the oven to 350°F. Line three baking sheets with parchment.
In a medium bowl, whisk the flour, ginger, cinnamon, cardamom, baking soda, and salt.
In the bowl of a stand mixer fitted with the paddle attachment, beat the butter and both sugars on medium-high speed until light and fluffy, about 3 minutes. Add the molasses, egg, and vanilla and continue to beat until incorporated, about 1 minute.

Reduce the speed to low, slowly add the flour mixture, and mix until just incorporated, about 1 minute. Shape the dough into a disk, wrap in plastic, and refrigerate until firm, about 1 hour.
Put about ⅓ cup granulated sugar in a small bowl. Using your hands, roll teaspoonfuls of dough into 1-inch balls. Roll each ball in sugar and arrange them about 2 inches apart on the lined baking sheets. Use the bottom of a glass to flatten the cookies slightly. Bake one sheet at a time until the cookies feel dry to the touch and are beginning to firm up (they'll still feel soft inside), 10 to 14 minutes. Cool completely on racks.

MAKE THE LEMON CREAM

With a hand mixer, mix the cream cheese and lemon zest in a medium bowl until smooth. Slowly add the confectioners' sugar and continue to mix until smooth.

ASSEMBLE THE COOKIES

Drop about 1 tsp. of the lemon cream in the center of a cookie, top with another cookie, and gently press them. Repeat with the remaining cookies. Store in an airtight container for up to 2 days.

A former Chez Panisse cook, Tasha DeSerio is now co-proprietor of Olive Green Catering in Berkeley, California. ◻

 Get the shopping list and game plan for this menu at FineCooking.com/extras.

All together now: The chicken, salad, pita chips, yogurt sauce, and peppers make a fine (and delicious) mess.

the classic....

Inked In

Crab cakes as we know them made their print debut in Crosby Gaige's 1939 *New York World's Fair Cook Book*. They were called Baltimore Crab Cakes, in honor of their place of origin.

Bigger Is Better

The key to delicious crab cakes is starting with nice, big chunks of crab (blue crab is traditional) and handling them gently. Look for crab labeled jumbo lump or backfin lump.

Spice It Up

It's not a classic crab cake without Old Bay seasoning, a traditional spice blend created in the 1940s that includes celery seeds, paprika, and black pepper.

Bread Matters

Fresh breadcrumbs (and eggs) are used as binders. But use just enough to hold the crabmeat together. Cook's hint: White sandwich bread yields the absolute best cakes—soft and flaky at the same time.

TRADITIONAL OR INNOVATIVE? For a side-by-side tasting to find the ultimate crab cake, we sought out the most delicious authentic Maryland crab cake we could find and then asked a superstar chef for his original interpretation. Susie Middleton, *Fine Cooking*'s editor at large and a Chesapeake Bay native, contributed the definitive classic, which also happens to be the recipe she grew up eating. Chef Eric Ripert of New York City's four-star seafood restaurant Le Bernardin gave us a delightfully fresh, modern version. The battle is on.

....the update

Over the Top
Toasted unsweetened coconut flakes sprinkled on top add a little crunch to these "cakes."

Prized Crustacean
Peekytoe crab is almost as treasured by chefs as lobster. For more on how this Maine crab got its name and made it big, see page 83.

Exotic Twist
For Chef Ripert, a quick soak in lime juice and coconut milk for the crab evokes the sunny beaches of the Caribbean.

Bottom Line
In a nod to the season, a sweet, spiced-up tomato chutney enhances the natural sweetness of the crab.

classic maryland crab cakes

You can find Old Bay seasoning in most supermarkets and seafood stores. Use just enough to give a hint of its presence or it will overpower the crab.

Serves 4

- 1 lb. jumbo lump or backfin lump crabmeat, fresh or pasteurized
- 1 large egg
- ¼ cup mayonnaise
- 1½ tsp. Dijon mustard
- 1½ tsp. Old Bay seasoning
- 1 tsp. fresh lemon juice
- ½ tsp. Worcestershire sauce
  Kosher salt
- 1¼ cups fresh breadcrumbs (from soft white sandwich bread, such as Pepperidge Farm)
- 1 Tbs. chopped fresh flat-leaf parsley
- 2 Tbs. unsalted butter
- 1 Tbs. olive oil
  Lemon wedges for serving

Drain the crabmeat, if necessary, and pick through it for shells (jumbo lump will not have shells). Put the crab in a medium mixing bowl and set aside.

In a small bowl, whisk the egg, mayonnaise, mustard, Old Bay seasoning, lemon juice, Worcestershire sauce, and ¼ tsp. salt. Scrape the mixture over the crab and mix gently until well combined. Gently break up the lumps with your fingers but do not overmix.

Sprinkle the breadcrumbs and the parsley over the mixture, and mix them in thoroughly but gently; try not to turn the mixture into a mash—it should still be somewhat loose. Cover with plastic wrap and refrigerate for 1 to 3 hours.

Shape the crab mixture into 8 cakes about 1 inch thick. In a 12-inch nonstick skillet, heat the butter with the olive oil over medium heat. When the butter is frothy, add the cakes to the pan (8 should fit comfortably). Cook until dark golden brown on the underside, about 4 minutes. Flip the cakes, reduce the heat to medium low, and continue cooking until the other side is well browned, 4 to 5 minutes. Serve with lemon wedges on the side for squeezing over the cakes.

"This crab cake is the real deal—no fussy stuff, no flavor disguises. Just pure, sweet crab meat, and lots of it."
—SUSIE MIDDLETON

Food Styling by Susan Sugarman

Photographs by Scott Phillips

lime-and-coconut-marinated peekytoe "crab cakes" with tomato chutney

In true restaurant fashion, you'll need a ring mold to build these "cakes" so that they hold their shape. See Test Kitchen, p. 81, for more information.
Serves 6

FOR THE TOMATO CHUTNEY

- 2 tsp. black peppercorns
- 1 tsp. coriander seeds
- 1 tsp. yellow mustard seeds
- 4 whole cloves
- 1 bay leaf
- 2 Tbs. canola oil
- ½ cup small-diced yellow onion
- 1 tsp. minced garlic
- 1 tsp. minced fresh ginger
- 3 cups peeled, seeded, and diced fresh tomatoes
- 1 Tbs. seeded, minced jalapeño
- 1 Tbs. granulated sugar
  Fine sea salt and freshly ground black pepper

FOR THE BASIL OIL

- 2 cups loosely packed fresh basil
- ½ cup canola oil

FOR THE CRAB

- 1 lb. peekytoe crabmeat (or substitute jumbo lump or Dungeness)
- 6 Tbs. fresh lime juice
- ¼ cup very loosely packed fresh basil, thinly sliced
- 3 Tbs. minced shallot
- 3 Tbs. coconut milk
- ¾ tsp. Espelette pepper (optional)
  Fine sea salt and freshly ground black pepper

FOR THE GARNISH

- ¼ cup unsweetened coconut flakes, toasted
- 6 small fresh basil tops

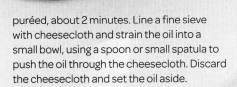

MAKE THE CHUTNEY

Cut a small square of cheesecloth and put the peppercorns, coriander seeds, mustard seeds, cloves, and bay leaf in the middle of the cloth. Gather the edges into a pouch and secure with twine.

Heat the oil in a 4-quart heavy-duty nonreactive saucepan over medium heat. Add the onion, garlic, and ginger and cook, stirring occasionally, until soft but not browned, 3 to 5 minutes. Reduce the heat to medium low and add the tomatoes, jalapeño, sugar, and the spice bundle. Cook, stirring frequently, until very thick and most of the liquid has evaporated, 25 to 30 minutes. Season to taste with salt and pepper, discard the spice bundle, and let cool.

MAKE THE BASIL OIL

Bring a medium pot of salted water to a boil over high heat. Prepare an ice bath by filling a medium bowl with several inches of ice water. Blanch the basil in the boiling water for 10 seconds. Drain and immediately plunge into the ice bath to cool. Drain again and gently squeeze out any water. Put the basil and the oil in a blender and process until puréed, about 2 minutes. Line a fine sieve with cheesecloth and strain the oil into a small bowl, using a spoon or small spatula to push the oil through the cheesecloth. Discard the cheesecloth and set the oil aside.

MARINATE THE CRAB

Pick over the crab to remove any cartilage or shells. Work with the crab gently, being careful not to break up the meat. Put the crab in a medium bowl and add the lime juice, basil, shallot, coconut milk, Espelette pepper (if using), a pinch of salt, and a few grinds of pepper. Gently toss to coat and let marinate for about 10 minutes at room temperature. Put the crab in a fine sieve over a medium bowl and drain for at least 5 minutes.

ASSEMBLE THE DISH

Put a 2½-inch-diameter ring mold in the center of a small plate, spread about 2 Tbs. of the chutney in the bottom, and top with ½ cup of the crab mixture. Carefully remove the mold. Repeat to make 5 more servings. Drizzle some basil oil around each plate, and garnish the top of each "cake" with toasted coconut flakes and basil tops. Serve immediately.

Susie Middleton lives and cooks on Martha's Vineyard, Massachusetts, where she contributes to Edible Vineyard. *Eric Ripert will host his own PBS show,* Avec Ripert, *this fall.* ◻

"Sure, I like crab cakes as much as the next person, but there's plenty of room to play around if you're a little creative. My 'cakes' are fun, fresh—slightly exotic."
—ERIC RIPERT

 Which is your favorite version? Go to Fine Cooking.com/extras and cast your vote.

Salad: *it's what's for dinner*

Almond-Crusted Chicken and Nectarine Salad with Buttermilk-Chive Dressing, recipe on page 76.

Get tonight's meal on the table in no time with these fast, fresh recipes.

BY MARYELLEN DRISCOLL

GREENS ARE IN. If you belong to a CSA or regularly visit your local farmers' market, you know what I mean. This is their season. So at my house, where we feast on what's fresh, salad now moves to center stage. A head of lettuce doesn't get stretched over a few nights; it's the meal.

almond-crusted chicken and nectarine salad with buttermilk-chive dressing

If you can't find chicken tenderloins, look for thin cutlets, which work just as well.

Serves 4

FOR THE DRESSING

¼ cup buttermilk

1 Tbs. sour cream

1 Tbs. white balsamic vinegar

½ tsp. honey

2 Tbs. extra-virgin olive oil

1 Tbs. thinly sliced fresh chives

Kosher salt and freshly ground black pepper

FOR THE CHICKEN

2 large eggs

1¾ cups sliced almonds

½ cup all-purpose flour

1½ lb. chicken tenderloins, pounded ¼ inch thick

Kosher salt and freshly ground black pepper

2-3 Tbs. vegetable oil

FOR THE SALAD

6 cups torn tender lettuce (such as butter lettuce, oakleaf, Red Sails) or arugula or both

2 small to medium ripe nectarines (or peaches), halved, pitted, and sliced ¼ inch thick

Kosher salt and freshly ground black pepper

MAKE THE DRESSING

In a medium bowl or liquid measuring cup, combine the buttermilk, sour cream, vinegar, and honey. Slowly whisk in the oil to blend. Stir in the chives and season to taste with salt and pepper.

COOK THE CHICKEN

Lightly beat the eggs in a wide, shallow dish. Pulse the almonds and flour together in a food processor until the almonds are chopped; transfer the almond mixture to another wide, shallow dish. Season the chicken on all sides with 1 tsp. salt and ¾ tsp. pepper. Dip one piece of chicken at a time in the eggs. Shake off the excess and dredge in the almond mixture, pressing lightly to help it adhere. Set aside on a wire rack.

Heat 2 Tbs. of the oil in a large skillet over medium heat until shimmering hot. Working in batches, cook the chicken until light golden brown on both sides and just cooked through, 3 to 4 minutes per side. Transfer the chicken to a paper-towel-lined plate when done. Between batches, remove any stray almonds from the pan and add more oil if necessary.

ASSEMBLE THE SALAD

In a large bowl, toss the lettuce, arugula, or both and the nectarines with about half of the dressing. Season to taste with salt and pepper. Divide among 4 dinner plates. Divide the chicken among the plates, overlapping the pieces on top of the salad. Drizzle additional dressing over the chicken and serve.

Photographs by Scott Phillips

pan-seared salmon with baby greens and fennel

If you have fleur de sel, use it to season the finished salad. The salt flakes are an appealing contrast to the sweet and citrusy dressing. **Serves 4**

FOR THE DRESSING

2½	Tbs. Champagne or white wine vinegar
2	Tbs. fresh orange juice
1	tsp. finely grated orange zest
	Kosher salt and freshly ground black pepper
¼	cup dried cherries
½	cup extra-virgin olive oil

FOR THE SALMON

4	6-oz. skinless salmon fillets, preferably center cut
	Kosher salt and freshly ground black pepper
1½	Tbs. extra-virgin olive oil

FOR THE SALAD

8	oz. mixed baby salad greens (about 8 lightly packed cups)
1	small fennel bulb, trimmed, halved lengthwise, cored, and very thinly sliced crosswise
	Kosher salt and freshly ground black pepper

START THE DRESSING

In a small bowl, combine the vinegar with the orange juice and zest, ¼ tsp. salt, and a few grinds of pepper. Stir in the dried cherries and set aside.

COOK THE SALMON

Season the salmon fillets on both sides with 1 tsp. salt and ¼ tsp. pepper. Heat the oil in a 12-inch skillet over medium-high heat. Cook the salmon, flipping once, until barely cooked through and a rich golden brown crust develops on both sides, 4 to 5 minutes per side. Set aside on a plate.

FINISH THE DRESSING

Using a fork or slotted spoon, remove the cherries from the orange juice mixture and set aside. Slowly whisk the ½ cup olive oil into the orange juice mixture until blended. Season to taste with salt and pepper.

ASSEMBLE THE SALAD

Combine the greens and fennel in a large bowl. Add about half of the vinaigrette to the salad, toss, and season to taste with salt and pepper. Divide the salad among 4 large plates or shallow bowls. Set a piece of salmon on each salad and sprinkle the cherries around the fish. Drizzle some of the remaining vinaigrette over each fillet and serve.

grilled steak salad with pineapple-ginger dressing

Look for peeled and cut fresh pineapple in the produce section of your supermarket; it's a great time-saver. **Serves 4**

FOR THE DRESSING

5	Tbs. pineapple juice
1	Tbs. soy sauce
1	Tbs. peanut oil
1	Tbs. Asian sesame oil
2	tsp. fresh lime juice
½	tsp. honey
½	tsp. finely grated fresh ginger
1	small clove garlic, minced
	Large pinch crushed red pepper flakes
¼	cup small-diced fresh pineapple
1	Tbs. finely chopped fresh cilantro

FOR THE STEAK

1	lb. flank steak
1½	Tbs. vegetable oil; more for the grill
	Kosher salt and freshly ground black pepper

FOR THE SALAD

6	oz. torn butter lettuce (about 6 lightly packed cups)
1	medium cucumber, seeded and thinly sliced
3	radishes, thinly sliced
	Kosher salt and freshly ground black pepper
¼	cup thinly sliced scallion (both white and light-green parts)

Heat a gas grill to medium high.

MAKE THE DRESSING

In a small bowl, whisk the pineapple juice, soy sauce, peanut oil, sesame oil, lime juice, honey, ginger, garlic, and pepper flakes to blend. Stir in the pineapple and cilantro.

COOK THE STEAK

Rub the steak with the oil and season with 1 tsp. each salt and pepper. Clean and oil the grill grates. Grill the steak, covered, until it has nice grill marks on one side, 5 to 6 minutes. Flip and reduce the heat to medium. Cook, covered, until done to your liking, an additional 4 to 5 minutes for medium rare. Transfer to a cutting board and let rest for 5 to 10 minutes.

ASSEMBLE THE SALAD

In a large bowl, toss the lettuce, cucumber, and radishes with about half of the dressing. Season to taste with salt and pepper. Divide among 4 large plates.
Thinly slice the steak across the grain and drape it over the greens. Drizzle some of the remaining dressing over the beef, sprinkle with the scallions, and serve.

Food styling by Michelli Knauer

spinach and artichoke salad with couscous cakes and feta

Quick-to-cook couscous cakes make this meatless main-course salad satisfying.
Serves 3

FOR THE DRESSING

- 2 Tbs. fresh lemon juice
- 1 Tbs. sour cream
- 1 tsp. finely chopped fresh mint
- 5 Tbs. extra-virgin olive oil
  Kosher salt and freshly ground black pepper

FOR THE COUSCOUS CAKES

- ¾ cup couscous
  Kosher salt
- 1 large clove garlic, peeled
- ¼ cup packed fresh flat-leaf parsley leaves
- ½ cup canned chickpeas, rinsed and drained
- 2 large eggs, lightly beaten
  Finely grated zest of 1 medium lemon (about 1½ tsp.)
- 3 Tbs. vegetable or canola oil

FOR THE SALAD

- 8 oz. baby spinach, washed and dried (about 6 lightly packed cups)

- 1 14-oz. can artichoke bottoms, drained, rinsed, and sliced
- 15 cherry tomatoes, halved
  Kosher salt and freshly ground black pepper
- 1 oz. crumbled feta (about ¼ cup)

MAKE THE DRESSING

In a small bowl, combine the lemon juice, sour cream, and mint. Slowly whisk in the olive oil. Season to taste with salt and pepper.

MAKE THE COUSCOUS CAKES

Put the couscous and 1 tsp. salt in a medium bowl. Add 1 cup boiling water to the couscous, cover the bowl with a pan lid or plate, and let sit for 4 to 5 minutes.

Coarsely chop the garlic in a food processor. Add the parsley and pulse until finely chopped. Add the chickpeas and 1 tsp. salt and pulse until coarsely chopped.

Uncover the couscous and fluff with a fork. Stir in the chickpea mixture, eggs, and lemon zest until well combined. Press the couscous mixture into a ¼-cup measure, smooth the top, and invert the measuring cup to release

the cake onto a plate. Repeat with the remaining couscous mixture to make 9 cakes.

Heat 1½ Tbs. of the vegetable oil in a large skillet over medium heat until shimmering hot. Add 5 of the couscous cakes to the skillet and use a spatula to lightly flatten the cakes so they're about ¾ inch thick. Cook, flipping once, until crisp and golden brown on both sides, 2 to 3 minutes per side. Transfer to a paper-towel-lined plate. Add the remaining 1½ Tbs. vegetable oil to the skillet and cook the remaining cakes the same way.

ASSEMBLE THE SALAD

In a large bowl, toss the spinach, artichokes, and tomatoes with about three-quarters of the dressing. Season to taste with salt and pepper and divide among 3 large plates. Top each salad with 3 couscous cakes, sprinkle each salad with feta, and drizzle with the remaining dressing.

Maryellen Driscoll is a Fine Cooking *contributing editor.* ◻

TEST KITCHEN

Tips/Techniques/Equipment/Ingredients/Glossary

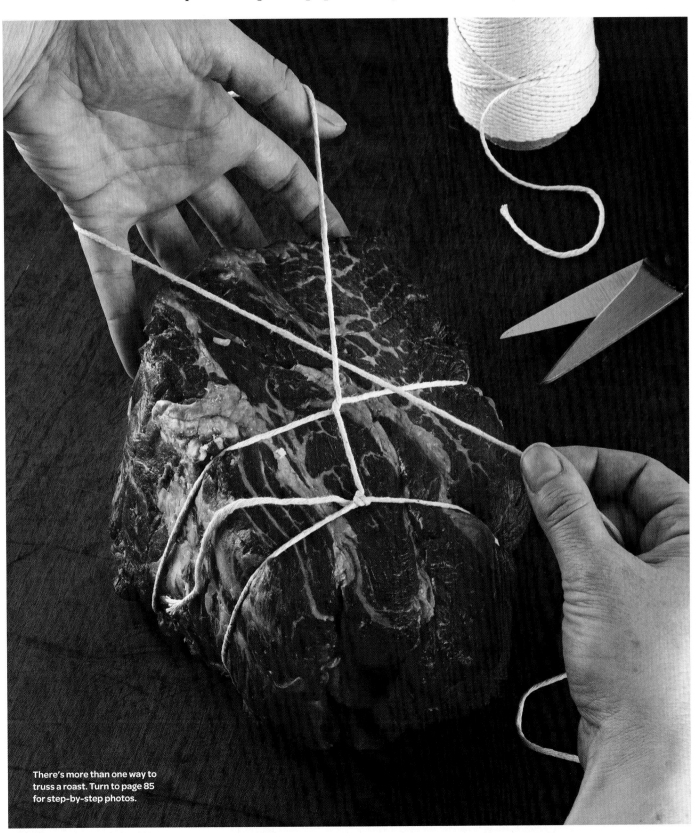

There's more than one way to truss a roast. Turn to page 85 for step-by-step photos.

ENGLISH-STYLE BEEF SHORT RIBS

COUNTRY-STYLE PORK RIBS

FLANKEN-STYLE
BEEF SHORT RIBS

Ribs for barbecue-braising

WHEN IT COMES TO RIBS on the grill, we usually think of baby backs or spareribs, but for our barbecue-braising recipes on page 54, we wanted meaty ribs with a high fat content that would hold up to long, slow, moist cooking.

Country-style pork ribs

Meatier and thicker than spareribs and baby backs, country-style pork ribs are actually blade chops from the shoulder end of the loin. They're available either bone-in or boneless and can be found in the meat section of most supermarkets.

Beef short ribs

Beef short ribs are generally cut in two styles: flanken and English. Flanken are cut across the bones, resulting in a strip of meat about ½ inch thick with several bone segments. English ribs are cut parallel to the bone, so each piece consists of one 2- to 4-inch segment of meat attached to one piece of rib bone. We tested the Vietnamese Short Ribs on page 61 with English ribs, but you can substitute flanken—just keep in mind that the cooking time may be shorter. Most supermarkets carry short ribs, but because they're not as popular during the summer months, you may need to special-order them.

—*Melissa Pellegrino and Jennifer Armentrout*

Is it done?

Two terms for knowing when to take the pot off the heat.

Fork tender: This term is used to describe the readiness of slow-cooked meat, like the barbecue-braised dishes on page 54. To gauge whether the meat is fully cooked, you just stick a fork in it. There are two ways to tell if it's fork tender. Pull on the fork—if the meat releases easily, it's done. Or you can gently twist the fork against the grain of the meat—if the meat pulls apart into strands, it's good to go.

Subscribe and save up to $58*

TREAT YOURSELF

☐ 1 year just $29.95 – **Save 30%***
☐ 2 years just $49.95 – **Save 42%***
☐ 3 years just $69.95 – **BEST BUY! Save 45%***

Send no money now. We will bill you later.

N 5 0 9 9 6 0 N

MR. / MRS. / MS. _____

ADDRESS _____ APT. # _____

CITY _____

STATE _____ ZIP _____ EMAIL (OPTIONAL) _____

The Taunton Press will send you occasional notices about noteworthy products and exclusive offers.

fine Cooking®
FineCooking.com/order

Savings off U.S. newsstand price. Above prices for U.S. and Canada (GST included). Payable in U.S. funds. International customers, visit FineCooking.com/order

© 2009 The Taunton Press

Treat a friend to *Fine Cooking*

☐ 1 year just $29.95 – **Save 30%***
☐ 2 years just $49.95 – **Save 42%***
☐ 3 years just $69.95 – **BEST BUY! Save 45%***

Send no money now. We will bill you later.

N 5 0 9 9 6 1 N

YOUR NAME: _____   **SEND GIFT TO:** _____

ADDRESS _____   ADDRESS _____

APT. # _____ CITY _____   APT. # _____ CITY _____

STATE _____ ZIP _____   STATE _____ ZIP _____

EMAIL (OPTIONAL) _____

The Taunton Press will send you occasional notices about noteworthy products and exclusive offers.

fine Cooking®

Savings off U.S. newsstand price. Above prices for U.S. and Canada (GST included). Payable in U.S. funds. International customers, visit FineCooking.com/order

© 2009 The Taunton Press

Ring molds

EXPLORE THE EQUIPMENT cupboard of any good restaurant, and chances are you'll find a stash of ring molds. These open-ended cylinders come in a variety of diameters and heights and are a chef's secret weapon for building towering creations like the peekytoe "crab cake" on page 73.

There are several ring mold options available. The most versatile are made of stainless steel or aluminum, so in addition to molding mile-high foods, you can also use them to bake tall cakes. They're available at restaurant supply stores (see page 89 for a mail-order source).

Chefs looking to balance their bottom lines have also been known to fashion their own ring molds from plastic PVC pipe (found in any hardware store). With a hacksaw, they can customize the molds to whatever length they want.

In that same spirit of do-it-yourself resourcefulness, we searched our test kitchen to see what other ring mold stand-ins we could find, and came up with two. First, a nesting set of biscuit cutters yielded a 2½-inch-diameter cutter—just the size we needed for the crab cakes. It wasn't as tall as a true ring mold might be, but it was tall enough. Then we noticed that a 8-ounce can of tomato sauce is the perfect diameter, and it's taller than a biscuit cutter. The only catch is to make sure you use a can with a rim on the bottom; otherwise, it's nearly impossible to remove the bottom with a can opener.

—*Jennifer Armentrout*

From left: double-sided biscuit cutter, PVC piping, stainless-steel ring mold, tomato sauce can.

Peekytoe crab

There's a rags-to-riches story behind the peekytoe crab, a favorite ingredient in high-end restaurants. These crabs, known more commonly as rock, sand, or bay crabs, used to be just a throwaway byproduct of the lobster industry. But that all changed when a marketing campaign by the Browne Trading Company in Portland, Maine, amped up the crab's appeal (and its price) by giving it a stylish, new name: peekytoe.

The name is derived from the word "picked," which is Maine slang for "pointed." The crabs have legs with a sharp point that turns inward, a "picked toe." In Maine, "picked" is often pronounced with two syllables, and eventually "picked toe" morphed into "peekytoe."

The small crabs themselves are too fragile to ship live, so they're cooked and picked prior to shipping. The delicate, sweet, white and pale-pink-speckled meat best lends itself to straightforward preparations where its flavor can really shine, as in Eric Ripert's Lime-Coconut-Marinated Peekytoe "Crab Cakes" with Tomato Chutney on page 73.   —*Melissa Pellegrino*

Nappé: This French word describes the consistency at which a sauce, especially a custard sauce, is thick enough to coat the back of a spoon and hold the shape of a line when a finger is drawn through it. The ice cream base on page 48 is a type of custard, and when it's nappé, it's ready to come off the stove.

—*Melissa Pellegrino and Jennifer Armentrout*

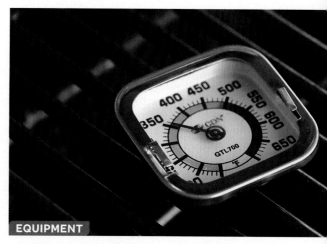

EQUIPMENT

Grill surface thermometer

KNOWING HOW HOT THE GRILL IS can be a little tricky. Even if your grill has a thermometer built into the lid, you still can't tell how hot it is down on the grate where all the cooking happens. That's why we were happy to discover this grill surface thermometer from CDN. Small and easy to read, it sits right on the surface of the grill grates. We grew to love it while testing the barbecue-braising recipes on page 54, all of which call for maintaining 350°F for up to several hours. See page 89 for a mail-order source. —*Melissa Pellegrino*

INGREDIENT

Harissa

Harissa is a spicy North African sauce or paste made of ground dried chile peppers, garlic, olive oil, and spices like coriander, caraway, and cumin. Primarily Tunisian, harissa is also used in Moroccan, Algerian, and Libyan cooking. Ranging in heat from mild to scorching hot, harissa is used as both a condiment and an ingredient that's stirred into couscous, tagines (stews), soups, and pastas.

Look for harissa in tubes, cans, or jars at well-stocked grocery stores and specialty markets (see page 89 for a mail-order source). Or try your hand at making a homemade batch, using this recipe.

TIPS

Taste nut oils before using

While all oils have a limited shelf life, nut and seed oils, like hazelnut, almond, sesame, and walnut, are more likely than others to turn rancid. The main reason is that they've sat too long on the shelf, either at home or in the market. We've purchased nut oils that had gone bad before they were opened. The lesson: Be sure to taste your oil before every use. An oil can be rancid without smelling bad, so don't just take a whiff—try it. If its flavor is the slightest bit unpleasant, discard it.

How to protect those pricey oils
Rancid oil is inevitable, but you can do a couple of things to delay it. Air, light, and temperature are the enemies, so...

Yields about 1 cup

- 6 **dried Anaheim or New Mexico chiles**
- 4 **dried chiles de Arbol**
- 1 **tsp. caraway seed**
- 1 **tsp. coriander seed**
- ¾ **tsp. cumin seed**
- 2 **medium cloves garlic, minced**
- ½ **tsp. finely grated lemon zest**
  Kosher salt
- 2 **Tbs. extra-virgin olive oil; more as needed**

Bring a kettle of water to a boil. Stem and seed the chiles and put them in a medium heatproof bowl. Add enough boiling water to cover the chiles and let soak until well softened, about 1 hour. Drain and squeeze out any excess water.

Meanwhile, in a small skillet, lightly toast the caraway, coriander, and cumin seeds over medium heat until fragrant, 2 to 3 minutes. Let cool slightly and then grind finely with a spice grinder.

Put the chiles, ground spices, garlic, lemon zest, ¾ tsp. salt, and 1 Tbs. warm water in a blender. With the motor running, gradually pour the oil in a steady stream through the feed hole in the blender cap; continue blending until a mostly smooth, paste-like sauce forms. If the sauce is too thick to purée, add warm water 1 Tbs. at a time to loosen. Transfer the harissa to an airtight container and top with a thin layer of olive oil. Store in the refrigerator for up to 2 weeks.

—*Melissa Pellegrino*

1. **Purchase** from a store that has high turnover; chances are the oil will be fresher when you buy it.
2. **Transfer** the oil to a metal or dark-glass container if it didn't come in one, in order to block light.
3. **Tightly close** the container to keep air out.
4. **Store** the oil in the refrigerator to keep it cool.

—*Jennifer Armentrout*

Two ways to tie meat

Tying keeps long-cooked meats, like the barbecue-braised dishes on page 54, from falling apart as they cook. The first method shown here is as easy as tying a slipknot. The second method is a little trickier, but once you get the hang of it, it's faster and it holds the meat together better.

INDIVIDUAL LOOPS

1 Cut several short lengths of butcher's twine. Wrap one piece around the meat and tie with a slipknot.

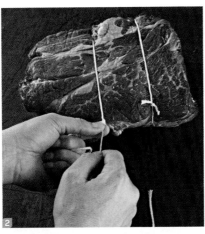

2 Cinch the slipknot snugly against the meat. Repeat, spacing the loops 2 to 3 inches apart.

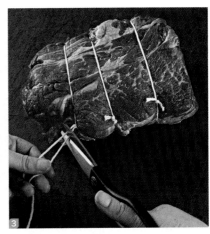

3 Trim the excess twine.

ONE LONG STRAND

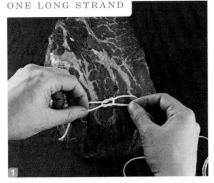

1 Cut a long piece of twine and tie the end of the twine in a single loop around one end of the meat, securing it with a square knot.

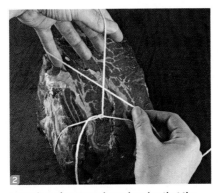

2 Loop the twine around your hand so that the loose end passes underneath the tied end.

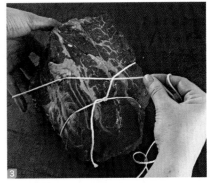

3 Slip this loop under and around the meat. Pull the loop snug, adjusting its position as needed.

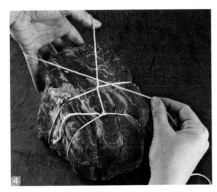

4 Repeat, spacing the loops 2 to 3 inches apart, until you reach a couple of inches from the end of the meat.

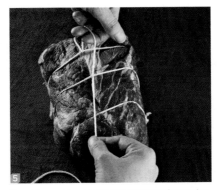

5 Turn the meat over and thread the twine under the loops, back to the starting end.

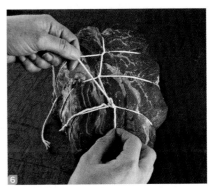

6 Secure the loose end to the tied end with another knot, and then trim any excess twine.

—*Jennifer Armentrout*

Make it Tonight

Just 30 minutes to dinner, start to finish.

grilled pork chops with sweet-and-sour onions

Garlic bread drizzled with a bit of olive oil is the perfect accompaniment.

Serves 4

4	¾-inch-thick bone-in pork loin chops (1¾ to 2 lb.)
¼	cup extra-virgin olive oil
1	Tbs. chopped fresh thyme
	Kosher salt and freshly ground black pepper
1½	lb. red onions (about 3 medium), peeled and cut into ¼- to ½-inch-thick disks
½	cup red wine vinegar
1	Tbs. granulated sugar

Prepare a medium-high fire on a gas or charcoal grill. In a medium bowl, toss the pork chops with 1 Tbs. of the oil, half of the thyme, 1 tsp. salt, and ½ tsp. pepper. Put the onions on a large plate and sprinkle with 2 Tbs. of the oil and 1½ tsp. salt. In a small bowl, whisk the vinegar, sugar, and the remaining thyme.

Grill the onions, covered, flipping once, until crisp-tender, 5 to 6 minutes per side. Return to the plate. Grill the pork, covered, flipping once, until firm to the touch and just cooked through, 3 to 4 minutes per side.

Transfer the pork to a large platter, brush with some of the vinegar mixture and tent loosely with foil. Heat the remaining 1 Tbs. oil in a large skillet over medium-high heat until it's shimmering hot. Add the onions and the remaining vinegar mixture and cook, stirring, until they absorb all of the liquid and take on a browned, glazed appearance, 3 to 4 minutes. Serve the pork chops with the onions.

—Tony Rosenfeld

tex-mex chicken with chiles and cheese

Serve with rice pilaf, or wrap the chicken in warm corn tortillas.

Serves 4

1¼	lb. boneless, skinless chicken breast halves, trimmed and sliced ¼ inch thick
1½	tsp. chili powder
½	tsp. ground cumin
	Kosher salt and freshly ground black pepper
½	cup all-purpose flour
3½	Tbs. unsalted butter
1½	cups fresh or thawed frozen corn kernels
1	medium jalapeño, seeded if desired and thinly sliced
1	large clove garlic, minced
2–3	medium limes, 1 or 2 juiced to yield 3 Tbs. and 1 cut into wedges
1	Tbs. chopped fresh oregano
1	cup grated sharp Cheddar

Position a rack about 4 inches from the broiler and heat the broiler to high. Toss the chicken with the chili powder, cumin, ¾ tsp. salt, and ½ tsp. black pepper. Lightly dredge the chicken in the flour and shake off any excess.

Melt 2½ Tbs. of the butter in a 12-inch ovenproof skillet (preferably cast iron) over medium-high heat. Add the chicken and cook, stirring occasionally, until browned, about 5 minutes. Transfer to a plate.

Add the remaining 1 Tbs. butter, the corn, jalapeño, garlic, and ½ tsp. salt. Cook, stirring, until the corn begins to brown lightly, 2 to 3 minutes. Add the chicken, lime juice, oregano, and ½ cup water. Cook, stirring, until the chicken is just cooked through, about 2 minutes. Sprinkle with the Cheddar and transfer the skillet to the broiler. Broil until the cheese melts and browns on top, about 3 minutes. Serve with lime wedges.

—Tony Rosenfeld

vegetables and tofu with spicy peanut sauce

On the Indonesian island of Java, this hearty, main-course salad—known as *gado-gado*—is sold by street vendors, who carry the ingredients on yoke-like poles, assembling each serving to order. It's surprisingly easy to make.

Serves 2 to 3

- 4 medium red potatoes (12 oz.), cut into ⅓-inch-thick slices
- 2 medium carrots (4 oz.), peeled and cut on the diagonal into ⅓-inch-thick slices
- 7 oz. package pressed, baked tofu (regular or Thai flavor), sliced into 1-inch-square pieces, ½ inch thick
- 1 small crown broccoli (7 oz.), cut into 1-inch florets
- 3 oz. green beans, trimmed and halved crosswise on the diagonal
- ½ cup natural unsalted peanut butter (smooth or chunky)
- 1 Tbs. soy sauce
- 1½ tsp. Asian chile paste, such as sambal oeleck; more to taste
  Kosher salt

Put a steamer basket in a large pot and fill the pot with water to just reach the bottom of the basket.

Put the potatoes in a single layer in the steamer basket, set the pot over medium-high heat, and bring the water to a boil. Cover the pot and cook for 4 minutes, then carefully remove the lid, move the potatoes to one side of the pot, and add the carrots in a snug, slightly overlapping layer. Cover the pot and steam until the carrots and potatoes are just tender, another 6 to 7 minutes. Transfer the potatoes and carrots to a platter. Put the tofu, broccoli, and beans in the steamer; cover and cook until the tofu is hot and the broccoli and

beans are just tender, about 4 minutes. Transfer to the platter with the other vegetables.

In a medium bowl, combine the peanut butter, soy sauce, chile paste, and ½ cup hot water from the pot. Whisk to combine, adding more water as needed to create a thick but fluid sauce. Add more chile paste and salt to taste. Serve with the sauce on the side.

—*Dabney Gough*

clams with basil broth

Quick and tasty: rich, tender steamed clams in an aromatic white wine broth. Serve with plenty of crusty sourdough bread for dipping.

Serves 4

- 4 lb. littleneck clams
- ¾ cup finely diced yellow onion
- ½ cup dry white wine
- 1½ tsp. minced garlic
- 2 Tbs. chopped fresh basil
  Kosher salt and freshly ground black pepper

Scrub the clams with a brush under cold water to remove any sand; rinse well. Discard any with cracked shells or open shells that don't close when tapped firmly against the counter.

In a 5- to 6-quart pot, combine the onion, wine, garlic, and 1 cup water; bring to a boil over high heat. Add the clams, cover, and steam until they open, about 5 minutes—begin checking the clams early to avoid overcooking.

Transfer the clams to serving bowls, discarding any that don't open. Stir the basil into the cooking liquid, season to taste with salt and pepper, and pour over the clams. Serve immediately.

—*Bonnie Gorder-Hinchey*

duck breasts with peaches and tarragon

If ripe fresh apricots are available, you can use them instead of peaches.

Serves 4

- 2 1-lb. boneless duck breasts
  Kosher salt and freshly ground black pepper
- 1 Tbs. unsalted butter
- 2 medium shallots, thinly sliced (½ cup)
- 6 Tbs. dry white wine or dry vermouth
- 6 Tbs. lower-salt chicken broth
- 3 medium peaches (or 6 medium apricots), pitted and sliced ½ inch thick
- 1 Tbs. chopped fresh tarragon leaves
- 2 tsp. mild honey, such as clover honey

Heat the oven to 425°F. Score the skin and fat on each breast without cutting into the meat. Season with ½ tsp. salt and ¼ tsp. pepper.

Heat a 12-inch ovenproof skillet over medium heat. Add the breasts skin side down and cook until the skin is browned and crisp, about 6 minutes. Flip and put the skillet in the oven. Roast until an instant-read thermometer inserted in the center registers 130° to 135°F for medium rare, 8 to 9 minutes.

Transfer the duck to a cutting board. Discard all but 1 Tbs. fat from the skillet. Swirl in the butter and return the skillet to medium heat. Add the shallots and cook, stirring often, until softened, about 2 minutes. Add the wine and simmer until reduced by half, about 2 minutes. Add the broth and simmer until reduced by half, another 2 minutes. Add the peaches, tarragon, honey, ¼ tsp. salt, and ½ tsp. pepper. Stir until the sauce is bubbling, 1 minute.

Slice the duck and serve with the fruit sauce.

—*Bruce Weinstein and Mark Scarbrough*

Photographs by Scott Phillips; food styling by Michelli Knauer, except pork chops and duck breasts, Jamie Kimm

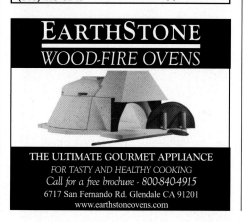

WHERE TO BUY IT

green beans, page 38

- **Hot (picante) pimentón de la Vera,** $9.95 for two 2.5-oz. tins, latienda .com, 800-710-4304.
- **Marcona almonds,** $8.95 for a 5.3-oz. jar, latienda.com, 800-710-4304.
- **Wooden boxes** courtesy of Rose Garbien at Bittersweet Ridge, Roxbury, Connecticut, 860-355-2644.

barbecue-braising, page 54

- **All-Clad LTD2 8-quart stock pot with lid,** $380, williams-sonoma.com, 877-812-6235. Note: LTD2 pots are not meant for use on charcoal grills but are safe to use on gas grills.
- **Weber Genesis S-310 stainless-steel grill,** about $900, weber.com for stores.
- **DBO Home Burl pasta bowl,** color Celery, $75, dbohome.com, 860-364-6008.

repertoire, page 26

- **All Clad 4-quart stainless-steel saucepan,** $184.95, cooking.com/fc, 800-663-8810.
- **Miu 7-inch stainless-steel mesh strainer,** $21.95, cooking.com/fc, 800-663-8810.
- **Mikasa Parchment soup bowl,** $14.99, mikasa.com, 866-645-2721.
- **KitchenAid 4-speed blender,** $99.99, shopkitchenaid .com, 800-541-6390.

ice cream, page 46

- **Cuisinart Pure Indulgence 2-quart frozen yogurt, ice cream, and sorbet maker,** $79.95, cooking.com/fc, 800-663-8810.
- **Lello 4070 Gelato Junior,** $194.29, amazon.com.
- **Large waffle cones** courtesy of Matt's Supreme Cones, mattscones.com, 800-888-2377.
- **The Perfect Purée of Napa Valley passionfruit concentrate,** 15-oz. jar for $17.50 plus shipping, perfectpuree.com, or 888-556-3707 for stores.

front cover

- **DBO Home Burl large round plate,** color Steamer, $98, dbohome.com, 860-364-6008.

drinks, page 36

- **Roost Marseilles small beverage dispenser,** $170, velocityartanddesign .com, 866-781-9494.
- **Pier 1 Imports stemless martini and wine glasses,** $2, pier1.com, 800-245-4595.
- **Domaine Ste. Michelle Brut,** $9.99 for a 750-ml bottle, wallywine.com, 888-992-5597.
- **Linie Norwegian Aquavit,** $34.99 for a 750-ml bottle, wallywine.com, 888-992-5597.

picnic, page 62

- **Ground sumac** (sumac powder), $3.99 for a 2-oz. package, kalustyans.com, 800-352-3451.
- **Black sesame seeds,** $4.99 for a 4-oz. package, kalustyans.com, 800-352-3451.
- **BioPlus Earth food containers** courtesy of Fold-Pak, fold-pak.com/products_bioplus.htm for stores.
- **All-Occasion Veneerware bamboo plates** and flatware, prices vary, bambuhome.com for stores.
- **Corn-based plastic containers,** ecoproducts.com/store.htm, or call 303-449-1876.
- **Seventh Generation natural paper napkins,** 500-count, $9.02, amazon.com.

test kitchen, page 81

- **CDN large grill surface thermometer,** $7.99, kitchen kapers.com, 800-455-5567.
- **Mustapha's Moroccan harissa,** $8.01 for a 10-oz. jar, chefshop .com, 800-596-0885.
- **2½-inch round ring mold,** $8.47, culinarycookware.com, 800-305-5415.

crab cakes, page 70

- **Peekytoe crabmeat,** market price, brownetrading.com, 800-944-7848.
- **Espelette pepper (piment d'Espelette),** $8 for a ½-oz. bag, adrianascaravan.com, 800-316-0820.
- **Medium shredded and desiccated unsweetened coconut flakes,** $6.99 for an 8-oz. bag, kalustyans.com, 800-352-3451.

menus, page 92

- **Wine recommendations** courtesy of Patrick Watson at Smith & Vine in Brooklyn, New York. For more wine ideas, go to smithandvine.com, or call 718-243-2864.

For more kitchen tools, go to **FineCooking.com/buy-it**

Photographs by Scott Phillips

Appliances

Chef's Choice *p. 9* Woo 'em with waffles! Prepare the world's most delicious waffles in 90 seconds! The Chef's Choice® unique Quad® baking system lets you choose the ideal flavor, texture, and color.
800-342-3255
www.chefschoice.com

Dacor *p. 80* Since 1965, Dacor® has redefined the modern kitchen with a collection that offers the best balance of style and performance. Dacor is in the details.
800-793-0093
www.dacor.com/hot

Earthstone Wood-Fire Ovens *p. 88* Wood-fired brick ovens for indoor and outdoor use. Can double as a fireplace. Great for baking, grilling, and roasting.
800-840-4915
www.earthstoneovens.com

Mugnaini's Wood-Fired Cooking *p. 88* Mugnaini, exclusive importers of Italian wood-fired ovens. Italian tradition, American technology. Dedicated to customer service in design, building support, and oven use.
888-887-7206
www.mugnaini.com

Rangecraft Manufacturing, Co. *p. 19* Specializing in the manufacture of a wide selection of high-quality metal range hoods, including copper, brass, and stainless steel. Quality finishes include matte, brushed, antique, mirror, or hammered.
877-RCHOODS
www.rangecraft.com

Viking Range *p. 2* If cooking is everything, the complete Viking kitchen offers everything you need - professional performance and impeccable design.
888-845-4641
www.vikingrange.com/wheretobuy

Cookware

Fissler USA *p. 19* For over 163 years, Fissler has been the European leader in innovative cookware. All products are manufactured in Germany and come with a lifetime warranty.
www.fisslerusa.com

Kuhn-Rikon Corporation *p. 9* Kuhn Rikon offers the finest in pressure cookers, specialty cookware, and distinctive kitchen tools to make a cook's life easier.
800-924-4699
www.kuhnrikon.com/fine

Peugeot Peppermill *p. 11* For all your entertaining needs, find some of the finest houseware products in the world at Swissmar, Contact us Today!
877-947-7627
www.psp-peugeot-usa.com

Cutlery

Japanese Chefs Knife *p. 13* Your online source for Japanese chef's knives for home cooking and the professional chef. Finest selections from the top brands: Masahiro, Misono, Fujiwara Kanefusa, Glestain
www.japanesechefsknife.com

Japanese Chefs Knife *p. 16* Your online source for Japanese chef's knives for home cooking and the professional chef. Finest selections from the top brands: Masahiro, Misono, Fujiwara Kanefusa, Glestain.
www.japanesechefsknife.com

Sointu USA *p. 11* Sointu USA created the market for Japanese knives in the US. Its collection of brands represents the very best of what is manufactured in Japan.
www.sointuusa.com

Gourmet Foods

Al Fresco All Natural Sausage *p. 5* Al fresco All Natural Chicken Sausage comes in 14 sumptuous flavors and has 70% less fat than traditional pork sausage. Live life with flavor.
www.alfrescoallnatural.com

La Tienda *p. 88* A window to the best of Spain. America's most comprehensive inventory of quality Spanish food selected by a knowledgeable and dedicated family. Immediate delivery.
888-472-1022
www.tienda.com

Texas Black Angus.com *p. 88* Absolutely the finest beef your ever tasted! No Hormones. All Natural. Delivered to your doorstep.
www.texasblackangus.com

Wisconsin Cheese *p. 95* Wisconsin cheesemaking has long been renowned for its unparalleled innovation and artistry. Discover many award-winning specialty and artisan cheeses, recipes and pairing ideas at EatWisconsinCheese.com
www.eatwisconsincheese.com

Ingredients

Bob's Red Mill Natural Foods *p. 11* Bob's Red Mill Natural Foods, Inc. is the nation's leading miller of stone ground whole grains. To learn more about our wholesome, delicious products visit
www.bobsredmill.com/fc

Bulk Foods *p. 88* Offering a wide selection of spices, nuts, dried fruits, and other ingredients.
www.bulkfoods.com

Char Crust Dry-Rub Seasoning *p. 19* Get the secret! Char Crust ® dry-rub seasonings for all meat & fish. Only Char Crust® *Seals In The Juices!* ® Turns you into a chef...instantly.
www.charcrust.com

Magic Seasonings *p. 16* Chef Paul Prudhomme's all-natural magic seasoning blends, sauces and marinades, pepper sauce, smoked meats, cookbooks, gift packs, sweet potato pecan pie, and much more!
800-457-2857
www.chefpaul.com

Kitchen Design & Tableware

A Cook's Wares *p. 88* We have what you need for your kitchen: The finest cookware, bakeware, cutlery, utensils and small appliances. Since 1981.
800-915-9788
www.cookswares.com

Plum Pudding Kitchen *p. 16* Your online source for "irresistibly Italian" Vietri dinnerware, flatware, glassware, and much more. Let us help you set a special table!
888-940-7586
www.plumpuddingkitchen.com

Kitchen Tools & Utensils

Bella Copper *p. 88* The world's leading heat diffuser/defroster plate provides superior heat conduction for more even cooking and faster defrosting. Available in solid copper or pure silver. A gourmet kitchen essential.
805-215-3241
www.bellacopper.com

GelPro *p. 16* Stand in comfort! Let's Gel was started with one simple goal, to make the time you spend standing in your kitchen more comfortable.
866-GEL-MATS
www.gelpro.com

Kerekes *p. 88* Your complete online source for professional chef's tools, cookware, bakeware, and cake decorating supplies used by top chefs at the finest restaurants and kitchens.
www.bakedeco.com

Schools, Travel & Organizations

Culinary Business Academy *p. 16* Extensive and comprehensive personal chef business knowledge and training from the world's recognized leader in the personal chef industry. Nobody offers what we offer.
800-747-2433
www.hireachef.com

Le Cordon Bleu *p. 13* Master the culinary arts. Earn the Grand Diplome in approximately nine months. Three- to five-week intensive courses and online hospitality programs are also available.
800-457-2433
www.cordonbleu.edu

Wines, Beverages & Accessories

Illy Espresso USA, Inc. *p. 7* Full selection of expertly roasted coffee, home-delivery coffee subscription programs, artist cup collections, and exceptional accessories and gifts. Free shipping on coffee orders over $50.
www.illyusa.com/finecook5

Woodbridge Winery *p. 96* For 25 years, we have aged our wines in small oak barrels and handcrafted each vintage. Woodbridge: Taste our small winery tradition™.
www.woodbridgewines.com

NUTRITION

Recipe	Calories (kcal)	Fat Cal (kcal)	Protein (g)	Carb (g)	Total Fat (g)	Sat Fat (g)	Mono Fat (g)	Poly Fat (g)	Chol (mg)	Sodium (g)	Fiber (g)
KOHLRABI, p. 15											
Kohlrabi-Radish Slaw with Cumin and Cilantro	120	80	2	10	9	0.5	6	2.5	0	90	4
HEARTS OF PALM, p. 22											
Hearts of Palm and Radish Coins with Shrimp (per piece)	30	15	2	1	2	0	1	0	15	65	0
Grilled Hearts of Palm, Radicchio, and Asparagus	190	140	7	7	16	3	10	1.5	10	800	3
Arugula with Hearts of Palm, Grapefruit, and Oil-Cured Olives	200	150	3	13	17	2.5	12	2	0	490	3
VICHYSSOISE, p. 26											
Classic Vichyssoise	300	160	7	30	18	11	5	1	65	210	2
HERBS, p. 32											
Penne with Zucchini, Fresh Herbs, and Lemon Zest	440	140	15	67	15	2.5	10	2	0	450	8
DRINKS, p. 36											
St. Cecilia Society Punch	270	0	1	30	0	0	0	0	0	0	2
Tenant's Harbor Punch	290	0	1	24	0	0	0	0	0	10	1
GREEN BEANS, p. 38											
Summer Bean Confetti Salad with Pickled Red Onion Vinaigrette	120	80	3	9	9	1	4	3.5	0	200	3
Fusilli with Green Beans, Pancetta, and Parmigiano	540	210	20	62	23	10	8	2.5	50	1270	6
Green Beans with Smoked Paprika and Almonds	120	70	4	12	7	1	5	1.5	0	290	4
Roasted Romanos and Tomatoes with Tapenade	190	150	2	8	17	2.5	13	2	0	550	2
Easy Tapenade (per 1 Tbs.)	45	40	0	1	4.5	0.5	3.5	0.5	0	135	0
Haricots Verts with Toasted Walnuts and Chèvre	180	130	6	8	15	3.5	4.5	7	5	340	3
Spicy Shrimp with Ginger-Garlic Long Beans	210	70	20	10	8	1	3	3.5	170	870	2
ICE CREAM, p. 46											
Double Vanilla Bourbon Ice Cream (per ½ cup)	350	230	4	22	26	15	8	1.5	215	75	0
Peach Mascarpone Ice Cream (per ½ cup)	610	478	9	32	52	29	15	2.5	290	110	1
Rocky Road Ice Cream (per ½ cup)	470	320	6	36	36	20	10	2	215	80	2
Rum Raisin Ice Cream (per ½ cup)	410	230	5	39	26	15	8	1.5	215	80	1
Strawberry Pound Cake Ice Cream (per ½ cup)	430	250	5	43	28	16	9	1.5	220	105	1
BARBECUE-BRAISING, p. 54											
Barbecue-Braised Bourbon Beef with Mustard Glaze	400	140	47	8	15	6	8	1	120	510	1
Barbecue-Braised Moroccan Lamb Shanks with Honey-Mint Glaze	610	100	52	77	11	3	4	2	130	1130	14
Barbecue-Braised Thai Chicken Legs with Lemongrass Glaze	370	170	34	15	19	5	7	4.5	105	970	1
Barbecue-Braised Country Spareribs with Beer and Mustard Glaze	560	310	35	22	35	13	15	3.5	130	660	2
Barbecue-Braised Vietnamese Short Ribs with Sweet Vinegar Glaze	580	280	50	25	31	11	14	3.5	110	1750	2
PICNIC, p. 62											
Brined Grilled Chicken Breasts with Red Chile Oil (with 1 Tbs. oil)	300	180	27	2	20	3	13	2.5	75	300	0
Bulgur Salad with Wilted Chard and Green Olives	270	160	5	25	18	2.5	13	2	0	850	7
Charred Peppers with Garlic and Sherry Vinegar	100	60	1	8	7	1	5	1	0	100	2
Toasted Pita with Black Sesame Seeds and Sumac (per piece)	50	20	1	6	2.5	0	1.5	0	0	105	1
Garlic-Yogurt Sauce (per 1 Tbs.)	25	20	1	1	2	0.5	1.5	0	0	50	0
Ginger-Spice Sandwich Cookies with Lemon Cream (per cookie)	150	50	1	24	6	4	1.5	0	25	55	0
CRAB CAKES, p. 70											
Classic Maryland Crab Cakes	340	200	23	9	23	6	7	7	140	890	0
Lime-and-Coconut-Marinated Peekytoe "Crab Cakes"	350	250	15	11	28	5	15	7	45	580	2
DINNER SALADS, p. 74											
Spinach and Artichoke Salad with Couscous Cakes and Feta	710	390	20	63	44	8	24	9	155	1580	9
Pan-Seared Salmon with Baby Greens and Fennel	620	330	41	14	38	4.5	25	6	105	650	4
Grilled Steak Salad with Pineapple-Ginger Dressing	360	190	33	8	22	6	9	5	60	760	1
Almond-Crusted Chicken and Nectarine Salad with Chive Dressing	680	370	50	31	41	6	23	10	200	700	7
TEST KITCHEN, p. 81											
Harissa (per 1 Tbs.)	50	15	2	6	2	0	1.5	0	0	55	1
MAKE IT TONIGHT, p. 86											
Clams with Basil Broth	140	10	18	8	1.5	0	0	0	45	360	1
Vegetables and Tofu with Spicy Peanut Sauce	530	260	30	41	29	4	0	0	0	1070	10
Tex-Mex Chicken with Chiles and Cheese	470	210	38	28	23	13	4	1.5	130	610	3
Duck Breasts with Peaches and Tarragon	310	130	25	17	14	4.5	6	1.5	140	300	2
Grilled Pork Chops with Sweet-and-Sour Onions	370	190	25	21	21	4.5	13	2.5	60	760	3

The nutritional analyses have been calculated by a registered dietitian at Nutritional Solutions in Melville, New York. When a recipe gives a choice of ingredients, the first choice is the one used. Optional ingredients with measured amounts are included; ingredients without specific quantities are not. Analyses are per serving; when a range of ingredient amounts or servings is given, the smaller amount or portion is used. When the quantities of salt and pepper aren't specified, the analysis is based on ¼ tsp. salt and ⅛ tsp. pepper per serving for entrées, and ⅛ tsp. salt and ¹⁄₁₆ tsp. pepper per serving for side dishes.

MENUS

dinner from the grill

Tenant's Harbor Punch
page 37

Brined Grilled Chicken Breasts
with Red Chile Oil
page 64

Grilled Hearts of Palm,
Radicchio, and Asparagus
page 23

Grilled Mixed Fruits with
Island Spices and Dark Rum
FineCooking.com

quick elegance

Duck Breasts with
Peaches and Tarragon
page 87

Green Beans with
Smoked Paprika and Almonds
page 44

Real Chocolate Mousse
FineCooking.com

To drink:
Bourgogne Rouge, 2006

vegetarian night

Classic Vichyssoise
page 27

Arugula with Hearts of Palm,
Grapefruit, and Oil-Cured Olives
page 23

Penne with Zucchini, Fresh
Herbs, and Lemon Zest
page 33

To drink: Austrian
Grüner Veltliner, 2006 or 2007

guys' night in

Toasted Pita with
Black Sesame Seeds and Sumac
page 66

Garlic-Yogurt Sauce
page 66

Barbecue-Braised Country
Spareribs with Beer and
Mustard Glaze
page 56

Kohlrabi-Radish Slaw
with Cumin and Cilantro
page 17

Whiskey Gingerbread Ice Cream
page 52

To drink: oatmeal stout or porter

late lunch

St. Cecilia Society
Punch
page 37

Hearts of Palm and
Radish Coins with Shrimp
page 22

Pan-Seared Salmon with
Baby Greens and Fennel
page 77

Peaches and Cream
Parfait
FineCooking.com

the new sunday roast

Barbecue-Braised Bourbon
Beef with Mustard Glaze
page 60

Basic Soft Polenta
FineCooking.com

Charred Peppers with
Garlic and Sherry Vinegar
page 67

To drink: Scotch ale
or dry stout

surf and turf

Clams with Basil Broth
page 87

Grilled Steak Salad
with Pineapple-Ginger Dressing
page 78

Ginger-Spice Sandwich Cookies
with Lemon Cream
page 68

To drink: Washington state
Syrah, 2002 to 2005

Photographs by Scott Phillips; wine recommendations by Patrick Watson at Smith & Vine, Brooklyn, New York

For wine, see Where to Buy It

RECIPE INDEX

VEGETARIAN: May contain eggs and dairy ingredients

MAKE AHEAD: Can be completely prepared ahead (may need reheating and a garnish to serve)

QUICK: Under 30 minutes

Gary Vaynerchuk

Unstuffing the wine world, one cork at a time.

BY LISA WADDLE

Fine Cooking: You're kind of crazy (no offense), unscripted, and loud on your low-budget Web show. How do you get more than 80,000 people to watch you every day?

Vaynerchuk: I know I'm high energy and in-your-face, and that can turn people off. But anyone who's watched more than three of my shows knows that I know a lot about wine.

FC: Who are these self-proclaimed "Vayniacs"?

Vaynerchuk: I love my fans. I think they're so passionate because I don't talk down to them. Look, I'm not trying to help people figure out which elevation in Argentina is perfect to grow Malbec; I'm trying to get them to understand that wine is one of the few luxuries in life that even doctors say we're allowed to enjoy. I want it to be more inclusive rather than exclusive, which wine has been for so long. I get emails from people in their twenties up to senior citizens.

FC: You describe wines as tasting like Skittles candy, sweaty socks, or Cinnamon Toast Crunch cereal, words you don't see in traditional tasting notes for wine. Are you trying to be flippant?

Vaynerchuk: I'm trying to rebrand wine. Most people look at the back of a bottle of wine and read, "aroma of currant leaves with a taste of slate." Yet they've never licked slate, so how can they know what that tastes like? I want to use descriptions everyone can understand. And it's not in my DNA to say I like a wine just because other critics do. If I think a wine is massively overrated or doesn't bring the thunder, I say so.

FC: "Bring the thunder"?

Vaynerchuk: That's my ultimate stamp of approval. My buddies and I started saying that when we were like 12 or 13—you made a basket or were good at Nintendo, you brought the thunder. One day it just slipped out on my Webcast and people loved it.

FC: When you rate a wine poorly, doesn't that hurt sales at your store?

Vaynerchuk: Ask my dad; he owns the place. Fortunately, he's very supportive of what I do. I can't say I like something if I don't. And I'm not asking people to trust me more than they trust the wine snobs. My message is, Don't trust anybody. Trust your own palate.

FC: Give me an example of one of your more memorable Webcasts?

Vaynerchuk: I went outside and tasted during a snowstorm, to show how temperature can affect wine.

FC: You've appeared on Ellen DeGeneres and Conan O'Brien; how does it feel to be a wine rock star?

Vaynerchuk: *I* think I'm bigger than Oprah, but I'm nobody. I'm confident, and I'm also very hungry. I think that saves my ass to some degree, that I'm this great contradiction.

FC: At what moment did you feel you had "made it"?

Vaynerchuk: I'm not there yet. My dream is to buy my all-time favorite team, the New York Jets. So I still have a lot to do.

Watch some of Gary's greatest hits at FineCooking.com/extras.

---

the dish

Name: Gary Vaynerchuk

Age: 33

Job: Hosts daily wine Webcast; director of operations at the Wine Library store

Started: 2006

Where: Springfield, New Jersey

Known for: New York Jets spit bucket

Find out more: tv.winelibrary.com

Illustration by Ward Schumaker

WISCONSIN BLUE

Never holds his tongue.

Not one for idle CHITCHAT. *Blue doesn't waste time with social pleasantries. When ordering a bottle of red, he neither asks the sommelier for advice nor requests to see the* WINE *list. Pinot noir it is. That's Blue. He's bold, determined, and opinionated. To not* LOVE *him is to not know him. And to not know him is a crying shame.*

He spent decades researching the right wood
for his wine barrels.

You can taste the results in just a sip.

Robert Mondavi believed that finesse and care were equal
ingredients to the grapes themselves. At the time, people
thought him a bit obsessive. Which is the very same reason
people drink Woodbridge by Robert Mondavi today.

His name is on the bottle. His story is in it.

WOODBRIDGE

by Robert Mondavi

Secrets to the
PERFECT OMELET

fine
Cooking

WE BRING OUT THE GOOD IN YOU

SUMMER ON THE GRILL
Shrimp, corn & lobster get smoky

Tomato heaven!
- Fresh tomato **sauce**
- Double-tomato **pizza**
- Cold tomato **soup**

30 minutes to tandoori chicken

POPSICLE COCKTAILS

How to make fresh feta

JG/SEPT 2009 • No.100
vw.finecooking.com

$6.95   CAN $7.95

09

7 44470 56529 1

GOOD CATCH
Seafood & corn
hot off the grill, page 42

Meet your new sous chef.

The Viking Professional Hand Blender makes quick work of everything from soups to smoothies with a powerful 300-watt motor. Ergonomic design and heavy-duty stainless steel add to the professional performance and appearance. Standard accessories include blending and whisk attachments plus a 35-ounce mixing cup. The optional chopper attachment chops nuts and herbs – and even dices vegetables. And for a limited time, you'll receive the chopper attachment ($30 value) FREE as a gift with purchase.

Visit vikingrange.com/wheretobuy to find a dealer near you.

Creative Kitchen, Inc.
3902 13th Avenue South, #2503
West Acres Mall
Fargo, ND 58103
888.404.5587
www.creativekitchenonline.com

Cooking.com
If It's Not In Your Kitchen, Try Ours.
www.cooking.com

CONTENTS

AUGUST/SEPTEMBER 2009 ISSUE 100

Cheese curds hang out on their
way to becoming homemade

CONTENTS

AUGUST/SEPTEMBER 2009 ISSUE 100

DEPARTMENTS

Cover and Contents photographs by Scott Phillips; illustration by Aude Van Ryn

MOST FOOD COMPANIES HAVE FORMULAS.
WE HAVE RECIPES.

Shown: grilled greek pizza with al fresco sundried tomato chicken sausage.

We've spent years in the kitchen—finding the perfect combinations of fresh, all natural ingredients—so that you only need minutes to turn our fully cooked, all natural chicken sausage into a healthy, delicious meal that you and your family will love. In fourteen gourmet flavors.

For healthy and delicious meal ideas from al fresco, including the recipe shown, go to:

alfrescoallnatural.com

al fresco

live life with flavor

70% less fat than pork sausage ✳ *All natural* ✳ *No artificial ingredients or preservatives*

The Big Conversation

AROUND HERE, many of our Monday-morning staff meetings start with a rollicking review of what we cooked and where we ate over the weekend. I'm never less than amazed at the enthusiasm and passion this crew has for food, which defines both their workdays and their downtime. Somebody will have made a dish I've never tried (perhaps their own cheese; see page 70), or discovered a farmstand I didn't know about. Somebody else will have been to a new restaurant or a local food event. They're an inspiration and an excellent resource, too, since these conversations often lead to great story ideas.

Of course, food does tend to be the main topic of conversation in these offices. But it's a pretty popular topic in a lot of places these days, from the front page of *The New York Times* to Twitter, where 140 characters is no barrier to some interesting recipe writing. Find us there, too, and on Facebook. And check out our Web site, where there's always an opinionated exchange going on in the forums. Our bloggers like nothing more than a lot of comments on their posts (don't miss The Food Geek, our resident food science guy, who thrills to the very idea of "why?"). And in the *Fine Cooking* Test Kitchen blog, we share each day's discoveries (and occasional failures).

I like to think we've given you plenty to talk about in this issue, from the irresistible platter of grilled shellfish and corn on our cover to a delicious way to preserve summer berries (page 18). And speaking of summer, don't miss the chance to make fresh tomato sauce (page 54) or mix a refreshing beer cocktail (page 32). So come join the conversation, or start one of your own.

Laurie Buckle, editor
fc@taunton.com

more *Fine Cooking*

ON THE ROAD
Join us for a delicious weekend of dining and drinking at the fourth annual Foxwoods Wine & Food Festival, August 28–30 in southeastern Connecticut. *Fine Cooking* editors and contributors will be hosting gala dinners and conducting seminars on everything from cocktail mixology to cake decorating. With more than 40 chefs at the stoves and some 500 wines and spirits available for tasting, this is New England's biggest culinary event. We'd love to see you! For more information, go to Fine Cooking.com/fwevent.

FOXWOODS FOOD&WINE FESTIVAL
sponsored by fine Cooking

SPECIAL ISSUES
We have two special issues coming to a newsstand near you. Look for contributing editor Ellie Krieger's latest, called *Quick & Fresh*. It features more than 75 deliciously good-for-you recipes. In addition, our Big Buy Cooking column is now a special issue, too. With dozens of fast and tasty recipes for your favorite warehouse foods, it's a food lover's guide to buying in bulk—and using it all up.

WEB
We love to grill—so much so that we've built a special grilling microsite just to share our best videos, tips, tools, recipes, and more. Check it out at FineCooking.com/grilling.

Your steak with béarnaise
just became the crème de la crème.

Culinary bliss awaits with Plugrá® European-Style
Butter as your secret ingredient. Create richer
sauces and creamier risottos for fare that is
truly *magnifique.*

PLUGRÁ
EUROPEAN STYLE BUTTER

Discover inspiration from the masters at www.plugra.com.

THE WINNER

Reader tip: Keeping produce fresh

To keep broccoli, asparagus, and herbs longer, treat them as you would cut flowers. Slice off about ¼ inch from the bottom of the stalks or stems and immediately put them in a jar of water and refrigerate. They'll be almost garden fresh when you use them.

—*Lynette L. Walther*
Camden, Maine

We want to hear from you. Give us your best tip and we'll reward you with a kitchen prize. Lynette is the winner of this Kataoka Tamahagane 8-inch chef's knife.

CALL OR WRITE: *Fine Cooking,*
The Taunton Press, 63 S. Main St.,
PO Box 5506, Newtown, CT 06470-5506.
Tel: 203-426-8171. Send an email:
fc@taunton.com.

A *Fine Cooking* weekend

A friend turned me on to *Fine Cooking* a while back, and I've loved every issue. The June/July 2009 issue is truly sublime. For Mother's Day weekend, I made a few of the barbecue-braised recipes, the classic crab cakes, and several of the ice creams. My family was in heaven. I just thought you should know someone is really enjoying all the hard work you put into your magazine.

—*Leah McIntyre*
Glen Mills, Pennsylvania

Roll call

I just received the June/July issue and wanted to say, Bravo! To get Eric Ripert, David Lebovitz, Bruce Aidells, Abigail Johnson Dodge, and James Peterson in the same issue is quite a coup. The recipes look amazing.

—*Zora Safir Hopkins, via email*

Fine *vegetarian* cooking?

I've been a subscriber for quite a while and recently decided to become a vegetarian. Do you have any plans to include more meatless recipes? Most vegetarian cooking magazines I have seen are short on delicious, foolproof vegetarian recipes that aren't casseroles.

—*Malcolm Norton*
Halifax, Nova Scotia

Editors' reply: We hear you and recognize that a lot of our readers are trying to reduce the amount of meat they eat. We're making an ongoing effort to include dishes that are vegetarian or can be made so with simple modifications. In this issue, for example, our Cook Once, Eat Twice feature stars a vegetarian Fresh Tomato Sauce that takes advantage of the abundance of ripe tomatoes in markets and gardens now. Two of the dishes made with this sauce, the grilled pizzas and a spicy curried chickpea and vegetable stew, are also vegetarian.

Frozen fruit

In your ice cream article "Scooped!" (June/July) you suggested that readers "resist the temptation to mix in whole fruit." I wondered why, and if there is a way to add chunks of fruit, like strawberries or peaches, as found in store-bought ice creams. I believe they add character and more flavor. Also, when adding peaches you say to "cook to soften." Exactly how do you cook them?

—*Patricia DeGeorges, via email*

Assistant food editor Melissa Pellegrino replies: We suggest avoiding fresh fruit because it can become icy and hard due to its high water content, as it often does in commercial ice cream. If you don't mind that texture, then by all means, add it—just keep the pieces small. As for cooking the peaches, simply cut up some peeled peaches and cook them over low heat in a small saucepan with a pinch of sugar until they begin to soften and break down, about 12 minutes.

Thumbs down

I've subscribed to *Fine Cooking* since the beginning and have rolled with the changes to this excellent publication. Sometimes it takes a bit of time to appreciate change, so I've given your latest incarnation a fair shot. I really want to like the new layout, but sadly I cannot get on board. The magazine is undoubtedly prettier, with plenty of pictures and a flashy layout, but harder to read. It is easy to flip through and look at the pictures, but I am rarely drawn to the text. Quality content has always separated *Fine Cooking* from the rest of the pack, which offer flash but little substance. Please keep it solid for the serious cooks who have loved your magazine over the years.

—*Peter Rauch, via email*

Thumbs up

I love your new look. I have read and subscribed to *Fine Cooking* for several years and I was surprised to see the negative reviews of your new format in the letters section. The pictures are great, the content as good as ever, and I found as many or more inspiring ideas that I can't wait to try. I was especially happy to see the Make It Tonight section. Thanks for the revamp and continued great magazine.

—*Colleen Cairncross, via email*

fine Cooking®

Editor	Laurie Glenn Buckle
Art Director	Don Morris
Senior Food Editor	Jennifer Armentrout
Senior Editor	Rebecca Freedman
Managing Editor	Lisa Waddle
Associate Editors	Laura Giannatempo Denise Mickelsen
Web Producer	Sarah Breckenridge
Assistant Web Producer	Sharon Anderson
Senior Copy/ Production Editor	Enid Johnson
Associate Art Director	Pamela Winn
Contributing Designer	Tannaz Fassihi
Photo Editor	Kelly Coughlan Gearity
Assistant Food Editor	Melissa Pellegrino
Editorial Assistant	Julissa Roberts
Editorial Interns	Evan Barbour Zoe Eisenberg
Editor at Large	Susie Middleton
Contributing Editors	Pam Anderson Abigail Johnson Dodge Maryellen Driscoll Tim Gaiser Sarah Jay Allison Ehri Kreitler Ellie Krieger Kimberly Y. Masibay Tony Rosenfeld Molly Stevens
Senior Managing Editor, Books	Carolyn Mandarano

Fine Cooking: (ISSN: 1072-5121) is published six times a year by The Taunton Press, Inc., Newtown, CT 06470-5506. Telephone 203-426-8171. Periodicals postage paid at Newtown, CT 06470 and at additional mailing offices. GST paid registration #123210981.

Subscription Rates: U.S. and Canada, $29.95 for one year, $49.95 for two years, $69.95 for three years (GST included, payable in U.S. funds). Outside the U.S./Canada: $36 for one year, $62 for two years, $88 for three years (payable in U.S. funds). Single copy, $6.95. Single copy outside the U.S., $7.95.

Postmaster: Send address changes to *Fine Cooking*, The Taunton Press, Inc., 63 South Main St., P.O. Box 5506, Newtown, CT 06470-5506.

Canada Post: Return undeliverable Canadian addresses to Fine Cooking, c/o Worldwide Mailers, Inc., 2835 Kew Drive, Windsor, ON N8T 3B7, or email to mnfa@taunton.com.

Printed in the USA.

Ed Schoenfeld ("Party in the Kitchen," page 62) is a restaurateur, Chinese food expert, and restaurant consultant who lives in Brooklyn. He is currently working with restaurateur Jeffrey Chodorow on Foodparc, a new European-style food hall scheduled to open in New York next spring.

• **My favorite food memory is...** making blintzes with my grandmother, eating two for every three I made.
• **The last thing I ate was...** a salami and scrambled egg sandwich on a roll.
• **My last meal would have to be...** foie gras, sea urchin, an aged porterhouse, and a perfect white peach.

Food writer, blogger, and cooking teacher Domenica Marchetti ("Get Saucy!," page 54) specializes in seasonal Italian home cooking. Her writing has appeared in *The Washington Post, Health,* and *Virginia Living,* among other publications. She has written two cookbooks and is working on her third, which will be about pasta.

• **Scrambled eggs or fried?...** Can I say poached?
• **My latest food discovery is...** cooking in a tagine.
• **My guilty food pleasure is...** steak fat.

Food scientist and cooking teacher Bonnie Gorder-Hinchey ("Feta," page 70) has more than 25 years of experience developing recipes and food products for companies such as Nestlé and General Mills. She teaches culinary, nutrition, and science classes at The Art Institute of Seattle.

• **My favorite spice is...** li hing mui (dried salted plum) because it's sweet, salty, and tangy all at once.
• **My favorite cookbook is...** anything from the early 1900s.
• **My latest food discovery is...** the smoker. We smoke everything.

Elizabeth Karmel ("Grilling Shellfish," page 42) is the executive chef of Hill Country in New York City. She teaches cooking classes and writes for several national publications. Her most recent cookbook, *Soaked, Slathered, and Seasoned: A Complete Guide to Flavoring Food for the Grill,* was published this past spring.

• **The strangest thing I've ever eaten is...** iguana in Oaxaca, Mexico.
• **My go-to weeknight dinner is...** what I call my back-pocket dinner—beer can chicken, grilled sweet potato chips, and grilled asparagus.
• **My favorite thing about my job is...** that it doesn't feel like a job.

Brian Preston-Campbell (stylist for "Cold Comfort," page 50) is a food stylist, writer, and the former sous chef at Mesa Grill in New York City. He was the food stylist for *Good Spirits,* which won a 2007 IACP award for food photography and styling, and he is the author of *Cool Waters: 50 Refreshing, Healthy Homemade Thirst-Quenchers.*

• **To a summer cookout, I would bring...** some of my homemade Irish draft ale.
• **The dish I most want to learn to cook is...** Texas barbecue beef brisket.
• **For breakfast, I eat...** chocolate chip waffles.

Mikey Price ("Eggplant Parmigiana," page 76) is the executive chef and owner of Market Table in New York City. He has cooked in many top New York restaurant kitchens, including The Harrison and The Mermaid Inn.

• **The last thing I cooked was...** honeydew gazpacho.
• **The dish I most want to learn to cook is...** authentic paella.
• **My favorite thing about my job is...** the immediate gratification I get from a full, happy dining room.

Eugenia Bone ("Summer Berries," page 18) is a cookbook author, food writer, and recipe developer who has written for *The New York Times, ForbesLife,* and *Sunset.* Her latest book, *Well-Preserved,* came out in May. She also writes a food blog of the same name for *The Denver Post.*

• **My favorite food memory is...** summer evenings in Provincetown gathering moon snails. My dad would cook them with olive oil, parsley, and lots of garlic.
• **My drink of choice is...** a Gibson martini with vodka and a little extra onion juice.
• **My culinary icon is...** my dad, Edward Giobbi.

Lew Bryson ("Beer Cocktails," page 32) is a beer and spirits writer who lives near Philadelphia. He is the author of four brewery travel guides and the managing editor of *Malt Advocate* magazine.

• **The strangest thing I ever drank was...** 60-year-old dandelion wine. It was like sunlight on the tongue.
• **I am currently obsessed with...** mustard. I have 26 mustards in my house right now, two of which I made myself.
• **My drink of choice is...** that I choose to have a drink.

Belgian illustrator Aude Van Ryn ("Lettuce Alone," page 22) works regularly for *The Guardian* as well as other international publications. She lives and works in London and exhibits at galleries around the world, including London, Brussels, and Tokyo.

• **My favorite ice cream flavor is...** my dad's lime sorbet. It's hard to get through the summer without it.
• **I'm currently obsessed with...** dried mangos. As soon as I open a pack, they're gone.
• **My last meal would have to be...** I don't want to think about that.

Photographs by, from top left: Elisa Herr; Christopher McNamara; Chris Cumming; Motofish Images; Jaime Tiampo; Rebecca Preston; courtesy of Market Table; Huger Foote; Dianne Baasch; Glyn Owen

fine Cooking®

National Advertising Manager	Patrick J. O'Donnell 203-304-3250 podonnell@taunton.com
Advertising Sales East Coast	Judy Caruso 203-304-3468 jcaruso@taunton.com
	Margaret Fleming-O'Brien 203-304-3530 mflemingobrien@taunton.com
Midwest	Mark Adeszko 312-629-5222 madeszko@aol.com
West Coast	Chuck Carroll 818-972-9650 cwcarroll@earthlink.net
Director of Advertising Marketing	Kristen Lacey
Senior Marketing Manager, Advertising	Karen Lutjen

Member Audit Bureau of Circulation The Audit Bureau

Senior Consumer Marketing Director	Beth Reynolds, ProCirc
Senior Consumer Marketing Manager	Melissa Robinson
Senior Manager Web Marketing	Robert Harlow
Business Managers	David Pond, Megan Sangster

The Taunton Press

Inspiration for hands-on living®
Independent publishers since 1975
Founders, Paul & Jan Roman

President	Suzanne Roman
EVP & CFO	Timothy Rahr
SVP & Chief Content Officer	Paul Spring
SVP, Creative	Susan Edelman
SVP & Chief Marketing Officer	Janine Scolpino
SVP, Advertising Sales	Karl Elken
SVP & Publisher, Book Group	Donald Linn
SVP, Technology	Jay Hartley
SVP, Operations	Thomas Luxeder
VP, Taunton Interactive	Jason Revzon
VP, Digital Content	Anatole Burkin
VP, Editorial Development	Maria Taylor
VP, Single Copy Sales	Jay Annis
VP & Controller	Wayne Reynolds
VP, Finance	Kathy Worth
VP, Human Resources	Carol Marotti
VP, Fulfillment	Patricia Williamson

Publishers of magazines, books, videos and online
Fine Woodworking • Fine Homebuilding
Threads • Fine Gardening • Fine Cooking
www.taunton.com

fine Cooking®

The Fine Cooking Culinary School

Let our experts help you take your cooking to the next level.

If you've ever wanted to go to culinary school, now's your chance. Become a member of FineCooking.com's CooksClub, and you're automatically eligible to enroll in our new online culinary school. Sign up for multiclass courses or single classes, and work at your own pace. In addition to *Fine Cooking*'s staff of experts, you'll learn from the best in the field.

Grilling is our first course, with master griller Fred Thompson. He'll take you from barbecue newbie to grill master in just 10 video classes, covering such topics as:

- How to set up your grill
- The differences between lump and briquette charcoal
- How to grill the perfect steak
- Real barbecue ribs and pork shoulder from your own backyard.

Future classes will include Knife Skills and Mastering Pies and Tarts.

Winner's Spotlight

Congratulations to Denise Jones and Veronica Vadakan, winners of our two recent online cooking challenges: Make It Mini and Waste Not.

For **Make It Mini**, cooks were asked to submit photos of dishes they had shrunk in size. Denise generated so many creative ideas for mini treats, it was hard to pick just one, but her chocolate cupcakes with lemongrass frosting were a standout. She wins a *Fine Cooking* Archive DVD, a copy of Ellie Krieger's *The Food You Crave* cookbook, and a Kyocera ceramic knife.

In the **Waste Not** challenge, we asked users to create dishes from the odds and ends that normally get thrown out or go bad before they can be used up. Veronica made a salad of dandelion greens, hard-cooked eggs, and bacon. She wins a $200 gift card to metrokitchen.com.

Look for other CooksTalk Challenges on Fine Cooking.com's home page, for more chances to win.

Fine Cooking eLetter

Sign up for the free FineCooking.com eLetter for a weekly look at what's new in our world. Get exclusive Web-only recipes, how-to videos, and advice from the experts.

More ways to join the conversation

Friend us on
facebook

Follow us on
twitter

To contact us:
Fine Cooking,
The Taunton Press,
63 South Main Street,
PO Box 5506, Newtown,
CT 06470-5506
Tel: 203-426-8171

Send an e-mail to:
fc@taunton.com

Visit:
www.finecooking.com

To submit an article proposal:
Write to *Fine Cooking* at the address above or
Call: 800-309-0744
Fax: 203-426-3434
Email: fc@taunton.com

To subscribe or place an order:
Visit www.finecooking.com/fcorder
or call: 800-888-8286
9am-9pm ET Mon-Fri
9am-5pm ET Sat

To find out about *Fine Cooking* products:
Visit www.finecooking.com/products

To get help with online member services:
Visit www.finecooking.com/customerservice

To find answers to frequently asked questions:
Visit www.finecooking.com/FAQs

To speak directly to a customer service professional:
Call 800-477-8727 9am-5pm ET Mon-Fri

To sell *Fine Cooking* in your store:
Call us toll-free at 866-505-4674, or
send an email to magazinesales@taunton.com

To advertise in *Fine Cooking*:
Call 800-309-8940
Or send an email to fcads@taunton.com

Mailing list:
We make a portion of our mailing list available to reputable firms. If you would prefer that we not include your name, please visit:
www.finecooking.com/privacy
or call: 800-477-8727 9am-5pm ET Mon-Fri

For employment information:
Visit www.careers.taunton.com

The Taunton guarantee:
If at any time you're not completely satisfied with *Fine Cooking*, you can cancel your subscription and receive a full and immediate refund of the entire subscription price. No questions asked.

Wisconsin Parmesan
Long live the Renaissance man.

He's down-to-earth yet always upscale. He can hold his own at a spaghetti feed, a neighborhood POTLUCK, or a black-tie affair. Meet PARMESAN. Never one to mistake a dinner fork for a salad fork, he enters the finest restaurants with a head-turning swagger typically set aside for celebrities and guys named Pierre. Parmesan. A good FRIEND to have on speed dial.

4TH ANNUAL FOXWOODS FOOD & WINE FESTIVAL

Featuring more than 40 celebrated Chefs and Wine & Spirits Experts

AUGUST 28, 29 & 30, 2009

GOVIND ARMSTRONG   DAVID BURKE   ALEX GUARNASCHELLI   ELLIE KRIEGER   MICHEL NISCHAN   MICHAEL SCHLOW   GARY VAYNERCHUK

Join us for what's guaranteed to be another sold-out weekend of fine wine, food and festivity at the 4th Annual Foxwoods Food & Wine Festival — a premier culinary event offering dynamic celebrity chef cooking demonstrations, wine seminars, a grand tasting and more.

For more information and to purchase tickets, please visit
foxwoodsfoodandwine.com or call 1-800-FOXWOODS

PLATINUM SPONSORS:

SILVER SPONSORS:

FOXWOODS FOOD & WINE FESTIVAL

sponsored by *fine* **Cooking**

MARKETPLACE

Shop Smarter, Eat Better

TRY THIS

Tomatillos

THIS DISTANT RELATIVE of the tomato is a staple of Mexican cooking, lending a tart, zesty flavor to sauces and salsas. Previously available only in Latin-American markets, tomatillos are now popping up in grocery stores across the country. Here's why you should try them.

What they are

Small, round fruits encased in a delicate, papery husk, tomatillos ripen to various colors, from yellow to red to purple. But they're most flavorful if harvested just before ripening, when they're vibrant green. Indigenous to Mexico and Central America, tomatillos ("little tomatoes" in Spanish) are also called husk tomatoes or *tomates verdes* (green tomatoes).

Why we love them

It's hard to resist their tangy, almost citrusy flavor, which turns slightly sweet with cooking.

Continued on page 16

Photographs by Scott Phillips; food styling by Michelli Knauer

Tomatillos are a perfect match for chile peppers, onions, and cilantro—all key ingredients in salsa verde, a popular Mexican sauce for grilled meats and fish. Tomatillos are also good with avocados, corn, lime, and scallions.

How to buy and store them

Look for firm fruits without blemishes and with their papery husks firmly attached. When fresh, tomatillos are a vibrant green color. Don't buy ones that have turned a yellowish green, as they're past their prime. Store tomatillos in their husks in a paper bag and refrigerate for up to a week.

How to cook with them

To prep tomatillos, peel the husk and rinse off the sticky residue it leaves behind. You don't need to remove the seeds. If eaten raw, tomatillos can be a little acidic and sharp-tasting (sometimes a good thing). When cooked, their flavor tends to mellow, letting their sweeter side shine. Toss raw chopped tomatillos in salads, or roast or grill them whole and add them to salsas and dips. You can also cut them into wedges before stirring into stews and braises, or sauté them in small chunks and add them to omelets or scrambled eggs.

—*Melissa Pellegrino*

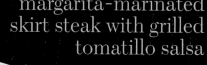
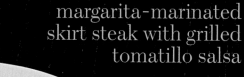

margarita-marinated skirt steak with grilled tomatillo salsa

Serves 4 to 6

FOR THE STEAK

- 2 limes
- ⅓ cup tequila
- ¼ cup canola oil
- 2 Tbs. chopped fresh cilantro
- 1 Tbs. Cointreau
- 2 medium cloves garlic, minced
- ⅛ tsp. crushed red pepper flakes
- 2 lb. skirt steak
  Kosher salt

FOR THE SALSA

- 1 Tbs. extra-virgin olive oil; more for the grill
- 1 lb. tomatillos (10 to 15), husked and rinsed
- 1 medium yellow bell pepper
  Kosher salt
- ½ ripe medium avocado, diced
- 2 Tbs. minced red onion
- 1 Tbs. chopped fresh cilantro
- 1 jalapeño, seeded and minced
  Freshly ground black pepper

MARINATE THE STEAK

Finely grate the zest from 1 lime and put it in a 9x13-inch baking dish. Finely grate 1 tsp. zest from the second lime and set aside for the salsa. Juice the limes. Add ¼ cup juice to the zest in the baking dish and mix 1 tsp. juice into the zest for the salsa.

To the baking dish, add the tequila, oil, cilantro, Cointreau, garlic, and pepper flakes; whisk to combine. Season the steak all over with ½ tsp. salt. Add it to the marinade and turn to coat. Cover with plastic wrap and refrigerate for 2 hours, turning the steak after 1 hour.

MAKE THE SALSA

Prepare a medium gas or charcoal grill fire. Scrub the grill grate with a wire brush and then wipe clean with a paper towel dipped in oil.

Rub the tomatillos and yellow pepper all over with the 1 Tbs. oil and season with ½ tsp. salt. Grill the tomatillos, turning occasionally, until they have good grill marks and are starting to collapse, about 6 minutes. Grill the pepper, turning occasionally, until charred all over, 8 to 10 minutes. Transfer the tomatillos to a plate and let cool. Put the pepper in a small bowl and cover with plastic wrap. Let sit until cool enough to handle.

Roughly chop the tomatillos and put them in a medium bowl. Peel the skin from the pepper, remove the seeds, and cut into small dice. Add the pepper to the tomatillos along with the avocado, onion, cilantro, jalapeño, and the reserved lime zest and juice. Season to taste with salt and pepper.

GRILL THE STEAK

Remove the steak from the marinade and pat it dry. Clean and oil the grill grates again. Grill the steak, covered, over medium heat until brown grill marks form on one side, about 5 minutes. Flip and cook until medium rare (130°F on an instant-read thermometer), 4 to 5 minutes more. Transfer to a cutting board and let rest for 5 minutes. Cut each steak crosswise into 2 or 3 pieces, and then thinly slice across the grain. Serve with the salsa on the side.

Make ahead: The salsa may be prepared up to 2 hours ahead.

Figs, Summer Squash, and Nectarines

Nine ways to use three seasonal ingredients we can't get enough of. *Fine Cooking* editors share some delicious ideas.

Summer Squash

Fettuccine with squash ribbons

Slice yellow and green squash in long, thin ribbons with a vegetable peeler or a mandoline. Then sauté some chopped sweet onions in olive oil until soft, add the squash, and cook until tender. Toss the mixture with cooked fettuccine and sprinkle with chopped fresh parsley.

—*Melissa Pellegrino*

Greek-style stuffed squash

Cut zucchini or yellow squash in half and scoop out some of the flesh. Bake in a 375°F oven until soft and starting to brown. Then fill with a mixture of sautéed ground lamb, chopped black olives, oregano, and a little tomato sauce. Top with crumbled feta and broil until browned on top.

—*Sarah Breckenridge*

Squash fritters

Grate 2 medium squash and let drain for 20 minutes. In a large bowl, whisk three beaten eggs with about ¾ cup flour, then mix in some crumbled feta or chèvre, the squash, and chopped fresh mint. Season with salt and pepper and thin with a little milk to a thick batter. Cook tablespoonfuls of batter in a hot oiled pan until golden brown on both sides. Serve with thick yogurt and harissa.

—*Lisa Waddle*

Nectarines

Spicy grilled nectarine salsa

Cut the nectarines in half, remove the pit, rub with olive oil, and grill over medium-high heat until soft and lightly browned. Then cut them into small dice and toss with diced red onion, minced habanero, chopped cilantro, and a vinaigrette of oil, lime juice, and honey. The salsa is great over seared scallops or grilled fish.

—*Melissa Pellegrino*

Nectarine ice cubes

Peel and pit the nectarines, slice them into wedges, and freeze in a single layer on a baking sheet. Once frozen, transfer to a plastic bag for easy storage. You can use the frozen nectarines to chill iced tea, fruit juices, or summer cocktails.

—*Denise Mickelsen*

Nectarines with Maraschino

Peel, pit, and cut the nectarines in wedges. Stir together some wine, Maraschino (a dry liqueur made with *marasca* sour cherries), and sugar, using about 2 Tbs. sugar for each 1 Tbs. of wine and liqueur. Add a squeeze of lemon juice. Macerate the nectarines in this mixture for at least 2 hours. Serve with fresh raspberries and a dollop of mascarpone or honeyed whipped cream.

—*Laura Giannatempo*

Figs

Marsala-baked figs

For an easy dessert, arrange whole figs in a shallow baking dish and add about ½ inch of sweet Marsala. Bake at 350°F, basting occasionally with the Marsala, until heated through. Serve drizzled with the Marsala and a little honey. Top with a dollop of half mascarpone and half heavy cream lightly sweetened and whipped to soft peaks.

—*Jennifer Armentrout*

Fig and grape compote

Simmer chopped figs and whole seeded Concord grapes (dig the seeds out with the tip of a paring knife) in a saucepan with a little red wine and some sugar until very soft and jammy. Serve with seared pork chops or as part of a cheese platter.

—*Sarah Breckenridge*

Figs with prosciutto and Parmigiano

Cut up a few small chunks of good Parmigiano and toss with a little aged balsamic vinegar. Cut some ripe figs in half and arrange them on a platter along with the Parmigiano and a few paper-thin slices of prosciutto. If you like, drizzle a few more drops of balsamic over the figs.

—*Laura Giannatempo*

Summer Berries

Turn the season's bounty into surprisingly versatile syrups.

BY EUGENIA BONE

FRESH, SWEET BERRIES ARE ONE OF SUMMER'S GREAT PLEASURES. Their season is short, so now is the time to buy them with abandon and make all those fruit salads and berry desserts you've been craving. Then turn them into delicious syrups and enjoy them for months to come. The technique is simple and with the master recipe, at right, you can make a syrup out of just about any berry.

Berry syrups are terrific on pancakes and ice cream or stirred into plain yogurt, rice pudding, and oatmeal. Or try brushing them over baked ham or a pork roast to create a sweet, fruity glaze. And for a delicious homemade soda, add one part syrup to two parts chilled seltzer water.

fresh berry syrup

This master recipe works well with a variety of summer berries. The thickness of the syrup will depend on the berries you use: Some are juicier, resulting in a thinner syrup, while others, like blueberries, have more pectin, yielding a thicker syrup. This method is for fridge storage only. To extend the shelf life, see the canning directions, opposite.

Yields 1 to 2 cups

- 3 cups fresh berries (such as blueberries, raspberries, strawberries, or blackberries), washed and trimmed as needed and halved if large
- 1–2 cups granulated sugar

Bring water to boil in a large pot fitted with a rack. Carefully, put 2 empty half-pint (8 fl. oz.) Mason jars and their lids and screw-on bands in the water and boil for 10 minutes to sterilize them. Remove the jars, lids, and bands with tongs and set on paper towels to drain.

In a medium heavy-duty saucepan, crush the berries with a potato masher. Add ¼ cup water (if using strawberries, add ½ cup water). Bring to a boil over medium-high heat, reduce the heat to medium low, and simmer until the berries are very soft and juicy, about 5 minutes.

Set a fine sieve over a bowl. Pour the berry pulp into the sieve and allow the juice to drip through. Gently press the pulp with a rubber spatula to extract as much juice as possible, but don't press so hard that you force the pulp through.

Clean the saucepan. Measure the juice and then pour it into the saucepan. For every ¼ cup juice, add ¼ cup sugar. Bring to a boil over medium heat, stirring to dissolve the sugar. Reduce the heat to low and simmer until the syrup is viscous but still runny, about 1 minute. Skim the foam with a spoon and pour the syrup into the sterilized jars. Put the jars on a wire rack and let cool to room temperature. Screw the lids and bands on and refrigerate the syrup for up to 2 weeks.

If the syrup thickens during storage, stir to loosen it before serving. Serve warm or at room temperature.

Flavor Twists

For a slightly more sophisticated syrup, try these flavor variations:

Lemon Blueberry
Add ½ tsp. finely grated lemon zest to blueberry syrup while still hot.

Raspberry Mint
Crush three sprigs fresh mint with the berries when making raspberry syrup.

Blackberry Thyme
Crush three sprigs fresh thyme with the berries when making blackberry syrup.

Strawberry Balsamic
Add balsamic vinegar to strawberry syrup (¾ tsp. per ½ cup syrup) while still hot.

 For a video on canning, go to FineCooking.com/extras.

Photographs by Scott Phillips

Canning Berry Syrups

IT'S EASY TO PRESERVE FRESH BERRY SYRUPS so they last well into the fall and winter months. All it takes is a quick sterilization of a few clean jars before you pour in the syrup, screw on the lids, and briskly boil for a few minutes. Here's the simple method, step by step.

The Method

If you're going through the extra step of canning, consider making a double batch; you'll have lots of syrup for your cold-weather pantry.

Bring water to a boil in a large pot fitted with a rack insert. Carefully put 4 empty half-cup (4 fl. oz) Mason jars (use 8 if you're doubling the recipe) or 2 empty half-pint (8 fl. oz.) Mason jars (use 4 if you're doubling the recipe) and their metal screw-on bands in the water and reduce the heat to a simmer; simmer until ready to use. Heat the lids in very hot water for 5 minutes to soften the flange. (Don't boil the lids when canning, as it might damage them and compromise the seal later.)

Remove the jars and rims with tongs, emptying the water from the jars **1**. Pour the syrup into the jars **2**, leaving about ¼ inch of headroom. Wipe the rims clean of any spilled syrup and affix the metal lids onto the jars with the screw bands. Turn the bands only fingertip tight; don't close them as tight as you can, or you may compromise the seal.

Put the jars in the pot fitted with the rack insert and add enough water to cover by 2 inches. Bring to a boil over high heat, and boil briskly for 10 minutes.

Transfer the jars to a rack. Allow them to cool for 12 to 24 hours. You should hear a popping sound as the vacuum seals the lid to the jar. When the syrup is completely cool, check the seals by pressing on the lids **3**. The lids should be taut and pulled down toward the inside of the jar. If a lid bounces when you press on it, the seal is imperfect, and you will have to repeat the canning pro-

cess with a new lid, or simply refrigerate the syrup and use within two weeks. You can also remove the bands and try to pick up the jars by holding onto the rim of the lids. If the lids are tight, your seal is good **4**.

Keep the bands in place when transporting the jars, but you do not need to store them with the bands on. Store in a cool, dark place for up to a year. Once a jar is opened, refrigerate the syrup for up to 2 weeks.

Eugenia Bone is the author of Well-Preserved, *published last May.*

Canning Tool Box

The only special tools you need for canning berry syrup are Mason jars and a canning rack (see Where to Buy It, page 93). You can reuse jars and bands that are not chipped or dented, but always use new lids (the flat metal disk with the rubberized flange).

Jars, bands, and lids

Pot

Rack

Tongs

French Bread

Making the most of a favorite food find
from a warehouse store. BY PAM ANDERSON

THE LURE OF A CRUSTY, freshly baked French loaf—or two
(yes, most big box stores sell them in pairs)—is irresistible. But
two pounds of bread is a lot to go through, no matter how many
sandwiches, crostini, or breadcrumbs you make. The trick is to
have a stash of delicious recipes that use it up in creative ways,
like a gingery summer berry trifle or a chilled fresh tomato and
bread soup with basil that's like summer in a bowl.

The Big Buy

What: French bread
(two-pack)
How much: 2 lb.
How to store: Keep
leftover bread in gallon-
size zip-top freezer bags
at room temperature
for up to two days. This
way, the crumb stays
fresh longer; the crust will
soften, but it will quickly
crisp up again if toasted
or heated in a warm oven.
To freeze bread, wrap it
in foil and put it in zip-top
bags. It will keep for up to
a month.

chilled fresh tomato, basil, and bread soup

Bread helps thicken this lovely summer
soup, and blanching the basil before
puréeing helps its color stay fresh-looking.
Serves 6

- ½ **lb. day-old French bread, crust
  removed, crumb cut into ¼-inch
  cubes (3 cups)**
  Kosher salt
- 1 **cup lightly packed fresh basil
  leaves; more for garnish**
- 2 **lb. ripe tomatoes, cored and
  chopped (5 cups)**
- 1 **large clove garlic, roughly chopped**
- 2 **tsp. sherry vinegar**
- ¼ **cup extra-virgin olive oil**

Position a rack in the center of the
oven and heat the oven to 350°F.
Spread the bread cubes on a rimmed
baking sheet and toast in the oven
until lightly golden and crisp, about
15 minutes.

Bring a medium pot of well-salted
water to a boil over high heat. Add
the basil and cook until wilted, about
30 seconds. Drain and run under cold
water. Pat dry with paper towels and
roughly chop.

In a blender, purée the basil, tomatoes, garlic, and 2 cups ice-cold water
for about 45 seconds. Strain through
a fine sieve to remove the solids and
return the purée to the blender.

Photographs by Scott Phillips; food styling by Michelli Knauer, except trifle, Safaya Tork

Add the bread, vinegar, and 2 tsp. salt and blend until puréed, about 2 minutes. The soup should be very smooth; if it's not, continue blending. Add the olive oil and process a few more seconds to combine. Divide among 6 soup bowls and garnish with basil sprigs, or refrigerate until ready to use. The soup can be refrigerated for up to 3 days.

plt salad

In this take on a BLT sandwich, prosciutto replaces bacon. Garlicky croutons are a delicious use for day-old bread.

Serves 6 to 8

- 7 oz. mixed salad greens, such as mesclun (10 lightly packed cups)
- 4 medium tomatoes, cored, cut into ¾-inch wedges (wedges halved crosswise if large), and lightly salted
- ½ cup fresh tender herb leaves, such as parsley, chives, chervil, tarragon, or a mix, torn or snipped if large
- ½ cup extra-virgin olive oil
- 6 thin slices prosciutto (about 3 oz.), cut lengthwise into ½-inch strips
- 2 cloves garlic, smashed and peeled
- 6-7 oz. day-old French bread (with crust), cut into ½-inch cubes
- 1 tsp. chopped fresh thyme
  Kosher salt and freshly ground black pepper
- 4 tsp. fresh lemon juice

Put the greens, tomatoes, and herbs in a large salad bowl.

Heat ¼ cup of the olive oil in a 12-inch skillet over medium heat. Add the prosciutto and cook, stirring frequently, until crisp and slightly darker in color, 4 to 5 minutes. With tongs or a slotted spoon, transfer to a plate lined with paper towels. Add the garlic to the skillet and cook, turning occasionally, until golden brown, 30 seconds to 1 minute; discard the garlic. Add the bread and thyme to the skillet and cook, stirring occasionally, until crisp and golden brown, 4 to 5 minutes. Toss with salt and pepper to taste.

Add the bread and prosciutto to the salad bowl. Drizzle the salad with the remaining ¼ cup olive oil and the lemon juice, and toss well. Season to taste with salt and pepper and serve.

summer berry trifle

Use any type of berry you like—just make sure you choose the ripest, tastiest ones available. The bread will soak up all their sweet juices.

Serves 10 to 12

- 1½ quarts mixed fresh berries (hull and quarter strawberries), plus extra berries for garnish
- ¾ cup plus 1 Tbs. granulated sugar
- 4 tsp. minced fresh ginger
- 1 lb. day-old French bread, crusts removed, crumb cut into ½-inch cubes (5 to 6 cups)
- ½ cup Grand Marnier or Cointreau
- 1½ cups heavy cream

Heat the berries and ¾ cup of the sugar in a 4-quart saucepan over medium-high heat, stirring occasionally, until they start to release juice but are still whole and intact, about 5 minutes. Stir in the ginger and pour the mixture onto a rimmed baking sheet to cool.

Meanwhile, in a large bowl, toss the bread with 5 Tbs. of the liqueur. In a chilled metal bowl with chilled beaters, whip the cream with the remaining 3 Tbs. liqueur and 1 Tbs. sugar to almost-stiff peaks.

In a 2- to 2½-quart clear glass bowl, layer in the following order: 1 mounded cup of bread cubes, 1 cup of berries and juices, and 1 cup of whipped cream. Repeat 3 times—you should

have 12 layers total. For the final layers, use all the remaining bread, berries (and their juices), and whipped cream. **Cover and refrigerate** until the juice has completely softened the bread, at least 4 hours or overnight. Garnish with fresh berries before serving.

Pam Anderson is a Fine Cooking *contributing editor. Her latest cookbook is* The Perfect Recipe for Losing Weight and Eating Great.

The three lives of a lettuce leaf

Wilted

Healthy

Keeping Fresh Greens Fresh

The science of cell structure helps explain why good lettuce goes bad. **BY BRIAN GEIGER**

IN THE DAILY STRUGGLE to eat healthfully, salads make it easy. They're economical, quick, and, because they're so easy to customize, almost always delicious.

The hard part is dealing with the disappointment of opening the crisper drawer and discovering wilted leaves. Or worse, a pool of green sludge. That's a quick way to discourage a nice graze. It's not difficult to keep lettuce happy; in some cases, you can even bring it back from the brink. But first you have to understand what's going on inside those leaves.

Under the microscope

Leaves are nature's solar panels, and salad greens are no different. The career goal of a leaf is to have as much surface area as possible with the minimum amount of volume, in order to capture sunlight, absorb carbon dioxide, and release oxygen. There's not a lot of extra structure, and for that reason, leaves are tender and delicate. The stems are the crunchy bit, because they are the internal pipes of plants: They facilitate

the exchange of nutrients between the leaves and the roots.

The crispness and color of lettuce are determined by the health of its cells. Every plant cell is surrounded by a cell wall, which provides the structure that helps give greens their crisp texture. Inside the cell wall, a semipermeable cell membrane (think of it as a filter) allows the exchange of fluids and gasses that keep the cell alive and productive. At the same time, the membrane contains the various functional parts of the cell, like

Illustration by Aude Van Ryn

Rotten

set next to each other in a grid. Inside each box is a balloon that can fill the box. If the balloons are filled so that they push against the sides of the boxes, you can squeeze the box structure and it's not going anywhere. If you squeeze hard enough, though, some of the balloons will pop. That pressure is what gives lettuce and other vegetables their crispness. By the same token, as lettuce ages, its cells leak liquid, which causes it to wilt.

Know when to fold 'em

The good news is that lettuce is designed to pull in nutrients from its surface. That makes it pretty easy to fix if you've let it wilt. Just soak the lettuce in cold water for a half-hour or so, and suddenly it's rejuvenated.

The cold-water trick is not magical, though. It won't heal rotting bits, it won't reverse cellular damage, and it won't get rid of damage from bacteria. So your lettuce still has to be in essentially good shape, even if it isn't crisp, before it can be resurrected.

How to tell? If a portion of the lettuce is much darker green or brown, if it's liquid rather than solid, or if it just doesn't look like lettuce anymore, throw in the towel. If it looks pretty much like lettuce except that it's limp, then you have a candidate for resuscitation.

As long as lettuce cells are whole, the lettuce is in good shape. Remember the balloon analogy? If the balloon is deflated but intact, no worries. However, if the balloon has popped, there's nothing you can do to fix it. You want to break up the cells when you're eating the lettuce, not when you're storing it.

Back, you bacteria

The two biggest threats to cell walls are physical stress and being exposed to liquid for too long. Physical stress because it directly damages the cell walls and makes them susceptible to bacteria, and water because it is a breeding ground for bacteria.

A cell's cytoplasm and vacuole contain all sorts of nutritious goodies. This is great for humans, since that's one of the reasons we eat salads. The flip side is that nutrition is also good for bacteria. Because bacteria are lacking in "chewing" and "puncturing" skills, they can't easily break through cell walls. But when cell walls become damaged, bacteria can move in and have a feast. And

bacteria are not on anyone's list of good salad components.

So buy salad greens that show no signs of damage. Rinse them just before eating, and handle them gently. A vigorous cleaning can cause damage from handling or by scraping dirt or sand across the leaves. Don't cut or tear the greens before you're ready to eat them.

Let's spend a moment on the tearing-versus-cutting debate. Some experts advise tearing greens into bite-size pieces, on the principle that cutting will damage the cells, while tearing will occur naturally between the cell walls without damaging the membranes. Others insist you should cut greens because in tearing them apart, you squeeze cells with your fingers, causing the cells to burst. I say: It doesn't matter. Just be as gentle as you can as close to eating time as you can.

Sound advice

Storage is much less controversial. Keep greens in an airtight container in the refrigerator. It's a good idea to wrap them in paper towels to absorb excess moisture (remember, too much water breeds bacteria) and to keep the leaves from touching the plastic directly (to prevent condensation).

Understanding your salad greens will help you keep them fresh, and keeping them fresh will help ensure that you'll eat them regularly. That will make you healthier, happier, and generally a better person. Between that and the fresh taste of a good salad, what more do you need?

Brian Geiger is a robotics project manager who explores the mysteries of food science here and in his blog at FineCooking.com.

chloroplasts, the little pockets inside each cell that hold chlorophyll and other chemicals. The chloroplasts' main job is to convert sunlight to chemical energy for the plant. It's also the chloroplasts that give lettuce its color—generally green or in the green-to-white range. Much of the volume of a cell is taken up by the cytoplasm and a sac called the vacuole, which holds most of the liquid that fills the cell. When plant cells are healthy and happy, the cells are filled to the brim with liquid, completing the structure that the cell wall started.

Pop goes the...lettuce

Sound confusing? Well, imagine a bunch of cardboard boxes with no tops or bottoms, all

crisp tips

● Store lettuce whole (uncut and untorn); it will last longer.

● Wrap lettuce in paper towels and keep in an airtight container in the fridge.

● Soak greens in cold water before serving to fill their cells with any water they've lost in their journey from field to table, making them as crisp as possible.

HOW TO MAKE

The Classic Omelet

A breakfast standard every cook should be able to prepare. **BY ALLISON EHRI KREITLER**

A CLASSIC FRENCH OMELET is pale on the outside (no browning at all) and creamy—ever so slightly under-cooked inside. Although it's a simple egg dish, you do have to pay attention to a few key steps to get it just right. With our basic recipe and step-by-step photos, you'll be on your way to delicious results in no time.

Step by Step to the Perfect Omelet

1 Cook until just set around the edge.

2 Scramble gently.

3 Turn off the heat as soon as the bottom has set.

4 Sprinkle the cheese down the middle.

5 Fold one-third of the omelet toward the center.

6 Fold again and flip onto a plate.

Photographs by Scott Phillips; food styling by Jennifer Armentrout, except right, Michelli Knauer

cheese omelet

If you prefer firmer eggs or if undercooked eggs are a concern, cook the omelet for another minute before adding the cheese. It will get a little brown, but the eggs will be cooked through.

Serves 1

½ Tbs. unsalted butter; more as needed

2 large eggs

⅛ tsp. sea salt or kosher salt

Freshly ground black pepper

¼ cup loosely packed grated Gruyère

Melt the butter in an 8-inch nonstick skillet over medium heat.

In a small bowl, lightly beat the eggs, salt, and a couple of grinds of pepper with a fork until the whites and yolks are completely mixed and the eggs are frothy. Pour the eggs into the skillet and let them sit, undisturbed, until the eggs are just beginning to set around the edges, 30 to 60 seconds **1**.

Gently scramble the eggs with a silicone spatula while shaking the pan back and forth **2**. Scramble and shake just until the eggs have set on the bottom but are still under-cooked on top, 45 to 60 seconds **3**. Turn off the heat and give the pan a few shakes to evenly distribute the eggs. Tap it once firmly on the stove to smooth the bottom of the omelet (use a heatproof cutting board if your stovetop is glass).

Sprinkle the cheese down the center third of the omelet **4** and run a spatula around the edge. You can use the spatula to smooth the top of the eggs if necessary. Let it sit for about 1 minute. The top of the omelet will still be loose and the bottom should have no color.

Fold a third of the omelet over the cheese **5**. Shake the unfolded third of the omelet up the side and slightly out of the pan. Invert the pan onto a plate to complete the final fold of the omelet **6**. It should be folded in three, like a letter. Rub the top with cold butter for shine, if desired. Serve immediately.

Allison Ehri Kreitler is a Fine Cooking *contributing editor.*

Filling Options

While cheese is traditional, you can fill an omelet with just about anything. Substitute any of these combos for the Gruyère in the basic recipe (aim for about ¼ cup filling per omelet).

- Crumbled goat cheese, sautéed shallots, and chopped fresh thyme
- Grated Emmenthal, sautéed mushrooms, and sautéed spinach
- Caramelized onions, cooked bacon, and chopped fresh marjoram
- Grated aged Gouda and lightly cooked asparagus thinly sliced on the diagonal

Great Finds

Our latest buys for the kitchen and table. BY DENISE MICKELSEN

Cool Tools

Swedish designer Jesper Stahl's kitchen tool collection is made from a glass-nylon blend, so each piece is lightweight, high-heat resistant, and nonstick. Now available in two new colors, titan silver and pacific blue, as well as in olive, tomato, and black. **$4 to $14 at kitchenart .com; 800-239-8090.**

Good to Grow

Perfect for the gardener-cook in your life, these lovely handmade seedpaper recipe bookmarks can be planted to grow fresh parsley, chives, basil, dill, or cilantro. Instructions and a recipe included. **$3.50 each at seedpapers.com; 505-989-7707.**

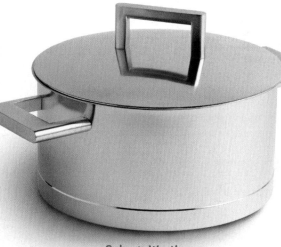

Fruit Forward

Global Gardens' delicious fruit Champagne vinegars are made with sparkling wine from Napa Valley's Domaine Chandon and real fruit purées (pomegranate, strawberry, and blood orange, to name a few). They're great in vinaigrettes, marinades, and sauces. **$14 to $20 at oliverevolution.com; 800-307-0447.**

Splurge Worthy

Demeyere, the high-end Belgian cookware brand, has partnered with UK architect John Pawson to create a sophisticated new line of pots and pans. Each piece is engineered for its specific task (sauté, boil, or sear), and Pawson's modern design makes this line as beautiful as it is functional. Shown, 2.3-quart saucepot with lid, $295. Other pieces, **$280 to $420 at bloomingdales.com; 800-777-0000.**

Take It to Go

Sagaform's new portable, folding charcoal grill means you can cook out anytime, anywhere. It's a modest 11 by 11 inches, and comes with its own shoulder bag for easy carrying. **$40 at halls.com; 888-425-5722.**

One of a Kind

Chicago-based artist and designer Susan Dwyer makes her ethereal gold-edged ceramic dinnerware by hand—no molds allowed in her studio—so each piece is unique. **$12 to $52 at upintheairsomewhere.com.**

Photographs by Scott Phillips

The Reading List

New must-buys for food lovers. BY KIMBERLY Y. MASIBAY

Rustic Fruit Desserts

Crumbles, Buckles, Cobblers, Pandowdies, and More

by Cory Schreiber and Julie Richardson

(Ten Speed Press, $22)

They say you can't judge a book by its cover, but I took one look at the luscious cobbler on the front of this slim volume and pretty much made up my mind. Happily, my intuition was spot on. This book is a pleasure.

The authors—two of Portland, Oregon's, most beloved chefs—deliver 70 unfussy recipes for good old-fashioned desserts. Most of them you'll want to devour promptly, but at the height of summer, when you've got fresh fruit up to your ears, the authors suggest keeping unbaked crisp or crumble toppings on hand in your freezer—then just bring home the fruit, and dessert is a snap.

Goat Song

A Seasonal Life, a Short History of Herding, and the Art of Making Cheese

by Brad Kessler

(Scribner, $24)

About a decade ago, novelist Brad Kessler and his wife moved to a 75-acre farm in the moun-tains of Vermont, where they planned to raise dairy goats. The couple knew nothing of goat herding, let alone living by na-ture's rules, so each day brought its share of dismay, discovery, and delight. In this spellbinding memoir, Kessler chronicles his adventures and his transforma-tion from urban writer to artisan cheesemaker, while also gracefully weaving in historical musings that illuminate the pastoral roots of our modern world. Fascinating, poetic, and erudite, this is a book that beckons the reader to return to its pages time and again.

The New Portuguese Table

Exciting Flavors from Europe's Western Coast

by David Leite

(Clarkson Potter, $32.50)

When award-winning food writer David Leite journeyed to Portu-gal to explore his native cuisine, he was struck by how different it was from the rustic Portuguese food he'd been raised on in New Jersey. Since his father's emigra-tion in the 1950s, new ingredi-ents and cooking techniques have flooded Portugal. Modern chefs are reinterpreting classic fare to delicious effect, borrow-ing flavors from India, Asia, and Africa. In the hands of one witty chef, for example, chicken in a pot becomes an aromatic grilled dish that Leite dubs Chicken out of a Pot and onto the Grill. He spotlights this new Portuguese fare and rounds out his recipe collection with plenty of classic family favorites, like spicy Grilled Shrimp with Piri-Piri Sauce, a Portuguese beach shack standard.

The Big Sur Bakery Cookbook

A Year in the Life of a Restaurant

by Michelle and Philip Wojtowicz, and Michael Gilson with Catherine Price

(William Morrow, $40)

Month by month, this magical book takes you through a year at a renowned restaurant perched along Highway 1 in rugged Big Sur, California. You'll find stun-ning photographs, essays about life in Big Sur, profiles of local purveyors, and a collection of inspiring monthly menus, with recipes. The Big Sur Bakery is all about down-to-earth fare made with the freshest, best ingredi-ents, so many of the recipes in this book are remarkably simple. There's nothing difficult about

making Braised Green Garlic; or Whole Rockfish, Scored and Charred; or Grilled Prime Rib Steak; or Roasted Apricots. The challenge for the home cook is in finding top-notch seasonal ingre-dients and then letting them sing.

Fresh Mexico

100 Simple Recipes for True Mexican Flavor

by Marcela Valladolid

(Clarkson Potter, $22.50)

Vibrant and deliciously feisty, the modern Mexican recipes in Marcela Valladolid's new cookbook are as irresistible as the young Tijuana-based chef herself. Valladolid is passion-ate about Mexican cuisine, but she's no stickler for tradition. Whether she's infusing an Indian technique with Mexican flavor (as in her Cilantro Tandoori Chicken), wrapping a tortilla around duck confit (for a Duck Burrito), or sneaking tequila into crème anglaise (for her Apricot-Tequila Ice Cream), Valladolid finds inspiration where others see culinary boundaries. Her accessible recipes emphasize fresh, easy-to-find ingredients and are perfect for summer— or anytime.

Kimberly Y. Masibay is a Fine Cooking *contributing editor.*

---

what we're reading now

The Spice Merchant's Daughter (Clarkson Potter, 2008), by cooking instructor Christina Arokiasamy, is a beautifully designed book that inspired me straight into the kitchen. Arokiasamy teaches how to buy, store, and cook with the spices, herbs, and chiles that she learned about from her mother, a spice trader and caring cook from Malaysia. I especially love her make-ahead spice pastes and rubs (or "cook's little helpers"), which are great for adding layers of flavor to simple home cooking. —Denise Mickelsen

Less Is More

For nutritionist Ellie Krieger, eating less meat is a good idea,
but summer cookouts can make that a challenge. She has a solution.

THE HEADY AROMA OF MEAT GRILLING over an
open flame never fails to ignite my appetite.
It's a built-in primal response, one that even
my vegetarian friends admit to having. That
intoxicating smell is the tease for the juicy,
charred, succulent flavor payoff to come
when it's time to dig in.

Trouble is, the kind and amount of meat
we're used to tossing on the grill—fatty
sausages, huge greasy burgers, and big
marbled steaks—are, to be blunt, nutritional
nightmares. They're loaded with bad-for-you
fats that are strongly linked to heart disease
and cancer, and those 12-ounce steaks are
way too big for our own good. On the flip side,
beef, pork, and lamb are packed with quality protein, key minerals like zinc and iron,
as well as essential B vitamins. So what's
a health-conscious carnivore to do? The
answer is simple: Choose a lean cut of meat
and eat less of it.

Go Lean In general, if it has the words
"loin" or "round" in the name, the meat is lean.
Beef sirloin, tenderloin, and bottom round
are all lean grilling classics, as are tri-tip and
flank steak. Pork tenderloin is nearly as lean
as skinless chicken breast. And pork and
lamb loin are good choices, too. Game steaks
like venison are nearly fat-free and fantastic
over an open flame. The key with all these
cuts is to cook them to only medium doneness, because they'll dry out if overcooked.

Portion Control Once you have the right
cut, the next step to eating meat sensibly is
to control your portions. The nutritionally
recommended portion of meat is 3 ounces
per serving. The problem is that if you see it
on a plate, it's downright depressing—about
the size of a deck of cards. My trick is to
make it *look* abundant. We eat with our eyes,
so rather than place a puny steak on a plate,
where it's dwarfed by the side dishes, slice
the meat thinly and pile it up on a piece of
grilled garlic bread to sop up the juices. Or
serve it mounded over whole-grain tortillas
as part of a steak taco dinner. Skewering
chunks of meat along with vegetables or fruit,
as I do in the Ancho-Marinated Pork and
Mango Skewers here, is another great way to
grill your meat but not eat too much of it. You

Serve it smart. For Ellie, a great
way to eat less meat is to skewer it.

get the perfect protein portion, but your plate
is dominated by two big, bountiful, meaty
skewers. It's all the primal satisfaction you
want with none of the downsides.

ancho-marinated pork and mango skewers

If you can't find ripe mangos, substitute pineapple.

Serves 4 (2 skewers per person)

¼	cup fresh orange juice
2	Tbs. fresh lime juice
2	Tbs. canola oil; more for the grill
2	tsp. dark brown sugar
2	tsp. pure ancho chile powder
2	medium cloves garlic, minced
	Pinch crushed red pepper flakes
	Kosher salt
1	lb. pork tenderloin, trimmed and cut into 1-inch cubes
2	medium ripe mangos, peeled, pitted, and cut into 1-inch cubes
8	skewers, 10 inches or longer, soaked in water for 30 minutes if wooden
1	Tbs. chopped fresh cilantro

In a medium bowl, whisk the orange juice, lime juice, oil, sugar, ancho powder, garlic, pepper flakes, and ½ tsp. salt. **Add the pork,** toss to coat, cover, and refrigerate for at least 1 hour or up to 4 hours.

Thread the pork and mango cubes onto the skewers, alternating them and beginning and ending with a piece of pork. Each skewer should have about 5 pieces of pork and 4 pieces of mango. **Prepare a medium** gas or charcoal grill fire. Scrub the grill grate with a wire brush and then wipe clean with a paper towel dipped in oil. Cook the skewers, turning once, until the meat is browned on the outside but still slightly pink in the center, about 8 minutes. Serve garnished with the cilantro.

Registered dietitian Ellie Krieger is a Fine Cooking *contributing editor.*

 Get more advice on fresh eating at FineCooking.com/fresh.

Mandolines

This time-saving kitchen tool lets you slice, julienne, and crinkle-cut like a pro. These three are a cut above. BY MARYELLEN DRISCOLL

TRANSFORMING A FEW POUNDS OF POTATOES into thin, even rounds for a gratin or shaving paper-thin slices of raw fennel for a salad takes great knife skills, not to mention patience. The alternative? A mandoline. It easily turns fruits and vegetables into uniform slices or julienne sticks of almost any thickness and size with speed and precision. It's safer to use than a hand-held slicer because it has legs for added stability. And don't forget the mandoline's inimitable talent: crinkle and waffle cuts. Here are our favorites among the dozen we tested.

how we tested

We tested 12 widely available mandolines, assessing each for ease of use, construction, performance, and safety. We were looking for sturdy mandolines with stable legs that resist skidding, intuitive assembly, super-sharp blades, and smooth functioning. We sliced potatoes into varying thick-nesses, from paper-thin to as thick as the mandoline would allow. We also sliced potatoes using the julienne and crinkle/waffle cut blades. We sliced and julienned carrots, shaved fennel, and sliced toma-toes and onions.

to buy or not to buy?

Do you really need a mandoline? Let's just say it comes in handy when making lots of thin, even slices or julienne cuts for any of these preparations (to name a few):

- Caramelized onions
- Gratins (potato, root vegetable, squash)
- Planks of zucchini, summer squash, or eggplant
- Fruit tarts
- French fries (crinkle, waffle cut, or straight)
- Shaved fennel, radish, apple, or hard cheeses for salads
- Onion rings
- Pickled vegetables
- Cole slaw
- Cucumber salad
- Vegetable stir-fries

THE ULTIMATE

De Buyer La Mandoline V Professionnelle

$190; Kitchenu.com

Priced at the fantasy level (but maybe you *deserve* it), this one's for the cook who wants a top-of-the-line mandoline. The extremely sharp V-shaped blade slices smoothly and effortlessly, even with ripe tomatoes —the only mandoline we tested that can make that claim. It sits on its side at a comfortable 45-degree angle, has a large food pusher, and the insertion and removal of the slicing blades is intuitive and straightforward. The design of the stainless-steel pusher is a standout —it's spring-loaded to maintain constant, even pressure on the food so you don't have to. And it feels sturdy and natural as you move it. You can set up the handle for right- or left-hand use. Clear markings at the top of the mando-line help you gauge the thickness of your cut, and the crank that adjusts the thickness is easy to access and operate. This model also comes with lots of bells and whistles: a straight-slicing blade, a blade for crinkle and waffle cuts, and three julienne blades—4 mm (3/16 inch), 7 mm (1/4 inch), and 10 mm (3/8 inch), all easy to install. The V Profession-nelle also comes with a demonstra-tion DVD and a large hard-plastic travel case.

ALL-AROUND CHAMP

De Buyer La Mandoline Swing
$90; Chefscatalog.com

Reasonably priced and user-friendly, this model is a great value for the money. The straight blades are razor-sharp and made for smooth slicing on almost everything except tomatoes and carrots. The spring-loaded pusher is easy to use and roomy enough to hold an average-size potato. This mandoline really excelled at crinkle and waffle cuts, but it doesn't have measured markings, so you have to guess as you adjust for thickness. The Swing comes with a double-sided blade that's straight on one side and serrated on the other (for crinkle and waffle cuts), and a double-sided julienne blade with 4 mm (³⁄₁₆ inch) and 10 mm (⅖ inch) widths. It's available in a variety of colors—orange, green, red, and black.

BEST BUY

Oxo Good Grips V-Blade Mandoline Slicer
$40; Oxo.com

This plastic model with a surprisingly sharp V-blade is a solid entry-level mandoline. It can slice in thicknesses from ¹⁄₁₆ inch to ¼ inch, create two widths of julienne cuts (⅛ inch and ¼ inch), make crinkle cuts (but not waffle), and even dice (⅛ inch and ¼ inch), a feature the other models do not have. The large pusher has an easy-to-grip shape that keeps your hand comfortably away from the blade. A color-coded dial makes it simple to set the thickness of a cut, but there are only four thickness settings. As a result, the french fries we made with this model were pretty thin. The blades store neatly under the unit.

Maryellen Driscoll is a Fine Cooking *contributing editor.*

Watch a video on how to set up and use a mandoline at Fine Cooking.com/extras.

Beer Becomes a Cocktail

Beer makes a great mixed drink—it goes down easy, plays well with others, and is the perfect thirst quencher. BY LEW BRYSON

BEER'S PRETTY FINE STUFF, IF YOU ASK ME. It has that great combination of sweet and bitter, a modest amount of alcohol (so you can drink a lot of it), and bubbles, which are never a bad thing. It's so simple: Open, pour, enjoy.

Then why mess with the easy pleasure of a tall, cool one by adding other ingredients? Because the results can be eye-openingly delicious. Call them beer cocktails, fettlers, *cerveza preparada* (prepared beer), or "just something I whipped up"—they're a great alternative to summer's more expected concoctions.

I started messing around with adding things to beer when I was in college. The cheap draft beer that was all we could afford tasted a lot better with a dose of ginger ale (I didn't know it then, but I was making what was essentially a Shandy).

My beer cocktails have gotten more sophisticated since then, but not a lot. They're intrinsically simple drinks. Because of the carbonation you can't shake them—just stir gently. And you want to keep the ingredient list short so you don't hide the character of the beer.

There are three ways to make a beer cocktail. You can enhance the beer with small amounts of nonalcoholic mixers, like fresh citrus juice, hot sauce, or spices. The Germans add a dollop of raspberry syrup to a piercingly tart Berliner Weisse beer. The simple Chelada, which hails from Mexico, features a light lager with a squeeze of fresh lime, served over ice in a salt-rimmed glass.

For a spicier, more robust version with soy, Worcestershire, and hot pepper sauces, check out the Michelada (recipe opposite).

Another option is to combine two beers that play well together. Guinness stout is a classic base for beer cocktails, as in the Black and Tan, which blends the burnt black bitterness of a stout, usually Guinness, with the smoother maltiness of a pale ale. In the Peach Melba Cocktail (recipe opposite), inspired by the classic dessert, I followed this idea and poured two fruit lambic beers together for a sweet, effervescent apéritif.

You can also boost your beer with the intense flavors and aromas of spirits or other alcoholic beverages, as in the elegant Black Velvet (Guinness mixed fifty-fifty with Champagne). My version, Eve's Black Heart (recipe below), mixes rich, dark Guinness with crisp, dry hard cider and a float of Calvados, or apple brandy. It's a knockout.

With the craft beer revolution in full swing and an exciting array of Belgian and British beers now available here, the options for creating new beer cocktails seem almost infinite. All it takes is imagination, a good beer store, a few adventurous friends, and a long afternoon to experiment. Pick out a few beers in varying styles (light lagers, brown ales, hoppy IPAs, dark stouts), have plenty of glassware on hand, some mixers, and ice, and you've got the ingredients for a new kind of cocktail party that'll have you mixing into the night.

eve's black heart

Similar to a Black Velvet, which is made with Guinness and Champagne, this beer cocktail has a double hit of apples from both hard cider and apple brandy. Hence, the name, derived from Eve's penchant for the forbidden fruit.
Serves 2

- 8 fl. oz. (1 cup) dry hard cider (such as Crispin brut or Farnum Hill semi-dry), chilled
- 1 14.9-fl.-oz. can Guinness draught, chilled
- 1 fl. oz. (2 Tbs.) Calvados

Divide the cider between two chilled pint glasses. To float the Guinness on top of the cider, pop the tab on the can, let it foam up, and then pour the beer slowly over the rounded back of a tablespoon measure held over each glass, stopping when almost full. Gently pour 1 Tbs. of the Calvados on top of each drink. Serve.

peach melba cocktail

Fruit lambic beers are tart Belgian brews fermented with wild yeasts and aged with crushed fruit or fruit juices. A mix of peach and raspberry lambics makes a drink that sounds like dessert but tastes like an apéritif.

Serves 1

- 6 fl. oz. (¾ cup) pêche (peach) lambic, such as Lindemans, chilled
- 2 fl. oz. (¼ cup) framboise (raspberry) lambic, such as Lindemans, chilled
- 1 thin slice lemon

Combine the two beers in a chilled 9-oz. Champagne flute. Gently squeeze the lemon slice over the drink and then add the slice to the drink. Serve.

the michelada

This beer cocktail is simple and delicious. For an even simpler version—the Chelada— salt the rim of an ice-filled pint glass, add light lager and fresh lime juice, and enjoy.

Serves 1

  Kosher salt
- ½ small lime
- 1 12-fl.-oz. bottle light lager, such as Corona or Modelo Especial, chilled
- 2 dashes Worchestershire sauce
- 2 dashes soy sauce
- 2 dashes hot pepper sauce, such as Cholula or Tabasco
  Freshly cracked black pepper

Pour 2 Tbs. salt into a small, wide dish. Wet the rim of a chilled pint glass with the lime. Dip the rim into the salt, margarita-style. Fill the glass with ice and squeeze the lime over the ice. Fill the glass with beer and then add the Worchestershire, soy, and hot sauce. Give a pepper mill a single twist over the ice. Stir gently until the drink takes on a uniform color. Serve immediately, with the remaining beer on the side for adding to the glass as you empty it. By the time you've finished, the heat of the drink will have subsided and you'll be ready for another.

Lew Bryson is a beer and whiskey writer based in Newtown, Pennsylvania.

For a bonus beer cocktail, go to FineCooking.com/extras.

play it by ear

Sweet corn on the cob is hard to resist, but there's a lot you can do with it off the cob, too. Here are five delicious ideas.

BY MARYELLEN DRISCOLL

ON OUR FARM, corn is a watched crop. First by the ravens eager to pluck the new tender sprouts. Then by Mooky, our brawny Lab, keen on scaring off any large-winged bird that hovers over the fields. And finally, we watch. We keep the weeds knocked back until the stalks grow enough canopy to shade them out. We greet the sight of the corn's emerging ears. We watch the tassel—the browning of the cascading silk a telltale mark of ripening.

Then, when we know it's time, we sample the results of all that watching and waiting. Raw. Right there in the field. Corn that fresh pops with a milky sweetness that dribbles down our chins, over our hands, and onto our T-shirts. There's no pot, no grill. No butter or salt. And definitely no table manners.

There's nothing quite like sinking your teeth into that first crop of summer corn. But the sweet, nutty, creamy qualities that make it so delicious are also what make it well suited to a surprising variety of dishes. Relish it on the cob, slathered in butter and stippled with salt. Then, cut it off the cob and try it in a spare and silky soup. Or in a fresh salad with cherry tomatoes and edamame, corn kernels are toasted in a skillet to tease out their nutty essence. Stirred into risotto, a creamy mash of grated corn makes this rich dish all the more luscious. The possibilities are endless, and the rewards for the long corn wait are sweet.

toasted corn, cherry tomato, and edamame salad

Toasting the corn in a skillet brings out its nutty flavor. You could also use grilled corn (see p. 39) in place of the skillet-toasted version.

Serves 4 to 6 as a side dish

- 1 cup frozen shelled edamame
- 5 Tbs. extra-virgin olive oil
- 2¼ cups fresh corn kernels (from about 3 medium ears)
- 2 Tbs. plain low-fat yogurt
- 2 Tbs. fresh lemon juice
- 1 tsp. clover honey
- ½ tsp. minced garlic
  Kosher salt
  Freshly ground black pepper
- 1 heaping cup quartered cherry tomatoes (about 15)
- ¼ cup very thinly sliced fresh mint
- ¼ cup very thinly sliced fresh basil

Cook the edamame according to package directions. Drain and set aside to cool completely.

Heat 1 Tbs. of the oil in a large skillet over medium heat. Add the corn and cook, stirring occasionally, until the kernels are golden brown in patches, about 9 minutes. Transfer to a bowl to cool.

In a small bowl or liquid measuring cup, whisk the yogurt, lemon juice, honey, garlic, and ¼ tsp. salt. Slowly pour in the remaining 4 Tbs. olive oil, whisking constantly until blended. Season to taste with salt and pepper.

In a medium serving bowl, combine the cooled edamame and corn, the tomatoes, and the herbs. Gently toss. Add half of the vinaigrette and gently toss. Add more vinaigrette and salt and pepper to taste. Serve at room temperature.

Corn: A Buyer's Guide

There are four types of sweet corn: standard sweet, sugar-enhanced, supersweet, and synergistic. You won't see these agricultural terms used at grocery stores or even at farmers' markets, but they help to explain the differences among them in terms of sweetness, tenderness, and how well they store.

If you really want to know what type of corn you're buying, ask the farmer. Just be prepared to try something new each time. The corn variety you saw on your last visit is probably not the same one you're going to find on your next. In general, the more sugary varieties of corn take longer to grow and appear later at the market.

Standard sweet
Common varieties include Butter and Sugar, with white and yellow kernels, and Silver Queen, with white kernels. This type of corn has a traditional corn flavor and texture, although sweetness varies among varieties. Its sugars are quicker to convert to starch, so it doesn't keep long after harvest.

Sugar-enhanced
Delectable, Kandy Korn, and Seneca Dancer are three popular varieties. Known for having a more tender texture than the standard type, sugar-enhanced corn is widely popular. Its degree of sweetness changes with the variety, but the conversion of sugar to starch is slower than that of standard sweet corn, so it holds up better.

Supersweet
Varieties include Sun & Stars and Xtra-Sweet. The most sugary of all, this type of corn has less true corn flavor and a firmer, almost crunchy texture, because the skin on the kernels is tougher. It holds its sweetness longer than any other type of corn, which is why you'll often see it in supermarkets, where the corn isn't typically freshly picked.

Synergistic
A popular variety is Serendipity. This type has both the tenderness of sugar-enhanced corn and the more pronounced sweetness of supersweet. It requires more time to mature than sugar-enhanced corn and can be watery if harvested too soon.

Silver Queen

Seneca Dancer

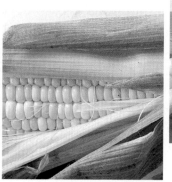

Supersweet

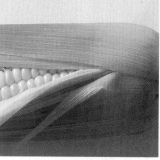

Serendipity

Photographs by Scott Phillips

risotto with corn, spicy sausage, and wilted arugula

Grating some of the corn to a mash and blending it with the rice makes a creamy foundation for this corn-studded risotto.

Serves 4 to 6 as a main course

- 6 cups lower-salt chicken broth; more as needed
- 3 medium ears fresh corn, shucked and halved crosswise
- 2 Tbs. extra-virgin olive oil
- 2 medium cloves garlic, minced
- 3 packed cups trimmed arugula
  Kosher salt and freshly ground black pepper
- 3 Tbs. unsalted butter
- 1 medium leek (white and light-green parts only), finely diced (about ¾ cup)
- ¼ lb. hot Italian pork sausage, casings removed and broken into chunks
- 2 cups arborio or carnaroli rice
- ½ cup dry white wine (like Pinot Grigio)
- ½ cup freshly grated Pecorino Romano; more for serving
- 2 Tbs. finely chopped fresh flat-leaf parsley (optional)

Heat the chicken broth in a medium saucepan over medium-high heat until very hot. Add the corn and cook until the kernels are just tender, 3 to 4 minutes. Transfer the corn to a cutting board and reduce the heat to keep the broth hot but not simmering.

Once the corn is cool enough to handle, slice the kernels off four of the pieces. Grate the kernels from the remaining two pieces using the large holes of a box grater. Discard the cobs.

Heat the olive oil and garlic in a large, heavy saucepan or medium Dutch oven over medium-high heat until the garlic is fragrant, about 2 minutes. Add the arugula and toss with tongs until wilted, about 1 minute. Season with a generous pinch of salt and pepper. Transfer the arugula to a cutting board, let it cool slightly, and then coarsely chop it. Wipe the pan clean.

Melt the butter in the cleaned pan over medium heat. Add the leek and a generous pinch of salt and cook, stirring occasionally, until softened, about 2 minutes. Add the sausage, breaking it apart with a fork or spoon into crumbles, and cook until no longer pink, 2 to 3 minutes. Add the rice and stir until the grains are well coated with fat and the edges become translucent, 1 to 2 minutes. Pour in the wine and stir until it's absorbed, about 30 seconds. Stir in the grated corn.

Ladle enough of the hot broth into the pan to barely cover the rice, about 1½ cups. Bring to a boil and then adjust the heat to maintain a lively simmer. Cook, stirring frequently, until the broth is mostly absorbed, 2 to 3 minutes. Continue adding broth in ½-cup increments, stirring occasionally and letting each addition be absorbed before adding the next.

After about 20 minutes, the rice should be just cooked but still fairly firm. At this point, add the whole corn kernels, chopped arugula, and another ½ cup broth. Continue to simmer and stir until the corn is warmed through and the rice is just tender to the tooth, an additional 1 to 3 minutes. Stir in another splash of broth if the risotto seems too thick. Remove the pot from the heat and stir in the cheese. Season with salt and pepper to taste. Serve the risotto immediately with a sprinkling of cheese and parsley, if using.

Food styling by Michelli Knauer

fresh corn fritters with charred tomato salsa

Try these as an appetizer (served with the salsa here), as a side with grilled chicken or fish, or for breakfast with maple syrup.

Yields about 26 bite-size fritters

4½ oz. (1 cup) all-purpose flour
¼ cup stone-ground yellow cornmeal
2 tsp. baking powder
1 tsp. sugar
½ tsp. table salt; more for sprinkling
½ cup whole milk
¼ cup sour cream
2 large eggs
1 cup fresh corn kernels (from about 1 large or 2 small ears of corn), coarsely chopped
1-1½ cups vegetable oil
1 recipe Charred Tomato Salsa (opposite)

In a medium bowl, stir the flour, cornmeal, baking powder, sugar, and salt. In a small bowl, whisk the milk, sour cream, and eggs. With a rubber spatula, gently stir the egg mixture into the flour mixture until just blended. Stir in the corn. Let sit for 10 to 15 minutes. Meanwhile, position a rack in the center of the oven and heat the oven to 200°F.

Pour the oil into a small, heavy frying pan, preferably cast iron, to a depth of ½ inch. Heat over medium heat until it's hot enough that a small dollop of batter sizzles when added. With a spring-lever miniature ice cream scoop or a tablespoon, scoop up a ball of the batter and gently release it into the hot oil. Add three or four more balls of batter to the hot oil, taking care not to crowd the pan. Reduce the heat to medium low so that the fritters cook gently. When golden brown on the bottom and barely cooked around the top edge, after 1 to 2 minutes, use a slotted spatula to turn the fritters and cook until golden on the bottom, 1 to 2 minutes longer.

Transfer the fritters to a wire rack set over a baking sheet, sprinkle generously with salt, and keep warm in the oven. Continue to cook the remaining batter in small batches, adding more oil as needed to maintain the ½-inch depth. Serve right away with the salsa.

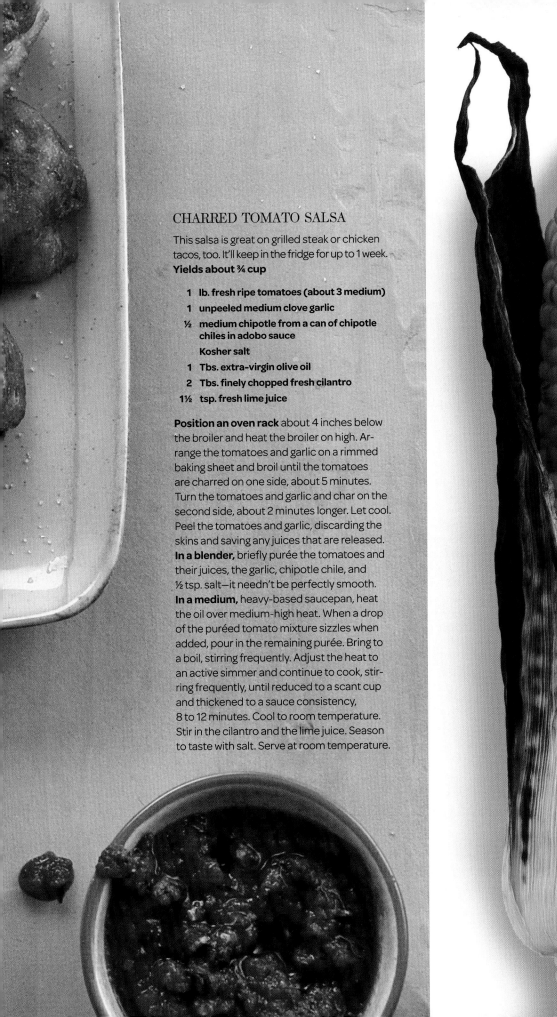

CHARRED TOMATO SALSA

This salsa is great on grilled steak or chicken tacos, too. It'll keep in the fridge for up to 1 week.
Yields about ¾ cup

- 1 **lb. fresh ripe tomatoes (about 3 medium)**
- 1 **unpeeled medium clove garlic**
- ½ **medium chipotle from a can of chipotle chiles in adobo sauce**
  Kosher salt
- 1 **Tbs. extra-virgin olive oil**
- 2 **Tbs. finely chopped fresh cilantro**
- 1½ **tsp. fresh lime juice**

Position an oven rack about 4 inches below the broiler and heat the broiler on high. Arrange the tomatoes and garlic on a rimmed baking sheet and broil until the tomatoes are charred on one side, about 5 minutes. Turn the tomatoes and garlic and char on the second side, about 2 minutes longer. Let cool. Peel the tomatoes and garlic, discarding the skins and saving any juices that are released. **In a blender,** briefly purée the tomatoes and their juices, the garlic, chipotle chile, and ½ tsp. salt—it needn't be perfectly smooth. **In a medium,** heavy-based saucepan, heat the oil over medium-high heat. When a drop of the puréed tomato mixture sizzles when added, pour in the remaining purée. Bring to a boil, stirring frequently. Adjust the heat to an active simmer and continue to cook, stirring frequently, until reduced to a scant cup and thickened to a sauce consistency, 8 to 12 minutes. Cool to room temperature. Stir in the cilantro and the lime juice. Season to taste with salt. Serve at room temperature.

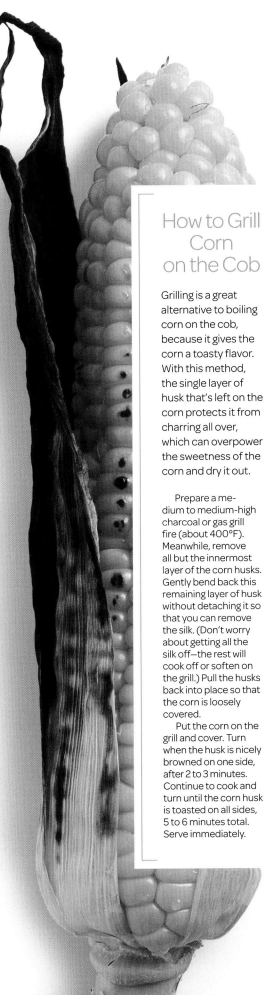

How to Grill Corn on the Cob

Grilling is a great alternative to boiling corn on the cob, because it gives the corn a toasty flavor. With this method, the single layer of husk that's left on the corn protects it from charring all over, which can overpower the sweetness of the corn and dry it out.

Prepare a medium to medium-high charcoal or gas grill fire (about 400°F). Meanwhile, remove all but the innermost layer of the corn husks. Gently bend back this remaining layer of husk without detaching it so that you can remove the silk. (Don't worry about getting all the silk off—the rest will cook off or soften on the grill.) Pull the husks back into place so that the corn is loosely covered.

Put the corn on the grill and cover. Turn when the husk is nicely browned on one side, after 2 to 3 minutes. Continue to cook and turn until the corn husk is toasted on all sides, 5 to 6 minutes total. Serve immediately.

summer corn soup with crisp prosciutto

Yields about 8 cups; serves 4 as a main course or 8 as a starter

- 3   very thin slices prosciutto
- 3-4   large ears fresh corn
- 4   Tbs. unsalted butter
- 1   medium yellow onion, chopped (about 1½ cups)
-    Kosher salt
- 2   cups lower-salt chicken broth
- 1½   cups medium-diced peeled red potato (from 2 to 3 medium)
-    Freshly ground black pepper
- 2   Tbs. coarsely chopped fresh basil

Position an oven rack about 4 inches below the broiler and heat the broiler on high. Arrange the prosciutto in a single layer on a small baking sheet and broil until it begins to curl, 1 to 2 minutes. Flip the prosciutto and broil until it appears dry-crisp and has curled a bit more, about 1 minute. Let cool, then finely chop or crumble by hand; set aside.

Slice the kernels off the corn cobs for a total of 3 cups corn. Reserve the cobs.

In a medium Dutch oven over medium heat, melt the butter. Add the onion and cook until softened and slightly golden, 5 to 7 minutes. Season with a generous pinch of salt.

Add 4 cups of water, the broth, potatoes, 1½ cups of the corn, the cobs, and 2 tsp. salt. Bring to a boil. Reduce the heat to medium low and simmer until the potatoes are tender, 10 to 15 minutes. Remove from the heat and discard the cobs.

Working in batches, carefully purée the soup in a blender, transferring each batch to a large heatproof bowl or large liquid measuring cup.

Pour the puréed soup back into the pot. Add the remaining 1½ cups corn and bring to a boil over medium-high heat. Reduce heat to medium low and simmer, stirring occasionally, until the corn kernels are tender, 3 to 5 minutes. Season to taste with salt and pepper. Garnish each serving with the crisped prosciutto and basil.

sweet corn cake with blueberry-lavender compote

A lavender-scented topping lends an elegant touch to this rustic cake. To cook the corn, boil it in lightly salted water until tender—3 to 5 minutes, depending on how fresh the corn is. You can skip sifting the cornmeal if you'd like a coarser texture in the cake.

Serves 10 to 12

FOR THE CAKE

- 6   oz. (12 Tbs.) unsalted butter, softened; more for the pan
- 4½   oz. (1 cup) unbleached all-purpose flour
- 2   tsp. baking powder
- ¼   tsp. table salt
- 2¼   oz. (½ cup) sifted stone-ground yellow cornmeal
- 1   cup cooked fresh corn kernels (from about 1 large ear)
- ½   cup sour cream, at room temperature
- ¾   cup granulated sugar
- 3   large eggs, at room temperature and lightly beaten

FOR THE COMPOTE

- 1   cup granulated sugar
- 2   tsp. dried lavender
- 1¼   cups cooked fresh corn kernels (from about 2 medium ears)
- 1   cup fresh blueberries

MAKE THE CAKE

Position a rack in the center of the oven and heat the oven to 350°F. Butter the sides and bottom of a 9x2-inch round cake pan. Fit a circle of parchment in the bottom of the pan and butter that as well.

Fresh Picked

When you're buying sweet corn, don't get hung up on varieties. Instead, keep in mind that timing is everything. Corn's sugars quickly turn into starch as the corn ages, so freshness should be your priority.

Buy To start, find a reliable source for locally grown produce—one that's closely linked to the fields where the vegetables are grown. Ideally, this means buying straight from the farm, either at a farmstand or a nearby farmers' market. Don't husk the corn before buying it. Instead, look for ears snugly wrapped in green husks that look vibrant, not dried out. Run your fingers along the ear. You should be able to feel plump, densely packed kernels up to or close to the tip.

Store At home, use fresh corn as soon as possible. If you must store it, don't remove the husk, which protects the corn from moisture loss. Wrap the ears in damp paper towels, seal them in zip-top bags, and store in the fridge for no longer than two days.

For sources, see Where to Buy It

Sift the flour, baking powder, and salt into a medium bowl. Whisk in the cornmeal; set aside.
Purée the corn kernels in a food processor until smooth. Strain the purée through a fine sieve, pressing with a rubber spatula to extract the liquid; scrape any purée off the bottom of the sieve into the liquid and then discard the remaining solids. Measure ¼ cup of the strained corn liquid and transfer to a small bowl (discard any excess liquid). Stir in the sour cream.
In a stand mixer fitted with the paddle attachment, beat the butter and sugar on medium-high speed until fluffy, about 2 minutes. Stop and scrape the sides of the bowl. On low speed, slowly pour in the beaten eggs, mixing until incorporated and stopping midway to scrape down the sides. (The mixture will be loose and curdled-looking.)

On low speed, add one-third of the flour mixture and mix until just blended. Add one-third of the sour cream-corn mixture and mix until just blended. Alternate adding the remaining flour and sour cream mixtures in two additions each. Do not overmix.
Scrape the batter into the cake pan and spread it evenly with a spatula. Bake until the cake is golden brown and springs back when lightly pressed in the center, 30 to 35 minutes. Transfer to a rack to cool for 10 to 15 minutes. Run a knife around the edge of the pan and then gently invert the cake onto the rack, removing the pan. Remove the parchment, turn the cake right side up onto the rack, and let cool completely.

MAKE THE COMPOTE
Combine the sugar and ⅔ cup water in a small saucepan. Bring to a simmer over medium-high heat, stirring frequently until the sugar has dissolved completely. Remove from the heat. Add the lavender and stir to combine. Let infuse for 10 minutes, then strain the syrup into a small bowl and let cool.
When ready to serve the cake, stir the corn and blueberries into the syrup. Cut the cake into wedges, and top each serving with about 3 Tbs. of the mixture, letting most of the syrup drain off the spoon before sprinkling the blueberries and corn over the cake.

Maryellen Driscoll is a Fine Cooking contributing editor. She and her husband own Free Bird Farm, in upstate New York. ◻

grilling shellfish

Lobster, shrimp, even oysters—they all take well to the grill, with sweet and smoky results. We show you how, and throw in three great

THERE ARE SO MANY GOOD REASONS to grill shellfish. Whether it's shrimp, lobster, clams, mussels, or oysters, grilling shellfish is as simple as can be—in most cases, a brush of olive oil and a sprinkle of salt are all you need in the way of prep—and it's a great way to serve a crowd. But the best reason is flavor. Nothing quite matches the sweet, intense, and slightly charred taste of shellfish when it's cooked on the grill.

The process is inherently easy, but there is something of an art to grilling shellfish. First, leave it in the shell, which protects the delicate meat and keeps it moist during cooking. Then grill it over relatively high, direct heat and cover the grill to keep the heat in; otherwise, the cooking time will be too long and the shellfish will get tough. Finally, pair it with a sauce of your choice (there are three tasty ones to choose from here) and you've got the makings of a perfect summer cookout.

grilled lobster

See Test Kitchen, p. 81, for directions on how to pick the meat from a cooked lobster.

Serves 4

- 4 whole live lobsters (1½ to 2 lb. each) or 4 frozen lobster tails, thawed
  Olive oil, as needed

Prepare the live lobsters as directed in Test Kitchen, p. 81.

Prepare a medium-high gas or charcoal grill fire. Brush olive oil on both sides of the lobsters and set them bottom side down on the cooking grates. Grill until the shells are bright red and the protein in the juices that seep from the shells turns white and coagulates, 8 to 10 minutes for a 1½-lb. lobster and 12 to 14 minutes for a 2-lb. lobster. (There's no need to turn the lobster over.) A thawed lobster tail will take about 8 minutes to grill.

Remove the lobsters from the grill and let cool for a few minutes. Serve warm with the dipping sauce of your choice (see pp. 48–49).

Note: With this method, you'll end up with a slight curve in the lobster's tail. If you want to keep the tail straight, thread a metal or bamboo skewer through the tail before grilling.

grilled shrimp

For tips on deveining shell-on shrimp, see Test Kitchen, p. 81.

Serves 4

- 1 lb. jumbo shell-on shrimp (16 to 20 per lb.), preferably deveined
- 2 Tbs. olive oil
  Kosher salt

Rinse the shrimp under cold running water. Dry the shrimp with paper towels and toss them in the oil to coat. Season with 1½ tsp. salt.

Prepare a medium-high gas or charcoal grill fire. When the grill is ready, use long-handled tongs to put the shrimp on the cooking grates, arranging them across the grates so they don't fall through. Grill, turning halfway through cooking, until the shrimp curl and become pink, 2 or 3 minutes per side. Transfer to a platter. Serve immediately with the dipping sauce of your choice (see pp. 48–49), or chill to use in a seafood salad or a cold shrimp cocktail.

Food styling by Michelli Knauer

mussels, clams, and oysters

This recipe serves four, but it's easily doubled or tripled. Plan on 6 shellfish per person, but buy more than that, since 2 or 3 out of every dozen may not open and will need to be discarded.

Serves 4

30 fresh mussels, clams, or oysters in the shell

Scrub the shellfish with a stiff brush under cool running water. If the mussels have beards, pull them off. Pat dry.

Prepare a medium-high gas or charcoal fire. When the grill is ready, set the shellfish directly on the cooking grate (oysters cupped side down). Grill until the shells pop open, the meat is plump, and the juices are boiling and sizzling in the shell, 3 to 7 minutes for mussels, 6 to 10 minutes for clams, and 4 to 6 minutes for oysters; there's no need to turn the shellfish. (Cooking times can vary widely, because the larger the shellfish, the longer it will take to cook; on the other hand, the fresher it is, the shorter the cooking time.) Remove the shellfish as they finish cooking, protecting your hands with tongs or hot pads. Discard any that don't open. Serve on the half shell with the dipping sauce of your choice (see pp. 48–49).

Oysters "R" Good All Year

There's an old wives' tale that oysters shouldn't be eaten in the hot summer months (any month that doesn't have the letter "r" in its name). Not true! Decades ago, when refrigeration was still primitive, the concern was probably valid. But with modern refrigeration, cooked oysters are perfectly safe in summer and, most would argue, raw oysters are, too, as long as they've been properly refrigerated.

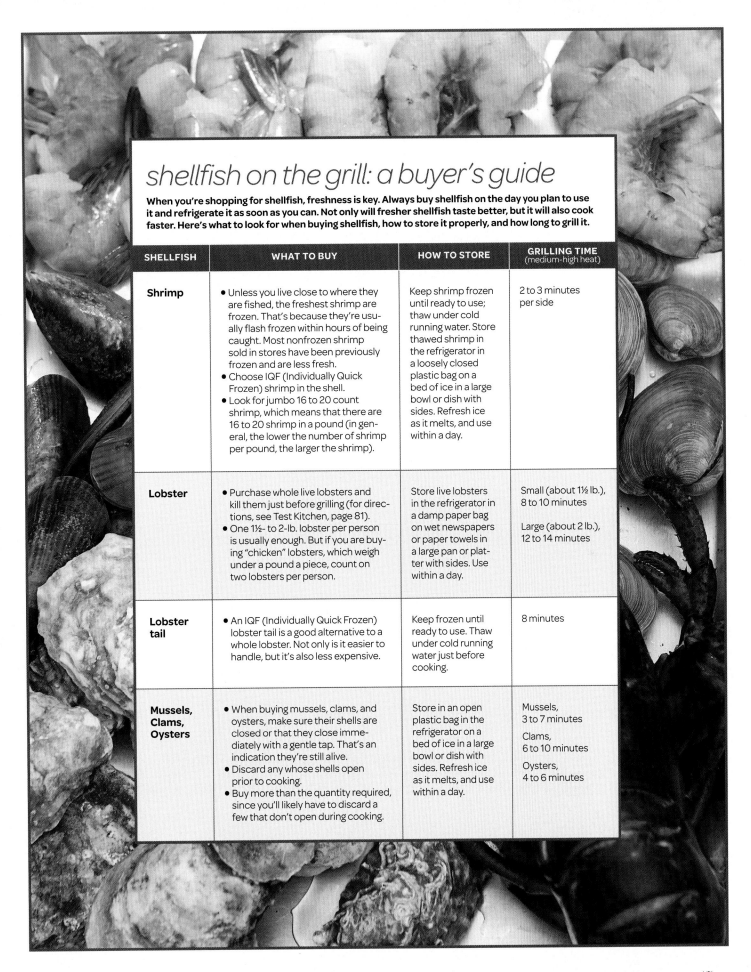

shellfish on the grill: a buyer's guide

When you're shopping for shellfish, freshness is key. Always buy shellfish on the day you plan to use it and refrigerate it as soon as you can. Not only will fresher shellfish taste better, but it will also cook faster. Here's what to look for when buying shellfish, how to store it properly, and how long to grill it.

SHELLFISH	WHAT TO BUY	HOW TO STORE	GRILLING TIME (medium-high heat)
Shrimp	• Unless you live close to where they are fished, the freshest shrimp are frozen. That's because they're usually flash frozen within hours of being caught. Most nonfrozen shrimp sold in stores have been previously frozen and are less fresh. • Choose IQF (Individually Quick Frozen) shrimp in the shell. • Look for jumbo 16 to 20 count shrimp, which means that there are 16 to 20 shrimp in a pound (in general, the lower the number of shrimp per pound, the larger the shrimp).	Keep shrimp frozen until ready to use; thaw under cold running water. Store thawed shrimp in the refrigerator in a loosely closed plastic bag on a bed of ice in a large bowl or dish with sides. Refresh ice as it melts, and use within a day.	2 to 3 minutes per side
Lobster	• Purchase whole live lobsters and kill them just before grilling (for directions, see Test Kitchen, page 81). • One 1½- to 2-lb. lobster per person is usually enough. But if you are buying "chicken" lobsters, which weigh under a pound a piece, count on two lobsters per person.	Store live lobsters in the refrigerator in a damp paper bag on wet newspapers or paper towels in a large pan or platter with sides. Use within a day.	Small (about 1½ lb.), 8 to 10 minutes Large (about 2 lb.), 12 to 14 minutes
Lobster tail	• An IQF (Individually Quick Frozen) lobster tail is a good alternative to a whole lobster. Not only is it easier to handle, but it's also less expensive.	Keep frozen until ready to use. Thaw under cold running water just before cooking.	8 minutes
Mussels, Clams, Oysters	• When buying mussels, clams, and oysters, make sure their shells are closed or that they close immediately with a gentle tap. That's an indication they're still alive. • Discard any whose shells open prior to cooking. • Buy more than the quantity required, since you'll likely have to discard a few that don't open during cooking.	Store in an open plastic bag in the refrigerator on a bed of ice in a large bowl or dish with sides. Refresh ice as it melts, and use within a day.	Mussels, 3 to 7 minutes Clams, 6 to 10 minutes Oysters, 4 to 6 minutes

bloody mary cocktail sauce

This tart and tangy sauce is a twist on a classic Bloody Mary cocktail. Rim your serving dish with celery salt before serving, if you like.

Yields a scant 2¼ cups

- 2 small lemons
- 1 small lime
- 1 cup ketchup
- 1 cup Heinz chili sauce
- 2 heaping Tbs. prepared white horseradish; more to taste
- 2 Tbs. vodka
- 1 Tbs. Worcestershire sauce
- 2 tsp. puréed canned chipotle chile in adobo; more to taste
- ⅛ tsp. celery salt; more to taste

Finely grate the zest from the lemons and then juice them. Juice the lime. In a nonreactive bowl, mix 3 Tbs. of the lemon juice, 2 Tbs. of the lime juice, and all of the zest with the ketchup, chili sauce, horseradish, vodka, Worcestershire, chipotle, and celery salt until well combined.

The sauce can be refrigerated for up to a week. Add more horseradish, chipotle, lemon juice, or celery salt to taste before serving.

Note: Chipotles come canned in adobo sauce. The easiest way to use them is to purée the whole can and store the mixture in an airtight container in the refrigerator for up to 2 weeks or in the freezer for up to 3 months. Use a small amount to add a sweet, smoky heat to everything from this cocktail sauce to mayonnaise, soups, and stews.

These three delicious dipping sauces work well with any grilled shellfish. Pick your favorite or make them all.

old bay dipping sauce

The flavors of a classic shrimp boil are combined in one dynamite melted-butter dipping sauce.

Yields about 1 cup

- 8 oz. (1 cup) unsalted butter, cut into 16 pieces
- 1 Tbs. Old Bay Seasoning
- 1 Tbs. grated shallot (about 1 large shallot)

In a small saucepan, bring 3 Tbs. water to a simmer over medium heat. Reduce the heat to low. One piece at a time, whisk in the butter, waiting until each piece is completely incorporated before

Clockwise from top left: Old Bay Dipping Sauce, Orange-Saffron Aïoli, Bloody Mary Cocktail Sauce

adding the next. Once the consistency begins to change from watery to creamy, with a pale yellow hue (after 4 or 5 pieces of butter have been whisked in), emulsification has begun. At this point, you can add 2 or 3 pieces of butter at a time, making sure they are almost fully combined before adding more. **Whisk in the Old Bay** and shallot. Turn off the heat but leave the pan on the burner to let the flavors develop. Serve warm. This sauce can be made up to 2 hours ahead and kept in a warm spot.

orange-saffron aïoli

This sauce is tailor-made for grilled mussels, but it's good with other shellfish, too. Omit the olives if you want a more delicate flavor.

Yields about 1 cup

- 1 **large orange**
  Pinch saffron, threads crumbled
- 2 **large cloves garlic, roughly chopped or grated**
- 1 **tsp. Dijon mustard**
- 1 **large egg yolk**
- ½ **cup extra-virgin olive oil**
- ½ **cup vegetable oil; more as needed**
  Kosher salt
- ¼ **cup pitted and finely chopped Niçoise olives**

Finely grate the zest from half the orange and then juice the orange. Put 1½ Tbs. of the juice in a small bowl along with the saffron, and let sit for 10 minutes.

In a food processor, combine the saffron mixture, orange zest, garlic, and mustard and pulse until the garlic is puréed, about 15 seconds. Add the egg yolk and process for 10 seconds. With the machine running, slowly pour the olive oil and vegetable oil through the feed tube until the sauce is thick and well combined. (If you like a thicker texture, add a little more vegetable oil.) Season to taste with salt.

Refrigerate the aïoli for at least 2 hours to let the flavors marry. (The aïoli will keep for 1 week in the refrigerator.) Fold in the olives just before serving.

Note: This recipe contains a raw egg yolk; if that's a concern, use a pasteurized egg instead.

Elizabeth Karmel is the author of Soaked, Slathered, and Seasoned: A Complete Guide to Flavoring Food for the Grill. ◻

Watch a video on preparing lobsters for the grill at FineCooking.com/extras.

Cold Comfort

Take a childhood favorite (remember Popsicles?), add vodka (or bourbon or sparkling wine), and freeze. The result? The coolest new cocktail party of the summer.

BY GENEVIEVE KO

bellini pops

The combination of ripe summer peaches and Prosecco makes for a sweet frozen treat that tastes a lot like the popular cocktail.

Yields 10 pops

16	to 18 oz. ripe peaches (about 4 medium), peeled, pitted, and chopped
¾	cup granulated sugar
2¼	tsp. fresh lemon juice
1½	cups Prosecco

Stir the peaches, sugar, and lemon juice in a medium saucepan. Bring to a boil over high heat, reduce the heat to medium, and simmer, stirring frequently, until the mixture is thick and syrupy, 10 to 15 minutes. Most of the peaches will have broken down, with some softened chunks remaining.

Transfer the mixture to a blender and blend until smooth. Add the Prosecco and blend briefly to incorporate it. Let the mixture cool to room temperature and then refrigerate until cold.

Divide the mixture among ten 3-oz. pop molds or wax-lined paper cups and freeze until just barely set, about 1½ hours. Insert craft sticks and freeze until firm, at least 6 hours more. When ready to serve, unmold or peel off the paper cups. The pops can be frozen for up to 3 days.

For sources, see Where to Buy It

bittersweet chocolate-bourbon pops

Dark chocolate and bourbon make for a truly decadent treat.
Yields 8 pops

½	cup granulated sugar
3½	oz. bittersweet chocolate (70% to 72%), chopped
2	Tbs. Dutch-processed cocoa powder
⅛	tsp. table salt
2	Tbs. good-quality bourbon (like Knob Creek)

Put the sugar, chocolate, cocoa powder, salt, and 2 cups water in a large saucepan. Bring to a boil over medium heat, whisking constantly. Transfer to a 4-cup glass measure (or any container with a spout for easy pouring). Let cool at room temperature for 30 minutes.

Stir in the bourbon and divide the mixture among eight 3-oz. pop molds or wax-lined paper cups. Freeze until just set, about 3 hours. Insert craft sticks and freeze until completely set, about 4 hours more. When ready to serve, unmold or peel off the paper cups. The pops can be frozen for up to 3 days.

lemon-vodka cream pops

A splash of citron vodka gives the classic cream pop a decidedly adult kick.
Yields 8 pops

3	or 4 medium lemons
1	cup heavy cream
1	cup whole milk
½	cup granulated sugar
⅛	tsp. table salt
2	Tbs. citron vodka

Using a vegetable peeler, remove all of the zest from 3 of the lemons in 3- to 4-inch-long strips. Set the lemons aside.

Combine the lemon zest, cream, milk, sugar, and salt in a large saucepan. Bring to a simmer over medium heat, stirring occasionally to dissolve the sugar, about 5 minutes. Remove from the heat. Let steep at room temperature, stirring occasionally, for 20 minutes.

Squeeze ⅔ cup juice from the reserved lemons (juice the fourth lemon, if necessary). Stirring constantly, pour the lemon juice into the cream mixture in a slow stream. Stir in the vodka.

Strain the mixture through a fine sieve into a 4-cup glass measure (or any container with a spout for easy pouring), pressing on the solids to extract as much liquid as possible. Divide the mixture among eight 3-oz. pop molds or wax-lined paper cups. Freeze until just barely set, 5 to 6 hours. Insert craft sticks and freeze until completely set, about 2 hours more. When ready to serve, unmold or peel off the paper cups. The pops can be frozen for up to 3 days.

Genevieve Ko is the co-author, with Pichet Ong, of The Sweet Spot: Asian-Inspired Desserts. ◘

Play It Cool
TIPS TO CHILLY SUCCESS

Shape Almost any mold—from classic cylinders to whimsical rockets—will work. Or keep it simple and use small wax-lined paper cups, which peel off easily.

Freeze To ensure that the pops freeze firmly, make certain your freezer is set to 0°F.

Serve You can pile a colorful selection of ice pops on a platter and pass it, or serve them individually in glasses (which do a good job of catching drips).

Food styling by Brian Preston-Campbell

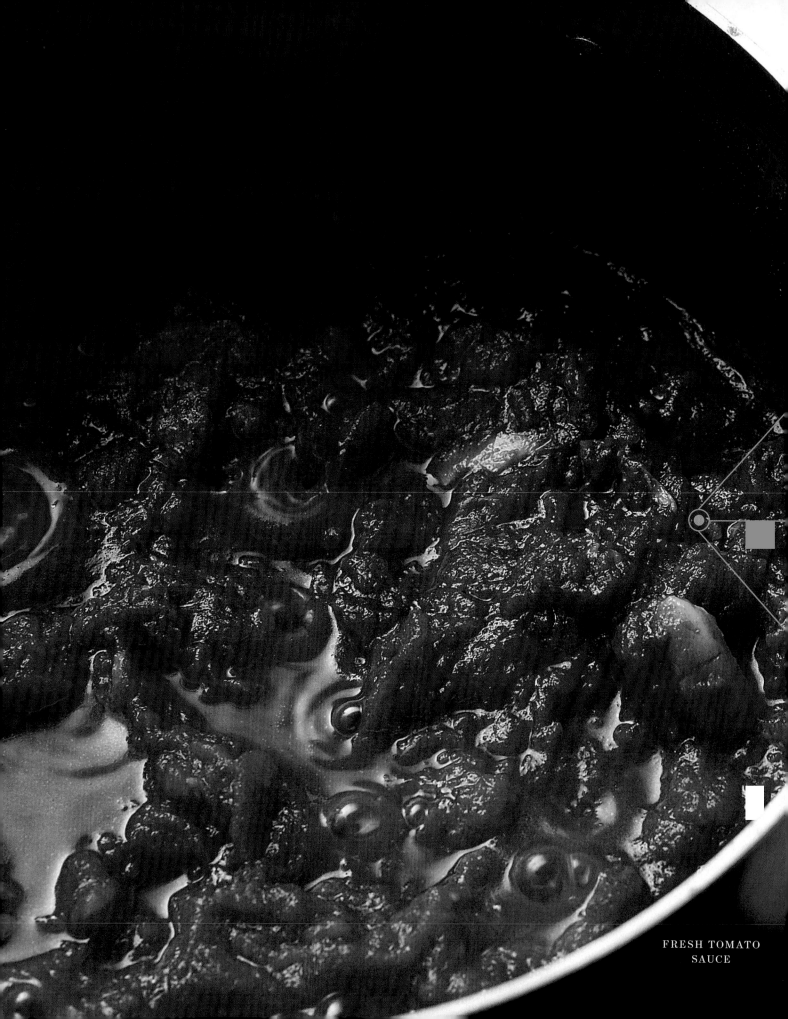

FRESH TOMATO
SAUCE

GREEK-SPICED
LAMB MEATBALLS
IN TOMATO SAUCE

CURRIED CHICKPEA
AND SUMMER
VEGETABLE STEW

GRILLED MUSHROOM
PIZZAS WITH
FRESH TOMATOES
AND ARUGULA

Get Saucy!

Turn those ripe-right-now tomatoes into a big pot of sauce; then make the most of it in three unexpected recipes.

BY DOMENICA MARCHETTI

I LOOK FORWARD to summer tomatoes the way some children feverishly anticipate Christmas morning, counting down the weeks until they appear at my farmers' market.

But just like a child surrounded with too many gifts, I admit to feeling a little overwhelmed by the bounty when tomato season is in full swing. I try my best to do right by them, serving tomatoes in salads, sandwiches, and savory tarts. But when all those red beauties start to overtake the counter, I pull out my biggest saucepan and get to work on a big batch of fresh tomato sauce.

The best tomatoes for sauce are Romas (also known as plum tomatoes), because they're meaty and have less water than other varieties. Once peeled and seeded, they cook into a richly flavored sauce in about an hour.

That big pot of sauce means some great weeknight meals. After I use some to top pasta for dinner the first night, it becomes the foundation for deeply flavored dishes like a curried stew loaded with summer vegetables, Greek-spiced lamb meatballs, and grilled pizzas topped with even more fresh tomatoes.

And because this sauce freezes so well, you can enjoy the essence of summer's flavors long after the last tomato plant has withered—insurance of the seasonal kind.

fresh tomato sauce

Yields about 8 cups sauce; serves 4, with leftovers

8	lb. ripe Roma tomatoes (about 40)
¼	cup extra-virgin olive oil
3	medium cloves garlic, crushed
2	tsp. kosher salt

Bring a large pot of water to a rolling boil. Rinse the tomatoes in cold water. With a paring knife, cut an X into the bottom of each tomato. (This will make it easier to peel the tomatoes once they're blanched.) Carefully lower about 10 tomatoes into the boiling water and leave them for 20 to 30 seconds. Use a slotted spoon to move them to a large bowl filled with ice water. Continue blanching the tomatoes in batches and transferring them to the ice water.

Use a paring knife and your fingers to remove the skin from the tomatoes—it should peel off easily. Cut the tomatoes lengthwise into quarters, core, and remove the seeds. Coarsely chop the tomatoes and transfer them to a bowl.

Heat the oil and the garlic in a 5- to 6-quart heavy-duty pot over medium-low heat until the garlic begins to sizzle and very lightly browns, 3 to 4 minutes. Carefully pour in the tomatoes. Raise the heat to medium high and bring the tomatoes to a boil. Stir in the salt, reduce the heat to medium, and let the sauce simmer, stirring occasionally, until the tomatoes have broken down and the sauce has thickened, about 1 hour. Remove from the heat and discard the garlic.

spaghetti with summer tomato sauce

Serve the sauce over pasta the first night and still have plenty left for the recipes on the following pages.

Serves 4

1	lb. dried spaghetti, or other pasta shape
	Kosher salt
2½	cups Fresh Tomato Sauce (recipe at left)
2	Tbs. chopped fresh basil leaves
	Freshly grated Parmigiano-Reggiano, for serving

Cook the pasta in boiling salted water according to package directions; drain. In a small saucepan, heat the tomato sauce over medium-low heat until just simmering. Off the heat, stir in the basil and salt to taste. Toss the pasta with the sauce and sprinkle with the Parmigiano.

Food styling by Michelli Knauer

Photographs by Scott Phillips

greek-spiced lamb meatballs in tomato sauce

Spice up the tomato sauce and you have a rich gravy in which to simmer fragrant lamb meatballs. Garnish with tangy feta and serve with a Greek salad and rice or pitas.

Yields 16 meatballs; serves 4

FOR THE MEATBALLS

	Nonstick cooking spray
1	cup fresh breadcrumbs, preferably sourdough
¼	cup low-fat milk
¾	lb. ground lamb, preferably shoulder meat
1	large egg, lightly beaten
2	Tbs. minced red onion
1	Tbs. minced fresh flat-leaf parsley
2	tsp. minced fresh oregano
1	tsp. minced garlic
½	tsp. dried mint
¼	tsp. ground cinnamon
¼	tsp. sweet paprika, preferably Hungarian
¼	tsp. ground allspice
	Kosher salt and freshly ground black pepper

FOR THE SAUCE

2	Tbs. extra-virgin olive oil
1	cup finely chopped red onion
2	tsp. finely chopped fresh oregano
1	fresh bay leaf
1	3-inch cinnamon stick
½	tsp. ground allspice
½	cup dry red wine
2	cups Fresh Tomato Sauce (recipe opposite)
	Kosher salt and freshly ground black pepper
4	oz. feta (preferably Greek), crumbled (scant 1 cup)

MAKE THE MEATBALLS

Heat the oven to 400°F and lightly coat a rimmed baking sheet with cooking spray. In a small bowl, combine the breadcrumbs and milk; let sit until the bread absorbs the milk, about 10 minutes.

Put the lamb in a medium bowl. Squeeze the excess milk out of the breadcrumbs and add them to the lamb. Add the egg, onion, parsley, oregano, garlic, mint, cinnamon, paprika, allspice, ½ tsp. salt, and a few grinds of pepper. With your hands or a rubber spatula, gently work the mixture together until thoroughly combined. Moisten your hands with cold water and shape the mixture into 16 balls (about the size of golf balls); arrange them on the baking sheet.

Bake the meatballs until cooked through and browned on top, 20 to 25 minutes.

MAKE THE SAUCE

Heat the oil in a large heavy-based saucepan over medium-low heat. Add the onion and cook, stirring frequently, until softened, about 8 minutes. Stir in the oregano, bay leaf, cinnamon stick, and allspice. Raise the heat to medium high and add the wine. Simmer for a minute or two until slightly reduced and then add the tomato sauce and ½ cup water. Bring the sauce to a boil and reduce the heat to medium low. Let the sauce cook at a gentle simmer, stirring occasionally, for 30 minutes. Add more water if it seems too thick.

Add the baked meatballs to the sauce, turning to coat them. Cover the pan partially and cook until the meatballs are heated through, about 5 minutes. Discard the bay leaf and cinnamon stick and season to taste with salt and pepper. Serve the meatballs and sauce sprinkled with the feta.

curried chickpea and summer vegetable stew

Transform the tomato sauce into an Indian-style vegetable stew that takes advantage of the season's bounty. Serve over basmati rice. You can also top it with the grilled chicken thighs on p. 89.

Serves 4 to 6

- 2 Tbs. peanut or vegetable oil
- 2 cups diced yellow onion
- 2 Tbs. minced fresh ginger
- 1 Tbs. minced garlic
- 1 medium eggplant, cut into ½-inch cubes (4 cups)
- 1 medium yellow summer squash, cut into ½-inch cubes (1¾ cups)
- 1 medium zucchini, cut into ½-inch cubes (1¼ cups)
  Kosher salt
- 1 tsp. garam masala
- ½ tsp. ground coriander
- ½ tsp. ground cumin
- ½ tsp. ground turmeric
- 1 small red hot chile, minced
  Freshly ground black pepper
- 1 15-oz. can chickpeas, with liquid
- 1½ cups Fresh Tomato Sauce (recipe on p. 56)
- 1 cup light coconut milk
- ¼ cup plus 2 Tbs. chopped fresh cilantro
- ¼ cup unsweetened shredded coconut, lightly toasted (optional)

Heat the oil in a large, deep skillet over medium heat until shimmering. Add the onion and cook, stirring frequently until soft and golden, about 15 minutes (reduce the heat to medium low, if necessary, to prevent the onion from burning). Stir in the ginger and garlic and cook for 2 minutes. Add the eggplant, yellow squash, zucchini, and ½ tsp. salt; stir to coat thoroughly. Cook over medium heat , stirring occasionally, until the vegetables are barely tender, 7 to 10 minutes.

Stir in the garam masala, coriander, cumin, turmeric, chile, 1 tsp. salt, and a few grinds of pepper. Cook until the spices are fragrant, 1 to 2 minutes. Pour in the chickpeas and their liquid, the tomato sauce, coconut milk, and 2 Tbs. of the cilantro.

Raise the heat to medium high and bring the stew to a boil. Reduce the heat to medium low and simmer, uncovered, until the eggplant and zucchini are completely tender but still hold their shape, and the sauce has thickened, 15 to 20 minutes.

To serve, ladle the stew into shallow rimmed bowls and sprinkle with the remaining ¼ cup cilantro and the toasted coconut (if using).

Fast Food

An easy dinner is guaranteed when you have a container's worth of this simple tomato sauce on hand. Here's how to keep it tasting great:

- Let cool and then transfer to an airtight container.
- Keep in the refrigerator for up to three days.
- Stash in the freezer for up to three months.

grilled mushroom, onion, and fontina pizzas with fresh tomatoes and arugula

To make the pizzas even faster, use refrigerated store-bought pizza dough. Before shaping, allow the dough to sit at room temperature until pliable, about 45 minutes.

Serves 4

- 1 recipe Pizza Dough (at right)
- 1½ cups Fresh Tomato Sauce (recipe on p. 56)
- 2 tsp. chopped fresh basil
- 4 large portobello mushroom caps, gills and stems removed
- 3 Tbs. extra-virgin olive oil; more for drizzling
  Kosher or sea salt and freshly ground black pepper
- 1 large red onion, sliced into ½-inch-thick disks
- 3 cups grated Fontina Val d'Aosta (9½ oz.)
- 2 medium yellow, purple, or orange tomatoes, sliced ¼ inch thick
- 2 cups baby arugula
- ½ cup loosely packed small fresh basil leaves
  Balsamic vinegar, for drizzling

Prepare a hot charcoal or gas grill fire. If using charcoal, spread the hot coals across half of the charcoal grate and leave the other half clear. If using gas, turn one of the burners to low to create a cooler zone. Scrub the grill grate with a wire brush and then wipe the grate with a paper towel dipped in oil.

While the grill is heating, shape the pizza dough. Put the dough on a lightly floured work surface. Knead it briefly to expel any air bubbles and then cut it into quarters. Cover 3 pieces with plastic wrap to prevent them from drying out. Using a rolling pin or your hands, flatten the dough into a 10-inch circle about ¼ inch thick. If at any point the dough resists rolling, set it aside to rest for a few minutes while you work another piece of dough.

Lightly dust a baking sheet with a little semolina or flour. Using your fingers, transfer the rolled-out dough to the baking sheet and cover with parchment. Repeat with the remaining 3 pieces of dough, shingling the dough between lightly dusted sheets of parchment. Cover the baking sheet with plastic wrap and refrigerate until ready to grill the pizzas.

Bring the tomato sauce to a simmer in a small pot over medium heat. Remove it from the heat and stir in the chopped basil. Keep warm.

When the grill is hot, brush the mushroom caps with 2 Tbs. of the olive oil and sprinkle with salt and pepper. Slide toothpicks or skewers horizontally into the onion disks to hold them together. Brush the disks with the remaining 1 Tbs. olive oil and season with salt and pepper. Arrange the mushrooms and onions on the hot side of the grill and cook until grill marks have formed, about 4 minutes. Flip and grill until they are well marked and tender, 3 to 4 minutes more for mushrooms,

1 minute more for onions (if the onions threaten to char, move them to the cool side of the grill). Let cool briefly, remove the skewers from the onions, and then coarsely chop the mushrooms and onions.

Have the pizza dough, sauce, toppings, and a clean baking sheet ready near the grill. Use your fingers to carefully transfer one of the dough rounds onto the grate over the hot part of the grill. Grill just until grill marks form on the bottom and the dough has begun to crisp and puff up a bit, about 2 minutes. (If you are able to fit 2 pizzas on the hot part of the grill at the same time, grill 2 at a time.) Using tongs and a wide spatula, move the crust, cooked side up, to the empty baking sheet. Spoon a thin layer of heated tomato sauce over the surface of the pizza. Scatter ¾ cup Fontina over the sauce, and then top with one-quarter of the mushrooms and onions.

Using tongs and a wide spatula, slide the pizza, raw side down, onto the cooler side of the grill. Cover and grill until the bottom is browned and crisped and the cheese has melted, 3 to 5 minutes. Using the tongs and spatula, transfer the pizza to a large dinner plate. Top with about 4 tomato slices and lightly season them with salt. Scatter about one-quarter of the arugula and basil over the pizza and drizzle with a little olive oil and balsamic vinegar.

Grill the remaining 3 pizzas in the same way, dividing the toppings evenly among them. Serve as soon as all of the pizzas have been grilled. (If you want the cooked pizzas to remain hot, put them in a 200°F oven as you finish them, but wait until just before serving to top with the tomatoes, arugula, and basil.)

PIZZA DOUGH

Yields about 1½ lb. dough

- 12½ oz. (2¾ cups) bread flour; more as needed
- 1¼ oz. (¼ cup) semolina flour; more for dusting
- 2 tsp. rapid-rise (instant) yeast
- 1½ tsp. fine sea salt
- 3 Tbs. extra-virgin olive oil; more for the bowl

Combine the bread flour, semolina, yeast, and sea salt in a food processor fitted with the metal blade. Pour 1 cup of cool water through the feed tube, pulsing as you pour. With the motor running, pour the oil through the feed tube and process until the dough comes together, about 1 minute.

Turn the dough out onto a clean work surface—you may or may not need to flour the surface, depending on how tacky the dough is. Knead the dough until it's smooth and elastic, about 2 minutes, and then gather it into a ball. Grease a large bowl with olive oil and put the dough in the bowl, turning to coat it with oil. Cover the bowl tightly with plastic wrap and leave in a warm place until the dough has doubled in size, 1½ to 2 hours.

Domenica Marchetti is a cooking teacher and cookbook author. Her most recent book is Big Night In: More Than 100 Wonderful Recipes for Feeding Family and Friends Italian-Style. ❑

Party
in the
Kitchen

Those who cook together, eat well together, especially when the menu's as fresh and fast as this one.

BY **ED SCHOENFELD**

WHEN IT COMES TO planning a party menu, I like delicious—it just has to taste good. And if the food's as much fun to make as it is to eat, guests will be happy helping out in the kitchen. That's my kind of party.

This is my kind of food, too—a modern mix of simple, fresh dishes with an Asian bent. The watermelon lemonade gets spiked with shochu, a Japanese (or sometimes Korean) spirit, while the pasta salad takes a new turn with snow peas, shiitake mushrooms, and sesame oil. A tasty twist on shrimp cocktail includes spicy mayo and crisp garlic breadcrumbs, and crunchy panko-breaded pork cutlets are topped with a Thai-inspired herb salad. Dessert is do-ahead (because your guests deserve a break by then): pineapple parfaits with mint, strawberries, and lychees. Like I said, easy and just a little exotic.

shochu watermelon lemonade

Shochu is a Japanese or Korean spirit typically distilled from barley, sweet potatoes, or rice. It has a light, slightly sweet, nutty flavor. You can substitute vodka, if you like.

Yields 8 cups; serves 8

- 4 cups peeled, seeded, and cubed watermelon (from about 4½ lb. unpeeled watermelon), plus thin wedges for garnish
- ¾ cup fresh lemon juice (from 4 or 5 lemons), plus thin lemon slices for garnish
- ¾ cup granulated sugar
- 1 cup shochu, chilled; more to taste

Purée the watermelon in a blender or food processor until smooth. Strain the purée through a fine sieve—you'll need 2 cups of watermelon juice. In a large bowl or pitcher, mix the watermelon juice, lemon juice, sugar, shochu, and 4 cups water until the sugar is dissolved. Refrigerate until well chilled, at least 2 hours and up to 6 hours.

When ready to serve, add more shochu to taste, if necessary. Serve in tall glasses filled with ice, garnished with a slice of lemon and a wedge of watermelon.

To drink

After cocktails, or with the meal, pour a Riesling with citrusy notes, like the Piesporter Goldtröpfchen Spätlese ($22). A smooth, mildly bitter lager such as Brooklyn Lager is a great beer option.

poached shrimp with spicy mayo and garlic breadcrumbs

To eat, guests dip each shrimp in the spicy mayo and then in the breadcrumbs.

Serves 8

- ½ cup vegetable oil
- 2½ Tbs. minced garlic
- 2 tsp. cornstarch
  Kosher salt
- 4 slices home-style white sandwich bread (such as Arnold or Pepperidge Farm)
- 1 Tbs. olive oil or melted butter
- 1 cup mayonnaise
- ⅓ cup finely chopped fresh cilantro
- ¼ cup finely chopped scallion
- 1 Tbs. minced jalapeño; more to taste
- 1 Tbs. fresh lime juice
- 2 lb. jumbo shrimp (16 to 20 per lb.), shelled, with tail segment left intact, and deveined

Make the breadcrumbs: Heat the vegetable oil in a small wok or saucepan over high heat until shimmering hot. In a small bowl, mix the garlic with the cornstarch and a pinch of salt. Put the garlic mixture in a fine sieve and shake to remove the excess cornstarch. Fry the garlic in the oil, stirring gently, until the garlic is light golden, about 1 minute. Immediately strain the garlic and oil through the sieve set over a bowl. Transfer the garlic to a paper-towel-lined plate, dab gently with paper towels to absorb excess oil, and let cool to room temperature. Reserve the garlic-flavored oil in the refrigerator for another use (such as vinaigrettes or grilled bread).

Heat the oven to 275°F. Pulse the bread in a food processor until the crumbs are uniform in size, 5 or 6 pulses. In a large bowl, mix the crumbs with the olive oil or butter until evenly coated. Transfer the crumbs to a rimmed baking sheet and bake, stirring once or twice, until golden brown, 20 to 30 minutes. Let the crumbs cool to room temperature. Transfer the crumbs to a medium, shallow serving bowl and stir in 1½ tsp. of the reserved fried garlic. Save the remaining garlic for the mayo.

Make the spicy mayo: In a small bowl, mix the mayonnaise, cilantro, scallion, jalapeño, lime juice, 1 tsp. salt, and the remaining 2 Tbs. fried garlic. Add more jalapeño and salt to taste. Transfer to a small serving bowl.

Cook the shrimp: Bring 7 cups of very well salted water to a boil in a 3-quart saucepan over high heat. Add the shrimp, stir once or twice, and poach until just cooked through, 1½ to 2 minutes (the water will not return to a boil). Drain the shrimp and let them cool for 10 minutes. Transfer the shrimp to a platter and serve them slightly warm or at room temperature with the mayo and breadcrumbs.

Make ahead: The breadcrumbs and mayo may be prepared up to 1 day ahead. Store separately in airtight containers; refrigerate the mayo.

Food styling by Michelli Knauer

Photographs by Scott Phillips

Start the party off right with addictive finger food and refreshing cocktails.

the dinner plan

- **2 days ahead:** Prepare the pineapple for the parfaits.
- **1 day ahead:** Make the spicy mayo and garlic breadcrumbs for the shrimp appetizer, and the dressing for the herb salad.
- **6 hours ahead:** Make the watermelon lemonade; toss the undressed herb salad.
- **4 hours ahead:** Bread the pork cutlets.
- **2 hours ahead:** Make the pasta salad.
- **1 hour ahead:** Macerate the strawberries.
- **Before serving:** Poach the shrimp; fry the pork cutlets; dress the herb salad; garnish the cocktails and parfaits.

Group cook: the more the merrier, and the faster dinner's done.

tonkatsu and mixed herb salad

Tonkatsu is a classic Japanese dish in which a thin pork cutlet is breaded and fried. It's typically served with shredded green cabbage, but here it's topped with a fresh herb salad (see recipe, opposite).

Serves 8

- 2½ lb. boneless center-cut pork loin, trimmed
- 2 medium cloves garlic, lightly crushed
  Kosher salt and freshly ground black pepper
- 1½ cups all-purpose flour
- 3 large eggs
- 3 Tbs. vegetable oil; more for frying
- 3 cups panko (Japanese breadcrumbs)
- 1 recipe Mixed Herb Salad with Honey-Lime Dressing (recipe opposite)

Heat the oven to 200°F.

Slice the pork into 16 equal pieces. Lay a sheet of plastic wrap over a piece of pork and pound until it's about ¼ inch thick. With a sharp knife, make tiny incisions at 2-inch intervals around the edge of the cutlet (this will help prevent it from curling as it cooks). Repeat with the remaining pork.

Rub both sides of each cutlet with the crushed garlic and then season generously with salt and pepper.

Put the flour in a wide, shallow bowl. Put the eggs in another wide, shallow bowl and beat them lightly with 3 Tbs. water, the oil, and ¾ tsp. salt. Put the panko in a third wide, shallow bowl. Working with one cutlet at a time, dredge the pork in the flour and then the egg mixture, shaking to remove excess. Dredge in the panko,

pressing the crumbs into the cutlet to help them adhere. As the cutlets are coated, transfer them to a rimmed baking sheet.

In a large, deep, straight-sided sauté pan (a cast-iron skillet works well), heat about ¼ inch of oil over medium-high heat until shimmering hot. Working in batches, cook 3 cutlets at a time, flipping once, until golden brown and cooked through, 2 to 3 minutes per side. Drain the cutlets on a paper-towel-lined baking sheet and keep warm in the oven until all of the pork is cooked.

Portion the cutlets among 8 dinner plates and mound the Mixed Herb Salad with Honey-Lime Dressing on top.

Make ahead: The cutlets can be breaded up to 4 hours ahead. Refrigerate until ready to fry.

MIXED HERB SALAD WITH HONEY-LIME DRESSING

A riff on the cabbage slaw traditionally served with tonkatsu, this salad goes the extra flavor mile with lots of fresh herbs, crunchy vegetables, and a tangy Thai-inspired dressing.

Serves 8

FOR THE SALAD

- 4 cups mixed mesclun greens
- 2 cups coarsely chopped bibb lettuce
- 1 cup very thinly sliced green cabbage
- 1 cup fresh basil leaves, preferably Thai basil, large leaves coarsely torn
- 1 cup fresh mint leaves
- 1 cup fresh cilantro leaves, coarsely chopped
- 4 small scallions (white and green parts), sliced into 1-inch lengths
- 1 cup cherry or grape tomatoes, halved
- ½ cup very thinly sliced red onion
- ½ cup very thinly sliced red bell pepper

FOR THE DRESSING

- 2½ Tbs. fresh lime juice
- 2½ Tbs. honey
- 2 tsp. fish sauce
- ⅛ tsp. minced garlic
- 2 Tbs. thinly sliced fresh red or green chile or both (optional)
  Kosher salt and freshly ground black pepper

MAKE THE SALAD

In a large bowl, combine the mesclun, lettuce, cabbage, basil, mint, cilantro, scallions, tomatoes, onion, and bell pepper.

MAKE THE DRESSING

In a small bowl, whisk the lime juice, honey, fish sauce, garlic, and chile, if using. Season to taste with salt and pepper.

Just before serving, toss the salad mixture with just enough of the dressing to coat the salad lightly—you may not need all of the dressing.

Make ahead: You can combine, cover, and refrigerate the salad ingredients up to 6 hours ahead. The dressing can be made up to 1 day ahead.

Clockwise from top left: Mixed Herb Salad with Honey-Lime Dressing; Sesame, Snow Pea, and Shiitake Pasta Salad; and Tonkatsu.

pineapple, strawberry, and lychee parfaits

Crushed fresh pineapple infused with mint serves as a refreshing base for summer berries and lychees in this cool parfait. (For more on lychees, see Test Kitchen, p. 81.) The leftover pineapple syrup would be great in rum cocktails or mixed with seltzer for a nonalcoholic drink.

Serves 6 to 8

- 2 medium ripe pineapples (about 3 lb. each)
- ¾ cup plus 2 Tbs. granulated sugar
- ½ cup small fresh mint sprigs; more for garnish
- 4 cups ripe strawberries, hulled, halved lengthwise if large
- 16 fresh lychees, shelled and pitted, or one 20-oz. can lychees, drained, rinsed, and halved lengthwise if large

Trim the pineapples and quarter them lengthwise. Cut away the cores and rinds of each quarter and cut the pineapple into 1½-inch pieces. Working in batches, pulse the pineapple in a food processor until crushed or about the size of grains of rice (it's fine if a few pieces are larger or smaller).

In a large nonreactive saucepan, bring ¾ cup of the sugar and 2 cups of water to a boil over high heat. Add the pineapple and let the mixture return to a hard boil. With a spoon, skim away and discard any foam that rises to the surface. Boil for 1 minute and then remove the pan from the heat. Add the mint sprigs and let the mixture cool to room temperature. Remove and discard the mint. Cover and refrigerate until well chilled, at least 4 hours and up to 2 days.

One hour before serving, in a small bowl, mix the strawberries with the remaining 2 Tbs. sugar and refrigerate.

To serve, drain the liquid from the pineapple in a sieve set over a bowl. Divide the pineapple into clear glasses, saving the syrup for another use. Top with the strawberries and lychees and garnish with a sprig of fresh mint.

Ed Schoenfeld is a chef, restaurant consultant, and Chinese food expert based in Brooklyn, New York. ❑

sesame, snow pea, and shiitake pasta salad

Two kinds of green peas, sesame, ginger, and soy give this earthy pasta salad bold flavor.

Serves 8

Kosher salt
- ½ lb. dried rolled, tubular pasta (such as cavatelli or strozzapreti)
- ½ cup frozen baby green peas
- 40 fresh snow peas (4 to 5 oz.), trimmed
- 3 Tbs. vegetable oil
- 1 cup thinly sliced yellow onion
- ½ lb. shiitake mushrooms, stemmed and sliced ¼ inch thick (about 3 cups)
- 1 tsp. minced garlic
- 1 tsp. minced fresh ginger
  Freshly ground black pepper
- 4 tsp. soy sauce
- 1 Tbs. rice vinegar
- 2 tsp. Asian sesame oil
- ¼ tsp. granulated sugar
- ½ cup thinly sliced scallions (white and green parts)
- 2 Tbs. toasted white sesame seeds

Bring a large pot of well-salted water to a boil over high heat. Add the pasta and cook until barely al dente, about 1 minute less than package timing. Add the green peas and cook for about 30 seconds. Add the snow peas, stir, and immediately drain the vegetables and pasta in a colander set in the sink. Rinse with cool water to stop the cooking. Drain well, toss with 1 Tbs. of the vegetable oil, and set aside.

Heat 1 Tbs. of the vegetable oil in a 12-inch skillet over medium heat. Add the onion, shiitake, garlic, ginger, ½ tsp. salt, and a few grinds of pepper. Cook, stirring occasionally, until the onions are opaque and the mushrooms have released their juices, 3 to 4 minutes—don't let the vegetables brown. Remove the pan from the heat, transfer the vegetables and any juices to a small bowl, and let cool to room temperature.

In another small bowl, whisk the remaining 1 Tbs. vegetable oil with the soy sauce, vinegar, sesame oil, and sugar.

In a large bowl, combine the cooled pasta and vegetables, scallions, and 1 Tbs. of the sesame seeds. Toss with the dressing and season to taste with salt and pepper. Serve at room temperature, garnished with the remaining sesame seeds.

Make ahead: You can prepare the salad up to 2 hours ahead.

Get a shopping list for this menu at FineCooking.com/extras.

MAKE YOUR OWN
FETA

From curds to whey and where they separate—
a step-by-step guide to a classic Mediterranean
cheese. BY BONNIE GORDER-HINCHEY

NOTHING COMPARES to the fresh taste of homemade cheese. And tangy, rich feta is one of the easiest to make at home. It's also an excellent "summer" cheese, the perfect partner to all those ripe tomatoes and gorgeous cucumbers available now.

Traditionally made with sheep's milk, feta is equally delicious when made from store-bought cow's milk. What gives it the distinctive sharp taste and crumbly texture is a week or more spent soaking, or aging, in a brine. Once you get your first taste of homemade feta, you'll agree it was worth the wait.

To understand the science behind cheesemaking, it's helpful to remember that it began as a way of preserving milk. You start by encouraging milk to curdle so that you can separate the solid portion (the curds) from the liquid (the whey). Rennet, a natural enzyme, is added to cause curdling. You also add live cultures

here in the form of yogurt—these "eat" the milk sugar (lactose) and produce an acid that lowers the milk's pH. That acidic environment, along with heat, helps the rennet curdle the milk.

Once the milk coagulates, you cut into it to let the whey flow out. The remaining whey is drained off by hanging the curd in cheesecloth for 24 hours at room temperature. Once drained, the cheese will have re-formed into a solid mass, ready to be cut into cubes and then sprinkled with salt to draw out any remaining whey. After three days, the cheese is put into a brine and aged for one to four weeks in the refrigerator.

Although the cheese is ready to eat after one week, longer aging results in firmer, saltier, and more flavorful feta. When you make your own, you control the flavor and intensity of the tang, so you can make a feta that's your idea of "just right."

homemade feta

To achieve the correct level of saltiness, be sure to weigh the salt; for more on this, see Test Kitchen, p. 81. Before starting, it's important to read the safety tips on p. 74. To learn more about lipase, calcium chloride, and rennet, see p. 74 as well.

Yields 1¼ lb.

FOR THE CHEESE

- ½ cup plain low-fat yogurt with live cultures
- 1 gallon whole pasteurized milk
- ¼ tsp. lipase powder, preferably calf
- ¾ tsp. calcium chloride
- ¼ tsp. liquid rennet
- 1½ oz. kosher salt (6 Tbs. if using Diamond Crystal; 3 Tbs. if using Morton)

FOR THE BRINE

- 2 oz. kosher salt (½ cup if using Diamond Crystal; ¼ cup if using Morton)

DAY 1: MAKE THE CHEESE CURD

Sterilize all the equipment you will need for this first day of work (see Safety First, p. 74). Clean all counters with hot soapy water or an antibacterial wipe.

In a small bowl, mix the yogurt with ½ cup of the milk.

In a deep 8- to 10-quart pot, heat the remaining milk over medium-low heat, stirring occasionally with a slotted spoon, until it registers 90°F on an instant-read thermometer, 10 to 12 minutes. Stir in the yogurt mixture. Turn off the heat (leave the pot on the burner), cover, and let sit for 45 minutes.

Meanwhile, in a small bowl with a soupspoon, stir the lipase with ¼ cup water until blended—it doesn't matter if the lipase stays a little lumpy. Let sit for 20 minutes. Stir in the calcium chloride and rennet until the mixture is smooth and blended.

Turn the burner under the milk mixture to medium low, add the lipase mixture and stir with a slotted spoon for 1 minute. Stop the movement of the milk with the spoon and hold a thermometer in the center of the milk—the temperature should be at least 96°F; if necessary, continue heating until it comes up to temperature.

Remove the thermometer, turn off the heat, cover the pot, and let sit undisturbed until the curd is firm and has a clean "cleave," 1 to 3 hours. To determine a clean cleave, wash your hands with soap and hot water and insert a finger (or a sterilized spoon) 1 inch diagonally into the curd and pull straight up. If the cleave is clean, the curd will split with sharp edges and whey will start to fill the split **1**.

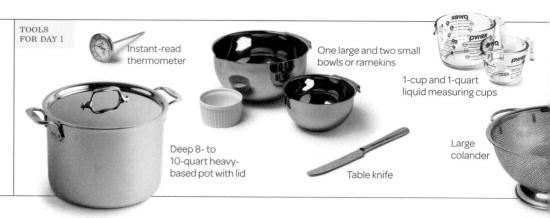

A Cheesemaker's Tool Box

It takes five days to ready the feta for brining. All tools must be sterilized to prevent unwanted bacteria from contaminating the cheese. **(To learn how to sterilize your equipment, see page 74.)** Here are the tools you'll need each day. All tools should be heatproof.

TOOLS FOR DAY 1

Instant-read thermometer

One large and two small bowls or ramekins

1-cup and 1-quart liquid measuring cups

Deep 8- to 10-quart heavy-based pot with lid

Table knife

Large colander

Photographs by Scott Phillips

CUT THE CURD

With a table knife, cut the curd all the way to the bottom of the pot in a ½-inch crosshatch pattern **2**. Turn the heat to low and heat for 5 minutes. Stir the curd with the slotted spoon and insert a thermometer; it should read at least 96°F. If not, continue heating, stirring occasionally, until the curds come up to temperature, increasing the heat to medium low, if necessary.

Turn off the heat, cover the pot, and let sit for 1 hour, stirring every 10 minutes to break up large chunks.

DRAIN THE CURD

Set a large colander over a large bowl and line it with 2 layers of cheesecloth. Pour the curd into the strainer and drain off the whey for 30 minutes **3**. Put 1 quart of the whey in a sterile 1-quart liquid measuring cup, cover, and set aside at room temperature.

Gather the ends of the cheesecloth and tie them loosely at the top of the curd **4**; then tie them around a long spoon or several chopsticks. Hang the bag inside the pot at room temperature for 24 hours **5**, loosely covering the top with plastic wrap. After 24 hours, you should feel a firm, solid mass of curds; if not, let the curd hang for another few hours and check again for firmness.

DAY 2: SALT THE FETA

Sterilize the equipment you'll need for this day of work. Clean all counters with hot soapy water or an antibacterial wipe. Untie the cheesecloth and transfer the feta to a cutting board.

Cut the feta into 2- to 3-inch pieces. If you see small, uniform, round holes throughout the cheese when you cut it, and it feels spongy, that means undesirable bacteria

have contaminated it and you should throw it out. Otherwise, arrange the squares in a single layer in a sterile shallow container with a tight-fitting lid. Sprinkle about ½ oz. salt over all sides of the cheese **6**. Cover and let sit at room temperature for 3 days. Turn the feta daily and resalt with ½ oz. salt on days 3 and 4. Each day, pour off the whey as it collects in the bottom of the container.

DAY 5: BRINE THE FETA

Sterilize a 3-quart covered container. Transfer the cheese pieces to the container—it's fine to stack them at this point. Stir the 2 oz. kosher salt into the 1 quart of reserved whey until it is dissolved. Pour this brine over the cheese, covering it completely. Cover and refrigerate for 1 to 4 weeks. The longer the feta is aged, the stronger the flavor and crumblier the texture will be.

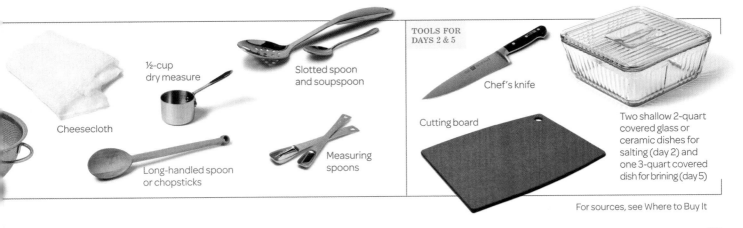

Cheesecloth

½-cup dry measure

Long-handled spoon or chopsticks

Slotted spoon and soupspoon

Measuring spoons

TOOLS FOR DAYS 2 & 5

Chef's knife

Cutting board

Two shallow 2-quart covered glass or ceramic dishes for salting (day 2) and one 3-quart covered dish for brining (day 5)

For sources, see Where to Buy It

Timeline: Making Feta

Making your own feta does take time, but much of it is hands off. Here's how you get from a gallon of milk to 1¼ lb. of cheese in less than two weeks (longer for a more intense cheese).

DAY 1	DAY 2	DAY 5	DAY 12

Mix ingredients and heat. Let sit until the curd firms. Cut, heat, and rest the curds again, then drain in cheesecloth for 24 hours.

Untie the cheesecloth and cut the feta into pieces. Salt and let sit at room temperature for three days.

Pour the brine over the cheese and let age for a week.

After a week, the feta is ready to taste. For a firmer, saltier cheese, continue to age it for up to three more weeks.

Cheese Science

Making your own cheese requires a few specialty ingredients: rennet, lipase, and calcium chloride. All are readily available online at sites like cheesemaking.com or thecheesemaker.com. Here's what each is and what it does:

Rennet An enzyme that sets, or curdles, the milk so that it becomes solid. Sold in liquid or tablet form, it must be kept refrigerated or it will lose its potency. Traditionally, rennet comes from the stomach of a calf, lamb, or goat, but today there are vegetarian versions available. All have the same coagulating ability.

Lipase An enzyme derived from animals that breaks down milk fat and creates feta's distinctive taste. Calf lipase produces the mildest flavor, while lamb lipase is used for the sharpest cheeses, such as Romano. It's sold in powder form.

Calcium Chloride Because pasteurization removes calcium from processed milk, you must add calcium chloride to aid coagulation. It is sold in liquid form and is necessary for a firm curd.

Safety First

Cheesemaking relies on good bacteria (the kind found in yogurt) as a preservative. But there are other types of bacteria you need to watch out for, to avoid illness. Basic home sanitizing measures can eliminate much of the danger. Follow these steps:

Clean counters with antibacterial wipes and wash your hands thoroughly before beginning (and throughout the process, as necessary).

Sterilize all equipment, in one of three ways:

1. Wash in hot, soapy water, rinse, and then submerge in boiling water for at least 10 minutes.
2. Steam by putting an inch of water in the bottom of a large pot, adding the equipment, covering the pot tightly, and boiling for 10 minutes. (If the cover doesn't fit, put aluminum foil over it to trap the steam.)
3. Use the sanitize setting on your dishwasher.

Do not use bleach in cleaning the equipment, as this can interfere with the chemistry of cheesemaking.

If at any point in the making or aging process you see small, uniform, round holes throughout the cheese, and it feels spongy, throw it out.

Details on food safety practices are available on the United States Food and Drug Administration's Web site at www.cfsan.fda.gov.

Bonnie Gorder-Hinchey is a food scientist and culinary consultant based in Seattle. ❑

 Take a feta-making class at FineCooking.com/extras.

The Cheese Plate

3 EASY IDEAS

- Top feta with extra-virgin olive oil and serve with olives and crusty bread (pictured).
- Drizzle feta with honey and cracked black peppercorns; serve with crackers.
- Dress feta with fresh herbs and lemon juice and bake at 375°F until golden on top; spread on crusty bread.

Eggplant Parmigiana

The real-deal Italian classic takes on a chef's rustic reinvention. May the best version win. **BY LAURA GIANNATEMPO AND MIKEY PRICE**

the classic...

Southern Exposure
It's commonly believed that eggplant parmigiana originated in southern Italy (Naples, to be precise), where eggplant is widely cultivated.

Bread Not
No breading in this parmigiana. In Italy, the eggplant slices are fried quickly in hot olive oil.

Slim Down
Forget big, chewy chunks of eggplant. To create slender, delicate layers for a lighter, more elegant dish, peel the eggplant and cut it into thin slices.

Say Cheese
Parmigiano-Reggiano is a key ingredient (it gives the dish its name after all). Made around Parma from raw cow's milk, it's a rich, hard cheese that's aged for at least 12 months.

Food styling by Michelli Knauer

Photographs by Scott Phillips

IF YOU THINK YOU KNOW EGGPLANT PARMIGIANA, think again. *Fine Cooking* associate editor and Italian native Laura Giannatempo gave us the definitive classic— a surprisingly lighter dish than most Americans are used to, since it skips the expected breading of the eggplant. Mikey Price, chef at New York's seasonally driven Market Table, contributed the competition: an addictive first course that features breadcrumb-coated zucchini ribbons rolled around an eggplant filling. It's going to be one tasty showdown.

...the update

Med Fusion
Eggplant parmigiana meets fried zucchini in an all-Italian celebration of the harvest season.

On a Roll
No layers here. Instead, thin zucchini ribbons create the perfect wrap.

Inside Story
It's inside the roll where eggplant marries with tomato sauce and Parmigiano-Reggiano to create the essence of eggplant parmigiana.

Nuts and Bolts
Toasted pine nuts mixed with the eggplant filling and sprinkled on top add a welcome textural variation.

"This is how we do it in Italy: no breading and no puddles of cheese, just thin layers of fried eggplant with homemade sauce, a little fresh mozzarella, and good Parmigiano-Reggiano. It doesn't get more authentic than this."

the classic...
eggplant parmigiana

Serves 6 as a first course; 4 as a main course

FOR THE EGGPLANT

2½ lb. eggplant (about 4 small or 2 medium-large)

Kosher salt

3 cups olive oil (or a blend of olive and canola oils)

FOR THE SAUCE

3 Tbs. extra-virgin olive oil

2 large cloves garlic, peeled and cut in half

3½ lb. plum tomatoes, peeled, seeded, and coarsely chopped, or two 28-oz. cans diced tomatoes (preferably San Marzano), drained

Kosher salt

12 large fresh basil leaves, torn in half

FOR ASSEMBLING

6 oz. fresh mozzarella, torn into ½-inch pieces

1¼ cups lightly packed freshly grated Parmigiano-Reggiano (3¼ oz.)

Salt the eggplant: Peel the eggplant and cut each crosswise into ¼-inch-thick slices. Cover the bottom and sides of a large colander with a few eggplant slices and sprinkle generously with salt. Top with more layers of eggplant and salt until you run out of slices (you'll end up with five or six layers). Let the colander sit in the sink or over a large bowl for at least 30 minutes and up to 2 hours.

The salt will draw out water and reduce the eggplant's ability to absorb oil.

Meanwhile, make the sauce: Heat the 3 Tbs. oil in a 10-inch skillet over medium heat. Add the garlic and cook until fragrant and barely golden, 1 to 2 minutes. Add the tomatoes and ½ tsp. salt. Raise the heat to medium high and cook, stirring occasionally, until the tomatoes begin to break down into a sauce, 20 to 25 minutes. If the sauce begins to dry up before the tomatoes break down, add warm water 1 Tbs. at a time. Lower the heat to medium and continue cooking, stirring occasionally, until you have a thick, chunky sauce, 5 to 10 minutes more. (Too much liquid in the sauce will make the finished dish watery.) Turn off the heat, remove the garlic, and stir in the basil leaves. Season to taste with more salt, if necessary, and set aside.

Fry the eggplant: Dry the eggplant by lining a large plate with a paper towel and setting a few slices on it. Top with another paper towel and layer on a few more slices. Repeat until you run out of slices.

Attach a candy thermometer to the side of a 3- or 4-quart saucepan. Add the olive oil and heat over medium-high heat. When the oil reaches 375°F, add as many eggplant slices as will fit comfortably in a single layer. Don't crowd the pan. If you don't have a candy thermometer, you can test the oil temperature by dipping a tip of one eggplant slice in the oil. If it immediately sizzles, the oil is ready.

Cook, turning once, until golden brown on both sides, about 2 minutes on the first side and 1 minute more on the second. Working quickly, pick up each slice with a slotted spoon and press the back of another large spoon against the slice to squeeze out as much oil as possible. Transfer to a plate lined with paper towels. Repeat until all the slices are fried, layering the fried eggplant between paper towels and adjusting the heat as necessary to maintain the frying temperature.

Assemble and bake: Position a rack in the center of the oven and heat the oven to 450°F.

Layer about one-third of the eggplant slices so they overlap slightly on the bottom of a 10x8-inch (or similar size) baking dish. With the back of a spoon or an offset spatula, spread about one-third of the tomato sauce in a very thin layer over the eggplant. Evenly sprinkle about half of the mozzarella and ⅓ cup of the Parmigiano over the tomato sauce. Make another layer with one-third of the eggplant, one-third of the tomato sauce, the remaining mozzarella, and ⅓ cup Parmigiano. Make one last layer with the remaining eggplant, tomato sauce, and Parmigiano. Bake until the cheese has melted evenly and the top is bubbly, with browned edges, 20 to 25 minutes. Let rest for at least 15 minutes before serving.

 Which version is your favorite? Go to FineCooking.com/extras and let us know.

...the update

eggplant parmigiana rolls with pine nuts and baby arugula

Serves 8 as an appetizer

- 4½ Tbs. plus ½ cup extra-virgin olive oil
- ½ medium yellow onion, cut into medium dice
- 1 clove garlic, chopped
- 3 cups peeled, seeded, and chopped fresh plum tomatoes (6 to 8 tomatoes)
  Kosher salt and freshly ground black pepper
- 2 Tbs. pitted and very coarsely chopped Kalamata or Niçoise olives
- 1 Tbs. capers, rinsed and coarsely chopped if large
- 1 Tbs. plus ½ cup vegetable oil
- 1 baby (Italian) eggplant (about ½ lb.) or ½ small regular eggplant, cut into large dice (2½ cups)
- 2 Tbs. finely grated Parmigiano-Reggiano
- 2 Tbs. toasted pine nuts
- 2 Tbs. fresh lemon juice (from 1 lemon)
- 1 Tbs. thinly sliced fresh basil
- 3 small zucchini (about 1 lb. total)
- 2 cups panko
- ½ cup all-purpose flour
- 2 large eggs, beaten
- 5 oz. baby arugula (6 lightly packed cups)
- ¼ cup shaved Parmigiano-Reggiano

Heat 1 Tbs. olive oil in a 3-quart saucepan over medium heat. Add the onion and garlic and cook until soft and slightly browned, about 3 minutes. Add the tomatoes, ¼ tsp. salt, and a grind of pepper and simmer, stirring frequently, until the tomatoes cook down to a dry sauce, 20 to 25 minutes, reducing the heat to medium low if necessary. Off the heat, stir in the olives, capers, ½ Tbs. olive oil, and salt and pepper to taste.

Heat 1 Tbs. each olive oil and vegetable oil in a 12-inch skillet over high heat. Add the eggplant and cook, stirring occasionally, until tender and well browned on several sides, 3 to 5 minutes. Transfer to a bowl and cool to room temperature.

To the eggplant, add the finely grated Parmigiano, 1 Tbs. of the pine nuts, 1 Tbs. lemon juice, the basil, and about half of the tomato sauce. Season to taste with salt and pepper.

Using a mandoline, slice the zucchini lengthwise about ⅛ inch thick. Select the 24 widest, longest slices and arrange them in a single layer on paper towels. Sprinkle lightly with salt and let sit until pliable, about 3 minutes—you can shingle the layers of zucchini between paper towels to save space. Pat dry. Arrange 3 slices of zucchini on a work surface, overlapping them lengthwise. Spread a heaping tablespoon of the eggplant mixture near one end of the zucchini ribbons and roll the zucchini around the filling to make a roll. Set aside, seam side down, and repeat with the remaining ingredients to make 8 rolls total. You may not need all the filling.

Put the panko, flour, and eggs in 3 shallow bowls. Lightly coat each roll in the flour, then dip it in the eggs, and coat in the bread-crumbs—it's fine if it isn't perfectly coated.

Heat the ½ cup olive oil and ½ cup vegetable oil in a 10-inch straight-sided sauté pan over medium heat. Working in two batches, fry the rolls until golden brown on all sides, 2 to 3 minutes per side. As each batch finishes, transfer to a paper-towel-lined plate and sprinkle lightly with salt.

While the rolls cook, reheat the remaining sauce in a small saucepan, adding about ¼ cup water, or enough to thin to a wet sauce.

Whisk the remaining 2 Tbs. olive oil and 1 Tbs. lemon juice in a small bowl. Toss the arugula with the dressing and season to taste with salt and pepper. Serve the rolls topped with the sauce, remaining pine nuts, and shaved Parmigiano, with the salad on the side.

Laura Giannatempo is the author of A Ligurian Kitchen: Recipes and Tales from the Italian Riviera. *Mikey Price is working on his first cookbook.* ❏

MIKEY SAID,

"I just plain don't like traditional eggplant parmigiana. But I do like the breading and frying part, so I kept that and changed everything else to make it fresher and more modern."

TEST KITCHEN

Tips/Techniques/Equipment/Ingredients/Glossary

Fresh lychees are a breeze to peel. To learn more about this exotic fruit, turn to page 82.

Lychee fruit

BENEATH THE SCALY SKIN of the lychee lies a delicate, juicy, fragrant fruit wrapped around a hard, inedible pit. With a sweet perfumed flavor and a texture a bit like a peeled grape, lychees (or litchis) are prized in many Asian countries, particularly China.

Lychees are readily available in cans, but if you see some fresh ones at the market—Asian markets are a great place to look—don't pass up the chance to try them. They're available from May to September.

Choose lychees that feel heavy for their size, with brittle, unblemished, reddish-pink to pinkish-brown skin. Store at room temperature for a few days, or in a plastic bag in the fridge for about two weeks.

Lychees are easy to peel—just pull the skin away with your fingernails. If eating out of hand, you can pop the peeled fruit into your mouth and spit out the pit, but if you need pitted lychees for a dessert like the Pineapple, Strawberry, and Lychee Parfaits on page 69, treat them as you would a peach: Run a paring knife around the pit to halve the fruit and then pry the halves from the pit.

—*Jennifer Armentrout*

Lobster 101

Unless you grew up near the New England shore, preparing and cracking a lobster may not be second nature. Here's what you need to know to become a lobster pro.

KILLING THE LOBSTER

No matter how you plan to cook your lobster, you should kill it first. While it's tempting to skip the execution part and just boil the live lobster—it'll die as it cooks, after all—that's a slow and cruel death. Here's the most humane way to quickly dispatch a lobster before cooking:

Chill the lobster in the freezer for 20 minutes—this numbs it and slows down its movements, making it safer to work with. Set the lobster on its back on a cutting board. Position the tip of a chef's knife in the middle of the lobster just below the claws, with the cutting edge facing the lobster's head (shown below).

In one swift motion, forcefully insert the point of the knife into the lobster and then chop down through the head, splitting it in half—this kills the lobster quickly. It isn't necessary to cut completely through the shell on the top of the head, and if you don't, the cooked lobster will look more appealing. The lobster may continue to move a bit, so cut off the rubber bands that bind the claws only after it has been cooked.

EATING THE LOBSTER

To eat the cooked lobster, you'll need a knife, a lobster cracker or nutcracker, and a seafood fork or pick.

A The knuckles and claws
1. Separate the knuckles and claws from the body in one piece by twisting them off or cutting with a knife. Separate the knuckles and claws at each joint.

2. Use a cracker to break open each piece. Remove the nuggets of meat with a seafood fork or pick.

B The tail
1. Twist the tail off the body of the lobster. If the lobster is female, you might get the bonus of bright red roe, which is edible. The greenish substance between the tail and body is the liver and pancreas, called the tomalley. Many consider it a delicacy, but toxins can be concentrated in it, and several public health agencies caution against eating it. If any sticks to the tail meat, wipe or rinse it off.

A

2. Bend the tail fins upward until they snap off. Check the fins for any morsels of meat to pick out.

3. Use a finger or a fork to push the tail meat out of the shell.

4. Make a shallow incision down the center top of the tail to expose the vein-like intestinal tract (it may be dark or clear). Flick out the tract with the knife tip, just as you would devein a shrimp.

B

C **The legs**

1. Snap the smaller legs off the body.

2. Pick out any morsels of meat from the body where the legs were. To get the bits of meat from the legs, bite down on a leg to loosen the meat, and then squeeze and suck the meat out between your teeth.

—*Melissa Pellegrino and Jennifer Armentrout*

TECHNIQUE

How to dice a mango

MANGOS CONTAIN A LARGE, FLAT SEED that doesn't separate readily from the juicy flesh, so the easiest way to handle a mango is to cut the flesh away from the seed. Mango flesh can be slippery, so leaving the skin on will help you get a grip.

INGREDIENT

Measuring kosher salt

Most of our recipes call for kosher salt by the teaspoon, but you might have noticed that our feta recipe on page 72 calls for the salt by weight. The reason for this is simple but important: From brand to brand, equal weights of kosher salt may not measure the same by volume. In the photo below you can see that 2 ounces of Morton salt is exactly ¼ cup, but 2 ounces of Diamond Crystal overflows an identical measuring cup. That 2 ounces actually fills a ½ cup measure perfectly. Why? Because Morton's crystals are denser than Diamond Crystal's.

When a recipe calls for a relatively small amount of salt, this distinction isn't very noticeable. Since this is the case with most of our recipes, we usually just call for salt by volume and leave it up to the cook to salt to taste at the end of a recipe. But the feta recipe requires a hefty 3½ ounces of salt. Depending on the brand, that's anywhere from 7 to 14 tablespoons, which is why we recommend going by weight for this recipe.

We prefer Diamond Crystal kosher salt for the lighter and flakier shape of its crystals. They stick to foods rather than bouncing off, and they blend better. Plus, Diamond Crystal is pure salt, with no anti-caking additive.　—J.A.

1 Balance the mango on one of its narrow sides, and then slice off one of the wide sides of the fruit. Try to cut as close to the seed as possible, usually about ¾ inch from the center. Repeat with the other wide side and then slice off the remaining strips of fruit from the narrow sides.

2 To dice the wide pieces of mango, cup one in your palm and use a paring knife to score the fruit into the dice size you want. Try to cut down to but not through the skin, and hold the mango with a kitchen towel to protect your hand in case the knife does pierce the mango skin.

3 Use your fingertips to pop the mango inside out and then use the paring knife to slice the cubes away from the skin.

4 To dice the narrow strips of mango, simply trim away the skin and cut.　—J.A.

Melted butter

OUR STORY ON GRILLING SHELLFISH (page 42) includes three dipping sauces, but you may want to keep it simple and just serve melted butter. Here are two ways to go.

Drawn butter is often served as a dipping sauce for shellfish, especially lobster. There's a lot of disagreement, though, as to what exactly drawn butter is. Most culinary references say it's clarified butter—that is, pure melted butter fat that's been separated from the milk solids and water that are present in whole butter. But talk to a few good chefs and you'll hear the argument that much of the flavor in melted butter comes from those milk solids, so they consider drawn butter to be simply melted butter seasoned with a little salt and pepper and maybe a bit of lemon juice.

Beurre monté is an emulsified butter sauce. When whole butter is melted, the butter fat tends to separate from the milk solids and water. But you can keep this from happening by whisking lumps of cold butter into a couple of tablespoons of extra-warm water. This emulsifies the butter as it melts, and separation doesn't occur. You can use beurre monté in a variety of ways; one of our favorites is as a poaching liquid for lobster and delicate white fish. It also makes a delicious sauce— just add some minced shallots, white wine, and lemon juice for a version of beurre blanc, a classic white wine butter sauce. Or you can add spices to make a dipping sauce, as we did in the Old Bay Dipping Sauce on page 48. If you'd like to make a plain beurre monté, just follow that recipe up to the point where the Old Bay and shallots are added, and season it with a little salt instead.

—*J.A. and M.P.*

Cutting corn off the cob

Removing corn kernels from the cob can be messy—they like to bounce off the cutting board and end up scattered all over the counter and floor. To keep those kernels in their place, insert the tip of the ear of corn into the center hole of a Bundt pan. Cut the kernels away from the cob in long downward strokes, letting them fall into the pan.

—*M.P.*

Deveining shrimp in the shell

The recipe for Grilled Shrimp on page 44 calls for unshelled shrimp, and that means the usual approach to deveining shrimp—splitting the shell to get to the vein—won't work. Fortunately, there's a way to devein shrimp without splitting the shell, and all it takes is a toothpick or a wooden skewer.

Bend the shrimp so the shell sections nearest the tail separate, exposing the flesh. Insert the skewer into the shrimp, digging in deeply enough to get under the vein. Lever the skewer to begin pulling the vein from the shrimp. If you're lucky, you'll get it on the first or second try. Once it pulls out completely, pinch off the end to separate it from the tail.

If the vein breaks at the first tail section, try the next one. Sometimes you can pull out just enough to grasp and finish the job with your fingertips before the vein break. —*J.A.*

Fish sauce

The Honey-Lime Dressing on page 67 and the Thai-Style Sirloin Steak on page 88 get a punch of flavor from fish sauce. This pungent amber-brown liquid is a mainstay in Southeast Asian cooking. Known as nam pla in Thai and nuoc nam in Vietnamese, fish sauce imparts a distinctive salty flavor to many of the region's dishes. Though its aroma is strongly fishy straight from the bottle, cooking mellows it considerably, as does combining it with other assertive ingredients, like lime juice, chile, and garlic.

Fish sauce is made from freshly caught fish that are too small for substantial eating, such as anchovies. The fish are packed between layers of salt in an earthenware vessel. A bamboo mat is placed over the final layer and topped with a weight to keep the fish in place. They are then covered with an airtight top and set in a warm sunny spot where they are left to ferment for nine months and up to a year. As the fish break down, they produce a brown liquid—the fish sauce—which is drained from a spigot at the bottom of the container. —*M.P.*

Ginger peeler

You may already know that when it comes to peeling ginger, scraping the edge of a spoon over the ginger works better than trimming with a paring knife—the knife cuts too deeply into the flesh, while the spoon just grazes the skin. Building on the spoon technique, Oxo has come up with this little ginger-peeling tool. It's not a vast improvement over a spoon, but it has a couple of advantages. The fat rubber handle is more comfortable and easier to grasp than a narrow spoon handle, and its slightly pointed tip helps you maneuver into the grooves between ginger knobs, especially the little ones. It also has a slightly sharper edge than most spoons. If you only occasionally peel ginger, you can stick with a spoon, but if you cook with it often—or if you're a kitchen gadget junkie—then you might want to add this one to your collection. —*J.A.*

TIP

The easy way to slice peppers

Even with a sharp knife, slick pepper skins can be difficult to slice through. Make it easier on yourself by arranging the pepper segments skin side down on the cutting board. This positions the soft, easier-to-cut flesh on top, with the tougher skin against the board, where it takes less effort to slice through with a little pressure.

—*Dabney Gough*

Complement the perfect BBQ while saving energy

COOKSTAR INDUCTION PRO

· "Keep Warm" function to double as a warming plate
· Light & portable with a frameless design for easy cleaning
· 1500 watt induction motor, UL safety certified
· Made in Germany with a 3 Year Warranty

Find a retailer near you by contacting us at
T 888-FISSLER E info@fisslerusa.com
Fissler. Perfect every time.

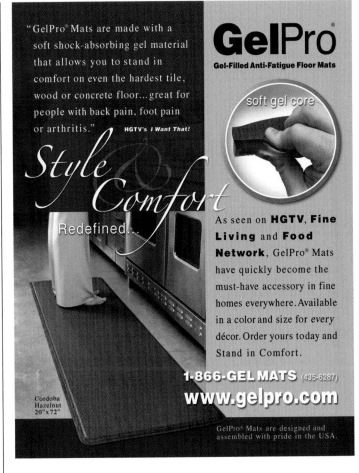

"GelPro® Mats are made with a soft shock-absorbing gel material that allows you to stand in comfort on even the hardest tile, wood or concrete floor...great for people with back pain, foot pain or arthritis." HGTV's *I Want That!*

GelPro®
Gel-Filled Anti-Fatigue Floor Mats

soft gel core

Style & Comfort
Redefined...

As seen on **HGTV**, **Fine Living** and **Food Network**, GelPro® Mats have quickly become the must-have accessory in fine homes everywhere. Available in a color and size for *every* décor. Order yours today and Stand in Comfort.

Cordoba
Hazelnut
20"x72"

1-866-GEL MATS (435-6287)
www.gelpro.com

GelPro® Mats are designed and assembled with pride in the USA.

Make It Tonight

Just 30 minutes to dinner, start to finish.

thai-style steak with red curry sauce and spicy carrot salad

You can find Thai red curry paste in the Asian section of your supermarket, or try an Asian market, which might have more brand options. Be sure to shake the coconut milk vigorously before you open the can.

Serves 4

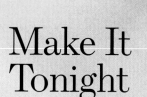

- 1½ lb. sirloin steak
-      Kosher salt and freshly ground black pepper
- 2 Tbs. canola oil
- 3 Tbs. fresh lime juice
- 2 Tbs. fish sauce
- 2 tsp. light brown sugar
- 6 medium carrots, peeled and grated
- ¼ cup tightly packed fresh cilantro, roughly chopped
- 1-2 jalapeño or serrano chiles, stemmed, seeded, and finely chopped
- ⅔ cup canned unsweetened coconut milk
- 1 Tbs. Thai red curry paste

Season the steak all over with 1½ tsp. salt and ¼ tsp. pepper. Heat 1 Tbs. of the oil in a large heavy-duty skillet over medium-high heat. Cook the steak, flipping once, until well browned outside and medium rare inside, 10 to 12 minutes total.

Meanwhile, put the remaining 1 Tbs. oil, 2 Tbs. of the lime juice, 1½ Tbs. of the fish sauce, and 1 tsp. of the sugar in a large bowl and whisk to combine and dissolve the sugar. Add the carrots, cilantro, and chiles and toss well to coat.

When the steak is done, transfer to a large plate, loosely cover with foil, and keep warm. Return the skillet to the stovetop over medium-low heat. Add ⅓ cup water and bring to a boil, scraping with a wooden spoon to release any brown bits. Add the coconut milk, curry paste, and the remaining 1 Tbs. lime juice, ½ Tbs. fish sauce, and 1 tsp. sugar; cook, whisking constantly, until thickened and fragrant, 4 to 5 minutes. Season to taste with salt and pepper.

Thinly slice the steak across the grain and transfer to plates. Spoon the sauce over the top and serve with the carrot salad on the side.

—Liz Pearson

Photographs by Scott Phillips; food styling by Michelli Knauer, except lemony orzo by Heidi Johannsen Stewart and falafel by Jamie Kimm

lemony orzo with tuna and artichoke hearts

No dry vermouth or white wine on hand? Deglaze the skillet with chicken broth or water instead.

Serves 4

	Kosher salt
1½	cups dried orzo (about 9 oz.)
1	Tbs. extra-virgin olive oil
1	small yellow onion, finely chopped
	Freshly ground black pepper
⅓	cup dry vermouth or white wine
1	14-oz. can artichoke hearts, drained and quartered
½	cup oil-packed sun-dried tomatoes, drained and thinly sliced
1	5-oz. can water-packed solid white tuna, drained
3	Tbs. crème fraîche or sour cream
3	Tbs. fresh lemon juice
3	Tbs. coarsely chopped fresh basil

Bring a large pot of well-salted water to a boil. Add the orzo and cook according to package timing until al dente. Drain well.

Meanwhile, heat the oil in a large skillet over medium heat. Add the onion, ½ tsp. salt, and ⅛ tsp. pepper and cook, stirring often, until deep golden brown, 7 to 8 minutes. Remove the skillet from the heat and add the vermouth or wine. Return the skillet to the heat and stir well, scraping up any browned bits from the bottom. Add the artichoke hearts and sun-dried tomatoes and cook just until tender and heated through, 2 to 3 minutes more. Off the heat, gently stir in the tuna.

Transfer the hot orzo to a large bowl and toss with the crème fraîche and lemon juice. Add the onion-artichoke mixture, 2 Tbs. of the basil, and salt and pepper to taste. Toss gently to combine. Spoon into bowls, garnish with the remaining 1 Tbs. basil, and serve.

—*Liz Pearson*

quick tandoori chicken thighs

The yogurt in this spicy marinade helps tenderize the chicken and brings lots of tangy flavor to the dish.

Serves 4 to 6

1	cup plain low-fat yogurt
2	Tbs. fresh lemon juice
1	Tbs. minced fresh ginger
2	tsp. minced garlic
1	tsp. ground turmeric
½	tsp. ground coriander
½	tsp. ground cumin
½	tsp. garam masala
	Kosher salt and freshly ground black pepper
8	skin-on, bone-in chicken thighs
	Vegetable oil for the grill

In a large bowl, whisk the yogurt, lemon juice, ginger, garlic, turmeric, coriander, cumin, garam masala, ½ tsp. salt, and several grinds of black pepper. Add the chicken thighs to the marinade and turn to coat them thoroughly. Cover and refrigerate while you heat the grill.

Prepare a medium gas or charcoal grill fire. If you are using a charcoal grill, spread the hot coals across two-thirds of the bottom grate and leave the remaining portion clear. If you are using gas, turn one of the burners to low to create a cooler zone. Scrub the grill grate with a wire brush and then use a paper towel to wipe it with oil.

Remove the chicken thighs from the marinade and wipe off the excess (don't worry if some remains). Put the chicken, skin side down, directly over the hot part of the grill and grill, covered, until the skin is browned, 3 to 4 minutes (don't leave the grill at this point because flare-ups may occur; if they do, move the chicken away from the flame).

Flip the chicken and grill until well browned on the second side, 3 to 4 minutes. Move the thighs to the cooler part of the grill and continue to grill, covered, until their internal temperature registers 165°F on an instant-read thermometer, 10 to 15 minutes more.

—*Domenica Marchetti*

falafel with tomato-cucumber salad

Falafel are usually deep-fried, but pan-searing these chickpea fritters is healthier (and not as messy). Serve them in pita bread, topped with thick yogurt or tahini sauce, if you like.

Serves 4

- 1 15-oz. can chickpeas, rinsed and drained
- 7 Tbs. extra-virgin olive oil
- 1 tsp. ground cumin
- ½ tsp. ground coriander
- Kosher salt and freshly ground black pepper
- 1 medium yellow onion, diced
- ½ cup plain fine dry breadcrumbs; more as needed
- 1½ cups cherry tomatoes, quartered
- 1 medium pickling cucumber or ⅓ English cucumber, halved and sliced ¼ inch thick
- 1 Tbs. fresh lemon juice
- 4 pitas, warmed

Heat the oven to 425°F.

In a food processor, pulse the chickpeas, 2 Tbs. of the oil, the cumin, coriander, 1 tsp. salt, and ½ tsp. black pepper into a chunky paste. Add the onion and breadcrumbs and pulse until the mixture tightens up. You should be able to easily form it into a patty—add more breadcrumbs as needed. Gently form the chickpea mixture into twelve ½-inch-thick patties.

Heat 2 Tbs. of the oil in a 10-inch nonstick skillet over medium heat until shimmering hot. Add 6 of the patties and cook until nicely browned, about 2 minutes. Flip and cook the other sides until browned, 1 to 2 minutes more. Transfer the patties to a baking sheet. Repeat with 2 Tbs. more oil and the remaining six patties. Bake the patties until heated through, about 5 minutes.

Meanwhile, toss the tomatoes and cucumber with the lemon juice, the remaining 1 Tbs. oil, and salt to taste.

Split the pitas and stuff them with the falafel and tomato-cucumber salad.

—*Tony Rosenfeld*

caramelized onion cheeseburgers

Burgers just got better with the addition of tender sweet onions, melted cheese, and tangy lemon-Dijon mayonnaise.

Serves 4

- 2 Tbs. extra-virgin olive oil; more as needed
- 1 large sweet onion, thinly sliced (about 2 cups)
  Kosher salt and freshly ground black pepper
- ⅓ cup mayonnaise
- 1 Tbs. Dijon mustard
- 1½ tsp. fresh lemon juice
- 1 tsp. finely chopped fresh rosemary
- 1 small clove garlic, minced
- 1½ lb. 85%-lean ground beef
- 4 slices Comté or Gruyère cheese
- 4 good-quality hamburger buns or rolls, split
- 12 fresh arugula leaves

Prepare a medium-high gas or charcoal grill fire. Alternatively, position an oven rack 5 to 6 inches from the broiler and heat the broiler to high. Line the bottom of a broiler pan with foil and lightly oil the perforated part of the pan.

Meanwhile, heat the oil in a 10-inch skillet over medium-high heat. Add the onion, ¼ tsp. salt, and ⅛ tsp. pepper; reduce the heat to medium low and cook, stirring occasionally, until deeply golden brown and tender, 15 to 18 minutes.

Combine the mayonnaise, Dijon, lemon juice, rosemary, and garlic in a small bowl. Season to taste with salt and pepper and set aside.

In a medium bowl, gently combine the beef with ¼ tsp. salt and ⅛ tsp. pepper. Form the beef into 4 patties (3½ inches in diameter) and make a deep depression in the center of each patty so the burgers keep their shape during cooking. Lightly sprinkle the patties with ¾ tsp. salt and ½ tsp. pepper. Grill or broil them on the prepared pan for about 4 minutes per side for medium, or until desired doneness. Top each burger with 1 slice of the cheese and grill or broil until melted, 30 to 60 seconds.

Toast the buns on the grill or under the broiler until golden, 30 to 60 seconds. Serve the burgers on the toasted buns with the caramelized onions, mayonnaise, and arugula.

—*David Bonom*

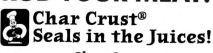

WHERE TO BUY IT

berry syrups, page 18

Tarnow sugar bowl and creamer, $36, williamssonoma.com, 877-812-6235. **Ball quilted-crystal Mason jelly jars**, cases of 12, $7.99 for 4 oz. and $9.49 for 8 oz., canningpantry.com, 800-285-9044. **Fagor America home canning kit**, $25, fagoramerica.com. **Locking tongs**, see Shellfish, below center. **Norpro canning rack**, $5.99, thekitchenstore.com, 800-458-2616.

corn, page 34

Stone-ground yellow cornmeal, $3.99 for 2 lb., old-mill.com, 877-653-6455. **Dried lavender**, $4.99 for 1 oz., Kalustyans .com, 800-352-3451.

omelets, page 24

All-Clad 8-inch nonstick skillet, $63.75, cooking .com/fc, 800-663-8810. **Oxo Good Grips tomato sauce spatula**, $7.99, bedbathand beyond.com, 800-462-3966.

party in the kitchen, page 62

Iichiko shochu, $21.99 for a 750-ml bottle, mainlywines.com, 877-247-4062. **Fresh lychees**, $26.25 for 2 lb. (when in season), melissas.com, 800-588-0151. **Colorways 4-piece medium bowl set**, in tonal black with glitter, $29.95, www .zak.com for stores, 509-244-0555.

From crateandbarrel.com, 800-967-6696: **Ona pitcher**, large, $26.95. **Hazel flatware**, $29.95 for a 5-piece place setting. **Nilsson small pitcher**, $26.95. **Nilsson dinnerware**, $69.95 for a 5-piece place setting. **Nilsson rectangular dish**, brown, $54.95. **Three-part square dish**, $29.95. **Lodge cast-iron round skillet**, $27.95. **Rings glasses**, 16 oz., $1.50. **Rings pitcher**, $7.95.

ice pops, page 50

Direction 9-oz. double old-fashioned glass, $8.95, crateand barrel.com, 800-967-6696. Small **Williams martini glasses**, $72 for a set of 4, williamssonoma .com, 877-812-6235. **Nachtman bistro Champagne flute**, $11.50, in Williams Sonoma stores only, 877-812-6235.

From prairiemoon.biz, 866-331-0767: **Freezer pop sticks**, $2.49 for a bag of 50. **Ice pops mold (10)**, $19.95. **Groovy freezer pop mold**, $11.95.

test kitchen, page 81

Oxo ginger peeler, $6.95, cooking.com/fc, 800-663-8810.

beer cocktails, page 32

Crispin hard apple cider brut, $6.99 for 4 bottles, store.wineconnect .com/harbor, 952-472-0648. **Farnum Hill semi-dry cider**, farnumhillciders.com for stores. **Lindemans framboise lambic** and **Lindemans pêche**, $9.69 each for a 25-oz. bottle, bevmo.com, 877-772-3866. **Spiegelau Tubes beer classics lager glass**, 2 for $29.90, glassware.riedel.com, 888-474-3335.

shellfish, page 42

Fresh lobster and other shellfish, market price, brownetrading.com, 800-944-7848. **Seafood scissors**, $9.95, williamssonoma.com, 877-812-6235. **Locking tongs**, 19½ inches long, $17.95, cooking .com/fc, 800-663-8810.

eggplant, page 76

The Gripper cutting board, 11x14 inches, $14.95, cooking.com/fc, 800-663-8810.

menus, page 96

Wine recommendations courtesy of Patrick Watson at Smith & Vine in Brooklyn, New York. For more great wine ideas, go to smithandvine.com, or call 718-243-2864.

feta, page 70

All-Clad stainless-steel 8-quart tall stock pot, $295, williamssonoma.com, 877-812-6235. **Five-piece measuring cup set by All-Clad**, $49.95, cooking.com/fc, 800-663-8810. **Twelve-cup vintage glass food storage**, $10.99, thecontainer store.com, 888-266-8246. **Stainless mixing bowls with pour spouts**, $39.95 for a set of 3, crateand barrel.com, 800-967-6696. **Maple deep wooden spoon**, 14-inch, $6.95, crateandbarrel.com, 800-967-6696. **White ramekins by Corningware**, $12.95 for set of 4, cooking.com/fc, 800-663-8810. **Cheesecloth**, $3.99, bedbathandbeyond .com, 800-462-3966. **Pyrex measuring cups**, 1 cup and 1 quart, $3.99 and $5.99, bedbathand beyond.com, 800-462-3966. **Henkels Pro S 10-inch chef's knife**, $139.95, cooking.com/fc, 800-663-8810. **Epicurean Chef Series cutting board**, 27x18 inches, $129.99, epicureancs.com, 866-678-3500. **Slotted spoon**, $9.95, crateand barrel.com, 800-967-6696. **Large Tovolo stainless-steel colander**, $19.99, target.com, 800-591-3869. **Taylor instant-read 1¾-inch dial thermometer**, $7.95, chefgadget.com.

For more kitchen tools, go to **FineCooking.com/buy-it**

Photographs by Scott Phillips

Appliances

Dacor *p. 99* Since 1965, Dacor® has redefined the modern kitchen with a collection that offers the best balance of style and performance. Dacor is in the details.
800-793-0093
www.dacor.com/hot

Earthstone Wood-Fire Ovens *p. 92* Wood-fired brick ovens for indoor and outdoor use. Can double as a fireplace. Great for baking, grilling, and roasting.
800-840-4915
www.earthstoneovens.com

Mugnaini's Wood-Fired Cooking *p. 92* Mugnaini, exclusive importers of Italian wood-fired ovens. Italian tradition, American technology. Dedicated to customer service in design, building support, and oven use.
888-887-7206
www.mugnaini.com

Viking Range *p. 2* If cooking is everything, the complete Viking kitchen offers everything you need - professional performance and impeccable design.
888-845-4641
www.vikingrange.com/wheretobuy

Cookware

A Cook's Wares *p. 92* We have what you need for your kitchen: The finest cookware, bakeware, cutlery, utensils and small appliances. Since 1981.
800-915-9788
www.cookswares.com

Fissler USA *p. 87* For over 163 years, Fissler has been the European leader in innovative cookware. All products are manufactured in Germany and come with a lifetime warranty.
www.fisslerusa.com

Kuhn-Rikon Corporation *p. 11* Kuhn Rikon offers the finest in pressure cookers, specialty cookware, and distinctive kitchen tools to make a cook's life easier.
800-924-4699
www.kuhnrikon.com/fine

Gourmet Foods

Al Fresco All Natural Sausage *p. 5* Al fresco All Natural Chicken Sausage comes in 14 sumptuous flavors and has 70% less fat than traditional pork sausage. Live life with flavor.
www.alfrescoallnatural.com

Char Crust *p. 92* Get the secret! Char Crust ® dry-rub seasonings for all meat & fish. Only Char Crust ® *Seals in the juices!* ® Turns you into a chef...instantly.
www.charcrust.com

La Tienda *p. 92* A window to the best of Spain. America's most comprehensive inventory of quality Spanish food selected by a knowledgeable and dedicated family. Immediate delivery.
888-472-1022
www.tienda.com

Plugra European Style Butter *p. 7*
www.plugra.com

Wisconsin Cheese *p. 13* Wisconsin cheesemaking has long been renowned for its unparalleled innovation and artistry. Discover many award-winning specialty and artisan cheeses, recipes and pairing ideas at EatWisconsinCheese.com
www.eatwisconsincheese.com

Ingredients

Bulk Foods *p. 92* Offering a wide selection of spices, nuts, dried fruits, and other ingredients.
www.bulkfoods.com

Magic Seasonings *p. 9* Chef Paul Prudhomme's all-natural magic seasoning blends, sauces and marinades, pepper sauce, smoked meats, cookbooks, gift packs, sweet potato pecan pie, and much more!
800-457-2857
www.chefpaul.com

Sugarcraft, Inc. *p. 92* Sugarcraft Inc., Hamilton, Ohio. We carry baking, cake decorating, candy, and cookie supplies, etc. We import specialty items!
www.sugarcraft.com

Kitchen Tools & Utensils

Bella Copper *p. 92* The world's leading heat diffuser/defroster plate provides superior heat conduction for more even cooking and faster defrosting. Available in solid copper or pure silver. A gourmet kitchen essential.
805-215-3241
www.bellacopper.com

Chester P. Basil's *p. 86* Maker of some of America's finest handcrafted wooden spoons, utensils, and boards. Uniquely shaped for superior function. Beautiful cherry wood tools. "Order today!"
www.cpbasils.com

GelPro *p. 87* Stand in comfort! Let's Gel was started with one simple goal, to make the time you spend standing in your kitchen more comfortable.
866-GEL-MATS
www.gelpro.com

House On the Hill *p. 92* Over 400 molds for springerle, speculaas, gingerbread, marzipan, fondant and cake decorating. Order now for holiday cookie baking. Catalog on request.
www.houseonthehill.net

Japanese Chefs Knife *p. 11, 13* Your online source for Japanese chef's knives for home cooking and the professional chef. Finest selections from the top brands: Masahiro, Misono, Fujiwara Kanefusa, Glestain.
www.japanesechefsknife.com

Jessica's Biscuit *p. 90*
www.e-cookbooks.com

Kerekes *p. 92* Your complete online source for professional chef's tools, cookware, bakeware, and cake decorating supplies used by top chefs at the finest restaurants and kitchens.
www.bakedeco.com

Plum Pudding Kitchen *p. 91* Your online source for "irresistibly Italian" Vietri dinnerware, flatware, glassware, and much more. Let us help you set a special table!
888-940-7586
www.plumpuddingkitchen.com

Schools, Travel & Organizations

Culinary Business Academy *p. 91* Extensive and comprehensive personal chef business knowledge and training from the world's recognized leader in the personal chef industry. Nobody offers what we offer.
800-747-2433
www.culinarybusiness.com

Foxwoods Food & Wine Festival *p. 14*
www.foxwoodsfoodandwine.com

Le Cordon Bleu *p. 9* Master the culinary arts. Earn the Grand Diplome in approximately nine months. Three- to five-week intensive courses and online hospitality programs are also available.
800-457-2433
www.cordonbleu.edu

Wine & Beverages

Blackstone Winery *p. 100*
www.blackstonewinery.com

Don Francisco's Coffee *p. 92*
www.dfcoffee.com

For direct links to all these advertiser websites in one place, please go to **finecooking.com/shopping**

NUTRITION

Recipes	Calories (kcal)	Fat Cal (kcal)	Protein (g)	Carb (g)	Total Fat (g)	Sat Fat (g)	Mono Fat (g)	Poly Fat (g)	Chol (mg)	Sodium (g)	Fiber (g)
TOMATILLOS, P. 16											
Margarita-Marinated Skirt Steak with Tomatillo Salsa	380	200	33	9	22	6	12	2.5	85	290	3
BERRIES, P. 18											
Fresh Berry Syrup (per 1 Tbs.)	50	0	0	14	0	0	0	0	0	0	0
BIG BUY: BREAD, P. 20											
Summer Berry Trifle	310	100	5	44	11	7	3	0.5	40	230	2
Chilled Tomato and Bread Soup with Garlic and Basil	210	80	5	26	9	1.5	7	1	0	600	2
PLT Salad	220	130	6	15	15	2.5	10	1.5	10	560	2
CLASSIC OMELET, P. 24											
Cheese Omelet	310	220	21	1	24	12	8	2	470	370	
GOOD LIFE, P. 28											
Ancho-Marinated Pork and Mango Skewers	250	80	25	20	8	2	4	1.5	75	120	2
BEER COCKTAILS, P. 32											
Eve's Black Heart	180	0	1	17	0	0	0	0	0	10	0
Peach Melba Cocktail	130	0	0	22	0	0	0	0	0	0	0
The Michelada	110	0	1	8	0	0	0	0	0	1170	0
CORN, P. 34											
Risotto with Corn, Spicy Sausage, and Wilted Arugula	530	170	18	73	19	8	7	2.5	25	610	3
Sweet Corn Cake with Blueberry-Lavender Compote	320	130	4	46	15	9	4	1	85	140	2
Corn Fritters with Charred Tomato Salsa (per fritter)	70	35	2	7	4	1	1.5	1	20	120	1
Charred Tomato Salsa (per 1 Tbs.)	20	10	0	2	1	0	1	0	0	75	1
Toasted Corn, Cherry Tomato, and Edamame Salad	200	110	5	18	13	1.5	8	1.5	0	65	3
Summer Corn Soup with Crisp Prosciutto	170	60	5	24	7	4	2	0.5	20	440	3
GRILLING SHELLFISH, P. 42											
Grilled Shrimp	140	70	18	0	8	1	5	1	170	610	0
Grilled Mussels, Clams, and Oysters	100	25	14	4	2.5	0.5	0.5	0.5	35	340	0
Grilled Lobster	170	35	31	1	3.5	0.5	2	0	155	480	0
Old Bay Dipping Sauce (per 1 Tbs.)	100	100	0	0	11	7	3	0	30	120	0
Bloody Mary Cocktail Sauce (per ¼ cup)	70	0	1	16	0	0	0	0	0	680	0
Orange-Saffron Aïoli (per 1 Tbs.)	130	130	0	1	15	2	9	4	15	330	0
ICE POPS, P. 50											
Lemon-Vodka Cream Pops	180	110	2	17	12	7	3.5	0	45	60	0
Bellini Pops	100	0	0	20	0	0	0	0	0	0	1
Bittersweet Chocolate-Bourbon Pops	120	50	1	19	6	2.5	0	0	0	35	1
TOMATO SAUCE, P. 54											
Fresh Tomato Sauce (per ½ cup)	70	35	2	8	4	0.5	2.5	0.5	0	150	2
Spaghetti with Summer Tomato Sauce	520	70	18	95	7	1	3.5	1.5	0	830	8
Curried Chickpea and Summer Vegetable Stew	300	110	11	40	13	4.5	4	2.5	0	520	12
Greek-Spiced Lamb Meatballs in Tomato Sauce	470	270	24	22	30	11	14	2.5	135	1040	4
Grilled Pizzas with Fresh Tomatoes and Arugula	950	450	38	90	50	19	24	4.5	95	1940	8
PARTY IN THE KITCHEN, P. 62											
Shochu Watermelon Lemonade	120	0	0	25	0	0	0	0	0	0	0
Shrimp with Spicy Mayo and Garlic Breadcrumbs	360	230	21	13	25	4	7	12	180	870	1
Tonkatsu and Mixed Herb Salad	350	130	35	20	14	4	6	2.5	130	450	2
Mixed Herb Salad with Honey-Lime Dressing	45	5	2	10	0	0	0	0	0	270	2
Sesame, Snow Pea, and Shiitake Pasta Salad	220	70	6	30	8	1	3	3.5	0	390	3
Pineapple, Strawberry, and Lychee Parfaits	160	5	2	42	0.5	0	0	0	0	0	4
FETA, P. 70											
Homemade Feta (per 1 oz.)	70	50	4	1	6	4	1.5	0	25	320	0
EGGPLANT PARMIGIANA, P. 76											
Classic Eggplant Parmigiana	580	460	13	21	52	11	33	5	25	320	9
Eggplant Parmigiana Rolls with Baby Arugula	250	170	5	16	19	3	12	2.5	55	170	3
MAKE IT TONIGHT, P. 88											
Lemony Orzo with Tuna and Artichoke Hearts	470	110	23	60	12	4	5	1.5	25	710	4
Thai-Style Steak with Red Curry Sauce and Carrot Salad	400	230	30	15	25	11	9	2.5	75	1300	3
Falafel with Tomato-Cucumber Salad	640	250	18	80	28	4	18	4.5	0	920	12
Quick Tandoori Chicken Thighs	210	120	21	1	13	3.5	5	3	80	105	0
Caramelized Onion Cheeseburgers	740	450	43	27	50	16	20	10	140	930	2

The nutritional analyses have been calculated by a registered dietitian at Nutritional Solutions in Melville, New York. When a recipe gives a choice of ingredients, the first choice is the one used. Optional ingredients with measured amounts are included; ingredients without specific quantities are not. Analyses are per serving; when a range of ingredient amounts or servings is given, the smaller amount or portion is used. When the quantities of salt and pepper aren't specified, the analysis is based on ¼ tsp. salt and ⅛ tsp. pepper per serving for entrées, and ⅛ tsp. salt and ⅟₁₆ tsp. pepper per serving for side dishes.

MENUS

the new clambake

Shellfish on the Grill
pages 44–46

Bloody Mary Cocktail Sauce
page 48

Toasted Corn, Cherry Tomato,
and Edamame Salad
page 36

Pineapple, Strawberry, and
Lychee Parfaits
page 69

*To drink: dry stout, like Guinness
Extra Stout (original)*

a summer saturday

Peach Melba Cocktail
page 33

Fresh Corn Fritters
with Charred Tomato Salsa
page 38

Ancho-Marinated Pork
and Mango Skewers
page 29

Orzo and Grilled Vegetables
with Feta, Olives, and Oregano
FineCooking.com

Summer Berry Trifle
page 21

*To drink: a delicate dry rosé, like
Commanderie de Peyrassol 2008*

brunch at home

Cheese Omelet
page 25

Mixed Fruit Salad

Buttermilk Pancakes
FineCooking.com

Berry Syrups
page 18

Bellini Pops
page 52

*To drink: a crisp sparkling wine,
like Brüder Dr. Becker
Scheurebe Sekt 2005*

friends for dinner

The Michelada
page 33

Poached Shrimp with Spicy Mayo
and Garlic Breadcrumbs
page 64

Margarita-Marinated Skirt Steak
with Grilled Tomatillo Salsa
page 16

Garlic Fries
FineCooking.com

Lemon-Vodka Cream Pops
page 53

the spice trail

Falafel with Tomato-
Cucumber Salad
page 90

Quick Tandoori
Chicken Thighs
page 89

Grilled Corn
page 39

Pistachio Peach Sundaes
with Crisp Phyllo Cups
FineCooking.com

*To drink: a pale bock, like
Smuttynose Maibock*

italian vegetarian

Chilled Fresh Tomato, Basil,
and Bread Soup
page 20

Classic Eggplant Parmigiana
page 78

Mixed Greens Salad

Strawberry-Balsamic Granita
FineCooking.com

*To drink: a dry yet fruity
effervescent red wine, like Medici
Ermete Concerto Lambrusco 2007*

Photographs by Scott Phillips; wine recommendations by Patrick Watson at Smith & Vine, Brooklyn, New York

RECIPE INDEX

VEGETARIAN: May contain eggs and dairy ingredients

MAKE AHEAD: Can be completely prepared ahead (may need reheating and a garnish to serve)

QUICK: 30 minutes and under

Diane Hatz

Changing the way people eat, with help from some barnyard friends. BY LISA WADDLE

the dish

Name: Diane Hatz

Age: 47

Job: Founder and creative marketing director at Sustainable Table, a nonprofit educational group that advocates sustainable eating

Started: 2003

Where: New York City

Known for: Producing animated spoofs of the movie *The Matrix,* to promote independent family farms

Find out more: sustainabletable.org

Fine Cooking: Everyone wants to eat better—what prompted you to make it your life's work?
Hatz: A mango. I live in New York's East Village, and one day I got up the nerve to go into a vegetarian health food store a few doors down from my apartment. I bought an organic mango, and it changed my life.

FC: How so?
Hatz: It was the sweetest, tastiest piece of fruit I'd ever eaten. I realized, "This is better for me, it's better for the environment, and it just tastes good." I wanted to share that.

FC: So how did you get from that mango to where you are now, running a nonprofit and making educational cartoons that reveal the darker side of corporate farming?
Hatz: I was describing how we all think our bacon and milk come from these sunny family farms, when in reality, the animals are in densely packed, unsanitary conditions. There's a huge disconnect between the fantasy we want to believe is true versus what's really going on. Someone said, "That sounds like the movie *The Matrix.*" With that, our movie wrote itself.

FC: Was the world ready for your message?
Hatz: *The Meatrix* launched in November 2003, right when the third *Matrix* film came out. We had 10,000 people watch our video in the first three days. Now it's in some 30 languages, including Tibetan and Swahili, and has been seen by more than 15 million people.

FC: Talk about viral videos! How else have you spread the word about the issues surrounding how food is raised or grown?
Hatz: We showed *The Meatrix* at Bonnaroo, the Woodstock-like annual music festival in Tennessee. I brought a 6-foot-tall cardboard cutout of Moopheus, the cow in the video that's based on the Laurence Fishburne character in *The Matrix.* I also rode a bio-fueled bus cross-country for a Pie Across America Tour.

FC: Why pie?
Hatz: To me, pies are a metaphor for something bigger. They represent a connection to local food, and they're meant for sharing.

FC: You've gone from fruit to film to pie—what's next?
Hatz: We're in the process of launching a How to Host a Sustainable Dinner Party kit that people can download from our Web site. It's based on the idea that by having people over and serving sustainable food—and we'll help you find out where to buy it—you can start a conversation about what it means and how to do it. Start with two people, and they tell six people, and so on.

FC: Is "sustainable" just the latest food buzzword?
Hatz: Sustainability is a way of life.

FC: So, where do you buy your meat?
Hatz: I've been a vegetarian for 21 years. It's a personal choice, not something I think everyone should do. The whole point of *The Meatrix* was to get people to buy sustainable meat.

Illustration by Ward Schumaker

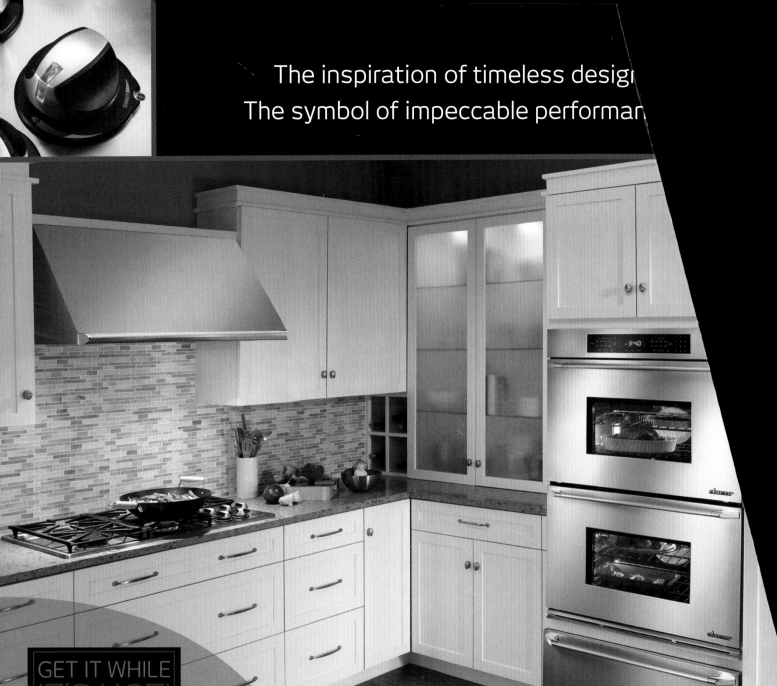

The inspiration of timeless design
The symbol of impeccable performance

The Renaissance® Wall Oven and Cooktop by Dacor. Timeless design
showcased by the Illumina™ Burner Control. And advanced features like
the RapidHeat™ Bake Element for faster pre-heating and remarkably even
temperature control. Inspiration is in the details. Dacor is in the details.

Visit **dacor.com/hot** or call 800.793.0093 for more details.

The Life of the Kitchen®

n.

ce.

* BEST FRIEND

GRANDPA'S WATCH *

OLD JEANS *

BLACKSTONE
WINERY
Merlot
CALIFORNIA

* HERE'S TO THE THINGS IN LIFE YOU CAN COUNT ON. BLACKSTONE WINERY.
All the awards, without the pretensions. That's why we're America's favorite Merlot.

THE ULTIMATE **FRENCH ONION SOUP**

fine Cooking

WE BRING OUT THE COOK IN YOU

SPECIAL SECTION

Thanksgiving Dinner
All the classics made easy!

Pie dreams
1 perfect crust
3 new ways to crimp
4 delicious fillings

COOKING WITH GRAPES

OCT/NOV 2009 • No.101
www.finecooking.com

Fresh pear pie with
dried cherries and
brown sugar streusel,
page 62

5 Sustainable fish
to buy & cook now

Reason to bake:
Crowd Control

UNBLEACHED
WHITE WHOLE WHEAT
FLOUR

Bakers everywhere know the real secrets to crowd-pleasing results.
The finest flour, a time-tested recipe, tips from your baking friends.

Whether you're an eager beginner, a devoted home baker,
or a seasoned pro, you'll find the resources to become the
very best baker you can be at King Arthur Flour.

You get so much more when you buy King Arthur Flour. See for yourself at **kingarthurflour.com/why**

CONTENTS

OCTOBER/NOVEMBER 2009 ISSUE 101

Classic French
Onion Soup, page 66

CONTENTS
OCTOBER/NOVEMBER 2009 ISSUE 101

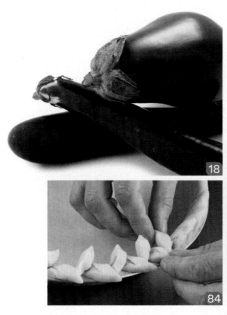

Ears, Tails, and All

Dare of the day: shrimp off a truck and a sauce so hot it came with a warning.

TRY ANYTHING NEW lately? A fruit you've never bought before? An unusual-sounding dish? A recipe with an unfamiliar technique? I go looking for these kinds of opportunities—but that wasn't always the case.

Raised in a food-conservative midwestern family, I grew up on steak and potatoes. There was chili and spaghetti, too, but there was no fish. And there were definitely no pig's ears. I ordered those last week at a buzz-worthy place called Animal on L.A.'s ever-evolving Fairfax Avenue. They were crispy, chewy, moreish. A few days before that, I bypassed the pizza my kids were having in favor of the garlicky lemon-butter shrimp with spicy sauce ("Very hot. No refunds.") from the window of Giovanni's shrimp truck on Oahu's North Shore. A favorite souvenir from a trip to St. Martin some years back is the memory of a beach picnic of hot pig's tail soup and cold beer.

Even if I occasionally have to talk myself into the food on my fork, I'm almost always glad I do. And even if I don't nail the dish I'm cooking the first time out, I'll get closer the next time. And the next.

This issue is filled with new things to try, persimmons, mackerel, and the wines of a place called Montsant among them. And it's packed with culinary challenges, including a tutorial on how to make the flakiest, most buttery piecrust ever. If you suffer from a fear of turkey (don't we all, at least a little?), I hope you'll feel empowered to take on the big bird once you've seen our all-you-need-to-know guide to the holiday meal in this month's expanded Repertoire column.

So why not make a salad with fuyu persimmons and fennel (page 16) or bake a bake-off worthy pie (page 56)? Heck, why not offer to make Thanksgiving this year (page 29)? Bet you'll be glad you do.

Laurie Buckle, editor
fc@taunton.com

more fine cooking

BOOKS

Assistant food editor Melissa Pellegrino adds "cookbook author" to her many accomplishments this month, with the release of *The Italian Farmer's Table,* which she wrote with her husband, Matthew Scialabba. It's the delicious story of the many months they spent working in the gardens and cooking in the kitchens of 30 *agriturismi*—small family farms—in northern Italy. Available in November; $19.95.

Contributing editor Ellie Krieger is following the success of her best-selling, award-winning cookbook, *The Food You Crave,* with *So Easy,* an irresistible collection of 150 quick and healthful recipes for every meal of the week. Don't miss her rush-hour dinners: a month of main courses that you can whip up in less than half an hour. Available in October; $29.95.

We, too, have a new book out this fall: *Absolutely Chocolate,* from the editors of *Fine Cooking,* is an absolutely decadent collection of all our best chocolate recipes, from Old-Fashioned Hot Fudge to Chocolate Pavlova with Tangerine Whipped Cream. Available in October; $29.95.

SPECIAL ISSUES

We have two new special issues hitting newsstands in October: *Sweet Cakes* (perfect for holiday baking) and *Parties!* (mix-and-match menus for every occasion). To order, go to FineCooking.com.

Perfection by the cup.

Just like your favorite barista, the Viking Professional 12-cup Coffee Maker knows that time and temperature are the secrets to perfect coffee. Our exclusive SureTemp™ system guarantees the correct amount of brew time at the perfect temperature for optimal satisfaction. The intuitive programmable display allows you to schedule each brewing and select the precise serving desired, while the double-wall stainless steel thermal carafe maintains the flavor and aroma for hours. And the removable water reservoir is the ultimate in convenience. $299.95 (Barista tip jar not included).

To find a dealer near you, visit vikingrange.com/wheretobuy.

THE WINNER

Reader tip: let the sun shine

If you have a plastic storage container that's been stained by foods like tomato sauce, leaving the container out in the sun for a few hours will remove the stains. The sun's ultraviolet radiation breaks apart molecular structures and changes the way color is reflected; this photochemical change makes the stains disappear. It also kills bacteria. —*Deanna Figueroa, Victoria, Texas*

We want to hear from you. Give us your best tip and we'll reward you with a kitchen prize. Deanna is the winner of this Chef's Choice premium electric food slicer, model 610.

CALL OR WRITE: *Fine Cooking,* The Taunton Press, 63 S. Main St., PO Box 5506, Newtown, CT 06470-5506. Tel: 203-426-8171. Send an email: fc@taunton.com.

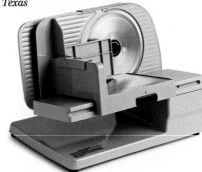

Lobster: two views

I wanted to commend you on "Lobster 101" in the August/September Test Kitchen. Killing a lobster before you cook it requires extra time and work, but simply throwing it into a pot of boiling water is indeed cruel. Thanks for having the gumption to tell it like it is and for encouraging your readers to be humane.
—*Ruth Lucas Wilson, via email*

Your story about how to kill a lobster is cruel and inhumane. I understand that not everyone wants to be a vegetarian, but to me, this article has crossed a line.
—*Martina Lerede, via email*

PVC usage

On page 83 of Test Kitchen in your June/July issue, it says that chefs sometimes use PVC piping as ring molds. Is this a food-safe option?
—*Barbara Goldstein, via email*

Editors' reply: PVC, like a lot of other plastics, is fine when used for cold food preparations, but it should not be used for hot food, especially if it isn't food-grade PVC. The concern is that chemicals may be released when non-food-grade PVC is heated higher than 140°F (although even then, it's a minute amount).

Beer alone

In your August/September issue you introduce us to beer cocktails ("Beer Becomes a Cocktail," page 32). I put those who mix a fine beer with lesser ingredients in the same category as someone who would paint a fine piece of wood or put ketchup on a steak. Make mine hoppy and make it a treat for all the senses, but please don't make my beer into something it never was meant to be.
—*Charles McEniry, Stoughton, Wisconsin*

Picture perfect

What a great cover photo on your August/September issue; I could almost smell the freshly grilled corn. The articles also meet your traditional high standards. I found lots of inspiration, as I do in all of your issues.
—*David Lilly, Los Angeles, California*

CORRECTIONS

Please note that in issues 97 through 100, the sodium content column on the Nutrition page should have read "mg" rather than "g." We apologize for any confusion.

Also, the food stylist for the August/September cover was Michelli Knauer.

fine Cooking

Editor	**Laurie Glenn Buckle**
Art Director	**Don Morris**
Senior Food Editor	**Jennifer Armentrout**
Senior Editor	**Rebecca Freedman**
Managing Editor	**Lisa Waddle**
Associate Editors	**Laura Giannatempo** **Denise Mickelsen**
Web Producer	**Sarah Breckenridge**
Assistant Web Producer	**Sharon Anderson**
Senior Copy/ Production Editor	**Enid Johnson**
Associate Art Director	**Pamela Winn**
Photo Editor	**Kelly Coughlan Gearity**
Assistant Food Editor	**Melissa Pellegrino**
Editorial Assistant	**Julissa Roberts**
Editorial Interns	**Evan Barbour** **Zoe Eisenberg**
Editor at Large	**Susie Middleton**
Contributing Editors	**Pam Anderson** **Abigail Johnson Dodge** **Maryellen Driscoll** **Allison Ehri Kreitler** **Ellie Krieger** **Kimberly Y. Masibay** **Tony Rosenfeld** **Molly Stevens**
Senior Managing Editor, Books	**Carolyn Mandarano**

Fine Cooking: (ISSN: 1072-5121) is published six times a year by The Taunton Press, Inc., Newtown, CT 06470-5506. Telephone 203-426-8171. Periodicals postage paid at Newtown, CT 06470 and at additional mailing offices. GST paid registration #123210981.

Subscription Rates: U.S. and Canada, $29.95 for one year, $49.95 for two years, $69.95 for three years (GST included, payable in U.S. funds). Outside the U.S./Canada: $36 for one year, $62 for two years, $88 for three years (payable in U.S. funds). Single copy, $6.95. Single copy outside the U.S., $7.95.

Postmaster: Send address changes to *Fine Cooking,* The Taunton Press, Inc., 63 South Main St., P.O. Box 5506, Newtown, CT 06470-5506.

Canada Post: Return undeliverable Canadian addresses to Fine Cooking, c/o Worldwide Mailers, Inc., 2835 Kew Drive, Windsor, ON N8T 3B7, or email to mnfa@taunton.com.

Printed in the USA.

Photograph by Scott Phillips

Frank Melodia ("Good Catch," page 68; "French Onion Soup," page 64) is a food stylist and recipe developer whose work regularly appears in *Redbook* and *Woman's Day*. When not styling or cooking, he tends his garden in Great River, New York.

• **My favorite food memory is...** eating a brioche stuffed with scoops of buffalo milk gelato, topped with whipped buffalo cream, for breakfast in Campania, Italy.

• **The strangest thing I've ever eaten...** fried scorpions in Thailand.

• **My favorite cookbook is...** my signed copy of *Mastering the Art of French Cooking* by Julia Child and Simone Beck. Julia signed it with a red pen.

Chris Santos ("French Onion Soup," page 64) is co-owner and executive chef of The Stanton Social in New York City. He also works as a food stylist and consultant on movies and is developing a line of chef's apparel with tattoo artist Michelle Myles.

• **My favorite kitchen tool is...** a hand-held immersion blender. I want to design a holster for it so it's always by my side.

• **I'm currently obsessed with...** making compound salts like olive salt, bacon salt, or jalapeño salt.

• **Pie or cake?** Cake. It's way more interesting than pie. And who's ever heard of a birthday pie?

Anne Willan ("French Onion Soup," page 64) is the founder of La Varenne cooking school. She has more than 30 years of experience as a teacher, cookbook author, and culinary historian. Her latest book, *The Country Cooking of France,* won two 2008 James Beard Awards.

• **Sweet or salty?** Salty. I'm a cook, not a pastry cook.

• **For breakfast, I eat...** muesli with pomegranate juice.

• **The dish I most want to learn to cook is...** those little "pearls" that are so popular in molecular gastronomy.

Jeanne Kelley ("Grape Crush," page 40) is a food writer, recipe developer, and food stylist. She is the author of the award-winning cookbook *Blue Eggs and Yellow Tomatoes* and lives in Eagle Rock, California, with her husband, two daughters, chickens, turkeys, and bees.

• **My favorite kitchen tool is...** my garlic press.

• **The last thing I cooked was...** grilled sourdough pizza with goat cheese, Aleppo pepper, and an herb drizzle.

• **My least favorite food is...** mayonnaise, unless it's homemade.

A former food editor and test kitchen director, **Nicole Rees** ("Pie Dreams," page 56) is currently the research and development manager for a baking ingredient company in Wilsonville, Oregon. *Baking Unplugged,* her most recent cookbook, was published in February.

• **My latest drink discovery is...** Founders Kentucky Breakfast Stout, which is aged in bourbon barrels. It tastes like coffee and beer in the best possible way.

• **My favorite herb is...** parsley. I can't cook without it.

• **My go-to weeknight dinner is...** my take on pasta carbonara, with tons of garlic, white wine, and of course, parsley.

Jay Weinstein ("Good Catch," page 68) is a New York City-based food writer, editor, cooking teacher, and cookbook author. His writing and recipes have been featured in *The New York Times, National Geographic Traveler,* and *Travel + Leisure.*

• **My favorite food memory is...** eating a peach I picked through the window of my car in Escondido, California. It was so ripe, the juice ran down my arm when I bit into it. No napkin was worthy of it.

• **My top food destination is...** Singapore.

• **My guilty food pleasure is...** imitation crab sticks mixed with mayo and Old Bay on a toasted hot dog roll.

fine **Cooking**

National Advertising Manager	Patrick J. O'Donnell 203-304-3250 podonnell@taunton.com
Advertising Sales East Coast	Judy Caruso 203-304-3468 jcaruso@taunton.com
	Margaret Fleming-O'Brien 203-304-3530 mflemingobrien@taunton.com
Midwest	Mark Adeszko 312-629-5222 madeszko@aol.com
West Coast	Chuck Carroll 818-972-9650 cwcarroll@earthlink.net
Director of Advertising Marketing	Kristen Lacey
Senior Marketing Manager, Advertising	Karen Lutjen

Member Audit Bureau of Circulation	The Audit Bureau

Senior Consumer Marketing Director	Beth Reynolds, ProCirc
Senior Consumer Marketing Manager	Melissa Robinson
Senior Manager Web Marketing	Robert Harlow
Business Managers	David Pond, Megan Sangster

The Taunton Press
Inspiration for hands-on living®
Independent publishers since 1975
Founders, Paul & Jan Roman

President	Suzanne Roman
EVP & CFO	Timothy Rahr
SVP & Chief Content Officer	Paul Spring
SVP, Creative	Susan Edelman
SVP & Chief Marketing Officer	Janine Scolpino
SVP, Advertising Sales	Karl Elken
SVP, Technology	Jay Hartley
SVP, Operations	Thomas Luxeder
VP, Taunton Interactive	Jason Revzon
VP, Digital Content	Anatole Burkin
VP, Editorial Development	Maria Taylor
VP, Single Copy Sales	Jay Annis
VP & Controller	Wayne Reynolds
VP, Finance	Kathy Worth
VP, Human Resources	Carol Marotti
VP, Fulfillment	Patricia Williamson

Publishers of magazines, books, videos and online
Fine Woodworking • Fine Homebuilding
Threads • Fine Gardening • Fine Cooking
www.taunton.com

Photographs by, from top left, Con Poulos, Baltz & Company, Michael Arden, Martin Kelley, Lisa Bell, Tuan Pu Wang

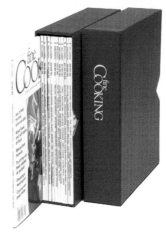

What's for (Thanksgiving) Dinner?

During the holidays, it's more pressing than ever to have the right answer to that question. At **FineCooking.com/thanksgiving** you'll find the tools, videos, and recipes for putting together a memorable feast:

MENU MAKER

Use this tool to build your custom menu from hundreds of recipes, complete with a tailored-to-you shopping list and timeline.

CREATE YOUR OWN RECIPE

Our exclusive recipe builder lets you put your own personalized stamp on Thanksgiving favorites. Create a stuffing, a potato gratin, or a fruit tart with your favorite flavors and add-ins, then print or share the recipe.

WATCH AND LEARN

Get quick video tips on brining or carving a turkey, the best tools for mashed potatoes, and how to blind bake a piecrust.

The Fine Cooking Culinary School

CooksClub members get an exclusive pass to *Fine Cooking*'s new in-depth how-to video series. Drop in for a single class, or take a multi-class series.

Starting in October, look for our 10-class course on pies and tarts with contributing editor Abigail Johnson Dodge. You'll learn:

- The basics of perfect piecrust
- An easy technique for lattice crusts
- Classic holiday pies
- From-scratch puff pastry tarts

Join CooksClub today for full access!

Winners' Spotlight

Congratulations to Brynne Valouch, winner of our Create Your Own Ice Cream Contest, which invited users to dream up concoctions based on David Lebovitz's simple ice cream formula (June/July 2009). The FineCooking.com community chose Brynne's **Spiced Sweet Potato Ice Cream** as the winner out of 10 wildly creative entries. Check out her recipe at FineCooking.com.

Brynne wins a Cuisinart Flavor Duo two-bowl ice cream maker.

fine Cooking®

To contact us:
Fine Cooking,
The Taunton Press,
63 South Main Street,
P.O. Box 5506, Newtown,
CT 06470-5506
Tel: 203-426-8171

Send an e-mail to:
fc@taunton.com

Visit:
www.finecooking.com

To submit an article proposal:
Write to *Fine Cooking* at the address above or
Call: 800-309-0744
Fax: 203-426-3434
Email: fc@taunton.com

To subscribe or place an order:
Visit www.finecooking.com/fcorder
or call: 800-888-8286
9am-9pm ET Mon-Fri
9am-5pm ET Sat

To find out about *Fine Cooking* products:
Visit www.finecooking.com/products

To get help with online member services:
Visit www.finecooking.com/customerservice

To find answers to frequently asked questions:
Visit www.finecooking.com/FAQs

To contact *Fine Cooking* customer service:
Email us at support@customerservice.taunton.com

**To speak directly to a customer service
professional:**
Call 800-477-8727 9am-5pm ET Mon-Fri

To sell *Fine Cooking* in your store:
Call us toll-free at 866-505-4674, or
email us at magazinesales@taunton.com

To advertise in *Fine Cooking*:
Call 800-309-8940
Or email us at fcads@taunton.com

Mailing list:
We make a portion of our mailing list available
to reputable firms. If you would prefer that
we not include your name, please visit:
www.finecooking.com/privacy
or call: 800-477-8727 9am-5pm ET Mon-Fri

For employment information:
Visit www.careers.taunton.com

The Taunton guarantee:
If at any time you're not completely satisfied with
Fine Cooking, you can cancel your subscription and
receive a full and immediate refund of the entire
subscription price. No questions asked.

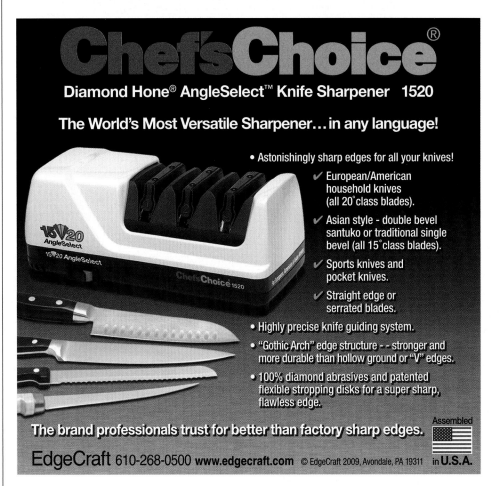

Your famous raspberry streusel just became legendary.

Culinary bliss awaits with Plugrá® European-Style Butter as your secret ingredient. Create higher cakes and flakier pastries for *pâtisserie* that are truly *magnifique.*

PLUGRÁ®
EUROPEAN STYLE BUTTER

Discover inspiration from the masters at www.plugra.com.

MARKETPLACE

Shop Smarter, Eat Better

TRY THIS

Persimmons

EASILY MISTAKEN for underripe tomatoes, these round, orangy-red fruits are popular the world over. Depending on the variety, persimmons can have smooth, custard-like flesh that tastes of banana and mango, or firmer flesh with notes of apricots and a mellow sweetness.

You can eat persimmons out of hand or add them to sweet dishes such as puddings, breads, cookies, and ice cream. They're also delicious in savory preparations like salsas and relishes, in salads, or sautéed as a side dish for roasted pork or lamb. So the next time you see them in the produce aisle, bring home a few and get a taste of what you've been missing.

Continued on page 16

What they are

Part of the genus *Diospyros,* which means "fruit of the gods" in Greek, persimmons are tree fruits grown in many countries, including China, Italy, the United States, and Japan (where they are considered the national fruit). They are in season from fall through winter and are an excellent source of fiber as well as vitamins A and C.

Persimmon varieties are divided into two categories, astringent and nonastringent. Astringent varieties, such as the acorn-shaped Hachiya, are tannic and sour when underripe; they should be eaten when very ripe and jelly-soft. Fuyu (shown on page 15) is the most common nonastringent variety; shaped like pincushions, they are smaller than Hachiyas and have fewer tannins, so they can be eaten both underripe and soft. The Fuyu has a subtle, crisp flavor reminiscent of apricots, while the Hachiya has tropical fruit notes and is very rich and sweet.

How to buy and store them

Look for fruit that is plump, heavy for its size, and vibrantly colored, with glossy skin. Avoid those with bruises, blemishes, or cracks. Keep the unripe fruit at room temperature, preferably in a brown paper bag, to help it ripen. If persimmons are already ripe and soft when you buy them, eat them right away or store in the refrigerator for no more than two days.

How to cook with them

Remove the core for both eating and cooking. The skin is edible, though you may want to peel it, because it can be a little waxy. Cut the fruit into wedges, slices, or cubes.

Ripe Hachiyas are often the persimmon of choice for sweet dishes. The firmer texture and subtly sweet flavor of Fuyus make them a good variety for savory preparations.

—*Melissa Pellegrino*

fuyu persimmon and fennel salad with hazelnuts

Serves 6

- 6 Tbs. fresh orange juice
- 2 Tbs. white wine vinegar
- 2 Tbs. minced shallot
- 2 tsp. finely grated orange zest
  Kosher salt
- ½ cup extra-virgin olive oil
- 4 medium ripe Fuyu persimmons, peeled, quartered, cored, and thinly sliced
- 2 medium bulbs fennel, trimmed, cored, and very thinly sliced or shaved with a mandoline or vegetable peeler
- ½ cup lightly packed fresh flat-leaf parsley leaves, coarsely torn if large

Freshly ground black pepper
- ½ cup toasted, peeled hazelnuts, chopped
- ½ cup shaved Parmigiano-Reggiano

Put the orange juice, vinegar, shallot, zest, and ¼ tsp. salt in a small bowl and let sit for 15 to 30 minutes to soften the shallot and meld the flavors. Gradually whisk in the oil.

In a large bowl, toss the persimmons, fennel, and parsley with enough of the vinaigrette to coat (you may not need all of it). Season to taste with salt and pepper. Divide among 6 salad plates and sprinkle with the hazelnuts and Parmigiano-Reggiano.

Pecans, Eggplant, Sweet Potatoes

Nine ways to use three seasonal ingredients we can't get enough of. *Fine Cooking* editors share some delicious ideas.

Pecans

Pecan-crusted fish fillets

Chopped pecans make a crunchy crust for any thin white fish fillet (think tilapia or sole). Dredge the fillet in flour, dip it in buttermilk, then coat with a mixture of finely chopped pecans, breadcrumbs, salt, and pepper. Cook the fillets in a little oil in a nonstick skillet until the crust is golden and the fish flakes.

—Lisa Waddle

Pecan butter

Combine chopped toasted pecans with a softened stick of unsalted butter, maple syrup, and a pinch of salt. Using waxed paper or plastic wrap, roll the pecan butter into a long, thin cylinder and chill in the refrigerator until firm. It's great on everything from pancakes and baked potatoes to steamed veggies.

—Juli Roberts

Sugar and spice pecans

Toast pecans on a baking sheet in a medium-hot oven. Mix light brown sugar, cayenne, kosher salt, and a few grinds of black pepper. Transfer the pecans to a large bowl and toss them with melted butter and the sugar-spice mixture. Line the baking sheet with foil, return the pecans to the sheet, and bake again until golden brown. The pecans will continue to crisp as they cool.

—Kelly Gearity

Eggplant

Roasted eggplant "sandwiches"

This bread-free sandwich is a favorite at my house. Stack sliced fresh mozzarella, torn fresh basil, and a slice or two of ripe tomato between thick slices of roasted eggplant, and serve with a fork and knife.

—Lisa Waddle

Grilled eggplant with cumin-coriander butter

Toast some whole cumin, coriander, and brown mustard seeds in a dry skillet until aromatic. Lightly crush the seeds in the pan (you can use the bottom of a small pot), then add a few tablespoons of butter to the pan and stir to melt. Pour the spiced butter over slices or wedges of grilled or roasted eggplant.

—Sarah Breckenridge

Marinated eggplant

For an easy appetizer, arrange grilled eggplant slices in a shallow bowl, add some sliced garlic, chopped fresh parsley and basil, and pour on enough good olive oil to soak the eggplant. Cover and marinate for 24 hours in the refrigerator before serving at room temperature.

—Laura Giannatempo

Sweet Potatoes

Sweet potato pancakes

Jazz up a breakfast favorite by adding cooled mashed sweet potato to the batter. I use my standard pancake recipe but include about ½ cup of mashed sweet potato for every 1 cup of flour. A touch of cinnamon and nutmeg is nice, too.

—Denise Mickelsen

Twice-baked sweet potatoes

Bake sweet potatoes until tender, then halve them lengthwise and scoop out the flesh, leaving a border of flesh so the skin holds its shape. Mash the flesh with either chipotle, lime juice, and sour cream or maple syrup, fresh thyme, and butter. Mound the mash back into the skins and bake until hot.

—Jennifer Armentrout

Sweet potato-leek soup

Sauté some sliced leeks in butter and oil until tender but not browned. Add sliced sweet potatoes and enough chicken broth to cover. Simmer with a bouquet garni (bay leaf, thyme, parsley, and black peppercorns in a cheesecloth pouch) until the potatoes are tender. Discard the bouquet and purée. Serve with a drizzle of cream and toasted pumpkin seeds.

—Melissa Pellegrino

Amore ®

A LITTLE LOVE GOES A LONG WAY™

Snuggle into Autumn with
hearty, healthy, seasonal cooking.
Concentrated Amore pastes are
convenient, fun to use, and all
natural. Give us a squeeze and
bring vibrant flavors, grown in
Italy, to your recipes.

Visit amorebrand.com
for more delicious recipes.

Creamy Bow Tie Casserole   Serves 6

1/4 cup Amore Tomato Paste
2 tsp Amore Pesto Paste
  or 1/4 cup chopped fresh basil
1 tsp Amore Garlic Paste
15oz container ricotta
1 cup milk

8oz bow tie pasta
Salt
4 oz mozzarella, cut into 1/2-dice
1 cup thawed frozen peas
1 cup halved cherry tomatoes
1 cup grated Parmesan

In a large bowl, whisk together the Amore Tomato, Pesto and Garlic Pastes with
the ricotta until smooth. Whisk in the milk. Cook the pasta
in a large pot of boiling salted water until tender.
Drain well. Toss the pasta with the tomato paste
mixture. Stir in the mozzarella, peas, cherry
tomatoes, and half of the Parmesan. Spread the
pasta in a buttered 8-inch square baking dish.
Sprinkle with the remaining Parmesan. Cover
with foil and bake in a 350°F oven for 30 minutes.
Uncover and bake 10 minutes more or until browned
and bubbly. Serve hot.

Apples and Pears

Make the most of the season's bounty—
turn it into sweet fruit butter.

BY ABIGAIL JOHNSON DODGE

NOW IS THE BEST TIME to buy (or pick) crisp, juicy fall apples and pears, so go wild at your local orchard or farmers' market and start cooking. Fruit butter—a sweet spread made from cooked-down fruit—is a great way to keep the flavors of the season on hand for weeks (or months, if canned). It's simple to make and utterly delicious.

Fruit butter is, of course, perfect for spreading on hot toast, muffins, or scones, but you can do much more with it. Use it to glaze lamb chops or pork tenderloin; make a quick sundae with vanilla or cinnamon ice cream, warm fruit butter, and toasted nuts; stir the butter into plain yogurt, cottage cheese, or oatmeal; or use it instead of mayonnaise on a turkey and cheddar panini. The possibilities are endless, though the season is not.

Top picks

There are many flavorful apple and pear varieties available nationally, and most of them make delicious fruit butters. Here are our favorites:

Apples: Honey Crisp, Ida Red, Rome Beauty, McIntosh, Cortland, Ginger Gold, Golden Delicious

Pears: Anjou, Concorde, Bosc, Bartlett

maple apple-pear butter

Cook the apples and pears with their peels, cores, and seeds to get every ounce of flavor from the fruit. Regardless of what pear variety you use, they must be ripe, or your butter may be unpleasantly grainy.

Yields 5½ cups

3½	lb. ripe pears
2½	lb. apples
3	cups apple or pear cider
1⅓	cups pure maple syrup
¼	cup firmly packed light brown sugar
1½	tsp. ground cinnamon
¼	tsp. ground cloves
¼	tsp. table salt
1	Tbs. lemon juice
1½	tsp. pure vanilla extract

Cut the pears into 1-inch chunks. Cut the apples in half or into quarters if large. Put the fruit and the cider in a very large pot (at least 7-quart capacity). Bring to a boil over high heat. Reduce the heat to medium low and simmer, stirring frequently, until the fruit is very soft when pierced with a knife, 40 to 60 minutes. Take the pot off the heat.

Set a food mill fitted with a fine sieve disk over a large bowl. (For more on food mills, see Test Kitchen, p. 83.) Purée the fruit in small batches, discarding seeds and skins.

Wipe out any remaining seeds or peels from the pot and pour in the purée. Add the maple syrup, brown sugar, cinnamon, cloves, and salt. Stir until well blended.

Bring to a boil over high heat. Reduce the heat to low or medium low to maintain a simmer. Using a large spoon, skim off most of the foam that rises to the surface during the initial simmering.

Continue simmering, stirring often with an angled spatula, making sure to scrape the bottom, corners, and sides of the pot, until the purée becomes thick and dark and the bubbling becomes slow and laborious (more like volcanic burps than bubbles), 1¾ hours to 2¾ hours. Be sure to stir toward the end of cooking to avoid scorching. To test for doneness, spoon a dollop of the butter onto a small plate and refrigerate for a minute or two. It should hold its shape with no water separating out around its edge.

Remove the pot from the heat and add the lemon juice and vanilla, stirring until well blended. Transfer the butter to a container, let cool to room temperature, and then store, covered, in the refrigerator for up to 3 weeks.

Note: For longer storage at room temperature, can the fruit butter. Transfer the hot butter to clean, hot canning jars, leaving ¼ inch of headspace in each jar, and follow the canning directions at FineCooking.com/extras, processing the butter for 10 minutes.

Abby Dodge is a Fine Cooking *contributing editor.*

The inspiration of timeless design.
The symbol of impeccable performance.

GET IT WHILE IT'S HOT!

FREE WARMING DRAWER or MICROWAVE when you purchase an eligible Dual-Fuel Range or Wall Oven/Cooktop combination. For a limited time. Offer ends December 31, 2009.

The Renaissance® Wall Oven and Cooktop by Dacor. Timeless design showcased by the Illumina™ Burner Control. And advanced features like the RapidHeat™ Bake Element for faster pre-heating and remarkably even temperature control. Inspiration is in the details. Dacor is in the details.

Visit **dacor.com/hot** or call 800.793.0093 for more details.

The Life of the Kitchen®

Fingerling Potatoes

Making the most of a favorite food find from a warehouse store. BY MELISSA PELLEGRINO

WHO KNEW YOU COULD BUY big bags of fingerling potatoes—those small, slender, somewhat finger-shaped spuds—in the produce section of your local warehouse store? They're such a tasty find. And we've got ideas to help you use them up—a hearty salad, a refined take on fish and chips, and a luscious braise. That's some pretty big flavor from some small potatoes.

The Big Buy

What: Fingerling potatoes (mixed varieties)
How much: 5-lb. bags
How to store: Potatoes should be stored in a cool, dark place, ideally between 45°F and 50°F. Never refrigerate raw potatoes because low temperatures will cause some of their starches to convert to sugars, which taste unpleasant and can lead to overbrowning during cooking. Smaller potatoes don't last as long as larger ones, so use fingerlings within a week, if you can. If they have begun to sprout, they are past their prime.

glazed fingerling potato salad with pancetta and warm mustard vinaigrette

Potatoes, crisp pancetta, and aged Gouda, along with some good-for-you greens, make for one delicious salad.
Serves 4

4	Tbs. unsalted butter
¾	lb. fingerling potatoes (7 or 8 medium), quartered lengthwise
	Kosher salt
2	oz. pancetta, cut into ¼-inch dice (⅓ cup)
5	Tbs. extra-virgin olive oil
2	Tbs. finely chopped shallot
3	Tbs. red wine vinegar
1	tsp. Dijon mustard
	Freshly ground black pepper
4	oz. escarole, torn into small pieces (6 cups)
½	cup shaved aged Gouda (1½ oz.)

Melt 2 Tbs. of the butter in a 10-inch straight-sided sauté pan over medium heat. Add the potatoes and enough water to just cover them (about 2 cups). Bring to a boil. Add 1 tsp. salt, cover the pan, reduce the heat to medium low, and cook, shaking the pan occasionally, until the potatoes are just tender, about 8 minutes. Uncover the pan, raise the heat to medium high, and add the remaining 2 Tbs. butter. Cook, shaking the pan occasionally, until all of the liquid has reduced to a glaze

and the potatoes are lightly browned, about 20 minutes more.

Meanwhile, cook the pancetta in an 8-inch nonstick skillet over medium heat, stirring occasionally, until crisp, 6 to 8 minutes. Transfer to a paper-towel-lined plate. Pour off any fat from the pan, return the pan to medium heat, and add ½ Tbs. of the oil. Add the shallot to the pan and cook, stirring, until tender, about 2 minutes. Stir in the vinegar and mustard and cook until the mustard is smooth, 30 seconds to 1 minute. Transfer the mixture to a small bowl and gradually whisk in the remaining 4½ Tbs. oil. Season to taste with salt and pepper.

Put the escarole and pancetta in a large bowl and toss with 3 Tbs. of the vinaigrette. Season to taste with salt and pepper. Divide the salad and the potatoes among 4 salad plates and sprinkle with the cheese. Drizzle with the remaining vinaigrette and serve.

braised fingerling potatoes with fennel, olives, and thyme

This rustic side dish is great with roasted lamb or pork.

Serves 4

- 3 Tbs. extra-virgin olive oil
- ¾ lb. fingerling potatoes (7 or 8 medium), cut lengthwise into ¼-inch-thick slices
- 1 small bulb fennel, trimmed and halved lengthwise, then cut lengthwise into ½-inch-thick slices
- 1 medium sweet onion, thinly sliced
- ½ cup lower-salt chicken broth

- 3 sprigs fresh thyme, plus 2 tsp. chopped fresh thyme for garnish
  Kosher salt and freshly ground black pepper
- ¼ cup pitted Niçoise olives

Heat the oven to 375°F.
Heat 1½ Tbs. of the oil in a 10-inch straight-sided sauté pan over medium-high heat. Add the potatoes and ¼ tsp. salt and cook, stirring occasionally, until the potatoes begin to brown, about 7 minutes. Transfer the potatoes to a plate.

Add the remaining 1½ Tbs. oil and the fennel to the pan with a pinch of salt and cook, stirring occasionally, until lightly browned, about 5 minutes. Add the onion to the pan and cook, stirring often, until starting to soften and lightly brown, 2 minutes more. Add the broth and bring to a boil. Gently nestle the potatoes into the fennel-onion mixture and add the thyme sprigs. Cover the pan and braise in the oven until the potatoes and fennel are tender, about 20 minutes.

Uncover the pan, add the olives, and continue to braise until most of the liquid has evaporated and the vegetables are meltingly tender, another 10 minutes. Remove from the oven, discard the thyme sprigs, and season to taste with salt and pepper. Garnish with the chopped thyme and serve.

fingerling potato galettes with chive crème fraîche and smoked trout

This elegant starter takes fish and chips to a whole new level.

Serves 4

- 8 oz. fingerling potatoes (about 5 medium)
- 2 Tbs. extra-virgin olive oil
  Kosher salt and freshly ground black pepper
- ¼ cup crème fraîche
- 2 Tbs. thinly sliced fresh chives
- ¼ tsp. finely grated lemon zest
- 12 small, thin slices smoked trout (about 4 oz.)

Heat the oven to 375°F. Line a rimmed baking sheet with a nonstick baking liner or parchment.

Using a mandoline or a sharp knife, cut the potatoes lengthwise into ¹⁄₁₆-inch-thick slices. Soak the 40 nicest, most even slices in a large bowl of cold water until pliable, about 20 minutes.

Drain the potatoes and pat dry with paper towels. Put them in a medium bowl and toss with the oil, 1 tsp. salt, and ½ tsp. pepper. Fan 10 potato slices into a 6-inch circle (like a flower) on the prepared sheet. Repeat with the remaining potato slices to make 4 individual circles. Cover the potatoes with parchment and set another baking sheet on top to keep the potatoes flat. Bake until tender, about 15 minutes. Remove the top baking sheet and the parchment and continue to cook until crisp and browned, 15 to 20 minutes more.

Meanwhile, in a small bowl, whisk the crème fraîche, 1½ Tbs. of the chives, the lemon zest, ⅛ tsp. salt, and ¼ tsp. pepper.

Carefully transfer the potato galettes to individual plates. Place one slice of trout on a potato circle. Add a dollop of crème fraîche, then another slice of trout, another dollop of crème fraîche, and a final slice of trout. Top with a small dollop of crème fraîche and garnish with some of the remaining chives and a grind of pepper. Repeat with the remaining galettes, trout, crème fraîche, chives, and pepper.

Great Finds

Our latest buys for the kitchen and table. **BY DENISE MICKELSEN**

Pop-Up Style

You'll have fun setting the table with these recycled paper placemats with pop-up cutouts. They do double-duty as place cards when you write your guests' names on them. Available in assorted styles, including scooter with groceries (shown). **$26 for a pack of 10 at publiqueshop .com; 415-305-1999.**

Get Spicy

Merquén, a smoky Chilean spice blend of ground cacho de cabra chiles, coriander, cumin, and salt from Etnia, a Chilean fair-trade company, is our new go-to flavoring. It's great on roasted veggies, pork, chicken, or beef, and in marinades and salsas. **$7 for a 1-ounce bottle at gourmetimportshop .com; 800-995-6530.**

The Low Down

Here's a kitchen fantasy (copper!) with a real purpose. Mauviel's new heavy-duty 12x16x2¼-inch shallow roasting pan has low sides for increased air flow around food, which promotes browning and crisping. The copper construction makes for superior heat conductivity, even cooking, and durability. **M'Heritage shallow roaster (copper and stainless steel), $450 at metrokitchen.com; 888-892-9911.**

Pour Pretty

Emile Henry's lovely new glazed pitcher is made from the same Burgundian clay as their ovenware, which means it's durable, holds temperature well (be it hot or cold), and is dishwasher safe. Available in six colors, including figue (shown). **Urban bistro 1-liter pitcher, $45; for stores, www.emilehenry .com; 302-326-4800.**

Fancy Foods

Sweet and savory vinegars, preserves, rubs, salts, sauces, teas, and cocoas are just some of the handmade items available from the Vervacious husband-and-wife team of Heidi and Mark Stanvick. We especially love the gingery sancho pepper sashimi dipping sauce and the delicate saffron fleur de sel. **From $7 to $19.50 at vervacious.com; 207-221-3590.**

Happy Chic

This colorful enamel and polished-nickel serving set from designer Jonathan Adler brings modern elegance and a touch of whimsy to your table. Available in blue, lime, and orange (shown). **Enamel serving set, $78 at jonathanadler.com; 800-963-0891.**

Joe to Go

Never settle for take-out coffee again with this handy French press and travel mug combo. Available in eight colors, including green (shown). **16-ounce Bodum travel press, $30 at bodumusa .com; 800-232-6386.**

IF YOU CAN FIND FRESHER INGREDIENTS YOU'RE ON A FARM.

Shown: greek salad with spinach & feta chicken sausage.

We've spent years in the kitchen—finding the perfect combinations of fresh, all natural ingredients—so that you only need minutes to turn our fully cooked, all natural chicken sausage into a healthy, delicious meal that you and your family will love. In fourteen gourmet flavors.

For healthy and delicious meal ideas from al fresco, including the recipe shown, go to:

alfrescoallnatural.com

al fresco ®

live life with flavor

70% less fat than pork sausage * All natural * No artificial ingredients or preservatives

Ingredient Temperatures

Think it doesn't matter if your butter and eggs are room temperature or right out of the fridge? Think again. BY BRIAN GEIGER

OCCASIONALLY, I AM IMPATIENT. I like to skip steps whenever I can, especially if those steps seem nonsensical. If it's time to make a cake, and the recipe says to let the ingredients come to room temperature before combining them, I used to think, "Come on. Surely there's no real reason I can't use the butter if it's a little firm?" Same with the eggs. Is moving them from the fridge to the countertop really going to make a difference?

When it comes to the science of baking, the answer is a resounding yes. Bake a cake with frigid butter and eggs and you'll end up with something resembling a pancake. That's why some recipes call for "room-temperature" ingredients, a frustratingly general concept, especially from a scientific point of view. Think about it: The temperature of a room varies wildly based on location, season, and availability of a heating or

cooling system. There must be a smarter way to gauge the temperature, right?

Better lift with butter

Let's start by looking at what we want the butter and eggs to do. First at bat, butter. One of the things that distinguishes it from liquid fats like oil is that butter has the ability to hold air. Many cake and cookie recipes tell

Subscribe and save up to $58*

TREAT YOURSELF

☐ 1 year just $29.95 — **Save 30%***
☐ 2 years just $49.95 — **Save 42%***
☐ 3 years just $69.95 — **BEST BUY! Save 45%***

Send no money now. We will bill you later.

N510160N

MR. / MRS. / MS.

ADDRESS   APT. #

CITY

STATE   ZIP   EMAIL (OPTIONAL)

FineCooking.com/order

The Taunton Press will send you occasional notices about noteworthy products and exclusive offers.

*Savings off U.S. newsstand price. Above prices for U.S. and Canada (GST included). Payable in U.S. funds. International customers, visit FineCooking.com/order

Treat a friend to *Fine Cooking*

☐ 1 year just $29.95 — **Save 30%***
☐ 2 years just $49.95 — **Save 42%***
☐ 3 years just $69.95 — **BEST BUY! Save 45%***

Send no money now. We will bill you later.

N510161N

YOUR NAME: **SEND GIFT TO:**

ADDRESS   ADDRESS

APT. #   CITY   APT. #   CITY

STATE   ZIP   STATE   ZIP

EMAIL (OPTIONAL)

The Taunton Press will send you occasional notices about noteworthy products and exclusive offers.

*Savings off U.S. newsstand price. Above prices for U.S. and Canada (GST included). Payable in U.S. funds. International customers, visit FineCooking.com/order

The Taunton Press
Inspiration for hands-on living®

||||

BUSINESS REPLY MAIL
FIRST-CLASS MAIL   PERMIT NO. 6   NEWTOWN CT

POSTAGE WILL BE PAID BY ADDRESSEE

®

63 S MAIN ST
PO BOX 5507
NEWTOWN CT 06470-9879

NO POSTAGE
NECESSARY
IF MAILED
IN THE
UNITED STATES

||||..||.|.||.|.|||.|.||.|.|.||..|.|||

THE MORE YOU GOT - THE MORE IT RISES NG" 65°

'TTER

"SLIGHTLY FIRM"

you to beat sugar into butter "until light and fluffy," which creates air bubbles. (This is called the creaming method.) The more bubbles you have, the higher the confection will rise. If your butter is too cold, though, the fat and sugar won't mix, resulting in few bubbles. (Butter that's too warm isn't good either—it will melt, so the bubbles won't have any support and will disappear.)

Research shows that it's best to bake with butter that's about 65°F, which is actually cooler than room temperature in most homes. So how do you tell if your butter is the right temp? Short of using an instant-read thermometer in a stick of butter, I like to use the thumb method. I learned this from

master baker Carole Walter, author of the cookbooks *Great Cakes* and *Great Cookies*. She suggests holding a wrapped stick of butter in your hand and pressing firmly with your thumb. There should be a slight indentation. She refers to this butter as "slightly firm," a more descriptive (and practical) phrase than "room temperature."

(A pie aside: If you're making a piecrust, though—as in the recipe on page 58—your butter needs are completely different. You want the butter very cold so that it remains in small solid pieces while being worked into the flour. These small pieces ensure a flaky crust, because they melt in the oven and leave steam pockets.)

The egg also raises

Eggs are also crucial in giving loft to baked goods. The white of the egg is 90 percent water and 10 percent protein; when you beat an egg, it's the protein that traps the air bubbles, and when incorporated into baked goods, these bubbles expand in the heat of the oven. Egg whites can be whipped up to eight times their volume, but this maximum air-trapping happens only when the eggs are warm; in warm eggs, the whites and yolks are looser, so it's easier to incorporate air into them (which is the whole point).

Warmer eggs are also better when you're mixing batter for cakes and cookies, because if you introduce cold eggs to a warmer butter-sugar mixture, the fat in the butter could harden. That would impede integration of the butter and eggs, which is why you're creaming them to begin with.

But you do want your eggs to be cold if you need to separate the whites and yolks. Cold eggs are easier to separate, so if your recipe calls for the yolks and whites to be separated, do it before warming the eggs.

Quick rescue

The good news is, if your eggs and butter are cold, it doesn't take long to bring them to a respectable baking temperature. With eggs, just fill a glass or bowl with warm water and submerge the eggs (in their shells) for 5 to

10 minutes. The water will bring the eggs up to temp in a hurry, with no risk of actually cooking them.

As for butter, some people like to stick it in the microwave, but I find that nuking does an uneven job. Instead, I cut the butter into smaller pieces (to increase its surface area), spread it on a plate or baking sheet, and leave it out on the counter. In about 20 minutes, it will be warm enough to bring your cakes to great heights.

Knowing the science behind ingredient temperatures makes me no less impatient when it comes time to mix up a cake. But knowing that cold eggs and butter will result in a dense, less tender cake tempers my haste—especially when the wait is shorter than an episode of *Firefly*.

Brian Geiger is a robotics project manager who was recently named the best piemaker in Charlottesville, Virginia. Follow his blog at FineCooking.com.

To chill or not to chill

Talk of leaving eggs or butter out at room temperature tends to raise red flags in the food safety department. Here's the straight story.

Butter can be left out on the counter (for easier spreading) without fear of food poisoning. However, most butter makers recommend refrigerating to maintain the best flavor. (It's pretty easy to spot rancid butter: It turns a deeper color and becomes less opaque.)

Eggs can carry salmonella, so the risks of not refrigerating are a bit higher. Markets in other countries regularly store eggs at room temperature, but the USDA recommends refrigerating them, because a colder temperature will inhibit the growth of bacteria. Since it's a simple matter of a quick soak in warm tap water to bring eggs in the shell up to temperature for baking (see Quick rescue, at left), it's best to keep them chilled.

He made California a world-renowned destination for wine.

Maybe he can do the same for your house.

Skeptics laughed when Robert Mondavi doggedly set out to prove that California wines could be quality wines. But today a glass of Woodbridge by Robert Mondavi may make you smile in a totally different way.

His name is on the bottle. His story is in it.

WOODBRIDGE
by Robert Mondavi

REPERTOIRE

How to Make
Thanksgiving Dinner

Your holiday meal just got a lot easier. Consider this your all-in-one guide to making a delicious, stress-free dinner on the big day. Everything you need to know is right here—simple recipes for all the classics (think juicy roast turkey with pan gravy, bread stuffing, mashed potatoes, and cranberry sauce), plus a cook's toolbox, a handy timeline, and plenty of tips so you can pull it off like a pro. **BY PAM ANDERSON**

Food styling by Allison Ehri Kreitler

holiday classics

dry-rubbed roast turkey with pan gravy

cranberry sauce with caramelized onions

bread stuffing with fresh herbs

rustic mashed potatoes

(For more side dish ideas and desserts, see the Recipe Index, page 97)

dry-rubbed roast turkey with pan gravy

Master the basics—turkey, gravy, stuffing, cranberry sauce, and mashed potatoes—and the rest will be easy. Trust us! Let the cooking begin with the big bird, which gets a salt rub. Leave it in the fridge overnight to season the meat and dry the skin so that it will get good and crisp. The gravy will come together while the cooked turkey rests.

Serves 12

- ½ **cup finely chopped fresh sage**
- 2 **Tbs. finely grated orange zest**
- 1 **oz. kosher salt (¼ cup Diamond Crystal or 2 Tbs. Morton); more as needed**

Freshly ground black pepper
- 1 **12-lb. all-natural turkey**
- 2 **large carrots, cut into 1- to 2-inch chunks**
- 2 **medium celery stalks, cut into 1- to 2-inch chunks**
- 1 **medium yellow onion, cut into 1- to 2-inch chunks**
- 1 **Tbs. extra-virgin olive oil; more as needed**
- ½ **cup dry white wine or vermouth**
- 1½ **cups lower-salt chicken broth**
- 1⅛ **oz. (¼ cup) all-purpose flour**

Season the turkey: In a medium bowl, mix the sage, zest, 1 oz. salt, and 1 Tbs. pepper.

Remove the tail, neck, heart, and gizzard from the turkey and reserve for making turkey broth, if you like (go to FineCooking.com for a recipe). Discard the liver. Remove and discard the plastic timer and any metal or plastic leg holders. Rinse and pat the turkey dry. Rub the spice mixture under the turkey's skin over the entire breast **1**, legs, and thighs, as well as in the cavity and over the wings. Set on a platter or pan large enough to hold the turkey and refrigerate uncovered overnight.

Roast the turkey: Position a rack in the bottom of the oven and heat the oven to 400°F. In a large bowl, toss the carrots, celery, and onion

Photographs by Scott Phillips

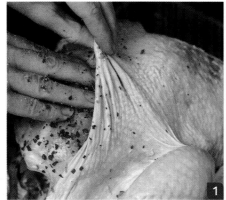

part of the thigh registers 175°F, an additional 1 to 1½ hours. During this phase, check the vegetables in the pan every 20 minutes or so: They should be brown, but if they or the drippings threaten to burn, add about ¼ cup water—you may need to do this several times.

When the turkey is done, protect your hands with silicone oven mitts or wads of paper towels and tilt the turkey so the juices in the cavity run into the roasting pan. Transfer the turkey to a carving board and let it rest for 30 to 40 minutes. Carve when ready to serve.

Make the gravy: While the turkey is resting, set the roasting pan over medium-high heat. Add the wine and cook, using a wooden spoon or heatproof spatula to loosen the brown bits, until reduced by about half, 2 to 3 minutes. Strain the contents of the roasting pan into a bowl, pressing on the solids to release the flavorful drippings. Discard the solids.

In a 1-quart liquid measuring cup, combine the broth with 1½ cups water. Tasting as you go, add enough of the pan drippings to the broth to make a flavorful yet not overly salted liquid—you may or may not use all of the drippings. Let sit until the fat rises to the surface. Skim off and reserve as much fat as possible.

Measure 4 Tbs. of the fat into a medium saucepan (supplement with olive oil if necessary) over medium heat. Whisk in the flour. Cook, whisking almost constantly, for 2 to 3 minutes. Whisk in about ½ cup of the broth. As soon as the broth thickens, whisk in another ½ cup. Repeat until the mixture stays relatively smooth, at which point you can whisk in the remaining broth **2**. Bring to a simmer and cook, whisking frequently, for 5 to 10 minutes to develop the flavor. The gravy will be on the thin side; if you prefer it thicker, continue simmering until thickened to your liking, but expect the flavor to concentrate as well. Season to taste with salt and pepper. Pour into a gravy boat and serve with the carved turkey.

with the oil. Put half of the vegetables in the center of a large flameproof roasting pan and put the rest in the turkey cavity. Tuck the wings behind the turkey's neck and tie the legs together with twine. Set a V-rack in the roasting pan over the vegetables. Put the turkey breast side down on the V-rack. Roast for 1 hour.

Remove the pan from the oven and baste the turkey back and sides with some of the pan drippings. With silicone oven mitts or two wads of paper towels, carefully turn the turkey breast side up and baste with more pan drippings. Continue to roast the turkey until an instant-read thermometer inserted in the thickest

T-Day Tip Sheet

Use an all-natural turkey. Avoid kosher birds (they're already brined and will be too salty) and "self-basting" birds (which are treated with fat solutions). Consider ordering your bird in advance.

Rub it in. Use an herb-zest-spice rub on the turkey for loads of extra flavor.

Let it rest. Let your turkey rest for 30 to 40 minutes before carving— the juices will redistribute into the meat, making it moist and tender. It also gives you time to finish preparing the meal.

Get the lumps out. For lump-free gravy, gradually whisk the broth into the roux. The liquid will thicken quickly and get gluey, so keep whisking in more broth, a bit at a time, until the gravy is smooth.

Cool it. Let the cranberry sauce cool to room temperature before serving so it has time to thicken properly.

Dry the bread. For the best stuffing, let the bread dry overnight so it can absorb all the other delicious flavors that make it stuffing; toasting the bread also boosts flavor.

Use the right potato. Russets are your best choice for fluffy mashed potatoes, due to their high starch content. Keeping the skin on adds flavor, texture, and nutrients.

 Ready for the advanced course? Try some variations on the recipes in this story (and find a recipe for homemade Turkey Broth) at FineCooking.com/extras.

Toolbox

Check to make sure you have these kitchen essentials on hand before you start cooking. (For mail-order sources, see page 93.)

- Medium and large bowls
- 1-quart liquid measuring cup
- Chef's knife
- Medium saucepan
- Sieve
- Large flameproof roasting pan
- V-rack
- Kitchen twine
- Baster
- Instant-read thermometer
- Carving board
- Wooden spoon or heatproof spatula
- Whisk
- Large rimmed baking sheet
- 12-inch skillet
- 3-quart baking dish
- 10-inch straight-sided sauté pan with lid
- 8-quart pot with lid
- Skewer or toothpick
- Food mill (see Test Kitchen, page 83), ricer, or stand mixer with paddle attachment

cranberry sauce with caramelized onions

Slow-cooked onions bring extra flavor to this simple sauce, and cloves add warmth.

Yields 2½ to 3 cups

1	**Tbs. vegetable or canola oil**
1	**large yellow onion, cut into medium dice**
⅛	**tsp. ground cloves**
	Kosher salt and freshly ground black pepper
1	**12-oz. bag fresh or thawed frozen cranberries, rinsed and picked over (3½ cups)**
1	**cup granulated sugar**

In a 10-inch straight-sided sauté pan or skillet, heat the oil over medium heat. Add the onions, cloves, a pinch of salt, and a grind or two of pepper. Reduce the heat to low, cover, and cook, stirring occasionally, until the onions are golden-brown and very soft, 20 to 25 minutes. Remove the lid, increase the heat to medium high, and cook the onions, stirring often, until deep caramel-brown, an additional 2 to 3 minutes.

Add the cranberries, sugar, a pinch of salt, and ½ cup water and bring to a simmer over medium-high heat. Simmer for 1 minute, then cover, turn off the heat, and let cool to room temperature.

The sauce may be prepared up to 3 days ahead and refrigerated. Return to room temperature before serving.

The Dinner Plan

You can work through most of Wednesday and still get dinner on the table by Thursday evening. Shop on your way home, and then follow this easy timeline.

1 DAY AHEAD	6 HOURS AHEAD	3 HOURS AHEAD	2 HOURS AHEAD	1 HOUR AHEAD	30 MINUTES AHEAD
Season the turkey and make the cranberry sauce; refrigerate. Cut the bread cubes for the stuffing and let them dry overnight.	Toast the bread cubes and cook the onions and celery for the stuffing.	Begin roasting the turkey.	Make the mashed potatoes and keep them warm; let the cranberry sauce come to room temperature.	Finish and bake the stuffing.	Let the turkey rest; make the gravy.

bread stuffing with fresh herbs

Skip the packaged stuffing mix and use day-old bread and fresh herbs for great flavor.

Serves 12

- 1 lb. crusty Italian or French bread, cut into ½-inch cubes (10 to 12 cups)
- 2 oz. (4 Tbs.) unsalted butter; more for the pan
- 2 medium-large yellow onions, cut into medium dice
- 2 medium celery stalks (or 3 celery heart stalks), cut into medium dice (¾ cup)
- 2 to 3 cups lower-salt chicken broth
- ⅓ cup finely chopped fresh flat-leaf parsley
- 1 Tbs. finely chopped fresh sage
- 1 Tbs. finely chopped fresh thyme
- 2 large eggs, lightly beaten
  Kosher salt and freshly ground black pepper

Spread the bread cubes in a single layer on a large rimmed baking sheet. Let dry overnight.

Position a rack in the center of the oven and heat the oven to 400°F. Bake the bread cubes until light golden-brown, 12 to 15 minutes.

Heat the butter in a 12-inch skillet over medium-high heat. Add the onions and celery and cook, stirring occasionally, until soft but not browned, 6 to 8 minutes. Let cool. (The recipe may be prepared to this point up to 6 hours ahead.)

In a large bowl, mix the bread cubes with the cooked vegetables, 2 cups of the broth, the parsley, sage, thyme, eggs, ¾ tsp. salt, and ½ tsp. pepper. If the liquid isn't immediately absorbed by the bread, toss occasionally for a few minutes until it is. If the liquid is immediately absorbed, toss in another ½ cup broth. The bread should be moist but not soggy. If necessary, add the remaining ½ cup broth.

Butter a 3-quart baking dish (13x9-inch works well). Transfer the bread mixture to the dish, cover with foil, and bake at 400°F until heated through, 25 to 30 minutes. Remove the foil and continue to bake until the top is slightly browned and crusty, about 20 minutes more.

rustic mashed potatoes

These are the real deal—creamy, buttery potatoes that get great texture from leaving the skins on. If you use a ricer or food mill (see Test Kitchen, p. 83, for more information on food mills) to mash the potatoes there will be small bits of skin in the finished dish. If you use a stand mixer, the skin will be in larger pieces.

Serves 12

- 5 lb. medium russet (Idaho) potatoes, scrubbed
- 2½ cups half-and-half
  Kosher salt and freshly ground black pepper
- 5 oz. (10 Tbs.) butter, cut into ½-inch pieces and softened

Put the whole unpeeled potatoes in an 8-quart pot and add enough water to cover. Cover and bring to a boil over high heat. Reduce the heat to medium low and simmer until the potatoes are tender when pierced with a skewer or toothpick, 25 to 30 minutes.

Cut the potatoes into chunks and pass them through a food mill or a ricer into a large heatproof bowl. Alternatively, put them in a stand mixer fitted with the paddle attachment. Cover the mixing bowl with a towel to contain any splashes and mix on low speed until mostly smooth, about 1 minute.

Add the half-and-half, 1 Tbs. salt, and 1 tsp. pepper and mix the potatoes by hand with a wooden spoon until smooth, light, and fluffy. Stir in the butter until melted. Season to taste with salt and pepper.

To keep warm for up to 2 hours, cover the bowl with plastic wrap and set it over (but not in) a pan of barely simmering water.

Pam Anderson is a Fine Cooking *contributing editor.*

The Soup Solution

Starting a meal with a bowl of soup can help you stay healthy and eat less. Here's why. BY ELLIE KRIEGER

WHEN I EAT, I WANT TRUE SATISFACTION. I don't want to leave the table uncomfortably stuffed, but I definitely want to feel fed. I consider it a good thing that I have the appetite of a real, active woman (life's better when you love to eat). But I also want to continue to fit into my favorite jeans and, of course, stay healthy. One way to reconcile these seemingly conflicting desires is with soup. Really.

There is serious research showing that if you eat a bowl of vegetable soup before a meal, you wind up eating less overall and—here's the best part—you feel just as satisfied. That's because with a light soup as a starter, you begin to feel full before you get to the other courses, so you eat fewer calories without even trying (read: no diets). And you can do so deliciously.

For the biggest fill-factor with the lowest caloric impact, a chunky vegetable soup, served hot, is your best bet. It's high in water and fiber (both known to promote a sense of satiety), yet it's light and relatively low in fat (as opposed to cream-based soups, for example). Plus, its temperature compels you to eat it slowly, allowing your stomach the time it needs to tell your brain you're full. And hearty bites of vegetables—rather than puréed veggies—make you chew longer, which also contributes to feeling full.

Besides their clear health benefits, vegetable soups are the perfect canvas for what's in season. This time of year, I love to make hearty, warming soups using a variety of gorgeous fall vegetables, like the ones in this recipe. The foundation of onion and carrots is enhanced with chunks of butternut squash and ribbons of kale in a broth infused with herbs and spices. In two words: satisfaction guaranteed.

"There is serious research showing that if you eat a bowl of vegetable soup before a meal, you eat less overall and you feel just as satisfied," says Ellie.

Good to Know

If you eat soup as a starter, you'll feel satisfied and eat less. Keep these guidelines in mind as you plan your meals:

Make it a vegetable soup. No high-fat meat or cream to keep the calorie count down.

Keep the veggies chunky. You'll need to chew longer, which will make you feel full more quickly.

Serve it hot. You'll eat more slowly, allowing your stomach time to tell your brain that you're full.

Photographs by Scott Phillips; food styling by Allison Ehri Kreitler;

autumn vegetable soup

You can refrigerate this soup for 3 days or freeze for 2 months. Feel free to substitute other fall vegetables or beans.
Yields about 8 cups; serves 6 to 8 as a starter

- 2 **Tbs. olive oil**
- 3 **medium carrots, cut into medium dice**
- 1 **large yellow onion, cut into medium dice**
- 2 **medium cloves garlic, minced**
- 2 **cups ½-inch-cubed peeled butternut squash (about half a 2-lb. squash)**
- ¼ **tsp. ground allspice**
  Pinch cayenne pepper; more to taste
  Kosher salt
- 1 **quart lower-salt chicken broth**
- 1 **14.5-oz. can no-salt-added diced tomatoes**
- 4 **sprigs fresh thyme**
- 2 **cups lightly packed, coarsely chopped kale**
- 1 **cup lower-salt canned chickpeas**

Heat the oil in a large soup pot over medium-high heat. Add the carrots and onion and cook, stirring occasionally, until they begin to soften, about 6 minutes. Add the garlic and cook for 1 minute more. Add the squash, allspice, cayenne, and 1 tsp. salt and stir to combine. Add the broth, tomatoes with their juice, and thyme. Bring to a boil, reduce the heat to medium, cover, and simmer for 10 minutes. Add the kale and the chickpeas and cook uncovered until the squash is tender and the kale has wilted, about 10 minutes more. Discard the thyme springs before serving. Season to taste with more salt and cayenne.

Registered dietitian Ellie Krieger is a Fine Cooking *contributing editor.*

hair and makeup by Nicole Bryl Make-Up New York; wardrobe by Julie Ewald

Remote Probe Thermometers

You'll always know when dinner is done with this handy kitchen tool. Here are our top picks.

BY NICKI PENDLETON WOOD

COOKING WITHOUT A THERMOMETER is like driving somewhere you've never been without a map (or more likely, a GPS). A thermometer takes all the guesswork out of knowing when food is properly cooked. And unlike using an instant-read thermometer, with a probe thermometer you don't have to open the oven door (which allows heat to escape) or poke multiple holes in your food (which lets flavorful juices leak out) to check for doneness.

What it is A probe thermometer consists of a thin metal rod (a probe) that's connected by a wire to a digital display. Insert the probe into the food, shut the oven door, set the display on the counter, and you're free to turn your attention elsewhere.

What it can do Most remote probe thermometers detect temperatures between 32°F and 392°F. An alarm (or series of alarms) tells you when your food is cooked to its target temperature. Some models include timers, and some have pre-programmed temperature settings for different meat types (set to USDA standards). Depending on the model's temperature range, consider using it for more-diverse kitchen tasks like candy-making, frying in oil, and even calibrating your oven.

What to look for For optimal control, choose a thermometer that has a manual setting or allows for variations in doneness. Models with magnetized displays that can be propped up (for easy reading on a countertop) or lie flat (for sticking to an appliance) are good. Among the many we tested, here are our favorites.

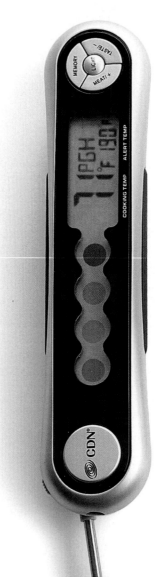

◀ TOP OF THE LINE

CDN 2-in-1 Probe Thermometer 2P212

$30; kitchenkapers.com

This model is perfect for the gadget-loving cook. Extra features abound: a pre-set list of meat types (options include duck and even ground veal), preferred "taste" settings from rare to well done (although this isn't available for pork, chicken, turkey, and ground meats; the manual setting from 32°F to 212°F lets you bypass this), and a color-coded display that shows how your food is progressing, from rare to well done. An early alert sounds 10 minutes before the food reaches the target temperature. There's another alert when it reaches its target and a third when the food is overcooked. There is also a programmable memory option. Two probes are included—one instant-read probe that folds out of the unit (great for grilling) and one remote probe for oven cooking. This model is unique in that it's backlit for nighttime cooking and has a generous five-year warranty.

how we tested

We evaluated 14 remote probe thermometers for design, construction, functionality, and extra features. We conducted side-by-side tests to monitor the temperature of ice water and boiling water, large pieces of cooked meat and poultry, hot oil for frying, and baked bread.

ThermoWorks Electronic Cooking Thermometer/ Timer TW362B

$21; amazon.com

ThermoWorks has updated its probe thermometer/timer. Responding to customer feedback, it has added an on/off switch to preserve battery life and modified the housing, which now props up the display for good visibility from a counter or lies flat for mounting on the side of the oven. With a temperature range of 32°F to 392°F, it's up to most common kitchen tasks, and the timer is a bonus. This model does not have pre-programmed temperatures for different foods. It comes with a one-year warranty.

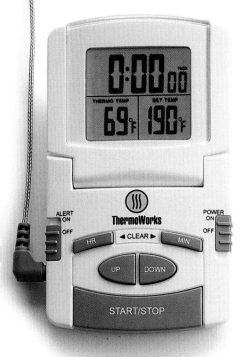

Taylor Gourmet Digital Cooking Thermometer with Probe and Timer

$21; target.com

If you're looking for a thermometer that gets the job done and looks good while doing it, then this is the model for you. The big stainless-steel display offers easy reading in dim light and from a distance, and its heft gives it a sturdy, reliable feel. The functioning is intuitive, the temperature range is a standard 32°F to 392°F, and it has a countdown timer with alarm as well as a one-year warranty.

Acu-Rite Digital Meat Thermometer 0993 STW

$14; found at Walmart stores

Not only does it come at a bargain price, but this model is intuitive enough to use straight out of the box. It measures degrees to a decimal point for added precision and has an impressive temperature range: −40°F to 572°F. There are no pre-programmed temperature settings. An alarm sounds when the thermometer hits its target temperature, both on the way up and on the way down—a useful

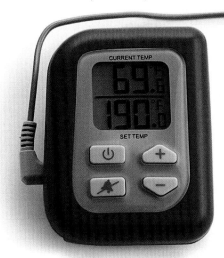

feature for more-complex tasks like tempering chocolate or regulating frying oil temperatures before and after adding food to the oil. The auto-shutoff feature is a standout, too—more thermometers should have it to preserve battery life. The probe is dishwasher-safe, and the silicone wire stays cool to the touch. The only shortcomings on this model are its bulky wedge shape and a magnet too weak to securely attach to the oven door. It comes with a one-year warranty.

Nicki Pendleton Wood is a cookbook editor and equipment tester based in Nashville.

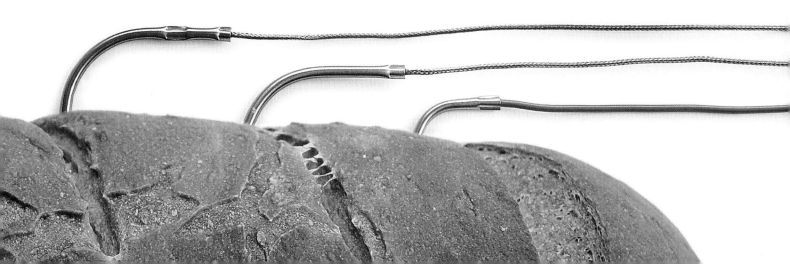

Montsant Rising

Red wines from the Montsant region are the next big thing from Spain (watch out, Priorat). So get drinking now, while the prices are still low and the quality just keeps getting better. BY DOUG FROST

THERE IS A SOAP OPERA PLAYING out in the Catalonian mountains of Spain. It's a case of sibling rivalry—a feud between the Priorat wine region, the crowned royalty of Spanish red wine, and its overlooked brother, Montsant. Priorat is one of only two regions in Spain with DOC (Denominación de Origen Calificada) classification, the country's highest honor. Montsant is a relatively new and unsung DO (Denominación de Origen) region, fighting for its due from the world's red wine drinkers. Priorat thinks its wines reign supreme. Montsant fans beg to differ. After all, Montsant shares climate, soil, grapes, and viticulture with Priorat, but little of its fame and fortune.

A star is born

Ten years ago, and for the previous century or two, the Rioja region was the king of Spanish reds. Things began to change in the late 1990s, when Priorat muscled its way into the ranks of the royals as its new vintners began making some of Spain's most powerful red wines. Guided by a small group of energetic 20-somethings, Priorat's wines were transformed from bulk, oxidized, fruitless stinkers into modern dandies. The young winemakers, sometimes even the children of the families who started the wineries, worked tirelessly to improve production methods, making small-batch, high-quality wines filled with rich, fresh fruit. The hand-tending of vines on the steep slopes of Priorat was back-breaking work, but it got the wines noticed.

In 2004, when Priorat was awarded its DOC status, it pushed fusty Rioja aside in an enological coup d'etat. In a decade or so, Priorat earned what had taken Rioja nearly two centuries to achieve: acclaim as Spain's representative to the pantheon of the world's great red wines.

Priorat's ascension caused no end of jealous teeth-gnashing and hair-pulling in other aspirational wine regions, like Ribera del Duero to the northwest. Priorat's closer neighbors were affected, too—nearby towns with political clout and proven winemaking skills managed to remain a part of the Priorat region, but other areas with lesser reputations or bulk wine operations were cleaved away and added to a new wine region called Montsant. This new region, established in 2001, gathered together the vineyards surrounding Priorat in a wide loop.

In the shadows

Today, Montsant remains in the shadow—literally and metaphorically—of the lofty Priorat vineyards. Montsant's insistence that its terroir is little different from Priorat's is dismissed by some, applauded by others. The fact of the matter is that while Montsant's vineyards might not be as starkly picturesque as Priorat's, Montsant has a lot of the same old, gnarled, wizened vines of Garnacha and Cariñena grapes that make for big, bold reds. It also has some newer transplants: Caber-

Illustration by Marta Antelo; photographs by Scott Phillips

net, Merlot, and Syrah, which make for very exciting, complex wines that rival Priorat's best offerings.

Kinder, gentler wines

Many of Montsant's vineyards consist of the same *llicorella* (slate) soils as Priorat's, but with some limestone, sand, and clay thrown in the mix. This soil gives the wines great flinty character and minerality. And Montsant's elevation—between 1,500 and 2,000 feet—means that its wines, while big and bold, are not as relentlessly powerful as Priorat's (which boasts elevations as high as 3,000 feet). But that's merely an issue of degree, or perhaps temperament. If Priorat is a marauding Godzilla, Montsant is more like King Kong gently holding Fay Wray.

Since Montsant's wines rarely evince the bombast and firepower of its DOC neighbor,

and often have lower alcohol levels, too, they are better suited for enjoying with food—when a little bombast goes a long way. Montsant wines function at the table the same way many Zinfandels do, but with a gentler demeanor and a typically tart finish that's very refreshing. This means that the wines complement a larger palette of foods, both bold and understated, like seafood, duck, steak, lamb, cheeses, and even pizza.

The next big thing

Slightly lower elevation is one reason Montsant wines cost less than those from Priorat—the land is a bit easier to work. Mixed soil is another reason, and DO status is yet another. But because Montsant is the next big thing in Spanish red wine, for now, prices are low and the quality is only getting better. Sure, the top wines of the area, such

as Celler Capçanes Cabrida (an intense yet well-balanced old-vine Garnacha), will set you back $75, but many well-made bottles from the region cost less than $30, and there are plenty for less than $20.

Montsant is still 10 or 20 years behind Priorat in transforming and modernizing its wineries. But the terroir, the grapes, and the promise are there—given a few years and dedication from the local winemakers, there is a good chance that Montsant will join Priorat on the throne of DOC royals. Until then, Montsant continues to shine in the reflected glory of its famous big brother, Priorat, at more comfortable prices. Which is why, if you're looking for amazing value in the world of wine, you should look to Spain. And within Spain, look to Montsant.

Doug Frost is a wine consultant and writer based in Kansas City, Missouri.

Montsant: A Buyer's Guide

To fully discover what Montsant has to offer, consider trying reds that range from bright and fruity to dark and earthy.

RICH, FRUITY, AND BRIGHT	DARK AND EARTHY

La Cova dels Vins Ombra 2007 ($17) Take one-third each of Cariñena, Garnacha, and Cabernet Sauvignon grapes, and you end up with a very pretty, supple Montsant wine.

Celler de Capçanes Mas Donis 2007 ($13) An incredible bargain from one of Montsant's top producers, this wine, made from old-vine Garnacha with a dollop of Syrah, bursts with tart fruit.

Acústic Montsant 2007 ($16) Bright and full of juicy red berry flavors, this is a delicious wine made with old-vine Cariñena and Garnacha grapes.

Celler Laurona Montsant 2004 ($35) Black cherries and spice feature in this very elegant blend of Garnacha, Merlot, Syrah, and Cabernet Sauvignon.

Can Blau 2007 ($14) This wine showcases the rich, supple side of Montsant. A blend of Cariñena, Syrah, and Garnacha, it has the full complement of the region's traditional grapes and a little dose of modern Syrah, too.

Agricola Falset-Marça Etim Selección 2006 ($15) One of the hidden secrets of Montsant (and a great value to boot), this wine is made from half Garnacha and half a blend of Cariñena and Cabernet Sauvignon.

Masroig Les Sorts Vinyes Velles 2005 ($35) Made from 50 percent Cariñena, 35 percent Garnacha, and 15 percent Cabernet Sauvignon, this is a chocolatey, earthy wine with raisin and smoky barrel notes.

Venus la Universal Dido 2007 ($33) An intense, earthy wine made from Garnacha, Cabernet, and Merlot, from the brilliant winemaker Sara Perez, daughter of Josep Lluís Pérez, one of Priorat's star vintners during the 1990s.

grape crush

It's time to fall in love with grapes all over again. Here are six unexpected recipes (think sweet *and* savory) for this season's harvest. BY JEANNE KELLEY

Grapes are one of those fruits we've gotten used to seeing in grocery stores all year long. But those bland, lifeless bunches bear almost no resemblance to the grapes you'll find in farmers' markets now. Like any fruit at its prime, fall grapes are as good as they come: plump, fragrant, juicy—literally bursting with flavor. Now is also when you'll come across the widest variety of grapes, from the familiar Red Flame to big, round Concords and petite, delicately sweet Champagne grapes.

frisée and grape salad with verjus and blue cheese

Use a colorful assortment of grapes for this elegant salad. Verjus is pressed unfermented juice from unripe grapes (for more information, see Test Kitchen, p. 83).
Serves 4 to 6

3 Tbs. verjus

2 Tbs. grapeseed oil

1½ Tbs. finely chopped shallot

8 cups lightly packed baby frisée or mixed salad greens, separated into leaves

2 cups mixed grapes, halved, and seeded if necessary

½ cup crumbled blue cheese, such as Point Reyes or Maytag (about 2 oz.)

Kosher salt and freshly ground black pepper

In a salad bowl, whisk the verjus and the oil. Add the shallot and let sit for 5 minutes. Add the frisée, grapes, and cheese and toss to combine. Season to taste with salt and pepper.

bulgur and grape salad with walnuts and currants

This wholesome whole-grain side dish is great with roast chicken or lamb. Enjoy it as is or with a crumble of goat cheese.

Yields about 5 cups; serves 6

- 1 cup medium bulgur wheat
- 1 cup seedless red grapes, cut in halves or quarters, depending on size, or Champagne grapes
- 1 cup small-diced celery (about 3 stalks)
- ⅓ cup chopped toasted walnuts
- ¼ cup packed coarsely chopped fresh flat-leaf parsley
- 3 Tbs. dried currants
- 3 Tbs. walnut oil, preferably roasted
- 3 Tbs. white balsamic vinegar
- 2 Tbs. minced shallot
  Kosher salt and freshly ground black pepper

In a small saucepan, bring 1 cup water to a boil over high heat. Stir in the bulgur, remove from the heat, cover, and let sit until the water is completely absorbed and the bulgur is tender and cooled to room temperature, about 1 hour. Transfer to a large bowl. Add the grapes, celery, walnuts, parsley, currants, walnut oil, vinegar, shallot, and ½ tsp. salt; toss well. Season to taste with more salt and pepper.

Grapes: A Buyer's Guide

Some of the recipes here call for specific types of grapes, but feel free to substitute whatever looks best at the market. Here's a quick roundup of the most common table grape varieties.

Red Flame grapes are sweet in flavor with a crunchy texture. They're ideal for both eating out of hand and cooking, as they keep their shape well and acquire a deeper flavor when heated.

Concord grapes have thick skins, juicy flesh, large seeds, and a strong strawberry-like flavor. They come in purple and white varieties and are ideal for juices and jellies.

Champagne grapes have delicate, sweet, pea-size berries that need gentle handling. These seedless grapes are not used in the homonymous French sparkling wine but are so named because they're thought to resemble tiny bubbles.

Green Thompson grapes are the top seller at the supermarket. Large and seedless, they have firm skins that make them very durable. Their mild flavor pairs well with citrus.

Muscat grapes usually have seeds and come in black and white varieties. Prized for their honey-floral flavor and perfume, they're used for both eating (they're delicious with cheese) and making wine.

Autumn Royal grapes have large, oval-shaped black berries. Sweet and straightforward, these seedless grapes pair well with salty foods like prosciutto and salted nuts.

Food styling by Kevin Crafts

moroccan-spiced seared scallops with green grape and lemon relish

Lemon zest cooked in salt water brings the flavor of preserved lemons to this succulent relish. Serve as a small plate or a light main course.

Serves 4

1	medium lemon
	Kosher salt
1½	cups seedless green grapes, quartered lengthwise and at room temperature
¼	cup extra-virgin olive oil
2	scallions, thinly sliced
2	Tbs. chopped fresh cilantro
2	Tbs. chopped fresh mint
1	tsp. ground cumin
1	tsp. sweet Hungarian paprika
1	tsp. ground turmeric
¼	tsp. ground cinnamon
¼	tsp. ground ginger
1½	lb. large all-natural "dry" sea scallops, side muscles removed
	Freshly ground black pepper

Using a vegetable peeler, remove the zest from the lemon in strips (yellow part only). Reserve the lemon. In a small saucepan, combine the lemon zest with ½ cup water and 1 tsp. salt. Bring to a simmer over medium-low heat and cook until the liquid reduces to about 1 Tbs., about 10 minutes. Drain, rinse, drain again, and pat dry. Finely mince the lemon zest and combine it with the grapes, 2 Tbs. of the olive oil, scallions, cilantro, and mint in a medium bowl.

In a small bowl, combine the cumin, paprika, turmeric, cinnamon, and ginger.

Pat the scallops dry. Season them liberally with salt and pepper and coat them with the spice mixture.

Heat 1 Tbs. of the olive oil in a 12-inch nonstick skillet over medium-high heat until shimmering. Add half of the scallops and cook, turning once, until seared on the outside but still translucent in the center, 1 to 2 minutes per side. Transfer to a warm plate. Repeat with the remaining 1 Tbs. oil and scallops.

Divide the scallops among 4 plates and serve with the relish. Cut the reserved lemon into quarters and squeeze over the scallops and relish. Serve immediately.

duck breast with saba and grapes

Reduced grape must (saba) boosts the grape flavor in this rich, sweet sauce (for more information on saba, see Test Kitchen, p. 83). Serve with wilted spinach and roasted turnips or potatoes.

Serves 4

4	small or 2 large boneless duck breasts (1¾ to 2 lb. total)
	Kosher salt and freshly ground black pepper
1½	cups seedless Autumn Royal or other purple or red grapes
¼	cup minced shallot
½	cup dry white wine
1	cup lower-salt chicken broth
3	Tbs. saba
1	Tbs. chopped fresh flat-leaf parsley

With a sharp knife, score the duck skin in a diamond pattern, being careful not to cut all the way through to the meat. Season the duck all over with salt and pepper. Put the duck skin side down in a cold 12-inch skillet. Cook over medium heat without moving, spooning off the excess fat occasionally, until the skin becomes light golden-brown, 8 to 9 minutes.

Loosen the duck from the pan with a spatula. Raise the heat to medium high and continue cooking, skin side down, until the skin is thin, crisp, and browned, about 4 minutes. Turn the duck and continue cooking until an instant-read thermometer registers 135°F in the thickest part of a breast for medium rare, about 10 minutes more. Transfer the duck to a plate.

Pour off all but 1 Tbs. of the fat from the skillet. Add the grapes and cook over medium-high heat, stirring often, until lightly browned but still firm, about 3 minutes. With a slotted spoon, transfer the grapes to the plate with the duck. Add the shallot to the skillet and cook until slightly softened, about 1 minute. Add the wine and cook, stirring up the browned bits, until all the liquid evaporates, 2 to 4 minutes. Add the chicken broth and saba and boil until the mixture reduces to ⅔ cup, 5 to 6 minutes. Season to taste with salt and pepper. Add the grapes, duck, and any juices from the plate to the skillet. Simmer gently for about 1 minute, turning the duck to coat it with the sauce. Thinly slice the duck and divide it among 4 plates. Spoon the sauce and grapes over the duck. Sprinkle with the parsley and serve immediately.

For sources, see Where to Buy It

Shop and Store

Try to find plump-looking grapes that have intact skins and are firmly attached to their stems. Store them in the refrigerator in a plastic or paper bag without washing them. They should last about a week. When ready to eat or use in a dish, wash grapes in a colander under running water.

custard tart with wine-poached grapes

Sweet, citrusy custard and a nutty almond crust make a perfect backdrop for the tender poached grapes in this elegant dessert. **Serves 8**

FOR THE CRUST

- 3½ oz. (7 Tbs.) chilled unsalted butter, cut into ½-inch pieces; more for the pan
- 3⅜ oz. (¾ cup) unbleached all-purpose flour
- ¼ cup toasted, slivered almonds
- ¼ cup granulated sugar
- ½ tsp. table salt
- 1 large egg yolk, chilled

FOR THE FILLING

- 2 large eggs
- 2 large egg yolks
- ½ cup granulated sugar
- 3 Tbs. fresh lime juice
- 3 Tbs. dry white wine, preferably Sauvignon Blanc
- ½ cup heavy cream

FOR THE TOPPING

- ½ cup dry white wine, preferably Sauvignon Blanc
- 2 Tbs. honey
- 2 Tbs. granulated sugar
- 1 Tbs. fresh lime juice
- 65 seedless red grapes (2¼ cups)

MAKE THE CRUST

Butter a 4x13½-inch rectangular fluted tart pan with a removable bottom. Combine the flour, almonds, sugar, and salt in a food processor and process until the almonds are finely chopped, about 40 seconds. Add the butter and pulse until the mixture resembles coarse meal, about 15 seconds. Add the egg yolk and process until moist clumps form. With lightly floured hands, press the dough evenly over the bottom and up the sides of the prepared tart pan. Freeze until firm, about 45 minutes.

Position a rack in the center of the oven, put a rimmed baking sheet on the rack, and heat the oven to 375°F. Bake the crust on the heated baking sheet until light golden on the bottom and golden-brown on the edges, about 15 minutes. Cool completely.

MAKE THE FILLING

In a medium heavy-duty saucepan, whisk the eggs, yolks, sugar, lime juice, and white wine until well blended. Cook over medium-high heat, whisking frequently, until the mixture boils and thickens, about 3 minutes. Transfer the filling to a medium bowl and let cool until warm.

Whisk the cream into the filling and pour the mixture into the baked tart shell. Bake at 375°F until the filling begins to slightly puff and bubble around the edges, about 15 minutes. Let cool to room temperature.

MAKE THE TOPPING

In a medium heavy-duty saucepan, boil the wine, honey, sugar, and lime juice over medium heat until the mixture reduces to a thick syrup and begins to darken slightly, 4 to 5 minutes—you should have about ¼ cup. Reduce the heat to low, add the grapes, cover, and poach gently over low heat until tender, about 3 minutes. With a slotted spoon, transfer the grapes to a dinner plate. Continue to boil the poaching liquid until syrupy, about 1 minute. Randomly place the grapes on top of the tart, pressing slightly into the filling. Gently brush the glaze over the grapes. Let the tart cool completely at room temperature for at least 4 hours before serving.

 Get information on hundreds of ingredients at FineCooking.com /ingredients.

braised chicken with gewürztraminer and grapes

Serve with brown rice or egg noodles and steamed green beans.
Serves 6

- 1   Tbs. olive oil
- 12   bone-in, skin-on chicken thighs, trimmed (about 3½ lb. total)
-     Kosher salt
- 1½   cups red or green seedless grapes or Muscat grapes
- 2   cups finely chopped yellow onion
- 2   medium cloves garlic, chopped
- 1   750-ml bottle medium-dry Gewürztraminer
- 2   cups lower-salt chicken broth
- 1   Tbs. chopped fresh thyme or 1 tsp. dried, crumbled
- ½   cup heavy cream
- 2   tsp. cornstarch
-     Freshly ground black pepper

Heat the oil in a 7- to 8-quart enameled Dutch oven over medium-high heat. Season the chicken generously with salt. Working in batches so as not to crowd the pan, sear the chicken, turning once, until golden-brown, 10 to 12 minutes per batch. Transfer the chicken to a large bowl.
When all the chicken is browned, pour off all but 2 Tbs. of fat. Add the grapes and cook until just tender, about 3 minutes. With a slotted spoon, transfer the grapes to a small bowl. Reduce the heat to medium and add the onions and a pinch of salt to the pan. Cook, stirring frequently, until tender, about 7 minutes. Add the garlic and cook, stirring, to soften, 1 to 2 minutes. Pour in the wine and simmer, stirring up the browned bits on the bottom of the pan, until the wine reduces by almost half, about 5 minutes.
Return the chicken to the pan, along with any accumulated juices. Add the broth and sprinkle with thyme. Bring to a simmer, reduce the heat to medium low, cover, and cook until the chicken is very tender, about 25 minutes. Transfer the chicken to a bowl.
Raise the heat to medium high and boil the liquid until reduced to about 2½ cups, about 12 minutes. In a small bowl, whisk the cream with the cornstarch, then whisk the cream mixture into the sauce. Cook, whisking constantly, until the sauce simmers and thickens to the consistency of heavy cream, 1 to 2 minutes. Season to taste with salt and pepper. Return the chicken to the pan. Simmer gently over medium-low heat until the chicken is heated through. Stir in the reserved grapes. The chicken skin will be soft—remove it prior to serving, if desired.

Note: This dish can be prepared 2 days ahead; cool, cover, and refrigerate the chicken and grapes separately.

Jeanne Kelley is a food writer, recipe developer, and food stylist who lives near Los Angeles. Her latest cookbook is Blue Eggs and Yellow Tomatoes. ☐

No changes to the classic Thanksgiving table allowed—except for the side dishes. Here, the familiar green bean casserole gets a new look with cremini mushrooms, sage, and pancetta.

flip sides

Modern makeovers for some favorite Thanksgiving side dishes—
from creamed onions to sweet potato casserole. BY SUSIE MIDDLETON

AT THANKSGIVING, NOSTALGIA RULES. If you're not careful to serve
all the usual suspects, you'll hear cries of "Where's the sweet potato casserole?" "What about the green beans?" "But we always have glazed carrots!"
As a cook, you're stuck between a rock and your desire to have fun in the
kitchen trying new things.

  Here's a plan that'll satisfy your craving for fresh flavors without letting
anyone down. (And no, we're not suggesting you give up the turkey or
mashed potatoes.) We've taken six traditional Thanksgiving side dishes and
given them modern makeovers. So everyone wins: Cooks are happy that
they can play a little, and guests get to have their favorites—just better.

green beans with crispy pancetta, mushrooms, and shallots

The onion-topped green bean casserole is a Thanksgiving mainstay. This version, while full of familiar flavors, is a bit more elegant, and dare we say it, a lot more flavorful.

Serves 8

Kosher salt

1½ lb. green beans, trimmed

2½ oz. thinly sliced pancetta (five or six ¹⁄₁₆- to ⅛-inch-thick slices)

3 Tbs. extra-virgin olive oil

6 medium cremini mushrooms, trimmed, halved if large, and very thinly sliced

2 medium-large shallots, halved lengthwise and very thinly sliced

¼ cup very thinly sliced fresh sage leaves

1 Tbs. sherry vinegar

½ tsp. Dijon mustard

Fill a large mixing bowl with ice cubes and water and set aside. Fill a 6- or 7-quart pot two-thirds full of well-salted water. Bring the water to a boil and boil the beans uncovered until tender to the bite, 4 to 6 minutes. Drain, transfer to the bowl of ice water, and let sit until cooled, about 2 minutes. Drain and pat dry.

Put the pancetta in a 12-inch nonstick skillet and cook over medium-low heat until crisp and browned, 10 to 12 minutes. Transfer to a paper-towel-lined plate and coarsely crumble. Remove the pan from the heat and let it cool slightly.

Add 2 Tbs. of the olive oil to the pan and return it to medium-high heat. Add the mushrooms, shallots, and ¼ tsp. salt and cook, stirring frequently, until both are nicely browned

and shrunken, about 5 minutes. Add the sage and cook, stirring, until fragrant, about 30 seconds. Take the pan off the heat and add the vinegar, mustard, and the remaining 1 Tbs. oil. Stir to combine.

Return the pan to medium heat, add the green beans and toss to combine and heat through, 2 to 3 minutes. Season to taste with salt. Transfer to a warm serving platter and garnish with the pancetta.

Make ahead: The beans can be boiled and refrigerated up to 6 hours ahead. The remaining ingredients can also be prepped up to 6 hours ahead and held in the refrigerator. An hour before finishing, remove the beans from the refrigerator to come to room temperature.

roasted turnips with maple and cardamom

For those who can't imagine turkey without a side of mashed turnips, here's a new take on the vegetable. An intriguing sauce laced with coriander and cardamom gives the dish surprising complexity.

Serves 8

3½ lb. purple-top turnips, peeled and cut into ¾-inch dice (10 cups)

3 Tbs. vegetable oil

Kosher salt

1 oz. (2 Tbs.) unsalted butter

3 Tbs. pure maple syrup

¼ tsp. pure vanilla extract

Generous pinch crushed red pepper flakes

¼ tsp. ground coriander

⅛ tsp. ground cardamom

1 tsp. fresh lemon juice

1 Tbs. finely chopped fresh cilantro (or a mix of parsley and mint)

Position racks in the top and bottom thirds of the oven and heat the oven to 475°F. Line two large, heavy-duty rimmed baking sheets with foil. In a mixing bowl, combine the turnips, oil, and 1½ tsp. salt. Toss to coat well. Divide the turnips between the two pans and spread evenly in one layer. Roast for 20 minutes. With a large spatula, flip the turnips. Swap the pans' positions and roast until tender and nicely browned on a few sides, 15 to 20 minutes. (The turnips on the lower rack may be done sooner than those on the upper rack.)

Meanwhile, melt the butter in a small saucepan over low heat. Whisk in the maple syrup, vanilla, and red pepper flakes, and then the coriander and cardamom, until the sauce is heated, 30 seconds. Remove the pan from the heat.

Transfer the turnips to a large mixing bowl. Gently reheat the sauce, if necessary, and stir in the lemon juice. With a heatproof spatula, toss the sauce with the turnips. Add half of the cilantro and salt to taste and toss again. Transfer to a warm serving dish and garnish with the remaining cilantro.

Make ahead: This dish can be made a day ahead. To reheat, put the dressed turnips (without the cilantro) in a large nonstick skillet and cover with a lid. Heat gently over medium-low heat until warmed through, stirring occasionally, about 15 minutes. Add the cilantro and season to taste with salt just before serving.

[THE TRADITION
boiled brussels sprouts]

brussels sprouts with toasted hazelnut butter

The lemon zest in the butter adds loads of bright flavor to the nutty sprouts. Suffice it to say, this delicious dish trumps the old one.

Serves 6 to 8

FOR THE BUTTER

- ⅓ cup hazelnuts (about 1 oz.)
- 2 oz. (4 Tbs.) unsalted butter, softened
- 2 tsp. finely grated lemon zest
- 1½ tsp. lightly chopped fresh thyme
- ½ tsp. honey
- Kosher salt

FOR THE BRUSSELS SPROUTS

- ¼ cup extra-virgin olive oil
- 1¾ lb. Brussels sprouts, trimmed and quartered or cut into 6 wedges if very large (about 6 cups)
- Kosher salt
- ½ cup lower-salt chicken broth

MAKE THE BUTTER

Heat the oven to 400°F. Put the hazelnuts on a small rimmed baking sheet. Roast in the oven until they are a deep golden-brown (the skins will be visibly splitting), 5 to 6 minutes. Wrap the nuts in a clean kitchen towel, cool for a couple of minutes, and then take the skins off by rubbing the nuts together in the kitchen towel while still warm. Don't worry about getting all of the skins off.

Let the nuts cool for about 10 minutes. Finely chop ¼ cup of the nuts in a small food processor. The nuts should be very finely ground, but not so much that they turn into nut butter. Coarsely chop the remaining nuts and set aside for a garnish.

Put the finely chopped nuts, butter, lemon zest, thyme, honey, and ¼ tsp. salt in a small bowl and mix with a spatula until well combined. Set aside or refrigerate if not using right away.

COOK THE BRUSSELS SPROUTS

Heat the oil in a 12-inch skillet over medium-high heat. Add the Brussels sprouts and 1½ tsp. salt and stir well. Reduce the heat to medium and cook, stirring occasionally and then more frequently as the sprouts begin to brown, until all of the sprouts are golden-brown on most sides and have lost their raw color (they will still feel firm), 15 to 18 minutes.

Add the broth and immediately cover the pan. Cook until the broth has reduced to a few tablespoons, about 2 minutes. Uncover, raise the heat to high, and boil off most of the remaining liquid, 1 to 2 minutes. Take the pan off the heat and add the hazelnut butter in spoonfuls; toss well. Season to taste with salt.

Transfer the sprouts to a warm serving dish and garnish with the reserved hazelnuts.

Make ahead: You can trim and quarter the Brussels sprouts several hours before cooking. The butter can be made and refrigerated (tightly wrapped) 2 days ahead. Store the extra nuts for garnish at room temperature.

Photographs by Scott Phillips

pomegranate-balsamic-glazed carrots

Glazed carrots never had it so good. Bright, fresh flavors and a little cayenne play well with the rich fare on the rest of the Thanksgiving plate.

Serves 8

- ¼ cup pure pomegranate juice
- 1 Tbs. balsamic vinegar
- 2 tsp. honey
- 1 oz. (2 Tbs.) unsalted butter
- 2 Tbs. extra-virgin olive oil
- 2 lb. carrots, trimmed, peeled, and cut into sticks about 2 inches long and ⅜ inch wide (see Test Kitchen, p. 83, for more information)
  Kosher salt
- ⅓ cup lower-salt chicken broth
- ⅛ tsp. cayenne
- 2 Tbs. lightly packed thinly sliced fresh mint

Combine the juice, vinegar, and honey in a liquid measuring cup and whisk. Cut 1 Tbs. of the butter into 4 pieces and refrigerate.
In a 12-inch skillet, heat the remaining 1 Tbs. butter with the olive oil over medium-high heat. When the butter has melted, add the carrots and 1½ tsp. salt and toss well to coat. Cook without stirring until the bottom layer of carrots is lightly browned in spots, 4 to 5 minutes. Using tongs, stir and flip the carrots and then leave undisturbed for 1 to 2 minutes to brown. Continue cooking, occasionally stirring and flipping, until most of the carrots are a bit browned in places and are starting to feel tender, an additional 3 to 5 minutes. Reduce the heat to medium if the bottom of the pan begins to brown too much.

Carefully add the chicken broth, cover quickly, and cook until all but about 1 Tbs. of the broth has evaporated, about 2 minutes. Uncover, reduce the heat to medium low, and add the pomegranate mixture (re-whisk, if necessary) and the cayenne. Cook, stirring gently, until the mixture reduces and becomes slightly glazy, about 1 minute. Take the pan off the heat, add the chilled butter, and gently toss with a heatproof spatula until the butter has melted, 30 seconds to 1 minute. Season to taste with salt and stir in about two-thirds of the mint. Serve in a warm shallow bowl or on a platter, garnished with the remaining mint.

Make ahead: Cut the carrots and prepare the rest of your ingredients up to 6 hours ahead. Cook the dish just before serving.

bourbon sweet potato and apple casserole with a pecan crust

This dish is nothing like the sweet potato casserole of old. Sautéed apples, a crunchy pecan crust, and spicy mashed sweet potatoes make for a sophisticated update.

Serves 8

3   to 3¼ lb. sweet potatoes (about 3 large)

2   oz. (4 Tbs.) unsalted butter; more for the pan

4   oz. toasted and very finely chopped pecans (1 cup)

1⅓ cups fresh breadcrumbs

2   Tbs. finely chopped fresh parsley
    Kosher salt

1   cup heavy cream

8   ¼-inch-thick slices fresh ginger, unpeeled and crushed

2   whole star anise

1   2- to 3-inch cinnamon stick

2   Tbs. plus 2 tsp. bourbon

1½ tsp. pure vanilla extract

1¾ lb. Granny Smith apples (about 3 large), peeled, quartered, cored, and thinly sliced

Bake the sweet potatoes: Position a rack in the center of the oven and heat the oven to 400°F. Line a rimmed baking sheet with aluminum foil. Prick the sweet potatoes all over with a fork and bake them on the sheet until completely tender when pierced with a fork,

55 to 60 minutes. Let rest until cool enough to handle. Meanwhile, if not working ahead, reduce the oven temperature to 375°F.

Discard the skins and put the flesh in a medium mixing bowl. With a potato masher, work the sweet potatoes until they're well mashed (they don't have to be perfectly smooth).

Make the crumb topping: Melt 2 Tbs. of the butter and combine with the pecans, breadcrumbs, parsley, and two big pinches of salt in a small bowl.

Infuse the cream: Combine the heavy cream, ginger, star anise, and cinnamon stick in a small saucepan. Bring to a full boil (watch carefully so that it doesn't boil over) and remove from the heat immediately. Let steep for 15 to 20 minutes. Strain through a fine sieve into a liquid measuring cup, pressing down on the solids with a spatula to extract all of the liquid. Stir in 2 Tbs. of the bourbon, the vanilla extract, and ¼ tsp. salt.

Cook the apples: In a 12-inch nonstick skillet, melt the remaining 2 Tbs. butter over medium-high heat. Add the apples, season with ¼ tsp. salt, and toss well. Raise the heat to high and cook, stirring frequently, until soft and lightly browned, 8 to 9 minutes. Lower the heat if the apples are getting too dark, but not so much that they soften without browning.

Turn off the heat, carefully add the remaining 2 tsp. bourbon and stir until it evaporates, a few seconds. Pour in ⅓ cup of the infused cream and stir until the apples have absorbed most of it, a few more seconds. Set the pan aside and let the apples cool for about 15 minutes, turning them occasionally to release steam.

Assemble the casserole: Butter a shallow 3-quart baking dish (9x13-inch works well). Add the remaining cream to the mashed sweet potatoes and mix thoroughly. Season to taste with salt. Arrange the apples across the bottom of the baking dish. Spread the sweet potato mixture over the apples in an even layer. Top with the pecan-crumb mixture.

Bake the casserole at 375°F until the crumb topping is dark brown (it will be browner around the edges) and the casserole is heated through, about 25 minutes.

Make ahead: You can bake and mash the sweet potatoes and make the crumb topping a day ahead (cover both and refrigerate). Bring the potatoes and crumb topping to room temperature before assembling the dish. You can also assemble and refrigerate for up to 8 hours before baking. Return to room temperature before baking.

creamy baked leeks
with garlic, thyme, and parmigiano

This simple recipe doesn't require the cook's attention at the last minute—but it will get the attention of your onion-loving guests. If possible, choose leeks that are all about the same size.

Serves 8

1	tsp. unsalted butter
	Kosher salt
8	medium-large leeks (ideally with several inches of white)
2	tsp. lightly chopped fresh thyme
1	cup heavy cream
2	large cloves garlic, smashed and peeled
⅓	cup finely grated Parmigiano-Reggiano

Heat the oven to 350°F. Rub the bottom of a shallow 10x15-inch (or similar) rectangular baking dish with the butter. Sprinkle ¼ tsp. salt over the bottom of the pan.

Cut the dark-green portion and all but about 1 inch of the light green off the top of the leeks. Peel away any tough or damaged outer leaves. Trim the ends by cutting the roots but leaving a bit of the base intact to hold the leek together. Cut each leek in half lengthwise. Gently wash each half under running water, fanning open the layers to rinse as thoroughly as possible. Pat the leeks dry and then arrange them cut side down in the baking dish. They should all fit snugly, but if they are crowded, turn a few on their sides. Sprinkle the thyme and ¼ tsp. salt over the leeks.

Heat the cream and garlic in a small saucepan over high heat. As soon as the cream comes to a rolling boil (watch carefully and don't let it boil over), remove the pan from the heat and let sit for 5 minutes. Pour the cream and garlic evenly over the leeks.

Cover the leeks with a piece of parchment cut to fit inside the pan.

Bake the leeks until the thickest ends are tender all the way through when pierced with a paring knife and the cream is almost entirely reduced, about 35 minutes. Sprinkle the leeks with the Parmigiano and salt to taste. Bake just until the cheese melts, an additional 1 to 2 minutes. Transfer the leeks to a warm serving platter.

Make ahead: You can wash and trim the leeks and arrange them in the buttered baking dish 6 hours ahead.

Susie Middleton is Fine Cooking's *editor at large. Her first cookbook,* Fast, Fresh, & Green: 125 Delicious Recipes for Veggie Lovers, *is due out in spring 2010.* ◘

Pie Dreams

A good pie is all about the crust. Learn the secrets to flaky, buttery perfection, then choose from four delicious fillings that are just right for the season. BY NICOLE REES

Fresh Pear Pie with Dried Cherries
and Brown Sugar Streusel, page 62

What makes a great piecrust? In a word: butter—even better, really good butter. Sure, lard or shortening produces a tender, flaky crust, but they can't compete with butter's flavor. Creamy, rich European-style butter is especially good. It has a higher fat content (and less water) than most American butters, so it's tastier and more supple to work with.

The good news is that a butter crust can be just as flaky as one made with lard if you make it the old-fashioned way—by hand, rubbing cold chunks of butter between your fingertips and into the flour. No pastry blender, no mixer, no food processor. This technique allows you to monitor the size of the butter pieces in

all-butter piecrust

This pie dough can be made ahead and refrigerated overnight or frozen (before or after rolling) for up to 3 months. Simply transfer the dough to the refrigerator the night before you plan to make pie, and it'll be ready to go.

Yields one 9-inch piecrust

- 6 oz. (1⅓ cups) unbleached all-purpose flour
- 1 tsp. granulated sugar
- ⅜ tsp. table salt
- 4 oz. (8 Tbs.) cold unsalted butter, preferably European style, cut into ¾-inch pieces
- 3 to 4 Tbs. ice water

MAKE THE DOUGH

To make the dough: Put the flour, sugar, and salt in a medium bowl and stir with a rubber spatula or a fork to combine. Add the butter to the bowl. Rub the cold chunks of butter between your fingertips, smearing the butter into the flour **1** to create small (roughly ¼-inch) flakes of fat **2**.

Drizzle 3 Tbs. ice water over the flour mixture. Stir with the spatula or fork, adding 1 Tbs. more water if necessary, until the mixture forms a shaggy dough that's moist enough to hold together when pressed between your fingers **3**.

With well-floured hands, gently gather and press the dough together, and then form it into a disk with smooth edges **4**. Wrap the dough in plastic and chill for at least 1 hour, but preferably 2 to 4 hours, before rolling.

the flour and creates flakes, rather than lumps, that remain in the dough when you roll it. As the crust bakes, the butter melts, creating steam pockets that leave behind a flaky texture. It's a classic method and one well worth bringing back.

Below, we take you through this easy technique step by step and then show you how to roll out the dough, transfer it to a pie plate, and blind bake it. From there, it's a simple matter of choosing the filling. Or maybe not so simple, since the choices range from coffee-toffee pecan, to spiced pumpkin, to pear and dried cherry, and finally cranberry-apple. Delicious indecision.

Food styling by Allison Ehri Kreitler, except piecrust opposite, Jennifer Armentrout

ROLL THE DOUGH

To roll the dough: Let the chilled dough sit at room temperature to soften slightly—it should be cold and firm but not rock hard. Depending on how long the dough was chilled, this could take 5 to 20 minutes. When ready to roll, lightly flour the countertop or other surface (a pastry cloth, silicone rolling mat, or parchment on a counter also works great) and position the rolling pin in the center of the dough disk. Roll away from you toward 12 o'clock, easing the pressure as you near the edge to keep the edge from becoming too thin. Return to the center and roll toward 6 o'clock. Repeat toward 3 and then 9 o'clock, always easing the pressure at the edges and picking up the pin rather than rolling it back to the center **5**.

Continue to "roll around the clock," aiming for different "times" on each pass until the dough is 13 to 14 inches in diameter and about ⅛ inch thick. Try to use as few passes of the rolling pin as possible. After every few passes, check that the dough isn't sticking by lifting it with a bench knife (dough scraper). Reflour only as needed—excess flour makes a drier, tougher crust. Each time you lift the dough, give it a quarter turn to help even out the thickness.

LINE THE PIE PLATE

To line the pie plate: Gently transfer the dough to a 9-inch pie plate, preferably metal, by folding it in half and unfolding it into the plate. Do not stretch the dough as you line the pan, or it will spring back when baked. Gently lift the outer edges of the dough to give you enough slack to line the sides of the pan without stretching the dough **6**.

Trim the overhanging dough to 1 inch from the edge of the pan. Roll the dough under itself into a cylinder that rests on the edge of the pan **7**.

To crimp the edge, have one hand on the inside of the edge, and one hand on the outside, and use the index finger of the inside hand to push the dough between the thumb and index finger of the outside hand to form a U or V shape **8**. Repeat around the edge of the pie plate, creating a crimped edge whose individual flutes are about an inch apart. (Turn to Test Kitchen, p. 83, for more ideas on decorative edges.) As you are going along, if you notice that the edge is not perfectly symmetrical and that the amount of dough you'll have to crimp seems sparse in places, take a bit of trimmed scrap, wet it with a drop or two of water, and attach it to the sparse area by pressing it firmly into place.

Prick the sides and bottom of the crust all over with a fork. Refrigerate until firm, about 1 hour or overnight. This will relax the dough and help prevent the edges from caving in.

 To see a video on crimping piecrust, visit FineCooking.com/extras.

BLIND BAKE THE CRUST

To blind bake the crust: Position a rack in the center of the oven and heat the oven to 425°F. Line the chilled piecrust with foil and fill it with dried beans or pie weights **9**. Bake for 15 minutes; remove the foil and the beans or weights. Reduce the oven temperature to 375°F.

Bake until the bottom looks dry but is not quite done and the edges are light golden, 5 to 7 minutes more **10**. Let cool on a rack while you prepare one of the fillings on pp. 62–63.

Blind-Baking Basics

Blind baking means baking an empty piecrust before adding a filling. Here's what you need to know:

WHY BLIND BAKE?

Blind baking gives the crust a head start, allowing it to firm up before the filling is added. This prevents the crust from getting soggy. Dried beans or pie weights help it keep its shape. Without them, the crust will rise and puff on the bottom or slide down the sides under the weight of the crimped edge.

HOW LONG?

In recipes where the filling doesn't need further cooking or cooks for a short period of time, such as cream pies or fruit tarts, the crust is usually blind baked until cooked through and golden-brown. But in recipes where the pie cooks for a while after adding the filling (like the ones here), it's best to blind bake the crust just part way so it won't overcook as it continues to bake with the filling.

REMEMBER TO CHILL

Don't be tempted to skip chilling a crust before blind baking it. Piecrusts baked right after shaping are warm enough for the butter to melt quickly in the oven, causing the edge to sink or even slump over the edge of the pie pan.

The Pie Baker's Tip Sheet

1. Cold butter For flaky piecrust, it's important to start with very cold butter, so that it doesn't melt while you work it into the flour. When this happens, butter becomes too thoroughly mixed with the flour, resulting in a mealy, crumbly crust rather than a flaky one. Freeze butter briefly if you have warm hands, live in a warm climate, or are making a very large batch of pie dough. It's also a good idea to chill the bowl and even the flour when making pie in warm weather.

2. Just enough water For a tender piecrust, don't add too much water. Water contributes to the development of gluten proteins. If you add more than necessary, the resulting crust may still be flaky, but it will be tough rather than tender. For

these reasons, trust your fingertips over your eyes: The dough should hold together when pressed between your fingers, although it will still look pretty shaggy.

3. Easy rolling Take the time before chilling the dough to form an even, circular disk with clean, smooth edges. This will make rolling out the dough much easier because the edges are less likely to crack.

4. Crisp crust Bake filled pies on a preheated, rimmed baking sheet and use a lightweight metal pie dish. Both will help set the crust quickly, preventing it from getting soggy. Baking on a sheet is also handy for catching bubbling juices.

From Crust to Pie

Turn the page for four irresistible filling options: pecan, pumpkin, apple, and pear.

Clockwise, from top:
**Coffee-Toffee Pecan Pie,
Ginger-Spice Cranberry-Apple
Streusel Pie, Jamaican-Spiced
Pumpkin Pie**

fresh pear pie with dried cherries and brown sugar streusel

A hint of spice lets the delicate flavor of the pears shine through, while the dried cherries are a welcome alternative to traditional raisins.

Serves 8

FOR THE STREUSEL

4½	oz. (1 cup) unbleached all-purpose flour
½	cup old-fashioned rolled oats
½	cup packed light brown sugar
¼	tsp. table salt
4	oz. (8 Tbs.) unsalted butter, melted

FOR THE FILLING

3	lb. ripe Anjou or Bartlett pears (5 or 6 medium), peeled and cored, cut lengthwise into 8 wedges and then crosswise into ½-inch slices (about 7 cups)
1½	Tbs. fresh lemon juice
⅔	cup granulated sugar
1⅛	oz. (¼ cup) unbleached all-purpose flour
¼	tsp. table salt
¼	tsp. ground cinnamon
⅛	tsp. freshly grated nutmeg
¾	cup dried tart cherries, coarsely chopped
1	blind-baked All-Butter Piecrust (recipe on p. 58)

Position a rack in the center of the oven, set a heavy-duty rimmed baking sheet on the rack, and heat the oven to 350°F.

MAKE THE STREUSEL

In a medium bowl, combine the flour, oats, sugar, and salt. Using your fingers, blend the butter into the flour mixture. The mixture will be moist. Set aside.

MAKE THE FILLING

In a large bowl, toss the pears with the lemon juice. In a small bowl, whisk the sugar, flour, salt, cinnamon, and nutmeg. Add the sugar mixture to the pears and toss well to combine. Stir in the cherries.

Mound the filling into the piecrust. Sprinkle the streusel topping over the pear mixture, pressing the streusel between your fingers into small lumps as you sprinkle.

Put the pie on the heated baking sheet and bake until the pastry is golden-brown and the filling is bubbly and thickened at the edges, 55 to 65 minutes. Rotate the pie halfway through baking, and if the pastry or streusel browns before the filling has thickened, loosely cover the top or edges of the pie as needed with a pie shield or a sheet of aluminum foil.

Transfer to a rack and cool completely before serving. The pie can be stored at room temperature for up to 2 days.

jamaican-spiced pumpkin pie

Coconut milk and spiced rum add an unusual and delicious twist to this pumpkin pie.

Serves 8

1	15-oz. can pure pumpkin purée
1¼	cups unsweetened coconut milk (full fat only, stirred or shaken well before using)
¾	cup packed light brown sugar
1	tsp. ground ginger
¾	tsp. ground cinnamon
½	tsp. table salt
⅛	tsp. freshly grated nutmeg
4	large eggs, at room temperature
2	Tbs. spiced rum, such as Captain Morgan
1	blind-baked All-Butter Piecrust (recipe on p. 58)

Position a rack in the center of the oven, set a heavy-duty rimmed baking sheet on the rack, and heat the oven to 425°F.

In a large bowl, whisk the pumpkin, coconut milk, sugar, ginger, cinnamon, salt, and nutmeg until smooth. Whisk in the eggs and then the rum, until the mixture is smooth. Pour the filling into the piecrust.

Put the pie on the heated baking sheet. Bake for 10 minutes and then reduce the oven temperature to 350°F. Bake until the center of the pie no longer wobbles when the pan is nudged (a slight jiggle is fine), an additional 45 to 55 minutes.

Transfer to a rack and cool completely before serving. The pie can be stored at room temperature for up to 2 days.

ginger-spice cranberry-apple streusel pie

Tart apples and cranberries are tempered with a nutty, sweet streusel and a hint of cardamom.

Serves 8

FOR THE STREUSEL

4½	oz. (1 cup) unbleached all-purpose flour
¾	cup packed light brown sugar
½	cup chopped lightly toasted walnuts
¼	tsp. table salt
3	oz. (6 Tbs.) unsalted butter, melted

FOR THE FILLING

4	tart baking apples, such as Granny Smith or Pink Lady (1½ to 2 lb.)
6	oz. fresh or thawed frozen cranberries (1¾ cups)
¾	cup plus 6 Tbs. granulated sugar
1	oz. (3½ Tbs.) all-purpose flour
1	Tbs. finely chopped crystallized ginger
¼	tsp. ground cardamom
¼	tsp. ground cinnamon
1	blind-baked All-Butter Piecrust (recipe on p. 58)

Position a rack in the center of the oven, set a heavy-duty rimmed baking sheet on the rack, and heat the oven to 350°F.

MAKE THE STREUSEL

In a medium bowl, combine the flour, sugar, walnuts, and salt. Using your fingers, blend the butter into the flour mixture. Set aside.

MAKE THE FILLING

Peel, quarter, and core each apple. Cut each quarter lengthwise into ¼-inch-thick slices and then cut each slice crosswise at ¼-inch intervals to make tiny rectangles. In a food processor, pulse the cranberries with ¾ cup of the sugar until coarsely chopped. In a large bowl, combine the remaining 6 Tbs. sugar with the flour, ginger, cardamom, and cinnamon, breaking up ginger clumps with your fingers. Toss in the cranberry mixture and apples.

Mound the filling into the piecrust. Sprinkle the streusel topping over the apple mixture, pressing the streusel between your fingers into small lumps as you sprinkle.

Put the pie on the heated baking sheet and bake until the streusel is deeply browned and the filling is bubbling vigorously at the edges of the pie, 65 to 75 minutes. Check every 20 minutes, and if the pastry edge or the streusel browns before the filling is done, loosely cover the top or edges of the pie as needed with aluminum foil.

Transfer to a rack and cool completely before serving. The pie can be stored at room temperature for up to 2 days.

coffee-toffee pecan pie

With notes of butterscotch, espresso, and bourbon, this is a pecan pie like no other.

Serves 8

3	oz. (6 Tbs.) unsalted butter
¾	cup packed dark brown sugar
¾	cup light or dark corn syrup
½	cup Lyle's Golden Syrup (see Test Kitchen, p. 83, for more information)
3	large eggs, at room temperature
2	Tbs. bourbon
1	Tbs. instant espresso powder
1	tsp. pure vanilla extract
¾	tsp. table salt
⅓	cup very finely chopped toasted pecans
2	cups toasted pecan halves
1	blind-baked All-Butter Piecrust (recipe on p. 58)
½	cup crushed chocolate toffee candy pieces, such as Heath or Skor

Position a rack in the center of the oven, set a heavy-duty rimmed baking sheet on the rack, and heat the oven to 375°F.

In a medium saucepan over medium heat, melt the butter and cook, swirling the pan occasionally, until the butter is brown, 3 to 5 minutes. Immediately whisk in the brown sugar, corn syrup, and Lyle's Golden Syrup until smooth. Remove the pan from the heat and let cool slightly. One at a time, whisk in the eggs. Whisk in the bourbon, espresso powder, vanilla, and salt. Stir in the chopped pecans.

Sprinkle half of the pecan halves in the piecrust, followed by the toffee candy pieces, and then the remaining pecan halves. Pour the syrup mixture over all.

Put the pie on the heated baking sheet and reduce the oven temperature to 350°F. Bake until set, 45 to 55 minutes, rotating the pan halfway through baking. When the pan is nudged, the center of the pie will no longer wobble, but the whole pie will jiggle just slightly, and the filling will bubble at the edges.

Transfer to a rack and cool completely before serving. The pie can be stored at room temperature for up to 2 days.

Nicole Rees is a food scientist and professional baker who lives in Portland, Oregon. ❑

French Onion Soup

The bistro classic squares off against a modern upstart. Which version will you choose? BY ANNE WILLAN AND CHRIS SANTOS

Big Cheese
Aged Gruyère is key to getting the bubbling crust of traditional French onion soup. Why? It's rich, smooth, and melts easily.

Rustic Roots
Before *soupe à l'oignon* made it to the bistros of Lyon and Paris, its likely origins were in a simple peasant meal of onions, broth, and stale bread.

Bold Yellow
Plenty of flavorful yellow onions cooked until deep brown are the secret to this classic.

The Morning After
In Paris, onion soup is eaten in the wee hours of the morning after a night on the town. Its presence on breakfast menus confirms its status as a cure for the common hangover.

THE CLASSIC

The grande dame of French cuisine, Anne Willan, shares her recipe for the ultimate classic. It's made with homemade beef broth and caramelized onions, and topped with oozing Gruyère cheese.

Small Fry
The soup dumplings are quickly deep-fried before the dish is topped with cheese and finished in the oven, in a nod to tradition.

On a Stick
In a sly reference to the classic, the dumplings are skewered with croutons, which stand in for the expected slice of bread.

It's a Wrap
Inspired by traditional Chinese soup dumplings, this update features onion soup wrapped inside a purse-like dumpling.

Freeze Frame
To make it easier to contain the soup inside the dumplings, the soup is frozen and then cut into small pieces.

THE UPDATE

Chris Santos's modern version comes straight from his menu at The Stanton Social on New York's Lower East Side. It's a whimsical idea that resembles Chinese soup dumplings more than it does any onion soup we've ever had.

french onion soup

Serves 6 to 8

- 2 oz. (¼ cup) unsalted butter, more for the baking sheet
- 4 medium-large yellow onions (about 2 lb.), thinly sliced (8 cups)
  Kosher salt and freshly ground black pepper
- 1 tsp. granulated sugar
- 1 small baguette (½ lb.), cut into ½-inch slices
- 2 quarts Roasted Beef Broth (recipe at right) or lower-salt canned beef or chicken broth
- 1 bay leaf
- 2 cups grated Gruyère

Melt the butter in a 4-quart pot over medium heat. Stir in the onions and season with 1 tsp. salt and a few grinds of pepper. Reduce the heat to low. Press a piece of foil onto the onions to cover them completely, cover the pot with a lid, and cook, stirring occasionally (you will have to lift the foil), until the onions are very soft but not falling apart, 40 to 50 minutes. Remove the lid and foil, raise the heat to medium high, and stir in the sugar. Cook, stirring often, until very deeply browned, 10 to 15 minutes.

Meanwhile, to make the croûtes (baguette toasts), position a rack in the center of the oven and heat the oven to 350°F. Butter a rimmed baking sheet and arrange the baguette slices on the sheet in a single layer. Bake until the bread is crisp and lightly browned, turning once, 15 to 20 minutes. Set aside.

Add the broth and bay leaf to the caramelized onions and bring the soup to a boil over medium-high heat. Reduce the heat to medium low and simmer for 10 minutes to blend the flavors. Discard the bay leaf and season to taste with salt and pepper.

To serve, position a rack 6 inches from the broiler and heat the broiler to high. Put 6 to 8 broilerproof soup bowls or crocks on a baking sheet. Put 2 or 3 croûtes in each bowl and ladle the hot soup on top. Sprinkle with the cheese and broil until the top is browned and bubbly, 2 to 5 minutes. Serve immediately.

Make ahead: The soup and croûtes can be made up to 2 days ahead. Store the soup in the refrigerator and the croûtes in an airtight container at room temperature.

ROASTED BEEF BROTH

Yields about 2½ quarts

- 5 lb. meaty beef or veal bones, such as shanks, knuckles, and ribs
- 2 medium carrots, cut into big chunks
- 2 medium yellow onions, quartered
- 1 bouquet garni (1 sprig fresh thyme, 1 bay leaf, and 4 parsley stems, tied with twine)
- 1 Tbs. black peppercorns
- 1 Tbs. tomato paste

Position a rack in the center of the oven and heat the oven to 450°F.

Put the bones on a large rimmed baking sheet and roast until beginning to brown, about 20 minutes. Add the carrots and onions and continue roasting until the bones and vegetables are very brown, 30 to 45 minutes more.

With a slotted spoon or tongs, transfer the roasted bones and vegetables to a stockpot, leaving any rendered fat in the pan. Add the bouquet garni, peppercorns, tomato paste, and 5 to 7 quarts cold water (enough to cover the bones and vegetables by a couple of inches) to the pot. Bring to a boil slowly over medium heat, reduce the heat to medium low or low, and simmer, uncovered, skimming the surface occasionally with a slotted spoon until the broth is flavorful and reduced enough to just barely cover the bones and vegetables, 4 to 5 hours.

Strain the broth into a large bowl, cover, and chill. Skim off any fat before using. The broth can be refrigerated for up to 3 days or frozen for up to 2 months.

ANNE SAYS,

"My classic is all about onions cooked until perfectly caramelized and meltingly tender; dark, rich beef broth; and melted cheese on top. Need I say more?"

french onion soup dumplings

Yields 40 dumplings; serves 8 to 10 as an appetizer

FOR THE "SOUP"

- 4 oz. (½ cup) unsalted butter
- 1 cup thinly sliced yellow or red onion (or a combination)
- ½ cup thinly sliced shallot (2 medium)
- 1 cup dry red wine
- 1 cup lower-salt beef broth
- 1 cup lower-salt chicken broth
- 2 Tbs. chopped fresh thyme
- 1 Tbs. aged balsamic vinegar
  Kosher salt and freshly ground black pepper

FOR THE CROUTONS

- ½ lb. dense, chewy bread, crust removed, cut into ¾-inch cubes (about 2 cups)
- 2 Tbs. extra-virgin olive oil
- ½ tsp. minced garlic (1 medium clove)
- ½ tsp. chopped fresh thyme
  Kosher salt and freshly ground black pepper

FOR THE DUMPLINGS

- 40 square wonton wrappers
- 1 large egg, lightly beaten
- 3 cups vegetable oil
- 1¾ cups grated Gruyère
  Kosher salt and freshly ground black pepper

MAKE THE "SOUP"

Melt the butter in a 12-inch skillet over medium-low heat. Add the onions and shallots and cook, stirring frequently, until they're a deep caramel color, 25 to 35 minutes.

Raise the heat to medium, add the wine, and cook until it has completely evaporated, 5 to 9 minutes. Add the beef and chicken broths and cook until the liquid is reduced by about half, 5 to 7 minutes. Add the thyme and vinegar, season to taste with salt and pepper, and cook 1 minute more. Remove from the heat and let cool. Line a 4½x8½-inch loaf pan with foil and pour the "soup" mixture into the pan. Freeze until solid, at least 4 hours but preferably overnight.

MAKE THE CROUTONS

Position a rack in the center of the oven and heat the oven to 400°F. In a large bowl, toss the bread with the olive oil, garlic, thyme, ¼ tsp. salt, and ⅛ tsp. pepper. Spread the croutons on a small baking sheet and bake, stirring occasionally, until golden brown, about 15 minutes. Let cool and then skewer 40 of the best-looking croutons with toothpicks (save the leftovers for another use).

MAKE THE DUMPLINGS

Working with about 10 wonton wrappers at a time, arrange them on a flat surface and brush the edges with the egg. Unmold the "soup" mixture from the loaf pan. Using a chef's knife, cut the frozen soup lengthwise into 4 long, even strips, and then cut each strip crosswise into 10 even pieces, to make 40 pieces total, each about ¾ inch square. Put one square in the center of each wrapper and fold up the edges, pressing to create a purse-like dumpling. Repeat to make 40 dumplings. Put the dumplings on a small baking sheet or tray and freeze until ready to fry.

Heat the vegetable oil in a 4-quart saucepan over medium-high heat until the temperature on a candy thermometer reads 365°F or until the oil begins to ripple and bubbles immediately when the edge of one dumpling is dipped into it. Have ready a tray or plate lined with paper towels. Add as many dumplings as will fit in the pan without crowding and fry until golden brown, 2 to 4 minutes. With a slotted spoon, transfer the dumplings to the paper towels. Continue frying the remaining dumplings.

Position a rack in the center of the oven and heat the oven to 450°F. Divide the dumplings among 8 to 10 small, shallow ovenproof gratin dishes and top with the Gruyère. Bake until the cheese is melted, 5 to 6 minutes. Stick a crouton skewer in each dumpling, sprinkle with a little salt and pepper, and serve.

Anne Willan is the founder of La Varenne cooking school. Chris Santos is executive chef and owner of The Stanton Social in New York City. ◻

Which version is your favorite? Go to FineCooking.com/extras and let us know.

CHRIS SAYS,

"My food is meant for sharing. But how do you share French onion soup politely? In my version, you get everything that's great about the classic—crispy bread, gooey cheese, and luscious soup—in one delicious bite."

Food styling by Frank Melodia

Good Catch

Five fish you can always feel good about buying—
and delicious things to do with them. BY JAY WEINSTEIN

Clockwise from left:
Pacific halibut, arctic char,
black cod, mackerel,
striped bass

Shopping at the fish counter can be confusing

these days. Which fish should you buy? What kinds are safe to eat? We've all heard the warnings about dwindling fish populations and fish farming's environmental costs, not to mention the news about mercury in large fish and the health consequences it poses. What's a cook to do?

Research is good; downloadable buying charts are accurate and exhaustive. But without those tools at hand, it's wise to have a fallback plan. With that in mind, here are five great-tasting sustainable fish that you can always buy (and eat) with peace of mind. They're plentiful, wild, and sustainably caught, and all have relatively low levels of mercury.

Some of these fish may be familiar (halibut) and others may not (mackerel), but all are easy to prepare and at their best when simply cooked, allowing their fresh, distinctive flavors to shine. No more wondering what to buy or how to cook it—and that's no fish story.

pan-seared arctic char with olives and potatoes

Serves 4

- 4 small red potatoes (about ¾ lb.), sliced ¼ inch thick
  Kosher salt and freshly ground black pepper
- 4 skin-on arctic char fillets (about 5 oz. each), scaled
- 3 Tbs. olive oil
- 2 sprigs fresh rosemary, each about 3 inches long
- ½ cup pitted Kalamata olives
- 3 Tbs. roughly chopped fresh flat-leaf parsley
- 1 Tbs. balsamic vinegar
- 4 lemon wedges

In a medium saucepan over high heat, bring the potatoes to a boil in enough salted water to cover them by 1 inch. Reduce the heat to a brisk simmer and cook until tender but not falling apart, about 5 minutes. Drain. Set aside.

Pat the fish dry and season with ½ tsp. salt and ¼ tsp. pepper. Heat 1½ Tbs. of the olive oil in a 12-inch nonstick skillet over medium-high heat until shimmering hot. Arrange the fish skin side down in the pan so the fillets fit without touching. Cook undisturbed for 3 minutes. Flip the fillets and cook until the fish is cooked through, an additional 2 to 3 minutes. With a slotted spatula, transfer the fish to a serving platter or plates.

Add the remaining 1½ Tbs. oil to the pan and heat until shimmering. Add the potatoes and rosemary and cook, flipping occasionally, until the potatoes are tender, 3 to 4 minutes. Add the olives, parsley, balsamic, and a pinch of salt and pepper and stir gently to heat. Arrange the potato mixture around the fish. Serve garnished with the lemon wedges.

ARCTIC CHAR

Why this fish Caught in Alaska and the Pacific Northwest, char was never threatened because it is a fast-reproducing fish that was largely ignored during the heyday of salmon. Now that overfishing and unsustainable farming practices have turned salmon into an eco-culinary mess, char is getting its share of attention. (If you can't find it wild, farmed arctic char is a good alternative because it's raised sustainably.)

Why we love it A distant cousin of salmon and trout, char has a mild salmon-like flavor and a beautiful pink color—the result of its natural diet, which includes tiny crustaceans like pink shrimp. Arctic char takes well to virtually any cooking method, and it's hard to overcook, since its fatty texture allows a good deal of elbow room.

steamed black cod with scallions and rice wine

You can substitute dry sherry if you can't find Shaoxing rice wine in an Asian market or a wine store. For a mail-order source, see Where to Buy It, p. 93.

Serves 4

- 1 **2-inch piece fresh ginger, peeled**
- 1 **tsp. reduced-sodium soy sauce**
- 1 **tsp. granulated sugar**
- 4 **skinless black cod fillets (about 4 oz. each)**
- 12 **scallions or spring onions, dark-green parts only, cut on the diagonal into 2-inch pieces**
- 2 **Tbs. canola oil**
- ¼ **cup Shaoxing (Chinese rice wine)**
- 1 **cup long-grain white rice, preferably jasmine, cooked according to package directions**

With a rasp-style grater, grate the ginger into a fine sieve set over a large bowl. Use the back of a spoon to press down on the pulp to release the juice; discard the pulp. Stir in the soy sauce and sugar. Add the fish, turn to coat, cover, and marinate for 20 minutes at room temperature.

Set a steamer (either western style or Asian bamboo) over a pot with at least 1 inch of simmering water. On a dinner plate that can fit in the steamer, arrange the fish so the fillets fit without touching (discard the remaining marinade). Distribute the scallions around the fish and put the plate in the steamer. Cover and steam the fish until just cooked through, 4 to 5 minutes.

Heat the oil in a small pan over medium heat and add the Shaoxing. Allow it to sizzle for just a few seconds and remove from the heat.

Divide the rice among 4 dinner plates. Top the rice with the fish and scallions (transfer directly from the steamer without attempting to remove the plate). Spoon the Shaoxing sauce over all and serve.

Food styling by Frank Melodia

FISH FACTS

BLACK COD

Why this fish Unlike the similarly textured Chilean sea bass, black cod is harvested from well-managed Alaskan fisheries, which impose strict catch limits to protect the species from depletion. So black cod populations are not threatened. It's different, though, for other types of cod, like Atlantic cod, whose worldwide populations have collapsed one by one, with only the northeastern United States population remaining, and Pacific cod, whose fisheries are sustainable but small.

Why we love it Called sablefish in Europe, black cod is one of the richest-tasting fish on the market. It is buttery and luxurious and nearly impossible to overcook. A cook's dream, black cod is incredibly versatile, lending itself to steaming and braising as well as roasting. It's delicious in light, delicate preparations (like the one here), but can also stand up to spicy, aggressive marinades.

Photographs by Scott Phillips

STRIPED BASS

Why this fish With fisheries predominantly on the eastern seaboard, striped bass has begun to rebound from overfishing in the 1980s, thanks to sensible fishing practices. As a result, its population is increasing every year. (If you can't find it wild, farmed striped bass is a good alternative because it's raised sustainably.)

Why we love it Striped bass has a delicate, almost grassy flavor that's similar to snapper but cleaner and less oily. Its delicate texture makes it well suited for sautéing, roasting, or steaming; grilling can be tricky, as the flesh tends to fall apart easily. It requires a little attention at the stove because it can quickly cross the line from juicy to overcooked. The method at right is easy, since you can keep an eye on the fish throughout the cooking process. Striped bass plays well with other gentle flavors like leeks and mushrooms, or it can be a vehicle for assertive, spicy flavors, from Indian to North African (as in this recipe).

crisp striped bass with preserved lemon, chickpeas, and couscous

Preserved lemon brings a bright, salty citrus note to this dish. For information on where to buy preserved lemon and harissa, see p. 93.

Serves 4

- 4 skin-on striped bass fillets (5 oz. each), scaled
  Kosher salt and freshly ground black pepper
- ¾ cup all-purpose unbleached flour
- 3 Tbs. extra-virgin olive oil; more for drizzling
- ¼ tsp. cumin seeds
- 2 cups seeded, diced fresh tomatoes
- 1 19-oz. can chickpeas, drained and rinsed (about 2 cups)
- 2 Tbs. chopped Moroccan preserved lemon (or 1 tsp. grated lemon zest)
- ½ cup chopped fresh cilantro, plus whole leaves for garnish
- 1 cup couscous, cooked according to package directions
  Harissa or other chile sauce to taste

Heat the oven to 200°F. Pat the fish fillets dry and season all over with ½ tsp. salt and ¼ tsp. pepper. Put the flour in a wide, shallow dish and lightly dredge the fish in the flour, shaking off any excess.

Heat the oil in a 12-inch nonstick skillet over medium-high heat until shimmering hot. Arrange the fish skin side down in the pan so the fillets fit without touching. Cook undisturbed for 4 minutes. With a spatula, peek under a fillet to see if the skin is golden-brown and crisp. If not, cook 1 minute more. Flip the fillets and cook until lightly golden-brown and just cooked through, an additional 1 to 2 minutes. Transfer to a wire rack set over a baking sheet and keep warm in the oven.

Reduce the heat to medium, add the cumin seeds to the skillet, and cook, stirring, until fragrant, about 10 seconds. Add the tomatoes, ½ tsp. salt, and 3 Tbs. water and cook until they become saucy, 3 to 4 minutes. Stir in the chickpeas and cook until heated through, about 3 minutes. Add the preserved lemon (or lemon zest) and chopped cilantro. Season to taste with salt and pepper.

Scrape a fork through the couscous to fluff it, and then divide it among 4 dinner plates. Place the fish skin side up on the couscous. Spoon on the chickpea mixture and garnish with the harissa and a scattering of cilantro leaves. If desired, drizzle extra-virgin olive oil over the fish at the table.

braised pacific halibut
with leeks, mushrooms, and clams

Clams give this dish a special briny flavor. Like all bivalves, clams help maintain marine ecosystems; Manila clams are a particularly good choice because they are sustainably farmed.

Serves 4

- 4 oz. (½ cup) unsalted butter
- ½ lb. oyster or hen of the woods mushrooms, thinly sliced (about 4 cups)
- 3 large leeks, white and light-green parts only, thinly sliced (about 4 cups)
  Kosher salt and freshly ground black pepper
- 3 cups lower-salt chicken broth
- 4 skinless Pacific halibut fillets (about 4 oz. each)
- 16 to 24 small clams, such as Manila or littlenecks, scrubbed
- 1 Tbs. finely chopped fresh flat-leaf parsley

Melt the butter over medium heat in an 11- or 12-inch straight-sided sauté pan with a lid. Add the mushrooms and leeks and season lightly with salt and pepper. Cook gently, stirring occasionally, until softened but not browned, 7 to 8 minutes. Add the broth, raise the heat to medium high, and bring to a boil.

Season the halibut with salt and pepper. Nestle the fish and clams among the vegetables in the skillet. Bring the broth back to a boil, cover tightly, and reduce the heat to low. Cook gently until the fish is just cooked through and the clams have opened, about 7 minutes. If all of the clams are not open, remove the fish and the open clams and continue cooking until the remaining clams open, another 2 to 3 minutes. Discard any clams that haven't opened by this time.

Serve the fish in warmed shallow soup bowls, topped with leeks and mushrooms, surrounded by clams and broth, and sprinkled with chopped parsley.

Fresh clues

When buying fish fillets, examine the flesh, which should be moist and glistening and without any large gaps. Dry-looking flesh is a sign of age.

Fresh fish should not smell strong or fishy but should have a mild, fresh scent suggestive of the sea.

When buying skin-on fillets, look for intact skin and make sure the scales were properly removed. Most fish skin is edible and delicious, especially when cooked until crisp.

ATLANTIC MACKEREL

Why this fish If ever there was a diamond in the rough, it's Atlantic mackerel. Prized by the Japanese for the robust flavor it delivers in sushi preparations, it has until recently been overlooked by American cooks, who have favored milder-tasting fish. But with its high omega-3 oil content, mackerel is a heart-healthy choice that's growing in popularity. Plus, the methods used to catch it don't damage the ocean's eco-system, so it's a good sustainable choice.

Why we love it Mackerel's rich, strong flavor is exactly why we like it. This assertiveness pairs well with complex ingredients like miso and soy (as in this recipe) and is complemented by citrus and bright vinaigrettes. It's delicious sautéed or roasted but too oily for poaching.

miso-roasted atlantic mackerel

Mackerel can be bony, so use tweezers or needle-nose pliers to remove any pin bones. Also, its oily nature causes it to develop a fishy flavor fast, so always buy the freshest fish possible and eat it the same day.

Serves 4

- ¼   **cup white or yellow miso**
- ¼   **cup honey**
- 1   **Tbs. toasted Asian sesame oil**
- 2   **tsp. reduced-sodium soy sauce**
- 8   **boneless, skin-on Atlantic mackerel fillets (3½ to 4 oz. each), scaled**
- 2   **to 3 Tbs. vegetable oil; more for the baking sheet**
- 4   **lemon wedges or slices**

In a large bowl, whisk the miso, honey, sesame oil, and soy sauce into a smooth paste. Add the mackerel fillets and toss to coat with the marinade. Marinate for 20 minutes at room temperature. Meanwhile, heat the oven to 350°F.

Wipe the marinade from the skin side of the fillets. Heat 2 Tbs. of the oil in a 12-inch cast-iron or nonstick skillet over medium-high heat. Working in batches to avoid crowding the pan, cook the fillets skin side down until the skin darkens and crisps slightly, 3 to 4 minutes. As each batch finishes, transfer the fillets skin side down to a lightly oiled baking sheet. Add the remaining 1 Tbs. oil to the skillet between batches if it seems dry. Once all the fillets are seared, put the baking sheet in the oven and bake until the flesh is flaky when poked with a paring knife, 5 minutes. Serve garnished with lemon wedges or slices.

Jay Weinstein is a New York City-based food writer and former chef. His latest book is The Ethical Gourmet. ❑

the wine life

For Paul Speck and his family, wine and food—both from one small piece of land in Ontario—are what it's all about.

BY DENISE MICKELSEN

PAUL SPECK, ONE-TIME CITY BOY turned philosopher turned winemaker, is tearing the foil from a bottle of sparkling wine as he gets ready for a Friday night dinner with his two younger brothers and their wives. It's a bone-dry sparkler from their family winery—Henry of Pelham Family Estate Winery in St. Catharines, Ontario—and with a splash of their Cabernet Franc ice wine, it makes for a killer cocktail.

Melissa, Paul's wife, is busy arranging "dessert": an all-Ontario cheese plate with fresh fruit and toasted nuts. Her menu for tonight—a juicy stuffed pork roast, beets with fresh goat cheese, sautéed broccoli raab, and a lentil salad—comes straight from neighborhood shops and farmers' markets, including a family-owned butcher shop across the street from her children's school.

It may be fall in St. Catharines, but there's still some warmth in the air, so Paul is cooking the garlic-and-herb-stuffed pork on a rotisserie. "I'm always trying new things on the grill," says Paul. "We have these big dinners together about once a month, so I've got plenty of chances to experiment. Planning the menus and the wines—ours or someone else's—is practically a family pastime."

Wine and food were not always Paul's passions. "I studied philosophy in college, and I actually wanted to be a lawyer in Toronto," he explains as he checks on the pork that's filling the patio with a rich, garlicky perfume. "But my dad asked me to come help run the winery, and it turns out I was lucky to be in this place at the right time." Whatever you want to call it—luck or fate or a father's wish—the timing

was ideal. Just as Paul began managing the family business (he'd later become the winery's president), the premium wine industry in Ontario began to take off. And as Henry of Pelham grew, so did Paul's passion for making wine. (For more, see The Wine Thinker, page 78.)

Making—and drinking—wine is much more than a job for Paul and his brothers: It's a lifestyle, one that includes good food. As they stand on the patio, sipping cocktails and nibbling on prosciutto and oil-cured olives before dinner, talk turns to a New Zealand rosé that Paul wants his brothers to try. "It's made from Cabernet Franc, which we grow, too. European-style grapes like Cab Franc, Chardonnay, and Riesling, they all grow well here and make wines that express this part of the world. That's key for us."

Plates are passed and filled, and more bottles are opened—Henry of Pelham's lush, fruity reserve Cabernet-Merlot blend is ideal with the smoky, grilled pork roast and gently bitter broccoli raab. The beet salad with goat cheese and toasted pecans is creamy and tangy and crunchy all at once, and earthy lentils and scallions get a kick from sherry vinaigrette.

Later, Melissa serves the cheese plate and Paul pours their Riesling ice wine. One cheese in particular, a buttery, cow's milk, washed-rind cheese called Niagara Gold, captures everyone's attention. It's made less than 10 miles from the winery, and it pairs perfectly with the cold, sweet wine. For Paul Speck and his brothers, this is what it's all about—great wine and food, all from this corner of Canada.

HARVEST DINNER

•

Tuscan-Style Roast Pork
with Rosemary, Sage, and Garlic

Sautéed Broccoli Raab
with Balsamic Vinegar

Beet Salad with Oregano, Pecans,
and Goat Cheese

Lentil Salad with Sherry Vinaigrette

*Henry of Pelham 2007 Barrel-Fermented
Chardonnay; 2006 Reserve Cabernet-
Merlot; 2008 Dry Rosé*

Ontario cheese plate with fresh fruit
Henry of Pelham 2007 Riesling Ice Wine

Recipes begin on the next page.

From far left: All in a day's work (if you can call it that). Paul Speck shares a toast with members of Ontario's liquor board. White wines in the tasting room. Melissa and Paul welcome his brothers, Matthew and Daniel, and their wives, Jillian and Louise, to their home for dinner. Why the name Henry of Pelham? The winery, which is on Pelham Road, was named after Henry Smith, son of Paul's ancestor, Nicholas Smith, who in 1794, settled the land upon which the winery sits.

Paul Speck believes that fine wine is grown, not made. After all, a bottle of wine is only as good as its grapes.

The land Henry of Pelham Family Estate Winery sits near the base of the Niagara Escarpment (the steep cliff over which Niagara Falls runs) in the Short Hills Bench sub-appellation of Niagara. "The soil is heavy clay with lots of limestone and shale sediment spread throughout," Paul explains. "The clay naturally restricts the root growth of the vines, which is a good thing. Low yields and small volume are perfect for growing premium wines. And the sediment gives the grapes—especially Riesling and Chardonnay—a great natural acidity and minerality."

The climate "We're sandwiched between Lake Ontario and the Niagara Escarpment, so there's a triangle of warm air from the lake and cool air from the escarpment flowing over the vineyards," says Paul. These conditions are ideal for growing both ice wine and red wine grapes, with temperatures as hot as 85°F in the summer, and as cold as 10°F in the winter.

The wines Three-quarters of the grapes that go into Henry of Pelham wines come from their own vineyards, which, for a small 225-acre winery (170 acres of which are under vine), is significant. The other quarter comes from neighboring vineyards in Niagara. "We will always be 100 percent Niagara. That way, when you buy our wines you're getting something special from this part of the world."

tuscan-style roast pork with rosemary, sage, and garlic

This juicy roast (shown on page 77) gets a flavorful, burnished crust from its time on a rotisserie grill. If you don't have a rotisserie, you can grill the pork over indirect heat for equally delicious results. Steer clear of pork loins labeled "extra tender" or "guaranteed tender," because they've been treated with sodium phosphate and water and will be too salty if brined.

Serves 6 to 8

FOR THE BRINED PORK

- 3 oz. kosher salt (¾ cup if using Diamond Crystal; 6 Tbs. if using Morton)
- ¼ cup packed light brown sugar
- 3 medium cloves garlic, smashed and peeled
- 3 large sprigs fresh rosemary
- 3 large sprigs fresh sage
- 1 3-lb. all-natural boneless pork loin, trimmed of excess fat

FOR THE HERB PASTE

- 8 medium cloves garlic, peeled
- ¼ cup fresh rosemary leaves
- ¼ cup fresh sage leaves
   Kosher salt and freshly ground black pepper
- 3 Tbs. extra-virgin olive oil

BRINE THE PORK

In a 3- to 4-quart saucepan, combine the salt, sugar, garlic, and herb sprigs with 2 cups of water. Stir over high heat just until the salt and sugar dissolve. Add 6 more cups of water and cool to room temperature. Transfer to a large container, add the pork, cover, and refrigerate for 8 to 18 hours.

MAKE THE HERB PASTE

Put the garlic, rosemary, sage, 1 Tbs. salt, and 1 tsp. pepper in a large mortar and pound to a coarse paste with the pestle. Add the oil and use the pestle to work it into the garlic paste. If you don't have a mortar and pestle, combine all the ingredients in a mini food processor and pulse into a coarse paste.

BUTTERFLY AND SEASON THE PORK

Remove the pork from the brine and pat it dry (discard the brine). Butterfly the pork loin by making a horizontal slit down the length of the loin, cutting almost through to the other side. Open the meat like a book. Spread half of the herb paste over the inner surface of the roast; then fold it back to its original shape. Tie the roast at 1-inch intervals with butcher's twine and then spread the remaining herb paste over the entire outer surface.

GRILL THE PORK

Set up a grill for indirect rotisserie cooking according to the manufacturer's instructions. Heat the grill to 350°F. When ready to cook, skewer the roast lengthwise on the rotisserie spit and let it rotate on the grill, covered, until an instant-read thermometer inserted near the center of the roast registers 145°F, 35 to 45 minutes.

If you don't have a rotisserie, set up your grill for indirect grilling. Heat the grill to 350°F. Put the roast in the cool zone on the grill, and cook as directed above, turning the roast about every 10 minutes.

Remove the roast from the spit if necessary and transfer it to a cutting board. Let stand for 5 minutes, remove the string, and slice thinly. Serve hot, warm, or at room temperature.

Make ahead: The pork must be brined 8 to 18 hours ahead. You can also butterfly and season the roast with the herb paste up to 4 hours before grilling. Refrigerate, but let sit at room temperature while you heat the grill.

Food styling by Allison Ehri Kreitler

Photographs by Scott Phillips

beet salad with oregano, pecans, and goat cheese

Beets and goat cheese are a classic pairing, but for a twist, try substituting blue cheese for the goat cheese and walnuts for the pecans.

Serves 6 to 8

8	to 10 medium beets (red, golden, or a combination)
3	Tbs. extra-virgin olive oil
3	Tbs. aged balsamic vinegar
	Sea salt or kosher salt and freshly ground black pepper
4	oz. soft goat cheese, crumbled
2	Tbs. chopped fresh oregano
¼	cup chopped lightly toasted pecans

If the beets have leaves and stems, trim off the leaves and all but ¼ inch of the stems. Wash the beets. In a large saucepan or stockpot fit with a steamer basket, steam the beets until a paring knife enters them easily, 30 to 45 minutes, depending on their size. Set aside until cool enough to handle but still warm.

Peel the beets; the skin will rub right off. Trim and discard the tops and tails and cut the beets into thick wedges. Transfer the beets to a large serving bowl and drizzle with the olive oil and vinegar. Season with a generous pinch of salt and pepper. Sprinkle the goat cheese, oregano, and pecans over the beets and serve.

Make ahead: You can cook, peel, and cut the beets up to 6 hours ahead. Refrigerate, and return to room temperature before finishing.

 For more information on Henry of Pelham Family Estate Winery, go to henryofpelham.com.

sautéed broccoli raab with balsamic vinegar

Mildly bitter broccoli raab is tempered with sweet balsamic vinegar, garlic, anchovies, and a touch of hot chile. Even if you think you don't like anchovies, don't leave them out—their flavor blends into the background and gives the dish a savory edge that is absolutely delicious.

Serves 6 to 8

- ¼ **cup aged balsamic vinegar**
  Kosher salt
- 2 **large bunches broccoli raab (2½ lb.), thick stems trimmed, leaves and florets rinsed well**
- 4 **medium cloves garlic, lightly crushed and peeled**
- 3 **Tbs. extra-virgin olive oil**
- 4 **oil-packed anchovy fillets, finely chopped**
- ¼ **tsp. crushed red pepper flakes**
  Freshly ground black pepper

In a small saucepan, boil the vinegar over medium-high heat until reduced by half, about 4 minutes. Set aside.

Bring a large pot of well-salted water to a boil over high heat. Have a large bowl of ice water ready. Blanch the broccoli raab in the boiling water for 3 minutes (the water needn't return to a boil). Drain it and transfer to the ice water to cool. Drain well and gently squeeze the broccoli raab to remove excess water.

Heat the garlic and oil in a large skillet over medium heat until the garlic begins to turn golden, 2 minutes; remove and discard the garlic. Add the anchovies, mashing them with the back of a wooden spoon until fragrant, 30 seconds. Add the pepper flakes and cook, stirring constantly, for 5 to 10 seconds. Add the broccoli raab and cook, stirring often, until tender and heated through, 3 to 4 minutes. Drizzle with the vinegar and season to taste with salt and pepper. Transfer to a platter and serve.

Make ahead: You can reduce the vinegar and blanch the broccoli raab up to 6 hours ahead. Leave the vinegar at room temperature and refrigerate the broccoli raab, returning it to room temperature before finishing the dish.

lentil salad with sherry vinaigrette

Ellen Smythe, Melissa Speck's aunt, gave her this recipe when she and Paul were first married. It's been a staple of the Specks' dinner parties ever since.

Serves 6 to 8

- 1 **lb. (2 ¼ cups) French green lentils (lentils du Puy)**
  Kosher salt
- ¼ **cup white wine vinegar or sherry vinegar**
  Freshly ground black pepper
- 6 **Tbs. extra-virgin olive oil**
- 4 **scallions, trimmed and thinly sliced**
- 1 **tsp. minced garlic**

Pick over and rinse the lentils and put them in a 4-quart saucepan. Cover them with 2 quarts cold water and add 2 tsp. salt. Bring to a boil over high heat. Lower the heat, partially cover the pot, and simmer until the lentils are slightly firm but tender and still intact, 20 to 30 minutes. Drain and run cold water over them. Drain again and transfer to a large bowl.

Sprinkle the lentils with the vinegar, 1 tsp. salt, and a few grinds of black pepper. Stir gently to combine, taking care not to mash the lentils. Stir in the oil, 1 Tbs. at a time, and finally, the scallions and garlic.

Let stand at room temperature for about 1 hour; then season to taste and serve.

Make ahead: For the best flavor, make this salad at least 1 hour and up to 3 hours before serving.

Recipes by Melissa Speck. Text by Fine Cooking *associate editor Denise Mickelsen.* ❑

For sources, see Where to Buy It

ontario cheese plate with fresh fruit

Paul often brings home Canadian cheeses from The Coach House Café and Cheese Shoppe, located on the Henry of Pelham property. For this dinner, Ontario cheeses take center stage (counterclockwise from front): Ramembert, a sheep's milk bloomy-rind cheese from Ewenity Dairy; Niagara Gold, a semisoft washed-rind cow's milk cheese from Upper Canada Cheese Co.; and a cow's milk smoked blue called Blue Haze, from Provincial Affineurs. Fresh fruit, olives, and toasted nuts round out the plate. Ice wine is the perfect accompaniment.

A kiss from the heart of Italy!

In the heart of Italy's majestic region of Umbria, the historic home of St. Valentine,
a young Perugina chocolatier was inspired to create Baci – Italian for kiss.
For nearly 100 years, passion for the Baci tradition remains unchanged.
Silky dark chocolate envelops a heart of gianduia, sprinkled with chopped hazelnuts
and crowned with a whole hazelnut. Each kiss is hugged by a love note
and wrapped in Baci's iconic silver and blue foil.

Available at fine stores everywhere.
www.perugina.com

PERUGINA
L'ARTE DEL GUSTO

Perugina is a proud sponsor of Public Television's "Lidia's Italy" with Lidia Bastianich   www.lidiasitaly.com

TEST KITCHEN
Tips/Techniques/Equipment/Ingredients/Glossary

Can you spot the recycled car parts in this photo? For the answer, turn to page 85.

Advanced crimping

CRIMPING A PIECRUST IS NOT ONLY DECORATIVE but also useful: It helps to hold up the edge of a single-crust pie. The pie story on page 56 covers the most basic crimping style. Once you get the hang of it, you can be more creative. Here are **three more ways** to crimp a crust:

Scalloped edge

Form a curve with your index finger on the inside edge of the dough and press the edge into gentle curves. Be sure that the scalloped edge is resting firmly on the edge of the pan and not hanging beyond it.

Rope edge

Using the side of your thumb or the flat edge of a table knife, press gently into the dough edge at a 45-degree angle (diagonal to the pan). Repeat every ½ to ¾ inch or so until you've come full circle. Be sure not to press all the way down to the pie plate, or you may sever the dough.

Wheat edge

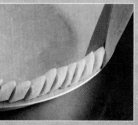 

Holding a pair of scissors at a 45-degree angle, snip the edge at ½- to ¾-inch intervals. With your fingertips, pull each segment in alternating directions toward the inside and outside of the pie. Pinch the tips of each segment into points and smooth each segment as needed.

—*Nicole Rees*

Photographs by Scott Phillips; food styling by Jennifer Armentrout

Watch the video! For a demonstration of these piecrust techniques, go to FineCooking.com/extras.

TECHNIQUE

Crispy duck skin

AS COLD-WATER CREATURES, DUCKS ARE WELL INSULATED, which is a nice way of saying that they have a lot of fat. Without proper attention to that fat, duck skin can cook up flabby. To avoid this, you need to score the skin and slowly render most of the fat. Not only does this method produce nice, crisp skin, but it also gives you duck fat to save for other uses, like roasting or sautéing potatoes.

With a sharp knife, cut a diamond-shaped cross-hatch pattern through the skin into the fat, making sure not to cut into the flesh.

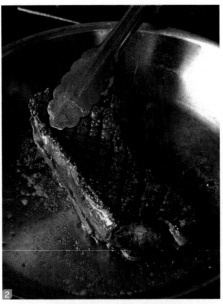

Slowly cook the duck skin side down over medium heat until much of the fat has melted out and the skin is rich amber-brown and crisp. Then turn and finish cooking the duck.

—Melissa Pellegrino

INGREDIENT

Lyle's Golden Syrup

A FAMILIAR PANTRY STAPLE in the U.K., Lyle's Golden Syrup is a full-flavored cane sugar syrup that's used as an ingredient in both baking and savory cooking, and as a topping for foods like pancakes and ice cream. In this issue, it lends its rich, caramelly flavor to the Coffee-Toffee Pecan Pie on page 63.

Pecan pie is traditionally made with corn syrup, but corn syrup lacks great flavor and often produces a slightly runny filling. Replacing some of the corn syrup with the thicker, sweeter Golden Syrup results in a more stable filling with better flavor.

Look for Lyle's Golden Syrup in your supermarket near the honey and maple syrup. You'll find it either in the traditional tin pictured here or in a plastic squeeze bottle. If your store doesn't carry it, see page 93 for a mail-order source. Store the syrup at cool room temperature. If crystals develop, heat the syrup before using to dissolve them.

—J. A.

EQUIPMENT

Recycled kitchen tools

Eco-friendly materials are big in the cookware market right now, and one of our favorite green lines is Lamson & Goodnow's GoodNow recycled cooking tools. The business end of each tool contains 90 percent high-carbon stainless steel recycled from old appliances and car parts. And though you'd never know it to look at them, the heat-resistant handles are made from 100 percent recycled paper compressed with nonpetroleum resin. Adding to their green pedigree, the tools are made in Lamson's 170-year-old Massachusetts factory, which is powered with hydroelectric energy produced from a river that runs through the factory grounds, and all of the manufacturing scraps are recycled.

The line includes assorted turners and spatulas, plus a potato masher. For handling delicate foods like fish fillets, you can't beat this 3x6-inch chef's slotted turner (a.k.a. fish spatula). Try using this tool with one of the fish recipes beginning on page 68. See Where to Buy It, page 93, to order.

—Jennifer Armentrout

Food mill: buy or don't buy?

A FOOD MILL IS ONE OF THOSE TOOLS YOU MAY NOT USE VERY OFTEN, but you'll be glad to have one when you need it. In this issue alone, two recipes call for a food mill: the Maple Apple-Pear Butter on page 20 and the Rustic Mashed Potatoes on page 33. Making apple sauce (or butter) and mashed potatoes are two of the three main uses for a food mill. The third is separating seeds and skins from tomatoes.

bowl hook

paddle

disk

hopper

crank

HOW IT WORKS

A bowl-shaped **hopper** holds the food to be milled. A **hook** and a handle help secure the hopper over a separate bowl to catch the milled food.

A hand-driven **crank** pushes an angled **paddle**, which smears and forces the food through a disk.

The **disk,** perforated with colander-like holes, strains the food, separating out the unwanted bits (seeds, skins, etc).

HOW TO CHOOSE A FOOD MILL

The best models feature deep hoppers and paddles that fit snugly against the disks. They come apart easily for cleaning and have interchangeable disks with various hole sizes, so you can control how finely strained your food is.

We particularly like two models. The Cuisipro food mill has three disks (2 mm, 3 mm, and 4 mm) and a little rotating scraper on the underside of the disk that knocks the food off as you turn the handle. The Rösle food mill comes with two disks (1 mm and 3 mm), and several other sizes are available for purchase. An antifriction pad between the paddle and disk makes it slightly easier to operate than the Cuisipro. To order either, see Where to Buy It, page 93.

COOK'S TIP:

If the disk becomes clogged during milling, turn the crank backwards, and the paddle becomes a scraper that clears the clog.

—J. A.

Perfect carrot sticks

In the Pomegranate-Balsamic-Glazed Carrots recipe on page 53, the carrots need to be cut in consistent widths to cook evenly. Here's the method we use.

Cut the peeled carrots into 2-inch lengths and then halve each piece lengthwise. Lay them cut side down on the cutting board and slice lengthwise about ⅜ inch thick.

—Susie Middleton

Saba and verjus

In the grape recipes beginning on page 40, we call for two out-of-the-ordinary ingredients, both related to grapes: saba and verjus. Here's the low-down on both.

Saba is reduced grape must (unfermented grape juice) from Italy. This brown, syrupy substance has a sweet, concentrated, almost prune-like flavor. Depending on region, dialect, or translation, it can go by several names: *saba* is from Sardinia, *sapa* is from Emiglia Romagna; in Apulia, the syrup is called *vin cotto,* and in yet another Italian region the same may be called *mosto cotto.* Other countries with wine-growing regions also have versions of this grape-must syrup—Turkey's is called *pekmez,* and in Palestine it's *dibs.* Whatever its name, enjoy the syrup with roasted grapes or pears, drizzled on strong cheeses such as Parmigiano-Reggiano or Gorgonzola, or brushed on roasted lamb or duck. Store in a dark place at cool room temperature.

A byproduct of wine production, **verjus** (French for "green juice") is unfermented, unripe grape juice. In the vineyard, clusters of unripe grapes are picked to allow other grapes on the same vine to ripen more fully for winemaking. The "thinned" grapes are pressed, resulting in a juice with a sweet-tart taste—something like a thin Sauternes with a lemonade finish. Verjus is lower in acid than vinegar but still adds bright flavor to foods. And because of its low acidity, verjus doesn't compete with the flavor of wine. It's great on green salads and in fruit salads, in sauces for chicken and fish, and it also makes a wonderful addition to a grape sorbet or granita. Opened verjus will keep in the refrigerator for up to two months.

Saba and verjus are both available at specialty foods stores or online; see Where to Buy It, page 93, for sources.

—*Jeanne Kelley*

Make It Tonight

Just 30 minutes to dinner, start to finish.

broiled chicken thighs with chipotle sauce

Roasted red peppers and spicy, smoky ground chipotle chiles make this sauce a knockout. Serve with roasted potatoes.

Serves 4

- 1½ tsp. ground cumin
- 1 tsp. packed light brown sugar
- ¾ tsp. ground chipotle chile
- ¼ tsp. ground cinnamon
  Kosher salt
- 8 boneless, skinless chicken thighs (about 1¾ lb.), trimmed
- 3 Tbs. olive oil
- 1 medium clove garlic
- 1 large or 2 small jarred roasted red peppers, drained
- 1 Tbs. coarsely chopped fresh cilantro

Position a rack about 6 inches from the broiler and heat the broiler on high. In a small bowl, combine 1 tsp. of the cumin, the sugar, ¼ tsp. of the chipotle, the cinnamon, and 1 tsp. salt. In a medium bowl, toss the chicken with 1 Tbs. of the oil, and then toss with the spice mixture.

Arrange the chicken on a rack set over a rimmed baking sheet lined with foil and broil until the chicken browns lightly on top, about 5 minutes. Flip the chicken and continue to broil until browned and cooked through, about 5 minutes more.

Meanwhile, coarsely chop the garlic and sprinkle it with ¼ tsp. salt. Using the flat side of a chef's knife, smear and mash the garlic and salt together to form a coarse paste. Transfer the garlic paste to a food processor and add the roasted red pepper, the remaining 2 Tbs. oil, the remaining ½ tsp. each of cumin and chipotle, and ½ tsp. salt. Purée into a smooth sauce.

Garnish the chicken with the cilantro and serve with the sauce.

—*Tony Rosenfeld*

smoked salmon hash with chive sour cream

If you're in the mood for "breakfast for dinner," serve this with a fried or poached egg on top. A fresh spinach salad makes a good side.

Serves 4

- 2 Tbs. extra-virgin olive oil
- 3 large red potatoes (about 1½ lb.), cut into ½-inch dice
- 1 small yellow onion, roughly chopped
- 1 small green bell pepper, stemmed, cored, seeded, and finely chopped
  Kosher salt and freshly ground black pepper
- ⅔ cup sour cream
- 2 Tbs. thinly sliced fresh chives
- 1½ Tbs. fresh lemon juice
- ½ tsp. Dijon mustard
- 1 4-oz. hot-smoked salmon fillet, skinned and broken into large flakes (about 1 cup)

Heat the oil in a 12-inch nonstick skillet over medium-high heat. Add the potatoes, onion, bell pepper, 1 tsp. salt, and ¼ tsp. pepper and cook, stirring often, until golden-brown, about 10 minutes. Reduce the heat to medium and continue cooking until the potatoes are tender, about 15 minutes more; season to taste with salt and pepper.

Meanwhile, combine the sour cream, 1 Tbs. of the chives, ½ Tbs. of the lemon juice, the mustard, ½ tsp. salt, and ⅛ tsp. pepper in a medium bowl and stir well; set aside.

When the potatoes are tender, gently fold in the salmon and the remaining 1 Tbs. lemon juice and continue cooking until heated through, about 2 minutes more. Transfer the hash to plates. Garnish with the remaining 1 Tbs. chives and serve with a dollop of the chive sour cream.

—*Liz Pearson*

Photographs by Scott Phillips; food styling by Safaya Tork, except beef ragù, Heidi Johannsen Stewart

beef ragù over spaghetti squash with garlic bread

Here, spaghetti squash is used like pasta to delicious effect, and a quick garlic bread rounds out the meal.

Serves 4

- ¼ baguette, halved lengthwise
- 1½ Tbs. unsalted butter, melted
- 6 medium cloves garlic
  Kosher salt and freshly ground black pepper
- 1 small (2½-lb.) spaghetti squash, halved lengthwise and seeded
- 1 Tbs. extra-virgin olive oil
- 1 lb. lean ground beef
- 1 small yellow onion, finely chopped
- 1 15-oz. can crushed tomatoes
- ¼ cup coarsely chopped fresh basil
- ¼ cup freshly grated Parmigiano-Reggiano

Heat the oven to 375°F. Arrange the bread cut side up on a foil-lined baking sheet. Brush it with the butter. Peel and chop the garlic. Divide the garlic in half and sprinkle one-half with a generous pinch of salt. Using the flat side of a chef's knife, mince and mash the garlic and salt together to form a smooth paste. Spread each piece of bread evenly with garlic paste and season with salt and pepper. Bake until light golden-brown and crisp, 12 to 14 minutes. Cut each piece in half to make 4 pieces total, and cover with foil to keep warm.

Meanwhile, arrange the spaghetti squash in a single layer in the bottom of a large, wide pot. (Don't worry if the squash halves don't lie completely flat in the pot.) Add ½ inch of water, cover the pot, and bring to a boil. Reduce to a simmer and cook until the squash is tender enough to shred when raked with a fork but still somewhat crisp, 15 to 20 minutes. Transfer the squash to a plate and set aside until cool enough to handle.

While the squash cooks, heat the oil in a 12-inch skillet over medium-high heat. Add the beef, the remaining chopped garlic, onion, ½ tsp. salt, and ¼ tsp. pepper; cook, stirring to break up the meat, until just cooked through, 5 to 6 minutes. Drain and discard the fat if necessary. Add the tomatoes, basil,

and ¼ cup water; stir well and bring to a boil. Reduce the heat to medium low and simmer for 10 minutes. Season to taste with salt and pepper.

With a fork, rake the squash flesh into strands, transfer to plates, and season to taste with salt. Ladle the beef ragù over the squash and garnish with the Parmigiano. Serve with the garlic bread.

—*Liz Pearson*

Continued on page 90

stir-fried pork with kimchi and shiitake

There are many types of kimchi (Korean preserved vegetables), but spicy napa cabbage kimchi is the most popular and the best version for this recipe. It can be found at Asian markets and in the produce section of some large supermarkets. Steamed short-grain rice makes a good accompaniment to this dish.

Serves 4

- 1   pork tenderloin (12 to 16 oz.), trimmed of silverskin and cut crosswise ¼ inch thick
- 1   Tbs. soy sauce
      Freshly ground black pepper
- 3   Tbs. peanut or canola oil
- 8   oz. fresh shiitake mushrooms, stems trimmed, caps cut into ¼-inch slices
- 6   scallions, cut into 1½-inch lengths
- 3   large cloves garlic, minced
- 16   oz. napa cabbage kimchi, drained and very coarsely chopped (about 2¾ cups)
- 3   Tbs. mirin (or 2 Tbs. sake or white wine plus 4 tsp. granulated sugar)
- 1   Tbs. Asian sesame oil
      Kosher salt
- ½   Tbs. toasted sesame seeds

In a medium bowl, toss the pork, ½ Tbs. of the soy sauce, and ⅛ tsp. pepper.

Heat 1 Tbs. of the oil in a 12-inch nonstick skillet over medium-high heat until you see the first wisp of smoke. Swirl to coat the pan, then add half of the pork and stir-fry until brown in spots and no longer pink, about 2 minutes. Transfer to a bowl. Add another 1 Tbs. of the oil to the skillet and repeat with the remaining pork.

Add the remaining 1 Tbs. of the oil to the pan and swirl to coat. Add the mushrooms and scallions and cook, stirring, until the mushrooms are shrunken in size and the scallions are wilted, 2 to 3 minutes. Stir in the garlic and cook until fragrant, about 30 seconds.

Add the kimchi, mirin, and the remaining ½ Tbs. soy sauce and cook, stirring frequently, until the liquid released by the kimchi is reduced to about ⅓ cup, about 3 minutes. (The amount of liquid released by the kimchi is somewhat unpredictable—if there is an excessive amount, cook until it reduces or spoon some of it off.) Add the pork and any accumulated juices and cook until heated through, 1 to 2 minutes more. Drizzle with the sesame oil and stir well. Season to taste with salt and pepper, sprinkle with the sesame seeds, and serve.

—*Dawn Yanagihara*

chocolate bark with ginger and pistachios

With a cup of coffee or tea, this is a quick and sweet end to dinner.

Serves 4

- 6   oz. bittersweet dark chocolate (70% to 72% cacao), chopped (1 cup)
- 2   oz. white chocolate, chopped (⅓ cup; optional)
- 3   Tbs. chopped salted pistachios
- 3   Tbs. chopped dried apricots
- 2   Tbs. chopped crystallized ginger

In a small bowl, melt the dark chocolate in the microwave on high for 1 to 2 minutes. Stir until smooth.

Line a baking sheet with a silicone baking mat or waxed paper. Spread the melted dark chocolate into an approximately 8x5-inch rectangle.

If using the white chocolate, melt it in the same manner as the dark chocolate and drizzle it in a zigzag pattern across the dark chocolate.

Sprinkle with the chopped pistachios, apricots, and ginger and press gently to set them into the chocolate. Chill in the refrigerator for 10 minutes. Break into pieces and serve. Store any leftovers in the refrigerator.

—*Bruce Weinstein and Mark Scarbrough*

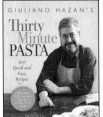

WHERE TO BUY IT

vineyard dinner, page 76

- **All-Clad marble cheese board** with three stainless-steel tools, $59.95, metrokitchen.com, 888-892-9911.
- **For more information about Ontario cheeses,** call Provincial Fine Foods, 877-487-7768, or go to aboutcheese.ca.

french onion soup, page 64

- **Revol 7-oz. porcelain au gratin dishes** (similar to the one on page 65), $12.95, surlatable.com, 800-243-0852.
- **3½-inch grooved toothpicks,** $10 for 2,000 at pickonus.com, 800-874-2587; call for smaller orders.

From 125west.com, 888-921-9378:
- **Pillivuyt 15-oz. onion soup bowl,** $25.
- **Demeyere John Pawson 4.2-quart casserole** with lid, $365.

piecrust, page 56

- **Johnson Rose pie pan,** 9x7½x1¼ inches, $2.40, kitchensupply direct.com, 866-601-5734.
- **Tapered rolling pin,** $14, williams-sonoma.com, 877-812-6235.

grapes, page 40

- **Rectangular tart pan,** 14x4½ inches, $18.95, cooking.com/fc, 800-663-8810.
- **La Tourangelle roasted walnut oil,** $12.99 for a 500-ml bottle, igourmet.com, 877-446-8763.
- **Burl plate** in oyster, $45, dbohome.com, 860-364-6008.

vegetable sides, page 48

All vintage items courtesy of Tillie's Antiques, 766 Main Street South, Woodbury, CT 06798, 203-263-2115.

For more kitchen tools, go to **FineCooking.com/buy-it**

Photographs by Scott Phillips

repertoire, page 29

- **Pyrex 1-quart measuring cup,** $5.99, bedbathandbeyond .com, 800-462-3966.
- **Corningware 3-quart baking dish,** $19.99, target.com, 800-591-3869.

From cooking.com/fc, 800-663-8810:
- **Amco nonskid metal mixing bowls,** set of three for $34.95.
- **Henckels 8-inch chef's knife,** $74.99.
- **All-Clad stainless-steel roasting pan** with rack, $159.99.
- **Cotton butcher's string,** $5.95.
- **Polder digital instant-read thermometer,** $14.99.
- **French 12-inch beechwood mixing spoon,** $3.95.
- **10-inch bamboo skewers,** pack of 100, $1.29.
- **Vollrath 18x13x1-inch jelly roll pan** (rimmed baking sheet), $9.95.
- **All-Clad 3-quart stainless-steel saucepan,** $159.95.
- **Vollrath 8-inch medium-mesh strainer,** $5.95.

From williams-sonoma.com, 877-812-6235:
- **Bulb baster,** $18.
- **Stainless-steel balloon whisk,** $12.
- **All-Clad 12-inch stainless-steel frying pan,** $135.
- **All-Clad 8-quart professional stockpot** with lid, $315.

From crateandbarrel.com, 800-967-6696:
- **All-Clad MC2 10-inch, 3-quart straight-sided sauté pan,** $179.95.
- **Reversible carve-serve board,** $49.95.

menus, page 96

Spanish wine recommendations courtesy of Kerin Auth at Tinto Fino in New York City.

drinks, page 38

For information on buying Spanish wines, go to tintofino .com or call 212-254-0850.

test kitchen, page 83

- **Saba,** $14.50 for a 9-oz. jar, gourmetsardinia.com, 713-621-6858.
- **Verjus,** $5 for a 375-ml. bottle, wolffer.com/store, 631-537-5106.
- **Rösle food mill,** $117, rosleusa .com, 302-326-4801.
- **Cuisipro Deluxe food mill,** $105, surlatable.com, 800-243-0852.

From amazon.com, 800-201-7575:
- **Lamson GoodNow 3x6-inch chef's slotted turner,** $29.99.
- **Lyle's Golden Syrup,** $5.75 for an 11-oz. bottle.

sustainable fish, page 68

- **Shaoxing rice wine,** $5.50 for a 750-ml bottle, asiamex.com, 636-272-0604.

From chefshop.com, 800-596-0885:
- **Mustapha's Moroccan harissa,** $8.01 for a 10-oz. jar.
- **Mustapha's preserved lemons,** $7.99 for a 300-gram jar.

Appliances

Chef's Choice *p. 13* Woo 'em with waffles! Prepare the world's most delicious waffles in 90 seconds! The Chef's Choice® unique Quad® baking system lets you choose the ideal flavor, texture, and color.
800-342-3255
www.edgecraft.com

Dacor *p. 21* Since 1965, Dacor® has redefined the modern kitchen with a collection that offers the best balance of style and performance. Dacor is in the details.
800-793-0093
www.dacor.com/hot

Earthstone Wood-Fire Ovens *p. 92* Wood-fired brick ovens for indoor and outdoor use. Can double as a fireplace. Great for baking, grilling, and roasting.
800-840-4915
www.earthstoneovens.com

MetroKitchen *p. 91* Metrokitchen.com, top brands for the professional chef in each of us. Free shipping, the web's best prices. Friendly, expert service on-line since 1998.
www.metrokitchen.com

Mugnaini Imports *p. 92* Mugnaini, exclusive importers of Italian wood-fired ovens. Italian tradition, American technology. Dedicated to customer service in design, building support, and oven use.
888-887-7206
www.mugnaini.com

Ninja Master *p. 11*
www.ninjakitchen.com

Rangecraft Manufacturing, Co. *p. 91* Specializing in the manufacture of a wide selection of high-quality metal range hoods, including copper, brass, and stainless steel. Quality finishes include matte, brushed, antique, mirror, or hammered.
877-RCHOODS
www.rangecraft.com

Viking Range *p. 7* If cooking is everything, the complete Viking kitchen offers everything you need - professional performance and impeccable design.
888-845-4641
www.vikingrange.com/wheretobuy

Zojirushi America Corporation *p. 9* Zojirushi manufactures top-of-the-line cooking appliances from rice cookers to breadmakers. Focusing on how our appliances fit into everyday lives for nearly 90 years.
www.zojirushi.com

Cookware

A Cook's Wares *p. 92* We have what you need for your kitchen: The finest cookware, bakeware, cutlery, utensils and small appliances. Since 1981.
800-915-9788
www.cookswares.com

Fissler USA *p. 11, 17* For over 163 years, Fissler has been the European leader in innovative cookware. All products are manufactured in Germany and come with a lifetime warranty.
www.fisslerusa.com

Kuhn-Rikon Corporation *p. 13* Kuhn Rikon offers the finest in pressure cookers, specialty cookware, and distinctive kitchen tools to make a cook's life easier.
800-924-4699
www.kuhnrikon.com/fine

MetroKitchen *p. 89* Metrokitchen.com, top brands for the professional chef in each of us. Free shipping, the web's best prices. Friendly, expert service on-line since 1998.
www.metrokitchen.com

Gourmet Foods

Al Fresco All Natural Sausage *p. 25* Al fresco All Natural Chicken Sausage comes in 14 sumptuous flavors and has 70% less fat than traditional pork sausage. Live life with flavor.
www.alfrescoallnatural.com

Galloway's Specialty Foods *p. 92* From everyday to gourmet! Galloway's carries a wide range of organic and gourmet foods for the chef who loves to explore. Shop online at www.gallowaysfoods.com
www.gallowaysfoods.com

Ghirardelli Chocolate *p. 99* The luxuriously deep flavor and smooth texture of Ghirardelli Premium Baking Chocolate delivers the ultimate chocolate indulgence. Visit www.ghirardelli.com for great holiday recipe ideas!
www.ghirardelli.com

John Wm. Macy's Cheesesticks *p. 87* Enrich any occasion with our all-natural sourdough CheeseSticks, CheeseCrisps and SweetSticks, made with fine aged cheeses and choice seasonings, then baked twice to "the perfect crunch!"
www.cheesesticks.com

La Tienda *p. 92* A window to the best of Spain. America's most comprehensive inventory of quality Spanish food selected by a knowledgeable and dedicated family. Immediate delivery.
888-472-1022
www.tienda.com

Ladd Hill Orchards *p. 92* Premium, Oregon-grown fresh or dried chestnuts and chestnut flour Gluten free. Certified organic by guaranteed organic certification agency.
www.laddhillchestnuts.com

Millie's Pierogi *p. 92* Handmade pierogi, made fresh and shipped fresh to your door! Cabbage, potato-cheese, cheese, prune, or blueberry fillings.
www.milliespierogi.com

Perugina *p. 82* Perugina: Maker of fine chocolate bars, pralines, hard candy, panettone, and Baci – Italy's iconic dark chocolate and hazelnut sweet.
www.perugina.com

Plugra European Style Butter *p. 14*
www.plugra.com

Ingredients

Amore *p. 19*
www.amorebrand.com

Bob's Red Mill Natural Foods *p. 17* Bob's Red Mill Natural Foods, Inc. is the nation's leading miller of stone ground whole grains. To learn more about our wholesome, delicious products visit www.bobsredmill.com/fc
www.bobsredmill.com/fc

Bulk Foods *p. 92* Offering a wide selection of spices, nuts, dried fruits, and other ingredients.
www.bulkfoods.com

Char Crust *p. 92* Get the secret! Char Crust ® dry-rub seasonings for all meat & fish. Only Char Crust® Seals In The Juices!® Turns you into a chef...instantly.
www.charcrust.com

Magic Seasonings *p. 11* Chef Paul Prudhomme's all-natural magic seasoning blends, sauces and marinades, pepper sauce, smoked meats, cookbooks, gift packs, sweet potato pecan pie, and much more!
800-457-2857
www.chefpaul.com

Sugarcraft, Inc. *p. 92* Sugarcraft Inc., Hamilton, Ohio. We carry baking, cake decorating, candy, and cookie supplies, etc. We import specialty items!
www.sugarcraft.com

The King Arthur Flour Co. *p. 2* The premier baking resource offering the finest ingredients, tools, recipes and education for all bakers. America's oldest flour company. 100% employee-owned; 100% committed to quality.
www.kingarthurflour.com/why

Kitchen Tools & Utensils

Bella Copper *p. 92* The world's leading heat diffuser/defroster plate provides superior heat conduction for more even cooking and faster defrosting. Available in solid copper or pure silver. A gourmet kitchen essential.
805-215-3241
www.bellacopper.com

Chester P. Basil's *p. 91* Maker of some of America's finest handcrafted wooden spoons, utensils, and boards. Uniquely shaped for superior function. Beautiful cherry wood tools. "Order today!"
www.cpbasils.com

deBuyer *p. 89* French manufacturer since 1830, de Buyer offers professional high-quality cooking and pastry utensils for lovers of flavor and gastronomy.
www.debuyer.com

Gel Pro *p. 17* Stand in comfort! Let's Gel was started with one simple goal, to make the time you spend standing in your kitchen more comfortable.
866-GEL-MATS
www.gelpro.com

House on the Hill *p. 92* Over 400 molds for springerle, speculaas, gingerbread, marzipan, fondant and cake decorating. Order now for holiday cookie baking. Catalog on request.
www.houseonthehill.net

Japanese Chefs Knife *p. 9* Your online source for Japanese chef's knives for home cooking and the professional chef. Finest selections from the top brands: Masahiro, Misono, Fujiwara Kanefusa, Glestain.
www.japanesechefsknife.com

Kerekes *p. 92* Your complete online source for professional chef's tools, cookware, bakeware, and cake decorating supplies used by top chefs at the finest restaurants and kitchens.
www.bakedeco.com

Vic Firth Gourmet *p. 9* All Vic Firth Gourmet wood pepper mills and salt mills are handcrafted in Newport, Maine from solid cherry or maple and have a Lifetime Guarantee.
www.vicfirthgourmet.com

Schools, Travel & Organizations

Culinary Business Academy *p. 9* Extensive and comprehensive personal chef business knowledge and training from the world's recognized leader in the personal chef industry. Nobody offers what we offer.
800-747-2433
www.culinarybusiness.com

Le Cordon Bleu *p. 11* Master the culinary arts. Earn the Grand Diplome in approximately nine months. Three- to five-week intensive courses and online hospitality programs are also available.
800-457-2433
www.cordonbleu.edu

Wines, Beverages & Accessories

Blackstone Winery *p. 100*
www.blackstonewinery.com

Twinings Tea *p. 5*
www.twiningsusa.com

Woodbridge Winery *p. 28* For 25 years, we have aged our wines in small oak barrels and handcrafted each vintage. Woodbridge: Taste our small winery tradition™.
www.woodbridgewines.com

NUTRITION

Recipes	Calories (kcal)	Fat Cal (kcal)	Protein (g)	Carb (g)	Total Fat (g)	Sat Fat (g)	Mono Fat (g)	Poly Fat (g)	Chol (mg)	Sodium (mg)	Fiber (g)
PERSIMMONS, P. 15											
Fuyu Persimmon and Fennel Salad with Hazelnuts	350	230	5	31	26	3.5	18	3	0	105	8
FRUIT BUTTER, P. 20											
Maple Apple-Pear Butter (per 1 Tbs.)	35	0	0	9	0	0	0	0	0	10	1
FINGERLING POTATOES, P. 22											
Glazed Fingerling Potato Salad with Mustard Vinaigrette	410	320	7	17	36	13	18	3	55	690	2
Fingerling Galettes with Smoked Trout	210	130	10	10	14	5	7	1	55	340	1
Braised Fingerlings with Fennel, Olives, and Thyme	210	120	4	22	13	2	9	1.5	0	290	4
TURKEY DINNER, P. 29											
Dry-Rubbed Roast Turkey with Pan Gravy	570	240	73	3	27	8	9	7	210	1130	0
Bread Stuffing with Fresh Herbs	160	60	6	22	6	3	1.5	1	45	320	2
Rustic Mashed Potatoes	290	140	6	33	16	10	4	0.5	45	340	3
Cranberry Sauce with Caramelized Onions (per ¼ cup)	90	10	0	21	1	0	0.5	0.5	0	25	2
GOOD LIFE, P. 34											
Autumn Vegetable Soup	120	40	5	16	4.5	0.5	3	1	0	250	3
GRAPES, P. 40											
Frisée and Grape Salad with Verjus and Blue Cheese	130	70	4	13	8	2.5	1.5	3.5	10	320	3
Bulgur and Grape Salad with Walnuts and Currants	220	100	5	29	11	1	2	8	0	115	6
Moroccan-Spiced Scallops with Grape and Lemon Relish	320	130	29	17	15	2	10	2	55	560	2
Duck Breast with Saba and Grapes	320	110	27	21	12	3	6	2	140	390	1
Braised Chicken with Gewürztraminer and Grapes	560	260	34	18	29	10	12	5	145	430	1
Custard Tart with Wine-Poached Grapes	390	190	5	46	21	11	7	1.5	180	180	1
VEGETABLE SIDE DISHES, P. 48											
Roasted Turnips with Maple and Cardamom	140	70	1	16	8	2.5	3	2.5	10	320	3
Pomegranate-Balsamic-Glazed Carrots	110	60	1	13	7	2.5	3.5	0.5	10	280	3
Green Beans with Crispy Pancetta and Mushrooms	110	70	3	8	8	1.5	5	1	5	410	3
Creamy Baked Leeks with Garlic, Thyme, and Parmigiano	170	110	2	14	12	7	3.5	0.5	45	105	2
Brussels Sprouts with Toasted Hazelnut Butter	190	140	4	10	16	5	9	1.5	15	270	4
Bourbon Sweet Potato and Apple Casserole	430	250	5	40	28	12	11	4	60	170	7
PIECRUST, P. 56											
Coffee-Toffee Pecan Pie	810	440	8	87	49	17	19	8	135	430	4
Jamaican-Spiced Pumpkin Pie	430	190	7	53	22	15	4.5	1	135	410	6
Fresh Pear Pie with Dried Cherries and Streusel	630	210	7	101	24	15	6	1	60	260	7
Ginger-Spice Cranberry-Apple Streusel Pie	610	220	6	94	25	13	6	4.5	55	190	4
FRENCH ONION SOUP, P. 64											
French Onion Soup	240	150	14	9	16	10	5	1	45	270	1
Roasted Beef Broth (per 1 cup)	40	15	5	1	1.5	0	0.5	0	0	15	0
French Onion Soup Dumplings (per 1 dumpling)	90	50	3	8	6	2.5	1.5	0	15	160	0
SUSTAINABLE FISH, P. 68											
Crisp Striped Bass with Preserved Lemon and Chickpeas	550	150	39	61	16	2.5	9	3.5	115	600	9
Pan-Seared Arctic Char with Olives and Potatoes	390	190	33	17	21	2	11	1.5	0	540	2
Steamed Black Cod with Scallions and Rice Wine	510	220	20	45	25	4.5	14	4.5	55	115	2
Braised Pacific Halibut with Mushrooms and Clams	480	250	40	17	28	15	7	2.5	125	460	3
Miso-Roasted Atlantic Mackerel	520	320	38	9	36	7	15	10	120	330	0
VINEYARD DINNER, P. 76											
Sautéed Broccoli Raab with Balsamic Vinegar	90	50	5	6	6	1	4	1	0	260	4
Beet Salad with Oregano, Pecans, and Goat Cheese	140	100	4	7	11	3	6	1.5	5	110	1
Tuscan-Style Roast Pork with Rosemary and Sage	290	140	32	2	16	4.5	9	1	85	1010	0
Lentil Salad with Sherry Vinaigrette	290	100	13	36	11	1.5	7	1	0	290	9
MAKE IT TONIGHT, P. 88											
Broiled Chicken Thighs with Chipotle Sauce	330	190	27	3	22	4.5	12	3.5	100	660	1
Stir-Fried Pork with Kimchi and Shiitake	340	160	23	17	18	3.5	8	5	55	1700	3
Smoked Salmon Hash with Chive Sour Cream	290	130	10	32	15	5	7	1.5	20	1030	4
Beef Ragù over Spaghetti Squash with Garlic Bread	370	170	26	27	19	8	8	1.5	80	410	6
Chocolate Bark with Ginger and Pistachios	380	170	6	45	19	11	7	1	0	80	6

The nutritional analyses have been calculated by a registered dietitian at Nutritional Solutions in Melville, New York. When a recipe gives a choice of ingredients, the first choice is the one used. Optional ingredients with measured amounts are included; ingredients without specific quantities are not. Analyses are per serving; when a range of ingredient amounts or servings is given, the smaller amount or portion is used. When the quantities of salt and pepper aren't specified, the analysis is based on ¼ tsp. salt and ⅛ tsp. pepper per serving for entrées, and ⅛ tsp. salt and ⅛ tsp. pepper per serving for side dishes.

Market Supper

Frisée and Grape Salad
with Verjus and Blue Cheese
page 42

Tuscan-Style Pork
with Rosemary, Sage,
and Garlic
page 78

Braised Fingerling Potatoes
with Fennel, Olives, and Thyme
page 23

Fresh Pear Pie with Dried Cherries
and Brown Sugar Streusel
page 62

*To drink: a lightly sweet blend of
Moscatel and Sauvignon Blanc,
like Gramona Gessami, 2008*

A Big Thanksgiving

Dry-Rubbed Roast Turkey
with Pan Gravy
page 30

Buttermilk Mashed Potatoes
with Chives
FineCooking.com

Brussels Sprouts with Toasted
Hazelnut Butter
page 52

Pomegranate-
Balsamic-Glazed Carrots
page 53

Wild Rice Bread Dressing with
Apple, Apricot, and Sage
FineCooking.com

Coffee-Toffee Pecan Pie
page 63

*To drink: a wine with medium
acidity and soft tannins, like
Wyatt Pinot Noir, 2006*

Soup and Salad

Autumn Vegetable Soup
page 35

Fuyu Persimmon and Fennel
Salad with Hazelnuts
page 16

———

French Onion Soup
page 66

Glazed Fingerling Potato Salad
with Pancetta and Warm
Mustard Vinaigrette
page 22

———

Curried Carrot Soup
with Cilantro
FineCooking.com

Beet Salad with Oregano,
Pecans, and Goat Cheese
page 79

*To drink, two wines for any night:
A classic Rioja like
Zuazo Gaston, 2006,
Vendimia Seleccionada
100% Tempranillo

or

A crisp, dry Albariño like
Mar de Vinas, 2008, Rias Baixas*

Breakfast
for Dinner

Smoked Salmon Hash
with Chive Sour Cream
page 88

Poached or fried eggs

Maple Apple-Pear Butter
page 20

Your Favorite Toast

To drink: Champagne Cocktails
FineCooking.com

Friday Night Easy

Beef Ragù over Spaghetti Squash
with Garlic Bread
page 89

Sautéed Broccoli Raab with Balsamic Vinegar
page 80

Chocolate Bark with Ginger and Pistachios
page 90

To drink: an Imperial Pilsner, like Birra Moretti

RECIPE INDEX

VEGETARIAN: May contain eggs and dairy ingredients

MAKE AHEAD: Can be completely prepared ahead (may need reheating and a garnish to serve)

QUICK: 30 minutes and under

Farmer Lee Jones

This Ohio-born, bow-tied farmer grows produce to order for chefs around the world. BY LISA WADDLE

Fine Cooking: Why do your fieldworkers wear lab coats and harvest with scissors?
Jones: Everything we grow is specifically requested by a chef and must be accounted for. Because a lot of our produce is delicate, we take extra care. We can't risk a crushed strawberry or a bent herb.

FC: Have you always farmed this way?
Jones: No, 40 years ago we were a traditional family farm. A hailstorm in the 1980s ruined our crops, and we couldn't repay our loans. I was nineteen when the banks foreclosed. The house, land, equipment, cars—it was all gone. We started over with six acres that I bought a few miles down the road. I quit college, and my mom and dad moved in with me.

FC: How did you come up with the idea of being a "personal farmer" to chefs?
Jones: My dad, Bob, and my brother, Bobby, and I had started selling our vegetables at the farmers' market in Cleveland. One day, a woman saw my zucchini and asked if I had any of the blossoms for sale. I went home and told my dad; he thought she was a kook—who eats flowers? But she kept asking and offering to pay, so I brought her some. Turns out she knew a lot of chefs, and soon enough they were asking for special items. The word spread.

FC: Are you still selling at the farmers' market?
Jones: About 5 years into the new farm, we were getting so many requests from chefs that my dad

said we needed to make a choice. I voted for regular customers, because chefs were 2 percent of the business and 80 percent of the aggravation. I got overruled.

FC: Any regrets?
Jones: We fill orders for up to 350 chefs each week, and sales have risen steadily. Now we're expanding beyond chefs to sell to the home gourmet. So I guess you should listen to your father.

FC: How many different vegetables, fruits, and herbs do you grow?
Jones: About 600 varieties, from White Icicle radishes to coconut thyme. But we've learned that every stage of a plant's life offers a different nuance, texture, flavor, and presentation on the plate. You can buy bok choy in seven stages, from micro to flowering, so that adds to the selection. Everything is grown using the best sustainable agriculture practices, hand-harvested, and shipped overnight. Twenty-four hours from ground to plate.

FC: Your methods are pretty high tech: bar-code tracking of every plant, a laboratory on site. Are you the farmer of the future?
Jones: Actually, we look more to the past for how we grow. We use crop rotation rather than chemical fertilizers to recharge the soil. Instead of buying new, we jury-rig old tractors, which are gentler on the soil. My dad says we're just trying to get as good as the growers were 100 years ago.

FC: If you weren't a farmer, what would you be?
Jones: Disappointed. I can't imagine being anything else.

the dish

Name: Lee Jones

Age: 48

Job: Co-owner of The Chef's Garden, which grows specialty produce for chefs worldwide, and of the nonprofit Veggie U, which brings healthy-eating classes to fourth graders nationwide

Started: 1983

Where: Milan, Ohio

Known for: Red bow tie and overalls

Illustration by Ward Schumaker

60% CACAO. 100% IMPRESSIVE.

BAKE WITH OUR DEEP, INTENSE CHOCOLATE FOR PURE PLEASURE IN EVERY BITE.

GHIRARDELLI® ULTIMATE DOUBLE CHOCOLATE COOKIES

Yield – 2 dozen cookies

1 bag (11.5 oz.) Ghirardelli 60% Cacao
   Bittersweet Chocolate Chips
6 Tbsp. (³/₄ stick) unsalted butter
3 eggs
1 cup sugar
¹/₃ cup all-purpose flour
¹/₂ tsp. baking powder
1 bag (12 oz.) Ghirardelli Semi-Sweet
   Chocolate Chips
1 cup (4 oz.) chopped walnuts

In double boiler over hot water, melt the bittersweet chocolate chips and butter. In large bowl with electric mixer, beat eggs and sugar until thick; stir in chocolate mixture. In small bowl, stir together flour and baking powder; stir into chocolate mixture. Gently mix in semi-sweet chocolate chips and walnuts.

Using a sheet of plastic wrap, form dough into two logs, each 2 inches in diameter and about 8 inches long. As dough will be very soft, use plastic wrap to hold dough in log shape. Wrap tightly. Refrigerate at least 1 hour or until firm.

Preheat oven to 375ºF. Unwrap dough; with sharp knife, cut into ³/₄-inch slices. Place slices 1 ¹/₂ inches apart on greased or parchment-lined cookie sheet. Bake 12 to 14 minutes or until shiny crust forms on top but interior is still soft.

Cool on baking sheet. Enjoy the moment of timeless pleasure.

MOMENTS OF TIMELESS PLEASURE.®

www.ghirardelli.com

* Her   * Miles Davis   * Him

* Here's to the things in life you can count on. Blackstone Winery.
All the awards, without the pretensions. That's why we're America's favorite Merlot.

2009 marks the 50th anniversary of Miles Davis' legendary album, Kind of Blue.

2009 Index

Covering issues 96–101. Page numbers followed by a letter indicate a foldout section.